The Days of Creation

History of Biblical Interpretation Series

4

ISSN 1382-4465

Deo Publishing

The DAYS *of* CREATION

A History of Christian Interpretation of Genesis 1:1–2:3

Andrew J. Brown

BLANDFORD FORUM

History of Biblical Interpretation Series, 4

ISSN 1382-4465

P.O. Box 6284, Blandford Forum, Dorset DT11 1AQ, UK

Printed by Henry Ling Ltd, at the Dorset Press, Dorchester, DT1 1HD, UK

British Library Cataloguing-in-Publication data
A catalogue record for this book is available from the British Library

ISBN 978-1-905679-27-0

Contents

Acknowledgments

This study began life as a PhD thesis at the University of Queensland, Brisbane, Australia. After nine and a half long years of study I completed the task in mid-2011. If I learned anything from the process, and I feel as if I certainly did, it was that anybody with any kind of intellectual aspirations in the Western world before about 1800 felt obliged to write a piece on Gen. 1:1–2:3, and these 'pieces' could run up to, in extreme instances, 800 pages of densely written text, often, inconveniently, in a language other than English. This was a foolish choice from a manageability point of view, but fascinating for all of that, and I feel as if this enterprise baptized me into a much fuller understanding of the Genesis text, of Christian teaching about creation, of biblical hermeneutics, and of the history of thinking about world origins in the West.

I would like first to thank my wife, Naomi, for not only tolerating this time-consuming undertaking but for actually, as is her gift, taking an active and intelligent interest in the whole study. She always remained confident that the task could be completed, and I thank her for her faithfulness and her faith in me.

I thank my supervisors at the University of Queensland, first Edgar Conrad, then Peter Harrison, and finally Philip Almond. I also received help from Davis Young, who read more than one draft and gave helpful comments, along with Ted Davis with his encouraging feedback in the later stages. I received language help from several friends and relatives, including Susan Richaudeau, Helen Bennett, Sue Kok, Alex Reynolds, Klaus and Gayle Gelewski, and Les Ball.

Finally, I would never have completed this study without the generous support of my employing church for 2005–2010, Murwillumbah Baptist Church in northeastern NSW, Australia, who granted me periods of part- and full-time leave with financial support, and whose members Andy and Jo Page and Joe and Joanne Biles provided quiet study areas. I would never have finished the work had it not been for their help.

Any mistakes that remain, as they say, are all mine!

Soli Deo Gloria.

Notes

I refer where it seems appropriate to ancient, medieval and Renaissance texts under translated titles in the interests of user-friendliness; scholars will recognize the works and readily call to mind the original titles, which I cite in the footnotes.

Unless otherwise noted, all translations are my own, and I have limited the citation of original text to the mention of strategic terms. Those interested in checking the original wording in full are invited to utilize the references given.

Abbreviations

ANE	Ancient Near East(ern)
Ecclus	Ecclesiasticus (Sirach)
LXX	Septuagint, the Greek translation of the Old Testament. The edition accessed is the LXX Septuaginta (LXT) (Old Greek Jewish Scriptures) edited by Alfred Rahlfs. Copyright © 1935 Württembergische Bibelanstalt/Deutsche Bibelgesellschaft (German Bible Society), Stuttgart. Copyright © 1998 BibleWorks, L.L.C.
MT	Masoretic text, the standard Hebrew Old Testament. The edition accessed is *Biblia Hebraica Stuttgartensia* (BHS), edited by K. Elliger and W. Rudolph of the Deutsche Bibelgesellschaft, Stuttgart, 4th edn, copyright © 1966, 1977, 1983, 1990 Deutsche Bibelgesellschaft (German Bible Society), Stuttgart. Copyright ©1998 BibleWorks, L.L.C.
NRSV	New Revised Standard Version of the Bible, Copyright © 1989 Division of Christian Education of the National Council of the Churches of Christ in the USA.
NT	New Testament
OT	Old Testament

Frequently Cited Works

ANF	*The Ante-Nicene Fathers,* edited by A. Cleveland Coxe. 10 vols. Buffalo: The Christian Literature Publishing co., 1885–96. Repr. Grand Rapids: Eerdmans, 1985–87. (This was based on *The Ante-Nicene Christian Library,* edited by A. Roberts and J. Donaldson. 24 vols. Edinburgh: T&T Clark, 1866–72.)
DECL	Döpp, Siegmar, and Wilhelm Geerlings, eds. *Dictionary of Early Christian Literature.* New York: Crossroad, 2000.
DGaL	Augustine's *De Genesi ad litteram*
DGLI	Augustine's *De Genesi ad litteram liber imperfectibus*
DGM	Augustine's *De Genesi contra Manichaeos*
HB/OT	Sæbø, Magna, ed. *Hebrew Bible/Old Testament: The History of Its Interpretation.* Vol. I, *From the Beginnings to the Middle Ages (Until 1300).* Part 1: *Antiquity.* Göttingen: Vandenhoeck & Ruprecht, 1996. Vol. I, part 2: *The Middle Ages.* Göttingen: Vandenhoeck &

	Ruprecht, 2000. Vol. II, *From the Renaissance to the Enlightenment.* Göttingen: Vandenhoeck & Ruprecht, 2008.
HHMBI	McKim, Donald, ed. *Historical Handbook of Major Biblical Interpreters.* Leicester: InterVarsity Press, 1998.
NPNF[1]	*A Select Library of Nicene and Post-Nicene Fathers of the Christian Church,* Series 1. Edited by Philip Schaff et al. 14 vols. New York: Christian Literature, 1886–90. Repr. Grand Rapids: Eerdmans, 1974–78.
NPNF[2]	*A Select Library of Nicene and Post-Nicene Fathers of the Christian Church,* Series 2. Edited by Philip Schaff and Henry Wace. 14 vols. Oxford: Parker, 1890–1900. Repr. Grand Rapids: Eerdmans, 1978–79.
ODCC	Cross, F.L., and E.A. Livingstone, eds. *The Oxford Dictionary of the Christian Church.* 2nd rev. ed. Oxford: Oxford University Press, 1983.
PG	*Patrologia graeca,* i.e. J.-P. Migne, ed. *Patrologiae cursus completus. Series graeca.* 162 vols. Paris, 1857–66.
PL	*Patrologia latina,* i.e. J.-P. Migne, ed. *Patrologiae cursus completus. Series latina.* 217 vols. Paris, 1844–64. Partly accessed via the Patrologia Latina Database (below).
RCFW	Backus, Irena, ed. *The Reception of the Church Fathers in the West.* 2 vols. Leiden: Brill, 1997.

Abbreviated Journal Titles

PSCF	*Perspectives on Science and Christian Faith*
WTJ	*Westminster Theological Journal*

Abbreviated Database Titles

CCEL	Christian Classics Ethereal Library, http://www.ccel.org.
CPT	The Digital Library of Classic Protestant Texts, Alexander Street Press, accessed via University of Queensland, http://solomon.tcpt.alexanderstreet.com.ezproxy.library.uq.edu.au.
ECCO	Eighteenth Century Collections Online, Gale Group, accessed via University of Queensland, http://galenet.galegroup.com.ezproxy.library.uq.edu.au/servlet/ECCO.
EEBO	Early English Books Online, Chadwyck-Healey, accessed via University of Queensland, http://eebo.chadwyck.com.ezproxy.library.uq.edu.au.
GB	Google Books, root URL http://books.google.com.
IA	Internet Archive, root URL http://www.archive.org.
PLD	Patrologia Latina Database, Chadwyck-Healey, accessed via University of Queensland, http://pld.chadwyck.co.uk.ezproxy.library.uq.edu.au.
TLG	Thesaurus Linguae Graecae, University of California at Irvine, accessed via University of Queensland, http://stephanus.tlg.uci.edu.ezproxy.library.uq.edu.au

1

Introduction

A long and obscure speech is wearying, but a brief and clear one delights.[1]
Isidore of Seville, *On Genesis*, Praefatio

Not long ago, browsing in a mainstream bookshop, I discovered a book entitled *The Genesis Enigma: Why the Bible Is Scientifically Accurate*.[2] Its author excitedly expounds the marvellous agreement he has discovered between the opening chapter of the Bible and the evolutionary history of the earth. I intend to show that history has witnessed hundreds of such harmonizing efforts, and the same would apply for a modern Genesis commentary, devotional work or chronology of biblical events. Genesis 1:1–2:3 continues to inspire new books, monographs, articles and essays every year, and the total literary output concerned with this chapter has been enormous.[3] Hence Richard Hess's grand claim: "This passage is arguably the single most reflected upon written text … in human history."[4] Genesis 1:1–2:3 is magnetic, unique, archetypal, universal, the starting point for numerous biblical themes, the anchor point for many aspects of Christian theology and the most famous cosmogony in Western literature.[5] Not even the dramatic advances of the scientific revolution, with its radically new perspective on the history of 'the heavens and the earth', have extinguished the appeal of this chapter.

[1] Prolixa enim et occulta taedat oratio; brevis et aperta delectate. Isidore of Seville, "Sancti Isidori Hispalensis Episcopi mysticorum expositiones sacramentorum seu quaestiones in Vetus Testamentum. In Genesin," in *PL* 83:208B.

[2] Andrew Parker, *The Genesis Enigma: Why the Bible is Scientifically Accurate* (New York: Dutton Adult, 2009).

[3] Throughout this study I have the full seven-day creation week of Gen. 1:1–2:3 in view. If at times I use the term 'Genesis 1' for short, this is not meant to minimise the importance of the content of Day 7 in Gen. 2:1–3.

[4] Richard S. Hess, "God and Origins: Interpreting the Early Chapters of Genesis," in *Darwin, Creation and the Fall: Theological Challenges*, ed. R.J. Berry and T.A. Noble (Nottingham: InterVarsity, 2009), 86.

[5] A cosmogony is an account or portrayal of the birth of the cosmos, or sometimes in practical usage, of the earth.

Defining the Enterprise

Recent years have witnessed a growing appreciation of the history of interpretation of such influential biblical texts. One way to understand both the cultural impact and, indeed, the meaning of a biblical (or non-biblical) text is to 'read its readings' – to discover what earlier readers have found in these words. This kind of study is commonly called 'reception history'. But because this is a technical term that needs defining, let me explain a little more carefully what I am setting out to do here. I am attempting a history of interpretation, or reception history, of Gen. 1:1–2:3, something near to what is expressed by the German term *Auslegungsgeschichte*.[6] I am distinguishing it from a *Wirkungsgeschichte* (history of impact), which traces the effects of a text further out into its hearing communities, for instance in the arts, or liturgy, or law, i.e. well beyond the bounds of the biblical commentary.[7] There is such a vast deposit of past interpretation of Gen. 1:1–2:3 that I have limited my study largely to 'bookish' interpretation: biblical commentaries, works of theology, literary renditions of the Genesis story, universal histories, and scientific or natural-philosophical explanations of the origin of the world. This limited scope already provides quite enough material to occupy one lifetime when it comes to such a core biblical text.

This enterprise is therefore a case study in reception history rather than an investigation of reception theory. Mark Knight differentiates the two by saying that reception history "considers concrete examples of reception without always being drawn into the consequences that these might hold for our understanding of interpretation, [while] the former focuses on the interpretative power of the reader in a more abstract and philosophical sense."[8] This book is very broad in historical scope, so I have concentrated on analysing specific examples of interpretation rather than theorizing more generally about reception. I nevertheless take on board Jonathan Roberts' warning that much existing reception-historical work has failed to ask "the accompanying hermeneutical questions."[9] So I try to couch my interpretive examples in their intellectual, historical and/or social contexts as space permits. But

[6] Hans-Josef Klauck et al., eds., *The Encyclopedia of the Bible and Its Reception* (Berlin: De Gruyter, 2009ff.), 1:xi.

[7] Mark Knight, "*Wirkungsgeschichte*, Reception History, Reception Theory," *JSNT* 33.2 (2010): 138; Jonathan Roberts and Christopher Rowland, "Introduction," *JSNT* 33.2 (2010): 132. *Rezeptionsgeschichte* would, as I understand it, cover both of the other terms.

[8] Knight, "*Wirkungsgeschichte*," 141.

[9] Jonathan Roberts, "Introduction," in *The Oxford Handbook of the Reception History of the Bible*, ed. M. Lieb, E. Mason, and J. Rowland (Oxford: Oxford University Press, 2006), 6.

this will need to be complemented by further exploration on the reader's part, lest this overview grow to the dimensions of some of the ancient tomes on Genesis!

This kind of study is not new, however. A thorough and complete survey of past interpretation of the creation week was published by Otto Zöckler in 1877–79. Indeed, it was standard practice for Renaissance, medieval and late-patristic scholars to review prior interpretations of Genesis 1 thoroughly and intelligently before or while undertaking their own. Reception history is not a fundamental innovation, though its attitude to its texts may sometimes differ. When we do 'reception history', we are surely asking what those before us thought about a text because we consider both their opinion and the text's meaning important. We gravitate especially to voices with whom we identify or whose authority we intuitively recognise, – or those whose impact on our world and its cultures is undeniable and compelling.

Philip Davies comments that there are two groups of biblical interpreters, those who interpret the Bible from within (the 'emic' perspective), who 'buy in' to the big story they find in the Bible, who feel a part of it. They may well believe in and even love the God they find portrayed there. This is essentially my own perspective, though my stance toward the portrayals is not necessarily uncritical. For this group, the importance of interpreting biblical texts and studying others' interpretations of them does not need much supporting argument.

The other group of which Davies speaks looks in at the biblical text from the outside (the 'etic' perspective), not from a sense of belonging but out of interest, perhaps, in a cultural artefact or historical phenomenon.[10] Even for the latter group, the Bible and its interpretive history is a relevant study, Davies argues. Two other reception-historical scholars credit the Bible with "an extraordinary intellectual history that has had an incalculable effect on modern culture, society and the individual sense of self."[11] More pointedly, the opening part of Genesis has been not only (probably) the most commented-on written text in human history, but also one of the greatest influences on Western thought over the last two millennia, and if we want to avoid a gaping ignorance about the course of Western history, thought and culture, not to mention Christian theology and the formation of the sciences concerned with origins, we simply cannot afford to ignore this particular interpretive story.

So this reception history of Gen. 1:1–2:3 constitutes a case study in biblical *hermeneutics* over a long timescale, demonstrating the degree to

[10] Philip Davies, "Reading the Bible Intelligently," *Relegere: Studies in Religion and Reception* 1.1 (2011): 146–49.

[11] Roberts and Rowland, "Introduction," 136.

which interpreters were willing to incorporate externally derived knowledge into their reading of Genesis and considering the effect of its inclusion. It is tantamount to an introduction to the major interpretive trends and strategies of Christian tradition era by era. More broadly, thanks to the great intellectual influence of Gen. 1:1–2:3, a study of its interpretation amounts to a case study in the *history of ideas*, not least the history of the development of science in the modern period. It is the crux text for the relationship between the Bible and science, and we might claim the same for science and religion generally.

The enhanced understanding of biblical hermeneutics that such an introduction offers can return its benefits for the present-day *exegesis* of Gen. 1:1–2:3, since the interpretive options available today have mostly already been examined at the bar of history. Any attempt at a literal, or concordist, or idealist treatment of the creation week should begin by becoming familiar with the long list of such attempts in the past and how they fared in the public arena.

Important Themes in this Story

I would anticipate three key themes for this study. First, it reveals the *depth* of the interpretive history of this Genesis text. Any way the modern reader reads this creation account is almost incapable of being truly new. It has been studied and interpreted inside out, and the main lines of present-day interpretation run much further back than we often realize. Efforts to harmonize Gen. 1:1–2:3 with current scientific research, for instance, run back for centuries; the day-age view is, if we count William Whiston's year-long days, above 300 years old. If we broaden the parameters to include accommodation to popular metaphysical understandings of the day, such efforts are as old as the Christian era itself. An enhanced awareness of this interpretive heritage should evoke humility in the present-day interpreter and may limit the time wasted exploring dead-end routes.

One evergreen interpretive issue has been the choice between literal and figurative approaches to the creation days, and whether figurative meanings refer to history, or to Christian character, to the metaphysical order, or to theological truths. Another long-term question is whether and how theology, philosophy or science ought to influence interpretation. And most of those who have read Gen. 1:1–2:3 throughout its history have come expecting truths from God through the vehicle of a revelatory text. We are therefore reminded of the continuity of this interpretive story, as study of this same text through different ages yields recurring themes.

Yet this depth has sometimes been read as uniformity, in ignorance of the great *difference* in interpretive situations between eras. The cultural, philosophical, religious and intellectual contexts of each major era were unique, with their own values, concerns and agendas; they came to Genesis asking very different questions. Even when a reader of Genesis came to an interpretive position that resembles one available today, the very different background of the day casts that outcome in quite a new light, warning us against premature correlation.

For instance, literal interpretations of the creation week as a familiar calendar week have existed since the patristic era. But when a Reformation thinker contended for a literal creation week, he was not resisting any day-age view, but Augustine's instantaneous creation, or Aristotle's eternal world. And Augustine's recruitment in support of a day-age view fails to appreciate the nature and context of his view. As Andrew Louth writes about the patristic era, these earlier periods are very different countries from those we inhabit.[12] This is a study in difference and diversity in interpretation, as well as continuity.

One final theme I would highlight is that of the historical *trajectory* of Gen. 1:1–2:3. It came in obscurity: it is barely referred to in the entire Old Testament (OT), two Exodus references excepted. It did not register strongly in the earliest centuries of Christian interpretation, yet interest grew, reaching an early climax around the turn of the fifth century AD, just about the time that the Christian church inherited the mantle of cultural leadership in the West from the decaying Roman Empire. Throughout the medieval era it remained a pivotal reference point not only for Christian understanding of world origins but for theology, moral and contemplative meaning and as a testing ground for true philosophy. Its authority in the Renaissance was unparalleled; for a time it became the reference point and framework for all knowledge about the physical world, as well as an enigmatic puzzle for mystical decoding.

But the early Modern era was a time of voyages by sea and land, investigations through microscope and telescope, and dissections of bodies and boulders. The data coming in from these multiplying sources became hard to accommodate within the terse lines of Genesis 1. This once powerful text by degrees lost control of natural-philosophical discourse, and slowly slipped to the margin of what became mainstream science, mainstream history, and mainstream anthropology. It remains a powerful and influential text within the Christian community, but its one-time dominance of the broader culture of the West has ended, though its sway remains strong in certain sacred subcultures, in church or synagogue. This is the story of the rise to the pinnacle of

[12] Andrew Louth, "The Six Days of Creation According to the Greek Fathers," in *Reading Genesis after Darwin*, ed. S.C. Barton and D. Wilkinson (New York: Oxford University Press, 2009), 40.

cultural authority, and then the long, slow decline, of a paradigmatic biblical text.

Related Studies and the Gap that Remains

This book narrates the history of Christian interpretation of the seven days of creation featured in Gen. 1:1–2:3. Avoiding the many points of detail in this section of Genesis that themselves have often aroused debate, I am concentrating instead on its form, asking: How was the framework of a seven-day week understood? How do such understandings make sense in the context of the interpreter's mindset, commitments, and social and historical setting? How can these examples help us to understand the interpretive process itself? How and why were particular treatments of Gen. 1:1–2:3 influential? What led some readers to opt for a literal understanding of the creation week, and others for a figurative one?

The early chapters of Genesis have already inspired similar histories of interpretation, as have smaller units within Genesis 1.[13] Studies relating to the past interpretation of Gen. 1:1–2:3 include the broad history by the late Catholic priest and physicist Stanley Jaki, which, though comprehensive and well-researched, suffers from a kind of triumphalist slant against concordism throughout.[14] A pertinent and ambitious article by Jack Lewis is frustrated by the inevitable length constraints of a journal article, yielding an often superficial result.[15] Others have sought to avoid this problem by being more selective of persons or by focusing on particular periods of history.[16] Frank Robbins' *The Hexaemeral*

[13] Within Gen. 1:1–2:3, see David Kenneth Jobling, "'And Have Dominion...': The Interpretation of Old Testament Texts Concerning Man's Rule over the Creation (Genesis 1:26, 28, 9:1–2, Psalm 8:7–9) from 200 B.C. to the Time of the Council of Nicea " (Th.D. dissertation, Union Theological Seminary, 1972); Jeremy Cohen, *Be Fertile and Increase, Fill the Earth and Master It: The Ancient and Medieval Career of a Biblical Text* (Ithaca, NY: Cornell University Press, 1989); Paul Vignaux, ed., *In Principio: interprétations des premiers versets de la Genèse* (Paris: Études Augustiniennes, 1973).

[14] Stanley Jaki, *Genesis 1 through the Ages* (New York: Thomas More Press, 1992); The problem with objectivity in Jaki's treatments of the history of science has been identified by others, e.g. J. Derral Mulholland, "Book Review: Planets and Their Inhabitants, a review of Planets and Planetarians by Stanley L. Jaki," *Journal for the History of Astronomy* 11 (1980): 68–69.

[15] Jack P. Lewis, "The Days of Creation: An Historical Survey of Interpretation," *Journal of the Evangelical Theological Society* 32 (1989): 433–55.

[16] K.E. Greene-McCreight, *Ad Litteram: How Augustine, Calvin, and Barth Read the "Plain Sense" of Genesis 1–3*, Issues in Systematic Theology (Frankfurt am Main: Lang, 1999); Robert Letham, "'In the Space of Six Days': The Days of Creation from Origen to the Westminster Assembly," *WTJ* 61.2 (1999): 149–74. For interpretations from the Eastern church in the patristic era, see Peter C. Bouteneff, *Beginnings: Ancient Christian Readings of the Biblical Creation Narratives* (Grand Rapids: Baker Academic, 2008). Some

Literature (1912) remains important for the patristic and medieval periods.[17] Complementary works focused on the same eras emerged from continental scholars as the twentieth century continued.[18]

Most comprehensive and extremely useful despite its age is Otto Zöckler's (1833–1906) *Geschichte der Beziehungen zwischen Theologie und Naturwissenschaft* (1877–79).[19] A theological professor at Greifswald from 1866, Zöckler was the leading spokesman on science and religion among late nineteenth-century orthodox German theologians and a leading early theological critic of Darwinism. Known for his even-handedness, his *Geschichte* was virtually unique at the time and remains the most thorough history of interpretation of the early chapters of Genesis up to his own time.[20] This work has naturally been superseded in historical terms by newer treatments of Genesis interpretation in the context of science and religion.[21] Numerous scholarly commentaries on

works devoted to individual interpreters or tight circles of interpreters are Louis Lavallee, "Augustine on the Creation Days," *Journal of the Evangelical Theological Society* 32 (1989): 457–64; Davis A. Young, "The Contemporary Relevance of Augustine's View of Creation," *PSCF* 40.1 (1988): 42–45; William S. Barker, "The Westminster Assembly on the Days of Creation: A Reply to David W Hall," *WTJ* 62.1 (2000): 113–20; Max Rogland, "*Ad Litteram:* Some Dutch Reformed Theologians on the Creation Days," *WTJ* 63 (2001): 211–33.

17 Frank Robbins, *The Hexaemeral Literature: A Study of the Greek and Latin Commentaries in Genesis* (Chicago: University of Chicago Press, 1912). The focus of another promising-sounding title is in fact Genesis 2–3: Gregory Allen Robbins, ed., *Genesis 1–3 in the History of Exegesis: Intrigue in the Garden* (Lewiston: Edwin Mellen, 1988).

18 E. Mangenot, ed., "Hexaméron," in *Dictionnaire de théologie catholique* (Paris: L. Letouzey, 1920), 6:2325–54; J.C.M. van Winden, "Hexaemeron," in *Reallexikon fur Antike und Christentum* (Stuttgart: Anton Hiersemann, 1988), 14:1250–69; G.T. Armstrong, *Die Genesis in der alten Kirche. Die drei Kirchenväter, Justinus, Irenäus, Tertullian*, Beiträge zur Geschichte der biblischen Hermeneutik (Tübingen: J.C.B. Mohr (Paul Siebeck), 1962); Monique Alexandre, *Le Commencement du Livre Genèse I–V: La version grecque de la Septente et sa réception*, Christianisme Antique (Paris: Beauchesne, 1988), 43–229.

19 Otto Zöckler, *Geschichte der Beziehungen zwischen Theologie und Naturwissenschaft: mit besondrer Rücksicht auf Schöpfungsgeschichte*, 2 vols. (Gütersloh: C. Bertelsmann, 1877–79).

20 Frederick Gregory, *Nature Lost? Natural Science and the German Theological Traditions of the Nineteenth Century* (Cambridge, MA: Harvard University Press, 1992), 112–14, 120–22, 128, 148, 158.

21 Michael Roberts, "Geology and Genesis Unearthed," *Churchman* 112.3 (1998): 225–55; Michael Roberts, "The Genesis of John Ray and His Successors," *Evangelical Quarterly* 74.2 (2002): 143–63; Michael Roberts, "Genesis Chapter 1 and Geological Time from Hugo Grotius and Marin Mersenne to William Conybeare and Thomas Chalmers (1620 to 1825)," in *Myth and Geology*, ed. L. Piccardi and W.B. Masse, GS Special Publications (London: The Geological Society, 2007), 39–49; Davis A. Young, "Scripture in the Hands of Geologists," *WTJ* 49 (1987): 1–34, 257–304; James R. Moore, "Geologists and Interpreters of Genesis in the Nineteenth Century," in *God and Nature: Historical Essays on the Encounter between Christianity and Science*, ed. D.C. Lindberg and R.L. Numbers (Berkeley: University of California Press, 1986), 322–50.

Genesis also remain important sources for the preceding history of interpretation.

Yet despite such sustained interest in the reception history of the creation week, a recent study that combines wide historical scope and analytical depth has been lacking.[22] In his essay in *Reading Genesis after Darwin*, Andrew Louth specifically points out this lack in relation to the patristic era.[23] While it is popular for modern day contenders for various literal and non-literal approaches to the days of creation to seek precedents for their views in Christian tradition, there remains a distinct lack of deep comprehension of those witnesses in their own context. 'Retrospective history' can lead us either to undervalue our predecessors' contribution or else to understand it anachronistically.[24] We must therefore make a serious attempt to understand these voices of history in their own contexts. As with genealogical studies, by getting to know our ancestors, we get to know ourselves. This study, then, is intended to integrate the best insights of the existing studies of the reception history of Gen. 1:1-2:3, to update older views, and to compensate for instances of superficiality, incompleteness or bias – and to offer the reader a useful reference point for further research on all aspects of the topic.

Reading Genesis before Darwin

Though focused on a confined part of the biblical text, this study is nevertheless very broad in historical scope, treating the most significant Christian interpretations from post-apostolic times down to around 1860, or in effect, Western, pre-Darwinian interpretation of Gen. 1:1–2:3. This limitation is not merely an expedient caused by the exponential trend in available sources and my length constraints. It is intended to address the area of greater ignorance, that concerning trends in science and religion prior to Darwin as compared to the period since. In the cult of the contemporary, the appetite for studying the past that makes sense of the present is lacking, and especially so before Darwin, or Luther, or Thomas Aquinas. Ironically, a recent volume with the title *Reading Genesis after Darwin* (2009) features multiple statements attesting that Darwin's *Origin of Species* (1859) did not greatly affect

[22] This interest is demonstrated in, e.g. Andrew Louth, ed., *Genesis 1–11*, Ancient Christian Commentary on Scripture (Downers Grove, IL: InterVarsity, 2001).

[23] Louth, "Six Days of Creation," 40 and note.

[24] Stephen Jay Gould, *Time's Arrow, Time's Cycle. Myth and Metaphor in the Discovery of Geological Time* (Harvard: Harvard University Press, 1987), 27. Concerning an important figure in our story, he asks, "How can we criticise Burnet for mixing science and religion when the taxonomy of his times recognised no such division and didn't even possess a word for what we now call science?"

interpretation of Genesis at the time, although it made a significant impact on Christian theology.[25]

The reality is that despite the cultural and intellectual impact of Darwin's *Origin*, the main lines of interpretation of the creation week were established prior to its appearance. Controversy over the compatibility of Genesis 1 and OT biblical chronology with an ancient earth had existed among scholars for a couple of centuries (not counting Aristotelian eternalism) before 1859. The current 'lively' creation-evolution debate "has been going on for more than three and a half centuries. Long before the publication of *On the Origin of Species* (1859) the role of the Bible as the key to the understanding of creation was already being questioned."[26] And when it came to the period around 1860, the more controversial work for the interpretation of Genesis 1 was not Darwin's *Origin*, but the edited volume *Essays and Reviews* (1860), which wrestled with the implications of historical criticism for the Bible.[27]

With this in mind I have chosen 1860 as the cut-off point for this study. The impact of Darwinism on the interpretation of Gen. 1:1–2:3 is both interesting or relevant, but took time to develop, and is best left for a follow-up to the present work. I have also chosen to focus on Christian interpretation as opposed to Jewish in view of limits of space and my own aptitude, although I mention some important Jewish antecedents to Christian interpretation of the creation week below, particularly the first-century Jew Philo, since his influence on patristic interpretation of Genesis is unparalleled. My concentration on the reception history of the seven-day creation framework, rather than the text's own features, also demands that I limit myself to the barest literary and philological analysis of Gen. 1:1-2:3 itself and altogether bypass

[25] Scott Mandelbrote, "Biblical Hermeneutics and the Sciences, 1700–1900: An Overview," in *Nature and Scripture in the Abrahamic Religions: 1700–Present*, ed. J.M. van der Meer and S. Mandelbrote (Leiden: Brill, 2008), 19; Richard S. Briggs, "The Hermeneutics of Reading Genesis after Darwin," in *Reading Genesis after Darwin*, ed. S.C. Barton and D. Wilkinson (New York: Oxford University Press, 2009), 58; John W. Rogerson, "What Difference Did Darwin Make? The Interpretation of Genesis in the Nineteenth Century," in *Reading Genesis after Darwin*, ed. S.C. Barton and D. Wilkinson, 75; John Hedley Brooke, "Genesis and the Scientists: Dissonance among the Harmonizers," in *Reading Genesis after Darwin*, ed. S.C. Barton and D. Wilkinson, 94, 97–98.

[26] Eric Jorink, "'Horrible and Blasphemous': Isaac La Peyrère, Isaac Vossius, and the Emergence of Radical Biblical Criticism in the Dutch Republic," in *Nature and Scripture in the Abrahamic Religions: Up to 1700*, ed. Jitse M. van der Meer and Scott Mandelbrote, Brill's Series in Church History (Leiden: Brill, 2008), 447.

[27] Mandelbrote, "Biblical Hermeneutics," 19–20; Frederick Gregory, "The Impact of Darwinian Evolution on Protestant Theology in the Nineteenth Century," in *God and Nature: Historical Essays on the Encounter between Christianity and Science*, ed. D.C. Lindberg and R.L. Numbers (Berkeley: University of California Press, 1986), 372–74.

the question of its oral or written origin, a topic thoroughly investigated elsewhere.[28]

I wish to do justice to the sheer complexity and unexpected qualities of this history while retaining the creative right to construct a coherent story, without which such a study dissolves into exhausting and irrelevant detail. I will not deliberately make use of any particular interpretive methodology or philosophy, yet happily acknowledge that my experience of life in Australia in particular Christian communities, my intellectual influences, social location and so forth will doubtless reveal themselves as the story unfolds. My praise or critique of other histories of interpretation will appear along the way as appropriate, and I will ultimately critique some ways in which the history of interpretation has itself been received and utilized in contemporary discussion.

The Nature of Genesis 1:1–2:3

The boundaries of the chosen text are fairly self-evident, since the account of the seven days of creation and God's cessation from creation forms a clear pericope or literary unit. Genesis 1:1–2 is included in the text under study because it is the necessary introduction to the creation week. On the other hand, Gen. 2:4a is not included in the present study because it is best understood as a title for what follows in Gen. 2:4b–4:26, in keeping with the argument that the *tōlēdōṯ* (תּוֹלְדוֹת) formulas in Genesis function as introductions rather than conclusions.[29] This is increasingly acknowledged by scholars specializing in the literary features of biblical texts, even though older historical-critical scholars have traditionally seen the first pericope in Genesis as concluding with the characteristically Priestly language of 2:4a.[30]

[28] As, for instance, does Calum M. Carmichael, *The Story of Creation: Its Origin and Its Interpretation in Philo and the Fourth Gospel*. Ithaca: Cornell University Press, 1996. For examples of a focus on Jewish reception of the creation week, see Justin Marston, "Jewish Understandings of Genesis 1 to 3," *Science & Christian Belief* 12 (2000): 127–50; Cohen, *Be Fertile and Increase*, 67–68.

[29] The *tōlēdōṯ* (תּוֹלְדוֹת) formulas may be found at Gen. 5:1; 6:9; 10:1, 32; 11:10, 27; 25:12–13, 19; 36:1, 9; 37:2.

[30] E.g. Gerhard von Rad, *Genesis*, rev. ed., Old Testament Library (London: SCM, 1972), 63; Claus Westermann, *Genesis*, 3 vols., vol. I (Minneapolis: Augsburg, 1984–86), 80ff; O. Speiser, *Genesis*, Anchor Bible (Garden City, NY: Doubleday, 1964), 14. See the insightful corrective of Terje Stordalen: "Genesis 2,4: Restudying a Locus Classicus," *Zeitschrift für die alttestamentliche Wissenschaft* 104 (1992): 163–77; and also Victor P. Hamilton, *The Book of Genesis Chapters 1–17* (Grand Rapids: Eerdmans, 1990), 3–8; Gordon J. Wenham, *Genesis 1–15*, Word Biblical Commentaries 1 (Waco, TX: Word, 1987), 49, 55–56; Brevard Childs, *Introduction to the Old Testament as Scripture* (Philadelphia: Fortress Press, 1979), 145; J.W. Wright, "Genealogies," in *Dictionary of the Old Testament: Pentateuch*, ed. T.D. Alexander and D.W. Baker (Downers Grove: InterVarsity, 2003), 348.

Genesis 1:1–2:3 is a highly structured text portraying a 'formatted', orderly creation, compared to the much more earthy, local, immediate garden scene that follows.[31] Following what might be understood as a prefacing summary (1:1) and a terse setting of the scene (1:2), the divine command that produces light (1:3) becomes the first of a series of creating and separating acts that occupy the six working days.[32] Day 2 (1:6–8) sees the formation of the firmament (רָקִיעַ, *rāqīa'*) that divides the existing water into upper and lower portions. Day 3 (1:9–13) features the twin productions of earth and separate sea(s) on the one hand and vegetation on the other. On Day 4 (1:14–19) a chiastic passage describes the formation of light-bearers (מְאֹרֹת, *m*ᵊ*'orot̲*) in the sky, that is, sun, moon, and (incidentally) stars. Living things that fill the realms of water and air are made on Day 5 (1:20–23). Finally, Day 6 first sees land-based animal life created, followed by the climax of human creation, which is enhanced with a poetic reflection, blessing, and provision of sustenance, and concludes with the 'very good' assessment (1:24–31). Day 7 (2:1–3) forms a different kind of climax, the cessation of God's work that testifies to the completeness of the task.

The content of each day is presented in a highly structured manner, usually consisting of a creative command, followed by its fulfilment, reported either in detail or in the simple, "and it was so."[33] In the first three days there follows the naming of entities produced, and all but the second day contain a positive assessment by God of the work achieved.[34] The final formulaic element, indispensable to the chapter's structure, is the time notice, "Evening and morning took place, day x."[35] Variations in the formulas used were often a spur for theological or metaphysical rumination by commentators. As commentators have often observed, Days 1–3 and Days 4–6 exhibit a considerable degree of correspondence to one another, so that the light created on Day 1 is assigned to the administration of the luminaries on Day 4, the expanse created on Day 2 is populated with birds on Day 5, likewise the "wa-

[31] Because Gen. 2:4–3:24 in its present context to some degree assumes and builds on Gen. 1:1–2:3, since it assumes for instance the presence of a basic 'earth and heaven', I have tended to refer in this book to Gen. 1:1–2:3 as 'the biblical creation narrative' in the singular. For the use of the plural 'creation narratives' to describe Genesis 1–3, see for example Bouteneff, *Beginnings*, ix.

[32] On Gen. 1:1, see Laurence A. Turner, *Genesis*, Readings (Sheffield: Sheffield Academic Press, 2000), 21.

[33] Each of the first six days begins with the words, וַיֹּאמֶר אֱלֹהִים, followed by a decree that begins with a jussive (or in v. 26, a cohortative) verb: יְהִי, v. 3, 6, 14; יִקָּווּ, v. 9; תַּדְשֵׁא, v. 11; יִשְׁרְצוּ, v. 20; תּוֹצֵא, v. 24; and נַעֲשֶׂה in v. 26.

[34] This appears in the formula, "And God saw that it was good", וַיַּרְא אֱלֹהִים כִּי־טוֹב.

[35] וַיְהִי־עֶרֶב וַיְהִי־בֹקֶר יוֹם אֶחָד. After Day 1 every other day has the ordinal ("second, third," etc.).

ters below" with fish, and the vegetated land of Day 3 is populated with plant-eating land animals and humans on Day 6.[36]

So God creates by differentiating what was uniform, so that both time and space are given an order that they had previously lacked. God is presented as the author of the great structures, cycles and tenants of the world. The very orderliness of Gen. 1:1–2:3 communicates this; God is pictured as creating the structure of time itself even as he occupies that time in constructive work. His labour is portrayed on the analogy of human labour; God must take time, even though God makes time. More recently OT scholars have emphasized that a deeper analogy is also at work, that of the consecration of a temple, such that the creation week implies the consecration of the cosmos as a great sanctuary for Yahweh, climaxing as he takes up residence ('rests') within it – a perspective that might help to redeem the importance of the oft-neglected seventh day in the eyes of Christian interpreters.[37]

The pericope of Gen. 1:1–2:3 is neatly self-contained, and quite soon acquired the Greek name 'Hexaemeron', meaning literally 'six days', with the six days of actual creative work in view. (The name could also apply to a biblical commentary or literary treatment of this theme, as we will see.)[38] This schema of creation across the span of seven days is almost entirely unique in the ancient world, with the nearest analogue appearing via a citation in the medieval lexicon of 'Suidas', which attributes to the 'Tyrrhenians' a belief in creation over six thousand-year periods in a sequence strongly resembling, and perhaps influenced by, the Genesis sequence.[39] The ANE creation myth most often compared since its discovery to Genesis 1 is *Enuma Elish*; but its well-known distribution across seven tablets reflects barely any

[36] As Laurence Turner notes, the correspondence is not quite exact, with seas per se only formed on Day 3: Turner, *Genesis*, 20.

[37] Moshe Weinfeld, "Sabbath, Temple, and the Enthronement of the Lord – The Problem of the Sitz im Leben of Genesis 1:1–2:3," in *Melanges bibliques et orientaux en l'honneur de M. Henri Cazelles*, ed. Andre Caquot and Mathias Delcor (Kevelaer: Butzon und Bercker, 1981), 504; B.C. Hodge, *Revisiting the Days of Genesis* (Eugene, OR: Wipf & Stock, 2011), 59-60; John H. Walton, *The Lost World of Genesis One: Ancient Cosmology and the Origins Debate* (Downers Grove, IL: IVP Academic, 2009), 72–92; M. Welker, "Creation, Big Bang or the Work of Seven Days?," *Theology Today* 52.27 (1995): 182–84.

[38] Its Latinized spelling, 'Hexameron', is sometimes seen. I will capitalize the term when I refer to the biblical narrative, and use lowercase 'h' when referring to the genre of literature concerned with the interpretation of that narrative. For a thorough discussion of the term, see van Winden, "Hexaemeron," 14:1251–52.

[39] Suidas, *Suidae Lexicon*, ed. Ada Adler, 4 vols. (Stuttgart: B.G. Teubner, 1967–), 4:609, and see C.F. Keil, "The First Book of Moses (Genesis)," in *Commentary on the Old Testament. 1. The Pentateuch*, ed. C.F. Keil and F. Delitzsch, trans. J. Martin (Edinburgh: T.&T. Clark, 1866; reprint, Grand Rapids: Eerdmans, 1973), 39–40, n. 32, http://books.google.com/books?id=F6NkmPGJKvIC.

structural correspondence with the Genesis days, barring human creation occurring on the sixth tablet, and does not represent a meaningful parallel.[40]

Even within Scripture, while references and allusions to the account in Gen. 1:1–2:3 are reasonably common,[41] clear mention of creation in the span of a week is limited exclusively to Exod. 20:11; 31:17, where it functions as the supreme warrant for Sabbath observance. But there are numerous indications both within Scripture, for instance in Exod. 24:15–18, where Yahweh summons Moses to meet him on Sinai, and in ANE narratives such as the *Gilgamesh Epic*,[42] that a sequence of six days followed by a climactic seventh day is an understood convention in ANE storytelling, suggesting that here in Genesis we are not dealing with historical reporting so much as with an ancient literary convention.[43]

The Interpretive Impact of Old Testament Translations

Few early Christian interpreters engaged with Gen. 1:1–2:3 in the original Hebrew. The Septuagint (LXX) or Greek translation of the OT was the Scripture of the early church. Until Jerome's innovative Latin translation from the Hebrew, begun about AD 390, the Latin translations used in the western areas of the Roman Empire were based on the LXX; then scholars depended on Jerome's version until the flourishing of Hebrew scholarship in the Renaissance.[44]

[40] James B. Pritchard, ed. *Ancient Near Eastern Texts Relating to the Old Testament*, 3rd ed. (Princeton: Princeton University Press, 1969), 68 and context.

[41] For instance Pss. 33:6–9; 74:16–17; 136:4–9; 148:3–10; and Isa. 45:12, 18 in the OT, and Matt. 1:1; 19:4; Mark 1:1; 10:6; John 1:1; 1 Cor. 11:7; 2 Cor. 4:6; Eph. 4:24; Col. 1:15; 3:10; Heb. 4:10; 11:3; Jas 3:9; and 2 Pet. 3:5–7 in the NT. Calum Carmichael suggests that John shapes a large part of his Gospel on the pattern of the seven days of creation: Carmichael, *Story of Creation*, vii, ix, 32ff.

[42] This device appears in *The Gilgamesh Epic* 11.127–31, 140–46, 215–18, 225–28; *Enuma Elish* 5.16–17; *Atrahasis Epic* 3.4.24–25; the *Eridu Genesis* 3.203; and the Ugaritic *Tale of Aqhat* AQHT A.1.1–17; 2.30–40, *Baal Cycle* 6.22–33 and *Keret Epic* KRT A.3.103–09, 114–20; 4.194–95, 207–11; 5.218–22. See Alexander Heidel, *The Gilgamesh Epic and Old Testament Parallels*, 2nd ed. (Chicago: University of Chicago Press, 1949), 85–86, 89; W.G. Lambert, A.R. Millard, and M. Civil, eds., *Atra-Hasis: The Babylonian Story of the Flood with the Sumerian Flood Story* (Oxford: Oxford University Press, 1969), 97, 143, 145; Pritchard, ed., *Ancient Near Eastern Texts*, 134, 144–45, 149–51; S.E. Loewenstamm, "The Seven-Day Unit in Ugaritic Epic Literature," *Israel Exploration Journal* 15 (1965): 122–33.

[43] For biblical examples, see Num. 19:11; Josh. 6:12–16, 20, and more generally, Job 5:19; Prov. 6:16–19. See Robert Gordis, "The Heptad as an Element of Biblical and Rabbinic Style," *JBL* 62.1 (1943): 18–21; W.M.W. Roth, "The Numerical Sequence x/x+1 in the Old Testament," *Vetus Testamentum* 12 (1962): 300–303.

[44] Eva Schulz-Flügel, "The Latin Old Testament Tradition," in *HB/OT*, vol. I, 1:652.

The LXX translation of our text is competent and straightforward, along with what Wevers calls "the tendency to level out or harmonize the text," which is most noticeable in the ironing out of perceived formal inconsistencies in the Hebrew text.[45] For instance, "and it was so" moves from Gen. 1:6 to 1:7, the approval formula, "and God saw that it was good", absent from Day 2 in the Hebrew, is added at Gen. 1:8 and a fulfilment description is inserted following the "It was so" of 1:9.[46] And in what looks like a theologically-motivated emendation, God is said to finish his work on the sixth day, rather than the seventh as it reads in the Hebrew.[47]

A final alteration in translation might seem fairly trivial, but had significant consequences for the future interpretation of our creation narrative. The LXX translators interpreted the first part of Gen. 2:5 as a continuation of the preceding sentence, yielding the meaning, "in the day that the LORD God made the heavens and the earth and every plant of the field before it existed on the earth, and every herb of the field before it had sprung up..."[48] This simple decision on punctuation and syntax committed interpreters of both Greek and Latin versions, even including Jerome's Vulgate, despite his recourse to the Hebrew text, to try to explain how vegetation could have been created in some way right back in Gen. 1:1 with the heavens and the earth.[49]

This translation therefore inadvertently lent support to a Platonic concept of the initial creation of living things in seminal or ideal form. When Gen. 1:11–13 attributed vegetation to Day 3, then, one option was simply to roll the days together and take them as instantaneous.[50] This forms part of the argumentative apparatus for Augustine's famous instantaneous creation, and demonstrates the significance of his and many other early scholars' dependence on the Greek and Latin versions. And by smoothing out the transition between what are normally

[45] Alexandre, *Commencement*, 45–46; A. Pietersma and B.G. Wright, eds., *A New English Translation of the Septuagint and the Other Greek Translations Traditionally Included under That Title* (New York: Oxford University Press, 2007), 1–5.

[46] This is also one of a handful of LXX variants that find support among the Genesis scroll fragments of Qumran, in this case 4QGen[k]. Martin Abegg, Jr., Peter Flint, and Eugene Ulrich, *The Dead Sea Scrolls Bible: The Oldest Known Bible Translated for the First Time into English* (Edinburgh: T&T Clark, 1999), 5–6; Pietersma and Wright, *Septuagint*, 6. The witness of the Qumran Genesis scrolls supports the general stability and integrity of our biblical Genesis text.

[47] John W. Wevers, "The Interpretative Character and Significance of the Septuagint Version," in *HB/OT*, vol. I, 1:96–97.

[48] ᾗ ἡμέρᾳ ἐποίησεν ὁ θεὸς τὸν οὐρανὸν καὶ τὴν γῆν καὶ πᾶν χλωρὸν ἀγροῦ πρὸ τοῦ γενέσθαι ἐπι τῆς γῆς καὶ πάντα χόρτον ἀγροῦ πρὸ τοῦ ἀνατεῖλαι....

[49] Jerome usually sided with the Hebrew against the LXX, as when he returned the word 'seventh' to Gen. 2:2.

[50] See on Augustine's exegesis of Gen. 2:4–5 in the following chapter.

deemed the two creation accounts of Gen. 1:1–2:4a and 2:4b–3:24, it encouraged the harmonization of the two accounts, most commonly by seeking to insert the events of the second, 'Eden narrative' into Day 6 of creation, e.g. the creation of Eve or the precise moment of the 'fall'.[51]

A View of the Landscape

Our story begins in the patristic period, where contrasting approaches to the Hexaemeron were taken by the major interpretive schools of that period. Augustine proved to be the most influential patristic interpreter in terms of subsequent reception of the creation days, and much of the following chapter is spent comparing medieval responses to his instantaneous creation proposal. This interpretive watershed, along with Aristotelian eternalism, persisted even into the Reformation era, while the seventeenth century witnessed the dawn of the idea of 'deep time' in the earth and cosmic history, as the first buds of the 'day-age' approach appeared in the soil of Platonic idealism. The harmonizing interpretations of Gen. 1:1–2:3 that matured in the eighteenth century, especially in conjunction with physical 'theories of the earth', occupy the next chapter. The last major chapter treats the mature concordism of the day-age theory of the nineteenth century, which competed with the non-concordist literalism of 'scriptural geology' and the non-concordist scepticism of more critically-oriented interpreters of Genesis to persuade a Bible-reading and geology-infatuated public, especially in Britain. This contest came to a climax at about the time of the publication of Darwin's *Origin of Species*, but not because of it. To this story of the long-term rivalry of literal and figurative interpretations of the creation week we now turn.

[51] Alexandre, *Commencement,* 43, and see also 45–46. See the modern critical edition, J.W. Wevers, ed. *Septuaginta Vetus Testamentum Graecum*, vol. I: *Genesis* (Göttingen: Vandenhoeck & Ruprecht, 1974), 75–83.

2

The Days of Creation in the Church Fathers

> Time will fail me should I wish to exhibit all the doubts and deliberations ... concerning the six days.[1]
>
> Anastasius of Sinai, *Anagogicarum contemplationum in Hexaemeron*

Introduction

Explicit Christian interpretation of the creation week first appears in the Apostolic Fathers and continues vigorously through the patristic period down to the late figures of Isidore of Seville and John of Damascus.[2] Allegorical interpretations were more prominent early, although Basil backed away from allegorical interpretation of Gen. 1:1–2:3. Augustine sought finally to incorporate allegorical meaning within the literal sense, bequeathing to the Middle Ages a sophisticated synthesis that was broadly matched by allegorical-literal compromise stances that finally emerged in the Eastern church. Meanwhile, theological readings sought clues in Gen. 1:1–2:3 to the constitution of the Trinity, and moral application found admonitions for faithful living through allegorical unfolding of the chapter's features. Nothing existed like the modern day-age figurative interpretation; there was a 'world-week' prophetic interpretation that took each creation day to represent one thousand years or so of world history, understood redemptively, but it did not necessarily exclude the ordinary, literal creation week, nor could it have been conceived of as something that explained pre-history. No pre-human history was contemplated. The interpretive

[1] Deficiet me tempus si velim in medium proferre sacrorum omnium asseclarum dubitationes et quaestiones de sex diebus. Anastasius of Sinai, "Anagogicarum contemplationum in Hexaemeron ad Theophilum libri undecim," in *PL* 89:859C.

[2] The patristic period is traditionally regarded as running from the earliest post-NT witnesses, the Apostolic Fathers, down to Gregory the Great (d. 604) and Isidore of Seville (d. 636) in the West, and John Damascene (d. <749) in the East: S. Döpp and W. Geerlings, eds., *Dictionary of Early Christian Literature* (New York: Crossroad, 2000), viii; Leo J. Elders, "Thomas Aquinas and the Fathers of the Church," in *RCFW* 1:337; J.W. Trigg, ed., *Biblical Interpretation*, Message of the Fathers of the Church (Wilmington, DE: Michael Glazier, 1988), 9.

terrain of the patristic era was a foreign country indeed, and we should be prepared to confront relatively unfamiliar creation week models and interpretive methods and motivations.

At the opening of the Christian era, the seven-day week was just becoming consolidated in the Roman calendar. The Romans had originally operated on an eight-day weekly cycle that pivoted on a market day. The change took place under the joint influences of Jewish Sabbatarianism and Near Eastern astrology, wherein each of the seven recognized planets of the time presided over its own particular day.[3] The sanctity of the seven-day week could only be reinforced by the Christian association of the day after the Sabbath with the resurrection of Jesus, an association often brought to bear on the meaning of the biblical creation week. The seventh day was the 'day of the Sun', the weekly high-point of Mithraism, then very prominent in Roman culture. The connection of this day with the resurrection of Jesus represents another of those cultural replacements of paganism by Christianity in these early centuries that might be read as either a victory of the latter over the former or else as an infiltration of the latter by the former.[4] While patristic Genesis commentary did not strive to justify the seven-day week, it operated within this fairly newly established temporal and social framework, doubtless with an ever present sense that pagan, astrological associations were competing with the biblical ones of creation and the Sabbath commandment.

The Existing Interpretive Smorgasbord

The earliest Christian interpreters had several available approaches for the interpretation of the days of creation in Genesis. The straightforward, literal understanding of the creation week chronology implied in Exod. 20:11 and 31:17 reappears in Josephus' *Antiquities of the Jews,* an apologetic recital of Jewish history that begins with creation. Josephus offers a straightforward and compact paraphrase of Gen. 1:1–2:3, seeing this passage as a matter-of-fact account of creation; it is only from Gen. 2:4 that "Moses ... begins to talk philosophically." Compared to the presumably historical nature of the six creation days, the anthropo-

[3] The recognised 'planets' were, from farthest to nearest, Saturn, Jupiter, Mars, Sun, Venus, Mercury, and Moon: F.H. Colson, *The Week: An Essay on the Origin and Development of the Seven-Day Cycle* (Cambridge University Press, 1926; reprint, Westport, CT: Greenwood Press, 1974), 18–19. This astrological background accounts for many weekday names in modern western languages and their order: Colson, *The Week*, 3–4, 19–20, 43–45; Eviatar Zerubavel, *The Seven Day Circle: The History and Meaning of the Week* (New York: The Free Press, 1985), 45.

[4] For a full discussion of the cultural interplay between the 'Lord's Day' (*Dominica* or κυριακὴ ἡμέρα) and the 'Day of the Sun', see Colson, *The Week*, 82–107.

morphic nature of Gen. 2:4ff. evidently required more sophisticated handling.[5] And close to hand were the NT references to elements of Genesis 1–3, such as Matt. 19:4–6 and 2 Cor. 4:6, that seemed to build theology on the platform of a literal understanding of the text.

But a quite different, figurative approach to the creation week already existed by this time. In certain Jewish writings classed within the Pseudepigrapha, the seven-day format of creation functions as the basis for speculation that a sevenfold or Sabbatarian key helps to explain eternal reality, or the structure of the heavens, or the overall structure of human history. The book of *Jubilees* (c. 150 BC), a midrash on Genesis and Exodus, extols the Sabbath through a mystical exploration of the number seven, which is built into the cosmos in the creation week and governs the unfolding history of the world.[6] Even the first day of creation features the creation of seven entities: heaven, earth, waters, spirits, abysses, darkness/night and light/day.[7] In *2 Enoch* 24–32, God reveals to Enoch[8] the events of creation, and while the seven-day framework of creation is somewhat obscured, it emerges that both the structure of the heavens and human nature are sevenfold.[9] Prior to this revelation, in chs. 3–20, Enoch is raised progressively through the seven heavens whose features clearly reflect the respective contents of the seven days of creation. According to one manuscript tradition, *2 Enoch* 33:1–2 then interprets the Hexaemeron prophetically as a structural framework for the entire course of providential history, i.e. a 'world-week', a model we will encounter again.[10] And in *4 Ezra* 6:38–54, curiously, the six days and one day of creation translate into geographical categories also, describing the relative proportions of dry land and sea respectively.[11] So the numerological potential of the seven-day scheme began in these writings to burst its original bounds and seemed to these writers to unveil the fundamental nature of reality.

More important than these for Christian interpretation of the Hexaemeron would be the emphatically non-historical strategy for deci-

[5] Josephus, "Antiquities," in *Josephus: Complete Works*, trans. W. Whiston (1736; reprint, Grand Rapids: Kregel, 1960), 25.

[6] J.H. Charlesworth, ed., *The Old Testament Pseudepigrapha*, vol. II (Garden City, NY: Doubleday, 1985), 55–58 (*Jubilees* 2.1–33). For further information see J.C. VanderKam, "Jubilees," in *Dictionary of New Testament Background*, ed. C.A. Evans and S.E. Porter (Downers Grove/Leicester: InterVarsity, 2000), 600.

[7] *Jubilees* 2.2. See the monograph Jacques T.A.G.M. van Ruiten, *Primaeval History Interpreted: The Rewriting of Genesis 1–11 in the Book of Jubilees*, Supplements to the Journal for the Study of Judaism (Leiden: Brill, 2000).

[8] I.e. the character mentioned in Gen. 5:21–24.

[9] J.H. Charlesworth, ed., *The Old Testament Pseudepigrapha*, vol. I: *Apocalyptic Literature and Testaments* (Garden City, NY: Doubleday, 1983), 140–55.

[10] Ibid., 156, also 191–200.

[11] Ibid., 536.

phering the creation days offered by the Alexandrian Jewish thinker Philo Judaeus (*c.* 20 BC–*c.* AD 50). Philo sought to bridge the worlds of traditional Judaism and Hellenistic philosophy in order to defend the honour of Jewish Scriptures and heritage, while adopting Hellenistic (specifically Stoic) methods for coaxing deep meaning from revered ancient texts whose archaic surface phenomena might be off-putting.[12] Philo did not come to Gen. 1:1–2:3 looking for historical data, but for revealed glimpses of the ontological structure of the universe, for timeless realities. In applying methods designed to dig below the literal surface of a biblical text such as this, he became, by historical accident, the pioneer of Christian allegorical interpretation of the creation week and of the Scriptures generally.

Philo's *De Opificio Mundi* (*On the Creation of the World*) was "[t]he first extant work in Greek dealing with the interpretation of the creation story in Genesis," according to Frank Robbins, who underlined Philo's role in initiating the hexaemeral literary tradition.[13] A number of exegetical traditions concerning Genesis appear to have begun with Philo. Number speculation, especially concerning the numbers six and seven, is prominent in *De Opificio Mundi,* as it is in the work of later figures such as Augustine.[14] Philo was the first to articulate a metaphysical significance in the unusual 'one day' (יוֹם אֶחָד, *yōm 'eḥād*) of Gen. 1:5; for him it indicates that the creation of Day 1 is not the material world but the perfectly unified intellectual world that forms the prototype for the material world.[15] Thus he introduces a material/immaterial dualism into the understanding of the creation account that frequently reappears in later treatments. Likewise he proposes that creation must be instantaneous, since the markers of the time that we know, the heavenly bodies, do not yet exist when creation begins. In other words, time itself is a created, not an eternal, entity.[16] He understands Moses as saying

[12] A.J. Hauser and D.F. Watson, eds., *A History of Biblical Interpretation* (Grand Rapids/Cambridge: Eerdmans, 2003), 15–16.

[13] Robbins, *Hexaemeral Literature*, 27; Folker Siegert, "Early Jewish Interpretation in a Hellenistic Style," in *HB/OT,* vol. I, bk 1:167.

[14] Philo, "On the Creation," in *The Works of Philo: Complete and Unabridged*, trans. C.D. Yonge (Peabody, MA: Hendrickson, 1993) (*De opificio mundi* 3.13–14; 30.89–43.128). Compare Augustine, "The City of God," in *NPNF*[1] 2:222–23 (Augustine, *De civitate Dei* 11.30–31); Augustine, *The Literal Meaning of Genesis*, trans. John Hammond Taylor, 2 vols., Ancient Christian Writers (New York: Newman Press, 1982), 1:104–107, 112 (*De Genesim ad litteram* 4.2.2–6; 4.7.14). See also Robbins, *Hexaemeral Literature*, 29. Philo's numerology is derived from Pythagorean (i.e. Hellenistic) philosophy, whereas that in *Jubilees* is characteristically Jewish and oriented towards the religious calendar.

[15] *De opificio mundi* 9.35; Jack P. Lewis, "Days of Creation," 435.

[16] *De opificio mundi* 7.26; Philo, "Allegorical Interpretation, I," in *The Works of Philo*, ed. C.D. Yonge (Peabody, MA: Hendrickson, 1993), 25 (*Legum allegoriae* 2.2).

> that the world was made in six days, not because the Creator stood in need of a length of time (for it is natural that God should do everything at once, not merely by uttering a command, but even by thinking of it); but because the things created required arrangement.[17]

So the six-day sequence is ideal rather than chronological. The seventh 'day' has a culminating role; while God ceases to create mortal creatures, he takes up his higher work of forming divine beings, which work alone deserves the blessing related in Gen. 2:3.[18]

Philo's amalgamation of Greek philosophy, specifically as manifested in Plato's *Timaeus,*[19] and the Hebrew Scriptures provided a unique precedent for later interpretations of the creation days. Philo, though a turn-of-the-era Alexandrian Jew, must be regarded as the founder of Christian non-literal interpretation of the creation week, as the Renaissance Jesuit scholar Suarez would testify many centuries in the future: "Indeed this opinion, that everything was created at once and that the first six days are to be interpreted as a kind of metaphor, originated from Philo Judaeus."[20] His impact on Alexandrian Christian exegesis is clear, and through Augustine, Philo's influence was transmitted to the Western church generally.[21]

The creation week therefore was already understood in these existing Jewish traditions as either a divine paradigm for history, or a revelation of ontological reality, or a numerological gateway to the rest of Scripture, or indeed as an explanation of the world's physical origin. The Christian church gradually began to explore these options and incorporate them into progressively more systematic and elaborate exegeses, homilies, poems and dogmatic treatises concerning the creation week, culminating in the great Genesis commentary of Augustine, the philosophical treatise of Philoponus, and the doctrinal meditations of Gregory the Great. Thus was the 'hexaemeron' born, this new genre of Christian literature concerned with expounding the meaning of the six days and explaining the origin of the present world. But the earliest attempts to expound the creation week had to wrestle with its meaning in the light of the implications of the Christian gospel, the

[17] *De opificio mundi* 3.13.

[18] *Legum allegoriae* 6.16–7.18.

[19] Samuel D. Giere, "A New Glimpse of Day One: An Intertextual History of Genesis 1.1–5 in Hebrew and Greek Texts up to 200 CE " (PhD diss., University of St. Andrews, 2007), 157.

[20] Hæc vero opinion, quod omnia simul create sint et quod primi sex dies per aliquem metaphoram sint interpretandi, initium habuit a Philone Judæo... Francisco Suarez, "Tractatus de opere sex dierum," in *Francisci Suarez opera omnia*, ed. D.M. André (Paris: L. Vivès, 1856), 3:55a, GB, http://books.google.com/books?id= a7sWAAAAQAAJ.

[21] Siegert, "Early Jewish Interpretation," 187–88; E.S. Sterling, "Philo," in *Dictionary of New Testament Background*, ed. C.A. Evans and S.E. Porter (Downers Grove: InterVarsity, 2000), 791.

phenomenon of the Christian church, the speculative explorations of the Jewish writers and Philo's philosophical, allegorical exposition.

The Earliest Interpretations of the Creation Week

The Christian doctrine of creation took time to gather momentum, and is mostly treated briefly and generally in the course of other patristic discussions, such as Justin Martyr's significant but passing mention of creation "out of formless matter" (ἐξ ἀμόρφου ὕλης) in his *First Apology,* and Tertullian's renunciation of the same within his *Against Hermogenes.*[22] The few early Christian interpretations of the days of creation are far from uniformly literal. Not just the prophetic books but all genres of the OT were expected to function prophetically, and the numerological sensitivities of the age meant that the seven-day week of Gen. 1:1–2:3 was ripe for such a prophetic interpretation.[23] The earliest surviving post-NT example of this approach occurs in *The Epistle of Barnabas* (<AD 135), one of the Apostolic Fathers. In *Barnabas* 15:4 the Hexaemeron serves as a paradigm for world history, once it is 'unlocked' with the interpretive key from Ps. 89:4 (LXX, Eng. 90:4) and 2 Pet. 3:8 that a thousand years is merely a day in God's perspective:

> Observe, children, what "he finished in six days" means. It means this: that in six thousand years the Lord will bring everything to an end, for with him a day signifies a thousand years. And he himself bears me witness when he says, "Behold, the day of the Lord will be as a thousand years." Therefore, children, in six days – that is, in six thousand years – everything will be brought to an end.[24]

The seventh day rest stands for a future millennial age; hence the Sabbath, so central in a Jewish work such as *Jubilees,* is re-appropriated as Christian eschatology.[25] "On that Sabbath, after I have set everything at rest, I will create the beginning of an eighth day, which is the begin-

[22] Justin Martyr, "The First Apology," in *ANF* 1:165; Justin Martyr, "Apologia," in *Die ältesten Apologeten*, ed. E.J. Goodspeed (Göttingen: Vandenhoeck & Ruprecht, 1915), ad loc, TLG. (*1 Apology* 10.2); Tertullian, "Against Hermogenes," in *ANF* 3:490–97 (*Adversus Hermogenem* 22–34).

[23] R.P.C. Hanson, "Biblical Exegesis in the Early Church," in *The Cambridge History of the Bible. 1. From the Beginnings to Jerome*, ed. P.R. Ackroyd and C.F. Evans (Cambridge: Cambridge University Press, 1970), 420–21, 449–51.

[24] "The Epistle of Barnabas," in *The Apostolic Fathers: Greek Texts and English Translations of Their Writings*, ed. M.W. Holmes, trans. J.B. Lightfoot and J.R. Harmer (Grand Rapids: Baker, 1999), 315. See the comments on the patristic attitude to such use of 'hermeneutical keys' in Christopher Hall, *Reading Scripture with the Church Fathers* (Downers Grove: InterVarsity, 1998), 152.

[25] See Heb. 4:1–11.

ning of another world."[26] This figurative understanding of the creation week, called the 'world-week' interpretation, is a specimen of what is called the 'periodization of history', which in Judaeo-Christian tradition divides history into (often regular) episodes in the unfolding plan of God for the world. Some of our earliest examples appear in Qumran scrolls 4Q504 (The Words of the Heavenly Lights) and apparently 4Q180–181 (The Ages of the World), along with the above-mentioned *2 Enoch* 33:1–2.[27]

The early Christian interpreter could readily enter this mode of thought and, drawing on Matthew 1, with its three sets of fourteen generations, and the six thousand years of Revelation 20, visualize a framework for divinely governed world history which in its stricter form equated each day of creation to one thousand years of history.[28] This prophetic model may reflect the apocalyptic impulse to emphasize God's governance of history in chaotic times. Its advocates usually interpreted the seventh day as the coming millennial age, and the 'eighth day' (ἡμέρα ὀγδόη, *hēmera ogdoē*) as eternity future.[29]

Irenaeus (c. 130–c. 200), a pivotal early Christian interpreter of the OT, depends on this world-week concept as he develops his millennial eschatology in *Against Heresies*.[30] "The day of the Lord is as a thousand years; and in six days created things were completed: it is evident, therefore, that they will come to an end at the sixth thousand year."[31] Irenaeus argues that the sentence of death upon Adam in the same day he eats the fruit (Gen. 2:17) proves true if that day is regarded as lasting

[26] *Barnabas* 15:8.

[27] Michael Wise, Martin Abegg, Jr., and Edward Cook, *Dead Sea Scrolls: A New Translation* (Rydalmere: Hodder & Stoughton, 1998), 238–39, 410–14; Giere, "New Glimpse," 140–41. Qumran is the location where the Dead Sea Scrolls were discovered.

[28] In Matt. 1, OT genealogies are subdivided into three equal sets of fourteen generations each, while Rev. 20:1-6 presents the thousand-year long or millennial reign of Christ.

[29] Among the considerable number of sources on this topic are: Gary W. Trompf, *The Idea of Historical Recurrence in Western Thought: From Antiquity to the Reformation* (Berkeley: 1979), 200–21; J. Daniélou, *The Theology of Jewish Christianity*, trans. J.A. Baker, The Development of Christian Doctrine before the Council of Nicaea (London: Darton, Longman and Todd, 1964), 390–404; Jonathan Z. Smith, "Ages of the World," in *The Encyclopedia of Religion*, ed. M. Eliade (New York: Macmillan, 1987), 1:130–31.

[30] For general background on Irenaeus, see James L. Kugel and Rowan A. Greer, *Early Biblical Interpretation*, Library of Early Christianity (Philadelphia: Westminster Press, 1986), 155–56; Joseph W. Trigg, "The Apostolic Fathers and Apologists," in *A History of Biblical Interpretation*, ed. A.J. Hauser and D.F. Watson (Grand Rapids: Eerdmans, 2003), 327ff.

[31] Irenaeus, "Against Heresies," in *ANF* 1:557 (*Adversus haereses* 5.28.3).

one thousand years.[32] Cyprian of Carthage (d. 258) includes the world-week interpretation of the creation week in a passage that compiles all the significant 'sevens' of Scripture.[33] Hippolytus of Rome (c. 170–c. 236), in his *Commentary on Daniel,* adds that Christ's first advent occurred in the middle of the sixth thousand, that is, about 5,500 years after creation, while the 6,000 year mark will initiate the 'Sabbath' of history, the millennial reign of Christ on earth with his saints. "Since, then, in six days God made all things, it follows that 6,000 years must be fulfilled."[34] This version of the world-week scheme was based on the longer OT chronology found in the LXX, which tallied about 5,500 years before the birth of Christ and supported an imminent expectation of the second advent of Christ. Because the LXX was to this time effectively the standard Christian OT, fathers both Eastern and Western typically saw themselves as living late in the 'sixth day' of history.[35]

A unique version appears in *The Banquet* by the Greek father Methodius (d. c. 311), wherein the creation week itself, not merely its symbolic pattern reflected in history, continues to the present time: "God, like a painter, is at this very time working at the world." "At the seventh thousand years, when God shall have completed the world, He shall rejoice in us."[36] This is an unusual blending of literal and figurative uses; the days of creation have actually *become* thousand-year ages within human history. In another work, Methodius reports with disapproval Origen's apparent disparagement of the world-week belief.[37] Patristic schemes in the more standard form climaxed with Augustine's

[32] *Adversus haereses* 5.23.2. He derives it from Justin Martyr, who in turn derives it from *Jubilees* 4.29–30. See Daniélou, *Jewish Christianity*, 391–92; Smith, "Ages of the World," 1:130.

[33] Cyprian of Carthage, "Exhortation to Martyrdom, Addressed to Fortunatus," in *ANF* 5:503.

[34] Hippolytus, "On Daniel," in *ANF* 5:179 (*Commentarii in Daniel* 4.23). For the Greek text, see Hippolytus, *Commentarium in Danielem*, trans. M. Lefèvre, Sources chrétiennes (Paris: Éditions du Cerf, 1947), ad loc., TLG. Daniélou observes that the attribution of this work to Hippolytus is disputed: Daniélou, *Jewish Christianity*, 401.

[35] For Eastern church examples, see Julius Africanus, "The Extant Fragments of the Five Books of the Chronography of Julius Africanus," in *ANF* 6:131, 137–38; Theophilus of Antioch, "Theophilus to Autolycus," trans. M. Dods, in *ANF* 2:120 (*Ad Autolycum* 3.28). For a Western example, see Lactantius, "The Divine Institutes," trans. William Fletcher, in *ANF* 7:211 (*Institutes* 7.14). More generally, see a strongly numerological use of the creation week in Victorinus of Pettau, "On the Creation of the World," trans. Robert Ernest Wallis, in *ANF* 7:342.

[36] Methodius of Olympus, "The Banquet," trans. W.R. Clark, in *ANF* 6:313, 344 (*Symposion seu convivium virginum* 2.1, 9.1).

[37] Methodius of Olympus, "Fragments on Creation," in *The Writings of Methodius, Alexander of Lycopolis, Peter of Alexandria, and Several Fragments*, trans. William R. Clark, Ante-Nicene Christian Library (Edinburgh: T.&T. Clark, 1883), 182.

conclusion to *The City of God*, which modelled a world-week interpretation that downplayed the specific thousand years per day equivalence.[38] This particular figurative application of the Genesis text survived beyond the patristic period, right through the Middle Ages and even influenced early Modern history-writing.

The later second-century figure Theophilos of Antioch offers the first really substantial (surviving) treatment of the days of creation in *To Autolycus* 2.10–18. Of sources mostly lost to us, Theophilos can already lament, "Many writers indeed have ... essayed to give an explanation of these things; yet ... they have emitted no slightest spark of truth."[39] The early part of Theophilos' exposition is quite physical and literal: the watery deep (Gen. 1:2) was initially dark because the newly made heaven was "like a lid" blocking out the eternal light above, but with the command, "Let there be light", the Word, "shining as a lamp in an enclosed chamber, lit up all that was under heaven."[40]

Yet with the gathering of waters into seas on Day 3, Theophilos increasingly turns to a morally driven allegorical exposition of the chapter. The sun serves as a type of God, while "the three days which were before the luminaries are types of the Trinity of God, and His Word, and His wisdom."[41] The land animals of the sixth day represent those who are not conscious of God but only of earthly things. But then Theophilos returns to a more natural explanation of the animal creation and a brief and literal treatment of the creation of human beings.[42] So even while Theophilos ventures into moral allegory, the creation days are taken seriously throughout as historical days in true sequence, with such literal ramifications as that plants were produced prior to heavenly bodies to demonstrate their independence from them.[43] This important early work of Christian apologetics sought to reinforce the reputation of the biblical creation account in the mind of a recipient/audience that respected contemporary Stoic accounts of the

[38] Smith, "Ages of the World," 1:130; Trompf, *Historical Recurrence*, 208. On the connection between belief in the world-week and early church millenarianism, see esp. Daniélou, *Jewish Christianity*, 390–404. For a late Eastern example, see E.A.W. Budge, ed., *The Book of the Cave of Treasures* (London: Religious Tract Society, 1927), 220–21.

[39] *Ad Autolycum* 2.12. This sort of comment begins to become very familiar indeed as one continues to read in this interpretive tradition. I have chosen to use the Greek spelling of this Greek author's name, following Louth, "Six Days of Creation," 40.

[40] *Ad Autolycum* 2.13.

[41] *Ad Autolycum* 2.15. This kind of allegory is known as tropology or moral interpretation. Robbins mentions both literal and moral aspects of the work: Robbins, *Hexaemeral Literature*, 36–39.

[42] *Ad Autolycum* 2.17–19.

[43] *Ad Autolycum* 2.15.

world's origin.[44] This work, along with a lost one of Hippolytus of Rome (c. 170–c. 236), represents an important source for the major hexaemeral works to come.[45]

Hippolytus' *Refutation of All Heresies* rebuts contemporary Gnostic ways of utilizing the days of creation. In their hyper-allegorical approach, the literal creation becomes as it were the smallest in a concentric set of semantic Russian dolls. Those who have 'eyes to see' may detect a series of greater meanings transcending the literal days, which come to signify material elements, powers, aspects of reason, levels in the metaphysical hierarchy, and events in the life of Christ.[46] According to Hippolytus, Simon Magus, the archetypal Gnostic, took the six days as six 'roots' (ῥίζα, *hriza*) or aspects of reason: mind/thought, speech/name, and reason/inspiration. The seventh day becomes the cosmic Christ, "the seventh power ... which came into being before all ages." These rational elements equate to the three created pairs of heaven and earth, sun and moon, air and water.[47] The six days or entities are elsewhere called powers (δύναμις, *dunamis*), so that they are not merely objects of creation but now agents in creation.

This seems agree with Irenaeus' description in *Against Heresies* of the beliefs of the Gnostic Ophites and Valentinians, where the 'Hebdomad' is again a brigade of heavenly powers rather than anything temporal.[48] Hippolytus attributes to Monoïmus the teaching, "The world, then, as Moses says, was made in six days, that is, by six powers," these powers themselves being inherent in the Seventh Power.[49] The enig-

[44] Kathleen McVey, "The Use of Stoic Cosmogony in Theophilus of Antioch's Hexaemeron," in *Biblical Hermeneutics in Historical Perspective: Studies in Honor of Karlfried Froehlich on His Sixtieth Birthday*, ed. M.S. Burrows and P. Rorem (Grand Rapids: Eerdmans, 1991), 58. The entire essay is vital for understanding the Stoic connections of Theophilos' treatment.

[45] Robbins, *Hexaemeral Literature*, 39; Eusebius of Caesarea, *The History of the Church from Christ to Constantine*, trans. G.A. Williamson (Harmondsworth: Penguin, 1965), 262 (*Ecclesiastical History* 6.22). See also Louth, "Six Days of Creation," 40–44; Bouteneff, *Beginnings*, 68–73.

[46] Hippolytus, *Refutatio omnium haeresium*, trans. Paul Wendland, Die griechischen christlichen Schriftsteller der ersten drei Jahrhunderte (Hildesheim: Georg Olms, 1977), 179; Hippolytus, *The Refutation of All Heresies ... with Fragments from his Commentaries on Various Books of Scripture*, trans. J.H. Macmahon and S.D.F. Salmond, Ante-Nicene Christian Library (Edinburgh: T.&T. Clark, 1878), 253 (*Refutatio omnium haeresium* 6.47).

[47] Catherine Osbourne, *Rethinking Early Greek Philosophy* (London: Duckworth, 1987), 238–41 (*Refutatio omnium haeresium* 6.13–14).

[48] Irenaeus, "Against Heresies," in 1:322, 355. Thomas Holsinger-Friesen, *Irenaeus and Genesis: A Study of Competition in Early Christian Hermeneutics*, Journal of Theological Interpretation Supplements (Winona Lake: Eisenbrauns, 2009), 58–59, 80–84, esp. n. 147.

[49] ἐν ἕξ ἡμέραις, τουτ᾽ ἐστιν ἐν ἕξ δυνάμεσιν, with a play on the preposition ἐν. Hippolytus, *Refutatio omnium haeresium*, 233, 279; Hippolytus, *The Refutation of All Heresies*, 319, 382 (*Refutatio omnium haeresium* 8.14.1–2, 10.17.3).

matic "three days before the sun and moon are created ... hint at mind and thought, that is, heaven and earth, and the seventh power, the unlimited one."[50] Oskar Skarsaune concludes on the basis of Hippolytus' report, "It is among Gnostic writers that allegorical exegesis of the six days of creation may have originated." Yet we ought not to underplay the contributions of Philo, *Jubilees* or *2 Enoch* to this development.[51]

Gnostic interpreters felt compelled in many cases to submit an interpretation of the early chapters of Genesis, implicitly acknowledging their authority,[52] while at the same time subverting their meaning by using them selectively and radically reframing their content. In keeping with their various degrees of derision for the material world, the step-by-step physical creation of Genesis 1 largely vanishes from view, as the chapter is effectively remythologized to speak cryptically of unseen orders of heavenly powers.

The Alexandrian School's Conceptual Creation Days

Christian scholars in Alexandria were the heirs of the large and ancient Jewish community in Alexandria. They were saturated in Hellenistic culture; they were astute by the philosophical standards of the Greco-Roman world, and had before them in Philo's work an example of a philosophically credible (that is, allegorical) handling of what might otherwise be regarded by the educated as a quaint Jewish fable, the creation week in Genesis. They were concerned to penetrate beneath the superficial 'veil' of the immediate language of the biblical text to access its true divine intent (σκοπός, *skopos*).[53] And their religiously and intellectually pluralistic environment brought them face to face with new permutations of Christianity that could force new debate over the meaning of Gen. 1:1–2:3.

It is perhaps an accident of history that leaves us with more commentary concerning creation from Clement of Alexandria (c. 150–215) than his teacher, Pantaenus, or his famous student Origen, whose commentary on Genesis was lost in anti-heretical purges of later years.[54] Second-century Alexandria was clearly a hotbed of Gnosticism, yet the Gnostic creation accounts of the Egyptian Nag Hammadi documents

[50] Osbourne, *Rethinking Early Greek Philosophy*, 240–41 (*Refutatio omnium haeresium* 6.14.2).

[51] Oskar Skarsaune, "The Development of Scriptural Interpretation in the Second and Third Centuries – except Clement and Origen," in *HB/OT*, vol. I, 1:416.

[52] Holsinger-Friesen, *Irenaeus and Genesis*, 43, 104.

[53] Frances Young, "Alexandrian and Antiochene Exegesis," in *A History of Biblical Interpretation*, ed. A.J. Hauser and D.F. Watson, 340.

[54] H.J. Vogt, "Origen," in *DECL*, 444–45.

On the Origin of the World and *Hypostasis of the Archons* as well as in Clement's *Excerpts from Theodotus* give little evidence of interest in the creation week of Genesis, in contrast with the numerological explorations seen in Hippolytus' *Refutations.*[55] It was nevertheless against a Gnostic background that Clement attempted to define a distinctively orthodox position on creation.[56]

In the *Miscellanies (Stromata),* Clement holds out the ideal state of *gnosis* (γνῶσις) as the Christian's goal.[57] In *Stromata* Book 4, Clement dabbles with a (meta)physical understanding wherein the days represent seven heavens which are separated from the 'Ogdoad' or the intelligible world (ὁ νοητὸς κόσμος, *ho noētos kosmos*) by the firmament.[58] Clement is cautious here, emphasizing that the ultimate meaning of the number seven in Scripture generally is that "the Gnostic ought to rise out of the sphere of creation and of sin."[59] In his treatment of the fourth commandment concerning the Sabbath day in *Stromata* Book 6, Clement points out that the number seven is fundamental in nature, with seven planets and seven days between phases of the moon, as well as conveniently breaking down the stages of human life.[60] So the sevenfold number of the creation days should be taken as a potent symbol, and not be mistaken for a historical descriptor. The process of creation is instantaneous for Clement as it was for Philo:

> For the creations on the different days followed in a most important succession; so that all things brought into existence might have honour from priority, created together in thought, but not being of equal worth. Nor was the creation of each signified by the voice, in as much as the creative work is said to have made them at once. For something must needs have been named first. Wherefore those things were announced first, from

[55] In *On the Origin of the World* the production of material creation is ancillary to the machinations of the demigod players. B. Layton, et al., *Nag Hammadi Codex II, 2–7...* 2 vols., The Coptic Gnostic Library/Nag Hammadi Studies (Leiden: Brill, 1982), 1:35, 53, 55, 57 (*On the Origin of the World* 14.42–44, 53–60).

[56] Everett Proctor, *Christian Controversy in Alexandria: Clement's Polemic against the Basilideans and Valentinians*, American University Studies. Series 7, Theology and Religion (New York: P. Lang, 1995), 1–4.

[57] Later fathers would avoid favourable use of the term.

[58] The numerological term Hebdomad (ἑβομάς) and its counterpart Ogdoad (ὀγδοάς), 'eight,' appear often in Hippolytus in association with Gnostic teaching: Hippolytus, *Refutatio omnium haeresium*, 161; Hippolytus, *The Refutation of All Heresies*, 233 (*Refutatio omnium haeresium* 6.32.8–9). See also the discussion on these terms in G.W.H. Lampe, *Patristic Greek Lexicon* (Oxford: Clarendon, 1961–68), 396, 934.

[59] Clement of Alexandria, "The Stromata," in *ANF* 2:438; Clement of Alexandria, *Stromata Buch I–VI*, trans. Otto Stählin, Die griechischen christlichen Schriftsteller der ersten Jahrhunderte (Berlin: Akademie-Verlag, 1985), 318–19 (*Stromata* 4.25.158–59).

[60] Clement of Alexandria, "The Stromata," 2:512–14; Clement of Alexandria, *Stromata Buch I–VI*, 501–06 (*Stromata* 6.16.137–45). The division of the human lifespan into periods of seven reappears in Augustine, *De Genesim contra Manichaeos*.

> which came those that were second, all things being originated together [ὁμοῦ, *homou*] from one essence by one power. For the will of God was one, in one identity. And how could creation take place in time, seeing time was born along with things which exist?[61]

As so often since, Gen. 2:4 provided the exegetical warrant for this instantaneous understanding of creation: "That … we may be taught that the world was originated, and not suppose that God made it in time, prophecy adds: 'This is the book of the generation: also of the things in them, when they were created in the day that God made heaven and earth.' For the expression 'when they were created' intimates an indefinite and dateless production."[62] Thus Clement, like Philo, found it prudent or natural in his Alexandrian intellectual setting to detach his theology of creation from the temporal framework in Gen. 1:1–2:3.[63] To have God creating over the span of a literal week would be metaphysically inconceivable, since time itself is being created along with the rest, and theologically difficult, as if God was unable to work more quickly.[64]

Origen (c. 184–c. 254) was one of the most notable scholars of the patristic church. Many of his works were lost in later purges, but his surviving work on Genesis that was not purely moral in its concerns is

[61] Clement of Alexandria, "The Stromata," 2:513 (*Stromata* 6.16.142.2–4). See Manlio Simonetti, *Biblical Interpretation in the Early Church: An Historical Introduction to Patristic Exegesis*, trans. J.A. Hughes (Edinburgh: T.&T. Clark, 1994), 65–66.

[62] Clement of Alexandria, "The Stromata," 2:514 (*Stromata* 6.16.145.4–5). For the reader's clarity, it is necessary to reproduce Gen. 2:4–7 in a modern version (NRSV):

> These are the generations of the heavens and the earth when they were created. In the day that the LORD God made the earth and the heavens, when no plant of the field was yet in the earth and no herb of the field had yet sprung up – for the LORD God had not caused it to rain upon the earth, and there was no one to till the ground; but a stream would rise from the earth, and water the whole face of the ground – then the LORD God formed man from the dust of the ground, and breathed into his nostrils the breath of life...

The punctuation is different from that of the text used by Clement and his contemporaries. Their instantaneous creation interpretation relied on running the clauses in v. 4 and v. 5a together to read something like, "These are the generations of the heavens and the earth when they were created, in the day that the LORD God made the earth and the heavens and every plant of the field before it had arisen on the earth ..." The LXX leans toward such a reading.

[63] However, the following passage, Gen. 2:4–3:24, pictures God in more obviously anthropomorphic terms.

[64] There is a statement in Clement's *Eclogae propheticae* that equates the days of Genesis 1 with angels, but it is not clear whether this is Clement's own position or that of a Gnostic opponent: Clement of Alexandria, "Eclogae ex Scripturis propheticis," in *PG* 9:725, line 715; Clement of Alexandria, "The Stromata," 2:514.

consistent with Clement's.[65] His apologetic work *Against Celsus* reveals that to him too it was unacceptable that God should have required six days to complete his creative work. It would be much like taking God's planting of the garden in Gen. 2:8 as a literal, physical act. Origen cites Ps. 32:9; 148:5 and Gen. 2:4 as evidence that creation was instantaneous, dismissing Celsus' mockery of the six-day creation and God's seventh-day rest as simplistic in its literalism.[66]

Origen's thrust in *On First Principles* Book 4 indicates the direction that his fuller exposition of the meaning of these 'days' might have taken. In this hermeneutical treatise he presents the three levels of meaning on which Scripture operates, and champions the goal of transcending the literal sense to contemplate God by means of the more spiritual senses. He goes so far as to scorn the historical and logical incongruities in the literal sense, holding that God placed them in the text to drive the reader towards a spiritual or figurative interpretation. Genesis 1:1–2:3 represents one of his prime examples: "Now what man of intelligence will believe that the first and the second and the third day, and the evening and the morning existed without the sun and moon and stars? And that the first day, if we may so call it, was even without a heaven?" Thus Origen essentially endorses Celsus' objection to the account as literally understood.[67] He concludes, "These are figurative expressions which indicate certain mysteries through a semblance of history and not through actual events."[68] Yet his belief that the world was "not yet ten thousand years old" reminds us that he makes no use of figurative creation days to represent long periods, nor had any sense of earth's having existed for immense ages.[69]

The discovery of the Tura Papyri in Egypt in 1941 has made Didymus the Blind's (c. 313–398) commentary on Genesis available to us. His exegesis is substantially Origenist, although Didymus does not mention Origen's name, and balances literal (πρὸς τὸ ῥητον, *pros to hrēton*) and allegorical (πρὸς τὴν διάνοιαν or πρὸς ἀναγωγήν, *pros to*

[65] His *Homilies on Genesis* range through the early chapters of Genesis largely by means of moral allegory, without close reflection on the meaning of the creation days: Origen, *Homilies on Genesis and Exodus*, trans. R.E. Heine, Fathers of the Church, a New Translation (Washington, DC: Catholic University of America Press, 1981).

[66] Origen, *Contra Celsum*, trans. H. Chadwick (Cambridge: Cambridge University Press, 1953), 367, 375–76 (Origen, *Contra Celsum* 6.50, 60); Origen, "Fragmenta in Genesim," in *PG* 12:97. Ps. 33:6–9 (LXX 32:6–9) says (NRSV): "By the word of the LORD the heavens were made, and all their host by the breath of his mouth ... For he spoke, and it came to be; he commanded, and it stood firm. " Ps. 148:5 simply says, "for he commanded and they were created. "

[67] *Contra Celsum* 6.60.

[68] Origen, *On First Principles*, ed. P. Koetschau, trans. G.W. Butterworth (Gloucester, MA: Smith, 1973), 288 (*De Principiis* 4.3).

[69] *Contra Celsum* 1.19.

dianoian or *pros anagōgē*) exposition of the text.[70] For Didymus too, the fact that three days of creation preceded the creation of the sun, along with 'the [single] day' of Gen. 2:4, were sure signs that the days of creation were never intended to be taken literally.[71] Where opponents point to the three days preceding the sun as a contradiction, Didymus directs them toward the allegorical sense; but if this should seem inadequate, he provides the reader with a defence of the literal understanding of the days, since sun and moon are not constitutive (ποιητικός, *poiētikos*), but only indicative (σημαντικός, *sēmantikos*), of the days.[72]

Yet Didymus cannot really see the work of God taking any time at all, for God functions outside of time. "We must not think of the six days as intended to be understood as a temporal duration, but as an apt way to describe the creative action of God and the power of the number."[73] The number six is most appropriate since it is the first of the perfect numbers (numbers that equal the sum of their factors). He continues, "By no means then let us say that with six revolutions of the sun six days passed – for the sun was not yet in existence in the first three days, but that concerning reason and pleasing harmony the number six has been taken."[74] In response to the potential challenge that, if the six days had merely symbolic value, our text might as easily read six hours, six months or six years, Didymus defends six days as short enough not to strongly imply the passage of time and long enough to appease the more simple-minded. Didymus clearly falls within the Alexandrian stream of thinking and presents a tempered later version of the exegesis of Clement and Origen.[75]

The famous Alexandrian theologian Athanasius (c. 297–373) also evinces a rather timeless concept of the creation process in two fleeting references in his *Orations against the Arians*. In the first, he indicates no more than that the productions are instantaneous *within* each of the six days. Yet his statement in the later section, "that no one creature was made before another, but all things originate subsisted at once together upon one and the same command," seems comprehensive. Athanasius'

[70] B. Neuschäfer, "Didymus the Blind," trans. M. O'Connell, in *DECL*, 174; Didymus the Blind, *Sur la Genèse*, trans. P. Nautin, 2 vols., Sources chrétiennes (Paris: Les Éditions du Cerf, 1976), 1:24, 74, 100.

[71] Ibid., 1:68–71, 94–95.

[72] Ibid., 1:68–71.

[73] [πε]ρὶ τῶν ἕξ ἡμερῶν δεῖ νοεῖν ὡς οὐ χρονικῆς ἕνεκα παρ[εκτάσε] ως παρειλημμένων ἀλλὰ λόγου οἰκείου τῇ δημιουργίᾳ το[ῦ θεοῦ] καὶ τῆς τοῦ ἀριθμοῦ δυνάμεως. Ibid., 1:92, and see 90–93.

[74] οὐχ ἵνα πάντως εἴπωμεν ὅτι ἐξάκις τοῦ ἡλίου κυκλεύοντος ἡμέραι ἓξ διεγένοντο, – οὔπω γὰρ ἦν γενόμενος ἥλιος ἐν ταῖς πρώταις τρισίν, – ἀλλ᾽ ὅτι λόγου καὶ ἁρμονίας χάριν ὁ ἕξ ἀριθμὸς παρειλήμφθη. Ibid., 1:92, 94.

[75] B. Neuschäfer points out that Didymus had moved in a much more orthodox direction christologically. Neuschäfer, "Didymus the Blind," 174.

main concern in this work is to affirm Christ as uncreated, against Arian teaching.[76] Such christological concerns were capable of entirely suppressing ordinary historical consideration of the creation days in patristic interpretation.[77]

Thus when Alexandrian Christian thinkers approached the account of the creation week, they sought metaphysical insights, theological signals, or prompts for piety; they did not perceive an unfolding series of physical creation events over earthly time. The Cappadocians, although admirers of Origen, would have a much more realist perspective on the creation week.

The Cappadocian Fathers' Literal and Philosophical Creation Days

The Cappadocian fathers, Basil of Caesarea, his younger brother Gregory of Nyssa, and Gregory Nazianzus, are credited with chief responsibility for engineering the victory of Nicene or Athanasian Christology over Arianism at the Council of Constantinople (381), after a vigorous century-long contest.[78] Concerning biblical exegesis, these three thinkers sympathized with Origen's quest to ascend from the literal biblical text to higher and more spiritual meanings. Yet Origen's influence is muted in the case of their writings on the creation week.[79]

It was perhaps within the last twelve months of his life that Basil (c. 330–379) preached his set of nine homilies on the Hexaemeron within a single week, and thus became author of the first Christian work exclusively concerned with the Hexaemeron. In his preaching Basil seeks to foster an understanding of creation that would lead to contemplation of God and to upright moral conduct. "By the sight of visible and sensible things the mind is led, as by a hand, to the contemplation of invisible things."[80] Yet despite this Basil makes only limited allegorical

[76] Athanasius, "Against the Arians (Orationes contra Arianos IV.)," in *NPNF*² 4:374–75, 381; Athanasius, "Orationes tres contra arianos," in *PG* 26:249, 252, 276 (*Orationes contra Arianos* 2.48–49, 60).

[77] E.g. Cyril of Alexandria, "Glaphyra," in *PG* 69:13, 16–17 (*Glaphyra in Genesim* 1.1–2).

[78] Geoffrey W. Bromiley, *Historical Theology: An Introduction* (Grand Rapids: Eerdmans, 1978), 138.

[79] For a thoughtful treatment of the creation works of Basil and the two Gregorys in light of their influence by Origen, a treatment that accounts for the apparent parting of the ways at this point, see J.F. Procopé, "The Christian Exegesis of the Old Testament in the Alexandrian Tradition," in *HB/OT*, vol. I, 1:538–40.

[80] Basil of Caesarea, "Hexaemeron," trans. Blomfield, in *NPNF*² 8:55 (*Hexaemeron* 1.6). The translation, "visible and sensible things," represents τῶν ὁρωμένων καὶ αἰσθητῶν, while "the contemplation of invisible things" represents τὴν θεωρίαντῶν ἀοράτων. See Basil of Caesarea, *Homélies sur l'Hexaemeron*, trans. Stanislas Giet, 2nd ed., Sources chrétiennes (Paris: Éditions du Cerf, 1968), 91, 103, 112. 'Theoria' is an im-

application of the creation account in Gen. 1:1–2:3, such as the illustrative use of plant and animal qualities to deliver moral lessons. Basil is deliberately literal and systematically exegetical in the work, claiming to understand the laws of allegory but instead opting to take all in the literal sense and "as it has been written."[81] He shows a clear interest in the constitution of the natural world, whose features are worthy of study and a motivation to praise: "Let us glorify the supreme Artificer for all that was wisely and skillfully made; by the beauty of visible things let us raise ourselves to Him who is above all beauty ..."[82]

While Basil never analyses the meaning of the days themselves, he takes them literally and assumes a progression between the works of different days. While the existence of days before the sun was an intolerable obstacle to a literal interpretation for Origen, Basil is untroubled:

> Since the birth of the sun, the light that it diffuses in the air, when shining on our hemisphere, is day; and the shadow produced by its disappearance is night. But at that time it was not after the movement of the sun, but following this primitive light spread abroad in the air or withdrawn in a measure determined by God, that day came and was followed by night.[83]

Later he adds, "Then [on Day 1] the actual nature of light was produced: now the sun's body is constructed to be a vehicle for that original light."[84] And the earth dried without the help of the sun on Day 3.[85] The philosophical distinction between essence and form made the light and what we would see as its source quite separable in Basil's mind. And time does not precede the moment of creation but is firmly in place from that moment on in his view, so that the creation process is clearly temporal.[86] Letham attributes a claim of instantaneous creation to Basil, perhaps recalling Basil's statement, "[I]f it is said, 'In the beginning God created,' it is to teach us that at the will of God the world arose in less than an instant, and it is to convey this meaning more clearly that other interpreters have said: 'God made summarily,' that is

portant concept for both Alexandrian and Cappadocian Fathers: Lampe, *Patristic Greek Lexicon*, 648–49.

[81] Basil of Caesarea, "Hexaemeron," 8:102; Basil of Caesarea, *Homélies sur l'Hexaemeron*, 480–82 (*Hexaemeron* 9.1). See also *Hexaemeron* 3.9.

[82] Basil of Caesarea, "Hexaemeron," 8:58; Basil of Caesarea, *Homélies sur l'Hexaemeron*, 134 (*Hexaemeron* 1.11). This restraint and return to worship do, however, follow paragraphs of content about the four elements, earth, water, air and fire, a possible fifth element pertaining to the celestial sphere, about the foundation of the earth and its possible position at the centre of the universe, and so forth.

[83] Basil of Caesarea, "Hexaemeron," 8:64 (*Hexaemeron* 2.8).

[84] Ibid., 8:83 (*Hexaemeron* 6.2).

[85] Ibid., 8:74 (*Hexaemeron* 4.5).

[86] Ibid., 8:55 (*Hexaemeron* 1.6).

to say all at once and in a moment."[87] But Mangenot correctly explains that it is "the elements of matter" that are thus simultaneously created, and then are organized "during the six cosmogonic days" which "are of twenty-four hours."[88] Basil therefore takes Gen. 1:1 as describing an initial, instantaneous creation event producing a basic heaven and earth to which detail is added in the course of six literal days.

Basil's brother Gregory (c. 335–c. 394) sought to continue and extend Basil's work after Basil's death. His *On the Making of Humanity* (*De hominis opificio*) made up Basil's omission of the creation of man, while his *On the Hexaemeron* defended Basil's interpretive stance in the abovementioned homilies.[89] There Gregory reminds critics of Basil's rather literal treatment of Gen. 1:1–2:3 of the limitations of Basil's popular audience, and sets out to provide a more philosophically sophisticated presentation of Moses' cosmogony that remains consistent with Basil's interpretation.[90] Gregory never explicitly denies the literal nature of the days of creation, but his Platonic view de-emphasizes their chronological aspect in favour of their ontological significance.[91] The "principles of things" are created instantaneously, and from them material forms develop according to the laws imposed by the Creator.[92] He answers the familiar objection to three days predating the creation of the luminaries by explaining that the first element to be created, fire, did the illuminating work and created by its orbiting motion the time intervals (τὰ χρονικὰ διστήματα, *ta chronika diastēmata*) of day and

[87] Letham, "Space of Six Days," 153; Basil of Caesarea, "Hexaemeron," 8:55 (*Hexaemeron* 1.6). Giet points out that Basil draws on the reading of Aquila in Origen's *Hexapla*, where Gen. 1:1 begins, Ἐν κεφαλαίῳ ἐποίησεν ὁ θεός: Basil of Caesarea, *Homelies sur l'Hexaemeron*, 112–13.

[88] "Il accepte la création simultanée des éléments de matière et son organisation durant les six jours cosmogoniques. " Mangenot, "Hexaméron," 6:2336.

[89] F. Dünzl, "Gregory of Nyssa," trans. M. O'Connell, in *DECL*, 263–65; Gregory of Nyssa, "Explicatio apologetica in Hexaemeron," in *PG* 44:61–124. There is now an English translation available at the website, http://www.sage.edu/faculty/salomd/nyssa/hex.html. It is attributed by Peter Bouteneff to Casimir McCambley: Bouteneff, *Beginnings*, 205.

[90] Gregory of Nyssa, "In Hexaemeron," 44:65A; Jaki, *Genesis 1*, 75.

[91] Gregory of Nyssa, "In Hexaemeron," 44:72C. 'Ontological' refers to things as timeless realities and may be contrasted with 'chronological', 'historical' or 'temporal'. Gregory's evident attraction to the higher truths hidden under the guise of the literal language of the creation account may betray Origen's influence, although scholars commonly regard Origenist influence as quite mitigated in this work: Gregory of Nyssa, "In Hexaemeron," 44:113B; Dünzl, "Gregory of Nyssa," 266; J. Quasten, *Patrology: The Golden Age of Greek Patristic Literature*, 4 vols. (Westminster: Spectrum, 1960), 3:264; Procopé, "Alexandrian Tradition," 541; Bertrand de Margerie, *An Introduction to the History of Exegesis. I: The Greek Fathers* (Petersham: Saint Bede's, 1993), 236.

[92] Mangenot, "Hexaméron," 6:2337; Jean Rousselet, "Grégoire de Nysse, avocat de ... Moïse," in *In Principio: Interprétations des premiers versets de la Genèse*, ed. Paul Vignaux (Paris: Études Augustiniennes, 1973), 101.

night until the luminaries had condensed from that dispersed substance.[93] This lends an aspect of historical reality to Gregory's otherwise rather noetic days, as Rousselet observes:

> By making of time an image of the timeless dialectic of God,...Gregory manages to justify *to the letter* (or 'literally') the cosmogony according to Moses, to justify *the days* as successive stages of the manifestation and ordering of the elements, stages on whose duration he does not give a verdict, but which are determined from the first by the circular movement of the fire.[94]

Yet the logical order of the creation days takes priority over the chronological, and the sequence (ἀκολουθία, *akolouthia*) of the days and their created contents is critical; the material parts of creation had to unfold in the given order by the very requirements of their nature, as in the case of the natural priority of fire.[95] Scripture itself reveals the divinely ordained and necessary *akolouthia* in the Mosaic account of these realities. There are two worlds, the 'noetic' or intelligible world, and the 'aesthetic' or sense-perceptible world, and Moses' account deals with the latter.[96] The creation days do have time-elapsing (διαστηματικος, *diastēmatikos*) reality in the 'aesthetic', material world, but ultimately reflect the logical order of creative works that occur in a momentary 'beginning' in the ideal realm.[97]

Gregory thus approached the instantaneous creation position we will later see in Augustine. While it is in a sense a literal interpretation rather than an allegorical one, its perspective is heavily metaphysical. In seeing creation as above all a timeless, conceptual structure in the mind of God and in his use of the Stoic concept of 'seminal principles' (in terms such as σπερματικῆς τινος δυνάμεως) to connect the instantaneous creation of everything with its unfolding through time,[98] Gregory

[93] Gregory of Nyssa, "In Hexaemeron," 44:64C, 76D–77B, 120A–B; Rousselet, "Grégoire de Nysse," 104. The Greek phrase cited occurs at 77B.

[94] Rousselet, "Grégoire de Nysse," 105. The emphasis is his. By 'noetic' I mean something that occurs in the mind, a mental construct or concept.

[95] Mangenot says, "[I]l expliqua la distinction des jours par la nécessité où Moïse était de mettre de l'ordre dans son récit" ([Gregory] explained the distinction of the days by Moses' need to set his story in order). Mangenot, "Hexaméron," 6:2337. The term ἀκολουθία, a typically Antiochene one, is abundant in the work: see for example Gregory of Nyssa, "In Hexaemeron," 44:68C, 81C, 85B–C, 116A, 118C. On this term's importance, see Frances Young, "Alexandrian and Antiochene Exegesis," 344. Another important 'sequence' term in the work, εἱρμός, may denote the chain of cause and effect in the Stoic sense: Lampe, *Patristic Greek Lexicon*, 421.

[96] Gregory of Nyssa, "In Hexaemeron," 44:76D.

[97] Ibid., 44:72A–B. This is a very important section of the work for grasping Gregory's thought.

[98] Gregory of Nyssa, "In Hexaemeron," 44:77D; van Winden, "Hexaemeron," 14:1262–63.

anticipated important later concepts of Augustine. Along with Basil, he helped to pave the way for the distinction of the initial creation of matter, pregnant with potential forms, and the differentiation and adornment of creation across the creation week, a scheme that would become typical of medieval theology.[99]

The third member of the Cappadocian trio, Gregory of Nazianzus (329–389), never treated the creation week in the same detail as the other two men, but shared with the other Gregory a dualistic view of creation wherein the angelic/intellectual creation precedes the earthly and material and the human Fall presumes an earlier fall of Lucifer. He seemed somewhat ambivalent regarding the reality of the days of Gen. 1:1–2:3: "So one thing is numbered first in the list of days, another second and third and so on, until we reach the seventh day, which brings work to an end. The events of creation are divided up by these days, ordered in accord with God's ineffable reasons, and not attributed all at once to the omnipotent Word, to whom merely thinking or speaking is a work completed." Like Gregory of Nyssa, while sympathetic to instantaneous creation, he apparently allows here a real sequence of chronological days to stand, though he perhaps finds it puzzling.[100]

The Antiochene and Syrian Traditions

The city of Antioch was a leading centre in the Roman world and quickly became an important centre for the newly planted Christian church.[101] We have already encountered the early figure Theophilos of Antioch, but the recognized 'school' of Antiochene biblical exegesis belongs to the late fourth and fifth centuries. This school of Christian exegetes centred in the Syrian region emphasized a literal approach to the Scriptures, attention to historical process and the narrative integrity

[99] Clemens Scholten however regards Gregory's work as akin to Origen's non-literal stance: Clemens Scholten, "Weshalb wird die Schöpfungsgeschichte zum naturwissenschaftlichen Bericht: Hexaemeronauslegung von Basilius von Cäsarea zu Johannes Philoponos," *Theologische Quartalschrift* 177.1 (1997): 2. A critical edition of Gregory's *Hexaemeron* has recently become available: Drobner, Hubertus R., ed. *Opera Exegetica in Genesim*, vol. I: *Gregorii Nysseni in Hexaemeron*, Gregrorii Nysseni Opera (Leiden: Brill, 2009).

[100] See his *Orations* 38.9–10, 44.3–4: B.E. Daley, ed., *Gregory of Nazianzus*, Early Christian Fathers (London: Routledge, 2006), 121, 156–57; Gregory of Nazianzus, "Orationes 38, 44," in *PG* 36:320–21, 609–12. See also pp. 415–23 of 'Peri Kosmon', the fourth poem in Gregory of Nazianzus, "Carmina dogmatica," in *PG* 37:397–522. This is translated in Gregory of Nazianzus, *On God and Man: The Theological Poetry of St. Gregory of Nazianzus*, ed. P. Gilbert, Popular Patristics (Crestwood, NY: St. Vladimir's Seminary Press, 2001), 48–52, http://books.google.com/books?id= 2ngq3Bd_YuMC.

[101] Acts 11:19–26; 13:1–2; 14:26–15:1, etc.

of the OT, guarded use of typology, and an ongoing battle against the perceived excesses of Alexandrian-style allegory.[102] Bringing a well-developed classical rhetorical perspective to the biblical text, they were particularly concerned by key aspects of Alexandrian interpretation:

> ... the allegorization of the narratives of creation, Paradise, the Fall, the Gospel stories, the resurrection of the body and the kingdom of God. This reveals an anxiety for the overarching story of the Rule of Faith – for what we might call "salvation history," and especially for the narratives that provided the beginning and ending of the biblical story.[103]

Despite the subsequent loss or destruction of the majority of their exegetical works, their surviving Genesis commentary sounds a steady note: creation across a series of ordinary days represents God's orderly creative method.[104] The hexaemeral narrative not only reflects an order in the mind of God but is taken seriously as a successive historical sequence. I believe that the influence of this interpretive school helped to temper the purely allegorical approach to the creation days of the earlier Alexandrians, a moderation apparent in the case of Didymus and the Cappadocians.

[102] Its pioneers included Eustathius of Antioch (c. 300–377), Diodore of Tarsus (d. < AD 394) and Eusebius of Emesa (c. 300–<359): see, respectively, Hauser and Watson, *Biblical Interpretation*, 47; T. Fuhrer, "Diodorus of Tarsus," in *DECL*, 175; R.B. ter Haar Romeny, "Eusebius of Emesa's Commentary on Genesis and the Origins of the Antiochene School," in *The Book of Genesis in Jewish and Oriental Christian Interpretation: A Collection of Essays*, ed. J. Frishman and L. van Rompay (Louvain: Peeters, 1997), 127–28; Lucas van Rompay, "Antiochene Biblical Interpretation: Greek and Syriac," in *The Book of Genesis in Jewish and Oriental Christian Interpretation: A Collection of Essays*, ed. J. Frishman and L. van Rompay, 109–10. For a good overview, including the relationship of Theophilos of Antioch to this school, see Sten Hidal, "Exegesis of the Old Testament in the Antiochene School with its Prevalent Literal and Historical Method," in *HB/OT*, vol. I, 1:543–68. Note esp. p. 544.

[103] Young, "Alexandrian and Antiochene Exegesis," 346; Hauser and Watson, *Biblical Interpretation*, 46.

[104] Barely any exegetical work on Genesis 1–3 has survived from Eustathius of Antioch, while a hexaemeron transmitted under his name is widely agreed to be inauthentic, and heavily dependent on Basil's *Hexaemeron*. (On the days of creation, cf. Pseudo-Eustathius, "Commentarius in Hexameron," in *PG* 18:712A–B, 712C, 717B with Basil of Caesarea, *Homélies sur l'Hexaemeron*, 196, 224, 254, 334–36 [*Hexaemeron* 3.3, 7; 4.3; 6.2–3].) J.H. Declerck, ed., *Eustathii Antiocheni, patris Nicaeni, opera quae supersunt omnia*, Corpus christianorum series Graeca (Turnhout: Brepols, 2002), 106–08; R. Devréesse, *Les anciens commentateurs grecs de l'Octateuque et des Rois*, Studi e Testi (Vatican City: 1959), 55; T. Fuhrer, "Eustathius of Antioch," in *DECL*, 220; Mangenot, "Hexaméron," 6:2337. Eusebius of Emesa's *Commentary on the Octateuch* survives in a recently identified Armenian manuscript: Eusebius of Emesa, *Eusèbe d'Émèse 1. Commentaire de l'Octateuque*, ed. V. Hovhannessian (Venice: 1980); Romeny, "Eusebius of Emesa's Commentary on Genesis," 127–28, 131. On Eusebius' reportedly literal approach to the Hexaemeron, see Robbins, *Hexaemeral Literature*, 97.

Acacius of Caesarea (d. 365) displays this Antiochene concern for both logical and chronological sequence in creation.[105] Creation was not instantaneous. "The things that came into existence on the sixth day did not yet exist on the fifth, nor the things of the fifth day on the fourth, nor the things of the fourth day on the third, nor the things of the third day on the second, nor the things of the second day on the first, nor the things on the first day before God began..."[106] The more technical *On the Creation of the World* of Severian of Gabala (d. c. 408) displays the same Antiochene sense of an orderly progression (ἀκολουθία) in creation:

> Come then, let us grasp the progression. For it is fitting, I think, that just as the lawgiver Moses himself comprehensively completed the account of creation in orderly sequence, we should make the connection between second things and first, and third things and second, and thus be approved, and [judged] to have passed on the explanation in an unconfused manner.... So first he made the upper heaven, second the earth, third the firmament, fourth he set the waters apart. That which he created first he adorned first.[107]

Likewise Theodore of Mopsuestia (c. 350–428), in the few surviving fragments concerning Genesis 1–3, also displays this consciousness of the six days as a chronological progression.[108] God "was on the first, and the second, and the third, and the fourth, and the fifth, and the sixth [day] always making something new, which he considered creation to lack."[109] Theodore limits the concept of instantaneous creation strictly to the 'heaven' and 'earth' of Gen. 1:1, which I take as equivalent to Basil's position that Gen. 1:1 teaches the instant initial creation of heaven, earth and the elements inevitably comprised therein, while

[105] G. Rowecamp, "Acacius of Caesarea," trans. M. O'Connell, in *DECL,* 4; Devréesse, *Les anciens commentateurs*, 105–06.

[106] Devréesse, *Les anciens commentateurs*, 107–08. My phrase 'systematically or methodically' represents the Greek, τάξει καὶ ὁδῷ.

[107] Severian of Gabala, "In mundi creationem," in *PG* 56:457–58. The words 'progression' and 'sequence' in this quotation both translate the important term ἀκολουθία. My translation may now be compared with the recent translation by Robert Hill: Severian of Gabala, "Homilies on Creation and Fall," in *Commentaries on Genesis 1–3*, ed. Robert C. Hill and Michael Glerup, *Ancient Christian Texts* (Downers Grove: InterVarsity, 2010), 48–49. On Severian, see P. Bruns, "Severian of Gabala," trans. M. O'Connell, in *DECL,* 531.

[108] I have worked from three text fragments, found in F. Petit, *Catenae Graecae in Genesim et in Exodum. I. Collectio Coisliniana in Genesim*, Corpus christianorum, series graeca (Turnhout: Brepols, 1986), 80–81; Theodore of Mopsuestia, "Fragmenta alia in Genesin," in *PG* 66:636; E. Sachau, *Theodori Mopsuesteni fragmenta Syriaca* (Lipsiae [Leipzig]: sumptibus Guilelmi Engelmann, 1869), 18–19.

[109] Petit, *Collectio Coisliniana*, 80; Theodore of Mopsuestia, "Fragmenta alia in Genesin," 66:636C.

these initial materials and spheres are given their detail, embellishments and occupants across the course of six natural days.[110]

The Antiochenes offer various justifications for a real six-day sequence. One kind of justification worked along physical lines, such as Theodoret of Cyrrhus' (393–466) explanation that the luminaries were created before animal life as a mitigation strategy, because the unapportioned light created on Day 1 would have overwhelmed creatures with organs of vision.[111] A more theological reason was that a step-by-step (κατὰ μέρος, *kata meros*) and orderly (ἐν τάξει, *en taxei*) creative method allowed God to better reveal himself to rational beings.[112] John Chrysostom (347–407) utilizes the same reasoning, and so anticipates Calvin's idea that God accommodates not the description of creation but his own creative activity to human capacity:

> It was … out of his loving kindness and goodness that he created everything; accordingly he created things in sequence [κατὰ μέρος] and provided us with a clear instruction about created things through the tongue of the blessed author, so that we might learn about them precisely and not fall into the error of those led by purely human reasoning.[113]

Some Antiochene commentators observe that the establishment of the day, along with the creation of plants, precedes that of the heavenly bodies in order to underline the fact that neither depends on the sun for its existence, but must be credited to the power of God.[114] That three (historical) days passed before the sun's creation is therefore something to boast about, rather than a cause for shame.[115] The Antiochene commentators therefore firmly retain the temporal factor in their concept of sequence (ἀκολουθία) and order (τάξις) in the creation week. Temporality is for them an essential element of the order of the universe once formed, yielding truly historical creation days.

Another group of writings on Genesis survives from leading Christian figures who lived east of Antioch, on the fringes of the Roman Empire, in the region now covered by Syria and upper Iraq. Roman control of these regions was partial and fluctuating, and their Christian

[110] Sachau, *Theodori Mopsuesteni fragmenta Syriaca*, 18; Mangenot, "Hexaméron," 6:2336.

[111] Theodoret of Cyrrhus, "Quaestiones in Octateuchum," in *PG* 80:96D (*Quaest. in Gen.* 16).

[112] This was the explanation of Gennadius I of Constantinople (c. 400–471): Gennadius, "In Genesin Fragmenta," in *PG* 85:1628C.

[113] John Chrysostom, *Homilies on Genesis 1–17*, trans. R.C. Hill, Fathers of the Church, a New Translation (Washington, DC: Catholic University of America Press, 1985), 44–45; John Chrysostom, "In Genesim (homiliae 1–67)," in *PG* 53:36, ll. 50–55.

[114] Severian of Gabala, "In mundi creationem," 56:433–34, 447, 449.

[115] Chrysostom, *Homilies*, 85; Chrysostom, "In Genesim (homiliae 1–67)," 58, l. 62ff. (Homily 6).

populations were further isolated by rejection for reasons of perceived christological aberration, either through Monophysitism, seen to too greatly meld the human and divine natures of Christ, or through Nestorianism, which was believed to separate the two natures too emphatically. Though ostracised, the works of this Syrian interpretive tradition, written in Syriac, are now being rediscovered and freshly appreciated beyond Eastern Christian communities.[116]

This indigenous Near Eastern line of Christian thought displays a commitment to the literal sense of the creation account related to that manifested at Antioch. The leading early Syrian exegete of Genesis is Ephraem (d. 373), who was the great beacon of Syrian biblical interpretation until the influence of Theodore of Mopsuestia swept through in the fifth century.[117] Ephraem adheres carefully to the literal sense in his commentary on Genesis: "So let no one think that there is anything allegorical in the works of the six days. No one can rightly say that the things that pertain to these days were symbolic."[118] He precludes not only any allegorization of the creation days but also an instantaneous creation – "that things that were made through [several] days were made in the blink of an eye."[119] Ephraem preserves the literal, concrete sequence of the creation days and naturally integrates the biblical account of creation with what was regarded as common knowledge about the physical world.[120]

Much Syrian Genesis commentary took the form of song; these Christians seem more naturally theological poets than biblical commentators. In Ephraim's *Hymn de Nativitate* 19, the seven days of creation (plus an eighth and even a tenth day!) combine to praise the Saviour in terms of their own christological symbolism or typology.[121] *Hymn de Fide* 6.13 calls the six days of creation to witness the central

[116] J. Frishman and L. van Rompay, eds., *Book of Genesis in Jewish and Oriental Christian Interpretation: A Collection of Essays* (Louvain: Peeters, 1997); Lucas van Rompay, "The Christian Syriac Tradition of Interpretation," in *HB/OT,* vol. I, 1:612–41; Van Winden, 'Hexaemeron', 1264–66; Zöckler, *Geschichte,* 1:170–75.

[117] Van Rompay, "Christian Syriac Tradition," 622; van Winden, "Hexaemeron," 14:1265.

[118] Ephraem Syrus, *Selected Prose Works*, ed. K.E. McVey, trans. E.G. Mathews and J.P. Amar, 91, Fathers of the Church, 91, a New Translation (Washington, DC: Catholic University of America Press, 1994), 74 (*Comm. in Gen.* 1.1).

[119] "neque fas est dicere in ictu (oculi) facta esse ea quae per dies facta sunt." R.M. Tonneau, *Sancti Ephraem Syri in Genesim et in Exodum Commentarii*, Corpus scriptorum Christianorum orientalium (Louvain: Peeters, 1955), 5.

[120] For instance, he explains in realistic terms why the luminaries must be created at dawn on Day 4: Ephraem Syrus, *Selected Prose Works*, 90–91 (*Comm. in Gen.*1.23–24).

[121] Ephraem Syrus, "Hymns on the Nativity," trans. J.B. Morris and A.E. Johnston, in *NPNF*^{2} 13. Edmund Beck lists this hymn as hymn 26 in his German translation: Ephraem Syrus, *Hymnen de nativitate (Epiphania)*, ed. Edmund Beck, Corpus scriptorum Christianorum orientalium (Louvain: Secretariat du Corpus SCO, 1959), 121–24.

role of the Son in creation, while in *Hymn de Virginitate* 51.1.1–4, days Two through Seven bring honour to the first day as a symbol of Christ, and the three days' service of primeval light typifies the three years of Christ's ministry.[122] In this material, then, the days of creation both symbolize Christ and join the hearers/singers of these hymns in rendering him praise, a use of the days in which rational or philosophical concerns move to the background. The same kind of christological typology of the creation days occurs in the poetic *Hexaemeron* of Jacob of Sarug (c. 449–521), who perceives a type of the resurrection in the appearance of the land from under the primordial waters, or the appearance of life in the sea.[123]

Yet the underlying picture of the creation week even in the Syrians' poetic works is consistently literal and temporal.[124] Narsai of Nisibis (399–502), who transmitted the heritage of Theodore of Mopsuestia to the later Nestorian (East Syrian) church, focuses on creation in his poetic homilies, where he too understands the six days literally: "[T]o instruct them [God] prolonged his work for six days. He could have created everything in a moment, but then his works would not have learned the power of his greatness."[125] Jacob of Sarug confesses that God indeed could have created the world instantly, but limited his work according to the world's ability to receive it:

> Not according to his ability did he create the creatures, when he created,
> But as they were capable of receiving existence,
> So that the works which came into being might give way to each other...
> And because of this [are] the first day and the second day,
> And the third, and fourth and fifth
> And the sixth day...[126]

[122] T. Kronholm, *Motifs from Genesis I–XI in the Genuine Hymns of Ephrem the Syrian with Particular Reference to the Influence of Jewish Exegetical Tradition*, Coniectanea Biblica OT (Lund: CWK Gleerup, 1978), 40, 42.

[123] T. Jansma, "L'Hexameron de Jacques de Sarug," *L'Orient syrien* 4 (1959): 29; Trigg, *Biblical Interpretation*, 185. Jacob belonged within the West-Syrian or Monophysite tradition, which owed less to the influence of Theodore of Mopsuestia.

[124] Van Winden, "Hexaemeron," 14:1266. For the combined influence of Ephraim and Theodore in the East Syrian school, see van Winden, "Hexaemeron," 14:1265; P. Gignoux, ed., *Homélies de Narsaï sur la Création*, Patrologia Orientalis (Turnholt: Brepols, 1968), 514f.

[125] Narsai of Nisibis, "On the Expression, "In the Beginning," and Concerning the Existence of God," in *Biblical Interpretation*, ed. J.W. Trigg, Message of the Fathers of the Church (Wilmington, DE: Michael Glazier, 1988), 217. See also Gignoux, ed., *Homélies de Narsaï*, 527, 553, 597, 607 (*On the Formation of the Creatures*, ll. 9–10, 427–28; *On the Formation of Creation and on the Persons of the Trinity*, ll. 205–13, 222, 367).

[126] Jacob of Sarug, "On the Establishment of Creation, Memra One, The First Day," in *Biblical Interpretation*, ed. J.W. Trigg (Wilmington, DE: Michael Glazier, 1988), 198–99.

The very ordering of the cosmos requires a six-day creative process, involving the separation of elements whose mingling or conflict would mean the breakdown of creation.

Jacob shared with Narsai an almost childlike conception of the cosmos as a disc-shaped earth shielded from the celestial light by a tent-like firmament.[127] This view of the cosmos may have been widespread in the Eastern Christian world, and famously survives in the detailed sixth-century exposition of Cosmas Indicopleustes.[128] Not in its more naive aspects, but in its lyrical and spiritual richness, the Eastern tradition's isolation from the ongoing development of Western biblical interpretation might be viewed as an unfortunate and impoverishing loss.

Eastern Influences in the Latin Fathers prior to Augustine

The Latin tradition whose influence would dominate later Western exegesis and theology began in the shadow of the Greek fathers, especially Origen. Called the first Latin exegete, Victorinus of Pettau (c. 230–304) helped introduce Origen's thought into the Latin sphere.[129] In *On the World's Formation* his treatment of the days of creation consists mostly of digressions on the numbers four and seven, which become gateways to other symbolic numbers throughout the Bible, the sevenfold structure of the heavens, the creative work and earthly life of Christ, and the great divisions of history.[130] Another western practitioner of Alexandrian-style exegesis was Hilary of Poitiers (c. 315–368), whose famous *On the Trinity* emphasizes the 'createdness' of creation in contrast to the Son's 'begottenness', explaining,

> the whole preparation of these things is co-eternal with God. For although, as Moses teaches, each act of creation had its proper order; – the making the firmament solid, the laying bare of the dry land, the gathering together of the sea, the ordering of the stars, the generation by the waters and the earth when they brought forth living creatures out of themselves; yet the creation of the heaven and earth and other elements is not separat-

[127] Jansma, "L'Hexameron de Jacques de Sarug," 17–19, 21, 24, 26, etc.; Jacob of Sarug, "Establishment of Creation," 193.

[128] Cosmas Indicopleustes, *Cosmae Aegyptii Monarchi Christiana Topographia, Sive Christianorum Opinio de Mundo*, ed. J.P. Migne, et al., vol. 88, PL.

[129] K.H. Schwarte, "Victorinus of Pettau," in *DECL*, 597. I have already mentioned him in connection with world-week thought.

[130] Victorinus of Pettau, "On the Creation of the World," 7:341–42. This short text is the basis for the following discussion.

> ed by the slightest interval in God's working, since their preparation had been completed in like infinity of eternity in the counsel of God.[131]

Luther understood Hilary to be advocating a purely instantaneous creation, while one Renaissance Catholic scholar pointed out that Hilary only claims instantaneous creation here for the contents of Gen. 1:1: heavens, earth and the basic elements of the universe.[132] Perhaps we are witnessing here a tempered Alexandrian perspective on creation that remains dualistic, locating creation first of all on a timeless, ideal plane, yet is moving nearer to the 'plain reading' of Gen. 1:1–2:3, without treating the two as mutually exclusive. Hilary belongs alongside Ambrose as helping to bequeath this twofold perspective on the creation week to Augustine.[133]

Ambrose's (c. 339–397) *Hexameron* (AD 389) is normally given limited treatment in the secondary literature because it depends heavily upon Basil's. As Robbins puts it, "The importance of the *Hexaemeron* of Ambrose lies in the fact that it, even more than the translation by Eustathius, introduced the ideas of Basil to the western church."[134] This dependence is manifest in both content and form, extending as far as the duplication of Basil's accidentally delayed teaching about bird life while treating the fifth day.[135] Transmission of an important Genesis

[131] Nam tametsi habeat dispensationem sui, secundum Moysen (Gen. I), firmamenti solidatio, aridae nudatio, maris congregatio, astrorum constitutio, aquarum terraeque in ejiciendis ex se animantibus generatio: sed coeli, terrae, caeterorumque elementorum creatio ne levi saltem momento operationis discernitur; quia eorum praeparatio aequabili penes Deum aeternitatis infinitate constiterat. Hilary of Poitiers, "De Trinitate or On the Trinity," trans. E.W. Watson, L. Pullan et al., in *NPNF*[2] 9:9:31–234; Hilary of Poitiers, "De Trinitate," in *PL* 10:457–59. Compare Athanasius, *Orationes contra Arianos*, mentioned above, as working on a very similar theme, as well as also inclining to an instantaneous creation.

[132] E.g. Martin Luther, *Lectures on Genesis: Chapters 1–5*, ed. J. Pelikan, 8 vols., vol. 1 (St. Louis: Concordia, 1958), 4, 37–38, 69. Luther obviously admires Hilary but feels compelled to part with both Hilary and Augustine on this point; Francisco Suarez, "Tractatus de opere sex dierum," 3:55A (*De opere sex dierum* 1.10.5).

[133] Richard A. Norris, Jr., "Augustine and the Close of the Ancient Period of Interpretation," in *A History of Biblical Interpretation*, ed. A.J. Hauser and D.F. Watson, 386. On Hilary's transmission of Origenism, see Christoph Jacob, "The Reception of the Origenist Tradition in Latin Exegesis," in *HB/OT*, vol. I, 1:682–89. For his medieval influence see Jacques-Guy Bougerol, "The Church Fathers and the Sentences of Peter Lombard," in *RCFW* 1:115.

[134] Robbins, *Hexaemeral Literature*, 58. See also Mangenot, "Hexaméron," 6:2338; Letham, "Space of Six Days," 153–54. Eustathius made a direct translation of Basil's work into Latin shortly after Ambrose preached his hexaemeral homilies. See Robbins, *Hexaemeral Literature*, 42.

[135] Compare Saint Ambrose, Bishop of Milan, *Hexameron, Paradise, and Cain and Abel*, trans. J.J. Savage, Fathers of the Church, a New Translation (New York: Catholic University of America Press, 1961; reprint, Ann Arbor, MI: UMI, 1997), 191ff. (*Hexameron* 5.8.12ff.) and Basil of Caesarea, "Hexaemeron," 8:96ff. (*Hexaemeron* 8.2ff).

interpretive tradition into the Latin sphere was important, but greater alertness to the redactional (editing) process allows us to appreciate Ambrose's hexaemeron as a work in its own right. Ambrose is in fact more sympathetic than Basil to 'spiritual' interpretation, adding to the moral lessons found in Basil's work a new, Christ-oriented variety of allegory.[136]

Ambrose nevertheless shares with Basil an explanation of the days of creation that hovers between instantaneous creation and a temporal approach to the creation week, finally favouring the latter. Day 1 is for Ambrose the primordial day, and in a sense God never has to create another, as the first one cycles on indefinitely. But Ambrose is not especially concerned to define the exact duration of the days of the creative week. He instead wishes to explain how a twenty-four hour cycle can be called simply a 'day' when it includes twelve dark hours – demonstrating that sometimes the questions we want to ask are not those that concern ancient authors.[137]

Ambrose at times uses language that suggests instantaneous creation, whereby "the Creator ... completed such a great work in the briefest moment ... so that the effect of His will anticipated the perception of time." He continues,

> Where, therefore, was there a delay, since you may read: 'For He spoke and they were made; He commanded and they were created'?[138] He who in a momentary exercise of His will completed such a majestic work employed no art or skill so that those things which were not were so quickly brought into existence; the will did not outrun the creation nor the creation, the will.[139]

Yet soon afterwards he is explaining that the term 'beginning' means "that at first He created heaven and earth; next, hills, regions, and the boundaries of the inhabitable world. Or we may understand that before He created the rest of the visible creatures, day, night, fruit-bearing trees, and the various kinds of animals He created heaven and earth."[140] And responding to the challenge that Ps. 148:5 implies instantaneous

[136] E.g. Ambrose, *Hexameron*, 282 (*Hexameron* 6.9.10). See the comment by Mangenot, "Hexaméron," 6:2338. Other differences from Basil are that Ambrose supplies some of his own natural philosophical data from classical sources, and completes the section on man omitted by Basil: van Winden, "Hexaemeron," 14:1263–64; Robbins, *Hexaemeral Literature*, 58–59.

[137] Lewis recognises this better than Letham on this occasion: Lewis, "Days of Creation," 447.

[138] The quotation is Ps. 148:5, to which Ambrose frequently returns.

[139] Ambrose, *Hexameron*, 8 (*Hexameron*, 1.3.8).

[140] Ibid., 11–12 (*Hexameron*, 1.4.12).

creation he says, "That could very well have happened. Yet Scripture points out that things were first created and afterwards put in order."[141]

So Ambrose's descriptions of creation in an instant only apply to the first stage of creation, that of heaven and earth (Gen. 1:1). Therefore Jaki says that Ambrose "was the first to formulate in the West" the idea "that first came the work of foundation ... and then the work of adornment."[142] While Mangenot attributes to Ambrose an initial [instantaneous] creation of 'matière élémentaire', and then its arrangement through six literal days, Ambrose finally seems to regard this as over-interpretation, and takes Basil's stance, that the earth was invisible, because "water flowed over it and covered it," i.e. not because matter was at that point fundamentally formless.[143]

The hexaemera of Basil, Gregory of Nyssa and Ambrose all appeared in a short space of time, representing a great crescendo of interest in the Hexaemeron that reached its peak in the Genesis work of Augustine of Hippo.[144]

Augustine's Quest for the Literal Meaning of Genesis

Augustine (354–430) is a towering figure in Christian history, and largely set the theological agenda for the millennium to follow. His fame is usually associated with his theological achievements, but he was also a highly significant biblical exegete who gave careful thought to his interpretive methods. He was in fact "the first orthodox Christian in the West to advance a comprehensive and original hermeneutic," explaining this most carefully in his *On Christian Doctrine*.[145] Patristic scholars are increasingly acknowledging the importance of biblical texts as governing sources for his thought, as compared, for example, with

[141] Ibid., 28–29 (*Hexameron*, 1.7.27). Note too the later triumphant comment, "The sun [is] ... younger than the green plant!"

[142] Jaki, *Genesis 1*, 82.

[143] Mangenot, "Hexaméron," 6:2338; Ambrose, *Hexameron*, 33–34 (*Hexameron*, 1.8.30).

[144] Comparison of 'publication dates' such as they are known reveals that many Genesis works, including Hexaemera, appear in a burst towards the end of the fourth century AD. Basil's appears in 378–9, followed immediately by Gregory of Nyssa's *Hexaemeron*: Dünzl, "Gregory of Nyssa," 264. Then followed John Chrysostom's *Homilies in Genesis* in 385 (Chrysostom, *Homilies*, 6) and Severian, *In mundi creationem,* about the same time. Harder to date but in the same vicinity are Diodore's *Commentary on the Octateuch* (d. <394) and the Genesis work of his student Theodore of Mopsuestia (any time from 393): P. Bruns, "Theodore of Mopsuestia," trans. M. O'Connell, in *DECL,* 563. Moving to the Latin works, in the same year as Ambrose's hexaemeral homilies, 389, came Augustine's first effort at a Genesis commentary, *On Genesis against the Manichaeans,* to be soon followed by his first attempt at a literal commentary on Genesis in 393.

[145] Frederick Van Fleteren, "Principles of Augustine's Hermeneutic: An Overview," in *Augustine: Biblical Exegete* (New York: Peter Lang, 2001), 1.

Neoplatonic influences or the literary interpretive methods learned in his rhetorical training.[146] So there is particular relevance in a close study of his exegetical labours over the opening of Genesis.

Genesis was profoundly important for Augustine and left its mark on many of his works, such as his famous *Confessions, On the Trinity* and *The City of God*. He also wrote a series of exegetical works specifically concerned with the opening chapters of Genesis, beginning with the allegorical *On Genesis against the Manichaeans* (389).[147] *On the Literal Meaning of Genesis, An Unfinished Book* followed in 393, while a figurative treatment of the creation account appears in Books 11–13 of the *Confessions* (between 397 and 401). And following the chief work, *The Literal Meaning of Genesis,*[148] (between 401 and 415), he wrote of creation finally in Book 11 of *The City of God* (c. 417–418).[149] We will need to consider Augustine's development of thought in relation to the days of creation across this series in order to understand his final position better.[150]

An allegorical approach to the creation week dominates the early *On Genesis against the Manichaeans.*[151] Augustine seeks to bypass Manichean objections to the literal sense, particularly the anthropomorphic presentation of God in Genesis 1–3, by presenting the seven days with their creative details as an allegory of (redemptive) human history. This is laid out in seven stages, running from Adam to Noah, then Noah to Abraham, Abraham to David, David to the exile of Judah and thence to the advent of Christ, with the seventh day representing the Messianic Age, all in classic world-week formulation, but without defining the periods in terms of years.[152] To expound the Genesis text in this prophetic way is appropriate, since "words can in no sense express how

[146] Ibid., 2–4, 7–9; John M. Norris, "Augustine's Interpretation of Genesis in the *City of God* XI–XV," in *Fourteenth International Conference on Patristic Studies*, ed. F. Young, M. Edwards, and P. Parvis (Oxford: Peeters, 2006), 207–208.

[147] W. Geerlings, "Augustine," in *DECL*, 62–63.

[148] Henceforth *DGaL* in the footnotes, for *De Genesi ad litteram*, and *Literal Meaning* in the main text.

[149] On the chronological details mentioned, see Roland J. Teske, "The Genesis Accounts of Creation," in *Augustine through the Ages: An Encyclopedia*, ed. O.S.A. Allan D. Fitzgerald (Grand Rapids/Cambridge: Eerdmans, 1999), 380–81.

[150] I have not yet seen a work that studies the progress of Augustine's interpretation of Genesis: Yoon Kyung Kim, *Augustine's Changing Interpretations of Genesis 1–3: From De Genesi contra Manichaeos to De Genesi ad litteram* (Lewiston, NY: Edwin Mellen Press, 2006).

[151] Augustine, *On Genesis: Two Books on Genesis Against the Manichees and On the Literal Interpretation of Genesis: An Unfinished Book*, trans. S.J. Roland J. Teske, Fathers of the Church, a New Translation (Washington, DC: The Catholic University of America Press, 1991), 68 (*De Genesi contra Manichaeos* 1.14.20).

[152] *De Genesi contra Manichaeos* 1.23.

God made and created heaven and earth and every creature," i.e. Augustine cannot yet see the way clear to a literal explanation.[153]

Earlier in the work, Augustine attempts to deflect Manichean scepticism about the passing of three days without the sun, concluding that "we are left with the interpretation that in that period of time the divisions between the works were called evening because of the completion of the work that was done, and morning because of the beginning of the work that was to come. Scripture clearly says this after the likeness of human works."[154] This is the nearest Augustine ever comes to anything like a modern 'day-age' theory, and it still is not very close. He is primarily seeking to qualify the human portrayal of God as needing rest, or requiring time to create, or having a physical form according to which the human being is modelled.[155] Augustine goes on finally to utilize the seven days as an allegory of the Christian's spiritual journey.[156] Allegory unlocks for Augustine a richness of meaning that transcends the literal narrative and its potentially demeaning picture of God.

Yet Augustine felt compelled to uncover a more literal sense, as seen in his unfinished hexaemeron of 393, although as he later reflected, "my inexperience collapsed under the weight of so heavy a load."[157] He found it difficult to read the creation days in a straightforward, historical sense:

> [H]ow could there be days before there was time, if time began with the course of the lights, which Scripture says were made on the fourth day? Or was this arrangement set forth according to what human frailty is used to and by the law of conveying exalted things to the humble in a humble fashion?[158]

In *The Literal Meaning of Genesis,* Augustine turned to confront the difficulties of a literal reading once again.[159] He flirts with a plainly literal understanding of creation in six ordinary solar days, considering the possible production of the first three days of creation in the sun's absence by means of an intermittent or orbiting light source, the kind

[153] *De Genesi contra Manichaeos* 1.23.41.

[154] *De Genesi contra Manichaeos* 1.14.20.

[155] Teske explains the connection between Augustine's apologetic endeavour and his interpretation of the creation days in this work quite fully: Roland J. Teske, introduction to Augustine, *On Genesis: Two Books*, 13–14, 19–26.

[156] *De Genesi contra Manichaeos* 1.25.43; see also Book 13 of his *Confessions*: Augustine, *Confessions*, trans. R.S. Pine-Coffin (Harmondsworth: Penguin, 1961), 311–46.

[157] Augustine, *On Genesis: Two Books*, 42. This comes from his late work, *Retractationes*. He had abandoned the unfinished commentary at Gen. 1:26.

[158] *De Genesi ad litteram liber imperfectibus* 1.3.8.

[159] His later treatment of the days of creation in *The City of God* adds nothing new to what appears in *DGaL*: Augustine, "The City of God," 2:208–23 (*De civitate Dei* 11.7–31).

of explanation advanced by Basil.[160] But this seems incomprehensible. "As for material light, it is not clear by what circular motion or going forth and returning it could have produced the succession of day and night before the making of the heaven called firmament, in which the heavenly bodies were made."[161] Augustine was keen not to commit Scripture to what he felt were rationally indefensible positions.[162]

Moreover, in the Latin Bible Augustine read, Ecclus 18:1 said, "He who remains for eternity created all things at once," while Ps. 32:9 appeared to confirm the suddenness of creation,[163] and Gen. 2:4–5 seemed to make 'day' the first created entity, itself incorporating the creation of vegetation. This reinforced Augustine's instinctive, Platonist inclination toward an idealist understanding of the term 'day' in Genesis.[164] "Hence," concludes Augustine, "I do not now appeal to another book of Holy Scripture to prove that God *created all things together*."[165] Another exegetical conundrum was that if each creation day needed creating itself, as this verse seemed to imply, God either had to create Day 7 when he was supposed to be resting, or else rest on an uncreated day.[166]

Augustine had in any case a theological difficulty with the suggestion that God in his perfection and power might require time to create

[160] Augustine, *Literal Meaning*, 1:37–38, 128–29 (*DGaL* 1.16.31, 4.21.38). Taylor's edition is used for all citations.

[161] *DGaL* 4.21.29. See also 1.12.24–25, 1.16.31, 2.14.28, the latter reading, "No one could conceive how the three days passed by before the beginning of the time that is reported as commencing on the fourth day." In his earlier commentary he had written, "I find no way that [days and nights] could be before the lights of the heaven were made" (*De Genesi ad litteram liber imperfectibus* 6.27).

[162] *DGaL* 1.19.38–39.

[163] *DGaL* 4.33.51–52; compare *De Genesi ad litteram liber imperfectibus* 1.7.28. Augustine accepted the LXX behind the Old Latin as inspired, and therefore accepted the apocryphal books as Scripture. See G. Bonner, "Augustine as Biblical Scholar," in *The Cambridge History of the Bible. 1. From the Beginnings to Jerome*, ed. P.R. Ackroyd and C.F. Evans (Cambridge: Cambridge University Press, 1970), 544–46; David F. Wright, "Augustine: His Exegesis and Hermeneutics," in *HB/OT*, vol. I, 1:719. The LXX reads ὁ ζῶν εἰς τὸν αἰῶνα ἔκτισεν τὰ πάντα κοινῇ, which speaks of God's creation of the sum total of things rather than of instantaneous creation. In the Latin versions this was rendered, qui vivit in aeternum creavit omnia *simul*, meaning 'at the same time'. See Taylor's comment, Augustine, *Literal Meaning*, 1:254. On Ps. 32:9, see above on Origen.

[164] According to Taylor, Augustine's Old Latin read, Cum factis est dies, fecit Deus caelum et terram et omne viride agri antequam esset super terram, i.e. "When day was made, God made heaven and earth and every green thing of the field before it appeared above the earth ..." Augustine, *Literal Meaning*, 2:328. For Augustine's discussion see *DGaL* 5.4.8, and also 4.33.52; 5.3.5–6. See also Lavallee, "Augustine on the Creation Days," 459; van Winden, "Hexaemeron," 14:1267.

[165] *DGaL* 5.3.6. Lavallee here inadvertently misquotes Augustine as saying, "I *do* now appeal to another book ..." Lavallee, "Augustine on the Creation Days," 460.

[166] *DGaL* 4.20.37

anything.[167] Regarding the creation of light, he protests, "It would be strange if this could have taken as much time to be done by God as it takes us to say it."[168] The creation of the earth and sea "should not be understood [to have been done] in periods of time, lest the ineffable power of God as he works should be involved in some slowness."[169] And importantly, God's rest on Day 7 must not be taken too literally: "Whatever evening and morning were in those days of creation, it is quite impossible to suppose that on the morning following the evening of the sixth day God's rest began. We cannot be so foolish or rash as to imagine that any such temporal good would accrue to the Eternal and Unchangeable."[170] The seventh day has no evening, because God's rest (or the rest he gives to creatures) is unending.[171]

So Augustine felt driven to find another interpretation to replace a plain, literal one, yet without lapsing into allegory, conscious that allegorical senses relied on a viable literal foundation of meaning. Augustine wrote in the *Confessions* about the hermeneutical task, and shows awareness there of a plurality of meaning in the Genesis text, even within the literal sense. Henry Chadwick writes, "Like most ancient writers, Augustine assumes that even matter-of-fact narratives are polyvalent."[172] To discover Moses' intended meaning is the ideal outcome, yet God's communication through Scripture may outreach the capacity of its human authors.[173] "From the words of Moses ... there gush clear streams of truth from which each of us ... may derive a true explanation of the creation as best he is able, some choosing one and some another interpretation."[174] Augustine therefore advocated humility and tentativeness in exegesis, as seen in the questioning and adaptive style of his commentaries.[175]

[167] *De Genesi ad litteram liber imperfectibus* 1.7.28.

[168] *DGaL* 1.10.19.

[169] *De Genesi ad litteram liber imperfectibus* 1.11.34.

[170] *DGaL* 4.18.34.

[171] *DGaL* 4.18.31.

[172] Gerald Bray, *Biblical Interpretation: Past and Present* (Downers Grove: InterVarsity, 1996), 126; Simonetti, *Biblical Interpretation*, 108; Henry Chadwick, "Augustine," in *A Dictionary of Biblical Interpretation*, ed. R.J. Coggins and J.L. Houlden (London: SCM, 1990), 67.

[173] Augustine, *Confessions*, 295–96, 300–03, 309 (*Confessions* 12.18, 24, 32). See Greene-McCreight, *Ad Litteram*, 71.

[174] *Confessions* 12.27, and see 12.31.

[175] *Confessions* 12.25. He held that inquiry is a better way than dogmatic assertion for treating "the hidden matters concerning natural things which we know were made by God," *De Genesi ad litteram liber imperfectibus* 1.1. See Young, "Augustine's View of Creation," 42, 45.

Spiritual benefit was another important criterion for a satisfactory interpretation: would it lead to love for God and neighbour?[176] God for his part had kindly 'accommodated' Scripture to address its readers according to their differing abilities; a person who cannot understand that the six days were repeated "without lapse of time," should leave that higher understanding to those equipped to grasp it, knowing that "Scripture does not abandon you in your infirmity, but with a mother's love accompanies you in your slower steps."[177] Finally, another indispensable interpretive criterion for Augustine was the 'Rule of Faith', an orthodox boundary that defined "an array of allowable interpretations."[178]

In *Literal Meaning*, then, Augustine reiterates that the ideal outcome is to identify "the meaning intended by the author. But if this is not clear, then at least we should choose an interpretation in keeping with the context of Scripture and in harmony with our faith." If context offers no help, we should at least choose "that which our faith demands," an edifying reading that satisfies the 'Rule of Faith'.[179] This is in effect a three-stage process of broadening interpretive options if the initial quest to discover the author's intention proves fruitless. He had developed a strategy for dealing with such dilemmas, and was about to implement it in the case of the days of creation.

As Augustine felt his way toward a more viable interpretation, he considered first the possibility that 'day' might have a metaphysical significance, referring "to the form of a thing created" while 'night' would refer "to the privation...of this form."[180] He had earlier accordingly understood 'heaven and earth' in verse 1 as named in anticipation of what formless matter was yet to become.[181] This formless state of matter is prior to its formation in a purely logical sense, not in time, so that we are already dealing here with instantaneous creation.[182] The ontological orientation of this idea was suited to Augustine's Platonist cast of mind, but Augustine finally abandons it as unable to explain

[176] Bonner, "Augustine as Biblical Scholar," 557; Greene-McCreight, *Ad Litteram*, 36; Thomas Williams, "Biblical Interpretation," in *The Cambridge Companion to Augustine*, ed. E. Stump and N. Kretzmann (Cambridge: Cambridge University Press, 2001), 67–68.

[177] *DGnL* 5.3.6. Note the use of the term 'accommodation' in Taylor's translation at *DGnL* 1.14.28. See also Greene-McCreight, *Ad Litteram*, 60–61.

[178] Greene-McCreight, *Ad Litteram*, 36. Augustine explicitly employs this principle by laying out the Apostles' Creed as his interpretive boundary as he begins his exegesis in his unfinished Genesis commentary: *DGLI* 1.2.

[179] *DGaL* 1.21.41.

[180] *DGaL* 4.1.1. He takes up this possibility (also found in *DGnM*) as early as 1.17.35 and does not finally abandon it until 4.26.43. See Taylor's note in Augustine, *Literal Meaning*, 247 n. 242. Cf. *DGLI* 10.32, 12.37, 15.51ff., *DGaL* 2.14.28, 4.1.1.

[181] *De Genesi ad litteram liber imperfectibus* 1.3.9, 1.4.12.

[182] *DGaL* 1.15.29.

how a seventh day could be 'made' without requiring God to work on his rest day.[183]

Augustine's final interpretation also involved instantaneous creation, but replaced his suggested metaphysical understanding with an ideal conception, making the creation week a logical sequence determined by the laws of number and perceptible only to the mind.[184] Taking an unexploited idea from Ambrose, Augustine argues that in reality the creation days constitute the one day recurring seven times.[185] The chronological aspect of the sequence fades away to leave an ideal or what Augustine calls a "causal connection":

> These seven days of our time, although like the seven days of creation in name and in numbering, follow one another in succession and mark off the division of time, but those first six days occurred in a form unfamiliar to us as intrinsic principles within things created. Hence evening and morning ... did not produce the changes that they do for us with the motion of the sun. This we are certainly forced to admit with regard to the first three days, which are recorded and numbered before the creation of the heavenly bodies."[186]

Augustine then argues that consistency then requires the extension of this implication to all seven days. He locates these seven rational, ideal creation days within angelic intellect(s). In Augustine's Neoplatonic framework, angels occupy the highest levels in the intellectual and metaphysical hierarchy, or 'great chain of being' that was perceived as linking the highest, God, right down through the created order to the humblest being.[187] Angels could not possibly be omitted from the Genesis account, "as if they were not among the works of God." By a process of elimination, and on account of the sequential priority given to 'day' in Gen. 2:4–5, Augustine concludes that the angels "are that light which was called, 'Day'."[188] This makes angels the very first work of creation and the object of the command in Gen. 1:3, after which their comprehension of all of God's (instantaneous) works of creation constitutes the rest of the creation week:

[183] *DGaL* 4.26.43.

[184] *DGaL* 4.33.52, 4.35.56. This is a shift from the apparent admission of a chronological element to the days in the *Confessions*, where Augustine sees the material forming of creation occurring in six days, since only material creation can change and thus show the effects of time. Without change, time does not pass: Augustine, *Confessions*, 12.12.

[185] *DGaL* 4.26.43, 4.33.52, 5.3.6, etc. Cf. Ambrose, *Hexameron*, 42–43 (*Hexameron* 1.10.37)

[186] *DGaL* 4.18.33. Compare *De Genesi ad litteram liber imperfectibus* 1.12.43, where Augustine allows that days 4-6 might be our familiar solar days. On 'causal connection', see *DGaL* 4.33.51.

[187] A. Lovejoy, *The Great Chain of Being* (Cambridge, MA: Harvard University Press, 1936; repr., New York: Harper, 1960), 59–61.

[188] *De civitate Dei* 11.9.

> The minds of angels, united to the Word of God in pure charity, created before the other works of creation, first saw in the Word of God those works to be made before they were actually made; and thus those works were first made in the angels' knowledge when God decreed that they should come into being, before they were made in their own proper natures. The angels also knew those works in their own natures as things already made, with a knowledge admittedly of a lower order called evening.[189]

Each day comprises three stages: knowledge in the Word of God (the preceding 'morning'), knowledge of things in themselves (evening), and reference to God in praise (the next morning).[190] Creation occurred as an instantaneous series of events in the rational world rather than as events taking time in the material world, even though it produced material creation. We might say that time happened in creation rather than creation happening in time.[191]

"Why, then," asks Augustine, reading our minds, "was there any need for six distinct days to be set forth in the narrative…? The reason is that those who cannot understand the meaning of the text, *He created all things together,* cannot arrive at the meaning of Scripture unless the narrative proceeds slowly step by step."[192] The seven-day scheme provided in the Bible pertains not to creation's performance so much as to its revelation to humans. The fact that the "framework of the six days of creation might seem to imply intervals of time," is an instance of the customary way in which Scripture speaks "with the limitations of human language in addressing men of limited understanding, while at the same time teaching a lesson to be understood by the reader who is able."[193] Not only this, but since in the conceptual world that Augustine shared with his Alexandrian forebears, mathematics reveals the fundamental structure of reality, the number six was ideal for expressing the perfection of creation: "God perfected all His works in six days

[189] *DGaL* 4.32.49.

[190] *DGaL* 4.22.39. The angels' knowledge of created things "in the Word of God" (= 'morning') and "in themselves" (= 'evening') might roughly equate to 'rational' and 'empirical' routes to knowledge, fitting the Platonic cast of Augustine's mind, for whom innate knowledge, especially as including divine revelation, is superior to but does not exclude knowledge gained through the senses. The latter remains legitimate so long as those who contemplate created things "rise up from a knowledge of a creature to the praise of the Creator": *DGaL* 4.28.45.

[191] This is despite some vacillation. In *DGaL* 4.31.48 Augustine appears momentarily to concede that the days represent a chronological sequence, but returns to a timeless creation in 4.32.50.

[192] *DGaL* 4.33.52.

[193] *DGaL* 5.6.19; *De Genesi ad litteram liber imperfectibus* 1.14.20, 3.8, 7.28.

because six is a perfect number."[194] Therefore our solar days are not identical in kind with the creation days of God, but analogous to them, a humble model of the far greater reality.[195]

Augustine's unique analysis of the days of creation may strike the modern reader as alien, forced, or unnecessarily complicated. Yet Robbins rightly explains it as a self-consistent, well thought-through system of teaching on creation.[196] It cannot be understood apart from an appreciation of Augustine's metaphysical inheritance. Henry Chadwick describes Augustine's conversion (intellectually) as a marriage of Neoplatonism and Christianity, with the latter transforming elements of the former.[197] Augustine's account of the six days of creation elevates the angelic or transcendent realm, prizing the essential and ontological over the physical, changeable, temporal realm.[198] Exegetical and theological factors may have forced Augustine to look for a more sophisticated interpretation of the days of creation, but his Neoplatonist metaphysic provides the basis for his particular rational solution.

Yet Augustine consciously decides at the beginning of *Literal Meaning* to explain Genesis 1–3 as "a faithful record of what happened" and "according to the plain meaning of the historical facts, not according to future events which they foreshadow."[199] How can this be called a literal interpretation, when he locates the creation days within angelic intelligence? Augustine answers this potential objection by defending the angelic comprehension of created things and their resulting praise of the Creator as "a truer evening and a truer morning."[200] In Augustine's metaphysic, the spiritual realm was not less real than the material one but more real. Although he takes 'day' metaphorically, this for Augustine remains literal exegesis, "reading the creation story as a creation story," rather than as the story of the church, Christ, or the individual believer's experience, *contra* those writers who understand this as

[194] *DGaL* 4.7.14. Six is the smallest number that is the sum of its factors (1+2+3=6 and 1x2x3=6).

[195] They "indeed recall the days of creation, but without in any way being really similar to them," *DGaL* 4.27.44.

[196] Robbins, *Hexaemeral Literature*, 64.

[197] Henry Chadwick, *Augustine*, Past Masters, ed. K. Thomas (Oxford: Oxford University Press, 1986), 25, 28–29.

[198] *De civitate Dei* 11.9.19 demonstrates the importance of 'principalities and powers', including angels, in Augustine's thinking.

[199] *DGaL* 1.17.34. Later he opposes the belief that actual history begins with Gen. 4:1, confirming the historicity of events narrated in Genesis 1–3, which he labels historical narrative: *DGaL* 8.1.1–3. In his less technical treatments, Augustine continued to permit himself a more allegorical approach: Simonetti, *Biblical Interpretation*, 107.

[200] *DGaL* 4.28.45.

an allegorical work.[201] For Augustine the narrated creation events are real, although the days exist as a moment on the boundary of the ideal and the world of human perception.

Yet Augustine's literal meaning certainly stretches the definition of 'literal' meaning and minimizes historical reality, and Augustine's defensiveness betrays his doubt about the literality of his own treatment, as he challenges his readers, "Whoever, then, does not accept the meaning that my limited powers have been able to discover or conjecture but seeks in the enumeration of the days of creation a different meaning, which might be understood not in a prophetical or figurative sense, but literally and more aptly, … let him search and find a solution with God's help."[202]

Augustine's *Literal Meaning* represents the climax of works on the early part of Genesis in the patristic period, and his hexaemeron provided the defining statement with which every medieval and Renaissance commentator on Gen. 1:1–2:3 would wrestle.[203] Though many subsequent interpreters would find his abstract rendition of creation insufficiently literal to warrant the label, preferring "a more concrete exegesis, representing the successive creations as the steps in a physical process," his authority was such that it was a long time before a Christian commentator on Genesis could safely ignore it.[204]

The Creation Week on the Brink of the Medieval Period

By the late patristic period, as the Roman Empire crumbled in the west and morphed into the Byzantine in the east, interpretation of the creation week settled into a general compromise between instantaneous creation and a literal progression of days. Allegorical readings from Alexandria had run up against the literal 'sequence' of the Antiochenes. The Cappadocian fathers had arrived at their compromise stances, a literal one with moral highlights in Basil's case, a philosophical rendition emphasizing ontological realities for Gregory of Nyssa. Basil's powerful example had led the allegorically-inclined Ambrose in a more literal direction regarding the Hexaemeron. And with Augustine's

[201] Williams, "Biblical Interpretation," 62, identifies this as non-allegorical. On the allegorical side see: Robbins, *Hexaemeral Literature*, 64; van Winden, "Hexaemeron," 14:1266; Lewis, "Days of Creation," 443.

[202] *DGaL* 4.28.45, also 1.20.40, etc. Greene-McCreight, *Ad Litteram*, 49. On p. 45 she refers to 'slippage' of the term 'literal' in Augustine's usage. See also C. John Collins, "How Old Is the Earth? Anthropomorphic Days in Genesis 1:1–2:3," *Presbyterion* 20 (1994): 125; Letham, "Space of Six Days," 156; Young, "Augustine's View of Creation," 42.

[203] I. Backus, ed., *The Reception of the Church Fathers in the West*, 2 vols. (Leiden: Brill, 1997).

[204] Robbins, *Hexaemeral Literature*, 77.

great Genesis commentary, Western patristic interpretation of Gen. 1:1–2:3 had reached its peak.

About the same time arose a tradition of Latin Christian epic poetry that incorporated the creation story into a broader epic narrative, with more or less poetic modification of the seven-day framework, and with more or less amalgamation with pagan origin traditions. This new genre was a significant conduit for interpretation of the creation story into the Middle Ages. Just as the medium of fiction may allow an author to say things that would seem objectionable in straightforward prose, the epic narrative genre permitted imaginative more reshaping of the creation story than Genesis commentary or doctrinal exposition.

Latin epic poems that retained the Genesis sequence of creation days were Cyprianus Gallus' *Liber in Genesin* (c. 550), the *Alethia* of Claudius Marius Victor (fl. 426) and Dracontius' *On the Praises of God,* although Marius Victor also tried to reconcile an instantaneous with a sequential creation.[205] Other poets used the Genesis narrative more freely. Hilary Arelatensis' (403–449) *Metrum in Genesim* abandons the creation week framework and resequences the creation events, as does Avitus' *Poematum de Mosaicae historiae gestis* (507), while in her *Cento,* modelled on Virgil, Proba (fl. 400) retains the sequence of six days but rearranges their content.[206] Hilary, Avitus, and the Byzantine churchman Georgios Pisides (d. c. 630), in his Greek epic poem, *Hexaemeron sive Cosmopoeia,* all incorporate Greco-Roman classical ideas into their re-imagined biblical account of origins.[207] These works were destined finally to influence the imagination of creation in the Renaissance.

Meanwhile the more literal line taken by the Antioch school had taken root in the Syriac sphere, and continued strongly right into the

[205] Cyprianus Gallus, "Incerti Auctoris Genesis," in *PL* 2:1097ff; Cyprianus Gallus, "Genesis. (Authorship Uncertain)," in *The Writings of Tertullian*, vol. III, *with the extant works of Victorinus and Commodianus*, ed. Alexander Roberts and James Donaldson, Ante-Nicene Christian Library (Edinburgh: T.&T. Clark, 1880), 18:293–300; Claudius Marius Victor, "Alethia," in *Commodianus; Claudius Marius Victorius*, ed. P. F. Hovingh, Corpus Christianorum Series Latina (Turnholt: Brepols, 1960), 130–36, esp. p. 130. (Also Claudius Marius Victor, "Commentariorum in Genesin libri tres," in *PL* 61:937–70.) Blossius Aemilius Dracontius, *Oeuvres*, ed. Claude Moussy and Colette Camus, 4 vols., vol. I. Louanges de Dieu [De laudibus dei], Livres I et II (Paris: Belles lettres, 1985), 1:156–69.

[206] Pseudo-Hilary, "S. Hilarii in Genesim ad Leonem Papam," in *Cypriani Galli Poetae Heptateuchos accedunt incertorum de Sodoma et Iona et ad senatorem carmina et Hilarii quae feruntur in Genesin, de Maccabaeis atque de Euangelio*, ed. R. Peiper, Corpus Scriptorum Ecclesiorum Latinorum (Vienna: Tempsky, 1881), 231–39, IA, http://www.archive.org/stream/corpusscriptorum24cypruoft. (Roberts regards the work as anonymous: H. Roberts, *Biblical Epic and Rhetorical Paraphrase* (Liverpool: Francis Cairns, 1985), 93); Avitus, "De Mosaicae Historiae Gestis," in *PL* 70:323–26; Proba, "Centones Virgiliani," in *PL* 19:803–06. Evans translates extracts: J.M. Evans, *'Paradise Lost' and the Genesis Tradition* (Oxford: Clarendon, 1968), 116–17.

[207] Georgius Pisides, "Hexaemeron sive Cosmopoeia," in *PG* 92:1426–80.

Byzantine/Muslim era with Jacob of Edessa (c. 633–708) and his successors, but in isolation from Western Christianity.[208] World-week schemes lived on, as in John of Damascus' (c. 675–c.749) respected *Exposition of the Orthodox Faith*.[209] His treatment of creation generally lined up with that of Gregory of Nazianzus, and he too accepted the creation of the angelic realm prior to that of the material world. Other interpreters such as the monastic Anastasius of Sinai (d. c. 700) were most interested in getting behind the literal sense of Gen. 1:1–2:3 to access truths about Christ via allegory, rather than attempting to attempt to explain the creation days historically or physically. Paul's statement in Eph. 5:32 was Anastasius' catch-cry: "This is a great mystery, but I am talking about Christ and the Church."[210]

But the most influential cosmogonic syntheses of the patristic era were both compromises between instantaneous creation and a historical creation week. This compromise in the Greek-speaking Eastern church seems to have represented a mollified Origenism. One such middle-ground commentator was Procopius of Gaza (c. 475–c. 536), who lived in Constantinople under the Byzantine emperor Justin I.[211] In keeping with the developing trend of his time, he was fond of collating others' opinions, sometimes making his own stance difficult to isolate, although he is often described as heavily influenced by the Cappadocians. Concerning Gen. 1:1–2:3, Procopius flirts quite seriously with the instantaneous creation of Origen's school, while using Antiochene-sounding terminology.[212] When explaining that the luminaries are created as lights are kindled for a banquet already prepared, seeming to imply progression, he adds, "And it is made clear that for the sake of order [τάξις, *taxis*] the number of these days has been employed and for our weakness, otherwise being unable to comprehend the creation

[208] See for example, Lucas van Rompay, "Development of Biblical Interpretation in the Syrian Churches of the Middle Ages," in *HB/OT*, vol. I, 2:559–77, esp. 561–62; E. ten Napel, "Some Remarks on the Hexaemeral Literature in Syriac," in *IV Symposium Syriacum (Groningen, 1984)*, ed. H.W.J. Drijvers, et al., Orientalia Christiana Analecta (Roma: Pont. Institutum Studiorum Orientalium, 1987), 63; van Winden, "Hexaemeron," 14:1265; Mangenot, "Hexaméron," 6:2337. Zahlten links Jacob of Edessa with a Cappadocian approach to Genesis 1, i.e. that of Basil and the two Gregorys: Johannes Zahlten, *Creatio Mundi: Darstellungen der sechs Schöpfungstage und naturwissenschaftliches Weltbild im Mittelalter*, Stuttgarter Beiträge zur Geschichte und Politik (Stuttgart: Klett-Cotta, 1979), 91.

[209] John of Damascus, "Exposition of the Orthodox Faith," trans. S.D.F. Salmond, in *NPNF*[2] 9:17 (*Expositio Fidei* 2.1).

[210] Anastasius of Sinai, "Hexaemeron," 89:856, 871.

[211] J.D. Douglas, ed., *The New International Dictionary of the Christian Church* (Grand Rapids: Zondervan, 1996), 806.

[212] Procopius of Gaza, "Commentarii in Genesin," in *PG* 87:21A. See van Winden, "Hexaemeron," 14:1261–62; Zöckler, *Geschichte*, 1:212; Robbins, *Hexaemeral Literature*, 57, 59; Mangenot, "Hexaméron," 6:2337.

of the things that came into being suddenly [ἀθρόως, *athroōs*]."[213] The further comment, "But some say that everything was made in chronological order for the teaching of the rational [λογικῶν, *logikōn*] powers," reflects Augustinian influence.[214] Like both Augustine and the Alexandrians, Procopius believes that numerological considerations govern why the work is described in six days and why the sun is created on the fourth.[215] Yet he seems to merge this idealist understanding with a literal Antiochene one: plants really arise before the sun, and the sun is formed on the fourth day out of the "essence of light" that was made on the first.[216] Procopius seems to represent an imperfectly synthesized Eastern view of the creation week that sat uneasily between logical and chronological alternatives.

The Alexandrian Christian philosopher John Philoponus (c. 490–c. 570) sought in his more sophisticated and better integrated *On the Creation of the World* (c. 546–549) to defend both the philosophical credibility of the Mosaic account of creation in Genesis and the viability of Basil's hexaemeral interpretation in the face of the stricter literalism of the competing Antiochene school represented by Theodore of Mopsuestia.[217] Philoponus takes Basil's ideas in a harmonizing direction, seeking to provide much more physical and metaphysical detail about the cosmos from the Genesis text, much as Gregory of Nyssa had. Clemens Scholten claims that the simplistic, flat earth world-picture of Syrian/Antiochene thinkers, explicitly described by fellow Alexandrian Cosmas Indicopleustes, drove Philoponus to demonstrate the harmony of the Mosaic account with a better-respected natural philosophy.[218]

In *On the Creation of the World,* Philoponus is able to imagine creation in more days than six, or less, but seems inclined towards an in-

[213] Procopius of Gaza, "Commentarii in Genesin," 87:85A, also 60D–61A.

[214] Ibid., 87:85B. See below on Augustine's hexaemeral interpretation.

[215] Ibid., 87:85D, 140B.

[216] Ibid., 87:80D, 85C, 88B.

[217] David C. Lindberg, "Science and the Early Church," in *God and Nature: Historical Essays on the Encounter between Christianity and Science*, ed. D.C. Lindberg and R.L. Numbers, 33, 38–41; Mangenot, "Hexaméron," 6:2337; Robbins, *Hexaemeral Literature*, 57–58; van Winden, "Hexaemeron," 14:1262; William A. Wallace, appendix to Thomas Aquinas, *Summa Theologiae: Latin Text and English Translation*, ed. Thomas Gilby, trans. W.A. Wallace, 60 vols., vol. 10: Cosmogony (1a. 65–74) (London: Blackfriars in conjunction with Eyre & Spottiswoode, 1964–76), 207. This is my source for the range of dates for the writing of *De opificio mundi*.

[218] Scholten, "Hexaemeronauslegung," 7–15. Scholten observes that this is the first work on Genesis with such a title, itself an indication of its harmonizing intention and the linking of Genesis to a particular view of the makeup of the cosmos. See also Jaki, *Genesis 1*, 95. Just how representative of Eastern Christian thought was that of Cosmas Indicopleustes is debated. See the analysis of Jeffrey B. Russell, *Inventing the Flat Earth* (New York: Praeger, 1991), 21-24, 33-35.

stantaneous creation.[219] His argument that the initial creation of Gen. 1:1 cannot be a process in time, since the agents of the measurement of time, the heavenly bodies of Day 4, do not yet exist, would naturally also apply to Days 1–3 of creation.[220] The rationale for a six-part creation is once again the perfection of the number six, which may express the combination of the single dimension of a line, the two dimensions of a plane, and the three dimensions of a solid; or it might reflect a sixfold hierarchy of entities rising from formless matter or a body without any qualities (ἄποιον, *apoion*), through the inanimate, the plant, that which can reproduce (τὸ ζώφυτον, *to zōphuton*), the irrational animal, and the reasoning creature.[221] For Philoponus, the more philosophically credible an explanation of the meaning of the six days, the less historical it was likely to be, and the more symbolic, expressing timeless, metaphysical realities.

The Western version of this temporal versus atemporal creation compromise softened Augustine's ideas under the influence of Basil and Ambrose. Gregory the Great (c. 540–604) helped to define the Western church's standard general doctrinal position on creation as the patristic period drew to a close. In his massive *Moralia in [J]ob* he treats the question of instantaneous creation almost accidentally as he sets out to explain how God can say in Job 40:10 (Vulg.) that he created the creature Behemoth 'with' Job.[222] There he reconciles the late-patristic synthesis of Augustine's instantaneous creation with a more straightforward reading of the creation week by distinguishing things' creation in their substance (*per substantiam*) from their creation in their particular, final forms (*per speciem*).[223] Creation 'at once' (*simul*) is a valid concept only as applied to the material substance of created entities. This is why, for instance, the heavenly bodies can be said to be created on Day 4 when the 'heavens' are created on Day 1. Such also is the relationship of the land of Day 3 to the 'earth' of verse 1, and it also explains the collection of the whole week's work within the 'day' of Gen. 2:4–5. This metaphysical distinction between form and matter

[219] Johannes Philoponus, *De opificio mundi*, trans. G. Reichardt (Leipzig: G.B. Teubner, 1897), 304, ll. 309–17, TLG. Van Winden's qualified description of Philoponus' move away from a literal-sounding beginning hints at the complexity of Philoponus' language and logic: van Winden, "Hexaemeron," 14:1262.

[220] Philoponus, *De opificio mundi*, 7–9, 305, ll. 303–308.

[221] Philoponus, *De opificio mundi*, 304–305.

[222] The verse is found at Job 40:15 in English versions. The Vulgate reads, *Ecce Behemoth, quem feci tecum.*

[223] Gregory the Great, *S. Gregorii Magni moralia in Iob libri XXIII–XXXV*, ed. Marci Adriaen, vol. 143B, Corpus Christianorum series Latina (Turnholt: Brepols, 1985), 1640–41 (*Moralia in Iob*, 32.12.16). Many later sources instead cite Book 32.10 concerning this argument of Gregory's, apparently citing texts with divisions that are different to Adriaen's.

was part of the mental fabric of Gregory's time, and applying this distinction to the creation week allowed the majority of subsequent medieval and Catholic Renaissance thinkers to reconcile Augustine's appealing theology of creation with the apparent realism of the creation week of Gen. 1:1–2:3.[224]

An important mediator of ideas between the patristic era and medieval Christendom was Isidore of Seville (c. 560–636). Genesis plays a part in several of his works, and his overriding goal is clearly to collate the best of patristic insight into these biblical mysteries.[225] Isidore's *On Genesis* was such a collation, acting as "the funnel by which the enormous output of the Fathers on Genesis was sifted and handed on to later times."[226] From the word 'beginning' on, Isidore interprets Gen. 1:1–2:3 allegorically in reference to Christ and the Christian quest for moral purification and spiritual elevation.[227] For Isidore, the birds of Gen. 1:20–22 represent "holy spirits soaring to the heavenlies," while the aquatic life of the same day represents people brought to new life through the sacrament of baptism.[228] Earlier writers such as Basil were quite amenable to finding moral allegories in the details of creation in this way, but with Isidore the method has come to truly predominate over a historical or literal approach.

The reference to 'the day' when God made heaven and earth (Gen. 2:4–6) leads Isidore to articulate an apparently Augustinian instantaneous creation.[229] Isidore shortly afterward returns to utilize the creation week to periodize world history in 'world-week' fashion, where the 'mornings' feature hopeful new acts of God, such as the raising up of King David (Day 4), and the 'evenings' represent some kind of decline, such as the corruption of the later kings of Israel and Judah at the close of the same day.[230] In this regard, too, Isidore's work formed an important hinge between patristic and medieval interpretation of Genesis.

[224] Pererius is a good Renaissance example: Benedictus Pererius, *Commentariorium et disputationum in Genesim, tomi quatuor, continentes historiam Mosis ab exordio mundi* (Cologne: apud Antonium Hierat, 1601; reprint, Vol. CA–29, series Catholic Reformation, Inter Documentation Co., Zug, Switzerland), 1:80. Gregory's voice is of chief importance for Pererius, and he quotes Gregory's statement at length. For an important medieval example, see Peter Lombard, "Sentences," in *PL* 192:675. (*Sentences* 2.12.2)

[225] Genesis plays an important role in his *Chronicon*: Isidore of Seville, "Sancti Isidori Hispalensis Episcopi chronicon," in *PL* 83:1019. His very brief summary of the creation week in this work sounds straightforwardly literal.

[226] Isidore of Seville, "In Genesin," 83:207B–209A; the quote is from Thomas O'Loughlin, "Christ as the Focus of Genesis Exegesis in Isidore of Seville," in *Studies in Patristic Christology*, ed. T. Finan and V. Twomey (Dublin: Four Courts, 1998), 145.

[227] See O'Loughlin, "Isidore of Seville," 156–57, 161–62.

[228] Isidore of Seville, "In Genesin," 83:211B.

[229] For instance, Mangenot, "Hexaméron," 6:2338; Zahlten, *Creatio Mundi*, 92.

[230] Claudio Leonardi, "Aspects of Old Testament Interpretation in the Church from the Seventh to the Tenth Century," in *HB/OT*, vol. I, bk 2:181–84.

Medieval writers such as Bede would follow Isidore's world-week ideas and his general allegorical approach more enthusiastically than his instantaneous creation.[231]

Conclusion

Augustine was "the chief authority of the medieval Latin writers on creation," and his treatment of the sequence of creation days was the most influential one to emerge from the patristic era.[232] His *Literal Meaning* would dominate the Genesis section of the classic annotated medieval Bible, the *Glossa ordinaria*, and thence the treatment of creation in Peter Lombard's *Sentences*. Augustine was a prime influence on Eriugena, Anselm, Bonaventure and Thomas Aquinas regarding exegesis of the creation week as in theology generally. He remains the chief ancient authority cited, although not always with agreement, in the Genesis commentaries of Luther and Calvin.[233]

Yet few Christian thinkers wholeheartedly adopted his noetic and instantaneous creation. It was usually tempered with a more 'realistic' reception of the daily sequence. Yet the immediate trend was not so much to deny the literalness of the creation week, but, exhibiting little interest in the surface meaning of the text, to delve promptly into the mysteries about Christ that the hexaemeral account was felt to conceal. These were the real gems that made the physical details of the text, such as solar days, seem trivial by comparison. Study of the creation narrative primarily as a (meta)physical cosmogony would await the resurgence of cosmogonic interest in connection with renewed attention to Plato's *Timaeus* in the twelfth century, with the associated revival of a sense of history and of nature.

[231] See E. Ann Matter, "The Church Fathers and the Glossa Ordinaria," in *RCFW* 1:87; Bede, *On Genesis*, trans. C. Kendall, Translated Texts for Historians (Liverpool: Liverpool University Press, 2008), 101; Aquinas, *Summa Theologiae*, 211–12.

[232] Robbins, *Hexaemeral Literature*, 64.

[233] Willemien Otten, "The Texture of Tradition: The Role of the Church Fathers in Carolingian Theology," in *RCFW*, 1:43; E. Ann Matter, "Glossa Ordinaria," 86; Bougerol, "Sentences," 115, 46, 50; Burcht Pranger, "Sic et Non: Patristic Authority between Refusal and Acceptance: Anselm of Canterbury, Peter Abelard and Bernard of Clairvaux," in *RCFW*, 1:169; Jacques-Guy Bougerol, "The Church Fathers and Auctoritates in Scholastic Theology to Bonaventure," in *RCFW*, 1:305–307; Elders, "Thomas Aquinas," 364; Eric Leland Saak, "The Reception of Augustine in the Later Middle Ages," in *RCFW*, 1:367–68. See the treatment of each of these figures in the following chapters.

3

The Days of Creation in the Middle Ages and Early Renaissance

> I left too, reflecting on the wisdom of some forgotten sage who had once said, "Chartres is the cathedral for those who do not believe." I walked slowly toward the windows of the west where pictures painted in gold, ruby, and sapphire light told the story of the first Christmas, and went out into the winter dusk.[1]

Introduction

The medieval era features a diversity of approaches to the early chapters of Genesis that befits its sensitivity to the multiple senses of Scripture, making the medieval literature that concerns Gen. 1:1–2:3 daunting and difficult to categorize.[2] It has more in common with the preceding, patristic era, than with Renaissance and Modern periods. To us it remains quite 'different' territory, unfamiliar in its interpretive values and methods. It was a period of virtually undisputed dominance for Genesis in questions of the world's origin and constitution. Other sources were not absent; many scholars were interested in reconciling Neoplatonism, and later in the period, Aristotelian philosophy with Genesis. Classical origins myths such as Hesiod's *Theogony*, Plato's *Timaeus* and Ovid's *Metamorphoses* were also familiar to medieval Christian scholars, and in a climate of reverence for sources of great age, were often taken quite seriously. Yet Scripture was the bar at which they had to answer, or at least had to be seen to answer. It was not

[1] Kenneth MacLeish, "Legacy from the Age of Faith," *National Geographic*, December 1969, 882.

[2] Yves-M. J. Congar comments that one could enlarge the list of medieval hexaemeral works almost indefinitely: Yves M.-J. Congar, "Le thème de *Dieu-Créateur* et les explications de l'Hexameron dans la tradition chrétienne," in *L'Homme devant Dieu: Mélanges offerts au Père Henri de Lubac*, Théologie 56–58 (Paris: 1963–64), 1:215–22.

until the seventeenth century that this authoritative status began to be openly questioned.

My chosen approach here is to follow Frank Robbins' suggestion: "The best index of the prevailing type of interpretation at this period is a comparison of their doctrines with those of Augustine on questions where a difference of opinion arose."[3] Such was the medieval regard for patristic tradition, and for Augustine in particular, that his unique understanding of the creation week is always taken seriously in medieval commentary on Genesis. Some writers adopt Augustine's instantaneous creation, where the 'days' of the creation week are 'intelligible' or mental realities. Others perceived the creation days as a sequence of real, sense-susceptible events involving historical succession. This meant limiting instantaneous creation to the appearance of primordial, undifferentiated matter after the example of Gregory the Great, and this became a common expedient for accommodating Augustine's view rather than controversially rejecting outright the teaching of such an esteemed father of the church.

But the very question of the nature of the days, temporal or not, pertained merely to the literal sense of the Genesis text. For many medieval writers, as for Isidore and Anastasius of Sinai, the literal sense was not the most interesting or important. Prophetic (world-week), christological and moral allegory were often more important to medieval scholars. Yet the literal meaning was generally acknowledged to be the interpretive starting-point and constitutes the primary reference point for our investigation. By the end of the period, a more natural and physical view of the world was restoring the prestige of the literal sense in biblical hermeneutics and prompting renewed interest in the creation week as an account of the physical origin of the world.

An Augustinian Creation in the Early Middle Ages

Instantaneous creation remained a persuasive option for early medieval Christian thinkers. Though Latin traditions dominated the medieval West, and were themselves dominated by Augustine's legacy, occasional Greek Christian influence might creep through, and in the case of Archbishop Theodore (d. 690) and Abbot Hadrian (d. 709), who hailed from the eastern Mediterranean, reinforced an instantaneous creation teaching. Their 'First Commentary on the Pentateuch' (PentI) treats the creation week simply as an expansion of the initial statement that God created the heavens and the earth.[4] A more temporal feel was

[3] Robbins, *Hexaemeral Literature*, 78.

[4] Bernhard Bischoff and Michael Lapidge, eds., *Biblical Commentaries from the Canterbury School of Theodore and Hadrian*, Cambridge Studies in Anglo-Saxon England (Cam-

meanwhile sustained in certain Christian epic poems of the early medieval era.[5] But a key Saxon figure who clearly responded to the Augustinian heritage was the Venerable Bede (c. 673–735), one of the 'gateway figures' who funnelled the deposit of patristic biblical learning into the medieval milieu.

Early in his commentary *On Genesis*, in full awareness of the major hexaemera of Basil, Ambrose and above all, Augustine,[6] Bede adopts the language of instantaneous creation. While humans build by laying a foundation and then courses of stone in turn, "God ... had no need of a delay of time." We are meant to understand from Gen. 1:1 that God created both heaven and earth simultaneously, i.e. the classical four elements, water, earth, and by implication, air and fire.[7] This is not Gregory's utterly formless initial matter, given form across the six days, which Bede would later adopt. The earth was only 'formless' in being concealed by water, as Basil and Ambrose had taught.[8] The pre-dawn light that preceded the sun's creation moved around the earth just as the sun would shortly, creating "without doubt a day of twenty-four hours."[9] Now we read further on, "It must be understood that everything he wanted came into existence faster than speech. It matters not at all what human speech names first in the class of created things that divine power fashioned collectively all at once."[10] But by this point in the commentary it is clear that he means that the objects of each creative *fiat* were brought into being instantly *on their respective days*.[11] Bede had sided with Augustine's predecessors Basil, Ambrose, and probably Athanasius, in holding to this qualified version of instantaneous creation.

bridge: Cambridge University Press, 1994), 205–206, 308–309; Beryl Smalley, *The Study of the Bible in the Middle Ages* (Oxford: Blackwell, 1952), 14–20; Robbins, *Hexaemeral Literature*, 12.

[5] E.g. the Saxon 'Caedmonian Genesis', dating sometime between 700 and 850. This Milton-like poem displays a poetic but realistic treatment of the sequence of the creation days: W. Kirkconnell, ed., *The Celestial Cycle* (Toronto: University of Toronto Press, 1952; reprint, New York: Gordian, 1967), 19–43. The works of Avitus, Dracontius and Cyprian were available in the times of Bede and Alcuin: Evans, *Genesis Tradition*, 141.

[6] Joseph F. Kelly, "Bede's Use of Augustine for His *Commentarium in principium Genesis*," in *Augustine: Biblical Exegete*, ed. Frederick van Fleteren and Joseph C. Schnaubelt (New York: Peter Lang, 2001), 193.

[7] Bede, *On Genesis*, 68.

[8] Bede, *On Genesis*, 71. (Compare Basil, *Hexaemeron* 2.1 and Ambrose, *Hexameron* 2.8.) For the distinction in Bede's own thinking, compare Mangenot, "Hexaméron," 6:2339; Zahlten, *Creatio Mundi*, 92–93.

[9] Bede, *On Genesis*, 73, 75, 83.

[10] Ibid., 89.

[11] This was noticed by Robert Grosseteste a few centuries later: Robert Grosseteste, *On the Six Days of Creation*, trans. C.F.J. Martin (Oxford University Press, 1996), 88.

Meanwhile, Bede enthusiastically perpetuated the patristic world-week tradition, connecting particular details of the creation days with corresponding aspects of the eras of redemptive history, following Isidore.[12] And before leaving the issue of the days altogether, he notes that while Gen. 2:4–5 could be understood as teaching the seminal creation of plants within the earth along Augustinian lines, it was simpler just to understand that 'day' in this text simply refers to the entirety of the creation week, wherein plants did not spring from the soil but appeared suddenly mature.[13] Thus Bede freed himself from one strained position of Augustine. But let us notice Bede's own particular priorities as he interpreted the creation account: he emphasizes that if the world was created in spring, as the vegetation would suggest; and indeed at the spring equinox, assuming that the first day and night were created equal; and if the moon was created full, and accordingly rose as the sun fell on the fourth day; then the following Sunday, or 'Day 8', would constitute the first ever Easter Sunday, and provide an immediate typological link to the resurrection of Christ – after all, the crowning point of interest for an interpreter such as Bede![14]

The legacy of fathers such as Augustine, Basil and Ambrose, conveyed through Gregory the Great, Isidore and now Bede, continued to propagate itself through the early Middle Ages via Carolingian scholars. Alcuin (c. 735–804), who has been called "the most important scholar of his age," produced a work on Genesis in the catechetical format known as the Quaestio which, typically for its time, prioritized lucid fidelity to the fathers rather than originality.[15] Following in Bede's train, Alcuin adopts certain well-established interpretations of Gen. 1:1–2:3: Gregory the Great's (and Bede's eventual) understanding that 'heaven' and 'earth' in 1:1 refer to a formless, mingled mass of the four elements fire, air, water and earth, to be formed over six natural days

[12] Bede, *On Genesis*, 100–05. The transmission of this idea from Augustine through Isidore, then Bede and on into the Middle Ages is reported among many others by M.-D. Chenu, ed., *Nature, Man and Society in the Twelfth Century: Essays on New Theological Perspectives in the Latin West* (Chicago: University of Chicago Press, 1968), 179 n. 135. I will say more about this in the subsequent section concerning history-oriented medieval works.

[13] Bede, *On Genesis*, 105–107.

[14] Ibid., 83, also 33–34. This works because Easter falls on the first Sunday after the first full moon after the spring equinox. Leonardi, "Old Testament Interpretation," 187. Note also that Bede still returns to the symbolic value of six as the perfect number: Bede, *On Genesis*, 96.

[15] The 'quaestio' dated back as far as (to use Genesis-related examples) Augustine's *Quaestiones in Heptateuchum* and Jerome's *Quaestiones hebraicae in Genesim*. See Gilbert Dahan, "Genres, Forms and Various Methods in Christian Exegesis of the Middle Ages," in *HB/OT*, vol. I, 2:221–22. The quotation is from Ulrich Köpf, "The Institutional Framework of Christian Exegesis in the Middle Ages," in *HB/OT*, vol. I, 2:157.

(because six is the perfect number!), an angelic creation and fall prior to the creation of the material world, and world-week historical allegory, with hopeful anticipation of the Sabbath rest to come.[16]

Further Genesis works followed from Alcuin's pupil Rabanus Maurus (c. 784–856), Claudius of Turin, Wicbod, Angelomus of Luxeuil (*fl.* c. 855), and Remigius of Auxerre (c. 841–908), whom Smalley represents as bringing a productive period of Bible commentary (or commentary compilation) to a close.[17] These scholars carefully adhered to patristic tradition, but there was one early medieval figure who stood out for his originality.

The Timeless Creation of Eriugena

The *De divisione naturae* or *Periphyseon* of John Scotus Eriugena (c. 810–c. 877), deemed "the most original mind of the Carolingian era,"[18] is regarded by Robbins as "perhaps the most important single work" in the post-patristic hexaemeral tradition.[19] Eriugena integrated Christian teaching on creation into a Neoplatonist metaphysic, in the process stretching the bounds of Christian orthodoxy. *De divisione naturae* is utterly comprehensive in its scope, attempting to explain not just physical nature but the whole of reality, tangible and intangible, including God, and even things that do not exist. He treats the creation week in Book 3, where he explicitly follows Augustine in offering a timeless, Neoplatonist interpretation of the Genesis creation account:

> For all these things ... were established all together and at once [ordained and constituted] for their own times and places, and in no case did the generation of any one of them into forms and species, quantities and qualities, precede by temporal intervals the generation of any other, but that they proceeded simultaneously, each according to its genus and species

[16] Alcuin, "Interrogationes et responsiones in Genesin," in *PL,* vol. 100:515ff. = *Interrogationes* 2–4, 25, 42–45. Note Bede's influence in Alcuin's explanation of Gen. 2:4, *Interrogationes* 45.

[17] Smalley, *Study of the Bible*, 44. See Rabanus Maurus, "Commentaria in Genesim," in *PL,* vol. 107:439–670; [Claudius of Turin], "In Genesim," in *PL,* vol. 50:893–1084 (On the attribution of this commentary to Claudius, see M.L.W. Laistner, "Some Early Medieval Commentaries on the Old Testament," *Harvard Theological Review* 46 (1953): 45; Congar, "Le theme de *Dieu-Createur,*" 1:217; Bray, *Biblical Interpretation*, 135); Wicbod, "Liber quaestionum super librum Genesis ex dictis sanctorum partum..." in *PL,* vol. 96:1105–68 (and see Leonardi, "Old Testament Interpretation," 188); Angelom of Luxeuil, "In Genesim," in *PL,* vol. 115:107–244 (and see Laistner, "Early Medieval Commentaries," 28–34); Remigius of Auxerre, *Remigii Autissiodorensis expositio super Genesim / cura et studio Burton Van Name Edwards*, Corpus Christianorum, continuatio mediaevalis (Turnhout: Brepols, 1999).

[18] Otten, "Texture of Tradition," 31.

[19] Robbins, *Hexaemeral Literature*, 73.

> and indivisible particulars, from their eternal reasons in which they subsist as essences in the Word of God. For the sixfold quantity of the six first days and their intelligible division is understood to refer to the causes of established things and of their first downrush simultaneously into the initial constitution of this world; and that which was made at once and all together by the Creator is distinguished, in the perfection of the number six, ... For all things were made in the twinkling of an eye.[20]

A preceding passage explains that the 'fiat' commands of God for each creation day signify "the [special] establishment of the primordial causes," or the second division of nature in Eriugena's scheme, the invisible powers that act as God's agents in producing all visible creation. The 'it was so' statements in turn signify "the procession of the same primordial causes into their effects through the genera and the species."[21] So the repeating textual formulas associated with the creation days represent logical stages in an instantaneous process of creation.

Eriugena's timeless creation is anchored in a timeless, emanationist theology. God creates by manifesting his own essential nature in certain 'primordial causes', and via them, in the lowest order of physical objects and beings.[22] By means of such humble forms the human intellect may grasp God; every created thing is a theophany.[23] This philosophy of creation is monistic in the sense that everything is ultimately a part of God, and emanationist in that all that exists emerges by necessity from the being of God, although Eriugena tries to retain a place for the will of God. Since everything that God wills must automatically and instantly occur, on the assumption that creation is eternally intended by God, creation exists in a kind of eternal present.[24] All things "are at the same time eternal and made in the only begotten Word of God".[25]

While Eriugena finds warrant for his interpretation in his forebear Augustine, his Neoplatonism, derived from Proclus via Pseudo-Dionysius and Maximus the Confessor, is more radical than Augus-

[20] Johannes Scotus Eriugena, *Periphyseon (De divisione naturae) Liber Tertius*, trans. I.P. Sheldon-Williams, Scriptores Latini Hiberniae (Dublin: The Dublin Institute for Advanced Studies, 1981), 209, 211. The brackets are present in both Sheldon-Williams' English translation and in his Latin original.

[21] Ibid., 205.

[22] Ibid., 171, 173. "[Eriugena's] interpretation of the six days' work is a reconciliation of the Scriptures with his own theory that the divine goodness proceeds from itself first into the ideal types, second into the larger subdivisions of corporeal things, and third into individual things": Robbins, *Hexaemeral Literature*, 73.

[23] Eriugena, *Periphyseon*, 195. A theophany is a manifestation of God, the term usually being applied to reported appearances of God in OT narratives.

[24] Ibid., 153.

[25] Ibid., 141.

tine's.[26] The temporal element of creation suggested by the six-day account is completely suppressed in Eriugena's ideal scheme. Eriugena understands himself, as did Augustine, to be interpreting the literal sense of the biblical text, "attempting, under God's guidance, to say a few things about only the creation of made things according to the historical sense," and he too deals with the created order of nature, but forces the Hexaemeron through such a potent metaphysical grid that its essence seems fundamentally changed.[27] We may find Eriugena's scheme alien, but it was a *tour de force* that helped introduce key Neoplatonic influences, such as the celestial hierarchy of Pseudo-Dionysius, into Western thought.[28]

Three Biblical Reference Works of the Twelfth Century

From the opening of the twelfth century, during a revival of Western intellectual culture, several new genres of Bible-related literature appeared whose effect was to standardize the collected deposit of patristic and early medieval biblical commentary. This rich commentary tradition was appended to the biblical text in what became the standard glossed Bible and compendium of biblical knowledge, the *Glossa ordinaria*, completed around 1130.[29] Not long afterwards, by extracting and combining the key discussions from his own running gloss, Peter Lombard developed his famous *Sentences*, which represented another new genre wherein exegetical comment was developed and systematized separately from the biblical text. This work prompted almost as much scholastic commentary as did the Bible itself.[30] Then Peter Comestor's *Historia scholastica* introduced an important new, historically

[26] Robert D. Crouse, "The Meaning of Creation in Augustine and Eriugena," in *Tenth International Conference on Patristic Studies, Oxford, 1987*, ed. E.A. Livingstone, Studia Patristica (Leuven: Peeters, 1989), 232. Yet Augustine's explanation in terms of angelic cognition is absent.

[27] Eriugena, *Periphyseon*, 197. This statement occurs as discussion begins on the second day of creation, and may be fairly local in its application to Eriugena's discussion. Sheldon-Williams actually believes that Eriugena instead proceeds to treat the text according to what Eriugena elsewhere describes as the 'scientific' sense: Eriugena, *Periphyseon*, 317 n. 344.

[28] Neil Lewis, "Robert Grosseteste and the Church Fathers," in *RCFW*, vol. 1:217–18. See also Backus, ed., *RCFW*, 1:xii.

[29] Margaret T. Gibson, "The Place of the Glossa Ordinaria in Medieval Exegesis," in *Ad Litteram: Authoritative Texts and their Medieval Readers*, ed. M.D. Jordan and K. Emery, Notre Dame Conferences in Medieval Studies (Notre Dame, ID: University of Notre Dame Press, 1992), 5; Gillian R. Evans, *The Language and Logic of the Bible: The Earlier Middle Ages* (Cambridge: Cambridge University Press, 1984), 37–47.

[30] Smalley, *Study of the Bible*, 64, 179, etc.; Gillian R. Evans, *The Language and Logic of the Bible: The Road to Reformation* (Cambridge: Cambridge University Press, 1985), 102.

arranged theological genre.[31] They all soon became standard references for biblical studies and greatly influenced, and now ably reflect, medieval thinking about the creation week.[32]

Each page of the *Glossa ordinaria* combines three kinds of text: a small portion of the Vulgate text of the Bible, the interspersed terse comments of the 'interlinear gloss', and the copious 'marginal gloss' that surrounds both. It was, in this particular form, "the 'normal tongue' (*glossa ordinaria*) of Scripture," a vivid example of medieval intertextuality, and the best available way to access patristic exegesis.[33] Augustine is the father whose creation thinking dominates the pages that relate to Genesis 1, which quote from his *Literal Meaning* his successive attempts to understand the creation days as literal solar days, then as lack of form (evenings) and the imparting of form (mornings), and then as a timeless process of angelic understanding.[34]

When the *Glossa* reaches Gen. 2:1–4, it again reproduces Augustine's endorsement of an instantaneous creation and merely 'intelligible' days, including his 'six is the perfect number' rationale, his efforts to clarify the meaning of God's seventh-day rest, and the sevenfold replaying of the prototypical first day.[35] Augustine's theory of creation days comprised of episodes of angelic comprehension is repeated in full.[36] The *Glossa* finally records the whole conclusion of *Literal Meaning* Book 4, where our solar days constitute a mere shadow or sign of the more real days that constituted the creation week.[37]

[31] Zahlten, *Creatio Mundi*, 94; Smalley, *Study of the Bible*, 200; Dahan, "Christian Exegesis of the Middle Ages," 211.

[32] See the comment relating to the *Glossa ordinaria* by Matter, "Glossa Ordinaria," 1:87. Surveys such as Robbins' and Jaki's bypass the *Glossa ordinaria* in particular.

[33] The quotation is from K. Froehlich, 'The Printed Gloss', introduction to K. Froehlich and M.T. Gibson, eds., *Biblia Latina cum Glossa Ordinaria: Facsimile Reprint of the Editio Princeps Adolph Rusch of Strassburg 1480/81*, 4 vols., vol. I (Turnhout: Brepols, 1992), xvi. Concerning intertextuality, E. Ann Matter says, "The *Glossa ordinaria* is a particularly good example of medieval intertextuality, the conscious borrowing and rearticulating of old material in a new form ": Matter, "Glossa Ordinaria," 1:109. Concerning access to patristic exegesis, see Gibson, "Place of the Glossa Ordinaria," 21.

[34] Froehlich and Gibson, *Glossa Ordinaria*, 1:9d, 10b–c. Page references refer to the reproduced text itself, which bears handwritten numbers. On Basil see Augustine, *Literal Meaning*, 37. (*DGaL* 1.16.31).

[35] Froehlich and Gibson, *Glossa Ordinaria*, 1:17a–18a, c. Cf. *DGaL* 4.11.21, 4.7.14, 4.18.31–33, 4.20.37.

[36] Froehlich and Gibson, *Glossa Ordinaria*, 1:18b–c. Cf. *DGaL* 4.22.39, 4.26.43.

[37] Froehlich and Gibson, *Glossa Ordinaria*, 1:18c–d. Cf. *DGaL* 4.35.56. Some of Augustine's comments relating to Gen. 2:4 from Book 5 follow, further supporting instantaneous creation, but in any case Augustine's position has by this point been clearly condoned: Froehlich and Gibson, *Glossa Ordinaria*, 1:19b–c. Cf. *DGaL* 5.1.1, 5.3.6, 5.5.12, etc.

Augustine's comments largely suffice in the *Glossa* for covering the literal sense of Gen. 1:1–2:3, but other levels of meaning are also treated as legitimate.[38] The world-week allegorical interpretation is presented via Isidore, who also contributes another allegorical interpretation of the days as a spiritual ascent to God.[39] Gregory supplies moral-spiritual thoughts, and Jerome's included comments are textual in nature.[40] Both Isidore and Alcuin contribute a model wherein the days of creation parallel the stages of human life.[41] So allegorical conceptions of the creation days, which might easily have been drawn from Augustine's other Genesis material, are in the *Glossa* associated with other writers, while it relies on Augustine solely for his discussion of the relationship of creation to time, a question associated with the literal sense of Genesis.[42]

Peter Lombard's (c. 1095–1169) famous *Sentences* (~1152) represent something of a mid-way step between running commentary or glosses and the theological 'summae' of the next century.[43] As the recognized standard theological reference work of the heart of the Middle Ages, it represents another telling example of mainstream Christian perspective on the creation week. Augustine is the chief patristic source for the *Sentences,* and the primary source for the section concerning creation is Augustine's *Literal Meaning,* accessed via the *Glossa ordinaria.*[44] The vital question here surrounds the tenability of Augustine's instantaneous creation view:

> Now certain of the holy Fathers who have very well scrutinized the words and mysteries of God seem to have written conflicting things on this point. Some indeed have handed down that everything was created once both in substance and form, as Augustine seems to have thought. Others have instead demonstrated and asserted that crude and formless initial matter, consisting of a mix and melee of the four elements, was created. Only then, through an interval of six days, were the various kinds of bodily things formed from that matter according to their particular types. Gregory, Jerome, Bede and many others commend and prefer this opinion, which seems more in accord with the Genesis Scriptures.[45]

[38] Augustine's contributions are sometimes labelled 'historice', and once, tellingly, 'historice, non temporaliter': Froehlich and Gibson, eds., *Glossa Ordinaria,* 1:9c, 10a–b, etc.

[39] Ibid., 1:12b, 13b–c, 14b–c, 16b–c.

[40] Ibid., 1:10b, c; 17a.

[41] Ibid., 1:9d, 16d.

[42] Note the reporting of Bede's conclusion on the basis of Gen. 2:4 and Ecclus. 18:1 that everything had to have been created at once in its 'causal substances': ibid., 1:18d.

[43] Smalley, *Study of the Bible,* 54.

[44] Bougerol, "Sentences," 1:115–20. Also Chenu, ed., *Nature, Man and Society,* 33.

[45] Lombard, "Sentences," 675 (*Sentences* 2.12.2) Note that I have translated the original 'commixtionem atque confusionem' as 'mix and melee' here.

Despite Augustine's authoritative weight and the theological attractiveness and philosophical simplicity of an instantaneous creation, the simplicity of a literal reading of the biblical account, the continued appeal of the Greek concept of a primordial chaos, and perhaps the sense that the majority position was more securely orthodox tipped the balances the other way for Lombard:

> When God in his wisdom made the angelic spirits, he made still other things, as the abovementioned Scripture, Genesis 1, makes clear, which says that *in the beginning God created heaven,* that is, angels, *and earth,* namely, the material of the four elements as yet mingled and unformed, which is called Chaos by the Greeks, and this was before any day. Next God distinguished the elements, and gave to individual things their proper and distinct types according to their kinds; which he formed not at once, as seemed best to certain of the holy Fathers, but through intervals of time and the measures of six days, as it seemed to others.[46]

Lombard proceeds to defend the use of the term *materia informis* for that initial matter, and limits the concept of instantaneous creation to its production.[47] The reality of his creation week explains why Lombard accounts for light before the sun in the literal, physical terms familiar from Basil and others.[48] But when he comes to mention the creation of man, Lombard unexpectedly reprises Augustine's instantaneous creation position, against his better judgment, as it were. "Moses, speaking to an ignorant and carnal people, restrained his mode of expression, speaking of God according to the analogy of the human, who completes his tasks through periods of time, while [God] himself performed his tasks at once."[49] Lombard therefore betrays a certain sympathy for Augustine's view, thought he perhaps felt it was difficult or unpopular or even unorthodox to overtly defend.

Lombard in this tract also articulates the classic medieval distinction between the work of 'distinction' (*distinctio*, or else *dispositio*), occupying the first three days, by which the four basic elements of fire, air, water and earth are set in their functional order, and the subsequent 'adorning' (*ornatio*) or 'equipping' of the separated elements with their details and inhabitants. Not only does this distinguish the initial creation (*creatio*) of Gen. 1:1 from what follows, but establishes the division of the creation week into corresponding sets of three days (*tridua*).[50] The bracketing off of the initial act of creation would make it easier in

[46] *Sentences* 2.12.1.

[47] *Sentences* 2.12.8. Compare Alcuin, *Interrogationes* 19.

[48] *Sentences* 2.13.6.

[49] Thus purely formal distinctions between things being presented in the guise of differences between days: *Sentences* 2.15.5.

[50] *Sentences* 2.14.6.

later centuries to incorporate the idea of a long-latent chaotic period into the formal theological structure perceived in Genesis 1. The recognition of two corresponding sets of three days, meanwhile, anticipates much later literary interpretations of Genesis 1, illustrating the principle of the 'depth' of this interpretive legacy.

Peter Comestor (d. c. 1179) was part of a trio of 'Paris Masters' that also included Peter Chanter and Stephen Langton. He taught at the cathedral school of Notre Dame 1160–78.[51] Comestor rates little mention in surveys of the hexaemeral literature, and his treatment of the creation week in his *Historia scholastica* is relatively brief.[52] But this omission again fails to acknowledge Comestor's influence in the medieval world, since the *Historia* quickly became a standard textbook in the schools and universities on a par with the *Glossa* and Lombard's *Sentences*.[53] While beginning his treatment of creation with John 1:1 in order to put Christ, the 'Word', in the foreground, Comestor treats the literal or historical sense of the biblical text as foundational for the allegorical and tropological senses, and so retains the historical aspect of the creation week using Lombard's tripartite formula:

> This creation ... Scripture expounds under the works of the six days, suggesting three [aspects], creation, arrangement and adornment. On the first day creation, and a certain arrangement; on the second and third, arrangement; during the remaining three, adornment.[54]

The initial creation of 'heaven and earth' includes both them and all that they contain at that stage, the contents of the empyrean heaven being the angelic hosts, and the contents of the 'earth' being the four elements.[55] This was all done instantaneously, but cannot be related instantaneously.[56] This was Augustine's argument for a wholesale instantaneous creation under a chronological guise, but Comestor's literal, physical account of the first day shows that Comestor does not extend this principle to the productions of the entire creation week.

[51] Smalley, *Study of the Bible*, 196–263; Bray, *Biblical Interpretation*, 141; Karlfried Froehlich, "Christian Interpretation of the Old Testament in the High Middle Ages," in *HB/OT*, vol. I, 2:505–10.

[52] But see Zahlten, *Creatio Mundi*, 94. Please note that I have referred in this section to the text of Peter Comestor, "Historia Scholastica," in *PL*, vol. 198:1053–1722. Froehlich criticises the quality of this text, noting the more recent edition, A. Sylwan, "Petrus Comestor, Historia Scholastica: une nouvelle édition," *Sacri Erudiri* 39 (2000): 345–82.

[53] Zahlten, *Creatio Mundi*, 94; Smalley, *Study of the Bible*, 179, 200; Dahan, "Christian Exegesis of the Middle Ages," 211.

[54] Hanc creationem ... sub operibus sex dierum explicat Scriptura, insinuans tria, creationem, dispositionem et ornatum. In primo die creationem, et quamdam dispositionem; in secundo et tertio, dispositionem; in reliquis tribus ornatum. Comestor, "Historia Scholastica," 198:1055A, 1056B.

[55] Ibid., 198:1055B.

[56] Sed quod simul factum est, simul dici non potuit. Ibid., 198:1056A.

When light is created along with heaven and earth on the first day, it slowly wanes and sets in the normal manner, then migrating under the earth, rises again to begin the second day, showing that we are dealing throughout with ordinary days.[57] But despite this trend in a realist direction, Augustine's instantaneous creation retained some dedicated defenders in the twelfth century.

Creation in the Commentary of the Twelfth Century

The twelfth century revival of learning produced a new surge of interest in Genesis, while Plato also came back into vogue, so that some thinkers sought to explain biblical creation in relation to the cosmogony in Plato's *Timaeus*.[58] A revived Platonism could have encouraged the positive reception of Augustine's legacy, but reactions to his instantaneous creation still ranged from the wholehearted adoption by Honorius of Autun to absolute rejection by Andrew of St. Victor. Other commentators meanwhile were more interested in non-literal levels of meaning, especially christological allegory.

Creation is handled allegorically in *On the Holy Trinity and His Works* by Rupert of Deutz (c. 1075–1129), such that the philosophical question of whether the days should be taken as time periods does not arise. For him the literal sense is the coarse veil of the old dispensation that is removed in Christ, allowing the light of more glorious realities to shine through.[59] He understands the speaking of the Word of creation to refer to the eternal procession of the Son from the Father, and Christ is also the 'Day' in which everything was made 'before it appeared' (Gen. 2:4–5).[60] Nevertheless many writers remained curious about the natural and philosophical implications of the Genesis text, and did engage Augustine's position, with writers earlier in the period more inclined to be favourable.

[57] Ibid., 198:1057D.

[58] M.-D. Chenu, "The Platonisms of the Twelfth Century," in *Nature, Man and Society in the Twelfth Century: Essays on New Theological Perspectives in the Latin West*, trans. J. Taylor and L.K. Little (Chicago: University of Chicago Press, 1968), 49–98. Regarding interest in Genesis, see Zahlten, *Creatio Mundi*, 86–101, esp. tables 4 and 5 in the appendices, which demonstrate a great multiplication of works relating to Genesis in the twelfth century.

[59] Rupert of Deutz, *De sancta Trinitate et operibus eius*, ed. R. Haacke, Corpus Christianorum, continuatio mediaevalis (Turnholt: Brepols, 1971), 1:125 (*De sancta Trinitate*, Prologue)

[60] *De sancta Trinitate*, Prologue; 1.20. He explains that in Christ the potentiality of everything that was yet to exist eternally resided.

The *Glossa ordinaria* offered the twelfth century a precedent for accepting instantaneous creation.[61] In the twelfth century, formal hexaemera began to re-emerge, one of the earliest being the *Expositio in Hexaemeron* of Peter Abelard (1079–1142), written at the request of Héloïse, his pupil and eventual lover.[62] Abelard is "generally considered the first important representative of scholastic theology."[63] His thinking and writing showed a flair and independence that made him the *cause celebré* of the Enlightenment and a controversial figure in his own day.[64] In the preface to the *Expositio in Hexaemeron*, Abelard describes Genesis' history of the creation as one of the most difficult parts of the OT to interpret.[65] He undertakes his exposition by means of a threefold approach, historical, moral and mystical, although the 'historical' interpretation of the days of creation often turns in a typological direction; references to water, for instance, frequently lead Abelard to meditations on baptism.[66] But he does address the issue of time in the creation week, in the context of explaining the formation of the firmament of Day 2:

> If anyone wants to know how great a lapse of time occurred here before [the waters] were made firm, wishing to understand what kind of day was that first one before the second, let him realize that those six days in which the world was completed ought by no means to be reckoned according to those days which we now experience by the sun's illumination, especially since in those first three days the sun had not yet been made. When, therefore, we estimate a day in these works of God ... we perceive a unique and different day according to the work of distinction, so that the first action of God is clearly called the first day, through which he initially worked, on the basis of which he could illumine us out of his knowledge ... we have interposed this, [so that] when [the reader] hears of one day or another spoken by the prophet, he might not understand those as delays of time, which we now experience in our days, but might refer

[61] Anselm of Canterbury (c. 1033–1109) seems hesitant to decide in his important *Cur Deus homo*: Anselm, "Why God Became Man," in *A Scholastic Miscellany: Anselm to Ockham*, ed. Eugene R. Fairweather, trans. E. Prout, The Library of Christian Classics: Ichthus Edition (Philadelphia: Westminster, 1982), 127. (*Cur Deus homo* 1.18).

[62] Peter Abelard, "Expositio in hexameron," in *PL,* vol. 178:729f; Eileen F Kearney, "Peter Abelard as Biblical Commentator: A Study of the Expositio in Hexaemeron," in *Petrus Abaelardus (1079–1142)* (Trier: Paulinus-Verlag, 1980), 199–200; Robert D. Linder, "Abelard (Abailard), Peter (1079–1142)," in *The New International Dictionary of the Christian Church*, ed. J.D. Douglas (Grand Rapids: Eerdmans, 1996), 3.

[63] Pranger, "Sic et Non," 1:170.

[64] Chenu, "Twelfth-Century Theology," xix; Kearney, "Peter Abelard," 199.

[65] The others are the Song of Songs and the vision of the living creatures and wheels at the beginning of Ezekiel.

[66] Abelard, "Expositio in hexameron," 178:731D; Kearney, "Peter Abelard," 200, 203–05.

> those different days to different works, however great the lapse of time in succession or operation in his own thinking.[67]

Earlier he interprets evening and morning as the conception of a specific thing in the mind of God, and then its material realization.[68] This interpretation in terms of a transition from the ideal to the real resembles Eriugena more than Augustine, although Abelard drew directly on Plato's *Timaeus* to help interpret the Genesis account.[69] In this Platonic framework, the days of creation are like the days of our experience only by analogy; the absence of the sun signifies the essential difference between the two. Abelard's moral and allegorical sections moreover feature the well-established understandings of the creation week according to (1) the six stages of history or 'world-week', (2) the stages of human physical life, and (3) the stages of the individual's experience of redemption.[70]

Some commentators of this period write as if they can hold to instantaneous creation and a literal creation week of time simultaneously. This seems to be a kind of cognitive dualism emerging from the Platonic distinction between the ideal and the real. It also may betray the assumption that the philosophically astute alone understand that the creation week is an accommodating literary device for the uninformed, who understandably take it literally. Arnold of Bonneval (d. c. 1160), a figure associated with the influential cathedral school at Chartres, adopts instantaneous creation in his *On the Works of the Six Days*. The opening meditation on the stability of creation through God's sustaining power really constitutes natural philosophy at the service of worship.[71] His exposition of the appearance of light in Gen. 1:3 offers a pair of similar allegorical expositions of the six days that seek to embrace both creation and individual spiritual progress. The second of the two is helpfully brief:

> The first day therefore is the institution of intellectual or spiritual natures; the second, the creation of visible, bodily things; the third, the distinction of things from one another, and the bringing of them to fruitfulness according to their kinds; the fourth, the illumination of the mind through the testimony of the Scriptures; the fifth, discernment between the appe-

[67] Abelard, "Expositio in hexameron," 178:745C–D.

[68] Ibid., 178:741B–C. See also Jaki, *Genesis 1*, 113.

[69] Kearney, "Peter Abelard," 202–03.

[70] Abelard, "Expositio in hexameron," 178:770C–773A; Trompf, *Historical Recurrence*, 213.

[71] Arnold of Bonneval, "De operibus sex dierum," in *PL*, vol. 189:1515A–1517A. A large extract from this section is conveniently translated in Chenu, *Nature, Man and Society*, 9.

> tites of the flesh and the spirit of reason; the sixth, the expression of the divine image and likeness in thought and action ...[72]

This curious variation on a moral allegory combines the creation of both invisible and visible realms with the spiritual progress of the individual.

Arnold seems to adhere to instantaneous creation as a defence against the teaching of eternal principles that might rival God, although he grants that angelic service of God predates the physical world.[73] He finds that Ecclus 18:1 affirms the instantaneous creation of "the entire creation, angelic and human, and every other individual thing," thought what God was able to assemble at once, we are only able to 'assemble', or we might say, put the pieces of the puzzle together, over time.[74] Arnold mocks the attribution of the passing of time to the creative process, and associates it with the dangerous speculation about a 'time before time' that preceded the Genesis creation and saw God performing other works, or featured some part of Lucifer's career. No, the Ecclesiasticus reference prohibits both pre-existent matter or beings and any duration of time in creation.[75] Instantaneous creation in this particular scenario actually represents the more theologically conservative option, in opposition to belief in pre-existent primordial matter, or a Miltonian, pre-historic, angelic drama.

Although we may detect a hint of conflict in Arnold's allegiance to instantaneous creation, that of Honorius of Autun (or Augustodunensis) (c. 1090–c. 1156) seems more confident. He assigns responsibility in turn to the Father for *creatio,* the Son for *dispositio,* and the Spirit for *vivificatio* or *ornatio*, the three phases of creation. Here Honorius interprets "In the beginning God created heaven and earth" to mean, "In a moment God made everything, corporal and incorporeal."[76] This seems to match the instantaneous creation presented in his *Elucidarium.*[77] Yet he proceeds to expound the meaning of the creative works that followed in very physical terms, right down to a light source remaining above the earth for twelve hours and then going below it for another twelve to produce the first, twenty-four hour day.[78] He points out the parallelism between the 'dispositions' of Days 1–3 and the corresponding 'ornamentations' of Days 4–6 before completing his expo-

[72] Arnold of Bonneval, "De operibus sex dierum," 189:1520B–C.

[73] Ibid., 189:1517A–B.

[74] Ibid., 189:1518A–B.

[75] Ibid., 189:1517B–1518A. The quotation is, of course, Ecclus 18:1 yet again.

[76] Honorius Augustodunensis, "Hexaemeron," in *PL,* vol. 172:254A–255A.

[77] Gillian R. Evans, "Masters and Disciples: Aspects of Christian Interpretation of the Old Testament in the Eleventh and Twelfth Centuries," in *HB/OT,* vol. I, 2:252.

[78] Honorius Augustodunensis, "Hexaemeron," 172:255C–256A.

sition through Gen. 2:1–3, all the while giving every indication that a real progression of creative days is in view.[79]

Honorius' subsequent analysis of history on a world-week format is by now expected, constituting a 'prophetic' exposition of the creation week.[80] But then Honorius turns to Augustine's opinion and endorses it wholeheartedly: "Yet God did not first make matter, and then form; but brought everything forth fully formed at once."[81] So why the preceding realistic and temporal-sounding creation week exposition? "[Scripture] narrates to the wise that God created all things together in one day on the one hand, but relates to those who are slower that God completed his works in six days: since indeed the more competent can hardly grasp that God in one day, even in a blink of an eye, is said to have created everything at once."[82] It emerges that the entire preceding 'historical' exposition merely constitutes an expedient for the humbler mind, which is not yet equipped to grasp the true nature of God's creative work![83]

By thus interpreting Honorius as committed to an instantaneous creation, I differ from Mangenot, who attributed the classic position of Gregory, Bede and Lombard to Honorius.[84] Indeed, we saw that he was able to utilize the classic *creatio-distinctio-ornatio* tripartite breakdown of the content of Genesis 1. This gives every appearance of a realist, temporal interpretation, but was understood by Abelard, Arnold and Honorius as a kind of façade on the passage, put there to aid the unsophisticated faithful. It should not be mistaken as these thinkers' final stance. The same is true in the *Glosses on Genesis* of another Paris master, Peter Chanter (d. 1197), who uses the above trio of categories in the normal manner in his glosses, but declares in his prologue that in contrast to "those who say that the world was created according to the distinction of six days, ... Augustine says that everything was created at once, as we shall say." This plays out in his commentary simply by the placement of Augustine's opinion last on various exegetical points pertaining to instantaneous creation. Chanter's regular use of the creation, disposition, and adornment creation categories must be understood

[79] Ibid., 172:257A–259A.

[80] Ibid., 172:259B–260A.

[81] Ibid., 172:260D.

[82] Ibid., 172:262D.

[83] The whole of chapters 4–5 of the work advocate this view, from which the above excerpts are taken.

[84] Mangenot, "Hexaméron," 6:2339; Zahlten, *Creatio Mundi*, 93.

within the context of this general Augustinian stance, and not as representing chronological progression.[85]

Yet the Neoplatonist revival did not drive every theologian in an idealistic direction. Another representative of the Chartres cathedral school was Thierry of Chartres (c. 1100–c. 1156).[86] Thierry's *Treatise on the Works of the Six Days* exemplifies the fact "that all members of the School of Chartres wanted to justify Genesis 1 with an eye on Plato's *Timaeus*."[87] Yet Thierry retained a real time progression in the creation week, perhaps under the influence of Aristotle's realism. He expresses the intention to leave aside the moral and allegorical interpretations which are openly available in patristic sources, to instead expound Genesis 1 in physical terms and [then] according to its literal sense.[88] The second, 'literal exposition' turns out to be highly abstract, abandoning the temporal framework of the days of creation for a decidedly atemporal Platonic idealism.[89] In the more concrete first exposition, the world's existence is first explained in terms of the four Aristotelian 'causes'.[90] Thierry's concept of the natural inter-relationships of the four elements, fire, air, water and earth, governs his explanation of the course of the days of creation through the remainder of this section.

When he comes to treat the 'temporal sequence' (*ordine temporum*) of the creation week, he reconciles instantaneous creation (Ecclus 18:1) with creation in six days by means of what was becoming the mainstream medieval solution, inherited from Gregory the Great: that initial, instantaneous creation was of primordial matter, while the six days pertain to the distinction of its various forms.[91] The interesting additional feature in Thierry's proposal is that this formation is self-driven through the inbuilt qualities of the four elements. The initial creation

[85] Petrus Cantor, *Glossae super Genesim. Prologus et Capitula 1–3*, trans. Agneta Sylwan, Studia Graeca et Latina Gothoburgensia (Göteborg: Acta Universitatis Gothoburgensis, 1992), 20–21, 43, 46 (*Glossae super Genesim* 1.2, 2.7–8)

[86] Zahlten, *Creatio Mundi*, 93; Chenu, "Twelfth-Century Theology," 8–9. The term 'school' here really has twin senses, the first being the idea of a cathedral-based institution of learning, and the second, a school of thought.

[87] The quotation comes from Jaki, *Genesis 1*, 109 n. 131. See also Chenu, *Nature, Man and Society*, 36; Evans, "Masters and Disciples," 251.

[88] Secundum phisicam et ad litteram. Thierry of Chartres, "Tractatus de sex dierum operibus," in *Commentaries on Boethius by Thierry of Chartres and His School*, ed. N.M. Häring (Toronto: Pontifical Institute of Medieval Studies, 1971), 555 (*De sex dierum operibus* 1).

[89] *De sex dierum operibus* 31–47. Chenu points out a similar phenomenon in the work of Allan of Lille: Chenu, *Nature, Man and Society*, 16.

[90] God is the efficient cause of the world; the wisdom of God, later equated with Christ, is its formal cause; its final cause is the benevolence of God, later equated with the Holy Spirit and thus embracing the whole Trinity; while the material cause or the medium used for creation is the stuff of the four elements: *De sex dierum operibus* 2–3.

[91] *De sex dierum operibus* 4.

of heaven (made of fire) and earth is the spark that ignites an automatic, developmental creative process: heaven by nature cannot stand still, and so as soon as it was created it began to revolve, producing the daylight that illuminated the earth for each subsequent day.[92]

The rest of the creation week unfolds inevitably from this first act of creation, as the fire heats up the air and through it the waters, so that vapours rise and form the firmament (Day 2), meanwhile reducing the volume of the waters and allowing land to appear (Day 3). The same heat energy penetrates the land and waters to produce life while the ascending vapours condense into stars, and so on. Robbins therefore describes the twelfth century "tendency to explain creation as a continuous physical process depending on the working out of natural causes," whose stirrings are seen in Abelard's treatment, as coming to a head in Thierry.[93] It is this very naturalism that encourages Thierry to take the days of creation seriously as temporal intervals and therefore to hold to the mitigated form of instantaneous creation.[94]

Another centre of learning in the twelfth century was the important abbey school of St. Victor in Paris, headed after 1133 by Hugh of St. Victor (1096–1141).[95] Hugh's advocated method of biblical study was first to master the literal sense, moving forward from the OT to the NT, and then to return primed up with Christian truth to decipher the allegorical meaning enciphered in the OT.[96] He clearly prizes the allegorical sense as the more valuable face of biblical revelation, intending his *On the Sacraments* "for those who are to be introduced to the second stage of instruction, which is in allegory."[97] Yet he dignifies the literal sense with its own validity, and a substantial part of his opening treatment of the creation week is literal.[98]

Concerning the creation days, Hugh grants that "the book of Genesis itself ... speaks so ambiguously about the work of the six days that it often seems to prove rather that all things were made simultaneously," leading some to "believe that this distribution of the six days in Genesis is mystical," and that created things were completed in the first moment. Yet he affirms a creation through intervals of time for the sake of

[92] *De sex dierum operibus* 5.

[93] Robbins, *Hexaemeral Literature*, 83.

[94] See the conclusion to the treatment of each day, citing the 'evening-morning' statement from the text, e.g. par. 6 on Day 1, par. 8 on Day 2, etc. Thierry's naturalistic account in some ways anticipates the early modern genre of 'theories of the earth.'

[95] Hugh of St. Victor, *Hugh of Saint Victor on the Sacraments of the Christian Faith*, trans. J.D. Deferrari (Cambridge, MA: The Mediaeval Academy of America, 1951), ix.

[96] Evans, "Masters and Disciples," 255–56; Smalley, *Study of the Bible*, 95.

[97] *On the Sacraments*, Prologue.

[98] R. Berndt, "The School of St. Victor in Paris," in *HB/OT*, vol. I, bk 2:491; Evans, "Masters and Disciples," 258; Smalley, *Study of the Bible*, 97.

the instruction of the rational creature.[99] Following the creation of matter, "In [the] first three days the frame work of this universe was arranged, and was distributed in its parts," leaving "the four elements of the world ... distinguished and arranged in their places.... Then followed the adornment of these, and this was done likewise in three successive days."[100]

The literality of Hugh's interpretation is confirmed as he questions whether God was occupied for the entirety of each creation day or instead did something at least on each of six days in a row: Hugh supports the former.[101] While the 'sacraments', or the spiritual or allegorical meaning bound up in the biblical narrative, remain Hugh's chief interest, eliciting moral interpretations of the various elements of creation, his historical approach puts him in company with his contemporary Lombard. They both limited instantaneous creation to the productions described in Gen. 1:1, as did Hugh of Amiens (d. 1164) in his historically-oriented, partial *Tractatus in Hexaemeron.*[102]

Two of Hugh of St. Victor's disciples would choose to focus on opposite halves of his dual hermeneutic. Richard of St. Victor developed its sacramental aspect, pursuing the spiritual and contemplative,[103] while Andrew of St. Victor (d. 1175) took Hugh's exegesis further in a literal direction. In the early Genesis section of his *Exposition of the Heptateuch* Andrew depends heavily on Hugh's prior work, yet Hugh's commitment to unfolding the 'sacraments' is missing, replaced by a Jerome-like attention to the Hebrew text. One scholar denies that this is mere appearance: "With the scriptural interpretation of the Victorines Jerome's method of exegesis acquired a new eminence during the twelfth century after being insignificant for a long time."[104]

Andrew shows signs of shaking off Augustine's exegetical influence. When Andrew comes to expound Gen. 2:4–5, his study of the Hebrew text leads him to posit a syntactic break between the two verses, such that verse 4 recapitulates what was created on the first day of creation alone, merely heaven and earth, while verse 5 relates only to what follows.[105] Andrew scorns Ecclus 18:1 for having tied many good

[99] *On the Sacraments* 1.1.2–3.

[100] *On the Sacraments* 1.1.24–25.

[101] *On the Sacraments* 1.1.16.

[102] Hugh of Amiens, "Tractatus in hexaemeron," in *PL,* vol. 192:1248D. (*Tractatus in Hexameron* 1.15). See Mangenot, "Hexaméron," 6:2339; Zahlten, *Creatio Mundi*, 93.

[103] Smalley, *Study of the Bible*, 106; Berndt, "School of St. Victor," 476–78.

[104] Berndt, "School of St. Victor," 491, see also 489.

[105] This is similar to Bede, although Bede felt free to accept a different meaning for 'day' in this verse compared with its usage in chapter 1, and thus able to refer to the entire creation week. Andrew retains the meaning of a literal day even in Gen. 2:4: Andrew of St. Victor, *Expositionem super Heptateuchum*, Corpus Christianorum, continuatio mediaevalis (Turnholt: Brepols, 1986), 26, ll. 696–706.

thinkers up in knots, so that they "unravel in a moment what they have woven in six days," interpreting Gen. 2:4 in a way that destroys the impression of a temporal succession created by the seven day framework.[106] Andrew thus defused an inherent tension in the mainstream interpretation represented by Lombard but, ominously, did so by disregarding a writing of recognized authority (Ecclesiasticus), while his literal and grammatical style of exegesis drew accusations of Judaizing.[107]

The Creation Week Re-Acquainted with Time

'World-week' belief, the use of the creation week as a prophetic framework explaining the course of redemptive history, continued to prosper through the Middle Ages at the hands of Isidore, Bede and their successors. This essentially allegorical interpretation was authorized by the understanding that scriptural revelation functioned on multiple levels, an understanding anchored in a worldview that perceived manifold correspondences between the different levels of reality, and motivated by the desire to find the Christ-oriented and redemptive meanings in OT texts. To quote Richard of St. Victor, "The work of creation was done in six days.... The work of the restoration of man can be completed in six ages. The six of the one repeat the six of the other so that he who was creator may be recognised as redeemer."[108] This long tradition is undoubtedly the ancestor of the periodization of redemptive history in modern-day dispensational thought.

Curiously, this historical kind of allegorical interpretation now began to be matched by a more historical use of the creation week, literally understood. Hugh of St. Victor observed in his *On the Sacraments*, "We must develop the story gradually as we proceed always to those works which follow in order," and cast his theological content in a historical format.[109] Here the creation week constitutes the first step in world history, and then shapes the presentation of the remainder, although the fact that the work of foundation took six days and that the work of restoration takes six ages is for Hugh indicative of their relative importance![110] We see the same awareness of history in the *Historia*

[106] Ibid., 27. Beryl Smalley translated Andrew's entire Prologue and discussion of Gen. 2:5, along with helpful comments: Smalley, *Study of the Bible*, 131–35.

[107] Ibid., 110, also 156, 163, 169–71.

[108] Richard of St. Victor, "Excerptionum allegoricarum libri XXIV", in *PL*, vol. 177:203 (*Exceptiones allegoricae* 2.1), quoted in Chenu, *Nature, Man and Society*, 180. As Chenu intimates, this statement strongly resembles that of his senior colleague: Hugh of St. Victor, *The Sacraments*, 26–27 (*On the Sacraments* 1.1.28).

[109] *On the Sacraments* 1.1.29.

[110] *On the Sacraments*, Prologue, 2–3.

scholastica of Peter Comestor, where biblical history provided the framework for a discussion of theology.[111]

Rupert of Deutz had a little earlier in his *On the Holy Trinity and His Works* also divided up history along Trinitarian lines:

> The work of the Trinity is in three parts, from the creation of the world up until its end. The first is from the appearance of first light up until the fall of the first man. The second, from the same fall of the first man up until the passion of the second man Jesus Christ, the Son of God. Third, from the latter's resurrection up until the consummation of the world [or 'age' – *saeculi*], that is the general resurrection of the dead. And the first belongs to the Father, the second to the Son, the third indeed is the special work of the Holy Spirit.[112]

This is like Hugh's juxtaposition of creation and redemption, but enhanced in Trinitarian terms, with a greater, eschatological role for the Holy Spirit.[113]

Joachim of Fiore (c. 1132–1202), an abbey in Calabria, the 'toe' of Italy, extended Rupert's Trinitarian reading of history by characterizing the OT era as the age of the Father, the NT era as the age of the Son, and anticipating an imminent era of the Spirit. The six-day creation week and the rest of the seventh, together with the seven-times-seven and culminating fiftieth of the OT jubilee cycle and other such periodic numbers, all fed into Joachim's quest to amplify the classic world-week scheme. His motivation was to study the correspondences between the ages of the Father and of the Son, or in effect between the two Testaments of the Bible, and then forward-project them to discover the further correspondences in his own historical context and make apocalyptic predictions about the near future. Although the world-week scheme retained a place for centuries beyond this time, Joachim's prophetic scheme may be taken as one of its fullest developments.[114]

[111] See Froehlich, "Christian Interpretation," 506; Chenu, *Nature, Man and Society,* 174 n. 124.

[112] Rupert of Deutz, *De sancta Trinitate,* 1:126 (*On the Holy Trinity,* Prologue, ll. 51–59).

[113] However, the chapter titles of the section on the Holy Spirit reveal a much more theological than historical emphasis: ibid., 1:100–18. By the theological term 'eschatological' I mean that which concerns the consummation of the saving plan of God, or 'last things'.

[114] See Joachim of Fiore, *Liber de concordia Novi ac Veteris Testamenti,* ed. E. Randolph Daniel, Transactions of the American Philosophical Society (Philadelphia, PA: American Philosophical Society, 1983). This edition reproduces Books 1–4 of the work, whose only clear use of Genesis may be found on p. 153: Froehlich, "Christian Interpretation," 514. E. Randolph Daniel points out that Book 5, Distinction 1 constitutes an exposition of the Genesis creation narrative: Joachim of Fiore, *Liber de concordia,* xxii. I was unfortunately unable to access the 1519 Venice edition or the 1964–65 reprint edition containing this book. I understand that critical editions of Joachim's works are forthcoming from

The Creation Week Re-Acquainted with Nature

Although we saw evidence of Aristotelian ideas in Thierry of Chartres, the thirteenth century was when Aristotelianism made an increasing impact on Western thought, functioning as an additional overlay on twelfth-century Platonism. It acted as a source of new categories, new terminology, new logic and new methods, shifting attention somewhat from the ideal and divine to the physical world.

This re-acquaintance with nature along Aristotelian outlines characterizes the *Speculum maius (Great Mirror),* the famous encyclopaedic work of Vincent of Beauvais (c. 1190–1265). Two of its volumes bear on the Genesis creation account, the *Speculum historiale* and the *Speculum naturale,* the latter, physically oriented work utilizing the Hexaemeron to accommodate all extant knowledge about the physical world, a use for which its divine authority and global reach made it especially suitable.[115] The debate over the nature of the creation days receives its greatest focus in the *Speculum naturale*, reminding us that Augustine's view and its mainstream, real-time alternative were understood as alternate views of real, historical creation pertaining to the literal sense of the text. Both sides of the debate are amply covered, but Augustine's instantaneous creation is granted greatest exposure and allowed to stand as the final word.[116]

Another, later medieval encyclopaedic work was the massive *Lectures on Genesis* of Henry of Langenstein (1325–97), a work popular in its day, although little known now.[117] The section of the work that concerns Gen. 1:1–2:3 embraces whatever was 'known' about all domains

the Centro Internazionale di Studi Gioacchimiti. For further insights into Joachim's thought, see Trompf, *Historical Recurrence*, 216–20; Smalley, *Study of the Bible*, 289–92; Evans, *Road to Reformation*, 12; Henning Graf Reventlow, *The Authority of the Bible and the Rise of the Modern World* (Philadelphia: Fortress, 1985), 25–29; G. Leff, *The Dissolution of the Medieval Outlook: An Essay on the Intellectual and Spiritual Change in the 14th Century* (New York: New York University Press, 1976), 133. Chenu mentions a third figure, along with Joachim and Rupert, who made an important contribution to this extrapolation of world-week thought: Anselm of Havelberg: Chenu, *Nature, Man and Society,* 191.

[115] William A. Wallace, appendix to Aquinas, *Summa Theologiae*, 212; N.H. Steneck, *Science and Creation in the Middle Ages: Henry of Langenstein on Genesis* (Notre Dame: University of Notre Dame Press, 1976), 21; Andrew Dickson White, *A History of the Warfare of Science with Theology in Christendom*, 2 vols. (New York: D. Appleton, 1896), 1:378.

[116] Vincent of Beauvais, *Speculum quadriplex, sive, Speculum maius*, 4 vols. (Graz: Akademische Druck- und Verlagsanstalt, 1964–65), 1:87–97 (*Speculum naturale* 2.15–29). Though appearing in the context of a much larger work, this treatment is worthy of a stand-alone Genesis commentary. A briefer treatment that covers the same ground and summarizes the arguments is found in Vincent of Beauvais, *Speculum*, 4:7–8. (*Speculum historiale* 1.16–18).

[117] Henry was a scholar in both 'arts' and theology who spent up to eight years lecturing on Genesis from shortly after his arrival at the University of Vienna in 1385: Steneck, *Henry of Langenstein on Genesis*, 10.

of the created order within the six-day framework, an approach that has precedents in the natural content of the hexaemera of Basil, Ambrose and beyond:[118]

> During the early Middle Ages the Venerable Bede, Isidore of Seville, Walafrid Strabo, and Rabanus Maurus all included long scientific discussions in their treatment of the six days, as did the Platonists of the twelfth and early thirteenth centuries: Bernard Silvester, Thierry of Chartres, William of Conches, Honorius of Autun, and Robert Grosseteste.[119]

Henry, the work's editor Steneck continues, found that "Chapter one of Genesis ... provides a convenient and familiar outline for pursuing a detailed analysis of the world, proceeding as it does from higher and more ethereal to lower and more earthly things.... The commentary on the six days of creation provides more than simply an excuse for doing science; it becomes a *way* of doing science.... Commenting on Genesis and on the minute details that go into bringing a universe into being is, in short, part of the laboratory process of medieval science."[120]

Henry interpreted the content of the creation days in Aristotelian terms of a descending order of causation that begins with the First Cause and extends down through the powers that move the stars, then the stars themselves, and down to the elements of the earthly world.[121] He utilized the familiar medieval breakdown of creation, distinction and adornment, and implies a literal stance in his discussion of the position in which the sun was created and the time of year of creation.[122] Henry saw the pattern of the days reflected in the cosmos, with the sun occupying the middle sphere of the seven planetary spheres that surround the earth, matching the literary position of the sun's creation on the fourth of the seven creation days.[123] And in a move that reminds us of Thierry of Chartres' naturalism and anticipates Renaissance 'long chaos' theories, Henry holds that the matter created *in principio* had by Day 3 already arranged itself by mass – earth, water, air, fire.[124]

Henry therefore exemplifies a new level of attention to the detail of the physical world, believing that the product of a full understanding of creation is a soul inflamed with admiration and love for the Creator.[125]

[118] Ibid., 6, 15.

[119] Ibid., 20ff. Henry's explicit sources include Augustine especially, but also Ambrose, Aristotle, Albert the Great and Hugh of St. Victor, while "Henry's immediate source for the literal interpretation and division of the six days is Nicholas of Lyra," ibid., 161 n. 13.

[120] Ibid., 55.

[121] Ibid., 38–39, 57, 90–92.

[122] Ibid., 29–30, 54–55.

[123] [E]st medius planetarium sicut quarta feria est media septa dierum: ibid., 64.

[124] Ibid., 74.

[125] Ibid., 141.

The physical world has become a worthwhile object of reverent interest and study, although much of his information about the natural world comes in fact from his traditional sources.[126] Henry stood as heir to the Augustinian tradition of uniting natural phenomena, metaphysics, philosophy and theology within the hexaemeral framework, in the belief that all knowledge is ultimately one.[127] Exegesis of the days of creation in Genesis was therefore a vital locus for the synthesis of knowledge of the natural world, all the way from the late patristic period and well into the early Modern period, as long as Christianity helped define the intellectual fabric of its society.

Medieval Pluralism in Robert Grosseteste's Hexaemeron

Robert Grosseteste (c. 1168–1253), the Franciscan teacher at Oxford after 1224, combined Platonist and Aristotelian philosophies, and well represents the medieval combinations of interests that are transcendental and natural, and of literal and figurative hermeneutical methods. Described as "the most learned man around 1230 in Latin Christendom," and as "one of the most wide-ranging, original minds of his time," Grosseteste's Platonist ontology was married to a biblical theology and monastic sympathies to produce a fondness for the spiritual senses of the biblical text.[128]

Grosseteste's *Hexaemeron* features an initial, literal exegesis of the works of each creation day, bolstered with abundant reference to previous authorities, including an emphasis on Greek fathers which was rare for the time.[129] Grosseteste then proceeds to the three spiritual senses: allegorical interpretation that concerns Christ and his church, moral interpretation concerning the progress of the soul in holiness, and occasionally anagogy, oriented toward the eternal future.[130] Yet he remains genuinely interested in the literal sense, often delving into the natural phenomena mentioned in the text (e.g. light) according to current knowledge and/or ancient authorities. Grosseteste sees numbers as a mystical key to the essence of reality, and inhabits the adamantine medieval realm of multiple correspondences between the worlds of nature, the human person, the Christian life, and so forth.

[126] Ibid., 142.

[127] Ibid., 145.

[128] The quotations are from Jaki, *Genesis 1*, 116; Froehlich, "Christian Interpretation," 516.

[129] Froehlich, "Christian Interpretation," 516; Smalley, *Study of the Bible*, 317.

[130] Grosseteste, *Six Days of Creation*, 66–68 (*Hexaemeron* 1.12.1–4).

This 'reflective' mindset fosters an interpretive pluralism that makes it challenging to isolate Grosseteste's position on the days of creation.[131] He returns repeatedly to the question of the right understanding of the days, with an ever-stronger leaning toward the Augustinian idea that they are stages of understanding in the angelic mind. The creation days in fact suggest to Grosseteste six aspects of creation according to which the Hexaemeron might itself be interpreted! The creation events may speak of: (1) A Platonic archetypal world, which is bound up in "the begotten wisdom of the Father"; (2) Angelic intellects; (3) The creation and formation of primordial matter; (4) The constitution of the church, which Grosseteste identifies as an allegorical line; (5) The perfecting of the soul through contemplation and good works, a moral interpretation; (6) "The making of this visible world in time over six days."[132] The ideal realm still retains the priority in this scheme, making Augustine's interpretation a natural final resting place, while the almost experimental incorporation of levels of interpretation into a six-level hexaemeral schema is reminiscent of Arnold of Bonneval. It might surprise the modern reader as 'different', that a literal and historical interpretation of the creation week only occurs here as option number six in Grosseteste's list!

Though Grosseteste can speak at times of a successive creation, his primary allegiance is to Augustine's theory of angelic knowledge:

> And those first seven days were completed at the same time in the minds of the angels: the awareness of the angelic minds of the distinctions of the creatures, and the resting of these distinctions in God was seven-fold.... Therefore the second day of the establishment of the firmament, and the third day, of the establishment of plants, occurred at one and the same time, together with the first day that was established. This could never be true if they were days of time. The remaining possibility is that they were days of the spirit, that existed together, and all were, in substance, one day. This could not be, unless they were in the light of the awareness of the mind of the angels.[133]

This interpretation takes pride of place for Grosseteste, who furthermore develops the symmetry of the days beyond the standard medieval forming (*distinctio*) and adorning (*ornatio*) pairing. Light is the dignified sole subject of Day 1, while the firmament, the seas and the

[131] Letham, "Space of Six Days," 160–61. Grosseteste's interpretive pluralism obviously frustrates Jaki, who believes that Grosseteste submerges "the essential meaning...into a flood of other possible meanings ": Jaki, *Genesis 1*, 117.

[132] *Hexaemeron* 1.3.1–8. Jaki, *Genesis 1*, 116–17; Letham, "Space of Six Days," 160.

[133] *Hexaemeron* 10.3.5, 10.4.2. See also *Hexaemeron* 5.12.1ff., where he combines Augustine's explanations of the creation days as stages of angel cognition (his third and final theory) and of alternate formation privation of form (his second). *Hexaemeron* 10.1.4 features a statement describing creation as successive.

land are made on the second and third days, they are then populated in the same order on Days 4–6. But the 'framework' by which Grosseteste prefers to understand the days of creation is as a set of seven with the luminaries occupying the noble centre position, with Days 1–3 featuring a series of descending dignity from light down to vegetable life, and Days 5–7 an ascending series "from the water creatures through animals and man to God's rest from his works. It is thus a fine matching: going down from each end to the middle, and going up from the middle to the ends."[134] The picture Grosseteste portrays is reminiscent of a Jewish menorah. Letham perceives here an anticipation "of what eventually became known as the framework hypothesis."[135] This is another way of saying that he is alert to the literary shape of the text. But in keeping with medieval interpretive pluralism, Grosseteste is able to encompass all the familiar figurative uses of the creation week in connection with human development, redemptive history and personal sanctification.[136]

Reconciling Augustine: The Great Masters of the Thirteenth Century

The thirteenth century produced two new genres of sacred writing: the Postilla, a development from the running gloss (or commentary), and the theological treatise known as the summa, a development from the *Sentences* of Peter Lombard and others. The pioneer of the summa was Alexander of Hales (c. 1170–1245), although his *Summa* is now attributed to certain of his students at his initiative.[137] More famous are the great summae of his scholastic heirs, Albert the Great and Thomas Aquinas, two of the three 'Great Masters' of medieval theology (along with Bonaventure).[138] Both wrestled with Augustine's instantaneous creation using the tools supplied by Aristotelian philosophy, while Bonaventure used his hexaemeral work to chart a contrasting path.

Albert the Great (1193–1280) dedicated a substantial part of his *Summa theologiae* to questions surrounding biblical creation, one section of which clearly responds to the equivalent section of Lombard's *Sentences*.[139] In it Albert committed himself to defending Augustine's in-

[134] *Hexaemeron* 5.1.2.

[135] Letham, "Space of Six Days," 161.

[136] *Hexaemeron* 8.30.1–31.2, 8.33.1, 9.9.4; Augustine, *On Genesis: Two Books*, 89–90. (*DGM* 1.43).

[137] Bougerol, "Auctoritates," 1:301; F.L. Cross and E.A. Livingstone, eds., *ODCC*, 35.

[138] Froehlich, "Christian Interpretation," 531.

[139] *Summa theologiae* part 2 contains the material pertaining to creation; Tractatus 11 is the part that answers to Lombard's *Sentences*, Book 2.12–15.

stantaneous creation as had the pioneer of the summa form, Alexander of Hales (c. 1170–1245).[140] Albert wanted to confirm the orthodoxy of Augustine's belief by reconciling it with the more mainstream position of Christian tradition and with the wording of Scripture.[141] This could defuse the potential threat of Augustine's arguably eccentric creation view to the authority of church tradition and its ability to speak with a coherent voice.[142]

In *Summa theologiae* Albert contemplates the classical chaos as a purely logical first step in God's creation. This allows him to accept the classical three-step creation of Gregory the Great and Jerome, where *creatio* produced a confused mass of the basic elements, to be arranged and beautified through the *distinctio* and *ornatio* stages, during Days 1–3 and 4–6 respectively. Albert admits here that while both instantaneous and mainstream creation positions are to be regarded as 'Catholic' or orthodox, the mainstream position harmonizes better with the literal meaning of Genesis.[143] Zöckler apparently took this as Albert's final stance on the matter, and understood him to mostly oppose Augustine's position, and Mangenot similarly, but I think more accurate the analysis of the Renaissance Catholic scholars Francisco Suarez and Marin Mersenne when they cited Albert as (mostly) in favour of Augustine's instantaneous creation.[144]

When he specifically treats simultaneous creation versus a real progression of time in the creation week, Albert supports the former case using Ecclus 18:1, the creation of man 'with' Behemoth in Job 40:10, and Augustine's general approach in *Literal Meaning*. Then he cites, not biblical, but philosophical objections to this position drawn from Aristotle and Boethius, who argued that anything that exists must have extension or 'measure' in time just as in space. Here he makes explicit his preference for Augustine's understanding that the days of creation pertain to a series of cyclical stages in angelic comprehension of crea-

[140] Alexander of Hales (called 'Alensis') is credited with an instantaneous creation position by Suarez, "Tractatus de opere sex dierum," 3:55B (*De opere sex dierum* 1.10.5)

[141] Albert the Great, *B. Alberti Magni ... Opera omnia*, ed. E. Borgnet, vol. 32: Summa theologiae pars secunda (Paris: L. Vivès, 1895), 507–34, http://albertusmagnus.uwaterloo.ca/webPages/downloading.html. (*Summa theologiae* 2.11.43–50). Albert's commitment to Augustine's view appears earlier in *Summa theologiae* 2.3.11.

[142] *Summa theologiae* 2.11.49.

[143] *Summa theologiae* 2.11.44. Augustine left much more room for this idea in his *On Genesis against the Manichaeans*, and it is this work that Albert cites under this question.

[144] Zöckler, *Geschichte*, 1:441; Mangenot, "Hexaméron," 6:2340. Compare Marine Mersenne, *Quaestiones celeberrimae in Genesim, cum accurata textus explicatione* (Paris: sumptibus Sebastiani Cramoisy, 1623), 685; Suarez, "Tractatus de opere sex dierum," 3:55B (*De opere sex dierum* 1.10.5). Both have in mind his other work, *Summa de quatuor coaequaevis*, while Suarez also mentions his commentary on Lombard's *Sentences*. See also John P. Dickson, "The Genre of Genesis 1," Centre for Public Christianity.

tion, seeing the physical world as created "in one indivisible now." No time delay intervenes in the *creatio – distinctio – ornatio* series.[145] The process of creation was instantaneous, although its expression to a human audience could not be.

Yet should Albert appear to be adopting eccentric opinion opposed both to the fathers and the letter of Scripture, he undertakes to prove that Augustine's angelic version of the creation week may be reconciled with both of these authorities. He explains that while Augustine interpreted the six days of creation as six cycles of angelic 'enlightenment' (*illustration*), Gregory and his fellow thinkers have simply envisaged six physical 'enlightenments', six phases of physical light shining on the earth.[146] Augustine's view of creation cannot be placed in contradiction to that of the other fathers, since they were talking about different things using the same terms. Augustine merely intended to make explicit something that is implicit within the Genesis text.[147] Albert is subtly permitting the more physical and timely view of creation to claim a certain legitimacy, while he confirms the legitimacy of his own right to adhere to Augustine's more sophisticated position. But the persisting tension within this stance warranted a further attempt at mediation between the opposing views of creation by Albert's student, Thomas Aquinas.

"The greatest medieval theologian" and the defining figure of scholasticism, Thomas Aquinas (1225–74) presents his understanding of material creation in Questions 65–74 of Part 1 of his *Summa theologiae*.[148] Thomas shares an Aristotelian philosophical framework with his teacher and fellow Dominican, Albert, along with a traditional heritage dominated by Augustine and the patristic and early medieval sources enshrined in the *Glossa ordinaria* and Lombard's *Sentences*.[149] In keeping with Augustine's *Literal Meaning,* but unusually before his own era, Aquinas' treatment of Genesis here is literal, which Beryl Smalley attributed to the realist influence of his Aristotelianism. For Thomas too, the question of whether the creation was an ideal sequence, or a real, historical succession concerns the literal meaning of the Genesis text,

[145] *Summa theologiae* 2.11.46.

[146] But Augustine's careful avoidance of mentioning 'night' in his explanation shows that he was thinking of a kind of enlightenment where renewed darkness was inappropriate – the 'days' of angelic enlightenment, never reversed by spiritual 'nights'.

[147] For the foregoing discussion, see *Summa theologiae* 2.11.49.

[148] The quotation is from Bray, *Biblical Interpretation*, 142. Aquinas also treats the Genesis creation account in his commentary on Lombard's *Sentences* and in the work *De potentia*. See Wallace's introduction, Aquinas, *Summa Theologiae*, 10:xx, xxiii.

[149] Wallace, appendix to Aquinas, *Summa Theologiae*, 10:211–18.

and not allegorical interpretations, and he wishes "to ascertain this [primary sense] as precisely as possible."[150]

Thomas' early questions about material creation are shaped by the question of Augustine's instantaneous creation. The formless stage of matter is only a logical or potential one, if no time elapsed in which it might exist in that state.[151] The light of Day 1 is not a formless state of luminous matter prior to its embodiment on Day 4 in Augustine's scheme, "For he does not admit a temporal succession in these works."[152] The dual appearances of heaven/s in Gen. 1:1, 8 and earth in 1:1, 10 are temporally fused also in the Augustinian model.[153] Using the disputation form as Albert did, Thomas first presents the affirmative case for instantaneous creation using Gen. 2:4–5a, Ecclus 18:1, Augustine's argument about the making of the seventh day, and the point that the works of God on the different days must have been fulfilled instantaneously, leaving each of the presumed twenty-four hour periods essentially idle. The negative case points instead to the repeated 'evening and morning' statements of the Genesis account. Compared to Albert's *Summa,* we observe a much diminished reliance of philosophical sources in relation to the creation week.[154]

Thomas' final synthesis in the *responsio* begins, "On this matter Augustine departs from other commentators," and sets out an even-handed comparison between the opposing positions:

> According to Augustine, the word *day* is interpreted as the knowledge of an angelic mind, and so the first day is the knowledge of the first divine work; the second day, of the second work, and so on.... And so the days are differentiated according to a natural sequence in the things known, and not to correspond to succession in knowledge or the things produced.... According to the other Fathers, however, these days and the succession of time in them reflect successiveness in the actual production of things.

Despite the fact that Augustine's and the mainstream views coincide in many ways, he must admit (unlike Albert) that a fundamental difference remains:

> For, according to the other writers, after the initial production of creatures there was a period of time when there was no light; likewise, the firmament was not yet formed; the earth not yet uncovered from the water; nor, the fourth point, the luminous heavenly bodies formed.

[150] Wallace, appendix to Aquinas, *Summa Theologiae,* 10:178.
[151] *Summa theologiae* 1.66.1.
[152] *Summa theologiae* 1.67.4; 1.70.1.
[153] *Summa theologiae* 1.68.1, 1.69.1.
[154] Albert the Great, *Summa theologiae,* 517–20. (*Summa theologiae* 2.11.46).

Thomas then explains the mainstream position with a fullness that suggests some sympathy on his part:

> God created all things *together,* with respect to their as yet unfinished substance. But considering the finishing that was effected by differentiation and ornamentation, this was not done *at* once .... It is not out of lack of power, in the sense that God needs time in which to act, that all things were not made distinct and ornamented at the same time; but rather so that an ordered pattern would be followed in things being fashioned.[155]

Yet like Lombard he allows Augustine the last word: "According to Augustine, this order of days should be attributed to natural ordering of the works assigned to the days."[156] This tentative and vacillating assessment of the validity of instantaneous creation, even harder than Albert's to finally pin down, has led to contrasting assessments, and is prone to misrepresentation by selective quotation. Whereas Jaki simply states, "Aquinas most emphatically states the instantaneous creation of all together," Zöckler was much closer to the truth when he observed Thomas' inclination to side with the mainstream against Augustine, but with a pronounced mildness of tone out of his great deference for Augustine.[157]

Thomas therefore ultimately endorses the mainstream creation, distinction, and ornamentation schema, explaining that each of the three primeval entities mentioned or implied in Gen. 1:1–2 enjoys one day of differentiation and one of ornamentation. Heaven, water, and earth began formless, in that heaven was dark, water was deep, and earth was *invisibilis vel inanis* (invisible or void).[158] Heaven is then differentiated into light and darkness on the first day, and adorned on the fourth with luminaries; water is divided by the firmament on Day 2 and then produces fish (and birds, on the common interpretation) on Day 5; and earth experiences its differentiation on Day 3 and its adornment with animal and human life on Day 6.[159] The literary and (for non-Augustinians) historical symmetry of the six days of creation finds here its clearest and best presentation to this point.[160] Thomas' synthesis of interpretations of the creation narrative in Genesis reveals an appreciation for the philosophical serviceability of Augustine's view, but at the same time the growing admission of its poor compatibility with the

[155] Thomas, *Summa theologiae* 1.74.2. Each of the block quotes comes from this section.

[156] Ibid.

[157] Jaki, *Genesis 1*, 120; Zöckler, *Geschichte*, 1:445; Letham, "Space of Six Days," 163; Lewis, "Days of Creation," 452.

[158] *Summa theologiae* 1.69.1.

[159] *Summa theologiae* 1.70.1; 1.74.1.

[160] Letham again points out another precedent for the modern 'framework hypothesis': Letham, "Space of Six Days," 163.

plain sense of the biblical text, and it ran against the intellectual trend towards greater realism and historical sensibility.

Bonaventure (1221–74), Paris master and head of the Franciscan order from 1257, although familiar with the philosophy of Aristotle, was critical in his use of it, and wary of trusting unenlightened human reason.[161] He composed an extensive commentary on Lombard's *Sentences* in which he more resolutely than Aquinas rejects Augustine's instantaneous creation.[162] There he taught that the standard belief that the matter of created things was created simultaneously, while they were formed in the course of the six ordinary days of creation, might seem less amenable to reason than Augustine's alternative, but had in its favour a submission to the light of faith.[163] But his best-known work related to the creation week is the incomplete *Collations on the Six Days*, a work put into writing by his audience and reflecting his resistance to "the Averroism being taught in the Paris arts faculty."[164] To borrow from Peter Chanter's well-known genre categories, this work functions as 'preaching' (*praedicatio*), whereas the *summae* and commentaries on the *Sentences* consisted of 'debate' (*disputatio*), helping to account for the radical difference between the two kinds of writing, evident even within Bonaventure's own works.[165]

The Hexaemeron provides the structure for Bonaventure's *Collations*; he intended to take each of the seven days of the creation week in turn, interpreted as seven 'visions', to represent the step-by-step ascent of the intellect to perfect contemplation of God. Thus Day 1 represents the vision of truth achieved through natural understanding – a legitimate but elementary step towards wisdom. Day 2 is the vision achieved through understanding lifted up by faith. Day 3 is the vision achieved through understanding instructed by Scripture. Day 4 represents the vision that comes through the intellect suspended in contem-

[161] Smalley, *Study of the Bible*, 312; Cross and Livingstone, eds., *ODCC*, 186.

[162] See Wallace, appendix to Aquinas, *Summa Theologiae*, 10:215; Mangenot, "Hexaméron," 6:2339. Concerning Bonaventure's *Breviloquum*, see Zöckler, *Geschichte*, 1:446.

[163] Congar, "Le theme de *Dieu-Createur*," 1:202 n. 254. The entire relevant passage is translated here by Congar (into French).

[164] Froehlich, "Christian Interpretation," 548; Congar, "Le thème de *Dieu-Créateur*," 1:206.

[165] Zöckler finds the contrast between the *Collations* and Bonaventure's *Sentences* commentary so great that he doubts the authenticity of the attribution of the former to Bonaventure: Zöckler, *Geschichte*, 1:446. However, other works of his also reveal a strong mystical bent, and I have not found his authorship of the work disputed amongst recent authors, e.g. Froehlich's essay. Bonaventure's editor perceives a change of attitude in Bonaventure akin to Aquinas' very late renunciation of his philosophical/theological efforts: Bonaventure, *Collations on the Six Days*, trans. J. de Vinck (Paterson, NJ: St Anthony Guild Press, 1970), 292 n. See also Froehlich, "Christian Interpretation," 553. On the kind of preaching represented in the *Collations*, see Dahan, "Christian Exegesis of the Middle Ages," 224–26.

plation, which is so characteristic of Bonaventure's thought in this work that it makes a fitting if inadvertent conclusion to it. The levels that remained to be treated under the headings of the fifth, sixth and seventh days were visions achieved through "understanding raised by prophecy," "understanding absorbed in God," and "understanding consummated in glory."[166]

Each of these 'days' comprises several 'collations', and each collation uses as a jumping-off point the pertinent text from Gen. 1:1–2:3, taking up the allegorical meanings suggested by its details and drawing them out in extensive and intricate detail to make the case for the pursuit of contemplative wisdom. There is rarely any literal interpretation of the days of creation as descriptions of the origin of our world.[167] Bonaventure indeed would see persistence with the literal sense for its own sake as a characteristically Jewish failure.[168] His treatment is not merely atemporal, in the philosophical manner of Augustine or Eriugena, but transcends the letter of the narrative through allegory, which is the better vehicle for spiritual illumination.[169]

But despite the multifaceted nature of Scripture in Bonaventure's conception, everything about this work is utterly systematic, structured and hierarchical.[170] His structure is often Trinitarian, so that it functions something like a base four set of logarithms, but Bonaventure's reverence for number as a key to reality means that other significant numbers often feature. Bonaventure may have avoided Augustine's instantaneous creation, but happily quotes Augustine in saying, "The number six is not perfect because God created the world in this number of days; but God created the world in this number of days because it is perfect."[171] Every layer of the complex structure of this work presumes the mysterious significance of number, the gateway to the ontological substructure of the world.

[166] Titles taken from de Vinck's helpful outline: Bonaventure, *Collations*, 399–400. The pertinent section in the text is *Collations* 3.24–31.

[167] Jaki protests, "The literal meaning of the six-day creation is nowhere considered," and, "The real world fares indeed very badly throughout the *Collationes*. " Jaki, *Genesis 1*, 125. Occasionally Bonaventure will make brief reference to the literal sense of the text, for instance, when he notes at the beginning of his treatment of the second day, "Literally speaking, this heaven is lofty, stable and visible," qualities which he develops in a cosmological sense for a few lines: *Collations* 18.1.

[168] *Collations* 19.7. This was the accusation levelled against Andrew of St. Victor, as I have mentioned.

[169] *Collations* 13.18–21. Bonaventure here describes a further four aspects of each of these recognised four levels of meaning in Scripture. See also *Collations* 2.27.

[170] *Collations* 2.19. See also 15.10.

[171] *Collations* 4.16. See also Augustine's *DGaL* 4.7.14.

This leads into another Augustinian feature, the periodization of history according to the creation week.[172] "As God created the world in six days and rested on the seventh, so also the mystical body of Christ has six ages, and a seventh that runs concurrently with the sixth, and an eighth."[173] Yet the Trinitarian historical scheme also appears later on: "The times of origin consist in the first seven days; the times of symbolism, in the span between the beginning of the world and Christ, when a new time begins ..."[174] This tripartite scheme, witnessed already in Rupert and also found in Thomas' *Summa,*[175] lends a somewhat eschatological feel to Bonaventure's discussion of his own time, where he seems to see the appearance of the mendicant orders as a climax in redemptive history, in a manner reminiscent of and perhaps influenced by Joachim of Fiore.[176]

The Late Medieval Synthesis: Nicholas of Lyra and Dionysius the Carthusian

Nicholas of Lyra (1270–1349) was a Paris-based Franciscan scholar and the author of the highly influential *Postilla litteralis super totum Bibliam* (1322–31) and its next-of-kin, the *Postilla moralis*. The former work, a running commentary on both Testaments, superseded the *Postilla* of Hugh of St. Cher (c. 1195–1263) and his fellow-workers as the standard supplement to the *Glossa ordinaria.*[177] The Postillas were the latest incarnation of running commentary on the Bible, and Lyra's *Postilla* came to be regularly printed alongside the Vulgate text of the Bible and the *Glossa ordinaria.*[178] A late-medieval biblical scholar would inevitably have studied the biblical text, the *Glossa* and Lyra's *Postilla* together. The *Postilla* was also the first biblical commentary to be printed (Rome, 1471–72) and was widely disseminated.[179] It forms a kind of

[172] I treat this phenomenon as it occurs in the patristic period early in the previous chapter.
[173] *Collations* 15.12ff.
[174] *Collations* 16.11.
[175] *Summa theologiae* 1.73.1.
[176] *Collations* 16.19; 22.9. Compare the comments about Joachim of Fiore in Leff, *Dissolution*, 133.
[177] Smalley, *Study of the Bible*, 272–74.
[178] Such glossed Bibles subsequently came to be published with additional comments and corrections upon the *Postilla* by Paul of Burgos (or Pablo de Santa Maria, b. 1341) and Matthias Döring of Thuringia: Philip D.W. Krey and Lesley Smith, eds., *Nicholas of Lyra: The Senses of Scripture*, Studies in the History of Christian Thought (Leiden: Brill, 2000), 11–12.
[179] Ibid.

exegetical bridge into the Reformation period, and its impact upon the exegesis of Luther is proverbial although not beyond dispute.[180]

The section of Lyra's *Postilla* that concerns Genesis 1–3 is programmatic for the rest of the work, giving it a rather theoretical character. The Hexaemeron was in fact the understood platform for a commentator of Lyra's time to work out and explain his metaphysical starting point for understanding the world, its Creator, humanity, and their inter-relationships.[181] Strongly influenced by Aquinas' *Summa*, Lyra expounds Days 1–4 of creation first in terms of Aquinas' belief that matter cannot exist without form, so that both must have arisen together. Then he recapitulates the interpretation of those four days from the standpoint that the initial creation was of generic matter, and the works of distinction consist of the giving of form to matter. Lyra ultimately prefers the latter, and assumes this metaphysical position throughout the rest of the *Postilla*.[182] The modern reader may share some of Jaki's frustration with the abstract nature of Lyra's "hylemorphistic explanations," but Lyra combats excessive abstractness when he rejects Augustine's seven 'days' of angelic cognition as 'far from the literal sense' and opts for literal days governed, in the case of Days 1–3, by a literal, primordial light.[183]

This literal approach to the days of creation, although embedded in a dominantly metaphysical explanation of Genesis 1–3, concords with Lyra's avowed literalism in this work. He "avoids discussion of issues that are not raised by the biblical text at hand, such as the creation and fall of the angels," and understands that the text of Genesis, according to its (divine) authorial intention, reveals the "historical reality" of "God's creation of form and matter."[184] Lyra's support for the more literal mainstream sequence of *creation – distinction – ornatio*, in contrast with Augustine's instantaneous creation, helped to ensure that it would be the chief view that the Middle Ages would bequeath to Renaissance scholarship. His *Postilla* also illustrates the medieval trend towards the priority of the literal sense, already long understood to include philosophical theorizing, and the increasing versatility of that sense, so that it

[180] The traditional saying is, *Si Lyra non lyrasset, Lutherus non saltasset,* meaning that if Lyra had not played the lyre, Luther would not have danced. Smalley dismisses the sentiment: Smalley, *Study of the Bible*, xvi. However, Luther certainly cites Lyra frequently in his Genesis commentary; see the following chapter.

[181] C. Patton, "Creation, Fall and Salvation: Lyra's Commentary on Genesis 1–3," in *Nicholas of Lyra: The Senses of Scripture*, ed. P.D.W. Krey and L. Smith (Leiden: Brill, 2000), 19.

[182] Ibid., 26, 42.

[183] Jaki, *Genesis 1*, 128, see also 126–29; Patton, "Lyra's Commentary on Genesis 1–3," 27.

[184] Ibid.

performs functions that might previously have been classed as allegorical or typological.[185]

Dionysius the Carthusian, or Denys van Leeuwen (1402–71), a Belgian by birth, provides an interesting overview of late medieval scholastic exegesis through his extensive biblical commentaries. His Genesis commentary considers opinions of Nicholas of Lyra alongside Thomas Aquinas, Albert the Great and Bonaventure, and through them Augustine, along with the medieval Spanish philosopher Avicebron, who like Averroes and Avicenna was a conduit for a new influx of Aristotelianism into late-medieval Europe. He also admired Pseudo-Dionysius the Areopagite, the unknown writer of mystical theological writings that were mistakenly attributed to Dionysius, Paul's convert in Acts 17:34.

Dionysius' consideration of Gen. 1:1 immediately raises the question of how the events of creation relate to time. He first establishes as non-negotiable the fact of the world's beginning at the hand of God. But the manner of that creation is a matter for legitimate debate, and the essential choice as Dionysius sees it is between Augustine's philosophically astute instantaneous creation of all things, and a creation "through intervals of days," i.e. in a literal creation week, an interpretation with the apparent sense of the biblical text and majority patristic opinion on its side.[186] The opinions of Albert and Thomas are taken seriously, and then comes the impressive clarity of Chrysostom's explanation:

> Moses in this way of speaking concisely explains and states by anticipation all that God later through six days performs, and afterward explains step by step what he initially presented in summary. And so by those two extremes, heaven and earth, he comprehends all the rest of the bodily things they contain. It is as if one said, "A builder made this house," and later added, "First he laid the foundation, then he set up the walls, and then he erected the roof." And thus what he says "in the beginning" is set forth and referred to the whole time of production of the works of the six days.[187]

It is not surprising that this for Dionysius represents the best available synopsis of creation in Genesis 1. But in the intellectual climate of his day it remained important for him to explain what kind of 'matter' was involved in creation, and he concludes that the four elements, earth, water, air and fire were created in a chaotic mixture on the first day, finding tacit endorsement for this particular stance above all in

[185] See the discussion of the senses of Scripture in Krey and Smith, eds., *Nicholas of Lyra*, 17.

[186] Dionysius the Carthusian. *Doctoris Ecstatici D. Dionysii Cartusiani in Sacram Scripturam Commentaria... Tomus I. In Genesim, Et Exodum (I-XIX)*. Monstrolii: Cartusiae Sanctae Mariae de Pratis, 1896, 1:17 (= Enarratio in cap. 1 Genesis – art. 6)

[187] Ibid., 1:20 (= Enarratio in cap. 1 Genesis – art. 6). See Jaki's mitigated praise: Stanley Jaki, *Genesis 1 through the Ages* (New York: Thomas More Press, 1992), 131.

certain statements from his (illusory) hero, the supposed Dionysius the Areopagite, which clinches the argument.[188]

A thousand years after Augustine's death, then, his position on creation still often set the parameters for discussion, the choice being essentially whether creation occurs over the first seven days of historic time, or outside of time altogether. Neoplatonic and Aristotelian concepts of the relationship of matter and form supplied the fodder for discussion. The key hermeneutical issue involved was which stance maintained the honour and integrity of Scripture, and in addition to that, what counted as a legitimate literal sense. For many thinkers, by this time, Augustine's stance finally failed both of these criteria. The ecclesiastical issue was how divergent opinion could be managed while maintaining consensus with the church, and counted against Augustine, for Dionysius, that in his exegetical method Augustine seemed willing to make Christian consensus a second priority to finding an explanation that seemed rationally sound.[189] Yet Augustine's solution would retain the admiration of a few of the more adventurous Renaissance interpreters we will encounter.

The Abstract Creation Week of Two Renaissance Platonists

Genesis continued to play a central role in the development of Western Christian thought as the Renaissance unfolded as illustrated in two key representatives of the southern Renaissance and the northern Renaissance respectively: Pico della Mirandola and John Colet. Both writers' interpretation of the Hexaemeron reflects a Platonist hermeneutic melded with hierarchical metaphysics, expressed in a palpable atmosphere of intellectual daring.

Italian humanist Pico della Mirandola's (1463–94) work, *Heptaplus,* subtitled *On the Sevenfold Narration of the Six Days of Genesis* (1489), is a philosophical *tour de force* from a classic Renaissance Man.[190] Mirandola was known for his prodigious learning despite barely surviving into his thirties. He quotes sources from the Bible and the church fathers through Plato, Aristotle, and Averroes to Indian Brahmans and Persian magi, but this Renaissance eclecticism is combined with a symbolic worldview and corresponding allegorical quest for truth that is thoroughly medieval. Mirandola's catch-cry could be 'oneness', reflecting

[188] Dionysius the Carthusian, *In Genesim*: 1:21–22 (= Enarratio in cap. 1 Genesis – art. 7).

[189] Ibid., 1:15 (= Enarratio in cap. 1 Genesis – art. 5).

[190] Pico della Mirandola, *On the Dignity of Man, On Being and the One, Heptaplus*, trans. P.J.W. Miller (Indianopolis: The Library of Liberal Arts, 1965), xxx.

his monistic view of reality as well as his belief that all philosophy and theology was ultimately compatible.[191]

From the outset, Mirandola takes the sevenfold structure of the creation account as his cue for its interpretation, a strategy we have already witnessed among medieval scholars such as Arnold of Bonneval and Robert Grosseteste. Indeed, the seven sections of the *Heptaplus* are not distributed each to a day of creation but each to a different hermeneutical approach to the passage.[192] The first four readings or 'Expositions' derive from his conception of reality in terms of four worlds. The first Exposition relates Genesis to the elemental or material world, the lowest level of both physical and metaphysical hierarchies. Mirandola's conception of the arrangement of chaotic primordial matter with form and through causes makes even this potentially concrete topic sound esoteric and non-physical.[193]

The second Exposition concerns the celestial world, the middle one in the hierarchy of existence, consisting of the ten spheres. The third Exposition features the angelic and invisible world, wherein ultimate reality proves to consist of intellect. "We have seen the nature of the angels created by God, turned to God by the spirit of love, and then enlightened by him and perfected by the light of intelligible forms."[194] The *Celestial Hierarchy* of pseudo-Dionysius is a clear influence again here, and there is an affinity with Augustine's theory of angelic knowledge. The nature of man is the topic of the fourth Exposition. In classic microcosm/macrocosm understanding, the human being comprises earthly, celestial and angelic worlds in possessing a physical body, rational soul and mediating spirit.

Mirandola's fifth Exposition then applies the creation days to the various worlds sequentially. Day 1 speaks of the intellectual, Day 2 of the celestial in terms of the intervening firmament, Day 3 of the elemental world in general terms. Days 4 and 5 then treat the occupants of the elemental world from highest to lowest, and finally we have humanity on Day 6. The sixth Exposition represents the text from Genesis as presenting the fifteen different ways in which things may be related to each other. There is an emphasis on unity, and Mirandola's approach is now moving towards moral (tropological) interpretation.

[191] "The concord of philosophies with each other, and with religion, is one of the most fundamental theses of Pico's writings. " Introduction by Paul J.W. Miller to ibid., xvii, xxvii.

[192] We saw a more modest version of this in Grosseteste, *On the Six Days of Creation*, 50–51 (*Hexaemeron* 1.3), Grosseteste himself following a precedent we have found in: Arnold of Bonneval, "De operibus sex dierum," 1520B–C.

[193] Jaki, *Genesis 1*, 139.

[194] *Heptaplus* 3.2–3.

Mirandola finally, in the seventh Exposition, reads the Mosaic text in an 'anagogical' fashion, expounding the world-week pattern of the plan of God in history, heading towards "the sabbath of the world and of the repose – that is, the felicity of the creatures." Mirandola expounds this ideal destiny in terms that may be traced to the founding father of Neoplatonism, Plotinus (c. 205–270): "Felicity I define as the return of each thing to its beginning," and, "The end of all things is the same as the beginning of all: one God, omnipotent and blessed."[195] Meanwhile Mirandola finds in the sun of Day 4 an indication that Christ was destined to come in the middle of the fourth millennium of the world's existence, and dates creation 3508 years before Christ.[196]

A short, biblical chronology clearly does not presume a literal interpretation of the days of creation. While Mirandola may imagine a creation week that is 168 hours long, the more vital role of the creation days in his mind is as symbolic gateways to multiple worlds, or better, the manifold faces of this one world. Because this multilayered reality is made by, upheld by and destined for re-immersion in one God, it is possible for one word or one statement to refer to all of its layers simultaneously, just as those layers reflect each other on every level:

> It is a well-contrived and admirable device of Moses … to use terms and to arrange his discourse so that the same words, the same context, and the same order in the whole passage are completely suitable for symbolizing the secrets of all the worlds and of the whole of nature.[197]

Allegorical interpretation is therefore the most natural and fitting approach to such a paradigmatic biblical text.[198] If Moses "treated anywhere of the nature and making of the whole world, that is, if in any part of his work he buried the treasures of all true philosophy as in a field, he must have done so most of all in the part where avowedly and most loftily he philosophizes on the emanation of all things from God, and on the grade, number, and order of the parts of the world."[199] Thus Mirandola defends Moses from accusations of a crude and unimpressive writing style or of philosophical irrelevance by demonstrating this text's true profundity, while he seeks to stimulate the worship and contemplation of God and of Christ, the true Sabbath.[200] His mystical, Platonic exposition recalls Eriugena's more than Augustine's, signifying

[195] *Heptaplus* 7.proem.

[196] *Heptaplus* 7.4.

[197] *Heptaplus* 2nd proem.

[198] "From this principle … flows the science of all allegorical interpretation." *Heptaplus* second proem.

[199] *Heptaplus* proem.

[200] *Heptaplus* proem and second proem.

a non-literal 'subculture' of Renaissance interpretation of Gen. 1:1–2:3.

John Colet (c. 1466–1519), "the most outstanding English humanist of his time," was educated in Paris and Italy and was thoroughly enmeshed in the Renaissance scholarly community, corresponding with the Italian Platonist Marsilio Ficino (1433–99) and interacting with Erasmus and Thomas More.[201] His approach to Genesis in his 'Letters to Radulphus' displays a similar Platonist orientation towards transcendent rather than material realities, but Colet goes further than Mirandola in explicitly disavowing the literal meaning of the days of creation.[202] With direct reference to Philo and periodic echoes of Augustine, Colet explains repeatedly that the days of the creation week are a device used by the 'poet' Moses to communicate truths about creation to the uncultivated Hebrews in order to motivate them to weekly rest and Sabbath observance.[203]

Colet's opinion of the Hebrews' cognitive abilities is unflattering, and consequently his estimation of Moses' accommodation to them is great; Moses was willing to present the elements of creation out of philosophical order, e.g. by presenting the formation of vegetation prior to that of the stars, for the sake of the spiritual or moral benefit of the simple-minded audience.[204] While there is a logical order in the creative events that is captured in this device of successive weekdays, there is in fact no passage of time involved:

> [It was Moses' intention] to begin his account with God, and to refer the origin of those divisions of the universe which all could see, and the arrangement of them, to God. He coupled with this also a distinction of works and days; in order to set before an uninstructed nation, with the sanction of religion, an example of working and resting, and lead them on to an imitation of God, the maker of the whole world.... [H]e represented God to have spent six days on the fabric of the universe, and to have rested on the seventh.... As I have mentioned, all these things were creat-

[201] Bray, *Biblical Interpretation*, 171; Cross and Livingstone, eds., *ODCC*, 312–13, 511; G.E. Duffield, "Colet, John (c.1466–1519)," in *The New International Dictionary of the Christian Church*, ed. J.D. Douglas and E.E. Cairns (Grand Rapids: Zondervan, 1978).

[202] John Colet, *Letters to Radulphus on the Mosaic Account of Creation [microform]: Together with Other Treatises*, ed. Joseph Hirst Lupton (London: G. Bell, 1876), IA, http://www.archive.org/details/MN41730ucmf_0. It is worth keeping in mind the different genre involved. A person is more likely to reveal his or her more daring thoughts in a private letter than a published work.

[203] Ibid., 9–10, 12, 23–24, 26–28.

[204] Ibid., 18–21. The reason why this is out of order has little to do with the physical dependence of vegetation upon sunlight, and more to do with Colet's understanding that the spheres of existence in the hierarchy of reality come out from God in order from higher to lower, and produce their inhabitants in the same order, so that 'heaven' must have produced stars before earth produced anything.

> ed simultaneously. For it is unworthy of God ... to suppose that He made first one thing and then another, as if He could not have made all things at once ...[205]

In Colet's scheme, Day 1 (Gen. 1:1–5) concerns the whole of creation, 'heaven' signifying form and 'earth' signifying matter, and the movement of the Spirit in verse 2, as well as the creation of light in verse 3, both signify the instantaneous application of form to matter. Day 1 is the eternal day, both an infinitesimal point and at the same time a universe above and beyond time. In it are wrapped up the remaining 'days' of creation.[206] The creative events of Day 1 are eternal 'events' – creation does not take place at a point in time, after a past eternity; creation is an eternal reality. This is more radical than Augustine, an eternal creation befitting the timeless emanation of the entire sense-perceptible, material world from God.

Colet's treatment of the subsequent creation days progresses to the detail of creation by category. Colet struggles for consistency here, but takes a course reminiscent of Mirandola's when he takes Day 2's events as a description of the creation of the second-order realm, the celestial realm of the planets. This demarcates the higher realm (or 'waters') of the angelic host, from the lower realm of this earthly world, whose dry land, seas, vegetation and all material components can be summed up, as with Augustine, as the 'waters below'.[207] The description from Days 3–6 uses more concrete language, according to the hearers' needs, now using terms like 'water' literally. The order of the narrative reflects the ontological order of creation, from the divine realm downwards to the less honourable material world. So the creation week is a conceptual scheme only, and not a historical one in any sense.[208] We see why Augustine's kind of instantaneous creation continues to be cited and rebutted in Renaissance Genesis commentaries: there was in fact a minority position amongst *avant-garde,* Platonist thinkers that maintained instantaneous creation and at times veered toward an unorthodox emanationism and eternal creation.[209]

Catholic Interpretations at the Dawn of the Reformation

Shortly after the turn of the sixteenth century there appear some Genesis works from the established church that I include here because they

[205] Ibid., 27.

[206] Ibid., 6–7, 12, etc.

[207] Acc. to Colet's translator and editor, Lupton: ibid., xxviii.

[208] Ibid., 10, 17, 22.

[209] "Colet ... conceives of a succession of emanations from the fountain of all Being: one needing to be finished, before another is begun. " Ibid., xxii.

do not obviously reflect the impact of the Protestant Reformation, but instead display a general continuity with what precedes. The *Commentary on Genesis* of Tommaso de Vio, Cardinal Cajetan (1469–1534), first appeared in 1531 as part of his Pentateuch commentary.[210] Cajetan was a Catholic scholar in the revived scholastic tradition of Thomas Aquinas, yet his approach to biblical exegesis displayed some more modern tendencies as well, such as a preference for the literal sense of Scripture, a willingness to critique the Latin Vulgate, and a rationalistic tone akin to Jerome's.[211] His Genesis commentary saw him "proceed to the boldest [limit] in opposition to the traditional styles of interpretation of his Church," apparently safeguarded by the patronage of Pope Clement VII.[212]

Cajetan's interpretation of the creation week constitutes the last prominent Catholic defence of Augustinian instantaneous creation and the chief target of opposed colleagues.[213] In his *Commentary,* Cajetan first explains the way the motion of the spheres produce light and darkness, and thus the twenty-four hour day, upon the earth. Refusing to contemplate any long, chaotic beginning, he draws from Gen. 2:4 the fact that heavens, earth and 'day' arise at the same time. It is the circular movement of the *primum mobile*[214] and the light-bearers it governs around the earth that produces the alternation of day and night. "So the beginning of time, of the *primum mobile*, and of the sun are one and the same, according to the order of nature."[215]

Now Moses speaks of a series of natural days such as are available to our senses. Yet from the first circular movement of the *primum mobile*

[210] Bray, *Biblical Interpretation,* 180.

[211] Concerning the Vulgate, take for example his rejection of the generation of birds from the water as based on a distorted translation of Gen. 1:20: Zöckler, *Geschichte,* 1:633.

[212] Ibid., 1:632. Zöckler proceeds to offer several examples. On Pope Clement VII, see Jared Wicks, "Catholic Old Testament Interpretation in the Reformation and Early Confessional Eras," in *HB/OT,* 2:618, 622.

[213] Pererius, *Commentariorium,* 1:79f; Mersenne, *Quaestiones celeberrimae,* 685–86; R.P. Cornelius a Lapide, *Commentaria in Scripturam Sacram. Tomus primus: in Pentateuchum Mosis* (Paris: Ludovicus Vivés, 1859), 50, IA, http://www.archive.org/stream/commentariainsc00lapigoog; Augustin Calmet, *Commentarius litteralis in omnes libros Veteris et Novi Testamenti. Tomi primi pars prima* (Paris: chez Pierre Emery, 1707; reprint, Venice: Typis Sebastiani Coleti, 1767), 87. The last two mention the Spanish Dominican theologian Melchior Canus (1509–60) along with Cajetan. See the references in Mangenot, "Hexaméron," 6:2340; Zöckler, *Geschichte,* 1:640.

[214] The outermost heavenly sphere, beyond the planets and driving their movement.

[215] Thomas de Vio Cajetan, *Opera omnia quotquot in Sacrae Scripturae expositionem reperiuntur,* vol. 1. Commentarii illustres planeque insignes in Quinque Mosaicos libros, Thomae de Vio Caietani, Cardinalis S. Xisti, in Quinque libros Mosis, iuxta sensum literalem, commentarii: et primum in Genesim (Rome: 1531; reprint, Hildesheim: Georg Olms Verlag, 2005), 6, ll. 14–17, GB, http://books.google.com/books?id=OwW0VNRfxHYC.

and the heavenly bodies, days run on indefinitely as an effect of the repetition of that first day. So Moses' pattern of days is an accommodative way of speaking, intended to reinforce the sanctity of the seventh day.[216] But accommodation is not fiction; Moses can arrange the works of creation in successive days because the aspects of creation bear fit proportion to one another, and fall into a logical sequence, just as do the days of the week:

> Therefore, because the things accomplished by God, distributed into six grades, were related to one another as if the things done in each grade were [so done] in individual days, and on the seventh the workman had rested upon achieving all, Moses, without fiction, accommodated all the things accomplished by God in the first instant, in which he created heavens and earth, appropriately related to each other in six grades of perfection, to six natural days and the rest of the seventh.[217]

Cajetan aligns himself with Augustine's general position here, without adopting his more demanding concept of stages in angelic knowledge. Cajetan's scheme is more physical and cosmos-oriented, but his ideal conception of the days is very compatible with Augustine's. Although the vast majority of later commentators will cite Cajetan disapprovingly on this topic, the Cambridge Platonist Henry More will rely on Cajetan as he sidesteps a literal interpretation of the creation days.[218] Meanwhile Spanish theologian Melchior Canus (1509?–1560) interpreted Ecclus 18:1 and Gen. 2:4–5 to mean that the work of creation had occupied one single, entire day, while the other creation days represented further recapitulations of that day for the sake of expounding new facets of creation. Canus thus acknowledged real chronological succession in creation, yet his attempted compromise would satisfy neither side.[219]

Naturalistic process rather than instantaneous beginning evidently characterized the Genesis-based *Cosmopoeia* (1535) of Augustinus Steuchus Eugubinus (1496–1549),[220] a work Zöckler characterizes as more radical again than Cajetan's. Eugubinus' exegetical models are Jerome and Mirandola, showing that he combines rationalism with a

[216] Ibid., 6, ll. 19–41.

[217] Ibid., 6, ll. 55–64. I have drawn on Jaki's translation of this section at certain points: Jaki, *Genesis 1*, 134.

[218] Henry More, *Conjectura cabbalistica* (London: James Flesher, 1653), 150, EEBO.

[219] This is according to Francisco Suarez, himself relying on the report of a third party. Suarez, "Tractatus de opere sex dierum," 3:81B–82A, 84A–86A (*De opere sex dierum* 1.12.2, 9–12).

[220] Eugubinus Augustinus Steuchus, *Cosmopoeia, vel de mundano opificio, expositio III capitum Genesis, in quibus de creatione tractat Moses ...* (Sebast. Gryphius, 1535).

mystical influence belonging to the Italian Renaissance.[221] According to Zöckler, Eugubinus strives to relate "the works of creation genetically to one another in the strictest possible way, and ... to portray the creative activity of God as a naturally mediated [activity]."[222] For instance, the sun exists from the first day, as with Cajetan, and its influence elevates vapours on Day 2 of creation, forming clouds and thus rain. The sun's warming influence dries out part of the earth's surface on Day 3, while fish are already coming into being in the seas on that day.[223] Eugubinus' openness to other ancient traditions makes him amenable to the common belief in "the emergence of the earth from a chaotic condition," supporting his perception of the creation week events as a natural cause-and-effect sequence.[224] While his interpretation was rarely cited favourably in this period, such a naturalistic interpretation of the creation account was destined to grow in popularity.

Conclusion

Frank Robbins characterized medieval exegesis of the Hexaemeron as a gradual defection from Augustine's abstractness towards "a more concrete exegesis, representing the successive creations as the steps in a physical process."[225] Yet early in the medieval period, Bede and Alcuin already felt it necessary to avoid a full alignment with Augustine, and their preferred position, Gregory's limitation of instantaneous creation to Gen. 1:1 and the initial material of the universe, remained the mainstream position of the Middle Ages, appearing in Lombard's *Sentences* and again in Lyra's *Postilla*. And pro-Augustinian stances are not limited to the early Middle Ages, but feature in the writings of Abelard and Honorius of Autun in the twelfth century and Albert the Great and Vincent of Beauvais in the thirteenth, while the most abstract, timeless treatments of creation appear at either end of the period with Eriugena and Mirandola.

However, Thomas Aquinas' decision not to endorse Augustine's viewpoint perhaps constituted a turning point. The literal sense was clearly coming into favour in the later centuries, and was destined to prevail in the era of the Reformation, and not only among Reformers. Cajetan and Calvin alike give evidence of this trend, while a more

[221] Zöckler, *Geschichte*, 1:634–35; Arnold L. Williams, *The Common Expositor: An Account of the Commentaries on Genesis 1527–1633* (Chapel Hill: University of North Carolina Press, 1948), 210–11; Jaki, *Genesis 1*, 157. Jaki regards him as a barely disguised pantheist.

[222] Zöckler, *Geschichte*, 1:635, see also 637–38.

[223] Ibid., 1:636.

[224] Ibid., 1:635.

[225] Robbins, *Hexaemeral Literature*, 77.

mystical stream of interpretation would survive to influence early Enlightenment understandings of the Genesis creation account. A growing realism in interpretation would in time confine the interpretive pluralism of the Middle Ages to certain, mystically-minded interpretive subcultures. The more literal study of the 'Two Books' of Scripture and Nature after the Reformation, in the light of new discoveries, both macroscopic and microscopic, would ultimately bring the issue of reconciling biblical creation with natural philosophy to crisis point.

4

The Days of Creation in the Era of the Reformation

> Among the excellent acts of that King, one above all hath the pre-eminence. It was the erection and institution of an order, or society.... I find in ancient records, this order or society is sometimes called Solomon's House, and sometimes the College of the Six Days' Works, whereby I am satisfied that our excellent King had learned from the Hebrews that God had created the world and all that therein is within six days: and therefore he instituted that house, for the finding out of the true nature of all things, whereby God might have the more glory in the workmanship of them, and men the more fruit in their use of them....[1]
>
> Francis Bacon, *New Atlantis,* 1626

Introduction

Bacon's allusion to the six days of the Hexaemeron typifies the Renaissance conception that the creation week of Genesis was global in its reach – that it described, reliably, the creation of the entire physical world, and that the phenomena of the physical world could be studied and accommodated within the hexaemeral framework. The following statement applies above all to the Hexaemeron:

> [T]he Bible, by virtue of its function as the organizing matrix for Christian civilization in the West, continued to serve as the all-encompassing referencing grid according to which the mushrooming empirical data about the ... physical world ... could be organized and classified.[2]

This applied to historical as well as physical data: "In its literal meaning the Bible was taken to present a total narrative of Earth's creation and of human history, including humanity's estrangement from God

[1] Francis Bacon, "The New Atlantis," in *Ideal Commonwealths* (New York: P.F. Collier, 1901), http://oregonstate.edu/instruct/phl302/texts/bacon/atlantis.html. The wording there is as written here, although it seems grammatically imperfect. See also Eugene M. Klaaren, *The Religious Origins of Modern Science: Belief in Creation in Seventeenth Century Thought* (Grand Rapids: Eerdmans, 1977), 95.

[2] W. Yarchin, "Biblical Interpretation in the Light of the Interpretation of Nature: 1650–1900," in *Nature and Scripture in the Abrahamic Religions: 1700–Present*, ed. J.M. van der Meer and S. Mandelbrote (Leiden: Brill, 2008), 45.

and a redemption through Christ..."[3] That is why this early Modern period, from the dawn of the Reformation until the eighteenth century, played host to several unique genres of literature related to Gen. 1:1–2:3.

The Genesis commentaries that were the subject of medieval and Renaissance scholar Arnold Williams' important study differed markedly from the modern version. They sought to accommodate every particle of human knowledge that pertained in any way to the created order, producing Genesis or even just hexaemeral commentaries of astonishing size, the pre-modern analogue of the encyclopaedia. We also witness the flowering of biblical chronologies, which combed the Bible for an absolute dating system for history, stretching back to creation. Closely allied were the 'universal histories', which utilized such a biblical chronological framework to incorporate all available historical knowledge into a total world history that often began with creation. Genesis also inspired mystical treatises, philosophical expositions, programmatic educational proposals (including Bacon's *New Atlantis*) and, towards the end of the period, the fascinating theories of the earth.[4]

For a time, the rapidly broadening horizons of Renaissance knowledge continued to find a home within Gen. 1:1–2:3, which functioned as a point of reference and a basis for the integration of diverse fields. Such was its authority that even counter-cultural ways of knowing, the mystical or hermetic approaches, typically gave a central profile to Gen. 1:1–2:3, as in the influential works of Jacob Böhme. "The amazing combination of Millenarian, mystical, rationalist, and scientific views" that Richard Popkin describes as the 'third force' of seventeenth century thought clearly held this paradigmatic biblical text in high regard, as it sought to nurture an upsurge of knowledge of the natural order in preparation for the imminent 'new age' of God.[5]

Peter Harrison has emphasized the connection between the predominance of a literal hermeneutic in early Protestant interpretation and the emergence of a non-symbolic, utilitarian and historical understand-

[3] Ibid., 43.

[4] See Martin Stevens and John Block Friedman, "Arnold Ledgerwood Williams," *The Chaucer Review* 7 (1973): 229–33. Williams' *The Common Expositor* is valuable source of information about Genesis commentary in this period. One example of a Genesis-influenced educational program is Johann Amos Comenius, 1592–1670, *Naturall Philosophie Reformed by Divine Light, or, A Synopsis of Physicks by J.A. Comenius....* (London: printed by Robert and William Leybourn, for Thomas Pierrepont, at the Sun in Pauls Church-yard, 1651), 9–17, EEBO. Bacon's *New Atlantis* is also an educational program of sorts.

[5] Richard H. Popkin, *The Third Force in Seventeenth-Century Thought* (Leiden: E.J. Brill, 1992), 119, also 106, 112–13.

ing of the natural world.[6] Compared to the multi-level perception of both word and world that characterized the Middle Ages and continued to survive in mystical works, the literal interpretation of word and world read both in a more uni-dimensional way.[7] The Reformers were convinced that God speaks simply in Scripture, such that the ordinary person might grasp its meaning.[8] The physical world likewise became an object of study for its own sake, and its usefulness for the service of humanity was analysed.

Meanwhile the Reformation itself suggested the possibility of questioning established authority, and the political and religious fragmentation of Europe in the wake of the Reformation and the Thirty Years War (1618–48) yielded regions where purveyors of new and heterodox ideas could survive and publish their ideas largely beyond the control of the Catholic Church. Combined with the undermining of ecclesiastical and then biblical authority went a growing confidence in the power of human reason to discover truth. Then the antiquarian interests of the age found new ancient sources that might steal attention from the Bible: while the works of Plato and Aristotle had performed this role in the Middle Ages, scholarly eclecticism could soon draw on the ancient writings of Persia, India and China, relativizing the role of Christian Scripture.

The effect of this independent kind of inquiry was to permit data from other sources to stand alongside that of Genesis and in time to feel that there was some fundamental difference between the kind of information provided by Genesis and what could be told from stars, stones and living things. Genesis 1:1–2:3 seemed to evince a different purpose than a comprehensive history of the world's origin, and seemed unable, like an 'old wineskin', to continue to accommodate the exponential expansion of new information from the cosmos and the microcosmos, from the New World and from new cultures. In Francis Haber's words, "The method of comparing historical data, ancient authorities, and the rapidly accumulating natural knowledge against Mosaic history and cosmogony quickly multiplied the area of discordant facts in the world of sixteenth-century scholarship."[9] The authority of Gen. 1:1–2:3 to speak of past and present realities re-

[6] Peter Harrison, *The Bible, Protestantism, and the Rise of Natural Science* (Cambridge, UK: Cambridge University Press, 1998), 107–108, 114–20.

[7] Where theistic belief is in view, we might say that the perspective on the world is dualistic, perceiving a visible, material realm and an invisible, spiritual one.

[8] By contrast, Renaissance Platonists such as Mirandola, Colet and Henry More remained committed to the multi-level nature of Scriptural meaning, usually feeling that the higher meanings were not really accessible to the common person.

[9] Francis Colin Haber, *The Age of the World: Moses to Darwin* (Baltimore: Johns Hopkins Press, 1959), 33–34.

mained for the present, but thinkers such as Descartes, Galileo and Burnet hinted that Genesis was not indispensable for framing a cosmogony or a cosmology. Early in the Renaissance period, natural philosophy had had to answer to Genesis. By 1700, Genesis was well on the way to having to answer to natural philosophy.

The Literal Creation Week of Early Reformed Scholars

The dawn of the Protestant Reformation is associated with a striking resurgence of interest in interpreting Genesis, with particular focus upon the six days of creation – a symptom perhaps of the new interest in understanding the physical world, but still by means of the authoritative source for such an understanding, the book of Genesis.[10] Literal interpretation predominated, representing the culmination of a trend first glimpsed in Andrew of St. Victor. The fact that medieval Jewish interpretation had moved in a literal direction to counter Christian allegorical teaching from the OT must also have influenced the Reformers, many of whom studied the Hebrew language, often with help from Jewish instructors.[11] This turn toward the literal re-emphasized the place of Gen. 1:1–2:3 as the first step in the Christian 'grand narrative' of redemptive history. Genesis took pride of place amongst the exegetical works of Luther, Calvin, Zwingli and many others. The Italian-born Reformer Peter Martyr Vermigli (1499–1562) characteristically emphasized that Genesis' teaching is absolutely foundational to the Christian structure of truth.[12]

The earliest Reformers to highlight the importance of Genesis belonged to the 'Rhineland school', comprising the Protestant humanists of Strasbourg, Basel and Zurich, one of whose founding figures was Ulrich Zwingli (1484–1531).[13] It was Zwingli's humanist conviction that language proficiency would expedite understanding of the true meaning of Scripture that led to the foundation of the Zurich 'Prophecy', a kind of daily OT exegesis class delivered by Zwingli in his church, the 'Great Minster', from 1525.[14] "Beginning with Genesis 1

[10] Harrison says that while nature was rediscovered in the twelfth century, it was interpreted according to written authorities until the sixteenth: Harrison, *The Bible, Protestantism*, 69.

[11] Hodge, *Revisiting*, 29.

[12] Pietro Martire Vermigli, 1499–1562, *In Primum Librum Mosis, qui vulgo Genesis dicitur* (Zurich: Christophorus Froschauer, 1579), 2, ll. 3–7; Zöckler, *Geschichte*, 1:690.

[13] Sophie Kessler Mesguich, "Early Christian Hebraists," in *HB/OT* 2:264–65; Peter Opitz, "The Exegetical and Hermeneutical Work of John Oecolampadius, Huldrych Zwingli and John Calvin," in *HB/OT* 2:432; R. Gerald Hobbs, "Pluriformity of Early Reformation Scriptural Interpretation," in *HB/OT* 2:454; I. Backus, "Ulrich Zwingli, Martin Bucer and the Church Fathers," in *RCFW* 2:639.

[14] I.L. Snavely, Jr., "Zwingli, Ulrich *(1484–1531)*," in *HHMBI*, 250–51.

and proceeding in a chronological-salvation history order, the series had reached 2 Chronicles 20 by the time of Zwingli's death in 1531."[15] Student notes taken from Zwingli's talks became the first output of Reformation exegesis of Genesis, appearing in 1527.[16] They were soon followed in the 1530s by more careful and thorough Genesis commentary from other Rhineland school exegetes: Conrad Pellican (1478–1556), Sebastian Münster (1488–1552), Johann Oecolampadius (1482–1531), Wolfgang Capito (1478–1541), and ultimately Calvin, figures all noted for their humanist training and sophisticated Hebrew scholarship.[17]

The Protestant teaching of the clarity of Scripture may be detected in Zwingli's break with interpreters (such as Mirandola) who treated Genesis as a kind of esoteric code embracing all philosophical truth. He emphasizes that Moses wrote Genesis very simply, such that even the ignorant and simple might understand it, and should be taken literally in the first instance. In Zwingli's democratic Protestant hermeneutic, Genesis too was an open book, the common property of every believer. Genesis 1 describes creation in terms of the work of a craftsman or artist who first roughs out his work and "then adds light, shadings and outlines."[18] This is an accommodated way of picturing creation; Moses is speaking 'anthropopathically' or according to human perceptions; this is the way a human builder works, though God is able to create everything with a single word of his power.[19]

Yet the seven-day creation week represents more to Zwingli than a mere accommodation of linguistic *expression* concealing an instantaneous creation, such as Colet conceived.[20] God accommodated his creative *action* itself to our comprehension by distributing his works among

[15] Opitz, "Oecolampadius, Zwingli and Calvin," 420–21.

[16] Hobbs, "Pluriformity," 455; Opitz, "Oecolampadius, Zwingli and Calvin," 422. As Opitz observes, these notes (Latin *Farrago*) do not constitute a full-blown commentary. They were edited by Leo Jud and Kaspar Megander.

[17] Hobbs, "Pluriformity," 482–83; Mesguich, "Early Christian Hebraists," 264–71; The pertinent works of the first three are Pellican's *Comm. in Libros V. et N.T.* (1532–39), 9 vols., Münster's *Annotations in omnes libros V.T.* (1535–46), and *D. Io. Oecolampadii in Genesim enarratio* (Basel, 1536), all works that proved difficult for me to access from the Southern Hemisphere.

[18] H. Zwingli, *Farrago annotationum in Genesim, ex ore Huld. Zuinglii per Leonem Iudae & Casparem Megandrum exceptarum*, ed. Rudolph Gwalther and Leo Jud, Opera D. Huldrychi Zuinglii, vigilantissimi Tigurinae ecclesiae antistitis (Zurich: Christoph Froschauer, 1545), 4a, CPT. Jaki, true to form, regards this as a felicitous beginning from which Zwingli subsequently departs: Jaki, *Genesis 1*, 141.

[19] Zwingli, *Farrago*, 4a. Zwingli in fact uses the Greek term ἀνθρωποπάθως here.

[20] Colet, *Letters to Radulphus*, 10, 12, 14, 27; Charles Blount, *The Oracles of Reason: Consisting of 1. A Vindication of Dr. Burnet's Archiologiae. 2. The Seventh and Eighth Chapters of the Same. 3. etc.* (London: n.p., 1693; reprint, New York: Garland, 1979), 68, 75–76.

the individual days.[21] Thus Zwingli clearly anticipates Calvin's better-known enunciation of this principle, and even though earlier Christian authors such as Ambrose and Chrysostom had extended the concept of accommodation to God's way of working in creation, the idea receives much clearer articulation with the Reformers and certain of their Catholic counterparts.[22]

Wolfgang Capito (1478–1541), one of the Strasbourg Reformers, likewise presents a literal creation week as a corollary of the clarity of Scripture in his theologically oriented *The Six-Day Work of God Displayed* (1539).[23] As against the speculations of a Mirandola or Eugubinus, a plain reading of the opening verses of Genesis will reveal the creation of all things by God *ex nihilo* by means of his co-eternal Word, meaning both his spoken command and his Son.[24] Capito rejects instantaneous creation and a compromise version resembling Melchior Cano's, reiterating, "This universe, as great as it is, was created out of nothing within six days, in this order, in which it is described as being created," crediting Luther for unveiling this straightforward interpretation.[25]

But though distinctly historical, Capito's six-day creation is strongly anti-naturalistic. He reluctantly concedes the use of pre-existing matter in certain of the works of creation, but earnestly resists any suggestion that the first-created matter implied by 'heaven and earth' (Gen. 1:1) had any inherent potentialities that contribute to the productions of the subsequent days, or that it could have pre-existed the absolute 'beginning' expressed in that verse.[26] Far from being a natural cause-and-effect series, the order of the creative days is counterintuitive, because the only condition at each stage for what follows is the absolute lack of

[21] See under Distinxit lucem a tenebris: ibid., 4b.

[22] Saint Ambrose, Bishop of Milan, "De Cain et Abel," in *PL* 14:352D–353A (*Cain and Abel* 2.6.23): Utique simul omnia fieri jubere potuit Deus: sed distinctionem servare maluit, quam nos in omnibus imitaremur negotiis, et maxime in vicissitudinibus gratiarum … ("God was certainly able to command eveything to come into being at once; but He chose instead to observe a distinction for the sake of our imitation in the affairs of life, and especially in changes of fortune."): Dionysius Petavius, "De sex primorum mundi dierum opificio," in *Dogmata Theologica Dionysii Petavii* (1650; reprint, Paris: L. Vivès, 1866), 4:174A, GB, http://books.google.com/books?id=ewwND6aisfgC. Chrysostom, *Homilies*, 44–45. See also Pererius, *Commentariorium*, 1:82B (*Commentariorium* 1.1.188).

[23] Wolfgang Capito, *Hexemeron Dei opus explicatum* … (Strassburg: per Wendelinum Rihelium, 1539), 6a–15b, CPT. Only every second page is numbered.

[24] Ibid., 16a–17b.

[25] Ibid., 107a. The quotation translates, *Hoc universum, quantum est, intra sex dies ex nihilo creatus est, hoc ordine, quo creatum esse scribitur.* Ibid., 106b.

[26] Ibid., 31a–32a, 40b–41a, 107a, 108a–b.

the next-created thing, such as the utter darkness that preceded the creation of light.[27]

Two of the premier Reformation theologians, Wolfgang Musculus (1497–1563) and Peter Martyr Vermigli, both seem less cautious than Capito about using the classical 'chaos' language, such as ὕλη (*hyle*) and variations on *rudis indigestaque moles* from Ovid's *Metamorphoses*.[28] In his *Commentary on Genesis* (1554), Musculus defends the progressiveness of creation through the analogy of human formation in the womb.[29] For him, a distinction between the creation of formless matter and the detailed work of the creation week is a way of refuting instantaneous creation. Both Musculus and Vermigli strictly rule out the 'insane and impious' idea of positing any pre-existence for this chaotic material, as Capito does, although Vermigli is willing to admit some degree of propensity for generation in the initially-created matter.[30]

Vermigli's posthumous *On the First Book of Moses* (1569) is representative of this group when it includes the creation of heaven and earth *within* the events of the first day of creation: "It is clear that three things were made on the first day: heaven and earth, and besides these, light."[31] This reduces the chaotic condition of v. 2 to little more than a logical step within the first creation day. To say as Robert Letham does, "There is no evidence that Vermigli understands the days of Genesis 1 as of twenty-four hours," is to fail to realize that the only remotely orthodox alternative available to these writers is an instantaneous creation in the tradition of Augustine.[32] Where that is refuted, a literal creation week made up of twenty-four hour days is assumed.[33] Never before had Genesis 1 been so clearly and simply interpreted in the universal terms of the fourth commandment (Exod. 20:11): "For in six days the LORD made the heavens and the earth, the sea, and all that is in them."

[27] Ibid., 108b–111a.

[28] Wolfgang Musculus, *In Genesim Mosis plenissimi commentarii* (Basel: per Ioannes Heruagios, 1554; reprint, Microform: Inter Documentation Co., Zug, Switzerland, 1985), 6; Vermigli, *In Primum Librum Mosis*, 2. For positive assessments of their significance, see Donald K. McKim, ed., *HHMBI*, 134; F. A. James, III, "Vermigli, Peter Martyr *(1499–1562)*," in *HHMBI,* 240; Hobbs, "Pluriformity," 457, 482.

[29] Musculus, *In Genesim Mosis*, 6.

[30] For the phrase see ibid., 4. More generally, Vermigli, *In Primum Librum Mosis*, 3.

[31] Tria perspicuum est fuisse condita primo die; Cœlum & terram, præterea lucem. Vermigli, *In Primum Librum Mosis*, 3b. See also Musculus, *In Genesim Mosis*, 4. There he says, Sic Moses hoc versu non scribit quale rerum confusionem deus discernendam & digerendam inuenerit, *sed qualiter primo die cœlum ac terram condiderit* (but the way in which he formed heaven and earth on the first day).

[32] Letham, "Space of Six Days," 169.

[33] Williams describes the virtual unanimity on this point at this time: Williams, *Common Expositor,* 43.

In 1535, Martin Luther (1483–1546) resolved to devote his remaining years to an exposition of the Pentateuch, and spent the next ten years lecturing his way through Genesis, finishing only three months before he died.[34] "The commentary on Genesis fills eight volumes, and represents nearly a quarter of his hermeneutical output," which is noteworthy for a NT professor.[35] Luther's teaching on Gen. 1:1–2:3 gives the impression that Nicholas of Lyra's *Postilla* is the 'set text' for his students and their handbook of traditional interpretation, e.g. for further detail on Augustine's instantaneous creation position, or for the classic 'creation, separation, adornment' demarcation of the creative work.[36] Augustine is one of Luther's favourite sources, as one might expect from an Augustinian friar, and he also reveres "the very excellent Hilary."[37] Every church father must however be brought to the bar of Scripture, and Luther's advice is "to read them with discretion."[38]

When this criterion is applied to Genesis, Luther feels constrained by his exegesis of the text to disagree with the instantaneous creation of Augustine and Hilary, despite regarding them as "almost the two greatest lights of the church."[39] The trend towards a predominantly literal interpretation of Scripture has reached an advanced stage in these early Protestant works, and Augustine's *Literal Meaning* seems to Luther a fundamentally allegorical or figurative undertaking.[40] The Reformation emphases on the clarity of Scripture and the priesthood of all believers implied that God did not intend the Genesis accounts to be comprehensible only to an intellectual elite. "Moses was writing for a people without learning or experience," and only wrote about things that were necessary for them to know, leaving aside esoteric facts like angelic creation and fall.[41] "His purpose is to teach us, not about allegorical creatures and an allegorical world but about real creatures and a visible world apprehended by the senses."[42] Augustine is implicitly reproved for his presumption:

> If, then, we do not understand the nature of the days or have no insight into why God wanted to make use of these intervals of time, let us con-

[34] Johannes Schwanke, "Luther on Creation," *Lutheran Quarterly* 16, no. 4 (2002): 1.

[35] Bray, *Biblical Interpretation*, 172.

[36] Luther, *Lectures on Genesis*, 4–5.

[37] Ibid., 21. On the late medieval Augustinian revival that forms an important backdrop to the career of Luther, see Saak, "Reception of Augustine," 1:367–404; Manfred Schulze, "Martin Luther and the Church Fathers," in *RCFW* 2:573ff.

[38] Luther, *Lectures on Genesis*, 61.

[39] Ibid., 4; Schwanke, "Luther on Creation," 1. Schwanke says, "Luther's doctrine of creation arises out of his study of Scripture," i.e. it is exegetically-driven.

[40] Luther, *Lectures on Genesis*, 4–5.

[41] Ibid., 23.

[42] Ibid., 5. This realism stands in dramatic contrast to the Platonic idealism of Mirandola and Colet.

> fess our lack of understanding rather than distort the words ... we assert that Moses spoke in the literal sense, not allegorically or figuratively, i.e., that the world, with all its creatures, was created within six days, as the words read. If we do not comprehend the reason for this, let us remain pupils and leave the job of teacher to the Holy Spirit.[43]

Luther therefore understands the newly created light of Gen. 1:3 as a physical light that performed the orbital illuminating role later to be taken up by the sun.[44] The 'evening' and 'morning' statements refer to "the natural day, which consists of twenty-four hours, during which the *primum mobile* revolved from east to west."[45] Luther's instinctive incorporation of the events of Genesis 2 into the creation account clinches the argument for him, for the creation of Eve from Adam and the naming of the animals, things that necessarily must have occurred on Day 6, were obviously "acts requiring time."[46] His speculation about whether creation took place in autumn or in spring, when the fruiting of the trees might suggest the former and the appearance of vegetation the latter, operates on the same literal basis.[47] Luther likewise refutes Aristotle's eternal world with the usual statement, based on the dual assumption of a literal creation week and a complete and reliable OT genealogical chain, "We know from Moses that the world was not in existence before 6,000 years ago."[48]

Nothing here would have been controversial at the time in mainstream Genesis commentary, and when Letham treats Luther as the first of the major exegetes in his survey who unambiguously adopts twenty-four hour creation days, he obscures the fact that aside from an impermissible Aristotelian eternalism and the minority that adhered to instantaneous creation, a literal creation week and a world only a few thousand years old had long been the standard understanding of Genesis 1 *where the literal sense was concerned*.[49] This literal sense formed the assumed basis for allegorical interpretations, including the world-week interpretation.

But like Zwingli's, Luther's concept of the literal sense had ample room for anthropomorphic language. In the wake of the Fall, God cannot be directly perceived by the human mind.[50] Therefore "God envelops Himself in His works in certain forms, as today He wraps

[43] Ibid.
[44] Ibid., 19.
[45] Ibid., 42.
[46] Ibid., 69.
[47] Ibid., 37–38.
[48] Ibid., 3.
[49] Letham, "Space of Six Days," 164.
[50] Luther is generally quite cautious about classical philosophy, especially about Aristotle's teaching about the antique past: Luther, *Lectures on Genesis*, 3–6.

Himself up in Baptism, in absolution, etc....For in His Word and in His works He shows Himself to us." Anthropomorphic language is necessary in speaking of God, because all of our knowledge of God and reference to God must now be mediated.[51] Hence the pictorial element in Gen. 1:1–2:3, whereby the work of creation is described in terms of the construction of a house or dwelling for humanity. Coming to Day 3 he says,

> He has built the first parts of the house. It has a most elegant roof, the heaven, though this is not yet fully adorned. Its foundation is the earth. Its walls on every side are the seas [standing higher than the land!]. Now He also makes provision for our sustenance, so that the earth brings forth herbs and trees of all kinds.[52]

Luther's plain, literal exegesis of the creation week finds consistent analogues amongst other sixteenth-century Lutheran commentary on Genesis, including Melanchthon's (1497–1560). The claim that Melanchthon held six-day and instantaneous creation in tension seems to have no basis. For example, his discussion of the question of the nature of the light before the sun involves compares the opinions of Basil, Gregory of Nazianzus and Ambrose, assuming all along the physical reality of such light and its temporal priority to the sun.[53] In his *Explicatio Geneseos inchoata* (1553), another German Reformer, Johannes Brenz (1499–1570) asserts that "heaven and earth did not exist eternally, but had a beginning, and were created *ex nihilo* by God," along with creation in six days, suggesting that the most vigorous alternative at the time was Aristotle's concept of an eternal world.[54] Instantaneous creation seems easier for Brenz to refute. Every indication is that the passage is to be taken literally, he says, and so there is no warrant for a retreat into allegory concerning the days of creation.[55]

[51] Ibid., 12–15.

[52] Ibid., 36. See also pp. 39, 47, 72–73. Despite Stanley Jaki's jaundiced view of Luther's Genesis exposition, this is not so very far from the Hebrews' 'world-tent' according to which Jaki himself understands Genesis 1: See Jaki, *Genesis 1*, 143–47, 271–74.

[53] Philip Melanchthon, "Commentarius in Genesin," in *Philippi Melanthonis opera quae supersunt omnia*, ed. C.G. Bretschneider, Corpus Reformatorum (Halle: C.A. Schwetschke, 1846), 13:769. Jack Lewis repeats this opinion from A.D. White, but Melanchthon's discussion of Ps. 32:6, 9 in his *Loci theologici*, as cited by White, merely emphasizes *creatio ex nihilo* in order to refute a Stoic view of eternal matter. The duration of creation is nowhere discussed in these paragraphs. Lewis, "Days of Creation," 449; White, *Warfare*, 1:8. See the passages cited by White: Philip Melanchthon, *Philippi Melanthonis opera quae supersunt omnia*, ed. C.G. Bretschneider and H.E. Bindseil, trans. Charles H. Hill, vol. 21. Loci theologici, Corpus Reformatorum (Brunswick: C.A. Schwetschke, 1854), 270–71, 637–38, GB, http://books.google.com/books?id= x6QMAAAAIAAJ.

[54] Johannes Brenz, *Explicatio Geneseos, inchoata primo die septembris, anno salvatis 1553* (Tübingen: Excudebat Georgius Gruppenbachius, 1576), 3–4, CPT.

[55] Ibid., 5.

John Calvin (1509–64) stands out in his time as a striking intellect whose precocious energies were applied not only to systematic theology, presented in his famous *Institutes*, but also to exegetical works that eventually covered almost the entire Protestant Bible, such that Philip Schaff called him "the founder of modern historical-grammatical exegesis."[56] An early emphasis in Calvin's commentary on Genesis is that humans have been "placed in this scene, for the purpose of beholding the glory of God."[57] Indeed, the essence of God is inaccessible otherwise: "For God – by other means invisible – ... clothes himself, so to speak, with the image of the world, in which he would present himself to our contemplation."[58] Creation, in Calvin's pictorial presentation, is not so much a house for the occupation of man as a stage or scene wherein man can indirectly contemplate God through its decorations and equipment.[59] Since the content of Genesis was divinely revealed to Moses, and these twin modes of natural and special revelation coincide in Genesis: "The intention of Moses, in beginning his Book with the creation of the world, is, to render God, as it were, visible to us in his works."[60]

Calvin's position on the days of creation is another plainly literal one, and he famously defends this reading in terms of the 'accommodation' of God in his self-revelation, which he expresses concerning 'the first day' in Gen. 1:5:

> Here the error of those is manifestly refuted, who maintain that the world was made in a moment. It is too violent a cavil to contend that Moses distributes the work which God perfected at once into six days, for the mere purpose of conveying instruction. Let us rather conclude that God himself took the space of six days, for the purpose of accommodating his works to the capacity of men.[61]

It is Calvin's stance that has loomed largest in modern-day Protestant discussions about the concept of accommodation in connection with the creation week.[62] And Calvin indeed makes several allu-

[56] Acc. to D.L. Puckett, "Calvin, John (1509–1564)," in *HHMBI,* 171–79. See also Bray, *Biblical Interpretation*, 177.

[57] John Calvin, *Genesis*, The Geneva Series of Commentaries (London: Banner of Truth, 1965), 62.

[58] Ibid., 60. Note that Luther had made a similar point.

[59] Ibid., 62–64.

[60] Ibid., 58.

[61] Ibid., 78. See also p. 103, on Gen. 2:1. The error here refuted is clearly known to Calvin to be the position of the figure of greatest traditional authority for him, Augustine. See Johannes Van Oort, "John Calvin and the Church Fathers," in *RCFW* 2:677–78. Calvin goes on in this passage to correct the assumption that the Greek text of Ecclus. 18:1 supports or requires an instantaneous creation.

[62] E.g. the quotation of Calvin's statement in Jaki, *Genesis 1*, 150–51; Letham, "Space of Six Days," 166; Lewis, "Days of Creation," 452–53.

sions to the accommodation principle in this early portion of his Genesis commentary. Reconciling Gen. 1:16 with the day's 'facts' of astronomy, Calvin says, "Moses wrote in a popular style things which, without instruction, all ordinary persons, endued with common sense, are able to understand ... he was ordained a teacher as well of the unlearned and rude as of the learned, [so] he could not otherwise fulfil his office than by descending to this grosser method of instruction."[63] The clarity of Scripture means that all may access God's truth, but highly educated minds find things described less precisely than they might prefer.

Yet Calvin's interpretive principle of literalism, and his corresponding suspicion of allegory, would never have suggested to him that the daily structure of the creation narrative might itself be an accommodating manner of speaking. Instead, God accommodated his manner of *working* to human needs, taking six days when he might have created everything in a moment, as some wrongly assert.[64] "The creation of the world was distributed over six days, for our sake, to the end that our minds might the more easily be retained in the meditation of God's works."[65] He adds shortly afterwards, "six days were employed in the formation of the world; not that God, to whom one moment is as a thousand years, had need of this succession of time, but that he might engage us in the consideration of his works."[66] We have seen that this concept had been enunciated as far back as Chrysostom and Augustine, but Calvin explains it with an unprecedented clarity that reflects a Reformation-era realism concerning the natural world.

The Reformed sphere continued to generate commentaries on Genesis as the sixteenth century drew to a close.[67] These works constituted the best of late sixteenth-century continental Protestant scholarship, and influenced English Protestant thinkers of the early seventeenth century. Protestant commentators on Genesis such as David Pareus (1548–1622) clearly had literal, twenty-four hour days in view as they assumed initially equal days and nights, indicating a creation at one or other of the equinoxes, and contemplated a physical cycle of light and

[63] Calvin, *Genesis*, 86–87.

[64] Greene-McCreight, *Ad Litteram*, 132–33. She notes that the actual term 'accommodating' appears in King's translation (the same one I use here) on p. 113, in Calvin's discussion of Gen. 2:8.

[65] Calvin, *Genesis*, 92. This is again much like Chrysostom's statement in Chrysostom, *Homilies*, 44–45.

[66] Calvin, *Genesis*, 105.

[67] E.g. Johannes Mercerus, *In Genesim Commentarius* (Geneva: ex typographia Matthaei Berjon, 1598); Hieronymus Zanchius, *De operibus Dei intra spacium sex dierum creatis opus* (Neustadt: 1591; reprint, Hanover, 1597). See Zöckler, *Geschichte*, 1:614–15, 696–97, 708–12; Williams, *Common Expositor*, 7–8, 10, 15, 275; Kirkconnell, ed., *Celestial Cycle*, 581. On their literal creation week, see Williams, *Common Expositor*, 43 n. 13.

darkness for the first three creation days. They rejected Augustine's figurative understanding as a failure to fully acknowledge God's power and Moses' communicative integrity, and affirmed that God took six days over creation to display his power, freedom and goodness as he brought things forth against the naturally expected order, e.g. light before the sun and vegetation before rain or human cultivation.[68]

Arnold Williams regards this Renaissance-style Genesis commentary, which incorporated not just theological but scientific knowledge under the authoritative framework of the Genesis creation narrative, as suffering final eclipse after the 1633 commentary of another continental Protestant, the Huguenot Andreas Rivetus (1572–1651), who also held to literal creation days.[69] But by this time the impetus of literal Protestant biblical interpretation had moved to Britain, where the many admirers of continental Protestant scholarship perpetuated their teaching of a creation 'in the space of six days.'

Burying Instantaneous Creation: Jesuit Scholars

Compared to the diversity in early sixteenth-century Catholic interpretation of Gen. 1:1–2:3, the chastened environment following the Council of Trent (1545–63) produced more conservative commentaries on Genesis. The following Jesuit commentaries reveal a determined campaign to debunk the instantaneous creation famously associated with Augustine and recently advanced by Cajetan.[70]

The Genesis commentary published in 1589 by the Jesuit teacher in Rome, Benedict(us) Pererius (Benito Pereyra) (1535–1610), the *Commentariorium et disputationum in Genesim,* is highly regarded for its time.[71] Pererius devotes a substantial section to the question whether the world was created through the period of six days or in a moment, showing the persistent importance of this question in late sixteenth-century Catholic scholarship.[72] He first describes the roots of the instantaneous understanding of the days from Philo through Procopius of Gaza and down to Cajetan, then explains Augustine's teaching about

[68] David Pareus, *In Genesin Mosis commentarius* (Frankfurt: In Officine Ionae Rhodii, 1609), 131–32, 154–56, 200; Williams, *Common Expositor,* 10, 17, 43, 255.

[69] Andraeus Rivetus, *Theologicae et scholasticae exercitations centum nonaginta in Genesin* (Leyden: 1633). Williams, *Common Expositor,* 10, 43, 258, 261.

[70] For a non-Jesuit Catholic work with the same stance, see also Ambrosius Catharinus, *Enarrationes R.P.F. Ambrosii Catharini politi senensis archiepiscopi Compsani in quinque priora capita libri Geneseos* (Rome: apud Antonium Bladum caerae apostolicae typographum, 1552; reprint, Ridgewood, NJ: Gregg Press, 1964), 23–25; Zöckler, *Geschichte,* 1:639–40; Wicks, "Catholic Old Testament Interpretation," 623.

[71] Jaki, *Genesis 1,* 160–61. Williams, *Common Expositor,* 16, 23, 258, 264.

[72] The section treats the question (*disputatio*), Utrum mundus per sex dierum intervalla, an simul totus uno temporis puncto sit conditis? Pererius, *Commentariorium,* 1:79–84.

the days in terms of angelic cognition, and acknowledges that Ecclus 18:1 accords well with the omnipotence of God.[73] Nevertheless the opposite position is unquestionably correct (*indubitatae veritatis*), being the position of almost all the fathers and doctors of the church, especially Gregory the Great.[74] If Moses had wished to describe to a 'rude Hebrew audience' that creation had occurred as Augustine conceived it, he could have done so much more clearly than the Genesis account appears, and without a scheme of days that risked being misrepresentative.[75] To understand Genesis 1 in this way makes a mockery of Moses' argument about the Sabbath in Exod. 20:11 and 31:17.[76]

Pererius then revisits the exegetical cruxes (Ecclus 18:1; Gen. 2:4; Job 40:15) and refutes the idea that creation through time impugns God's omnipotence, instead saying in conventional fashion that creation through a period of time displays more clearly the relationships (*ordo* & *connexio*) between created things and their dependence on God. The initial creation displays God's omnipotence, the acts of distinction show his wisdom, and those of adornment his goodness. Creation, then, was not instantaneous, but took place item-by-item (*particulatim*) through six days. Pererius notes the argument that creation in six days was necessitated by the profound significance of the number six, but feels that this reasoning "perhaps will not satisfy the mind of learned scholars."[77] Finally Pererius treats the 'world-week' teaching at considerable length, cautioning against its use as a tool for predicting the future.

Another learned Jesuit, Francisco Suarez (1548–1617), composed a *Treatise on the Work of the Six Days,* an impressive, comprehensive treatment of the theology of the six days of creation utilizing a scholastic style of argumentation.[78] Its flavour is that of the typical Renaissance commentary of the era of the Reformation: traditional and well-read, yet with little attempt to incorporate current developments in natural philosophy. Augustine's brand of instantaneous creation and his spiritual interpretation of the six days of creation loom even larger in Suarez' treatment than in Pererius', and Suarez stands emphatically against its modern exponents despite Aquinas' vacillating example.[79]

[73] Ibid., 1:79B.

[74] Ibid., 1:80A.

[75] Pareus made a very similar argument.

[76] Haec autem ratio Mosis, quis non videt quam infirma, futilis, & frivola, si Deus non per sex dies, sed simul & uno temporis moment ores omnes fecisset? Pererius, *Commentariorium*, 1:80B.

[77] Docti lectoris animum fortasse non explebunt.

[78] The pertinent section is Suarez, "Tractatus de opere sex dierum," 3:53–87 (*De opere sex dierum* 1.10–12). I am not aware of the original date of publication of the work.

[79] *De opere sex dierum* 1.10.5.

Suarez is concerned that the sequence of events in the creation week demands real succession in time, since some of the things that are created are said to be formed not *ex nihilo* but from some pre-existing material, as when the human being is made from the dust (*limus*) of the ground on Day 6, or the land and sea are separated on Day 3, presupposing existing land and sea.[80] Likewise, the rationale for the given number and content of the six days is hard to unravel on the supposition that the days are 'spiritual' or 'intelligible' – a kind of cognitive sequence revealing an ascending series or a graduated hierarchy in creation.[81] How does a newly separated firmament reveal an incremental improvement beyond the 'heavens' created in Gen. 1:1, or why would the separation of land and sea come between the firmament's formation and the luminaries of Day 4?[82] But Suarez' fundamental objection is that such a 'metaphorical' interpretation of what is clearly a historical narrative distorts its plain, literal sense and threatens its clarity.[83] A more distinctively Catholic feature is his continual emphasis on the general consensus of the fathers, which he felt weighed heavily against Augustine's innovative interpretation.[84]

In 1616 Cornelius a Lapide (1567–1637) produced his commentary on the Pentateuch, which formed a part of his immense and renowned 'Great Commentary' on the whole Bible.[85] There he objects that Augustine's teaching of instantaneous creation "utterly defeats the simple and historical narration of Moses" and fails to "sufficiently explain himself, as to whether he is bringing this forward as the mystical sense or the literal one."[86] To interpret the successive days as successive stages in

[80] Ibid., 1.10.6–7; 1.12.9.

[81] Ibid., 1.10.24; 1.11.41; 1.12.8.

[82] Ibid., 1.11.37; 1.12.8.

[83] Ibid., 1.10.5; 1.12.4–5.

[84] He denies or mitigates the support of Hilary of Poitiers, Athanasius, Procopius and others for Augustine's position: *De opere sex dierum* 1.10.5, 1.10.21, 1.11.33, 1.11.38, 1.12.3.

[85] Gerald Bray calls him "the most popular Catholic commentator of his age," and his 'Great Commentary' on the whole Bible, of which this work forms a part, is well-represented in libraries to the present day: Bray, *Biblical Interpretation*, 183. For other perspectives, see Pierre Gibert, "The Catholic Counterpart and Response to the Protestant Orthodoxy," in *HB/OT* 2:764–66; F.J. Crehan, "The Bible in the Roman Catholic Church from Trent to the Present Day," in *The Cambridge History of the Bible. 3. The West from the Reformation to the Present Day*, ed. S.L. Greenslade (Cambridge: Cambridge University Press, 1963), 215–17.

[86] Lapide, *In Pentateuchum Mosis*, 50B. The quotations in their context read, "Verum contrarium docent omnes alii Patres, idque omnino evincit simplex et historica narratio Mosis .... Quare jam erroneum est dicere, omnia uno die esse producta, licet id senserit Cajetanus et Melchior Canus, quem citat Bannes 1 *p*. Q. 74, art. 2; S. Augustinus ergo dubie, et disputando loquitur in quæstione, ut ipse ait, tunc difficillima, nec satis seipsum

the enlightenment of angelic intellects is pious and helpful, believes Lapide, but only when carefully identified as a mystical and not as the literal meaning of the Genesis text.[87]

Lapide's treatment of the question is necessarily brief, given his ambitious scope, but the concise treatment by Dionysius Petavius (Denis Pétau) (1583–1652) in the relevant section of his *Dogmata theologica* (vol. IV, 1650) seems to reveal a decline in the perceived importance of this issue.[88] Petavius regards the instantaneous creation view as generated by a misguided speculativeness that overlooks the simple meaning of Scripture, and re-emphasizes that it is not the narrating of the action but the action itself that was accommodated to human capacity. The relative brevity and serenity of Petavius' treatment suggests that the issue of instantaneous creation was less pressing by 1650.

These Catholic commentaries are truly impressive for their scholarship and rhetorical power. Yet the last-mentioned, Petavius, was one of the last of his kind. Christian commentary on Genesis would henceforth be increasingly affected by new natural-philosophical views of the universe, while those thinkers who were seeking to account for the origin of the world would from this time increasingly take their cues from sources other than the text of Genesis.[89]

The Hexaemeral Literary Tradition in the Renaissance

Earlier I mentioned the literary re-imagining of the creation week in the late-patristic Latin poets. This tradition survived the early medieval period, as demonstrated by the 'Saxon Genesis'.[90] The late fifteenth-century development of the printing press provided the instrument with which Renaissance classicism was able to rejuvenate and disseminate these epic hexaemeral poems. For example, the creation poems of Dracontius, Hilary, Marius Victor, Avitus and Cyprian were published as *In Hexamerone* by Parisian publisher Fréderic Morel (1523–83) in 1560.[91] Morel also translated and published the hexaemeral work of the

explicat, an hæc adferat pro mystico, an pro litteralis sensu." Note the identification of Cajetan and Canus.

[87] Ibid. Lapide also cites world-week belief from the Fathers with apparent approval: ibid., 77A. See also Gibert, "Catholic Counterpart," 765–66.

[88] Petavius, "De sex primorum mundi dierum opificio," 4:171–74 (Q. 5) For this publication date for the fourth volume, see Cross and Livingstone, eds., *ODCC*, 1067. The work was incomplete at his death.

[89] Jaki concludes his discussion of Petavius along such lines: Jaki, *Genesis 1*, 168.

[90] A.N. Doane, *The Saxon Genesis: An Edition of the West Saxon Genesis B and the Old Saxon Vatican Genesis* (Madison, Wis.: University of Wisconsin Press, 1991).

[91] Williams, *Common Expositor*, 27.

Byzantine Georges Pisides.[92] So it is not surprising that it was a friend of Morel, the French Huguenot, Guillaume de Salluste Du Bartas (1544–90), whose poems, *La Sepmaine* (1578) and *La Seconde Semaine* (1584, unfinished), combined to form a model creation-and-fall epic poem, a literary genre that bound together what was known of the natural world within the historical framework of the biblical Genesis account.[93]

Du Bartas only briefly treats the rationale for a six day duration of creation, and in an irenic tone that suggests a relative absence of controversy on the point:

> Not, but he could haue, in a moment made
> This flowry Mansion where mankind doth trade,
> Spred Heau'ns blew Curtains & those Lamps haue burnisht,
> Earth, aire, & sea; with beasts, birds, fish have furnisht:
> But, working with such Arte so many dayes,
> A sumptuous Pallace for mankinde to raise,
> Yer man was made yet; he declares to vs,
> How kind, how carefull, and how gracious,
> He would be to vs being made ...[94]

The immediately preceding doublet captures Du Bartas' perspective on the creation days:

> And so in *Sixe Dayes* form'd ingeniously
> All things contain'd in th' UNIVERSITIE.[95]

God took so long as a week on the work of creation to show his ongoing care for his creatures and to remind human beings not to rush important tasks but to take the time necessary to do them well!

Du Bartas' poem shares with the mirror literature an encyclopaedic approach to creation, as the flora of Day 3 and the fauna of Day 5 are expanded from the very basic Genesis 1 description into two considerable lists. But the natural world continues to be interpreted via biblical revelation, so that Du Bartas defends the reality of waters above the firmament just as Luther had done. He also rejects Copernicanism, whose intellectual foothold in Europe was still tentative at the time.[96]

[92] G. Banderier, "A 'Fortunate Phoenix'? Renaissance and Death of the Hexameron (1578–1615)," *Neuphilologische Mitteilungen* 102, no. 3 (2001): 255–56.

[93] Evans, *Genesis Tradition*, 142; Kirkconnell, ed., *Celestial Cycle*, 570–71. On pp. 47–58, Kirkconnell offers some pertinent extracts from Du Bartas' very long work.

[94] Guillaume de Salluste Du Bartas, *Du Bartas His Deuine Weekes and Workes...* trans. Joshua Sylvester, 3rd ed. (London: Humfrey Lounes... 1611), 13–14, EEBO.

[95] Ibid., 13. See also the reference on p. 10 to the testimony to the six-day duration of creation in the giving of the law at Sinai, as related in Exod. 20:11.

[96] Ibid., 54, 95–96, 106; Kirkconnell, ed., *Celestial Cycle*, 51–54; John Dillenberger, *Protestant Thought and Natural Science* (London: Collins, 1961), 26–28.

A characteristic Renaissance feature of *La Sepmaine* is the elaboration of the initially formless state of the earth by means of classical images of the primordial chaos as expressed in Ovid's *Metamorphoses*. Ovid (43 BC–AD 17), one of the great Roman poets, by means of this work bequeathed to the Modern West a key deposit of classical mythology.[97] During the Renaissance, the appetite for classical ancient sources was not limited to Christian Scripture. In historian Gordon Davies' words, "The Renaissance rediscovery of classical learning had made a profound impression upon European scholars, and many classical writers came to be regarded as almost infallible oracles."[98] The rediscovery of powerful images of the primordial world such as Ovid's led to their melding with concepts from the Genesis creation account in Renaissance literature.[99] Du Bartas' heavy reliance on Ovid's *Metamorphoses*, despite his clear *creatio ex nihilo* stance, helped popularize the incorporation of the classical chaos into the interpretation of Gen. 1:1–2.[100]

La Sepmaine's best-known heir appeared in Restoration England: John Milton's (1608–74) *Paradise Lost* (1667), the outstanding Renaissance example of the biblical epic. The treatment of the six days of creation forms only a limited part of it, so that it also represents a step in the dissolution of the Renaissance hexaemeron into other genres.[101] The work represents a synthesis of the accumulated traditions surrounding Genesis, and its epic form reflects the particular biblical consciousness of the age.[102]

Milton's poem embeds the creation week in a broader, pre-existing angelic drama, itself daringly prefaced by a timeless chaos.[103] Milton appears to view the creation days themselves quite literally, since the pre-solar light circles the earth as a radiant cloud, bathing it in daylight.[104] Yet an Augustinian style of argument is used to justify the six-day description:

[97] Ovid's *Metamorphoses* may be readily accessed online. For an English version, see http://classics.mit.edu/Ovid/metam.1.first.html and for the Latin, see http://www.thelatinlibrary.com/ovid/ovid.met1.shtml.

[98] Gordon L. Davies, *The Earth in Decay: A History of British Geomorphology, 1578–1878* (London: Macdonald, 1968), 18.

[99] Roberts, "Genesis Chapter 1," 41.

[100] Du Bartas, *Deuine Weekes and Workes*, 2, 7–8; Williams, *Common Expositor*, 27f. Banderier speaks of more than 200 printings or editions by 1632! Banderier, "Fortunate Phoenix," 252.

[101] Ibid., 264, 266.

[102] Williams, *Common Expositor*, 4; Leland Ryken, "Paradise Lost and its Biblical Epic Models," in *Milton and Scriptural Tradition*, ed. J.H. Sims and L. Ryken (Columbia, MO: University of Missouri Press, 1984), 47.

[103] John Milton, *Paradise Lost* (1667; reprint, Books That Have Changed Man's Thinking; Geneva: Edito-Service S.A., n.d.), 125-126 (*Paradise Lost* 7.151–53, 189–91).

[104] *Paradise Lost* 7.243–48, 355–62.

Immediate are the acts of God, more swift
Than time or motion, but to human ears
Cannot without process of speech be told,
So told as earthly notion can receive.[105]

This potentially undercuts the apparent literalism of the poetic treatment, although these instantaneous acts are probably understood to occur on separate days of time. After the Son has used golden compasses to circumscribe the world's circle in "the vast profundity obscure," creating heaven and earth, Milton expands the content of the remaining days with additional detail, angelic responses and so on, in a manner reminiscent of the hexaemera of Basil or Ambrose or the Latin poets.[106] The emphasis is on the immediacy of the response to the fiats of God, as all that has been called into existence instantly appears, demonstrating the power of his Word.[107]

Assessments of *Paradise Lost* see it as a kind of last hurrah: "His epic would outdo all previous treatments of the story in the sheer comprehensiveness of its vision ... *Paradise Lost* is ... the culmination of the myth's development."[108] Williams concludes towards the end of *The Common Expositor,* "Milton wrote not only the greatest of the hexameral epics but also the last."[109] "After Milton, the hexameral epic and the scriptural drama, which had been such a strong current in European literature since Du Bartas, practically ceased."[110] After him, no work of the same kind and quality would emerge, and indeed the very worldview that undergirded it was about to fracture. One of the marks of the hexaemeral literature, that it was at the same time "not only theological but also scientific," meant that the schism that was about to pull the two apart, destroying the 'medieval synthesis', would make it an unviable genre.[111]

Hence the briefly revived genre of the Renaissance hexaemeron represented the convergence of a Christian, biblically-determined world view and the Renaissance impulse to access and imitate classical literary models, now made readily available through the printing

[105] Ibid., 7.176–79.
[106] Ibid., 7.225–32ff.
[107] E.g. ibid., 7.285–86, 313–16, 453–56.
[108] Evans, *Genesis Tradition*, 219.
[109] Williams, *Common Expositor*, 264.
[110] Ibid., 259.
[111] Ibid., 261; Kirkconnell, ed., *Celestial Cycle*, xxvii. V.H.H. Green said, "The Reformation and Renaissance had between them shattered the medieval synthesis.... Neither religion nor culture provided the new society with a true focal point. National ambitions and economic greed thus injected an individualistic and class-conscious society with the seeds of its own decay." V.H.H. Green, *Renaissance and Reformation: A Survey of European History between 1450 and 1660*, 2nd ed. (London: Edward Arnold, 1964), 28.

press.[112] Its preoccupation with Genesis reflects humanity's fascination with origins, especially its own origins, while the unique authority of the Bible meant that its creation narratives still provided the explanatory paradigm. The melding of the biblical creation framework with classical cosmogonies was about to yield an entirely new genre of origins speculation, the theory of the earth, but its initial impact on exegesis would chiefly affect perceptions of the condition of the earth *before* the creation week began, not yet generally the reception of the creation days themselves.

Alternate Stances: Genesis One Encrypted

Despite the trend towards prioritizing the literal sense of Genesis, there persisted an alternative impulse to take the opening chapters of Genesis as a symbolic gateway to the fundamental elements of reality, following the example of earlier figures such as Clement and Origen in the patristic era, Eriugena in the early medieval, and Mirandola early in the Renaissance. It found an amenable home in Popkin's 'third force' in seventeenth century philosophy, as distinct from both "Cartesian rationalism and British empiricism," an eclectic and mystical strain that ultimately melded with the other two to give birth to modern science. Inquisitive and superstitious, Christian yet often heterodox, it was a quest to found perfect human knowledge in light of a millennial vision. Its traces are clear in many of the century's prominent minds, such that even Newton himself, while establishing a mechanistic model for the present operation of the cosmos, could invest great energies in futuristic interpretations of Bible prophecy.[113] Even his key concept of gravitation, a force mysteriously operating at a distance in the absence of any physical cause-and-effect linkage, fits very comfortably in a 'third force' context.

This line of thought employs an allegorical approach to the biblical text based on a mystical perception of manifold correspondences between the various levels of reality, whether physical, metaphysical, spiritual, moral, or even chemical. In one sense the heir to medieval allegory, it constituted a kind of underground revolt against the literalism so prevalent in this period. It represented a commitment to recondite knowledge, not located in the outward form of the written word but communicated from God or accessed in the transcendent realm

[112] Banderier, "Fortunate Phoenix," 256; Kirkconnell, ed., *Celestial Cycle*, 509, see also vi, xiii, xix, 491; Robbins, *Hexaemeral Literature*, 57, 89; Evans, *Genesis Tradition*, 142 and preceding pages; Roberts, *Biblical Epic*, esp. 92ff.; Williams, *Common Expositor*, 27.

[113] Popkin, *Third Force*, 90, 103, 113–15, 119.

through spiritual channels.[114] This matrix provides the necessary background for understanding several interpretations to be expounded in the following paragraphs: Böhme's superstitiously reverent mystical reading of Genesis 1, a Platonist-allegorical reading such as Henry More's, and even Isaac de la Peyrère's *Preadamitae*, a representative of that *avant-garde* early Modern literature that effectively undermined the scope and relevance of Genesis.

An early Protestant figure, Jacobus Brocardus, with his *Mystica et prophetica libri Geneseos interpretatio* (1580), may have helped to sow such seeds within the Protestant sphere. This scarce work represents a non-literal handling of the creation days, apparently in the service of an apocalyptic version of the world-week schema.[115] More influential was the curious and obtuse treatment of Genesis by Jakob Böhme (c. 1575–1624). Renaissance figure Paracelsus' (1493–1541) 'alchemical' philosophy featuring the 'salt-sulphur-mercury' triad is a recognisable feature of Böhme's writing, as is the original residence of the dual principles of good and evil in the nature of God, a concept Zöckler ascribes to the mystic Valentin Weigel (1533–88).[116] Böhme's unique contribution is to integrate a complex mystical and metaphysical understanding of the universe with the authoritative text of Genesis.

The earlier of his two works pertaining to Genesis 1 is *Aurora oder Morgenröthe im Aufgang*, which became so waylaid in discussing the nature of the stars in connection with Day 4 of creation that it remained unfinished.[117] His rather parochial interpretive key in this work seems to be the phonology of the words of the Genesis text in the German language.[118] The German syllables function as ciphers for his Gnostic, dualistic worldview, wherein the material world constitutes a physical scum resulting from the conflict of Lucifer with God, and reality is comprised of a bewildering web of correspondences.

The later work, *Mysterium Magnum, or an Exposition of the First Book of Moses Called Genesis* (originally 1624), is clearer concerning the creation days and more obviously related to Genesis 1 in its structure, although it too operates on multiple levels and shares the same

[114] See for example Popkin's comments on the Quaker Samuel Fisher: Popkin, *Third Force*, 103, 355–57.

[115] Williams, *Common Expositor*, 21, 43; Zöckler, *Geschichte*, 1:731. Note that Williams counted four editions from 1580–93, but Zöckler lists a 1575 edition also. I was unfortunately unable to gain direct access to Brocardus' work.

[116] Ibid., 1:726–30. One is reminded of the Manichean teaching of the patristic era.

[117] Jakob Böhme, 1575–1624, *Aurora. That is, the day-spring. Or dawning of the day in the Orient or morning-rednesse in the rising of the sun. That is the root or mother of philosophie, astrologie & theologie from the true ground...* trans. John Sparrow (London: printed by John Streater, for Giles Calvert, etc., 1656), EEBO. The preface is dated to 1612, which gives some idea of the date of original publication.

[118] Ibid., 405ff.

Manichaean or Gnostic derision for the physical world. Böhme briefly permits a certain literal sense to the Genesis text, but quickly moves to his preferred perspective, in which the days act as symbols representing ideal concepts, or successive material manifestations or productions of the Divine Nature via the agency of the breathed-out Word:

> That God hath created Heaven and earth, and all things in six dayes, as Moses saith; is the greatest Mystery, wholly hidden to the externall Reason: there is neither night, Morning or Evening in the Deep above the Moone; but a Contiuuall [*sic*] Day from the beginning of the outward world even until the End of the same. And albeit the Creation was finished in such a time as in the length of six dayes: yet the dayes-workes have a far more Subtle [or abstruce] meaning: for the Seven Properties are also understood therewith; Six whereof belong to the Active Dominion to good and Evill; and the Seventh (viz. the Essence) is the rest: wherein the other properties rest, which God hath expressed, and made visible. We have in the Dominion of the Planetick Orbe the figure, how the six properties of the Active life (which rest in the Seventh) have in six dayes introduced and manifested themselves out of the inward Spirituall world in an externall visible world of foure Elements ...[119]

The seven 'properties' mentioned are primarily chemical in nature, including the Paracelsian salt, sulphur and mercury, and they correspond also to the influences of the seven planets, and so on to other levels. This material creation is repeatedly associated with the fall of Lucifer: "The beginning is the first motion: which came to passe when Prince Michael fought with the Dragon; when he was spewed out with the Creation of the Earth: for even then the Enkindled Essence (which with the Enkindling did Coagulate it selfe into Earth and stones) was cast out of the internall into the externall.... Thus by the Separation, viz. of the light and darknesse; and by the expelling of Prince Lucifer, we are to understand the Creation of the first day."[120] The six days are really recapitulations of the first, and that first finds its prototype in the eternal Divine Nature: "For in the Eternall natures birth there is an Eternall day; whatsoever God hath manifested, and made visible in six diversalls, which are called dayes-workes, that standeth in the Eternall nature in six distinct degrees in the Essence, viz. in the Seventh Property ..."[121] Böhme's creation week is essentially ontological rather than temporal – a seven-sided cipher symbolizing the rather regrettable seven-part emanation of the Divine Nature into materiality.

[119] Jakob Böhme, *Mysterium magnum, or An Exposition of the First Book of Moses called Genesis* ... (London: printed and are to be sould by Lodowick Lloyd ... 1656), 49, EEBO.

[120] Ibid., 50–52.

[121] Ibid., 54.

Böhme's hallucinatory take on Genesis 1 was a seminal new entry in this mystical interpretive stream and would resurface in the alchemical/Paracelsian and Neoplatonist circles of seventeenth-century England and in German theosophy into the eighteenth century. As Roy Porter explains, "Paracelsianism was translating Genesis into alchemical language, and so establishing an important tradition of chemical speculation on the formation of the Earth."[122] Robert Fludd (1574–1637) was an early exponent of this "mystico-chemical interpretation of Genesis" in the English scene, although his treatment relates less to the actual text of Gen. 1:1–2:3 than does Böhme's *Mysterium Magnum*.[123]

Less mystical than Fludd was Johann Amos Comenius (1592–1670), who in *Naturall Philosophie Reformed by Divine Light* (1651 [1634]) takes Genesis 1 as his authoritative text and methodological starting point, believing that neglect of this text in favour of pagan (i.e. Aristotelian) sources was the downfall of natural philosophy.[124] He finds suggestions of a system of 'physicks' in Genesis 1, and for him, the events of the creation week unfold in a natural development once the three necessary principles, matter, spirit and light, are in place. God's approbation of the goodness of the light in Gen. 1:4 means, "he saw that all things would now proceed in order," or by natural cause and effect, through the course of an apparently literal creation week.[125] In contrast to Descartes or Galileo, Comenius used the 'two books' of God's revelation, the Bible and nature, in close conjunction and complete complementarity, and so treated Genesis 1 as paradigmatic for establishing a physical cosmology.[126]

Such symbolic or mystical treatments naturally tended to minimize the historical aspect of the creation days, establishing another precedent for future interpretations that would, for scientific or other reasons, seek to escape from a creation week of seven literal days. Sir Thomas

[122] Roy Porter, *The Making of Geology: Earth Science in Britain 1660–1815* (Cambridge: Cambridge University Press, 1977), 14.

[123] Zöckler calls him 'the English Böhme': Zöckler, *Geschichte*, 1:732. The relevant works are Robert Fludd, *Utriusque Cosmi Maioris scilicet et Minoris Metaphysica, Physica atque Technica Historia* (Oppenheim: 1617); Robert Fludd, *Mosaicall philosophy Grounded upon the Essentiall Truth, or Eternal Sapience / written first in Latin and afterwards thus rendred into English by Robert Fludd, Esq.* (London: printed for Humphrey Moseley... 1659), EEBO. See Katherine B. Collier, *Cosmogonies of Our Fathers. Some Theories of the Seventeenth and Eighteenth Centuries* (New York: Columbia University Press, 1934; reprint, New York: Octagon Books, 1968), 25–32. The quoted phrase is from Paolo Rossi, *The Dark Abyss of Time. The History of the Earth and the History of the Nations from Hooke to Vico* (Chicago: University of Chicago Press, 1984), 8.

[124] Comenius, *Naturall Philosophie*, unpaginated introduction.

[125] Ibid., 11, 19, 102. E.g. see the 'six dayes' reference on p. 19 and 'seven dayes' reference on p. 102.

[126] H.J.M. Nellen, "Growing Tension between Church Doctrines and Critical Exegesis of the O.T.," in *HB/OT*, vol. 2:825; Popkin, *Third Force*, 109.

Browne, in his *Religio Medici* (1642), noncommittally describes a current minority belief that "there went not a minute to the World's creation ... those six days ... make not to them one moment, but rather seem to manifest the method and Idea of the great work."[127] The preface to the Paracelsian *Oriatrike* (1662) of Jean Baptiste van Helmont (1577–1644) seems to manifest the same general attitude to the creation days.[128] For these fringe thinkers Genesis retained its role as the primordial and principal revelation concerning the natural world, but functioned in a purely mystical way.[129]

This metaphysical and cabbalistic, rather than physical and historical, interest in the Genesis text, survived well beyond the turn of the eighteenth century, especially in the theosophical movement.[130] It was a quest to understand the basic fabric of the present world using all the resources of both empirical and enigmatic, hidden knowledge. The Newtonian Nehemiah Grew (1641–1712) shows himself inclined in his *Cosmologia Sacra* (1701) to understand the days along cabbalistic or symbolic lines. He comments rather casually that most take the days literally, while some understand them as years or ages, and others would see the days as a heuristic device to help limited human minds grasp an instantaneous creation. God's omnipotence meant that creation could take any length of time or none.[131]

The same systematizing impulse that had produced the Cartesian and Newtonian schemes also yielded attempts to build physical systems on an explicitly scriptural foundation. *Physica vetus & vera* (1702) by Edmund Dickinson uses the Hexaemeron as the framework for a long and obscure explanation of the atomistic substructure of the universe in

[127] Sir Thomas Browne, *Religio Medici the Fourth Edition, Corrected and Amended...* (London: printed by E. Cotes for Andrew Crook ... 1656), 97, EEBO. (*Religio medici* 45). I have used the wording of Williams, *Common Expositor*, 43. Williams' discussion of this point is muddied by what I can only interpret as a typographical error: "Nearly all the commentaries mention their [I think he must mean 'the'] belief that the work of the days was but a manner of revealing the creation." He goes on to describe this belief, and at the end of the same paragraph, says, "No, God took six literal days for the creation of the world. With the single exception of Brocardus, every commentator I have read is determined that the Mosaic account be taken literally."

[128] Jean Baptiste van Helmont, 1577–1644, *Oriatrike, or, Physick Refined* (London: printed for L. Loyd, 1662), EEBO. The preface is unpaginated, but the quotation appears in image #11a–b in the electronic version.

[129] Klaaren, *Religious Origins of Modern Science*, 61.

[130] Rudolf Steiner, 1861-1925, *Genesis: Secrets of Creation: The First Book of Moses: Eleven Lectures given in Munich, 16-26 August 1910* (Forest Row: Rudolf Steiner Press, 2002).

[131] Nehemiah Grew, *Cosmologia Sacra: or A Discourse of the Universe as It Is the Creature and Kingdom of God ....* (London: W. Rogers, 1701), 194, 249, ECCO. Some writers have mistaken Grew as a simple literalist: Collier, *Cosmogonies*, 145; Jaki, *Genesis 1*, 184–85.

the tradition of Democritus, recently revived by Gassendi and Boyle, but melded with "a strangely old-fashioned, hermetic-cabbalistic secret wisdom."[132] Any sense of history is lacking, and the days of creation do not function as real measures of time. In a similar vein, John Hutchinson would shortly attempt in *Moses' Principia* (1724) to expound a Mosaic cosmic system in contrast to those of Descartes or Newton, reading the creation week narrative through strongly metaphysical glasses, as would his disciple Samuel Pike with his *Philosophia Sacra* (1753).[133] This alternate stream of thought maintained a degree of influence almost throughout the eighteenth century; John Wesley, for one, was one of the Christian thinkers showing the impact of Hutchinsonian ideas.[134]

Alternate Sources: Genesis One Excluded

Other key seventeenth-century thinkers placed their confidence in the power of reason more than in mystical revelation. Here René Descartes (1596–1650) parted ways with Comenius and company, effectively dispensing with Genesis as a serious source for understanding the world's origin. Prefacing his theory of cosmic formation in chapters 6–15 of his Treatise on Light, he portrays what follows as a 'fable', and then continues,

> Allow your thought to wander beyond this world to view another, wholly new, world, which I call forth in imaginary spaces beyond it … let us not try to go all the way, but rather enter it only far enough to lose sight of all the creatures that God made five or six thousand years ago, and after stopping there in some definite place, let us suppose that God creates anew so much matter all around us that, in whatever direction our imagination may extend, it no longer perceives any place that is empty." "From the first instant of their creation, He [God] causes some [particles] to start moving in one direction and others in another, some faster and others slower.... For God has established these laws [of nature] in such a marvelous way that … the laws of nature are sufficient to cause the parts

[132] Even Collier's chapter summarizing Dickinson's work is somewhat exhausting: Collier, *Cosmogonies*, 149–65. The quotation is from Zöckler, *Geschichte*, 2:199 (… einer sonderbar altmodischen, hermetisch-kabbalistischen Geheimweisheit …)

[133] John Hutchinson, *Moses's Principia. Of the Invisible Parts of Matter; of Motion: of Visible Forms* ... (London: J. Bettenham, 1724), 34–37, 98–99; Samuel Pike, *Philosophia Sacra: or, The Principles of Natural Philosophy. Extracted from Divine Revelation* (London: printed for the author, and sold by J. Buckland ... 1753), 105–15, ECCO.

[134] Dillenberger, *Protestant Thought*, 157–58; Collier, *Cosmogonies*, 176, 179.

> of this chaos to disentangle themselves and arrange themselves in such a good order that they will have the form of a most perfect world.[135]

Thus might all cosmic bodies form in 'vortices' by natural processes alone from an initial *plenum* of fluid matter created and set in motion by God.[136] The hypothesis was presented as what we would call a 'thought experiment' and not a reality, but this manoeuvre of 'saving the appearances' functioned as a 'lip service' justification for the fact that he "wholly ignored the Mosaic account."[137]

Thus Descartes set a precedent for eighteenth-century naturalistic models of cosmology by Maupertuis, Kant, and finally Laplace, whose *System of the World* (1796) did not even mention a Creator. In fact, since Copernicus' *De revolutionibus* (1543) and the development of his heliocentric theory of the solar system through the work of Tycho Brahe (1546–1601), Johannes Kepler (1571–1630), and Galileo Galilei (1564–1642), the Christian-Aristotelian cosmology connected to Genesis had faced a new rival.[138] A more empirical operator than Descartes, Galileo, in his 'Letter to the Grand Duchess Christina' (1615), sought a clear demarcation of spheres and limited biblical authority and reliability to matters of faith, calling upon Augustine's *Literal Meaning* to urge that biblical proofs should not decide the relative merits of physical theories.[139] Galileo evidently found the 'Book of God's Works' clearer for his purposes than the 'Book of God's Word'. The compatibility of the two books was not yet overtly disputed, but the question of the relationship between the two sets of data was becoming urgent. Should extrabiblical data be ignored, or incorporated into a biblical framework, or considered separately but alongside the biblical information? Descartes and Galileo modelled the possibility of excluding

[135] René Descartes, *The World and Other Writings*, ed. Stephen Gaukroger, Cambridge Texts in the History of Philosophy (New York: Cambridge University Press, 1998), 21–23. See also Gaukroger's introduction.

[136] The Latin term *plenum* implies the belief that there was no such thing as a vacuum in nature, and every part of the universe contains some kind of matter. This is a key difference between Cartesianism and Newtonian physics, which assumes on the reality of a vacuum.

[137] Collier, *Cosmogonies*, 33. On the meaning of the phrase, 'saving the appearances', see http://davidlavery.net/Barfield/encyclopedia_barfieldiana/lexicon/Saving.html, accessed 4/1/10, and more fully, P. Duhem, *To Save the Phenomena: An Essay on the Idea of Physical Theory from Plato to Galileo*, trans. E. Doland and Ch. Maschler (Chicago: University of Chicago Press, 1969).

[138] Collier, *Cosmogonies*, 13–24.

[139] Galileo Galilei, "Letter to Madame Christina of Lorraine, Grand Duchess of Tuscany, Concerning the Use of Biblical Quotations in Matters of Science," in *Discoveries and Opinions of Galileo*, ed. Stillman Drake (Garden City, NY: Doubleday, 1957), 173–216. For the particular use of Augustine's *Literal Meaning,* see pp. 175–76, 194, 198, and 206, where he makes use of *DGaL* 2.18.38, 1.21.41, 2.9.21 and 1.18.37–1.19.38 respectively.

Genesis 1 from controlling or even contributing substantially to hypotheses of the world's physical origin its physical constitution.

But such an exclusion was still not typical for the time. The important and well-connected Catholic intellectual, Marin Mersenne (1588–1648), in his *Quaestiones celeberrimae in Genesim* (1623), "the vastest commentary on Genesis 1 ever published," shows himself to be a wholehearted believer in the unity of natural and biblical knowledge.[140] He "wanted to find in Genesis all the results of modern physical research," and "turned the explanation of the literal meaning into a scientific commentary."[141] His treatment of the nature of the days of creation is quite brief, and after he cites figures for and against instantaneous creation, the discussion ends with and probably implicitly favours Thomas' mediating position.[142] But Mersenne's commentary is the first on Genesis that clearly wrestled with the Copernican model of the solar system, as well as with Tycho Brahe's compromise model.[143] Williams attributes this to Galileo's recent discoveries, while Jaki attributes Mersenne's final, geocentric conclusion to Galileo's first condemnation by Catholic authorities only seven years before.[144] Thus Mersenne's Genesis commentary is probably the first to reckon seriously with the extrabiblical, empirical data characteristic of the scientific age and to attempt to incorporate it into a biblical framework.[145]

A different rationale for the exclusion of the early chapters of Genesis from speaking decisively on physical nature and primordial history was brewing. The philosophy and methods of biblical criticism began to come into view in the mid- to late-seventeenth century, in a story related in numerous histories of biblical interpretation.[146] The Penta-

[140] The quotation is from Jaki, *Genesis 1*, 170. Williams, p. 7, notes that publication gives out after Genesis 6 for this reason. See also Cross and Livingstone, eds., *ODCC*, 906; Collier, *Cosmogonies*, 16–17; Williams, *Common Expositor*, 179, 263; William B. Ashworth, Jr., "Catholicism and Early Modern Science," in *God and Nature: Historical Essays on the Encounter between Christianity and Science*, ed. D.C. Lindberg and R.L. Numbers (Berkeley: University of California Press, 1986), 138–39.

[141] Nellen, "Growing Tension," 826.

[142] Mersenne, *Quaestiones celeberrimae*, 685. Such is Mersenne's style in the sections I saw, with frequent citation of tradition, limited inclination to state an explicit opinion, and a discursive structure that can make it difficult to pin down his point or find the transitions between topics.

[143] Ibid., 899–900, 919. Browsing the lengthy section on models of the planetary system makes plain both the importance of the issue at this time and the pressure that Mersenne feels to conform to Catholic or Papal decrees.

[144] Williams, *Common Expositor*, 189; Jaki, *Genesis 1*, 171.

[145] Williams, *Common Expositor*, 258, 262, 268.

[146] See for instance Arthur McCalla, *The Creationist Debate: The Encounter between the Bible and the Historical Mind* (London: Continuum, 2006), 34; Bray, *Biblical Interpretation*, 237–40; Richard H. Popkin, "Cartesianism and Biblical Criticism," in *Problems of Cartesi-*

teuch generally and not least the early chapters of Genesis quickly became a focus of the historical kind of biblical criticism that succeeded the technical analysis of textual evidence. Bolder thinkers began to raise doubts about the origin and reliability of the foundational 'Mosaic' documents, and not merely of later scribal copies. Richard Popkin describes the typical succession of critical claims, where "denial of the authenticity of the existing biblical text" was followed by "denial of the Mosaic authorship of the Pentateuch ... and the denial of the Bible as the framework for human history."[147]

One thinker who took this path was Isaac de La Peyrère (1596–1676), a French Protestant with a millennial vision centred on the restoration of the Jewish nation. La Peyrère was not the first but was certainly the most infamous early advocate of the pre-Adamite theory, which allowed that some presently existing races, especially those in newly discovered, far-flung lands, had not descended from Adam.[148] This idea had been brewing throughout the seventeenth century in a Dutch context famous for freethinking, and which was well familiar with pagan sources suggesting that non-Hebrew races boasted a deep antiquity.[149] La Peyrère's *Men before Adam* barely mentions the book of Genesis, but his willingness to contemplate human races not derived from Adam inevitably undercut the seemingly universal scope of Genesis 1–11 and rendered it merely a parochial story.[150] The authority of the early chapters of Genesis was just as threatened by this kind of restriction of their applicability as by aspersions against their authorship credentials or, in time, their factual reliability. The Bible had seemed to embrace every field of human knowledge, and Genesis to ably comprehend the world's origin. The disturbing sense was now arising "that there was an entire realm...where the Biblical tradition had nothing to say."[151] That there could be races, or continents, or even entire populated worlds unaccounted for by Genesis induced either dismissiveness, defensiveness or, progressively, an unfolding worldview crisis, a paradigm shift concerning divine revelation and biblical authority.

anism, ed. T.M. Lennon, J.M. Nicholas, and J.W. Davis (Kingston and Montreal: McGill-Queen's University Press, 1982), 64.

[147] The latter move was part of La Peyrère's limitation of the creation of Adam and Eve and the Flood to the history of the Jews alone. Ibid., 64.

[148] Isaac de La Peyrère, 1594–1676, *Men before Adam: or a Discourse upon the Twelfth, Thirteenth and Fourteenth Verses of the Epistle of the Apostle Paul to the Romans* (London: n.p., 1656), EEBO. This was first published in Latin in 1655, but circulated in manuscript form from 1641: Popkin, "Cartesianism and Biblical Criticism," 64.

[149] Jorink, "Horrible and Blasphemous," 432–38.

[150] Philip C. Almond, "Adam, Pre-Adamites, and Extra-Terrestrial Beings," *Journal of Religious History* 30, no. 2 (2006): 166–68. Almond depends for his synopsis of La Peyrère on R. Popkin, *Isaac La Peyrère (1596–1676)* (Leiden: Brill, 1987).

[151] Dillenberger, *Protestant Thought*, 136.

The denial of Mosaic authorship of the Pentateuch naturally constituted a fundamental challenge to the reliability of Genesis. Richard Popkin suggests that Hobbes' denial of the same in his *Leviathan* (1650) was likely inspired by La Peyrère's writing(s) circulating in manuscript, among a circle that included Marin Mersenne and Hugo Grotius, from 1641.[152] Such a denial became one arrow in the quiver of the loosely related group gathered under the name 'deism', a growing freethinking movement of late seventeenth-century Britain. One writer defines 'deists' as "theistic naturalists critical of revealed religion."[153] English deists attacked the exclusive claims of Christianity, such as the deity of Christ, the idea of messianic prophecy, or the revelatory origin and absolute reliability of Scripture, and sought to show that scriptural statements were historically conditioned and subject to error. Genesis, hitherto seen as the primordial document of the human race and a unique revelation of the otherwise unwitnessed earliest history of the world, was an obvious target for deistic doubt. English commentary of this period is often polemically geared towards refuting 'infidelity' or 'atheism', seeking to explain biblical creation in a rationally acceptable manner that corresponded with observations made in the 'Book of Nature.'

The ensuing decades would witness increasingly sophisticated attempts to identify and extract the original written sources whose strands were believed to together have made up the Genesis text. Just as other sources of knowledge about the external world were coming online, whether heavenly, terrestrial or cultural, the biblical one was becoming the subject of critical doubt and investigation, tending to accelerate its exclusion from questions of physical origins.

The Literal Creation of Early British Protestants

The literal interpretation of the creation week reached a peak in British Protestant interpretation of the early seventeenth century, prior to the nascent scepticism mentioned above. This dominant literalism was the

[152] See esp. ch. 33 in Thomas Hobbes, *Leviathan*, Revised student ed., Cambridge Texts in the History of Political Thought (Cambridge: Cambridge University Press, 1996). The radical Dutch thinker Baruch Spinoza certainly owned a copy of La Peyrère's *Pre-Adamitae* and systematized his scepticism in his *Tractatus Theologico-Politicus* (1670): Popkin, "Cartesianism and Biblical Criticism," 64–66; Baruch Spinoza, *Tractatus Theologico-Politicus*, trans. Samuel Shirley (Leiden: E.J. Brill, 1989). Cf. Richard Simon, *A Critical History of the Old Testament* (London: Walter Davis, 1682), EEBO. See p. 41 on the creation narratives. See Bray, *Biblical Interpretation*, 240.

[153] Wayne Hudson, *The English Deists: Studies in Early Enlightenment*, The Enlightenment World: Political and Intellectual History of the Long Eighteenth Century (London: Pickering & Chatto, 2009), 1–27, and p. 34 for the definition quoted. See also Reventlow, *Authority of the Bible*, 185–222.

offspring of the overwhelmingly literal example of continental Protestants. It was normal for Protestant Genesis commentaries from around this time, both British and continental, to emphasize the six-day span of creation.[154] In time this usage was adopted, probably thanks to Calvin's influence, into creedal documents such as the *Irish Articles of Religion* (1615),[155] compiled by James Ussher, and subsequently in the Westminster Confession, finalized in 1648, as follows:

> It pleased God the Father, Son, and Holy Ghost, for the manifestation of the glory of his eternal power, wisdom, and goodness, in the beginning, to create, or make of nothing, the world, and all things therein, whether visible or invisible, in the space of six days, and all very good.[156]

Since the Westminster Confession became the base document for the subsequent Savoy Declaration (1658) of the Congregationalists, and the London (1689) and Philadelphia (1688) Confessions of the Baptists, the 'six day' phrasing was carried directly over into these documents.[157]

The need for present-day would-be Presbyterian ministers to signify their assent to this creed has produced a vigorous contemporary debate in United States Presbyterian circles over whether the 'Westminster divines' would have intended the phrase "in the space of six days" literally.[158] Speaking historically, it hardly seems possible to conclude anything else. This phase of British Genesis commentary represents the pinnacle of literalism in the entire history of Christian exegesis, and examples of such plainly literal statements abound in mainstream works. The fact that this stance is taken in opposition to Augustine's instantaneous creation, rather than in order to resist any 'day-age' or periodic understanding of the creation days, is important but does not alter the case.[159] Literal days were uncontroversial precisely because

[154] See esp. Calvin, *Genesis*, 78; Luther, *Lectures on Genesis*, 38. There it is used to describe the position denied by Hilary and Augustine, a negative employment of the phrase, but one that may have been picked up in Protestant tradition.

[155] Philip Schaff, *The Creeds of Christendom*, 3 vols. (Grand Rapids: Baker, 1966), 529.

[156] *Westminster Confession of Faith* 4.1. For the wording, I have used "Westminster Confession of Faith, With Amendments by The Presbyterian Reformed Church of Australia" (Strathpine North, QLD, Australia: Covenanter Press, 1982). See Letham, "Space of Six Days," 171; Cross and Livingstone, eds., *ODCC*, 1473.

[157] Schaff, *Creeds*, 611, 718, 738; Louis Lavallee, "Creeds and the Six Creation Days," *Impact* 235 (1993) http://www.icr.org/article/364/.

[158] See for instance David W. Hall, "What Was the View of the Westminster Assembly Divines on the Creation Days?," in *Did God Create in Six Days?*, ed. J.A. Pipa and D.W. Hall (Taylors, SC: Southern Presbyterian Press, 1999; reprint, Tolle Lege Press, 2005), 43–54; Barker, "Westminster Assembly," 113–20; J.V. Fesko, "The Days of Creation and Confession Subscription in the OPC," *WTJ* 63 (2001): 235–49.

[159] Letham, "Space of Six Days," 172. See also Barker, "Westminster Assembly," 114–15.

there was no perceived viable alternative at the time, provided Augustine's and Aristotle's views were duly dispatched.

One of the earliest British figures to employ such explicit, 'space of six days' phrasing was the Puritan William Perkins (1558–1602), in his *An Exposition of the Symbole or Creed of the Apostles* (1616).[160] "Some may aske," says Perkins, "in what space of time did God make the world? *I answer,* God could have made the world, and all things in it in one moment: but he began and finished the whole worke in six distinct days." The summary of the creation week that follows is unambiguously literal, with the conclusion, "Thus in sixe distinct spaces of time, the Lord did make all things."[161] Letham and another participant in recent Presbyterian debates, William Barker, feel as if they spy in this phrasing an openness to less concrete days, but Perkins' position remains thoroughly literal; though the light of the first three days is produced by other means than the sun, the creation days were the first seven of the days that we live with today.[162]

As the 'leading Puritan theologian of his generation', Perkins may have helped to entrench 'space of six days' as a stock phrase in subsequent English commentary, e.g. in the *Medulla theologiae* of William Ames (1576–1633), Perkins' one-time pupil and another important Puritan theologian.[163] In 1631, George Walker wrote in his *History of the Creation,* "For the highest heaven, and the rude matter, the earth, were created in the first moment of time, and all other things in the space of six dayes, as the history most plainly teacheth," though the individual works of creation only took a moment.[164] Bishop Simon Patrick uses the Westminster phrase in his own Genesis commentary, while it also appears explicitly in certain of the 'universal histories' and is implicitly supported in others.[165]

[160] William Perkins, *An Exposition of the Symbole or Creed of the Apostles, according to the Tenour of the Scripture, and the Consent of Orthodoxe Fathers of the Church,* The Workes of that Famous and Worthy Minister of Christ, in the Universitie of Cambridge, Mr. William Perkins (London: printed by John Legatt, Printer to the Universitie of Cambridge, 1616), 141–47, section title 'God's Counsel', CPT.

[161] Perkins, *Exposition,* 143.

[162] Letham, "Space of Six Days," 170–71; Barker, "Westminster Assembly," 117.

[163] Letham, "Space of Six Days," 171–72; Lewis, "Days of Creation," 453; McKim, ed., *HHMBI,* 231; see also Cross and Livingstone, eds., *ODCC,* 1064; Bray, *Biblical Interpretation,* 167. Similar wording appears in Nicholas Gibbons, *Questions and Disputations concerning the Holy Scripture....* (London: imprinted by Felix Kyngston, 1601), 45, EEBO.

[164] George Walker, *The History of the Creation* (London: printed for John Bartlet ... 1631), 6–7. See also the same case made, pp. 10–11, 16.

[165] Simon Patrick, *A Commentary on the First Book of Moses, Called Genesis* (London: Ri. Chiswell, 1695), 11; Dionisius Petavius, *The History of the World: Or, An Account of Time* (London: printed by J. Streater ... 1659), 1, EEBO; Thomas Stackhouse, *A New History of the Holy Bible, from the Beginning of the World, to the Establishment of Christianity*

Andrew Willet's (1562–1621) commentary, *Hexapla in Genesin* (1605), proclaims its most unique feature in its title, that is, its sixfold approach to interpreting the biblical text, which surely implies a correspondence to the six days of creation. For each biblical chapter, Willet offers 1) an overview of the chapter, 2) a treatment of variations between texts and translations, 3) explanation of a range of exegetical details using the long-established 'question and answer' format, 4) an exposition of doctrinal issues, 5) apologetic rebuttals against objections to the text, and, 6) a moral or spiritual application of the text. In this regard Willet's approach might represent a restrained application of the principle explicit in Mirandola's *Heptaplus*: that the days of creation signify the appropriate number of interpretive methods that should be applied to their own textual location. This surely is a specimen of 'difference', although Willet's version avoids the polyvalence of Mirandola's and Arnold of Bonneval's versions.[166]

Willet also treats the nature of the creation days, objecting that an instantaneous creation cannot be reconciled with a truly literal understanding of the 'days' of Gen. 1:1–2:3, nor is required by Gen. 2:4 once 'day' in that verse is recognized as simply meaning 'time'.[167] This principle of literal interpretation was a hilltop standard for these writers; Scottish controversialist Alexander Ross' (1590–1654) stated reason for rejecting instantaneous creation is, "Moses' narration is historicall, and therefore he speaketh of sixe distinct dayes ... if wee vnderstand Moses in this place allegorically, then wee must make this whole historie an allegorie."[168]

Willet also refutes traditional claims by Egyptians, Greeks and other peoples of ancestries stretching back up to 100,000 years: "All these are lying fables, seeing by iust computation of yeares it is found, that the

.... 2nd rev. ed., 2 vols., vol. I (London: printed for Stephen Austen, 1742–44), 12, ECCO; John Adams, *A View of Universal History, from the Creation to the Present Time* .... 3 vols., vol. I (London: printed for G. Kearsley, 1795), 1, ECCO; *An Universal History, from the Earliest Account of Time to the Present* .... 20 vols., vol. I (Dublin: 1744–47), 100, 106, ECCO.

Literal creation week treatments that don't use the exact phrase include: Gervase Babington, *Certaine Plaine, Briefe and Comfortable Notes upon Everie Chapter of Genesis* (London: for Thomas Charde, 1592), 6r; John Lightfoot, *A Few, and New Observations upon the Booke of Genesis* (London: printed by T. Badger, 1642), 2, EEBO; Henry Ainsworth, *Annotations upon the First Book of Moses, called Genesis* ([Amsterdam]: Imprinted [by Giles Thorp], 1616); Christopher Cartwright, *Electa thargumico-rabbinica; sive, annotationes in Genesin* .... (London: Typis Guil. Du-gard: Impensis Sam. Thomson ad insigne equi candidi, in Coemeterio Paulino, 1648), CPT.

[166] Willet followed this work with further 'hexaplas' on Exodus, Leviticus, Daniel and Romans: McKim, ed., *HHMBI*, 144.

[167] Andrew Willet, *Hexapla in Genesin* (Cambridge: John Legat, 1605), 26, EEBO.

[168] Alexander Ross, *The First Book of Questions and Answers upon Genesis* (London: Nicholas Okes, 1620), 28.

world hath not yet continued since the first beginning thereof, 6000 yeares."[169] But while this short time span for world (and earth) history was the common view, world-week belief was received cautiously by these writers, perhaps because it was ultimately the outcome of an allegorical method of interpretation, even though an apocalyptic impulse might have worked in its favour. Willet attributes world-week belief to Jewish tradition and calls it "more curious than profitable".[170] The Puritan Henry Ainsworth (1571–1622) shows a wary openness to the world-week teaching, also attributing it to his Jewish sources, in his *Annotations upon the First Book of Moses, called Genesis* (1616).[171] Others such as Ross express no sympathy for the world-week concept.[172]

Literal treatments of the creation days in English commentary continue through the century virtually undiminished, as for example in the discussion of the 'day' of Gen. 1:5 by both John Richardson in 1655 and George Hughes in 1672.[173] The *Commentary upon the Three First Chapters of the First Book of Moses called Genesis* (1656) of John White describes the non-solar light of the first three days literally with no sign of defensiveness.[174] The legendary starting dates for creation of John Lightfoot and James Ussher arise out of the same mindset.[175] The literal creation week concept of figures such as these 'Westminster Divines', recently argued vigorously by David Hall, is in fact a simple truism; so long as Augustine and Aristotle were kept at bay, there was no rival to a literal creation week for these writers; they imagined no other historical duration for the creation days than twenty-four hours.[176]

[169] Willet, *Hexapla*, 20. Near the beginning of the dedicatory epistle to King James I that prefaces the work, Willet similarly states, "This worthie historie containeth the space of 2368 yeares, aboue halfe the age of the world, from the first to the second Adam. "

[170] Ibid., 3.

[171] Ainsworth, *Annotations*, on Gen. 1:31. See also the consistent approach to the eternal Sabbath in the world's future, as Ainsworth subsequently treats Gen. 2:1–3. The work is unpaginated.

[172] Ross, *First Book*, 30.

[173] John Richardson, 1580–1654, *Choice Observations and Explanations upon the Old Testament....* (London: printed by T.R. and E.M. for John Rothwell, 1655), EEBO. See p. 1 of each of the two main sections. George Hughes, 1603–67, *An Analytical Exposition of the First Book of Moses* (n.l.: n.d., 1672), EEBO.

[174] John White, 1575–1648, *A Commentary upon the Three First Chapters of the First Book of Moses called Genesis* (London: printed by John Streater ... 1656), 1:11, 23–24, 32–33, EEBO. Like Hughes, White displays an interest in the nature and duration of the chaos.

[175] See below.

[176] Hall, "Westminster Assembly Divines," 43–54; Williams, *Common Expositor*, 43; Philip C. Almond, *Adam and Eve in Seventeenth-Century Thought* (Cambridge: Cambridge University Press, 1999), 82; Harrison, *The Bible, Protestantism*, 122ff. On the Presbyterian debate, compare Hall with Barker, "Westminster Assembly," 115; Letham, "Space of Six Days," 174.

The Hexaemeral Framework of the Mirror Literature

'Mirror literature' arose in the Middle Ages, a branch of encyclopaedic works that sought to catalogue all earthly phenomena and beings within the hexaemeral framework drawn from Genesis 1. The global nature of the creation account in Genesis allowed it to structure the explanation of all that was known about the natural world. The 'mirror' in the title of such works implied the program of showing the world (where nature was the subject) as it really was, in all its diversity. The title 'reflects' the medieval symbolic view of reality, so amenable to allegory and symbolism, within which both words and things readily signified other things.[177] The prime time for the mirror literature was from the twelfth to the sixteenth centuries. The classic medieval example of the *Speculum maius* or 'Great Mirror' of Vincent of Beauvais begot such Renaissance heirs as William Caxton's *Mirrour of the World* (1480) and Lambertus Danaeus' *The Wonderfull Woorkmanship of the World* (1578).[178]

John Swan's *Speculum mundi* (1635) is an important early Modern example, and its full title explicitly identifies the work as a hexaemeron. Swan tries to cover all fields of natural knowledge under the umbrella of the creation week: plants, for instance (along with mineralogy in an appendix), are discussed under the rubric of Day 3, astronomy under Day 2 and Day 4, and land animals under Day 6. There are also new external data coming into consideration, such as travellers' reports of a tall mountain in Japan and a volcanic one in the Philippines, and observations of a new 'star' in the constellation Cassiopeia.[179] But we do not yet see any sign that new data was bringing the Genesis account or received biblical chronology into question.

Swan too is committed to the literal interpretation of this Mosaic history. Hence he cannot accept the reading of the light of Day 1 as representing angels; this would be "to leave the literal sense (which is to be followed in the History of the creation) and to cleave unto Alle-

[177] Harrison, *The Bible, Protestantism*, 114, 120, 161, 183, etc. These references mostly treat ramifications of the loss of this perspective from the Renaissance and Reformation forward.

[178] Ritamary Bradley, "Backgrounds of the Title Speculum in Mediaeval Literature," *Speculum* 29, no. 1 (1954): 100–15; Williams, *Common Expositor*, 30; Kirkconnell, ed., *Celestial Cycle*, 613; and on Vincent, see Cross and Livingstone, eds., *ODCC*, 1441, and the section, "The Creation Week Re-Acquainted with Nature" in the chapter on the Middle Ages, above.

[179] John Swan, *Speculum Mundi or A Glasse Representing the Face of the World....* 4th ed. (London: printed by J.R. for John Williams, 1670), EEBO, 34, 46. The 'new star' was the supernova observed by Tycho Brahe in November, 1572, which threatened Aristotelian cosmology because the latter philosophy did not countenance any change in the heavens beyond the sphere of the moon.

gories."[180] Swan argues at some length against an instantaneous creation, providing three moral reasons why God took a week to create the world: to humble humans with the realization that other entities preceded them in creation; to demonstrate God's care for people, in so carefully preparing their place of occupation; and to encourage people to take sufficient time and care over their tasks.[181]

But Swan's interest is historical as well as natural, and he also subdivides the world's history into seven periods according to the model of the creation week, although rejecting a strict allotment of 1000 years to each period as incompatible with the studied results of chronographers such as Scaliger, Ussher and Raleigh.[182] Swan claims to have worked out his own biblical chronology in another work, in which he (like Ussher) arrived at an interval of exactly 4000 years between creation and Christ's advent, but he denies that the world's history can be limited to 6000 years, wary of attempts to predict Christ's Second Coming.[183]

The Creation Week in Chronologies and Universal Histories

Scholars of the Renaissance period displayed an increasing appropriation of sources old and new, normally combined with a continued commitment to the unique authority of the biblical text, along with church tradition in the case of Catholic thinkers, and processed within an atmosphere of ever-growing confidence in the power of human reason. Renaissance efforts to locate creation chronologically were pioneered by Joseph Justus Scaliger, a French Huguenot who in 1583 "established the modern science of chronology" through publication of his *De emendatione temporum*.[184] It was Scaliger who established that Herod the Great had died in 4 BC, bequeathing to subsequent generations the idiosyncrasy that Jesus was born several years 'before Christ'.[185] His date of 3950 BC for creation was not the first such date to be offered, since the time envisaged for creation had ranged from the implied date of 3761 BC of Jewish reckoning up to dates above

[180] Ibid., 22.

[181] Ibid., 19–20.

[182] He also refers to Genesis commentators such as Calvin, Pareus, Ainsworth and Willet.

[183] Swan, *Speculum Mundi*, 472–84 (*Speculum Mundi* 9.6–7). Anticipations of the soon return of Christ and warnings against such speculations alike dot the entire course of this interpretive history, and exhibit a natural association with the world-week tradition.

[184] James Barr, "Why the World Was Created in 4004 BC: Archbishop Ussher and Biblical Chronology," *Bulletin of the John Rylands Library* 67 (1985): 584; Cross and Livingstone, eds., *ODCC*, 1240.

[185] Barr, "Archbishop Ussher," 578.

5000 where the extended chronology of the LXX was in view.[186] However, Scaliger introduced a new level of scholarship in chronological study, to be quickly followed by further technical works on the topic by Petavius and others, complete with "abundant and specific" dating of the original creation.[187]

The enterprise of biblical chronology provided the technical basis in turn for the 'universal histories', which attempted to account for all known human history using a biblical framework. The creation story usually provided the starting point for both kinds of works, which in practice could blend into one another. Arnold Williams explains, "English chroniclers, historians and geographers frequently follow the practice of Orosius and the Byzantine historians by beginning with the creation of the world."[188] We might also think of Peter Comestor's *Historia scholastica* and the historically-oriented works of Rupert of Deutz, Hugh of St. Victor and Joachim of Fiore in the Middle Ages. This use of the creation account assumes both the historical intention and the historical accuracy of the biblical chronological data, and its 'transferability' into a universal chronology. Earlier schemes assumed a literal creation week, while in later works the application of a short biblical chronology might be limited merely to the human race, in contrast to a much older natural order. Biblical chronologies tended to absorb world-week belief, particularly when calculations for the earth's age showed the potential, based on the Hebrew text tradition, to yield a creation date around 4000 BC.

Sir Walter Raleigh's (c. 1554–1618) universal history, *The History of the World* (1614), begins with such a thorough, commentary-style treatment of creation that Robbins cites it as an early modern representative of the hexaemeral genre.[189] That is, Raleigh's treatment functions as a full biblical commentary on the creation account. Drawing upon a very broad range of sources, both Christian and classical, Raleigh treats philosophical and theological questions typically associated with Genesis 1.[190] Each of the initially undistinguished features of creation was destined to undergo differentiation during the creation week, so that just as the waters divided into higher and lower on Day 2 and

[186] Ibid.: 580–82. I have naturally expressed these dates in modern terms for the reader's convenience.

[187] Petavius, whom we have already encountered, wrote his major work *De doctrina temporum* (1627) to correct and expand on Scaliger's work, and offered the date 3983 BC for creation. Ibid.: 581, 583; Cross and Livingstone, eds., *ODCC*, 1240. The quoted words are from Almond, *Adam and Eve*, 83.

[188] Williams, *Common Expositor*, 30.

[189] Robbins, *Hexaemeral Literature*, 89–90, 102; Williams, *Common Expositor*, 37.

[190] See Charles Stinger, "Italian Renaissance Learning and the Church Fathers," in *RCFW* 2:477.

the earth was distinguished as land masses on Day 3, initially-dispersed light was distinguished into luminaries on Day 4.[191] The first three days are named as such in anticipation of the functions of the luminaries from Day 4: "For that space of the first three days which preceded the sun's creation, or formal perfection, when as yet there was not any motion to be measured, and the day named in the fifth verse, was but such a space, as afterwards by the sun's motion made a civil or natural day." The first three creation days, then, are the same length as the truly solar days to follow.[192]

The Anglican churchman John Lightfoot (1602–75) achieved legendary status when he specified that on Day 6 of creation, "Man [was] creat'd by the *Trinity* about the third houre of the day, or nine of the clocke in the morning."[193] He added in his own chronological work, *A Chronicle of the Times* (1647), that the sin of the first couple took place at about noon, and the confrontation with God in the cool of the day at about 3pm, "and so fell *Adam* on the day that he was created."[194] This compression of the events of Genesis 2 into the sixth day of Gen. 1:24–31 was a normal interpretive assumption at this time; the inclusion of the Fall within this day's events was something of a high-tide mark.[195] The claim that Lightfoot published a universal creation date of 23rd October, 4004 BC at 9am, a claim going back at least to A.D. White's *History of the Warfare of Science with Theology*, seems to represent a conflation of Lightfoot's statement with one of James Ussher's, since Lightfoot alludes to an equinoctial, September (Jewish *Tishri,* i.e. new year) creation rather than one in October.[196] Lightfoot's chronology calculates a specific interval between creation and the Flood of 1656

[191] Sir Walter Ralegh, *The History of the World* (1614; reprint, The Works of Sir Walter Ralegh, Kt., vol. II, London: Burt Franklin, 1829), 14–15, 18.

[192] Ralegh, *History of the World*, 15 (quotation), 19–20. Raleigh also retains the threefold medieval division of creation, distinction and ornamentation: ibid., 23–24. (*History* 1.1.29)

[193] Lightfoot, *New Observations*, 4.

[194] John Lightfoot, *A Chronicle of the Times, and the Order of the Texts of the Old Testament* (London: John Clark, 1647), 4, EEBO. Philip Almond observes that there was a well-established tradition, stemming back to Augustine, of locating the Fall on the same day as the creation of humans: Almond, *Adam and Eve*, 166.

[195] Lightfoot, *New Observations*, 6.

[196] White, *Warfare*, 1:9. Thorough study will demonstrate the number of subsequent authors that repeat this claim of White's, but my search of several creation references in the edition of Lightfoot's works that White cites, that of Pitman, has not uncovered any clear evidence warranting White's specific wording: *The Whole Works of the Rev. John Lightfoot: Master of Catharine Hall, Cambridge*, ed. John Rogers Pitman, 13 vols. (London: printed by J.F. Dove, 1822), 2:10ff., 335; 4:63–67, 97, 112.

Philip Almond, in a personal communication, reminded me that the *Tishri* dating could represent a harmonization of creation with the Jewish New Year. This would be consistent with Lightfoot's Hebraic expertise.

years, an oft-mentioned consensus figure resulting from the integration of the antediluvian lifespans according to the Hebrew text, and yielding the cluster of creation dates around 4000 BC.[197]

Such specificity regarding the beginning of history indicates unquestioning confidence in the Bible as a reliable historical source, and a commitment to the literal interpretation of that history, employed in the service of burgeoning Renaissance scholarship. Yet this interest in the world's history, albeit viewed as the arena of God's redemptive work, is a this-worldly orientation when compared with earlier medieval commentary. R.A. Muller rightly points out, "These interests in chronology, geographical data and collation of texts ... place Lightfoot's methods squarely into the context of seventeenth-century hermeneutics .... Nor was the primary issue addressed the date of creation or the age of the world, but rather the literal historical meaning of the text. Thus biblical chronology ... belongs to the same hermeneutic as the detailed collation and critical establishment of the text."[198]

A younger fellow Anglican clergyman (and eventual bishop) was James Ussher (1581–1656). Through the eventual attachment of his chronology to the King James Bible, Ussher has become (in)famous for the endeavour to establish the date of creation, though his contribution was hardly unique.[199] James Barr has complained, "Modern works on biblical chronology may mention him but they make no attempt to understand him," although he was "a highly careful and rational person 'of an erudition rarely matched by that of his critics'."[200] Ussher's immortality reflects the quality and success of his efforts when judged by then-current goals and principles of biblical chronology.[201]

Ussher's *Annals of the Old Testament* (1650) is in fact another universal history, extending to the fall of Jerusalem in AD 70, the bulk being devoted to Greek and Roman history.[202] Ussher's 'Epistle to the Read-

[197] Barr, "Archbishop Ussher," 581–82.

[198] R.A. Muller, "Lightfoot, John (1602–1675)," in *HHMBI*, 209–210.

[199] See Stephen Jay Gould, ed., "Fall in the House of Ussher," in *Eight Little Piggies* (London: Jonathan Cape, 1993); C.L.E. Lewis and S.J. Knell, eds., *The Age of the Earth from 4004 BC to AD 2002*, GS Special Publications (London: Geological Society, 2001), 2–3; John G.C.M. Fuller, "Before the Hills in Order Stood: The Beginning of the Geology of Time in England," in *The Age of the Earth from 4004 BC to AD 2002*, ed. C.L.E. Lewis and S.J. Knell, GS Special Publications (London: The Geological Society, 2001), 19–22.

[200] Barr, "Archbishop Ussher," 575. The internal quotation is from the essay, John D. North, "Chronology and the Age of the World," in *Cosmology, History, and Theology*, ed. Wolfgang Yourgrau and Allan D. Breck (New York: 1977).

[201] See Fuller, "Before the Hills," 15–24.

[202] Barr, "Archbishop Ussher," 581. For the English version, with his NT chronology, see James Ussher, *The Annals of the Old Testament. From the Beginning of the World* (London: printed by E. Tyler, for J. Crook ... and for G. Bedell ... 1658), 1, EEBO.

er' defends the possibility of firm knowledge of the time of creation, apparently already a controversial stance, and reprises the long Christian tradition of biblical history/chronology, from Theophilos of Antioch down to Pareus and Petavius. The annals' brief reference to the events of the creation week date their beginning to "the entrance of the night preceding the twenty third day of *Octob.* in the year of the Julian calendar 710," i.e. a partial year 4004 BC.[203] In little over a page, Genesis 1 is finished with, in duly literal manner, and the history proceeds. Of Ussher's sophisticated task of arriving at such a date and dating scheme, the prefacing Epistle gives some indication, and Ussher's later work, *Sacred Chronology,* completed and published after his death, gives the technical argument.[204]

The Christian world-week tradition manifests itself in the *Annals* in two ways. First, it acts as an influence in Ussher's creation-date selection. Satisfied that the birth of Christ can be accurately dated to 4 BC, Ussher is attracted to a chronological solution that puts creation exactly 4000 years earlier.[205] He divides his treatment of history into seven 'Ages of the World', with their 'hinges' at well-established key moments in God's redemptive work, for example, the dedication of Solomon's temple, which in Ussher's scheme occurs exactly 1000 years before Christ's birth. The neatness of his solution reinforced Ussher's evident confidence that he had unravelled the chronological mysteries of history. Jaki can barely conceal his scorn for this example of "literalism in its conceivably strictest form," but Barr was much more historically aware, notwithstanding his belief in the ultimate wrong-headedness of Ussher's enterprise:

> In Ussher's time biblical chronology was hovering on the brink between the older and the modern world. To him, as to many earlier scholars, the Bible presented a perfect replica of history: it did not tell everything, but everything it told was absolutely correct .... On the other side one must say that Ussher's work represented ... a very 'rational' approach to the questions. He worked almost entirely from precise data, biblical or extrabiblical.[206]

So Ussher combines Renaissance rationalism, with a burgeoning collection of ancient sources for history at its disposal, with Reformation 'biblicism', an implicit faith in the biblical record, allowing him to confidently present a comprehensive description and chronology of

[203] Ussher, *Annals*, 1; Jaki, *Genesis 1,* 178. Gould's analysis of Ussher's creation date and its critics supports my suggestion that Lightfoot's 9am has been rolled together with Ussher's claim by some authors: see Gould, "Fall in the House of Ussher," 185.

[204] Barr, "Archbishop Ussher," 597.

[205] Ibid.: 578; Almond, *Adam and Eve*, 86.

[206] Jaki, *Genesis 1*, 179; Barr, "Archbishop Ussher," 599–601.

world history based on the Bible's (partial but reliable) chronological framework.

The same mindset sustained the labours of Jacques-Bénigne Bossuet (1627–1704), then tutor to the crown prince of France, who in 1681 published his *Discours sur l'histoire universelle.* His bold championing of the antiquity and literal truth of the Bible has galled some, but it was a well-argued, conservative Catholic position by the standards of the time, and consistent with Bossuet's responsibilities for the education of the French prince and his people.[207] Seeing Genesis as the ancient and sole reliable account of the world's origin among a mass of fables, Bossuet interprets the creation days literally: "Moses has taught us that this mighty architect ... wanted to do [his work] in stages and to create the universe in six days, to show that he does not act out of necessity or blind impetuosity."[208] Earlier, he describes history as beginning with the "grand spectacle" of "God creating heaven and earth through his word" in 4004 BC.[209]

Bossuet subsumes the traditional seven-part, world-week periodization of history, centred on the figures of Adam, Noah, Abraham, Moses, Solomon, Cyrus, and finally Jesus himself, into a scheme of twelve epochs that provide more proportionate sections once all accessible extrabiblical history is included.[210] The present, Christian era becomes the seventh and consummate stage in human history, unlike most earlier world-week schemes, which saw the seventh as a future, millennial age.[211] Such a move makes Bossuet somewhat more innovative than he first appears, and may have influenced the future day-age schemes of Buffon and de Luc in the eighteenth century, since they both utilized this humanistic adjustment to the traditional world-week pattern. In any case, Bossuet's influential *Discours* represented one of the crowning examples of the genre, making him, "one of the mediators between the ancient and the modern approaches to history."[212]

Yet the clock was ticking for this kind of comprehensive explanation of world history that reconciled all available external historical data with the Bible. "This very openness of Ussher (and others) to extra-

[207] Jacques-Bénigne Bossuet, *Discourse on Universal History*, ed. Orest Ranum, trans. Elborg Forster, Classic European Historians (Chicago: University of Chicago Press, 1976), 114. For negative assessments, see Jaki, *Genesis 1*, 182–83; White, *Warfare*, 1:27, also 12, 154, 240.

[208] Bossuet, *Universal History*, 114–15.

[209] Ibid., 9.

[210] Ibid., 109. Here Bossuet gives his rationale for the modification.

[211] Ibid., 108, 375–76. There is little eschatological atmosphere in Bossuet's treatment of the seventh age, unless it consists in his glorification of the French state as initially realized (to the salvation of the Church) under Charlemagne in AD 800.

[212] Ibid., xi.

biblical truth was, in the next half-century, to alter the balance," changing the way biblical truth was received.[213] Interest in the field remained strong, as seen in the fact that the English translation of Petavius' chronology appeared in the same year, 1659, as Isaac Vossius' *Dissertation on the True Age of the World,* and Georg Horn's reply of the same title.[214] Isaac Newton too maintained a scholarly interest in biblical chronology.[215] Vossius' work was driven by the need to deal with the indigenous national chronology of the Chinese nation uncovered by Jesuit missionaries there, which he did by reverting to a longer, LXX-based world chronology. Yet this concession hinted that both the creation account and the Bible generally were destined soon to lose their power of veto in the sphere of history as in other areas of knowledge under the pressure of new and sometimes barely compatible data from extrabiblical sources.[216]

Hints of Deep Time in Figurative Creation Week Understandings

The seventeenth century was a time of intellectual ferment, and the synthesis of the traditional biblical cosmogony of Genesis and the pagan traditions of Ovid, Hesiod and others was producing a new way of looking at the world's origin. The Dutch Arminians Hugo Grotius (1583–1645), Simon Episcopius (1583–1643), and later, Philippus van Limborch (1633–1712) and Jean Le Clerc (Clericus) (1657–1736), all pondered the nature and duration of the original chaos to which such classical sources pointed.[217] Hints from certain church fathers such as Gregory of Nazianzus had also fostered medieval speculation that the angels might have a history that predated the physical creation. Incorporating this idea of a primordial angelic drama, the Dutch Arminians also adopted the medieval differentiation between initial creation and subsequent distinction and adornment of the world through six days.

[213] Barr, "Archbishop Ussher," 603.

[214] McCalla, *Creationist Debate*, 42–46. Petavius' treatment, originally written in 1627, takes the creation week literally as would be expected.

[215] For the assumption that this was a mental aberration, see Jaki, *Genesis 1*, 177. Contrast Reventlow, *Authority of the Bible*, 335–36.

[216] Rossi, *Dark Abyss*, 137–50.

[217] Hugo Grotius, "Annotationes in Vetus Testamentum," in *Hugonis Grotii Opera omnia theologica in tres tomos divisa : ante quidem per partes, nunc autem conjunctim & accuratius edita* (London: Prostant venalia apud Mosem Pitt, 1679), 1, EEBO; Simon Episcopius, *M. Simonis Episcopii institutiones theologicae, privatis lectionibus Amstelodami traditae*, ed. Étienne de Courcelles (Amsterdam: Ex typographico Ioannis Blaeu, 1650), 345–49, CPT (*Institutiones theologicae* 4.3.1–3); Philip van Limborch, *Theologia Christiana* (1686), 120, CPT (*Theologia Christiana* 2.20.4); Jean Le Clerc, 1657–1736, *In Genesin*, Mosis Prophetae Libri Quinque (Amsterdam: 1710), 1, 7.

Their combination of the two ideas would add to the legacy of the Christian epic poets of late antiquity a powerful impetus to the Miltonic imagination of the primordial world.

As a result, this era witnessed an increasing belief that the 'chaos' stage of earth's origin had a long duration. This 'long chaos' idea penetrated the English intellectual scene and began to manifest itself in various written works and biblical commentaries, such as Matthew Hale's *Primitive Origination of Mankind* (1677) and Simon Patrick's *A Commentary upon the First Book of Moses, called Genesis* (1695), becoming pervasive by century's end.[218] As interpreters of Genesis began to feel the strain of debating either rationalistic hypotheses of the world's origin such as Descartes', or new empirical data about fossils and strata, comets and stars, some would find in the long chaos the means for countenancing these new ideas within the framework of Genesis 1.

Augustine's instantaneous creation had for more than a millennium been the recognized, Christian alternative to a simple, literal creation week. It was particularly tempting to those with a Neoplatonist bent like Augustine's, although thinkers like Eriugena and Mirandola pressed it beyond the bounds of Christian orthodoxy. Its staying power was proved in the allegiance of a first-rank Catholic commentator like Cardinal Cajetan, although it was driven underground in the course of the sixteenth century. This figurative approach, widely available in creation-related documents of the Christian tradition, proclaimed that it was possible to read the days of creation as a rational or logical, rather than historical, sequence – an ideal pattern expressing an order in creation that was ontological rather than chronological.

Another survival from patristic times was the world-week scheme, which (on a Hebrew Bible chronological reckoning) had not yet run out of time, although those suspicious of Jewish, Catholic or allegorical interpretation generally hesitated to openly endorse it. It appealed to those inclined to an apocalyptic and deterministic view of history. It amounted to another demonstration that a non-literal and yet still chronological meaning could be applied to the creation week. Thus far, it had been used as a key to human history, a kind of interpretive frame pinned at key points to the widely recognized 'grand narrative' of the Bible. But once indications of deep antiquity in nature began to emerge, the world-week tradition may also have functioned as a clue

[218] Matthew Hale, *The Primitive Origination of Mankind, Considered and Examined according to the Light of Nature* (London: printed by William Godbid for William Shrowsbery, 1677), 293–95, EEBO; Patrick, *Commentary*, 11. For instance, it not only formed the basis for Thomas Burnet's famous *Sacred Theory of the Earth*, but was often shared by Burnet's critics, e.g. John Keill, *An Examination of Dr. Burnet's Theory of the Earth....* (Oxford: printed at the Theater, 1698), 34. See also Roberts, "Genesis of John Ray," 147–48.

to the possibility of applying a chronological six-part scheme inspired by the Hexaemeron to *pre*-history.

The mystical and cabbalistic stream of Genesis interpretation in the sixteenth century also tended to direct attention away from the literal sense of the days of creation. I have already mentioned Brocardus, and Katherine Collier credits another maverick Renaissance thinker, Guillaume Postel (1510–81), with the origin of the modern view that the formation of the present world took a longer-than-normal creation week, citing Postel's *De universitate*.[219] Yet Postel's position on the source of light for the three days prior to the sun's creation seems to be the concrete one belonging to his time, and William Bouwsma's biography on Postel speaks only of his use of the world-week tradition in an apocalyptic fashion akin to Joachim of Fiore.[220] There seems to be no clear sixteenth-century example of the chronological expansion of the creation week *exclusive* of a literal 168-hour week. But a revived Neoplatonism and cabbalistic tendency was inclining some of the more daring thinkers of the day towards a completely atemporal creation.

Thomas Browne's 1642 testimony to the existence of a Platonist-sounding instantaneous creation alternative is confirmed by the Cambridge Platonist Henry More (1614–87).[221] More's *Conjectura cabbalistica* (1653) is a threefold exposition of the first three chapters of Genesis. His daring use of the term 'cabbala' for these expositions demonstrates his mystical orientation and his belief that the Genesis text is cryptic and requires unlocking to access its deeper mysteries. As with Mirandola, More's Genesis interpretation combines a Renaissance breadth of learning with an apologetic purpose; More wishes to refute the sceptical perception of the inadequacy of Mosaic philosophy, the product of a mistaken focus on "the meer *letter* of *Moses*." More intends to reveal the very best of philosophy concealed within "the more inward and mysterious meaning of the text."[222] Just as Moses' threefold communi-

[219] On Brocardus, see Williams, *Common Expositor*, 21, 43, and on Postel, Collier, *Cosmogonies*, 318, 450, etc.

[220] Ibid., 343. William J. Bouwsma, *Concordia Mundi: The Career and Thought of Guillaume Postel (1510–1581)*, ed. Oscar Handlin, Harvard Historical Monographs (Cambridge, MA: Harvard University Press, 1957), 281–83.

[221] The Cambridge Platonists of the early to mid-seventeenth century avoided both "the dogmatic Calvinism of the Puritans and the materialism of Hobbes," displaying a rationalism that presaged deism in some ways, yet tempered with a mystical Christianity reminiscent of their medieval heritage. Arthur Pollard, "Cambridge Platonists," in *The New International Dictionary of the Christian Church*, ed. J.D. Douglas and E.E. Cairns (Grand Rapids: Zondervan, 1996), 183.

[222] More, *Conjectura cabbalistica*, pages 2–3 of unpaginated prefatory letter. This drive towards exegetical ἀποκάλυψις (revelation) accords entirely with More's obvious Platonism: "For what is the divine wisdome, but that steady comprehension of the *Ideas* of all things …?" (page 5 of unpaginated preface to the reader).

cation in Genesis 1 vindicates religion "from that vile imputation of ignorance in philosophy, … so does it also justifie those more noble results of free Reason and Philosophy from that vulgar suspicion of Impiety and Irreligion."[223] But More frees Reason and Philosophy from the shackles of the Bible's literal sense at the price of prioritizing a hidden meaning that is difficult to access or sustain once the supporting structure of a Platonist view of the world is removed, potentially alienating the ordinary reader.

More's first 'cabbala' is the literal one, reading like a Jewish targum, and dedicated to 'natural philosophy'.[224] The days of creation are taken quite literally, enumerated as "the first natural day," "the second natural day", and so forth.[225] The light of the first day appears in the east and moves west, and three days indeed pass before the sun is made, teaching us not to give the credit due to the First Cause to secondary ones, as when people assume that plant life is impossible without the sun's light. Creation is a tent-like structure whose floor is made first, followed by the canopy of the firmament.[226]

'The Defence of the Threefold Cabbala' which follows reveals that the literal sense of the text is received here under quite a serious, yet familiar, proviso: "*Loquitur lex iuxta linguam humanam,* That the law speaks according to the language of the sons of men."[227] This is the familiar accommodation principle, here applied with a comprehensiveness that effectively subordinates the 'literal cabbala' to the 'philosophick cabbala' in truth terms. For instance, More's explanatory comment on Gen. 1:14 within 'The Defence of the Literal Cabbala' notes, "how easily the fancie of the rude people admit of days without a Sun."[228] His comment on Gen. 1:3 in the same 'Defence' shows that he sees this is a quite deliberate and appropriate accommodation by the text, but that this device should not waylay those who know better, for whom the philosophical and moral senses will prove more convincing and pertinent.[229]

The second, 'Philosophick Cabbala', reveals More's actual conception of the cosmos and its origin, where creation out of primordial matter is cast in terms generally familiar from Augustine and the

[223] More, *Conjectura cabbalistica*, page 11 of unpaginated preface to the reader.

[224] Ibid., page 10 of unpaginated preface to the reader. Both Henry Ainsworth (1616) and Christopher Cartwright (1648) in their Genesis commentaries displayed a great regard for the Jewish Targums and the targumic method. See also McKim, ed., *HHMBI*, 144–45.

[225] More, *Conjectura cabbalistica*, 3–4.

[226] Ibid., 2–5.

[227] Ibid., 102.

[228] Ibid., 120.

[229] Ibid., 115.

twelfth-century Platonists. The 'heaven and earth' of Gen. 1:1 are not physical entities. By 'heaven' or 'light' is meant "the whole comprehension of intellectual Spirits," including human and animal souls and seminal forms of all life; 'Earth' represents merely material creation's potentiality for existence. 'Evening' and 'morning' represent the passive and active metaphysical principles whose union produces, day by day, the various parts of the cosmos.[230] By Day 4 in More's 'philosophick' scheme we reach the production of the material universe, specifically the stars and planets, including Earth, although the 'garnishing' of the latter was anticipated within the description of Day 3.[231] This reminds us of the way More's Platonist ancestors John Colet and Mirandola related the creation account to the material, terrestrial world only from Day 3.[232] That this scheme of interpretation of the six days of creation is meant to deal with the reality we occupy is clear from his statement that after the six days there is no further creative act by God.[233]

Proceeding to 'The Defence of the Philosophick Cabbala', we find the implications of this scheme for the days of creation made explicit:

> As the Matter of the Universe came out in the second day, so the contriving of this Matter into Sunnes and Planets, is contained in this fourth day, the *Earth* herself not excepted, though according to the Letter she is made in the first day.... Nor will this at all seem bold or harsh, is we consider that the most learned have already agreed that all the whole Creation was made at once.[234]... So that the leisurely order of days is thus quite taken away, and all the scruples that may rise from that *Hypothesis*. Wherefore I say, the *Earth* as one of the *primary Planets* was created this fourth day.[235]

A few lines earlier he had spelled out what such a view of creation required hermeneutically:

> You are to understand that these *Six numbers,* or *days,* do not signify any order of time, but the nature of the things that were said to be made in them. But for any thing in *Moses* his *Philosophick Cabbala,* all might be

[230] Ibid., 23, 25.

[231] Ibid., 27–29. More accepts the Cartesian scheme of cosmogenesis, and with it the Copernican model of the universe, so that the earth is not the centre of the universe, but instead one of the planets, and thus mobile: More, *Conjectura cabbalistica*, 29, 149–52.

[232] Note that Arnold of Bonneval's hybrid literal-mystical reading of the creation week connects the production of bodily and visible creation (*corporalis et visibilis rerum creatio*) with Day 2 of creation: Arnold of Bonneval, "De operibus sex dierum," 1520B–C.

[233] More, *Conjectura cabbalistica*, 34.

[234] More cites Rabbi Moses Egyptus, Philo, Procopius of Gaza, Cardinal Cajetan, Augustine, and the schools of Hillel and Shammai in support of instantaneous creation here.

[235] More, *Conjectura cabbalistica*, 149–50.

made at once, or in such periods of time, as is most suitable to the nature of the things themselves.[236]

The fact that More envisages the formation of suns and thence planets in Cartesian 'vortices' suggests that such processes would require a long period of time.[237] More does not explicitly connect the necessary 'periods of time' to corresponding creation days, which would have been a little unnatural in his quite idealist reading of the Genesis narrative. But this combination of a Cartesian conception of the development of the cosmos with a Platonic idealist interpretation of the creation days may have aided the germination of the eventual day-age view. Creation days detached from a strictly literal reading might either remain quite non-temporal or be 're-historicized' as periods of earthly time much longer than days.

A protest published a few years later by Matthew Hale hints that a figurative conception of the creation days was indeed crossing the boundary from the ideal world to the real. Hale rebukes speculations that "the computation of the whole by Six Days was only by a kind of Analogical Expression to give Mankind a distinction by the Order of Production…the Divine Author by this distribution of Days did not intend any determinate portion of Time, much less days or times conformable to the length of our Days, but certain Mysterious Numbers of Times," as "vain Conjectures, introduced meerly to exclude an intermixture of a supernatural concurrence in the speedy production and formation of things." Hale saw any stretching of the creation days as a slippery slope, since the need to explain the creation events naturalistically would require "a dimension or computation much larger than our Days, and possibly than our Months, or Years, or Ages."[238] For him, allowing an indefinitely long chaotic period prior to creation was safer than playing fast and loose with the Genesis narrative, since "the perfecting of the World in its formal order and *constitutum* seems to be in the compass of six Natural Days."[239]

In light of these few indications, then, I would regard the period around 1650 as witnessing the gestation of the modern interpretation that interprets the days of creation as long periods of earthly, prehistoric time.[240]

[236] More, *Conjectura cabbalistica*, 148. "*Moses* his *Philosophick Cabbala*" is an obsolete way of expressing the possessive case, i.e. Moses' *Philosophick Cabbala*.

[237] Ibid., 152.

[238] Hale, *Primitive Origination*, 307.

[239] Ibid., 293–95.

[240] For another possible instance see Rhoda Rappaport, *When Geologists Were Historians 1665–1750* (Ithaca, NY: Cornell University Press, 1997), 139–40.

The Role of Genesis One in Early Modern Geotheories

Katherine Collier notes that by around 1690, when the heliocentric model of the solar system had won the day, astronomers might explore the cosmos relatively free from dogmatic or exegetical restraints, and "the emphasis changed from a discussion of the universe as a whole to a consideration of the earth in particular."[241] Thus there arose 'theories of the earth' or to use Martin Rudwick's term, 'Geotheories', whose aim "was to emulate on a terrestrial scale the achievement of Newton in the realm of celestial mechanics. It was to discover the one and only true explanation of how the earth works.... Theory of the Earth was in effect a scientific *genre* ..."[242] In the context of the Christian society of the day, someone presenting a 'geotheory' in order to explain the physical origin of the world necessarily took a stance towards the cosmogony in Genesis 1. Such stances ranged from strict conformity to the creation sequence in Genesis 1 to effective disregard of the creation week. Contrary to what we might expect, the earliest example of a modern geotheory fell at the latter end of the spectrum.

The prevailing framework for cosmology around 1600 was biblically influenced, to be sure, but much of its content was supplied by the Aristotelian physics that had merged with the biblical worldview in the High Middle Ages. This geocentric Aristotelian cosmology, with its immutable heavens and planets embedded in spheres and orbiting the earth in compounded circular motion, faced increasing questioning as the seventeenth century proceeded.[243] Descartes' pioneering new cosmology was strictly mechanistic and stood independent from Aristotle and the Bible alike.[244] God need simply create uniform matter, and the laws of nature would progressively introduce structure into it. Descartes' cosmology also included a specific earth theory, expounded in Part Four of his *Principles of Philosophy* (1644). While the world was not really formed naturally, "but was created directly by God," said Descartes, its present state made sense if its formation was imagined as occurring naturally within a 'vortex' of rotating matter."[245] His subsequent account of the earth's development makes no reference to the Genesis account, and thus offered a suggestive example of how the

[241] Collier, *Cosmogonies*, 133–34.

[242] Martin J.S. Rudwick, *Bursting the Limits of Time: The Reconstruction of Geohistory in the Age of Revolution* (Chicago and London: University of Chicago Press, 2005), 133–34. The rise of the genre did, however, predate Newton's cosmological model.

[243] Another aspect of Aristotelian physics, its four element system, proved very durable and remained in common use in Genesis treatments well into the modern era.

[244] Descartes, *The World*, xxii.

[245] René Descartes, *Principles of Philosophy*, ed. V.R. Miller and R.P. Miller (Dordrecht: D. Riedel, 1983 [1644]), 179.

origin of the earth might be accounted for in terms of natural laws and physical properties alone.[246]

The Dane Nicolaus Steno (1638–86) is renowned for his early recognition of the organic nature of fossils, his seminal suggestions about the formation of rock strata, and his prescient sense of an earth history.[247] His *Prodromus* (1669) offered a model to explain the physical development of the local landscape of Tuscany.[248] It features a six stage development process that might betray a hexaemeral influence, perhaps via the tradition of a world-week periodization of history, although Steno's scheme is concerned instead with terrestrial pre-history.[249] Steno seems to build his hypothetical history on the basis of his observations, and then try to bring it into line with Genesis.[250]

In the first of the six stages, the land starts out inundated, as Gen. 1:1–7 tells us, with non-fossiliferous strata formed directly by God, yet in the kind of level position that a reader might put down to natural precipitation from a fluid. The duration of this first state is not clear from nature but it is from Scripture, says Steno. In stage two, the land is a dry plane, and being undermined to produce enormous caverns. Steno links this with the watering of the earth in Gen. 2:10–14. The third stage, when the earth has a rough surface due to the collapse of the caverns, might seem to imply a connection with Day 3 of creation, although Steno simply cites Gen. 7:19–20 to establish that the antediluvian earth had mountains.[251] The fourth stage sees the earth re-inundated in the Deluge, which transports the remains of living things and deposits them as high as the mountaintops. In stage five, the land, once again above water level, could have been altered further by the

[246] Ibid., 179–288. Descartes frames this as a 'false hypothesis', pp. 181, 288.

[247] Ashworth gushes, "His proposal that the surface of the earth contains the evidence of its own history … is as brilliant an insight as one can find in this marvellous century." Ashworth, "God and Nature," 145. See also McCalla, *Creationist Debate*, 19–20, 27; John C. Greene, *The Death of Adam: Evolution and Its Impact on Western Thought* (Ames: Iowa State University Press, 1959), 48–53; Davies, *Earth in Decay*, 64–67; Stephen Toulmin and June Goodfield, *The Discovery of Time* (London: Harper & Row, 1965), 88–90; Rossi, *Dark Abyss*, 16–19, etc.; Rappaport, *Geologists*, 99, 104, 106, etc.; Davis A. Young and Ralph Stearley, *The Bible, Rocks and Time: Geological Evidence for the Age of the Earth* (Downers Grove: InterVarsity, 2008), 53–57.

[248] Nicolaus Steno, *The Prodromus of Nicolaus Steno's Dissertation concerning a Solid Body Enclosed by Process of Nature within a Solid*, trans. J.G. Winter, University of Michigan Humanistic Series/Contributions to the History of Science (New York: Macmillan, 1916; reprint, New York: Hafner, 1968). The *Prodromus* is thus an introduction to a larger work related to fossil formation.

[249] Dennis Dean, "The Age of the Earth Controversy: Beginning to Hutton," *Annals of Science* 38 (1981): 438; Cohn, *Noah's Flood*, 77.

[250] Rossi, *Dark Abyss*, 18. For the whole series, see Steno, *Prodromus*, 262–69.

[251] On the connection with Day 3 see Collier, *Cosmogonies*, 395.

formation of new caverns, whose further collapse in stage six leaves the landforms we see today.[252]

The structuring of Steno's scheme in matching pairs of three stages is little more than an unconscious aesthetic echo of the Genesis creation account, since it does not align with the content of the six days, though it is suggestive of Noah's Flood.[253] His model in fact lends itself to extrapolation from the two cycles presented to an indefinite number of 'geological' cycles of uplift and erosion, in contrast with the one-off nature of Genesis events. Nevertheless Steno's model, in league with the speculative *Mundus subterraneus* (1664–65) of Athanasius Kircher, helped inspire many subsequent earth theories and debates about the nature of the Flood.[254]

Several letters that passed between the learned Anglican clergyman and courtier Thomas Burnet (1635–1715) and Isaac Newton (1642–1727) upon initial publication of Burnet's *Sacred Theory* (treated below) clarify the difference in their stances on the nature and function of the six-day Genesis account. Rhoda Rappaport introduces this correspondence thus:

> Those naturalists who began to contemplate some extension of the time-scale usually stayed within the biblical framework by posing a traditional question: were the six days of Creation to be interpreted as twenty-four hour days? When Newton and Burnet discussed the matter, they agreed that days need not be taken literally, but neither saw much to be gained by extending "days" to "years." As Burnet put it, could land and sea separate in less than a year? "I thinke not, in a much longer [time]."[255]

But Burnet and Newton were not in fact in agreement. Newton had initially speculated that the chaotic globe might have begun to develop an irregular surface and subterranean caverns, and to differentiate into land and sea areas, as the sun heated the equatorial regions more than the polar areas.[256] "And all this might ye [i.e. the] rather bee, because at first wee may suppose ye diurnal revolutions of ye Earth to

[252] This summary is based on his written description, but also relies on his simpler, six-part diagram.

[253] Gould points out the cyclical aspect of Steno's scheme, in that the six-part diagram shown in linear form in the translation used here first appeared as two pairs of three steps side by side, making the parallels clear: Gould, *Time's Arrow*, 52–55.

[254] Ezio Vaccari, "European Views on Terrestrial Chronology from Descartes to the Mid-Eighteenth Century," in *The Age of the Earth from 4004 BC to AD 2002*, ed. C.L.E. Lewis and S.J. Knell, GS Special Publications (London: The Geological Society, 2001), 26–32; Porter, *Making of Geology*, 18, 30, 86; Davies, *Earth in Decay*, 138–39.

[255] Rappaport, *Geologists*, 193. "Newton first admired Burnet's theory … , then formulated his own ideas, and finally gave his approval to Whiston's," Porter, *Making of Geology*, 62.

[256] The influence of Steno and probably Kircher seems clear.

have been very slow, soe yt ye first 6 revolutions or days might containe time enough for ye whole Creation …"[257] In a letter dated 13th January, 1681, Burnet reproves Newton, saying, "But methinks you forget Moses (whom in another place you will not suffer us to recede from) in this acct of ye formation of ye Earth; for hee makes ye seas & dry land to bee divided & ye Earth wholly formd before ye Sun or Moon existed."

Burnet is right, but he does not share these standards of Newton's. Whereas Newton wishes to render a philosophical account of Genesis 1, Burnet believes this impossible due to its heavily accommodated nature: "As for Moses his description of ye formation of ye Earth in ye first chap. of Genesis … yt tis a description of ye present forme of ye Earth, wch was its forme alsoe then when Moses writ, and not of ye primaeval Earth wch was gone out of being long before."[258] If the creation account really only describes the present form of the earth, it is of no use at all in crafting a cosmogony, helping to explain why Gen. 1:1–2:3 will play no role in Burnet's *Sacred Theory*.

Burnet then tackles his potential critics in a hypothetical conversation, challenging them to admit that the original chaotic sphere of Gen. 1:2 yielded only the earth and its atmosphere (the 'sublunary sphere'), and that the heavens already existed before Day 4. If they concede these, Burnet feels he has proved "yt ye distinction of 6 dayes in ye Mosaical formation of ye world is noe physical reality, seing one of ye 6 you see is taken up wth a non-reality, ye creation of these things yt existed before … neither is this draught of ye creation physical but Ideal, or if you will, morall." Burnet then plays his best anti-literal card, concerning the 'firmament' formed on Day 2: "If you make ye firmament to bee ye Atmospheare … & ye vapours above it to bee ye celestial waters, … wth all my heart: but then how are ye Sun Moon & stars placd in this firmament?" Burnet therefore concludes that the firmament is "noe physical reality," and that the description of creation in Genesis 1 is "onely Ideal, accommodated to ye present Terraqueous forme of ye Earth," while it is Genesis 2 that actually constitutes a record of physical creation.[259]

Burnet cannot see even year-long creation days as sufficient for the processes recorded within the days, and imagines year-long nights as hard on the life forms made. "These things, Sr," says Burnet, "& some others of this nature I would suggest to those Divines yt insist upon ye

[257] Isaac Newton, *Correspondence*, ed. H.W. Turnbull et al., 7 vols., vol. II (Cambridge: published for the Royal Society at the University Press, 1960), 322.

[258] Ibid., 322–23.

[259] Ibid., 324. For a much later example of the same kind of proposal, see James Challis, *Creation in Plan and Progress* (Cambridge: Macmillan, 1861), 56–59, GB, http://books.google.com/books?id=3e4rAAAAYAAJ.

hypothesis of 6 dayes as a physical reality, wch even many of ye Fathers as I remember have allowed to bee onely an artificial scheame of narration, they supposing ye creation to have been momentaneous."[260] Burnet's own scheme seems to reveal here the idealist influence of his teacher Ralph Cudworth and his fellow Cambridge Platonists, and firmly rules out the relevance of Genesis 1 for generating a geotheory.[261]

Unlike Burnet, though, Newton does not abandon "ye necessity of adhereing to Moses his Hexameron as a physical description,"[262] offering various analogies for how a fluid chaos could solidify irregularly, yielding the land and sea of the Genesis account, rather than Burnet's platonically perfect sphere. As Scott Mandelbrote explains, "Newton was uneasy about the way in which Burnet appeared to use the technique of accommodation in order to dismiss the Mosaic account."[263] Newton's own accommodation principle was more constrained than Burnet's: "As to Moses I do not think his description of ye creation either Philosophical or feigned, but that he described realities in a language artificially adapted to ye sense of ye vulgar."[264] Newton notes that Burnet's cosmogony makes a mockery of the creations of Day 3, since it has no room for seas, and of Day 5, since without seas there cannot be sea creatures.

Newton instead imagines our solar system emerging from a single chaotic mass, aided by the laws of gravity, wherein the proto-sun begins to shine and the earth, oceans and atmosphere settle into their layers by weight during an extended creation week.[265] The sun, moon and stars of Day 4 are described according to appearance, and a little poetically, he admits, but given the need for a true, succinct, theological description of creation events that was accommodated to the vulgar, no-one could improve on Moses' account.[266] Newton thus offers an up-to-date 'developing chaos' understanding of Genesis 1.

But without a true earth whose rotation could be the measure of 'days' before Day 3, Days 1 and 2 of creation could be of any length at all. If God imparted to the earth from Day 3 a steadily accelerating rotation on its axis, such that the first revolution or day took one of our years, then three revolutions or days made up another solar year,

[260] Newton, *Correspondence*, 325.
[261] Rossi, *Dark Abyss*, 33.
[262] Newton, *Correspondence*, 327.
[263] Scott Mandelbrote, "Isaac Newton and Thomas Burnet: Biblical Criticism and the Crisis of Late Seventeenth-Century England," in *The Books of Nature and Scripture*, ed. R. Popkin and J. Force (Dordrecht: Kluwer, 1994), 158.
[264] Newton, *Correspondence*, 331.
[265] Ibid., 332.
[266] Ibid., 333.

five the next, and so on, the creation days would be much longer than solar days, but by the 183rd year the day would be its present length. Far from agreeing with Burnet's abandonment of real, temporal creation days, Newton refined his own concrete understanding of the hexaemeral account, which he regarded as a component of the pure, primordial religion revealed by God to Moses.[267] In being willing to alter the duration of the creation days, while maintaining their historical reality, Newton distinguishes his approach from the purely ideal ones of Burnet or Henry More and so represents a key pioneer of the 'day-age' approach.

The Impact of Burnet's Theory on Creation Week Belief

Burnet proceeded to publish *The Sacred Theory of the Earth* (1680–81), an explanation of the origin "of the *sublunary world,* ... which rose out of a Chaos about six thousand years ago."[268] Burnet assumes an initial, uniform 'chaos', situated in a Cartesian vortex, and theorizes that it would settle out by weight and thus take terrestrial form, developing a smooth, habitable crust, a global paradise.[269] This process of formation implies a considerable passage of time, and the completion of this antediluvian world is the starting-point for the familiar six-thousand-year biblical chronology, which Burnet applies to the earth alone.[270] Under the parching influence of the sun, the crust of this ideal early world dried out, contracted, and finally broke up and collapsed into the underlying watery abyss in the cataclysm of the biblical Deluge, producing the present form of the world, which Burnet perceives as a genuine wreck.[271] The Bible's influence on Burnet's scheme is substantial, chiefly consisting of the Genesis Flood story and the description in 2 Pet. 3:5–7 of a past world destroyed by the Flood and another, future de-

[267] Mandelbrote, "Isaac Newton and Thomas Burnet," 158–59. See also Gould, *Time's Arrow*, 38–41.

[268] Thomas Burnet, *The Sacred Theory of the Earth, containing an Account of the Original of the Earth, and of All the General Changes which It Hath Already Undergone, or Is to Undergo, till the Consummation of All Things* (Glasgow: R. Urie, 1753), 2, GB, http://books.google.com/books?id=-aQvAAAAYAAJ. It was first published in Latin as *Telluris theoria sacra* (1680–81), and then in English as *The Sacred Theory of the Earth* 1684–89: Collier, *Cosmogonies*, 68–69ff.

[269] Burnet, *Sacred Theory*, 55–65 (*Sacred Theory* 1.5–6)

[270] Ibid., 2, 8–9, 34–35, 55, 57 (*Sacred Theory* 1.1–2, 4–5). See also Blount, *Oracles of Reason*, 75. The cited section of Blount's work is a translation of two chapters from Burnet's *Archaeologiae philosophicae*. See below.

[271] Burnet, *Sacred Theory*, 65–74, 135–47 (*Sacred Theory* 1.6, 11); Blount, *Oracles of Reason*, 73.

struction by fire.[272] But the Hexaemeron plays no part in the scheme, nor are the two compatible; for instance, the distinction of sea and land found in Day 3 of the creation week appears only after the Flood in Burnet's scheme.[273]

The reason becomes clear in his subsequent *Archaeologiae philosophicae* (1692), where Burnet explicitly denies that Genesis 1–3 offers any useful information about the origin of the physical world. I agree with Roy Porter that Burnet published an idea so controversial for the time "in Latin mainly to prevent the vulgar at home from reading it," although the deist Charles Blount would soon translate the critical chapters into English in his *Oracles of Reason* (1693).[274] Burnet in *Archaeologiae philosophicae* describes the Genesis narrative as so drastically 'accommodated' to the limited understanding of Moses' popular audience that it features a rash of unacceptable conceptions of nature. Its geocentric account is out of step with the new astronomy, in which the earth is revealed to be "a blind and sordid particle of the Universe" and the "scum of nature," which we recognize by now as classic Gnostic language.[275] The Mosaic text describes things not only according to their present-day appearance, but in terms of erroneous popular conceptions, such as the belief that rain came from a storehouse of heavenly water above the firmament.[276]

Burnet also explains that the acts of creation allotted to the different days would in fact require very different amounts of time to complete, in some cases vastly overrunning the span of a single day: acts such as the formation and filling of ocean basins or the formation of stars.[277] While scholars have debated the possible presence of day-age thinking here, Burnet is not a concordist; he thinks the Hexaemeron irrelevant for his purposes.[278] In the same context, Burnet applauds Augustine's understanding of the creation week as a didactic device, so that Moses "spins out" his account of creation to six days in order to end with a Sabbath. To actually comprise the creation of the entire universe with-

[272] Collier, *Cosmogonies*, 79. The same Creation/Deluge/Conflagration tripartite scheme is used notably in John Ray, *Three Physico-Theological Discourses* (London: printed for Sam Smith, 1693).

[273] Dean, "Age of the Earth," 445.

[274] Porter, *Making of Geology*, 32. Note that the later, full translation leaves out the offending section: Thomas Burnet, *Doctrina antiqua de rerum originibus: or, An Inquiry into the Doctrine of the Philosophers of All Nations, concerning the Original of the World....* (London: printed for E. Curll, 1736). I primarily refer to Blount's translation.

[275] Blount, *Oracles of Reason*, 55.

[276] Ibid., 54, 68, 75.

[277] Ibid., 71–72.

[278] Compare Toulmin and Goodfield, *The Discovery of Time*, 146; Rappaport, *Geologists*, 193.

in a space of six days is inconceivable to Burnet.[279] Yet, as an account instituted 'morally' (ἠθικῶς)[280] rather than 'physically' (φυσικῶς), it serves its purpose admirably, and while it is analogous to other nations' accounts of origins, it avoids their descent into myth and polytheism.[281] The six-day pattern of creation possesses no ultimate significance here beyond a noble moral or ethical motive. But his cosmogony may, like Steno's, represent an aesthetic survival of the creation week pattern; as Stephen J. Gould pointed out, the career of planet Earth, illustrated on the frontispiece of *Sacred Theory*, is divided into seven stages, beginning with the formless, chaotic globe, and ultimately returning to the same state via a final conflagration.[282]

One of the first to respond critically to Burnet's *Sacred Theory* from a biblical point of view was Herbert Croft, Bishop of Hereford, in *Some Animadversions upon a Book intituled The Theory of the Earth* (1685).[283] He showed that Burnet's theory did not merely bypass the Mosaic account, including completely omitting the heavenly productions of Day 4, but positively contradicted it in postulating an antediluvian earth with no visible seas, and nowhere for aquatic life to live.[284] A more fundamental problem was the time lapse implicit in the natural settling of the primordial chaos: "I think I may securely affirm it could not settle in one, two, or three, or thirty months time; much less in one, two, or three days time; in which *Moses* relates the Heavens and Earth with the Sea to be framed, and the Earth to be clothed with Grass, Herbs and Trees."[285] Croft had certainly caught Burnet's meaning.

Erasmus Warren's *Geologia* (1690) makes the same complaint about the formation of the earth's crust, whereas in Genesis, "that glorious Work is expresly limited to *Six Days*."[286] Thus philosophy, the handmaid of divinity, usurps her mistress.[287] Warren protested, "*The Theory of the Earth* … pends too hard against the Sacred Scriptures, and ad-

[279] Blount, *Oracles of Reason*, 71, 73.

[280] Blount's version has ἠδικῶς, but I have followed the reading in the original edition: Thomas Burnet, *Archeologiae philosophicae, sive Doctrina antiqua de rerum originibus* (London: typis R. Norton, 1692), 314. These terms as representing distinct aspects of philosophy have classical antecedents and appear with this sense (in their adjectival form) for example in the writings of Diogenes Laertius: see on ἠθικος, Henry G. Liddell and Robert Scott, *Greek-English Lexicon*, 9th ed. (Oxford: Clarendon Press, 1940), 766.

[281] Blount, *Oracles of Reason*, 74–76.

[282] Gould, *Time's Arrow*, 21–22, 41–50.

[283] Davies, *Earth in Decay*, 72–73.

[284] Herbert Croft, *Some Animadversions upon a Book Intituled The Theory of the Earth* (London: printed for Charles Harper... 1685), 2–3, 150–155, 178, EEBO.

[285] Ibid., 158.

[286] Erasmus Warren, *Geologia: or, A Discourse concerning the Earth before the Deluge* (London: R. Chiswell, 1690), 48–50, 57–58.

[287] Ibid., 26.

vances to an intrenchment upon Divine Revelation ... that most Divine and Infallible Truth which was spoken by GOD; and therefore to be infinitely reverenc'd of Men."[288] Croft had similarly rebuked Burnet for "not resting satisfied with *Moses's* History of the Creation."[289] Warren admits the possibility of a cabbalistic approach to the Hexaemeron, but insists that cabbala must never undermine the plain, literal meaning. Certainly, God would not have obscured the Ten Commandments, of all biblical revelation, with cabbalistic mysteries. The six day statement of the fourth commandment therefore stands as the conclusive witness to a literal creation week.[290]

From a different philosophical angle, John Beaumont preferred to believe in a static cosmos, wherein the earth created complete from the start: "I must confess, if any Tergiversation were to be allow'd from the Text of *Moses*, I should be more enclin'd to think, that either the World being eternal, or ... at least, that the time of its Rise or Creation, being indefinite ... *Moses,* as a divine Legislator, substituted a Time for its Creation or Rise, and the *Modus* of it ... thereby to carry on a Doctrine for the Good and Salvation of Man." This sounds at least as adventurous as Burnet, but Beaumont finally adds, "I should more readily follow the Opinion of *Austin* [Augustine] ... that God created all things in an instant, without any succession of time."[291] Beaumont is more interested in digging down to the mystical/cabbalistic significance of the numbers featured in the Genesis narrative, all the while announcing his conformity to orthodoxy.[292] Although Dennis Dean said, "For John Beaumont...Biblical chronology was unsubstantiated and far too short," Beaumont offers no proposal here for long creation days, but only a dabbling with both eternalism and instantaneous creation.[293]

Thomas Robinson's *New Observations* (1696) also tackles Burnet's *Sacred Theory*, and represents a strange Renaissance synthesis of the Bible, medieval Aristotelianism, Neoplatonism, Paracelsian mysticism,

[288] Ibid., 42.

[289] Croft, *Some Animadversions*, 178.

[290] This notwithstanding that Warren, like Burnet, understands the process of creation in terms of Cartesian vortices. Warren,*Geologia*, 58–66. For him the sun is not created instantly on the fourth Day, but reaches maturity and effectiveness then. Perhaps this is the kind of admission Burnet had in mind when he wrote to Newton. See above on their correspondence.

[291] John Beaumont, *Considerations on a Book Entitled the Theory of the Earth* (London: printed for the author, and are to be sold by Randal Taylor ... 1693), 19–20.

[292] Ibid., 174–75. Such submission was offered with differing levels of sincerity and of dread by the various writers of the time!

[293] Dean, "Age of the Earth," 444; Beaumont, *Considerations*, 174–75. I have not checked the correspondence with John Locke that Dean also cites.

and Cartesianism.[294] Porter saw this bizarre kind of synthesis as a dying breed by Robinson's time. "Theories of this kind were rooted in the Hermetic, alchemical and mystical currents associated with Paracelsus, Fludd, Gabriel Plattes and Kircher. But by the end of the seventeenth century they were ignored or rejected..."[295] Nevertheless Robinson's offering displays a Platonic willingness to renegotiate the meaning of the Genesis days already glimpsed in Henry More. His first three operating premises are (1) "That this Natural World was created in a Natural Way, by the Agency of Second Causes; God Almighty concurring with them by his Direction," 2) "That the work of the Creation cou'd not, in a natural way, be compleated in so short a time as six days; for as it cannot be easily imagined that all the Solid Strata and Beds of Iron cou'd be digested into such good order, as we find them in," nor animals and plants grow to full maturity, such that Adam can eat "Ripe fruit in Paradise," and all the animals appear before him, and (3) "It may then be taken for a granted Principle, that by the six days work is meant the six distinct Productions; and by the Evening, and the Morning, is meant the Principles of Activity and Passivity, which were the Instrumental Causes of these Productions."[296]

Robinson's symbolic interpretation clearly belongs to the minority tradition of figurative interpretation of the creation days. His symbolic or cabbalistic orientation liberates Robinson to conclude that the process represented by the days of creation, though still sequential, might as easily have been much longer than a literal week as instantaneous.[297] His subsequent description of the creation process is full of the markers of a mystical Renaissance interpretation. The 'light' of Gen. 1:3 is treated as a fundamental principle of reality and crucial agent for the rest of the creative process; the 'darkness' of Gen. 1:2 represents the chaotic mass of passive matter, which undergoes 'fermentation' as the active principles or 'plastick powers' are set to work by God, generating life.[298] In the hierarchy of reality, the material earth, residing at the centre of the nested spheres, represents only the rubbish or dregs of the

[294] Compare Katherine Collier's comments about Robert Fludd: Collier, *Cosmogonies*, 31. Rossi says, "The themes of the Hermetic tradition and of Mosaic philosophy, often solidly joined to alchemistic ideas ... penetrated broadly ... into seventeenth-century culture," Rossi, *Dark Abyss*, 11. See also Harrison, *The Bible, Protestantism*, 270–71.

[295] Porter, *Making of Geology*, 70–71. Harrison describes this mystical tradition as something of a medieval survival, but by now "the last gasp of a dying world view. " Harrison, *The Bible, Protestantism*, 209–11.

[296] Thomas Robinson, *New Observations on the Natural History of This World of Matter and This World of Life ... Grounded upon the Mosaick System of the Creation and the Flood....* (London: printed for John Newton ... 1696), EEBO.

[297] Robinson expresses sympathy for cabbalism at one point at least: ibid., image 8b.

[298] Ibid., 20–26, 95ff. They also generate 'fossils' within the earth, so that Woodward and Steno are mistaken to think of them as once-living organisms: ibid., 105, 109, 112.

whole process.[299] The Cartesian part of the theory matches Burnet and Descartes himself, while the disdain for the material is again reminiscent of the Manichaeism of Böhme.[300] Robinson joins both Beaumont and Burnet in treating the creation days very freely and non-literally.

The naturalist and clergyman John Ray (1627–1705) used the tripartite arrangement familiar from Burnet's *Sacred Theory* in his *Three Physico-Theological Discourses* (1693): Creation, Deluge, and final Conflagration. It is a less ambitious and all-encompassing work than Burnet's, and seeks to understand the present form of the earth in the light of its fossil organisms. As in Burnet's *Sacred Theory,* the chaos produced by the initial creative act settles out into its respective elements, land covered by water and then air, in accordance with their relative densities.[301] It is not clear in Ray's scheme whether the orderly world arises out of the chaos *before* or *within* the six days of creation.

Ray cannot easily see where the formation of fossils of sea creatures fits into the biblical account. The Flood did not last long enough to deposit these fossils at high altitudes, since some fossil sea creatures had apparently lived, bred and died *in situ.* "If we stick to the letter of the Scripture-History of the Creation, that the Creation of Fishes succeeded the Separation of Land and Sea, and that the six days wherein the World was created, were six natural Days and no more, it is very difficult to return a satisfactory Answer" to the question of the origin of fossils. Yet if the land was only gradually uncovered by water after the creation, beginning with a small patch sufficient for Adam and Eve to inhabit, there would be time for shellfish and such like to breed and die and be fossilized even at what are now high altitudes.[302] This concept of a diminishing ocean became basic to the majority of geotheories going into the eighteenth century, such that Rudwick calls it 'the standard model'.[303]

Ray's correspondence reveals his conviction of the organic origin of fossils, and that they could not have been generally flood-deposited, as John Woodward had recently proposed.[304] But the logical consequences of these conclusions when combined "seem to shock the Scripture-History of ye novity of the World" and the widespread presumption of the impossibility of species extinction. He concedes the earth's antiquity, with its embedded fossils, but takes a stand "that ye race of mankind

[299] Ibid., 6–7, 9. See also the diagram in images 72 and 73 of this electronic version. Note also the Paracelsian 'salt, sulphur and mercury' triad, pp. 12, 99.

[300] Ibid., 22–24.

[301] Ray, *Three Physico-Theological Discourses*, 8–10.

[302] Ibid.

[303] Rudwick, *Bursting the Limits*, 172–74.

[304] See the following chapter for further comment on Woodward.

is new upon ye heart [*sic*], & not older then ye Scripture makes it."[305] The Hexaemeron clearly has greater influence in Ray's work than in Burnet's, with a focus on the formation of the land masses and ocean basins in conjunction with Day 3 (Gen. 1:9–11), as well as the creation of living things on Days 5–6.[306] Yet the Hexaemeron is under strain here, is being used selectively, and is already in retreat as an explanatory framework for the earth's origin. Scholars of the Royal Society were now finding their novel information about the world's origin less from Genesis and other ancient texts and more from close observation of nature.

The German polymath Gottfried Wilhelm Leibniz' (1646–1716) influential late seventeenth-century theory of the earth constituted "both a continuation and a criticism of Descartes's project," born of a concern about "the relationship between Descartes's account and the biblical narrative."[307] Leibniz' geotheory portrays the earth as a one-time sun whose surface formed a glassy crust, which suffered undermining, collapse, and upheaval, accompanied by catastrophic advance and retreat of the ocean waters. Such upheavals were repeated many times and in various localities, i.e. Steno's cycle could be pluralized.[308] "In effect, Leibniz disregarded time in any measurable sense when he wrote about the pre-human history of the earth."[309] Leibniz points out the two great physical agents involved in the formation of the earth, fire and water, in the creation account in the references to the formation of light and darkness (Gen. 1:3–4) and then the separation of wet and dry (Gen. 1:9–11), respectively, while the Deluge tradition clearly affected his concept of catastrophic rise and fall of the seas.[310] Despite these few nods in the direction of Genesis, Leibniz' scheme is quite naturalistic, the initial act of creation excepted, setting the tone for eighteenth-century geotheories.[311]

[305] John Ray, *Further Correspondence of John Ray*, ed. R.W.T. Gunther, Ray Society Publications (London: printed for the Ray Society, 1928), 260, 266, 277–78. He shortly afterwards offers Edward Lhwyd a synopsis of the same 'retreating ocean' cosmogony that features in *Three Physico-Theological Discourses*: Ray, *Further Correspondence*, 266–67.

[306] Ray, *Three Physico-Theological Discourses*, 10–45. Mountains are not signs of a world in collapse, *contra Burnet,* but of God's caring and useful design: ibid., 35.

[307] Gottfried Wilhelm Leibniz, *Protogaea*, trans. Claudine Cohen and Andre Wakefield (Chicago: University of Chicago Press, 2008), xx–xxi. The work was first publicised in condensed article form in the *Acta Eruditorum* in 1693 and in further articles in 1706 and 1710, until finally being published in full posthumously in 1749. See Andre Wakefield, introduction to Leibniz, *Protogaea*, xxxvii–xxxviii; Rappaport, *Geologists*, 208.

[308] Leibniz, *Protogaea*, 4–7, 10–17.

[309] Rappaport, *Geologists*, 196. See also Vaccari, "European Views," 30.

[310] On the agency of fire and water, see Andre Wakefield, introduction to Leibniz, *Protogaea*, xxi; Zöckler, *Geschichte*, 2:180.

[311] Zöckler makes the connection with the mechanistic scheme of Descartes at this point also: Zöckler, *Geschichte*, 2:179. "He must have been aware of the dangerously

William Whiston's New Genesis-Based Geotheory

This brings us to the important work of William Whiston (1667–1752), one of Newton's foremost disciples. In his *New Theory of the Earth* (1696), Whiston acknowledges his debt to Burnet, but wishes to offer an improved model for the earth's origin that is fully compatible with both the Genesis account of creation and the new Newtonian cosmology. The function of the heavens had been explained, it was felt, and now the world awaited a corresponding Newtonian explanation of the earth.[312] Whiston intended to prove that there is no need to oppose "the Obvious and Natural, to the Rational and Philosophick Interpretations of the Holy Scriptures."[313] Not only Newton's mechanics, but also Newton's lengthened creation days as they appeared in the correspondence with Burnet, would play their part in the *New Theory,* while Halley's recent investigation of cometary phenomena clearly also made a contribution.[314] In the section dedicated to explaining the Mosaic account of creation, Whiston immediately proposes:

> The Mosaick Creation is not a Nice and Philosophical account of the Origin of All Things; but an Historical and True Representation of the formation of our single Earth out of a confused Chaos, and of the successive and visible changes thereof each day, till it became the habitation of Mankind.[315]

In other, modern words, the Mosaic account does not treat the origin of things scientifically, but in historical, common-sense terms, just as Newton held. Nor does it treat the origin of the entire universe, a misconception that "seems to have been the principal occasion of men's Mistakes and Prejudices about this whole History," but only of planet Earth (as Burnet held!).[316] Both principles are bound up in the idea that the creation account is expressed from an earthly observer's point of view.[317] "The Sacred Penmen ... condescend still to the Apprehensions and Capacities of Men, and speak of the *Being* of things as they constantly *Appear* ..."[318] This should resolve perceived contradic-

materialistic character of this thesis," Andre Wakefield, introduction to Leibniz, *Protogaea,* xxviii.

[312] Mandelbrote, "Isaac Newton and Thomas Burnet," 162; William Whiston, *A New Theory of the Earth, from its Original, to the Consummation of All Things....* (London: R. Roberts, 1696), EEBO.

[313] Ibid., 76–80.

[314] Young, "Scripture in the Hands of Geologists," 17.

[315] Whiston, *New Theory*, 3. "The Scripture did not intend to teach men Philosophy, or accommodate itself to the true and *Pythagorick* [i.e. Copernican] System of the World," ibid., 19, 38.

[316] Ibid., 14.

[317] Ibid., 19.

[318] Ibid., 22.

tions between what is known of the natural world and Moses' presentation.[319] Whiston seeks an interpretive golden mean, neither taking the Mosaic History as an accurate ('scientific') portrayal of the cosmos, nor as "a meer Mythological and Mysterious reduction of the visible parts of it to six periods or divisions," in order to establish Sabbath practice for the Jews. No, what we have is "*An Historical Journal or Diary ... of the visible Works of each Day, such ... as an honest and observing Spectator on the Earth would have made...*"[320]

Why, then, does Whiston regard the traditional, absolute (i.e. philosophical) understanding of the creation account as unsustainable? "Such Notions," he believes, are "but the effects of ignorance of the frame of the World, and of the stile of Scripture; of an unacquaintedness with the Works, and thence an inability of judging concerning the Word of God relating to them."[321] Those who suppose that an initial chaos gave birth to the whole universe must explain how all the stars were flung out, against the rule of gravity, from one centre, to such immense distances as presently separate them, and, if one would include this process within the six days of creation, in only a few hours![322]

An even more pressing problem for Whiston is a sense of disproportion between the time required for the creation of earth and its accoutrements in the Hexaemeron versus that required for the formation of the entire rest of the cosmos.[323] The increasingly apparent vastness of the universe had made a deep impression on the scholars of the Royal Society. Such a mismatch between means and ends risked making God's creative work look foolish or absurd.[324] The received idea of creation, Whiston admits, belonged more naturally to the old, geocentric conception of the universe, with stars unappreciated, no other inhabited worlds envisaged, and everything existing for man, lord of the earth:

> While all this ... was the current Philosophy, 'tis not very surprising that the *Mosaick* History that we are now upon was understood in the Vulgar Sense, and seem'd not wholly disagreeable to the presumed Frame of Nature.... Those greater degrees of Knowledge which the Providence of God has in this Age afforded us, make such Opinions intolerable in the present, which were not so in the past Centuries.[325]

[319] Ibid., 2, 7, and esp. 61ff.
[320] Ibid., 30.
[321] Ibid., 39.
[322] Ibid., 36–38.
[323] Ibid., 51.
[324] Ibid., 41,57.
[325] Ibid., 58–59. Whiston and many of his contemporaries imagined with a striking certainty, considering the evidence available to them, that the universe was filled with habitable and indeed, inhabited, planets.

Astronomy had evidently played a key role in sapping the settled view of biblical creation. How could the universe have been made chiefly for man when the vast majority of the stars revealed by the telescope were not visible to the naked eye, and many comets' erratic orbits would deny them to human view for whole generations together?[326] No, it was the Genesis account, rather than creation per se, that Whiston believed was anthropocentric in its focus.

The readiest objection to Whiston's proposed limited scope for creation concerned the creation of sun, moon and stars on Day 4, and Whiston has a solution ready. Since the Hebrew lacks a verbal form to represent the pluperfect, he defends the interpreter's right to infer such a sense for the perfect (Qal) form of the verb where context demands it. Hence Gen. 1:16 may be translated, "And God had (before) made two great lights ..."[327] Should the reader not accept this grammatical argument, which would qualify as literal interpretation, he proposes an alternative idea with a long heritage: that this is an instance of biblical accommodation to the 'vulgar apprehensions of men', a phenomenological or figurative way of speaking. This is not opening the door to unrestrained allegory; after all, we know how to distinguish between use of figures of speech and allegory in everyday conversation![328] Whiston remains sensitive about this one point "wherein this intire Theory ... seems to recede from the obvious Letter of Scripture," but feels that it is warranted by the interpretive circumstances.[329]

Whiston limits the scope of the creation account not only spatially, being exclusively earth-focused, but also in terms of time. The chaos from which the earth originates predates the six-day creation week, meaning that Whiston, like many of his immediate predecessors, understood Gen. 1:1–2 as a preliminary statement to the events of the six days, and found room in the 'formless and void' earth of verse 2 to accommodate classical statements about primeval chaos.[330] Whiston interpreted this data to mean that the primeval earth was originally a comet![331] The converting of the comet's erratic path into the regular orbit of the new earth was one of the few direct acts of God in crea-

[326] Ibid., 69–70.
[327] Ibid., 14–15.
[328] Ibid., 17, 26–27.
[329] Ibid., 14.
[330] Ibid., 4–6, etc.
[331] Ibid., 32–33, 69ff. This is one specimen of the importance that recent discoveries assumed in the theoretical schemes of the day. Whiston believed that "a *Planet* is a *Comet* form'd into a regular and lasting constitution," which included a circular orbit: ibid., 74–75.

tion.[332] His detailed explanation of the unfolding of the days of creation presents a mostly natural sequence of events precipitated by the supernatural stabilization of the primeval earth's orbit. The cometary atmosphere settled out, creating a crust on the earth much as Burnet conceived it, and by the fourth day the atmosphere was clear enough to allow the full appearance of the sun and moon from the earth's surface.[333] Meanwhile the oceans had condensed and run into place, and the sun's warming influence had stirred to life the seeds of plants and animals created and implanted in land and seas by God. The crowning event, the creation of humans, also required a direct act of God.[334]

The chief biblical objection to Burnet's scheme had been that it simply did not have time to occur within the span of a literal creative week. Whiston's solution resembles Newton's earlier idea: while the earth's annual revolution around the sun initiated the creation week, its diurnal motion did not begin until afterwards. This meant that Whiston's creation days are each one year long.[335] Thus Burnet's kind of cosmogony is reconciled with the Genesis account with the aid of Newtonian astronomy. Unlike Burnet, Whiston associates the apparent damage that the ideal original earth had suffered with the Fall and the beginning of diurnal motion, although a double near miss by another comet would produce the later inundation of the Flood.[336] Creation and the Flood continue to be dated according to Ussher's highly regarded chronology, which Whiston amends slightly to suit his own scheme.[337] So Whiston's sophisticated model had systematized, within the booming genre of geotheory, a serious literal-figurative understanding of Genesis that boasted strong Newtonian credentials, lengthened the creation days to leave room for natural development, and took recent discoveries into account, while excluding the cosmos from the scope of the Hexaemeron.

Conclusion

The end of the seventeenth century witnessed important new trends that were still in early development, trends well represented in Whiston's thinking. He draws his knowledge both from the Bible and from

[332] Ibid., 223–24. There were six such direct acts in all, including the original creation of matter, the creating of the seeds of life, and the formation of complete human beings on Day 6: see pp. 222–29. Whiston programmatically limited the number of such 'miracles' in the creation week: ibid., 95.

[333] For the full description of the unfolding of the days, see ibid., 220–56, also 158–62.

[334] Ibid., 253.

[335] See esp. ibid., 79–90.

[336] Ibid., 102, 126–54, 173, 260, 278.

[337] Ibid., 123ff., 167.

natural sources. He regards Genesis highly and employs it quite deliberately, yet cuts back its once global application. His defence of its historicity at the same time concedes its philosophical shortcomings. His physical theory harmonizes Genesis with natural phenomena in a way that is contemporary and sophisticated, yet married to its moment and destined for eventual obsolescence. Arnold Williams encapsulated the progressive secularization of knowledge that was underway:

> The total result was to push the Genesis material into an ever smaller corner of the intellectual picture. Undoubtedly this growing secularization of interest and expansion of material for thought is what is ultimately responsible for the disappearance of the commentary on Genesis written in the manner of the sixteenth and early seventeenth centuries. Genesis ceased being a historical document or a scientific handbook.[338]

Yet this breakdown would take time; Whiston had made a stand for the synthesis of Genesis and the philosophy of the earth's origin, and such efforts would continue to appear throughout the following century, even as the 'abyss of time' opened up beneath them.

[338] Williams, *Common Expositor*, 268.

5

The Days of Creation and the Ambition of Reason in the Eighteenth Century

> Some drill and bore
> The solid earth, and from the strata there
> Extract a register, by which we learn,
> That he who made it, and revealed its date
> To Moses, was mistaken in its age.[1]
>
> William Cowper, *The Task* (1785)

Introduction

The new century opened to a burgeoning confidence in human reason. Isaac Newton had cemented the heliocentric cosmos into place, offering gravity as a powerful explanatory concept for its physical behaviour. Burnet and other early geotheorists offered hope that the earth's past might soon be as well understood according to natural law. Science as we understand it was still in gestation; those who worked in fields that we would today recognize as falling within natural science regarded their study as either 'natural history', where concerned with collection, classification and description, or as 'natural philosophy', where they sought explanation in terms of physical causation.[2] Denis

[1] William Cowper, *The Task: A Poem. In Six Books. To which is Added, Tirocinium: or, A Review of Schools*, New ed. (Philadelphia: printed for Thomas Dobson, etc., 1787), 64f., GB, http://books.google.com/books?id=StE0AAAAMAAJ (*The Task,* Book 3, 'The Garden', ll. 150–54). This interesting quotation, which shows a reasonably early wrestling with the deep time implications of proto-geology, has appeared in numerous histories of science or ideas, e.g. Collier, *Cosmogonies*, 141–42; White, *Warfare*, 222; W. Neil, "The Criticism and Theological Use of the Bible 1700–1950," in *The Cambridge History of the Bible. 3. The West from the Reformation to the Present Day*, ed. S.L. Greenslade (Cambridge: Cambridge University Press, 1963), 257; Michael Roberts, *Evangelicals and Science*, Greenwood Guides to Science and Religion, ed. Richard Olson (Westport, CT/London: Greenwood Press, 2008), 81.

[2] Peter Harrison, "'Science' and 'Religion': Constructing the Boundaries," *Journal of Religion* 86, no. 1 (2006): 81–85; Rudwick, *Bursting the Limits,* 52–55. Often cited is the

Diderot's 'Map of the System of Human Knowledge' from his 1749 *Encyclopédie* (1751–65) subordinates certain fields of 'science' under the grand category 'philosophy'. Theology, natural and revealed (i.e. Scripture-based), forms a discrete category of philosophy in Diderot's map, compared to the 'Science of Nature' and the 'Science of Man', and is related there to 'religion' and thence to 'superstition', or abused religion.[3] These demarcations were becoming harder and faster, as resistance developed to any move of 'theology' out of its box, to transgress into the 'sciences'. But the human instinct for a unified worldview is a strong one, and thinkers with a theistic mindset were not always willing to screen off their findings in nature from their theological convictions.

Interpretive accommodation of Genesis to prevailing currents of thought had happened as long as Genesis had existed, especially once interpreted outside of its source milieu. In the patristic and medieval eras, Neoplatonism, Pythagoreanism, Gnosticism and Aristotelian philosophy influenced or in some case overwhelmed Genesis interpretation. In the Renaissance too, philosophical influences were important, including Neoplatonism, atomism and Cartesian varieties. Philosophical frameworks influence everything we think we see around us or read in a biblical text, and it is vital to gain some understanding of the prevailing philosophies of an age in order to appreciate what is unique and different about the biblical interpretations yielded by that age. The descending trajectory of influence of Gen. 1:1–2:3 in the eighteenth century reflects the burgeoning Renaissance interest in nature, the empiricist movement in the seventeenth century, and the antiquarian instinct that turned from human relics to those of past natural events. The influx of newly discovered data from beyond the Atlantic, beyond the moon, below the microscope and below the earth's crust made accommodating natural data increasingly important in Genesis interpretation in this century.

To craft a concordist or semi-concordist rendition of Gen. 1:1–2:3 involved admitting that the interpretation of the biblical data could not and/or should not happen in complete isolation. It had to take note of what might be known from external sources.[4] Some thinkers would

use of 'sciences' in W. Whewell, *History of the Inductive Sciences* (London: John W. Parker, 1837).

[3] The map is reproduced in translation in Rudwick, *Bursting the Limits*, 50–51. For a more graphic representation, see http://quod.lib.umich.edu/d/did/tree–french.html, and for the French original, http://quod.lib.umich.edu/d/did/graphics/tree.french.jpg.

[4] I am reminded of an article, Allan J. Day, "Adam, Anthropology and the Genesis Record – Taking Genesis Seriously in the Light of Contemporary Science," *Science & Christian Belief* 10, no. 2 (1998), 115-143. This title would be truer to the content of the article if it read, "Taking Contemporary Science Seriously when Reading Genesis. "

object strongly, either dismissing the relevance or reliability of the Genesis account, distinguishing it utterly from nature, so that the two could not be compared, or else esteeming it so highly above the wavering, human conclusions of natural philosophy that the latter seemed irrelevant to the one true and divine source. But the opposite, concordist impulse predominated in the interpretation of Genesis in the era of the Enlightenment. Some theologians worried that the consideration of external considerations from natural philosophy or philosophy proper had the effect of distorting the natural intention of the language of Genesis. The counter-argument was that to interpret Genesis in isolation from external data could leave it trapped in obsolescence, and force Christian scientists and natural philosophers to choose between the Book of Nature and the Book of Scripture, two sources that ought to be found consistent in their mutual derivation from the one God.

The 'balance of power' between the Book of Nature and the Book of Scripture was shifting, however, in the Western mind. The older scenario was that a cosmogony or philosophy should come to Genesis for authorization, and such authorization was still often sought in the eighteenth or even the nineteenth century in Christian or church-dominated circles. But this was becoming rarer. Carl Linnaeus' famous *Philosophia botanica* made very little reference to Genesis; Baron D'Holbach's avant-garde *Le systeme de la nature* (1770–71), none. Genesis clearly had nothing to say about the geography of the New World, and it was fading out of universal histories as the century progressed. Theories of the present functioning of the physical earth could rely upon the authority of Copernicus and Newton, and theories of its past on Descartes or Burnet or Whiston. By 1800, then, a scientific or historical work needed to justify any mention of Genesis, rather than its neglect, and literal interpretations of Genesis account were buttressed with scientific and historical data for their verification. The mantle of authority had shifted to human reason and the deposit of its natural data and conclusions, soon destined to be labelled 'science.' The marginalization of Gen. 1:1–2:3 in reference to the material realm and physical origins was well underway.

There is a risk here: the contemporary Western mind, steeped in more than three centuries of natural-scientific 'revolution', is inclined to recognize (and then to dismiss) only those interpretations of Gen. 1:1–2:3 that pertain to the physical origin of the world. But the early Modern mental landscape was more fluid than ours, and physical and metaphysical, chemical and occult, and philosophical and theological concerns tended to blend. Ways of accessing knowledge were in formation and in dispute. Some thinkers approached the Genesis text expecting clues to the essential constitution of the world, or the earliest documentary evidence to the infancy of human society.[5] Others found mysteries of angels and demons, or symbols of the emergence of the ideal into materiality. More concretely, Gen. 1:1–2:3 could still function as the anchor point for certain fields of human knowledge such as cosmology, cosmogony or human history at the beginning of the eighteenth century. The period was awash with competing knowledge agendas; by the end of the century, some, such as hermetic mysticism, had been driven to the margins, while others, such as the study of nature, were rising to supremacy.

The eighteenth century ended with a simpler central set of interpretive options than it had possessed at the beginning of the century. The approach to Gen. 1:1–2:3 that rose to dominance in the wake of the new awareness of both history and the material world that developed in the Renaissance milieu was the approach that sought clues to the origin and history of the physical world itself. R.G. Collingwood spoke of the rise of the 'historical imagination': "Since the time of Descartes, and even since the time of Kant, mankind has acquired a new habit of thinking historically." This habit "has permeated and to some extent transformed every department of thought and action."[6] Although biblical chronology would finally be 'broken' to make way for process and change in nature, said Francis Haber, "the constant pressure of the Christian view of historical process on views of natural process helped to preserve a genetic outlook in terms of concrete, actualistic time…it held the potential in readiness until the geologists discovered the real chronology of the earth in fossil strata and could substitute a scientific for a theological series of epochs."[7]

Just as antiquarians unearthed relics of antique civilizations, fossilized life forms began to be read as the remains of real organisms, in some cases looking radically different than known living species. When seen by persons with a 'sense of history', the very thing encouraged by this Christian heritage, they began to speak of earth's own hitherto unsuspected antiquity. In one recent summary, "As the late eighteenth century became the early nineteenth century, lines of evidence from various areas of research, including geognosy, Earth physics, physical geography, and … fossils, converged in an intellectual development that produced the modern geohistorical perspective," with an Earth "not only of great age, but the product of contingency."[8]

[5] Johann Gottfried Herder, *Reflections on the Philosophy of the History of Mankind: Abridged, and with an Introduction, by Frank E. Manuel* (Chicago: University of Chicago Press, 1968). This was originally published as *Ideen zur Philosophie der Geschichte der Menschheit* (1784–1791).

[6] R.G. Collingwood, *The Idea of History* (Oxford: Clarendon, 1946), 232.

[7] Haber, *Age of the World*, 10, 291–92.

[8] Yarchin, "Biblical Interpretation," 48–49.

For an age interested in the physical origin of the world, in a terrestrial history, Genesis would be most commonly read as a cosmogony, an approach admittedly that accords well with its surface presentation. This realistic approach to Genesis had precedents in Antiochene and Cappadocian patristic exegesis, but with growing recognition of a developmental rather than static past existence of the cosmos and the earth, readers expected Genesis to give indications of this terrestrial history, the prequel to human history.[9] The popularity of 'theories of the earth' demonstrates that this newly historical mind was turning with interest not just to the human past but also to the terrestrial and cosmic past. Timeless 'natural history' was about to become a true 'history of nature', and Genesis was at risk of marginalization as learning, speculation and sheer autonomous confidence in reason increased. Meanwhile the modest suite of eighteenth-century Genesis commentaries tended to be unadventurous concerning the creation days, with a restrained concept of an initial chaos, adherence to six literal days, and limited reference to geotheoretical debates.[10]

The Influence of Whiston's New Theory and the Defence of Moses

Burnet's Cartesian geotheory had been controversial specifically because of its neglect of the Mosaic account, and Whiston had sought to remedy this by articulating a modified Burnetian scheme in harmony with Genesis, in terms both of creation and the Flood. He had achieved this concord by limiting the scope of the creation account to the earth and its immediate atmosphere, and moreover simply to the

[9] The eternal world of Aristotelian philosophy was the ultimate in a static picture of the universe. On account of the apparent stability of the world following creation in the Genesis imagery, the two accounts had been accepted as generally compatible, with the simple but strong exception of a quite sudden and supernatural creation *ex nihilo* perceived in Genesis 1. Some saw Plato's version of creation (as in the *Timaeus*) even more compatible with Genesis on this count. As Aristotle passed out of popularity, we might see echoes of competing ancient Greek philosophies in alternatives that arose: either a cyclical version of world history, related to Stoic belief in cycles of destruction and re-emergence, or a naturalistic, atomistic kind of development that had roots in Epicurean belief, and reappeared in Cartesianism.

[10] See for example Matthew Henry, *Exposition of the Old and New Testaments* (1708–10), CCEL, http://www.ccel.org/ccel/henry/mhc1.Gen.ii.html (esp. on Gen. 1:31.); Calmet, *Commentarius litteralis*, 87; Jacques Joseph Duguet and Joseph Vincent Bidel d'Asfeld, *Explication litterale de l'ouvrage des six jours mêlée des reflexions morales* (Brussels: Francois Foppens, 1731), 45–48, http://books.google.com.au/books?R6cGAAAAQAAJ; William Wall, *Critical Notes on the Old Testament....* (London: printed for C. Davis, 1734), 5–6, ECCO. Among secondary treatments, see Rossi, *Dark Abyss*, 197 on Calmet; Zöckler, *Geschichte*, 2:131–32; Christoph Bultmann, "Early Rationalism and Biblical Criticism on the Continent," in *HB/OT*, vol. 2:877.

conversion of the earth into a form fit for human habitation (thus allowing it a pre-history not related in Genesis). He had also lengthened the creation days into years, providing time for natural processes of formation to unfold. The enthusiasm at this point in history for the classical concept of the primordial 'chaos', best seen in the early stanzas of Ovid's *Metamorphoses*, made a developmental model of the world's origin seem very natural, and a chaos-oriented reading of Genesis was the very soil in which the geotheories of Burnet, Whiston and others thrived. "The whole schemata of original chaos followed by development was an essential part of the eighteenth century worldview," as Michael Roberts puts it.[11] Whiston's liberties with the 'days' of Genesis 1 were just one example of this tendency towards a gradualistic creation model.

Whiston's revamped Burnetian theory, utilizing Newton's powerful model of the cosmos and ostensibly harmonizing with the early chapters of the Bible, took root in Germany through a faithful treatment by Dethlev Clüver, and in direct translation, and achieved significant continental recognition.[12] It constituted the primary Genesis-oriented alternative to Woodward's scheme, although one British critic, John Witty, protested that Whiston's model played fast and loose with Genesis:

> If Moses's History of the Creation is not to be literally interpreted, then neither is that of the Fall; and if the Fall is a piece of Mythology, then so is the Redemption; and if the Redemption is a Fable, then welcome Deism, and farewel reveal'd Religion.[13]

Witty announces his intention "to re-assert Moses's right in the Hexaemeron to a simple Historical Dress; and to take off those Exceptions which have been made against the obvious Exposition of the History of the Creation.... I hope [to] vindicate Moses in his obvious Exposition, and therein break up ... one of the very strongest holds of Deism."[14] Confessing his supreme regard for the Mosaic history of creation, unique on account of its divine source and unparalleled historical witness to the subject matter of creation, Witty proceeds with a

[11] Roberts, "Genesis Chapter 1," 42.

[12] Dethlev Clüver, *Geologia sive philosophemata de Genesi ac structura globi terreni, oder: Natürliche Wissenschafft von Erschaffung und Bereitung der Erd-kugel: Wie nemlich nach Mosis und der ältesten Philosophen Bericht aus dem Chao, durch mechanische Gesetze der Bewegungen, die Erde sey herfür gebracht worden....* (Hamburg: Liebezeit, 1700). See Zöckler, *Geschichte*, 2:157–60; Vaccari, "European Views," 30.

[13] John Witty, *An Essay towards a Vindication of the Vulgar Exposition of the Mosaic History of the Creation of the World* (London: J. Wyat, 1705), [i], ECCO.

[14] Ibid. [v–vii].

three-part argument for the continued validity of "the vulgar Exposition of the Mosaic History of the Creation of the World."[15]

First, Witty argues that creation proceeded by the direct operation of God, to the exclusion of natural law. This, he says, has been the traditional position for Jews and Christians until recently and remains the majority position. Therefore [natural] philosophy, which deals in the realm of natural law, cannot comment on it, and the biblical account of creation stands on its own terms. Assuming, as is normally accepted, that "God Almighty was pleas'd first to create the World in a Chaotic condition, and thence ... to reduce it to what it is at present," motion must be involved, and where motion, time, and therefore why not six days as the necessary period?[16]

Second, even if one should hold that natural law did in fact operate to some extent within the creation week, the uncertain and changeable field of philosophy still lacks the right to sit in judgment on clear and certain scriptural testimony. The Bible is the only account of our original happiness and of how we lost it in the Fall, and thus is the only candidate to be considered as God's revelation to man of these things.[17] The biblical account has no case to answer in regard to the claims of natural philosophy. The Mosaic History may be taken as "*a plain, tho' general Account of the Creation of the whole material World out of nothing; and of the method God Almighty took in bringing it in the time specify'd by* Moses *into the form we find it in at present.*"[18]

Third, even if one should still allow natural philosophy some hearing, the biblical account stands up perfectly well to any query it can make. To prove this point, Witty enunciates a cosmogony of his own, although he disowns it more than once, declaring himself happy to take the Genesis account at face value. He simply offers this third option for apologetic purposes, to satisfy those who have an excessive regard for philosophy. He goes as far as he can to meet Whiston, accepting Whiston's definition of the Hexaemeron as "*an Historical Journal or Diary of the Mutations of the Chaos,*" so long as the 'chaos' is extended "to the utmost limits of the material Creation, and making the six Days mention'd by *Moses* of the same extent with those we have at present." This was despite his own developmental scheme in which "Sun, Moon and Stars" took "considerable time" to achieve their full form once motion was first impressed on matter.[19]

[15] Ibid., 1–4. In other words, we would say "the popular understanding of the Mosaic history..."

[16] Ibid., 7–9. We recognize the argument here that motion or action and time are mutually necessary.

[17] Ibid., 26–29.

[18] Ibid., 40.

[19] Ibid., 41–43.

While this solution could hardly have satisfied Whiston, Witty worries that his own orthodoxy will be suspected, and repeats his confidence that the 'most vulgar' interpretation of the Mosaic account is fully defensible.[20] Beneath the rhetoric, Witty is not so far from Whiston in portraying a six-day creation that mostly proceeds by natural cause and effect, with a few miraculous exceptions such as the special creation of human beings. For instance, "On the first Day, [the stars] were tending towards a collection, being able to shew in the Centres of their Vortices some little of a dim Light; on the second, they grew better, so as to have some power upon their Planets in making 'em atmospheres; on the third, they grew better still, being considerably assistant in raising the Vegetable Kingdoms; and on the fourth, their Work was done, they broke into that splendor with which they now comfort the whole Creation."[21] Witty's treatment therefore represents a conversation with Whiston that casts the earth's development out of chaos in a Cartesian rather than Newtonian form.[22]

Between Burnet, Whiston and Woodward, the parameters for geotheoretical debate in Britain had been established for a long time to come. Porter reminds us that in 1727, "Swift saw to it that the ivory-towered Laputians in *Gulliver's Travels* were discussing Whiston's Deluge theory."[23] Even Cotton Mather, probably the leading North American intellectual and theologian of the time, presented Whiston's theory as one strong option for interpreting Genesis 1 philosophically, in the first phase of his work on his mammoth *Biblia Americana* between 1693 and 1706.[24] But he does so a little nervously, evidently concerned that this stance's orthodoxy might be in doubt, and offers, remarkably, Dickinson's atomistic rendition of Genesis 1 as an apologia for the philosophical strength of Moses' cosmogony in its own right, as if Dickinson had not radically recast it![25] Back in the western Europe of the 1740s, "the theories of Burnet and of Whiston still flourished and were treated as worthy of serious consideration, especially in Germa-

[20] Ibid., 135, 148.

[21] Ibid., 111.

[22] Although Katherine Collier calls Witty 'the Anticartesian', Witty's *Essay* describes the nature of light and the formation of stars/planets inside their vortices in Cartesian terms: ibid., *Essay*, 59–64, 69–75; Collier, *Cosmogonies*, 166.

[23] Porter, *Making of Geology*, 63, 87. See Jonathan Swift, *Travels into Several Remote Nations of the World…by Lemuel Gulliver….* (Dublin: 1727), 14–15, ECCO.

[24] R. Smolinski, ed., *Biblia Americana: Cotton Mather* (Grand Rapids: Baker, 2010), 51ff.

[25] Ibid., 3–5, 67–70, 79–97, 338–82.

ny."[26] The Frenchman Buffon's in-depth treatment of the three figures in 1749 shows how potent these models remained by mid-century.[27]

Amongst mid-century British works, Whiston's influence is clear in Benjamin Parker's *A Survey of the Six Days Works of the Creation* (1745), where year-long creation days are connected with the paradise-like state of the antediluvian earth, though Parker defends the universal scope of the hexaemeral narrative.[28] The anonymous author of *A Critical and Practical Exposition of the Pentateuch* (1748), identified by later authors as one Jam[i]eson, also offers a Whistonian explanation.[29] He too limits the scope of the creation narrative to the earth alone, and like Whiston feels that to have five days spent forming the earth and only one on the entire remainder of the universe is ludicrously out of proportion.[30] His tone is derogatory: "The vulgar scheme of the Mosaic creation, represents all things from first to last, so disorderly and unphilosophically, that it is entirely disagreeable to the wisdom and perfections of God."[31] Though God can achieve his work in a moment, creatures cannot, and some events that must fit into Day 6, such as the naming of the animals, cannot fit into a natural day but "must have been a work of some considerable time."[32] The long-day view here seems ready to leave its Whistonian moorings, with a precedent now well established for accommodating a longer earth and cosmic history within the creation week framework.[33] When persons such as

[26] Collier, *Cosmogonies*, 190.

[27] Rossi credits Buffon (in his 1749 geotheory) with enforcing discussion of this trio on historians of science ever since, but Buffon's work is more a symptom of this trend than the cause: Rossi, *Dark Abyss*, 8.

[28] Benjamin Parker, *A Survey of the Six Days Works of the Creation* (London: printed for the author; Benjamin Stichall; and sold by R. Baldwin and J. Jefferies, 1745), 6–14, 24–26, 33–34, 79 n. The earth forms over the course of this extended creation week as the four elements settle out from an initial, indefinite chaos: Parker, *Six Days Works*, 4, 16, 18–20, 38.

[29] For the attribution, see Wilhelm Martin Leberecht de Wette, *A Critical and Historical Introduction to the Canonical Scriptures of the Old Testament*, trans. Theodore Parker, 2 vols. (Boston: Charles C. Little and James Brown, 1843), 1:29; Thomas Hartwell Horne, *An Introduction to the Critical Study and Knowledge of the Holy Scriptures*, 4th ed., 4 vols. (Philadelphia: E. Little, 1825), 2:762, GB, http://books.google.com.au/books?id=icFC AAAAIAAJ.

[30] [Jamieson], *A Critical and Practical Exposition of the Pentateuch, with Notes, Theological, Moral, Philosophical, Critical, and Historical...* (London: Printed for J. & P. Knapton, 1748), iii–vi, ECCO.

[31] Ibid., vi b.

[32] Ibid., vi b, 4b.

[33] The author also mentions world-week belief when discussing Gen. 1:31. Speaking of the 6000 years of "the Hebrew doctors," he scoffs, "But with equal reason might they have supposed it to last six millions of years or ages. " I think it would be a mistake to see any suggestion here of a truly deep-time perspective on creation; he is just dismissing what was a rapidly withering medieval-Renaissance manner of periodizing history.

Buffon and de Luc, convinced of the earth's deep history, sought to harmonize this with biblical creation, they would utilize Whiston's precedent, taking the days of creation non-literally and yet still temporally, rather than as purely ideal entities.

The Bearing of Diluvial Theories on the Interpretation of Genesis One

One of the key questions during the early eighteenth century concerning the world's origin was whether the processes involved in the production of the world as it presently stood, inferred by their present remains, could be accommodated within "the Scripture-History of ye novity of the World," to borrow John Ray's phrase.[34] The relative capabilities of the agencies of fire and water were already under consideration by this time, from Kircher's subterranean fire and Hooke's earthquakes to the waters of the Flood of Noah and of the original chaotic ocean.[35] The fossils which were by now mostly accepted as the remains of living creatures had evidently usually been deposited in water-borne sediment too, and John Woodward's *An Essay Towards a Natural History of the Earth* (1695) offered an extremely short-timescale diluvial (Flood-based) explanation for their deposition.[36] Woodward accounted for the production of the earth in its present configuration, mountain-top shells and all, *within* known history as set out in Scripture and other ancient sources, forestalling the need to locate the processes of its production before biblical history or within the creation week. As long as the Deluge appeared to explain the earth's present surface, strata and fossil contents, a traditionally young earth combined with a literal creation week remained a viable understanding of terrestrial origins.

Beginning with Swiss scholar J. Scheuchzer's 1704 Latin translation, Woodward's theory was translated into various continental languages and penetrated the European mind deeply, making "the problem of the great Flood ... a truly burning question" in the first half of the eighteenth century."[37] If the Flood could account for presently observed landforms, strata and fossils, then the creation week could simp-

[34] Ray, *Further Correspondence*, 260.

[35] Rappaport, *Geologists*, 204f.

[36] John Woodward, *An Essay Toward a Natural History of the Earth* ... (London: R. Wilkin, 1695; reprint, Arno Press, 1978). For a contemporary study of Woodward, showing Woodward's debt to Steno, and comparing their relative merits, see J. Arbuthnot, *An Examination of Dr Woodward's Account of the Deluge* (London: printed for C. Bateman ... 1697).

[37] Vaccari, "European Views," 30–32; Zöckler, *Geschichte*, 2:170; Rappaport, *Geologists*, 156, 200.

ly be taken literally. "With what amounts to a shrug," says Rappaport, "J.J. Scheuchzer...admitted that "days" could mean anything from years to seconds; having no way to be sure of the meaning, he judged it best 'to accept the common hypothesis'."[38] Scheuchzer knew that the days of Genesis had been and could be taken figuratively and applied to longer periods of time, but as a diluvialist he felt under no pressure to do so. The same factor may help explain the easy retention of a literal creation week in a work such as the widely-read *History of the Heavens* (1740) by French abbot Noël Antoine Pluche.[39]

Bishop Robert Clayton, writing in 1754, rejected gradualistic models of the formation of the earth's topography into mountains and ocean basins by a retreating sea (offered by Frenchmen Le Cat and Buffon) as incompatible with the implied brevity of the Mosaic account: "There does not seem to have been sufficient Time, according to the Mosaical account, for the Formation of Mountains by the tedious Operation of the Flux and Reflux of the Sea.... So that we must either give up the Mosaical Account, or theirs."[40] He rejected Whiston's year-long days as in conflict with the Genesis narrative, in preference for ordinary twenty-four hour days and a Deluge that effected major morphological change.[41] Clayton's critic Alexander Catcott offered a quite different 'hyper-tectonic' model wherein the hollow shell of the earth cracked on Day 3 of creation and at the Deluge, allowing large quantities of water to pass through.[42] But he retained the same literal creation week, along with a sympathy for the world-week understanding of (coterminous) human and planetary history.[43]

Thus conservative interpreters proved able to re-subject turn-of-the-century geotheories to the Genesis version of events. As late as 1780, the naturalist J. Silberschlag in his *Geogenie* still rejected any stretching of the creation days, accounting for the strata of the earth's crust by means of the Deluge, a stance that would survive in the 'scriptural

[38] Ibid., 194.

[39] Noël Antoine Pluche, *The History of the Heavens, Considered according to the Notions of the Poets and Philosophers, Compared with the Doctrines of Moses...* 2 vols., vol. II (London: printed for J. Osborn... 1740), 2:239–57, ECCO; Zöckler, *Geschichte*, 2:172, 175.

[40] Robert Clayton, *A Vindication of the Histories of the Old and New Testament. Part II. Wherein the Mosaical History of the Creation and Deluge is Philosophically Explained...* (Dublin/London: reprinted for W. Bowyer, and sold by R. Baldwin, and M. Cooper, etc., 1754), 10, 13, ECCO.

[41] Ibid., 53–60, 74ff.

[42] Alexander Catcott, *Remarks on the Second Part of the Lord Bishop of Clogher's Vindication of the Histories of the Old and New Testament....* (London: sold by E. Withers, etc., 1756), 35, 42, 66–68, 77–79, ECCO; Collier, *Cosmogonies*, 234–41; Young, "Scripture in the Hands of Geologists," 21–23.

[43] Catcott, *Remarks*, 93–96. Cf. Clayton, *Vindication*, 73.

geologies' of the nineteenth century.[44] But a serious weakness in Woodward's diluvial model had been that it necessarily required the deposition of the content of the diluvial slurry in order of specific gravity. The evidence of the earth would not prove to be so simple: strata and fossils under investigation exhibited neither arrangement in order of specific gravity, nor the (relative) simplicity that would indicate their production by a single, though massive, geological event.[45] When the Deluge did not seem to be able to account for observed phenomena, other world-forming solutions were sought, and among biblical interpreters, both long chaos and long creation day options were pursued, either in earnest or as a protective guise.

Departures from Diluvialism

In the words of geologist Davis Young, "Diluvialism was not the aberrant theory of a fringe group; it was mainstream natural history and was espoused by some of the ablest naturalists of the time."[46] The French Huguenot Louis Bourguet (1678–1742) generally supported Woodwardian diluvialism in his *Mémoire sur la Théorie de la Terre* (1729), believing that all strata were formed by deposition in water, yet attributing sedimentation to more than one event.[47] Rappaport reports that Bourguet had come under pressure from Leibniz and Antonio Vallisnieri (1661–1730), both believers in some degree of 'deep time', and therefore made allowance for a year-long or longer creation day.[48] Vallisnieri himself "stated that the strata of the mountains had been due to the action of several floods.... [I]n his book, *De' Corpi Marini* (1721)...he attacked the rigidity of traditional Earth histories based on the Biblical chronology by reducing the role of the Deluge ... [and thus] paved the way for the future establishment of a relative chronology for the formation of mountains ... no longer strictly linked to the two Biblical stages of Creation and Deluge."[49]

The role of the Deluge was therefore being increasingly relativized, leading eventually to its employment as the last in a series of catastrophes, then in the nineteenth century its restriction to a mere superficial

[44] Zöckler, *Geschichte*, 2:188–93.

[45] Rappaport, *Geologists*, 156, 160, 200.

[46] Young, "Scripture in the Hands of Geologists," 23. Zöckler names Büttner and Stahl as among German supporters of the diluvial model in this period: Zöckler, *Geschichte*, 2:170.

[47] Vaccari, "European Views," 32; Zöckler, *Geschichte*, 2:175–76; Rappaport, *Geologists*, 158.

[48] Rappaport, *Geologists*, 195–96.

[49] Vaccari, "European Views," 32. Luigi Ferdinando Marsili was an Italian diluvialist who came around to the plurality of ancient catastrophes: ibid., 32–33.

influence on the landscape, and finally its disappearance from mainstream geology. The second half of the eighteenth century meanwhile witnessed a developing consensus about the major divisions of the earth's strata, which was the subject of studies by Johann Gottlob Lehmann (1719–67), Georg Christian Füchsel (1722–1773) and Abraham Gottlob Werner (1749–1817) in Germany, Giovanni Arduino (1714–95) in Italy and Pyotr Simon Pallas (1741–1811) in Russia. They described the earth's crust as composed of 'primary mountains', the crystalline, igneous rocks that were found at the highest elevations in European mountains and understood to underlie the rest, 'secondary mountains', which were sedimentary in nature and fossil-bearing, positioned on the flanks of the primary mountains, and eventually 'tertiary mountains', a less consolidated set of sedimentary deposits overlying the secondaries. The Flood was occupying an ever smaller part of such explanations, usually connected with merely the latter stages of strata formation.

Further impeding the viability of a diluvial model was the growing awareness of volcanic regions in Italy and central France. The pioneering French naturalists Jean-Étienne Guettard (1715–86), Nicholas Desmarest (1735–1815) and Jean-Louis Giraud-Soulavie (1752–1813) discovered in the central French regions of Auvergne and Vivarais volcanoes whose formation had evidently involved multiple active episodes separated by long periods of erosion, and all complete before human memory or the construction of man-made (e.g. Roman) structures.[50] The impression of deep time imparted by accumulated volcanic formations reached British audiences through accounts of active Italian volcanoes: Patrick Brydone's *Tour through Sicily and Malta* (1773) and William Hamilton's *Campi Phlegraei* (1776).[51] References to the obviously contentious and sometimes arbitrary implications of these sources begin to appear in English writings in the same decade.[52]

[50] E.g. Rudwick, *Bursting the Limits*, 203–26; Young and Stearley, *Bible, Rocks and Time*, 79–80; Karl Alfred von Zittel, *History of Geology and Palaeontology to the End of the Nineteenth Century*, trans. Maria M. Ogilvie-Gordon (London: Walter Scott, 1901), 39–40, GB, http://books.google.com/books?lr=&id=0z28AAAAIAAJ.

[51] The latter work is the source of the impressive colour sketch of a lava flow at night that adorns the cover of Rudwick, *Bursting the Limits*, 36, 119–22, also 667. See also Dean, "Age of the Earth," 451–52; Davies, *Earth in Decay*, 99; Porter, *Making of Geology*, 99,159. Brydone's report of Canon Recupero's assumptions about Mt. Etna's development would be criticised for its faulty logic, but appears to have still been influential. See for example the complaint by Andrew Ure, *A New System of Geology....* (London: Longman, Rees, Orme, Brown, & Green, 1829), xlv, http://books.google.com.au/books?id=MULPAAAAMAAJ.

[52] E.g. Richard Watson, *An Apology for Christianity in a Series of Letters, Addressed to Edward Gibbon, esq., Author of The Decline and Fall of the Roman Empire* (Cambridge:

The explanatory shortfall of Noah's Flood left an evidently very busy prior earth history to be biblically accounted for in terms either of the chaos prior to the creation week, or of the creation week itself (or even the period between the creation week and the Deluge). Rudwick explains:

> When, in the course of the eighteenth century, it seemed to savants to be increasingly likely that the earth had existed long before the few millennia of recorded human history, the "days" of creation were simply reinterpreted ... as periods of distinctive character but indefinite extension. Alternatively, the initial act of creation out of "chaos" [or better, *of* the chaos] was assumed to have been followed by an unrecorded period of vast but indefinite duration, before the humanly more important events of the rest of the narrative.[53]

I have nuanced Rudwick's words here, because an eternal chaos prior to any creative action of God was not mainstream Christian belief, Milton's vagueness notwithstanding. The chaos was seen as the first-stage product of God's creative work, prior to the more specific acts of the creation week.

The developing chaos concept of late seventeenth-century geotheories, aided by Woodward's alertness to the agency of water in fossil and strata formation, mutated into the eighteenth-century diminishing ocean model of the formation of the earth's crust. Rudwick finds "geotheories based on a falling global sea level [to be] so general" that he labels them "the *standard model*."[54] This model achieved supremacy over simple diluvialism "by midcentury," when attribution of the stratified formations to "the biblical Flood had been generally abandoned. However, Woodward's basic idea of a sequential deposition or precipitation of the Secondary formations, from a proto-ocean that had subsided gradually to its present level, remained intact."[55]

This diminishing ocean model received added impetus from Swedish intellectuals such as Emanuel Swedenborg (1688–1772), Anders Celsius (1701–44), and Carl Linnaeus (1707–78), encouraged by the local phenomenon of the progressive fall in the level of the Baltic Sea.[56]

printed by J. Archdeacon printer to the University, for T. and J. Merrill, and J. Woodyer ... 1776), 255, 262, GB, http://books.google.com/books?id= 3MAvt_UW4XwC.

[53] For the first two options, see Rudwick, *Bursting the Limits*, 117.

[54] Ibid., 173.

[55] Ibid., 175–76.

[56] Rappaport, *Geologists*, 226–28; Zöckler, *Geschichte*, 2:170; Vaccari, "European Views," 33. Linnaeus defends the diminishing ocean model in his 1744 speech: Carl Linnaeus, 1707–78, "Oratio de Telluris habitabilis incremento (1744)," in *L'Équilibre de la Nature*, ed. Camille Limoges, trans. B. Jasmin, L'Histoire des Sciences: Textes et Études (Paris: Librairie Philosophique J. Vrin, 1972), 29–55. See esp. sections 27, 44–45, 97. The

In the final edition of his *Systema naturae*, Linnaeus wrote, "I can find no relic of a deluge, but many of the greatest antiquity [of the earth]."[57] His *Philosophia botanica* merely attests the fixity of species and the original creation of one male and female pair of each, without making any further reference to the Genesis text, despite Greene's reference to a reconciling scheme.[58] For a naturalist of the stature of Linnaeus to have largely avoided handling the Genesis texts is a telling example of the divergence between sacred history and earth history that was well underway on the Continent by the mid-eighteenth century.

While 'primary rocks' might be treated as original to creation or as the earliest precipitations from the primordial ocean according to this scheme, and the early 'geognost' Lehmann might still attribute secondary mountains (*Flötzgebirge*) to the Deluge, the more refined diminishing ocean model of Pallas merely allowed that the superficial 'tertiaries' had a diluvial origin.[59] It can hardly be emphasized enough that the primordial ocean and the Deluge were seen as entirely distinct causes connected to different stages of earth history, and their frequent conflation under the rubric, 'diluvialism', only clouds the picture. The geological teaching of the famous Werner assumed a diminishing ocean model when he taught the step-by-step precipitation of the various rock types in turn from the primordial fluid, a model that became known as Neptunism, which could stand virtually independent of Genesis.[60] Where such a series of depositions was imagined to occur sequentially prior to the creation week, i.e. where a long initial chaos was differentiated in proto-geological terms, the result was what came to be called the ruin-restitution or 'gap theory', to be treated below.[61]

Benoît de Maillet's (1656–1738) *Telliamed* was published posthumously in 1748, although it had been quietly circulated for some time.[62] The title 'Telliamed', ostensibly that of the 'Indian philosopher'

falling sea level in the Baltic is now interpreted as a rise in the level of the land itself in the wake of its relief from Ice Age glaciation.

[57] The saying is 'Diluvii vestigia cerno nulla, aevi vetustissimi plurima.' Haber, 159–60; Rupke, *Great Chain*, 57–58; 'Review of The Testimony of Natural Theology to Christianity by Thomas Gisborne (London, 1818),' *Quarterly Review* 41 (January 1819), 54.

[58] Carl Linnaeus, *Philosophia botanica* (Vienna: Ioannis Thomae Trattner, 1755), 80, 99. See Greene, *Death of Adam*, 133, 136.

[59] Rudwick, *Bursting the Limits*, 176–77.

[60] Ibid., 175.

[61] Charles Lyell, *Principles of Geology* (London: John Murray, 1830–33; reprint, Philadelphia: James Kay, Jun. and Brother, 1837), 57–64, GB, http://books.google.com/books?id=AOcJAAAAMAAJ; von Zittel, *History of Geology*, 34–38; Rudwick, *Bursting the Limits*, 90–94, 173–80; Young and Stearley, *Bible, Rocks and Time*, 71–76; Dean, "Age of the Earth," 449; Vaccari, "European Views," 34.

[62] Benoît de Maillet, *Telliamed: or, Discourses between an Indian Philosopher and a French Missionary, on the Diminution of the Sea, the Formation of the Earth, the Origin of Men and Animals....* (London: T. Osborne, 1750), ECCO. See Andre Wakefield, introduction to

of the subtitle, was clearly a thinly disguised self-reference, being simply de Maillet's own name spelled backwards. De Maillet envisaged diminution of the oceans through evaporation into space, estimated the rate involved, and extrapolated it backwards to establish an (immense) age for the earth.[63] His broader cosmology is a distinctly Cartesian, eternalistic, cyclical one, in which our earth constitutes a burnt-out sun and will one day return to being a sun.[64] The present diminution of earth's waters thus becomes a tiny slice of time in a virtually eternal process.[65] De Maillet portrays these ideas, rather appropriately, as those of an Indian philosopher, 'Telliamed', who converses with the ostensibly anonymous French writer over a course of six discourses entitled, 'Day One', 'Day Two' and so on.[66] This is, I think, an ironic gesture in the direction of the hexaemeral literature, since the content of these discourses only sporadically corresponds to the content of the creation days.[67]

De Maillet explains the days of creation as a metaphorical scheme, not as if "they were accomplished in the Space of Six Days, or of six Revolutions of our Globe round its Center." The absence of the sun in the creation account before Day 4 is (as usual) the clue that, "the Word *Day* is in that Part used improperly, metaphorically, and to signify the Succession with which the Supreme Intelligence executed the different Works there mentioned."[68] He confesses a general kind of correspondence between the shapeless initial mass, darkness upon the deep, the Spirit's motion on the waters, and the separation of the waters of the Genesis account, and the earth's actual physical development. De Maillet describes land as initially forming under the water, and vegetation appearing as the waters retreat, followed by animal and finally human life. Each increasingly complex order of life arises from the prior, simpler one, which was a genuinely evolutionary picture of life's development. De Maillet offers it self-consciously, however, as an

Leibniz, *Protogaea*, xxviii; Greene, *Death of Adam*, 346, n. 320; von Zittel, *History of Geology*, 33.

[63] De Maillet, *Telliamed*, 128–29. A quick calculation on the basis of the present height of Mt. Everest, compared with his stated rate of diminution, produces a figure near ten million years. The translation by A.V. Carozzi is from the original and restores the figure of two billion years that was originally in the manuscript. See Rappaport, *Geologists*, 229; Young, "Scripture in the Hands of Geologists," 258; Dean, "Age of the Earth," 447.

[64] De Maillet, *Telliamed*, 4, etc.

[65] Ibid., 176–205.

[66] Ibid., xlvii–lii.

[67] One example of such isolated exceptions is the treatment of human origins under 'Day Six'.

[68] Ibid., xxxvi f., 281.

idea that many will think it absurd, and his description does little to avoid confirming this impression.[69]

De Maillet does not sound sure that a satisfactory concord between such a developmental picture of world origins and the Bible is achievable, since if this globe is the work of the sea, it seems to follow that "you must renounce the History of the Creation, such as we read it in *Genesis*."[70] But things are not really so bleak: "It would be easy to shew, that if the system of *Telliamed* concerning the Origin of the Earth, is not entirely conformable to the Mosaic History of the Creation, yet it is not absolutely contrary to it."[71] In reality, his explanation of earth origins had not simply abandoned the traditional brief timescale, the Mosaic Deluge, and literal creation days, but had overthrown any discrete beginning to the world such as Gen. 1:1–2:3 presents and had evacuated the sequence of the days of all but the vaguest meaning.

Just as gradualistic and virtually as eternalistic, but now prioritizing the agency of heat, the 'Theory of the Earth' of Georges Louis Leclerc, comte de Buffon (1707–88), also appeared in 1749.[72] Buffon has been described as "the leading French naturalist of his day," and the geothery that opens his massive *Histoire Naturelle* as the most influential mid-century entry in the genre.[73] Buffon avoids making connections with the biblical creation texts, with the Leibnizian exception of relating the separation of light and darkness in Gen. 1:4 to the detaching of opaque proto-planets from the luminous sun, as solar material thrown into orbit by the impact of a comet. The earth, then, cools to its present form from an initially molten state, an idea Buffon owes and attributes to Leibniz.[74] Water eventually condenses upon the earth's surface, and by the action of the seas the strata are laid down much as Steno explained. The various kinds of life have a near-simultaneous origin, and

[69] Ibid., xxxv, 281; Leibniz, *Protogaea*, 14–15. See prior treatment of Leibniz and notes for documentation of the publication history of *Protogaea*. On his evolutionary ideas, see Peter J. Bowler, *Evolution: The History of an Idea* (Berkeley: University of California Press, 1984), 65. See also Zöckler, *Geschichte*, 2:239–40. Zöckler regards de Maillet as the main figure in the formation of the 'Descendenz' or evolutionary idea prior to Lamarck.

[70] De Maillet, *Telliamed*, xxxiii. Likewise, an eternal world "seems to combat what the Scriptures teach us concerning the Origin of the World. " Ibid., xxxiv.

[71] Ibid., xxxiv–xxxv.

[72] Rossi, *Dark Abyss*, 85. I have utilised Georges Louis Leclerc Buffon, Comte de, *Barr's Buffon. Buffon's Natural History, Containing a Theory of the Earth, a General History of Man,...From the French. With Notes by the Translator*, 10 vols., vol. I (London: printed by J. S. Barr, 1792), ECCO.

[73] E.g. McCalla, *Creationist Debate*, 56; Rappaport, *Geologists*, 250; Porter, *Making of Geology*, 105; Collier, *Cosmogonies*, 204.

[74] Buffon, *Buffon's Natural History*, 1:75–114, 144f., 184; Leibniz, *Protogaea*, 6. For general background and the relationship to Leibniz, see Rappaport, *Geologists*, 242; Rudwick, *Bursting the Limits*, 142; Toulmin and Goodfield, *The Discovery of Time*, 146; Andre Wakefield, introduction to Leibniz, *Protogaea*, xxxvii–xxxviii.

sea and land have exchanged places in the past and steadily continue to do so.

Buffon distances himself from Burnet and Woodward and objects that Whiston's extraordinary 'system' "has…strangely blended the divine knowledge with human science."[75] Any physical explanation of the Deluge, he claims, mistakenly allows philosophy to meddle with what the Bible describes as a miracle.[76] Buffon's interpretation of the past exclusively on the analogy of present processes leaves unique and unrepeatable events such as the Flood out of consideration, a move intended more to safeguard 'physical inquiry' from clerical interference than to protect biblical miracles from the intrusion of philosophy.[77] Buffon's conclusion goes beyond a merely antique earth towards eternalism: "It is impossible to doubt … that an infinite number of revolutions, particular changes and alterations, have happened on the surface of the globe." The 'revolutions' envisaged include the repeated interchange of land and sea, an idea with a legacy stretching back to Aristotle.[78] Our lives represent a mere instant by comparison, "a single fact in the history of the acts of the Almighty."[79] This "profoundly ahistorical" theory owes nothing to the biblical creation account, but exemplifies the "increasingly naturalistic," and importantly, dynamic rather than steady-state, Enlightenment perception of the earth's physical development. Enlightenment thinkers "began to view the Earth increasingly as a theatre of active processes," rather than a completed, changeless edifice constructed by God for the residence of humanity.[80]

[75] Buffon, *Buffon's Natural History*, 1:127–28. Whiston's theory was evidently still a potent force, and certainly has echoes in Buffon's own, in particular in the role of a comet in the constitution of the solar system.

[76] Ibid., 1:153–54.

[77] Ibid., 1:40.

[78] Sister Suzanne Kelly, "The Rise of Historical Geology in the Seventeenth Century," in *Toward a History of Geology*, ed. C. Schneer (Cambridge, MA: MIT Press, 1969), 219.

[79] Buffon, *Buffon's Natural History*, 2:253–54.

[80] Porter, *Making of Geology*, 109–10; Rossi, *Dark Abyss*, 56, 64–65; Rappaport, *Geologists*, 208. The 'profoundly ahistorical' comment belongs to Rudwick, *Bursting the Limits*, 148–49. In 1750 another Frenchman, Le Cat, offered another diminishing ocean model that seemed to have moved close to the later gap theory, with the geological ages fitted into Genesis 1 prior to the creation week. Tidal influences of the sun and moon, he thought, undermined the solid surface of the globe, leaving a mere shell, and then the surface completely collapsed into the abyss thus created, leaving 'a new chaos', a world perished in water as in 2 Peter 3, "from which a renewal of the planet then followed," Zöckler, *Geschichte*, 2:176. For more on Le Cat, see Collier, *Cosmogonies*, 224–25; Porter, *Making of Geology*, 101, 105, 109, 117.

Expanding the Creation Week: Examples Prior to Mid-Century

Defying the impetus to sharply distinguish natural and theological kinds of knowledge, which was Denis Diderot's plea in his *Encyclopédie*, was the quest to clearly distinguish theology and philosophy, was the quest by some to seek a harmony between Genesis and natural data by expanding the duration of the days of creation.[81] Where diluvialism and a literal creation week were no longer believed tenable, persisting faith in the Mosaic record might yield concordist interpretations of Gen. 1:1–2:3. In the wake of the pre-1700 pioneers of the long creation day option comes the scientific paper, 'An Attempt to Find the Age of the World by the Saltness of the Sea' (1715) by Edmund Halley (1656–1742), an important early member of the Royal Society.[82] On the way to suggesting a natural mechanism for establishing terrestrial chronology based on accumulation of salt in the oceans, Halley opens his argument as follows:

> There have been many Attempts made to ascertain, from the Appearances of Nature, what may have been the Antiquity of this Globe of *Earth*; on which, by the Evidence of Sacred Writ, *Mankind* has dwelt about 6000 Years; or according to the *Septuagint*, above 7000. But whereas we are there told that the Formation of *Man* was the last Act of the CREATOR, 'tis no where revealed in Scripture how long the Earth had existed before this last Creation, nor how long those five Days that preceded it may be accounted; since we are elsewhere told, that in respect of the Almighty a thousand Years is as one Day, being equally no part of *Eternity:* Nor can it well be conceived how those Days should be to be understood of natural Days, since they are mentioned as Measures of Time before the Creation of the Sun, which was not till the fourth Day. And 'tis certain *Adam* found the *Earth*, at his first Production, fully replenished with all sorts of other *Animals*.[83]

Halley's overt polemical purpose is not directed at a short biblical chronology, but opposition to Aristotelian eternalism. "[T]he forego-

[81] Denis Diderot, "Mosaïque et chrétienne philosophie," in *Encyclopédie, ou dictionnaire raisonné des sciences, des arts et des métiers*, ed. Denis Diderot and Jean le Rond D'Alembert (Paris: Briasson, David, Le Breton, Durand, 1765), ARTFL Encyclopédie Projet (winter 2008 edition), Robert Morrissey (ed), University of Chicago, http://artfl.uchicago.edu/cgi-bin/philologic31/getobject.pl?c.78:16.encyclopedie1108. The *Encyclopédie* article on Genesis is about four lines in extent, whereas the article 'Déluge' by Nicolas-Antoine Boulanger, incorporating all of the big names in geotheory at the time, from Burnet, Whiston, Woodward on down, is long and thorough.

[82] Davies, *Earth in Decay*, 98.

[83] Edmund Halley, "An Attempt to find the Age of the World by the Saltness of the Sea," in *The Philosophical Transactions (from the year 1700 to the year 1720) Abridg'd and Dispos'd under General Heads. Vol V. containing Part I. The Anatomical and Medical Papers, Part II. The Philological and Miscellaneous Papers*, ed. Henry Jones (London: G. Strahan, etc., 1721), 216, http://books.google.com/books?id=o1AVAAAAQAAJ.

ing Argument ... is chiefly intended to refute the ancient Notion, some have of late entertained, of the Eternity of all Things; though perhaps by it the world may be found much older than many have hitherto imagined."[84] An eternal, and therefore uncreated, world was a greater contradiction to biblical creation than an older than expected world with a definite beginning. Still, Halley is evidently conscious of breaking with the young-earth tradition, and is loath to have his stance mistaken for an eternalistic one.

Roy Porter unearthed a little-known geotheory entitled *Earth Generated and Atomized* (1715) by one William Hobbs.[85] It combines empirical observation of a certain coastal district of southern England with an organic view of the earth as a whole, complete with its own 'heartbeat'.[86] Hobbs denies that it is possible to sequentially list the creation of the parts of a growing organism; all parts develop simultaneously.[87] Therefore "the designe of Moses, was not so much to ascertaine, an exact Mechanick, or literall Order, for makeing the Heavens, and the Earth; as to convince and Assure us, That they were made, & Not Eternall."[88] The chronological framework of Gen. 1:1–2:3 is a kind of anthropomorphism, "as when parts, passions, and Members are ascribed, to the Creator of all Things ... only to Sute or adapt Things, to the weak capacity of humane understanding." On the analogy of the statement in 2 Peter 3 that a thousand years with the Lord are as one day, "it is very probable, That the first Three Dayes, might at least be as many hundred times Longer than now they are."[89]

Hobbs was convinced that the strata were formed level by precipitation from the primordial chaotic fluid, while organisms were incorporated into these strata as they died.[90] Once hardened, the strata were evidently disrupted and heaved upwards, forming land masses, a process captured in the creation description of Day 3.[91] Thus the earth probably existed "many hundred years ... before it was fully formed ... all great Animalls were generated before the Hills were raised ... whilst the hills & Mountains were *gradually* buding forth." Yet the absence of remains of terrestrial flora and fauna from deeper strata show that the

[84] Ibid., 218–19. Burnet shared the same concern: Stephen Jay Gould, ed., "On Rereading Edmund Halley," in *Eight Little Piggies* (London: Jonathan Cape, 1993), 168–79.

[85] William Hobbs, *Earth Generated and Atomized*, ed. Roy Porter (London/Ithaca: British Museum/Cornell University Press, 1981 [1715]); Roberts, "Genesis of John Ray," 147; Roberts, "Genesis Chapter 1," 41.

[86] Hobbs, *Earth Generated and Atomized*, 53f., 61f.

[87] Ibid., 40–41.

[88] Ibid., 42.

[89] Ibid., 110–11.

[90] Ibid., 39.

[91] Ibid., 47–50.

land areas were not elevated above sea level until after sea creatures had existed for some time. Therefore "these Trees and Land Animalls must be generated after the Rocks were hardened."[92] Woodwardian-style diluvialism is inadequate: "the waters of the Deluge ... could not naturally ... dissolve the Rocks and Mountains of the Earth, and mingle and immass the shells thereinto ..."[93] Hobbs thus forms an interesting amalgam of old and new, an organic earth full of vivifying influences and Paracelsian principles, and an up-to-date theory of truly organic fossils and strata deposition. These factors together led Hobbs to a liberal treatment of the creation days that is significant as a specimen of an intelligent layman's home-grown, eclectic, early Modern interpretation of Gen. 1:1–2:3.

On the basis of connections such as the appearance of land on Day 3 or the appearance of life on Days 5–6, a diminishing ocean geotheoretical model could be incorporated into a more systematic day-age or periodic day interpretation of the creation week. This could also be done using geotheoretical models oriented to the agency of heat rather than water, sometimes called 'Plutonist' models. Vallisnieri included earthquakes and subterranean fires among his possible agencies of geological change, and another Italian, Anton Lazzaro Moro (1687–1764), offered a purely Plutonist theory of the earth.[94] Having rejected diluvialism, he proposed a harmonizing scheme whereby eras in earth history equated to the days of creation.[95] Particularly important were the appearance of land on 'Day 3' by means of volcanic uplift and the flourishing of life on Days 5–6 as conditions on land settled down.[96]

Thus Moro's 1740 *De' crostacei* represents a significant step forward in the development of a day-age harmonizing interpretation of Genesis, where the additional time apparently required to explain present terrestrial phenomena, assuming the insufficiency of the Deluge, is found within an ostensible pre-human scriptural history, within a figuratively expanded creation week.[97] "Although each day was thus an epoch, Moro could not estimate duration, and he used phrases like 'hundreds of years' and 'thousands of years'."[98] This was a significant

[92] Ibid., 111–12.

[93] Ibid., 113, also 150.

[94] Vaccari, "European Views," 33. He was in fact the first to distinguish 'primary' and 'secondary' mountains, to be followed by Arduino and Lehmann: Rossi, *Dark Abyss*, 83; Davies, *Earth in Decay*, 106.

[95] Rappaport, *Geologists*, 221.

[96] Collier, *Cosmogonies*, 188–90.

[97] Rappaport, *Geologists*, 195, 223–25. Rossi notes that Moro's work preceded that of de Maillet, Buffon, Guettard and Boulanger: Rossi, *Dark Abyss*, 85. See his whole section, pp. 75–85.

[98] Rappaport, *Geologists*, 224.

step further away from a literal interpretation of Genesis 1 than Whiston had taken, and married a figurative scheme of the days to a punctuated geological account, thus paving the way for later interpretations.

Therefore the instinct for periodization belonging to the ancient world-week tradition of allegorization of Gen. 1:1–2:3 was being repositioned *prior* to human history. The earth's physical formation, rather than human and redemptive history, was now broken up into periods of something in order of a thousand years, and punctuated by crises that produced a dramatic change from one state into the next. The world-week, combined with deep time and the diluvial carry-over of catastrophic change, yielded the day-age concordist approach to Gen. 1:1–2:3. Augustine had shown that the days could be figurative even within the literal sense; the Renaissance Platonists had revived a similar perspective, and Whiston had formally offered a scheme of semi-literal, expanded creation days. Now Moro had passed right through the door opened by Whiston, using the creation week to periodize a primitive geological history of earth.

The Fading Flower: Eighteenth-Century Biblical Universal Histories

The instinct to periodize *human* history, however, was not yet at an end. Universal histories maintained considerable vigour in the early eighteenth century, but their traditional commitment to the primacy of the biblical framework of history was under the relativizing pressure of an ever-expanding awareness of the multiplicity of ethnic traditions of indigenous origins. The relative importance of the biblical creation account was destined steadily to diminish when compared with the histories or chronologies of the seventeenth century, in which the creation week often constituted an important first period in the history of the world.

One indication of this decline of the importance of biblical creation in the universal histories was that some authors would bracket off biblical creation as not falling within the definition of history. Nicolaus Lenglet Dufresnoy's *Chronological Tables of Universal History*, published in France around 1743, treated aspects of the creation period with some impatience, declaring, "But … this cannot be called history … we must … attend to what is really historical," and begins his genuine history with the Deluge.[99] Creation recedes to single sentence statements for each of the creation days in Thomas Hearne's *Ductor historicus*

[99] Nicolas Lenglet Dufresnoy, *Chronological Tables of Universal History, Sacred and Profane, Ecclesiastical and Civil; from the Creation of the World…* (London: printed for A. Millar, etc., 1762), ii–v, ECCO.

(1704–5).[100] Frenchman Antoine-Yves Goguet begins his historical coverage in the post-diluvian era, while OT events continue to function as "an expedient framework" for the structuring of ancient history, in the tradition of earlier histories such as Bossuet's. Tamara Griggs explains, "By choosing to begin not with Creation, but with the "first ages" after the Flood, Goguet made sure that the workings of God in the world and in the history of mankind took a back seat to the story of how humans established and perfected laws, arts, and sciences over time."[101] A less abrupt approach was to extract the creation week from the main text and treat it in a preface, as Samuel Shuckford elected to do.[102]

Sometimes the treatment of creation in a universal history was brief precisely because it was conservative. Dom Augustine Calmet's long *Histoire Universelle* (1735–47) treats creation warmly and concisely, displaying the traditional belief about the time involved in creation: it takes place *dans l'espace de six jours*, from the initial material of formless, chaotic matter, with no word about how long that matter remained formless.[103] When Thomas Stackhouse in *A New History of the Holy Bible* (1742–44), describes creation as "successive and gradual," he still means that it occurs "in the Space of *six Days*."[104] He explicitly adheres to Ussher's chronology, as does John Adams, while Calmet offers his own 4000 BC creation chronology.[105] When Stackhouse describes creation days as gradual, it is because the rival view is still that of an instantaneous creation.[106]

It was common to emphasize the chaos more than Calmet's simple mention. Shuckford's mini-hexaemeron describes how the Earth was initially "a confused and indigested Mass of Matter" for an indefinite period, "But God in six days reduced it into a world."[107] Stackhouse adopts an emphatic long-lasting chaos concept, following Burnet, and

[100] Thomas Hearne, *Ductor Historicus: or, A Short System of Universal History, and an Introduction to the Study of It*, 2nd ed., 2 vols., vol. I (London: printed for Tim. Childe ... 1704–1705), 225–26, ECCO.

[101] Tamara Griggs, "Universal History from Counter-Reformation to Enlightenment," *Modern Intellectual History* 4 (2007): 240–42. Goguet's work was titled, *De l'origine des loix, des arts, et des sciences, et de leurs progrès chez les anciens peuples* (1758).

[102] Samuel Shuckford, *The Sacred and Prophane History of the World Connected, from the Creation of the World to the Dissolution of the Assyrian Empire* ... 3 vols., vol. I (London: printed for R. Knaplock ... 1728–30), xxxv, ECCO. See Collier, *Cosmogonies*, ch. 20, 193–203.

[103] Augustin Calmet, *Histoire universelle, sacrée et profane: Depuis le commencement du monde jusqu'à nos jours*, vol. I (Strasbourg: Jean Renaud Doulssecker, 1735), 1–2. Likewise, Adams, *Universal History*, 1.

[104] Stackhouse, *New History*, 1.12. See Roberts, "Genesis Chapter 1," 42.

[105] Adams, *Universal History*, 1; Calmet, *Commentarius Litteralis*, xxxiii.

[106] Stackhouse, *New History*, 1:13.

[107] Shuckford, *Sacred and Prophane History*, 1:xxxv–xxxvi.

evidences belief in a pre-existing angelic order as did the early Dutch Arminians.[108] The earth's formation out of the chaos through the creation week follows the familiar 'settling chaos' model, with the sun and its six planets forming from their respective 'chaoses' and simultaneously reaching completion on the fourth day.[109] Stackhouse combines his literal creation week with a strong chaos concept without embarrassment and limits the scope of the creation account to our solar system. Hence Michael Roberts is mistaken to treat long chaos and literal creation week beliefs as mutually exclusive in this context.[110]

The question of valid sources for a universal history was up for debate. John Adams begins his history gravely,

> An authentic account of the creation of the world, and of the primitive state of man, is only to be found in the sacred records. There we are informed by Moses, the most ancient of all historians, that after the earth, by the immediate operation of the supreme Being, was gradually fitted, in the space of six days, for the habitation of man, Adam and Eve ... were then created.[111]

Moses' record is the most ancient "extant" record available in Shuckford's view, but he describes what other ancient records say about origins, treating them as generally reconcilable with the Mosaic record.[112]

A similar stance appears in the anonymous and enormous *An Universal History*, a work that from its first volume's publication in 1736 took until 1768 to complete in its final sixty-six volumes. Griggs reports that the first volume's author was George Sale, and Jaki regards it, along with Calmet's *Histoire Universelle*, as "the last major attempt to pigeonhole history, geological and political, into biblical chronology."[113] The substantial treatment of cosmogony in the preface begins with a long survey of pagan cosmogonies, arranged so as to finish with those ancient witnesses who believe "that the world had a beginning, being absolutely produced by GOD out of a state of non-existence, and ... liable to dissolution," i.e. who are nearest to a biblical metaphysic.[114]

[108] Stackhouse, *New History*, 1:1–3.

[109] Ibid., 1:5–7. Stackhouse limits the creation account to the earth, moon, sun and the planets of the solar system out to Saturn, which was the outermost known planet until William Herschel's discovery of Uranus in 1781.

[110] Roberts, "Genesis Chapter 1," 42. Perhaps by 'rigid six days', Roberts means those views that incorporated even Gen. 1:1–2 within the first day of creation.

[111] Adams, *Universal History*, 1.

[112] Shuckford, *Sacred and Prophane History*, 1:xxxviii ff.

[113] Griggs, "Universal History," 229, 234; Immanuel Kant, *Universal Natural History and Theory of the Heavens*, trans. S.L. Jaki (Edinburgh: Scottish Academic Press, 1981), 249, n. 225.

[114] *An Universal History*, 1:64–71.

"And now," says Sale at this point, "we come to the only authentic and genuine history of the creation; which has been left us by *Moses,* and carries with it all the marks of truth and probability, even though it be regarded only as a human composition, and separate from divine authority."[115] A summary of the events of the creation week follows this important concession, wherein "GOD, in the space of six days, disposed and reduced [the original chaos] into the present form of the world." He continues,

> This is the substance of what *Moses* has delivered concerning the creation of the world; which being short, and rather suited to the capacities of the people he designed to instruct, than written for the satisfaction of a philosophic enquirer, has left room for various explications, and the setting up of several very different hypotheses.[116]

The principle of accommodation therefore leaves room for the enterprise of geotheory, and Sale proceeds to survey the schemes of Descartes, Burnet and Whiston before offering his own personal cosmogony, based on the classic natural settling of the chaos through the creation week.[117] Then comes the bone of contention:

> Whether all this was really done in the space of six days, has been a question; some ... thinking it much too short for such a work, and others too long, supposing, that the world was created in a moment, and that *Moses* extends it to six days, the better to help the imagination of the people, that things may seem to rise in some order and method, and to take off any image of haste, or precipitancy. But we cannot see any reason to depart from the letter of *Moses* in this particular, the creation being described by him being not the creation of the substance of all things out of nothing, which was most probably the effect of one individual act, but the formation of one world, or system only, out of matter before created.[118]

We are at a significant point, hinted at already in More's *Conjectura Cabbalistica*: the reality of the creation days continues to be a point for debate, but the traditional alternative of instantaneous creation, still uppermost in Sale's mind, is about to give way to the new alternative, a 'deep time' perspective that will make six days seem too short a time for creation, rather than too long. Signs of development in the natural world would accumulate at an ever-accelerating rate, and a materialist focus submerge the Platonic idealism integral to the instantaneous creation position. The Genesis account was being safeguarded by being

[115] Ibid., 1:72. It seems that the defence of Moses' general credibility was already entailing the surrendering of a strict claim for his divinely inspired authority.

[116] Ibid., 1:73–74.

[117] Ibid., 1:85–88.

[118] Ibid., 1:100. The exact overlap with Stackhouse's work suggests Stackhouse's possible dependence upon this work.

limited in its scope, applied only to the earth or the solar system. But this shrinking sphere diminished its grandeur, and no well-known universal history after the mid-seventeenth century would again give such prominence to the issue of cosmogony or to the Genesis account.

Eighteenth-Century Mystical Interpretation of Genesis

Benjamin Parker in 1745 spent the closing section of his above-mentioned *Survey of the Six Days Works* opposing a 'mystical Divinity' (we might say Gnostic) that allegorizes the food provided on Day 6 and makes the first 'Adam' a purely spiritual and sexless being who 'fell' into physicality.[119] His comments are addressed to the Rev. William Law (d. 1761), who was connected with Methodism and respected for his piety, but for Parker represents all the dangers and excesses of 'enthusiasm'.[120] Law was heir to that mystical stream of theology that found hidden and deeply significant meanings in the early chapters of Genesis, specifically through Jacob Böhme.[121] This stream is sometimes labelled 'theosophy', defined in the *ODCC* "in its wider application ... [as] any intuitive knowledge of the Divine," covering "a number of religious and philosophical systems closely akin to pantheism and natural mysticism. Thus the teaching of Buddha, Plotinus, and the Gnostics in antiquity, and of John Scotus Eriugena, J. Boehme (the 'Teutonic Theosopher'), E. Swedenborg, and others in more recent times may be called Theosophy."[122] It is perhaps testament to the prestige of Genesis in these circles that the last three figures all offered significant interpretations of Genesis. Two of Böhme's eighteenth-century theosophical disciples were Emanuel Swedenborg and F.C. Oetinger.

Emanuel Swedenborg (1688–1772) first published his eccentric interpretation of Genesis in the *Arcana Coelestia* in Latin in eight volumes from 1749. Swedenborg was a brilliant polymath who in earlier scientific works had anticipated important discoveries usually associated with later figures such as Herschel, Kant and Laplace. He had also offered a mechanistic model of the formation of the universe in the tradition of Descartes in his 1734 *Principia*.[123] Following a spiritual crisis in the period 1743–45, however, Swedenborg became increasingly immersed in the mystical vision of Christianity which appears in the *Arcana*. Swe-

[119] Parker, *Six Days Works*, 266ff.

[120] See esp. ibid., 274–76, 285–86. Pp. 276–85 feature an extensive quote from John Locke on the dangers of enthusiasm, of which Parker names Wesley and Whitefield as examples.

[121] The connection is explicit at ibid., 274.

[122] Cross and Livingstone, eds., *ODCC*, 1364–65. The article goes on to apply the term more strictly to the movement initiated by Madame Blavatsky.

[123] Collier, *Cosmogonies*, 182–84.

denborg testified to contact with spirits and angels, to which he refers regularly in the *Arcana,* and believed himself both initiated into heavenly secrets and commissioned to reveal these to the world through his writings.[124] His mysticism translates into a purely allegorical treatment of Genesis and Exodus in the *Arcana.* The days of creation in Swedenborg's scheme are stages in the regeneration or enlightenment of man, culminating in the 'celestial man' of the seventh day.[125] "Scarcely anyone" amongst the regenerate reaches the seventh state.[126] It is clear from early on that Swedenborg sees himself as one of the privileged few, not an uncommon feature of mystical experience.

Swedenborg's interpretation of the Genesis text represents a sort of radicalized medieval style of moral or existential allegory at a time when literal readings mostly held the field. He regards the literal sense as barren and dead, a mere cover for the true mysteries. His lack of citations makes it impossible to know how dependent the widely read Swedenborg was on the allegorical tradition of the church, and he paints his exegesis as an original revelation. One motivation of his interpretive approach may be a perception that the turn to the literal sense that had occurred during the Renaissance and Reformation threatened to render the OT irrelevant to the Christian reader.[127] Personally Swedenborg seems to be reacting against his own Enlightenment rationalism in a hyper-spiritual direction. The resemblance of his teaching to earlier figures such as Böhme is distinct, though not explicit, and his 'fantastic journey' certainly takes him beyond the bounds of the Christian orthodoxy of the day into realms of Gnostic or Manichaean dualism wherein the physical world and the spiritual world are a mutually necessary, corresponding, eternal pair of entities.[128]

The influence of Böhme and Swedenborg sowed the seed for a German stream of theosophy that would eventually yield the ruin-restitution interpretation offered by J.G. Rosenmüller and others, wherein the six days' work is a reconstruction of Nature, destroyed through the fall of the ruling angels.[129] Part of this stream, F.C. Oetinger (1702–82) characterized the six days of creation in terms of six 'supermechanical powers' by which God performs his creative

[124] Emanuel Swedenborg, *Arcana Coelestia: The Heavenly Arcana Contained in the Holy Scripture* ... (New York: Swedenborg Foundation, 1982), 1:2–3, 37, 39 = sect. 35, 59, 67.

[125] Ibid., 1:6, 36, 45 = sections 12, 62, 85.

[126] Ibid., 1:7 = sect. 13.

[127] Ibid., 1:1–2 = sections 1–4.

[128] Zöckler, *Geschichte,* 2:205–208.

[129] "Without the fall of the first angel," Oetinger taught, "the creation of this world cannot be understood. " Ibid., 2:204–205, also 499, 511–12.

work, with one of these predominating in each day's work.[130] The creation week exists in merely our perception; creation is in fact an instantaneous reality to God.[131]

The mystical variety of interpretation is a curiously persistent thread in the story of the interpretation of Genesis 1, always autonomous and eclectic in spirit, and yet curiously consistent across its various manifestations. Judged by their self-understanding, mystical approaches should not 'evolve' between individuals at all, in that they are usually felt to be personal revelations of and/or from the Divine. Yet the historical reality is that their concepts, too, flow down from person to person, as can be seen in the ongoing influence of a Pseudo-Dionysius or a Böhme in subsequent, analogous revelations.

The Rise of the Ruin-Restitution Hypothesis

By the late eighteenth century, the Newtonian (and Copernican) view of the world had prevailed completely in the Western mind, and with it came a dawning understanding of the truly abyssal vastness of the cosmos. This was threatening to a Western mind that had a relatively compact and bounded image of the universe. (Whether or not it meant a demotion for the earth is disputed; the centre of the Aristotelian universe, after all, was where the coarsest of matter accumulated in a kind of metaphysical exile from the heavenly realms spread out on all sides. Others are more positive: "It was, to be sure, a place of corruption, but above all, it was the place of God's redemptive work. It was the abode of man, the special object of God's concern.")[132] Meanwhile investigation of the earth's strata was revealing that this 'stone book', only one volume of 'the Book of God's Works', had numerous chapters, long and complex, and telling of marvellous, unsuspected ancient characters. Between a young earth and a stubborn Aristotelian eternalism, a third

[130] Friedrich Christoph Oetinger, 1702–82 and Julius Hamberger, *Die Theologie aus der Idee des Lebens abgeleitet und auf sechs Hauptstücke zurückgeführt* (Stuttgart: J.F. Steinkopf, 1852), 142, GB, http://books.google.com/books?id=d3orAAAAYAAJ.

[131] Ibid., 143 and note.

[132] Dillenberger, *Protestant Thought,* 26. For the negative view, see D.R. Danielson, "The Great Copernican Cliché," *American Journal of Physics* 69:10 (2001): 1029–35. I suspect that within a generally Aristotelian conception of the universe in the late Middle Ages, there would have been a range of evaluations of the dignity of the earth; those with Gnostic tendencies tended to have the most demeaning views of earth, and the fact that Danielson can show such a low view outlasting the demise of the Aristotelian cosmology in Thomas Burnet (ibid., p. 1033) suggests that this did not spring from an Aristotelian cosmology alone.

way was arising: that of deep, but not bottomless, time.[133] This 'temporalizing' of nature has been much commentated on by historians; Nicolaas Rupke describes it as a new perspective on the 'great chain of being' described by Lovejoy, now changed from an ontological structure, as it were a vertical order, to a temporal one, in effect laid horizontally to run through time.[134]

Some practical factors in this development in western Europe were the revived tradition of epic poetry, with its awareness of Ovid's chaos; the same idea as it had crept into late medieval Genesis commentary, helped by the distinction between *creatio, distinctio* and *ornatio*; the speculations of Arminian theologians such as Episcopius and Limborch about the chronological priority of the angels to human creation, in order for the devil to be devilish in time to tempt Eve in the Garden of Eden; and finally, natural studies in fossils that suggested whole forms of life had risen and fallen before any human existed to note their existence. The combined influence of these factors inclined educated British thought, quite open to Dutch influence in the middle and late seventeenth century, to adopt the teaching of a 'long chaos' preceding the creation week, but following the evidently original creation of Gen. 1:1. The 'formless and void' state of the earth in Gen. 1:2 seemed to permit interpretation as a state of indefinite duration.[135]

This long chaos belief, no longer controversial by about 1750, formed the foundation for the ruin-restitution hypothesis, which inferred that the 'formless and void' condition of earth described in Gen. 1:2 resulted from malicious demonic action or else divine judgment for angelic sin – an interpretation backed up by parallel appearances of the Hebrew word pair תֹהוּ וָבֹהוּ *(tohu wabohu)*, seen in Gen. 1:2, in contexts speaking of devastation (Isa. 34:11; Jer. 4:23). This was the 'ruin-restitution' interpretation ably defended in a moderate form by Ger-

[133] Rudwick, *Bursting the Limits*, 117–18, 130–31; Rappaport, *Geologists*, 190; Gould, *Time's Arrow*, 42ff; Dean, "Age of the Earth," 435–41; Gould, "On Rereading Edmund Halley," 175–77.

[134] Nicolaas Rupke, *The Great Chain of History: William Buckland and the English School of Geology (1814–1849)* (Oxford: Clarendon, 1983), 3, 169–72; Lovejoy, *Great Chain of Being*, 244ff.

[135] John Wesley, *Explanatory Notes on the Old Testament*, 3 vols., vol. I (Bristol: Wm. Pine, 1765), http://jcsm.org/StudyCenter/wesley_commentary/genesis.htm; John Gill, *An Exposition of the Old Testament, ... Vol. I. Containing, I. Genesis. II. Exodus. III. Leviticus. IV. Numbers* (London: printed for the author; and sold by George Keith, 1763–65), 4–5, ECCO; William Dodd, *A Commentary on the Books of the Old and New Testament*, 3 vols., vol. 1 (London: printed for R. Davis, L. Davis, and T. Carnan and F. Newbery, Jr., 1770). He attributes the idea to John Locke; see his comments on Gen. 1:1, 2, 4. The essay prefixed to Dodd's commentary, 'Fragment on the Books of the Old Testament. By the late Gilbert West, Esq.,' incongruously disowns the poetic or philosophical absolute chaos, rebukes Whiston for a scheme that is incompatible with the Mosaic history, and defends the literalness of the six days at length.

man Lutheran scholar J.G. Rosenmüller (1736–1815) in his 1776 *Antiquissima telluris historia,* and clearly a well-established interpretive option among continental thinkers even before this.[136] Rosenmüller was clearly convinced of the antiquity of the earth, but could not imagine that this former earth had existed purely for the sake of shellfish and such like, and imagined that angels were the original beneficiaries.[137] It was probably their judgment that left the former world devastated, after which followed the six-day creation about which we read in Genesis:

> Moses relates that all of these things were done in the space of six days, where natural days are to be understood ... although the earth made by him was for a long time uninhabitable, it was then in the space of six days adorned and equipped with all things, that it might be a home for man.[138]

Rosenmüller's formal ruin-restitution theory was a definite step beyond the vague long-chaos theory, and also clearly distinguished from a periodic day position by an emphasis on literal creation days.[139] The ruin-restitution interpretation was reinforced by a perception among savants that a very different former world or terrestrial epoch had preceded our own, with a catastrophic transition between the two. Rather than equating this transition with Noah's Flood, this dramatic interface was increasingly located prior to human history and the present order of created life, as in Johann F. Blumenbach's *Totalrevolution* (1790).[140] For the naturalist who retained a reverence for the Christian revelation, Rosenmüller's ruin-restitution interpretation, placing as it did the great overthrow of the 'former world' not *within* biblical and human history but *before* it, offered a timely strategy for reconciling the Mosaic record

[136] Joseph Needham, treated below, discusses it in 1769 as a familiar interpretive option. Rosenmüller was professor of theology first at Erlangen and then at Leipzig from 1786–1815. His sons, E.F.K. Rosenmüller and Johann Christian Rosenmüller (1771–1820) themselves achieved a name, the former as a theologian and the latter researching the bear caves of Bavaria: Rudwick, *Bursting the Limits*, 351–52, etc.

[137] Johann Georg Rosenmüller, *Antiquissima telluris historia* (Ulm: Jo. Conradi Wohleri, 1776), 37, GB, http://books.google.com/books?id=j38UAAAAQAAJ.

[138] Sex dierum haec omnia facta esse Moses tradit, vbi dies intelligendi sunt naturals...terram etiam ab eo esse creatam, denique sex dierum spatio ita sit exornata et omnibus rebus instructa, vt hominum esset domicilium. Ibid., 47. Confronting the chief objection to this proposal, that Gen. 2:1 and Exod. 20:11 speak of the creation of all things within the space of six days, Rosenmüller responds that not the the whole creation of every entity but its *completion* should be attributed to the day in which it features: ibid., 66–67. For the earlier devastation of the earth, see ibid., 30–36, 39.

[139] He would be followed therein by W.F. Hetzel in a 1780 work and likewise by Johann A. Dathe in 1781, and in time by Thomas Chalmers' 'gap theory' in the English-speaking world. See Zöckler, *Geschichte*, 2:513; Mangenot, "Hexaméron," 6:2341. The introduction of a fuller demonological emphasis into the ruin-restitution idea would await certain nineteenth-century German theosophers, including the famous Schelling: Zöckler, *Geschichte*, 2:516.

[140] Rudwick, *Bursting the Limits*, 298–99.

with the growing consciousness of naturalists of a "vast abyss of time."[141] It avoided aligning the content of the days of creation with geological events, yet proposed a more general harmony between geological history and Genesis by inserting that history between Gen. 1:1 and 1:3. Therefore I define the ruin-restitution hypothesis and its mainly Anglophone cousin the gap theory as 'semi-concordist', as opposed to the full concordism of a day-age or periodic day approach.

Genesis 1 as the Primordial Human Document

The title of Rosenmüller's *Antiquissima telluris historia* reveals a perspective characteristic of this era. This was to see Genesis as the most ancient written document in existence and the sole testimony to the most ancient events, those of the creation week, with a reliability that could only be due to divine inspiration. This was the mindset that drove the traditional kind of universal history, already mentioned. However, the growing popularity of the ruin-restitution scheme revealed an emerging awareness of a pre-historic development of the earth and its plant and animal life.

In philosophical terms, this development was systematized in an important work by the Romantic German philosopher Johann Gottfried Herder (1744–1803), in his *Ideas toward a Philosophy of Human History* (1784–91). The work describes the formation of the earth in terms compatible with the common picture of development out of chaos, or what would soon become Laplace's nebular hypothesis. It then followed a kind of 'emergent evolution' theory in describing life developing in stages that were really ascending steps of the "great chain of being." Finally human beings appeared, "a link between two worlds, the natural world out of which he has grown and the spiritual world which through him ... is realizing itself on the earth."[142] Herder's innovation was to formalize this differentiation of human and earth history, and furthermore, to integrate the two histories in a horizontal unfolding of the chain of being in a manner destined by God.[143]

In an earlier and lesser-known work of Herder, we find the initial chapters of Genesis represented as the primordial document (*Urkunde*) of humanity, a prototype that contained and symbolized all mysteries, a cryptic key to be deciphered. The work is *Älteste Urkunde des Mensch-*

[141] Among relevant works that use a phrase like this in their titles, see Claude C. Albritton, *The Abyss of Time* (San Francisco 1980); Rossi, *Dark Abyss*. The phrase is drawn from the later work of Buffon, to be treated below.

[142] Collingwood, *The Idea of History*, 89.

[143] Herder, *Reflections*, 87–88; Rupke, *Great Chain of History*, 4, 57. On the enduring concept of the chain of being, clearly an influence on Herder's thought here, see Lovejoy, *Great Chain of Being*.

engeschlechts (1774–76).[144] Herder's fame relates to the Romantic movement, a reaction to continental Enlightenment rationalism, rather than to his biblical exegesis, and Anglophone discussions of the history of interpretation rarely mention this ambitious treatment of the first six or so chapters of Genesis. Its value is certainly debated; Christoph Bultmann says, "It is surprising in its enthusiasm, fails in most of its arguments, but nevertheless, it leaves the exegete with some good ideas." He alludes, as does Otto Zöckler, to a degree of fame surrounding the work that a reader of English histories of biblical interpretation would never suspect.[145]

The *Älteste Urkunde* strikes the reader as part agitated polemic against virtually all recent interpretations of Genesis prior to his own, and part intuitive and enraptured imaginative participation in the creation account, governed by Romantic sensibilities. On the one hand, Herder condemns the various cosmogonic (or geotheoretical), metaphysical, theosophic and even theological interpretations of Genesis 1 for overwhelming and obscuring what is in itself a simple, clear picture of creation, and thus blaspheming a revelation from God (*Offenbarung*).[146] On the other, Herder's treatment of the creation account seeks to empathetically enter the spirit of the easterner (*Morgenländer*) through whose eyes the creation scene is viewed.[147] Genesis 1 is not for him an analytical presentation of creation but an intuitive, felt, impressionistic portrait (*Bild*) or play or poetic piece (*Stück*). It is more to be felt than thought about. Its prime motif is the eruption of light into horrific and boundless darkness, i.e. the transition from Gen. 1:2 to 1:3. On "Let there be light," Herder proclaims, "With a single, mighty word, so terse and gentle, is all the preceding, fearful darkness banished.... In the face of the ancient night gleams a ray of divinity."[148] His hermeneutic is both aesthetic and realistic.[149]

[144] Reventlow reports that this work had something of an earlier incarnation in *Über die ersten Urkunden des menschlichen Geschlechts. Einige Anmerkungen* (betw. 1764–69): Henning Graf Reventlow, "Towards the End of the 'Century of Enlightenment': Established Shift from *Sacra Scriptura* to Literary Documents and Religion of the People of Israel," in *HB/OT* 2:1044.

[145] Christoph Bultmann, "Creation at the Beginning of History: Johann Gottfried Herder's Interpretation of Genesis 1," *JSOT* 68 (1995): 27; Zöckler, *Geschichte*, 2:224.

[146] Johann Gottfried Herder, *Älteste Urkunde des Menschengeschlechts*, 2 vols., vol. I (Riga: J.F. Hartknoch, 1774), 3–20. The relevant statements can be found throughout this section.

[147] On this see John W. Rogerson, *Old Testament Criticism in the Nineteenth Century: England and Germany* (London: SPCK, 1984), 17. Both this and the previous point receive comment in Dillenberger, *Protestant Thought*, 191–92.

[148] Herder, *Älteste Urkunde*, 1:27. Compare the opening passages of Haydn's *Creation*, treated below.

[149] See the substantial hermeneutical evaluation in Hans Frei, *The Eclipse of Biblical Narrative: A Study in Eighteenth and Nineteenth-Century Hermeneutics* (New Haven: Yale Uni-

Herder here is in no mood to answer questions about the relationship of the creation days with real periods of time. He believes that to make such harmonizing attempts is to misconstrue and distort, with Western methods, what is a fundamentally different, Eastern work. It simply does not invite physical questions and defies what we would call scientific correlation: "Light – three days before the sun! Heaven – the beautiful roof between waters and waters, a sea-vault and countertheatre for the earth! Earth, dry land, flowers and plants – while there is still no sun! Mountain and valley, as well as diurnal rotation – while there is still no sun!"[150] The point is clear: we cannot take this account as a blow-by-blow physical chronicle of creation. Later he puts it positively: "You see that this is the simplest daily table [*Tageregister*]; it provides you nothing other than a sense-oriented view [*sinnliche Ansicht*] ... what use to physics is such a list of names?"[151] The weekly framework is a form that corresponds to the simple perceptions of the ancient, Eastern audience the original Genesis had in view. "God...works six days like a workman" as a model (*Vorbild*) for happy and balanced human life in society.[152] This ancient piece of writing, when the distorting perspective of the 'cosmos-makers' and 'metaphysicians' is removed, appears as "the beautiful source [*Urkunde*], Institute of Work and of Rest, as a great, profound allegory of God."[153]

Assessments are mixed. Zöckler criticized Herder's lapse into symbolic mysticism, since he later in the work treats Genesis 1 cabbalistically as a 'hieroglyph' or mystical symbol, while he appreciates his demolition of natural-philosophical interpretations of Genesis 1.[154] Bultmann regards Herder as retaining an undervalued "philosophical intensity" and regard for "the 'poetic' character of the text."[155] As a specimen of biblical exegesis, this work on Genesis is conceited and erratic, yet stimulating and refreshing in its aesthetic feeling for the creation scene. Historically, Herder proposes an ambitious alternate

versity Press, 1974), 83–101. Frei praises Herder for his overall retention of a realistic sense of biblical narrative when it was being lost elsewhere. Bavinck instead sees Herder's work as a step down the road to mythical interpretation: Bavinck, *In the Beginning*, 115. Zöckler characterizes it as a 'Poetisirungsversuch' or 'poetizing enterprise', as opposed to 'mythicizing', 'rationalizing' and such approaches, Zöckler, *Geschichte*, 224–25.

[150] Herder, *Älteste Urkunde*, 1:6.

[151] Ibid., 1:12.

[152] Ibid., 1:92.

[153] B. Altaner and A. Stuiber, *Patrologie*, 9th ed. (Freiburg: Herder, 1978), 94. Herder is sometimes credited with the presentation of the creation week as two corresponding pairs of three days: Bruce Waltke, "The Literary Genre of Genesis, Chapter One," *Crux* 27 (1991): 5; Bavinck, *In the Beginning*, 102. We saw in the chapter on medieval works that in fact this awareness goes back at least to Lombard's *Sentences* 2.14.6.

[154] Herder, *Älteste Urkunde*, 1:227–28; Zöckler, *Geschichte*, 2:230–33.

[155] Bultmann, "Herder's Interpretation," 32.

interpretive approach in contrast to outdated traditional interpretations, arrogant, all-embracing world-systems and mystical treatments.[156] "Herder's main intention," according to Reventlow, "was to refute by a sort of apologetic the rationalistic criticism of the Bible, even though keeping his distance from Orthodoxy."[157] Concerning the days of creation, we see an early reaction against modern concordism that values history and yet finally is non-literal, ideal, and anthropomorphic in its understanding of the creation days. Ironically, if we were to see some influence here of Kant's separation of perception and reality, in Herder's very different approach in the later *Reflections,* with a much more realistic focus, we might see the impact of the physical cosmogony of Kant's early *Universal Natural History and Theory of the Heavens* (1755).[158]

The title of J.G. Eichhorn's (1752–1827) *Urgeschichte* (1779) also suggests a certain primordiality. But whereas Herder's treatment in the *Aelteste Urkunde* held myth and history somewhat in tension, Eichhorn's approach, influenced both by Herder and also his teacher J.D. Michaelis, takes the concept of myth from the classical philologist C.G. Heyne and applies it to creation in Genesis, thus settling on one of Herder's twin poles.[159] This is Eichhorn's rendition:

> Read it as two historical works of the old world … the air of its age and country breathes in it. Forget the age you live in, and the knowledge it affords you…. The first rays of the glimmering light of reason do not harmonise with the clear light of broad noon…. In particular its language must not be treated like that of a cultivated and philosophic age … it is like the world in its childhood…. It is like a painting, or the language of poetry … according to the language of this book, God produces every thing directly, without availing himself of the course of nature and certain intermediate causes … it had not been ascertained, by long-continued inquiry, that all events are connected into a series of intermediate causes. Therefore it stops with God, the ultimate cause.[160]

If the spirit of the *Morgenröthe* or dawn of the world breathes through Genesis, the spirit of Herder is certainly felt in this passage, his Romantic aesthetic orientation here melded with the cultural supremacy of the Enlightenment. Eichhorn's student and editor Philip Gabler (1753-1826) echoed Eichhorn's high esteem for the Genesis cosmogony when he said, "Concerning the main subject matter, there is no

[156] Herder, *Älteste Urkunde*, 1:224–25.

[157] Reventlow, "Century of Enlightenment," 1048.

[158] Kant, *Universal Natural History*; Reventlow, "Century of Enlightenment," 1048.

[159] Reventlow, "Century of Enlightenment," 1051; Frei, *Eclipse*, 159–60; Rogerson, *Old Testament Criticism*, 17; Bray, *Biblical Interpretation*, 248; McCalla, *Creationist Debate*, 87–88.

[160] De Wette, *Critical and Historical Introduction*, 31–32.

denying … that none of the ancient cosmogonies … can be even vaguely compared with the Mosaic cosmogony. It is the simplest and loftiest conception, and the one most nearly appropriate to even the most penetrating modern observations about the course of nature."[161] Similarly, J.F.W. Jerusalem (1709–89) concluded his exposition of the Genesis 1 creation narrative in terms that sound very much like Herder and Eichhorn, saying that this account bears all the hallmarks of the childhood of human civilization, and represents the most authentic account from the earliest history of man.[162]

Pioneering Concordist Proposals

Not all could heed Herder's call to stick to the feeling of the Genesis text and ignore its physical statements, nor were all satisfied that the account described simply the last renovation of the earth, as the ruin-restitution hypothesis proposed. Genesis 1:1–2:3 seemed to describe the original and unique creation of the earth, and other Christian thinkers persuaded of 'deep time' began anew to review the possible range of meaning permissible for the 'days' of Gen. 1:1–2:3, beyond simple twenty-four hour periods.[163] The periodic model of 'world-week' thought, wherein the creation days represented periods of human history of about a thousand years each, must have echoed in minds looking for a way to relate Genesis to a long pre-human earth history. And lengthened creation days had already been contemplated by Newton, Ray, and Whiston and others prior to 1700, and the idea persisted, for instance in correspondence from Quaker Thomas Story to a colleague, sometime between 1724 and 1741, that suggested "that "days" were an accommodating way of speaking, meaning 'certain

[161] Frei, *Eclipse*, 274. Gabler went on to publish his own *Neuer Versuch über die Mosaische Schöpfungsgeschichte aus der höhern Kritik. Ein Nachtrag zum ersten Theil seiner Ausgabe der Eichhorn'schen Urgeschichte* (1795). He followed Eichhorn's line to some degree and utilised the methods of higher criticism, but the work fell into almost total obscurity: Reventlow, "Century of Enlightenment," 1058–62.

[162] J.F.W. Jerusalem, *Betrachtungen über die vornehmsten Wahrheiten der Religion*, 3 vols., vol. II, part 2 (Braunschweig: Fürstl[ich?] Waisenhaus = Buchhandlung, 1779), 612–13, http://books.google.com/books?id=_VBbAAAAQAAJ. Zöckler finds stylistic similarities to Herder: Zöckler, *Geschichte*, 2:499. See below for more information on Jerusalem.

[163] Rappaport, *Geologists*, 193; Rudwick, *Bursting the Limits*, 122; Dean, "Age of the Earth," 444–45, 454; Lewis and Knell, eds., *Age of the Earth*, 6; Toulmin and Goodfield, *The Discovery of Time*, 146f; C.C. Gillispie, *Genesis and Geology: A Study in the Relations of Scientific Thought, Natural Theology and Social Opinions in Great Britain, 1790–1850* (New York: Harper & Row, 1951; reprint, with a foreword by Nicolaas A. Rupke and a new preface by the author, Cambridge, MA: Harvard University Press, 1996), 224. Virtually any work that features Buffon or de Luc will discuss their figurative use of the creation days of Genesis.

long & competent periods of time, & not natural days'."[164] Yet Moro's work remained little known, and with allegiance to Whiston's long days deteriorating, the trail went a little cold.[165]

Now a lengthened creation week would begin to be articulated anew in connection with geological eras, initially within the theoretically-driven context of geotheory rather than as a result of empirical observation.[166] William Yarchin reports that historian August Ludwig von Schlözer in his *Vorstellung einer Universalgeschichte* (1772) "suggested that each 'day' of Genesis 1 might be understood symbolically as a sequential stage in the geological and biological development of Earth."[167] Otto Zöckler credited the German cleric, apologist, and Enlightenment savant J.F.W. Jerusalem with the origin of the 'concordist' or day-age theory "in a modern, that is geologically-motivated, form," wherein "the six days were to be understood as 'six main revolutions' (*sechs Hauptrevolutionen*) or 'time periods' ... during which God ... had ... reformed (*umgebildet*) the chaotic original state of the world."[168] Jerusalem assumes that Moses narrates the earth's recent recovery from the latest 'ruin' simply as its one-time emergence from chaos. A text that is global when seen from within is shown to actually be local in its application to the real world and its history.[169]

Jerusalem in fact combines a geologically-informed ruin-restitution theory with an idealist tendency to interpret the Genesis days as merely logical categories and the week as a heuristic framework. He manifests a strong sense of accommodation and a persistent desire to take the Genesis account literally, as far as Moses' own intentions are concerned.[170] He finds in Genesis 1 a "sequence of ... development, and indeed in six periods or days, according to the six main classes in which reason ... still ... imagined it."[171] Taken on its own terms, Moses' intention in Genesis is a description of creation that is universal in terms

[164] Rappaport, *Geologists*, 194–95.

[165] On Moro, see ibid., 225–26.

[166] Kenneth L. Taylor, "Buffon, Desmarest and the Ordering of Geological Events in Époques," in *The Age of the Earth from 4004 BC to AD 2002*, ed. C.L.E. Lewis and S.J. Knell, GS Special Publications (London: The Geological Society, 2001), 39–45. Note the reference to Vaccari's point that Italian authors as well as Buffon and Desmarest were using this 'epoch' terminology as far back as the 1760s and even before.

[167] Yarchin, "Biblical Interpretation," 49.

[168] Zöckler, *Geschichte*, 2:499–500.

[169] Jerusalem, *Betrachtungen*, 2.2:561–652, 579–80, 610.

[170] Ibid., 2.2:568–73, 612–13. Peter Simon Pallas is cited on p. 571 and seems to have had particular influence.

[171] Ibid., 2.2:581.

of space, absolute in time, and intends literal days.[172] Historian Frederick Gregory concludes, "Jerusalem's treatment of Genesis revealed that wherever the biblical record defied common sense, its literal meaning was to be abandoned," although the tone of the work itself does not seem especially sceptical.[173]

Prior to von Schlözer or Jerusalem, the English Roman Catholic priest Joseph Needham presented his original theory of interpretation of Gen. 1:1–2:3 to the world in *Nouvelles Recherches* (1769).[174] Volume II begins with an open letter to Buffon that implies that Needham has acted as an exegetical guide for the naturalist, and as the first person to explain the creation week as a figurative schema, provided the idea behind Buffon's *Époques* of 1778.[175] Needham's subsequent explanation is not yet a geologically informed day-age schema, but a philosophical undertaking that interprets the days as successive periods of the world's development. As a Catholic cleric, Needham ostensibly cannot form a view that undermines church tradition, and so grounds his figurative interpretation in the 'universally respected' authority of Augustine, who "in his commentaries on Genesis, totally abandoned the letter of Scripture."[176] He thinks to speak for the church as he grants Buffon an exegetical sanction:

> You see, *Monsieur*, that concerning the literal sense of Scripture, if your reasons drawn from the nature of things themselves are strong and pressing, that you can depart from the letter in explaining Moses' history of the creation, and can do it without exposing yourself to [ecclesiastical]

[172] Ibid., 2.2:612–13. I was not able to locate Zöckler's specific quotations in the text, and note that he was citing a slightly later edition of the work, from 1785, where Jerusalem may have more explicitly offered a day-age solution.

[173] Gregory, *Nature Lost?*, 27; see also Dillenberger, *Protestant Thought*, 179–80.

[174] Joseph Needham and Lazzaro Spallanzani, *Nouvelles recherches physiques et métaphysiques sur la nature et la religion, avec une nouvelle théorie de la terre, et une mesure de la hauteur des Alpes ... par M. de Needham*, 2 vols., vol. II (London/Paris: Lacombe, 1769), ECCO. Deciphering the authorship of the overall work is not simple, but it appears that Spallanzani may be the author of vol. I concerning microscopic discoveries, with Needham as translator, while Needham is the direct author of vol. II. These biographical details come from Roberts, "Genesis Chapter 1," 43. See also Jacques Roger, *The Life Sciences in Eighteenth-Century French Thought*, ed. Keith Rodney Benson, trans. R. Ellrich (Stanford: Stanford University Press, 1998), 414–17, GB, http://books.google. com/books?id=_LY1bpIsrEgC.

[175] Il y a long-tems que j'ai cette opinion, & quoique je sois le premier qui ai avancé cette explication: Needham, *Nouvelles recherches*, 2:16. See also p. 5 for a similar statement. It is hard to tell whether Needham is disguising precedents for a figurative creation week, is ignorant of any, or does not recognize anything in the past truly analogous to his own. For an explanation of Buffon's *Époques*, see below.

[176] Ibid., 2:6–14.

censure. It is therefore permissible to understand by the six days, any six periods whatsoever, and not only six revolutions of twenty-four hours.[177]

And for Needham the creation days are indeed revolutions, metaphysical cycles. His observation of the fact that evening precedes morning on each of the creation days draws him into an interpretation which has Platonic affinities.[178] The evenings and mornings constitute a kind of ontological spiral, a development out of absolute non-being whereby the world progresses into a higher state of being, then regresses somewhat ('evening'), then on the next 'morning' advances yet further ahead, until creation reaches its culmination.[179] The initial creation of chaotic matter is the first emergence of being from utter non-being, expressed in the critical 'evening' of Gen. 1:5.[180] From there the creation account describes a 'scale' (*échelle*) of events, as the four elements are differentiated, dispersed and reassembled, and a second, ascending scale of life that culminates in humankind.[181] As with Herder a few years later in his *Reflections*, the chain of being has become a ladder of progress for the ascent of life.

This is admittedly not the literal sense of the creation account, admits Needham, but the intellectual one, most pertinent to the Christian 'Philosophe'.[182] He interprets the creation account as "a picturesque description" or "the tableau of Moses," which presents things as they appear for the benefit of its human audience, and does not concern the formation of the universe beyond our solar system.[183] Other stars and their systems could be far older than ours.[184] There was nothing better "*than an unknown and enigmatic day which precedes the sun and the natural day*" to express this metaphysical spiral by which the world came into being.[185] Therefore the first day of Gen. 1:5 "could not refer to a natural day of twenty-four hours, … [but] it is necessary to take these six terms of creation as six periods of unknown length of

[177] Ibid., 2:15–16. The same warrant is offered researchers of nature generally on pp. 75–76, 80.

[178] Ibid., 2:1–2, etc.

[179] Ibid., 2:23–25.

[180] Ibid., 2:1–2, 17, 20, 24, 56. I have no evidence for Needham's use of Le Clerc. But Le Clerc's ideas were clearly well known and perpetuated amongst more 'progressive' thinkers and commentators on Genesis, as we have seen, and his commentaries were still being reprinted well into the eighteenth century.

[181] Ibid., 2:20–22, 57.

[182] Ibid., 2:16.

[183] Ibid., 2:19, 23, 61, etc.

[184] Ibid., 2:61–67.

[185] *qu'un jour inconnu & inusité qui précède le soleil & le jour naturel.* Ibid., 2:24 (italics his). Needham attributes the phrase to Augustine.

time," their duration proportionate to the degree of progress expressed therein.[186]

Needham extends his argument by citing figurative uses of 'day' and 'evening/morning' throughout Scripture, and claiming that we still live in the seventh day of rest.[187] Although writing prior to Rosenmüller, Needham examines and finally rejects an alternative harmonizing option that is quite recognisable as the 'ruin-restitution' theory, and which supposes "that the earth described by Moses as formless and dark, was then arising from a revolution which had reduced it to ruins."[188] But while he does accept extended creation days, Needham regards the quest to date the age of the earth as presumptuous, and the vast chronologies suggested by philosophers as folly: "The days of Moses are probably periods which extend beyond twenty-four hours, but no-one has any proof that they must extend to thousands of years."[189] Enough time is merely required to allow the elements to settle out, take their places and bring forth their living populations.[190] He may lay the exegetical groundwork for Buffon's *Époques*, but the age of the earth in Buffon's conception is more definite and more generous in scope than Needham's.[191]

Buffon's Époques

The later volume of Buffon's *Histoire Naturelle* entitled *Les Époques de la Nature* (1778) signals a dramatic change in approach from his earlier geotheory. His cosmogony has clearly undergone development and refinement in the intervening time, and he this time dares to put figures on the earth's age that clearly defy traditional biblical chronology. But most significantly for us, his stance toward the Genesis text changes, and he opts instead to engage with it in a concordist manner, the very thing for which he had earlier castigated Whiston.

The *Époques* is structured according to the seven great epochs into which Buffon divides earth history. They are based upon the same Leibnizian conception of the cooling of an initially incandescent terres-

[186] Ibid., 2:24–25.

[187] Ibid., 2:67–75.

[188] De supposer que la terre décrite par *Moyse* comme informe & ténébreuse, sortoit alors d'une revolution qui l'avoit mise en ruines: ibid., 2:58, and see 54–60, 76–79. As Needham rejects this option, he makes a rather careless statement that "six thousand, or sixty thousand, or sixty million or billion years " form a mere infinitesimal part of eternity. This is quoted in an article by Michael Roberts, who perhaps mistakes this for Needham's own stance. Ibid., 2:54; Roberts, "Genesis Chapter 1," 43.

[189] Needham, *Nouvelles recherches*, 2:60–61; von Zittel, *History of Geology*, 34.

[190] Needham, *Nouvelles recherches*, 2:81–82.

[191] The age of the universe is another matter. Needham seems to contemplate quite an immense antiquity for it.

trial globe derived from the sun as was his earlier 'Theory'. The first Epoch saw the planets form as molten globes orbiting the sun, having been struck off it by the impact of a comet.[192] The basic, glassy structure of the earth, i.e. all plutonic rock, was formed by the solidification of such a molten globe in the second Epoch.[193] The third Epoch saw the condensation of the world's oceans from the atmospheric vapours of the early earth.[194] Aquatic life that could withstand high temperatures already inhabited the seas during this period.[195] It ended with the submersion of almost the entire globe, while the fourth Epoch featured the gradual retreat of the seas accompanied by volcanic action.[196] A more intelligent level of animal life appeared during this period.[197] The fifth Epoch saw the reign of the megafauna whose remains were then being discovered in far northern regions of the world.[198] The sixth Epoch then witnessed the separation of the continents through crustal collapse, and other dramatic changes such as the inbreaking of the Mediterranean Sea through what are now the Straits of Gibraltar.[199] As nature settled in its present state of near-rest, the seventh Epoch of human civilization opened, more or less corresponding to biblical history from the creation of man onward.[200]

Buffon conceives of a total world history of 75,000 years or so, although his consistency and/or clarity on this point are not absolute.[201] It was a bold step away from conformity to traditional chronology. The division between the span of human history and that of earth history is clear from the outset. Even earliest human civilization is nothing

[192] Georges Louis Leclerc Buffon, Comte de, *Les époques de la nature*, 2 vols. (Paris: de l'Imprimerie royale, 1780), 1:78ff., GB, http://books.google.com/books?id=d4sNAAAAQAAJ.

[193] Ibid., 1:122ff.

[194] Ibid., 1:171ff.

[195] Ibid., 1:177–78.

[196] Ibid., 2:1ff. Thus Buffon's new geotheory, unlike his first, had come to terms with the 'diminishing seas' genre of cosmogonies: Rudwick, *Bursting the Limits*, 173.

[197] Buffon, *Les époques de la nature*, 2:48.

[198] Ibid., 2:49ff.

[199] Ibid., 2:85ff. esp. 95. See also Rudwick, *Bursting the Limits*, 146.

[200] Buffon, *Les époques de la nature*, 2:164ff., also 162–63.

[201] Ibid., 1:125. The text abounds with references to multiples of five thousand years. Compare the table reproduced from this work in Rudwick, *Bursting the Limits*, 148. The figures offered there for the duration of life on earth and its first appearance can be combined to yield a present age for earth of 74,832 years. See Young and Stearley, *Bible, Rocks and Time*, 83. Other secondary sources cite Buffon's terrestrial age as 75,000 years (Collier, *Cosmogonies*, 209; Toulmin and Goodfield, *The Discovery of Time*, 146; McCalla, *Creationist Debate*, 56), 50,000 years (Jaki, *Genesis 1*, 188), 70,000 years (Greene, *Death of Adam*, 74), 85,000 years (Dean, "Age of the Earth," 452) and even 100,000 years (Mangenot, "Hexaméron," 6:2340)! Much of this variation is due to different ways or counting or starting-points or end-points. The order of magnitude is clear.

in comparison with the vastly ancient times when oceans covered the continents.[202] Ancient human traditions may be useful sources of information about the origin of human civilization, they can tell us nothing useful about *earth* history.[203] Therefore it is necessary to pay attention to physical facts, such as the bulging shape of the earth, its interior heat, and the glassy nature of its essential rocks, which confirm for Buffon the planet's consolidation from a molten mass.[204] Then one must study fossil monuments and understand what they can tell about the cooling and drying earth.[205]

But Buffon anticipates the protest, "How can you make this great antiquity that you attribute to matter accord with the sacred traditions, which only grant six or eight thousand years to the world? However strong your proofs, however well-founded your arguments, however clear your facts, are not those related in the holy Bible all the more certain? Is not contradicting them impugning God, who has been kind enough to reveal them to us?"[206] Buffon replies, "The more deeply I penetrate Nature, the more deeply I admire and profoundly respect its Author," and prepares to lay out "the key facts that the divine interpreter has transmitted to us concerning creation," in order to show that data from the natural world "can only add a new degree of clarity and of splendour" to the light of God's truth.[207]

Ostensibly, then, Buffon's new concordist turn is motivated by apologetic concerns. Some commentators feel, however, that the biblical or theological elements in this new work sit very lightly on its basic viewpoint, and Rudwick thinks he may detect a parody of the creation week.[208] Buffon holds that the period of chaos implied by Gen. 1:2, which by every indication in the text (such as the imperfect forms of the three verbs in that verse) is indefinite, constitutes the first Epoch, an "emphatic pause between the general production of matter and the

[202] Buffon, *Les époques de la nature*, 1:5. See also the reference to 'successive development', p. 68.

[203] Rappaport, *Geologists*, 261–62.

[204] Buffon, *Les époques de la nature*, 1:9–25. This class of evidence is glassy (Fr. *vitrescible*) in nature, which shows a debt to the Leibnizian type of geotheory.

[205] This is the '*calcinable*' class of evidence, i.e. calcium carbonate as opposed to silica-based.

[206] Comment accordez-vous, dira-t'on, cette haute ancienneté que vous donnez à la matière, avec les Traditions sacrées, qui ne donnent au monde que six ou huit mille ans? Quelque fortes que soient vos preuves, quelque fondés que soient vos raifonnemens, quelque évidens que soient vos faits, ceux qui sont rapportés dans le Livre sacré ne sont-ils pas encore plus certains? Les contredire, n'est-ce pas manquer à Dieu, qui a eu la bonté de nous les révéler? Buffon, *Les époques de la nature*, 1:54.

[207] Ibid., 1:54–55.

[208] McCalla, *Creationist Debate*, 1:56; Zöckler, *Geschichte*, 2:186; Rudwick, *Bursting the Limits*, 148–49.

production of particular forms."[209] Then the appearance of light, which was commanded in an instant but was not executed in an instant, constitutes the second Epoch.[210]

Buffon digresses after identifying Gen. 1:2–3 with his first two epochs to dwell on the meaning of the 'days' of that chapter. Whereas God could have created everything in an instant, had he wanted to employ the full potential of his omnipotence, he only wished on the contrary to space his work out across intervals. In the 'deprived' language (*langue pauvre*) of Genesis 1, 'day' proves to be the nearest term for describing *six intervalles de durée*. Their non-relation to our present days is confirmed by the passing of three before the sun's appearance, as well as the fact that they begin with evening and finish with morning. He continues,

> These six days, therefore, were not solar days similar to ours, nor days of light.... Nor were these days equal, for they would have been 'proportioned' to the work.[211] These are thus only six spaces of time; the sacred Historian has not determined the duration of each, but the sense of the narrator seems to make it so long, so that we can demonstrate the meaning just as much is required by the physical truths that we have.[212]

Buffon continues, tellingly, "Why then exclaim so strongly about this borrowing of time that we only take to the degree that we are forced to it by the demonstrative knowledge of the phenomena of nature?"[213] This is the unspoken creed of the concordist enterprise: the interpretation of the biblical data is to some degree conditioned by the pressure of data from other sources.

By this point, having offered quite a pioneering, day-age model for interpreting Genesis 1, Buffon abandons the exegesis of the chapter. It would have been difficult to complete, since the first Mosaic day, with the creation of light, equated to Buffon's second Epoch, so a direct correspondence that lasted through Day 7 was already impossible.[214] But along the way, Buffon reveals more about his hermeneutical stance toward the Genesis text, which involved a full-blown principle of accommodation:

[209] Buffon, *Les époques de la nature*, 1:56–57.

[210] Ibid., 1:58–59. It is worth noting here Rudwick's observation that Buffon's seven 'epochs' are points rather than periods, 'milestones' on the road of time: Rudwick, *Bursting the Limits*, 143.

[211] We noticed above that Needham also thought of the days this way.

[212] Buffon, *Les époques de la nature*, 1:62.

[213] Ibid., 1:62–63. This is the stratagem condoned by Needham.

[214] Collier similarly notes that shellfish appear in Buffon's third epoch: Collier, *Cosmogonies*, 207.

> It must be remembered that [God's] divine inspiration has passed via the organs of man; that his word to us has been transmitted in a deprived language, lacking precise expressions for abstract ideas, so that the Interpreter of this divine word has often been obliged to use words whose meanings are determined by circumstances.[215]

He shortly adds to this internal factor, divine accommodation, the external factor of concordance with nature and reason; while obliged to Scripture, we are also obliged

> to allow ourselves to depart from the letter of this holy tradition when the *letter kills,* that is, when it appears directly opposed to sound reason and the truth of the facts of Nature; for all reason, all truth come equally from God, there is no difference between those which he has revealed to us and those which he has allowed us to discover by our observations and our researches; ... it is for this reason that his Interpreter has only spoken to the first humans, again so ignorant, in a common sense.... Everything in Moses' story is set to the range of the people's intelligence; everything in it is represented according to the common man, for whom it wasn't a case of demonstrating the true system of the world, but it was enough to instruct (him) about what he owed to the Creator ...[216]

Buffon compounds the argument by expounding the all-too-humble conception of the physical universe that the audience of Genesis would, according to Buffon, have held.[217] But now the scientific revolution has providentially appeared at a time of cooling piety to bring people's loyalty back to God with a new revelation of his glory. "Besides," he continues, "I have only taken the liberty of this interpretation of the first verses of Genesis to achieve the greater good, which would be to forever reconcile natural science with that of theology. To me they can only appear to be in contradiction, and my explanation seems to demonstrate this."[218] If his interpretation seems too free for certain literalistic minds, "I beg them to judge me by the intention, and to consider that my system for the Epochs of Nature, being purely hypothetical, cannot harm revealed truths, which are such unchangeable axioms, independent of every hypothesis, and to which I have submitted and do submit my thoughts."[219] Thus Buffon finishes his apologetic section with an obligatory tip of the hat to revelation in the tradition of Descartes.

[215] Buffon, *Les époques de la nature,* 1:59.

[216] Ibid., 1:63, 64, 67.

[217] Ibid., 1:64–67.

[218] Ibid., 1:68–69. It may require a better reader of French than me to tell whether the subtle double meaning that seems to reside in this last sentence as I have translated it resides in the original.

[219] Ibid., 1:69.

Buffon's impact on subsequent thought was substantial. While he represented the destined-to-pass cadre of earth theorists in his endeavour to combine universal origins with the earth's physical history, he was a pioneer thinker in the natural sciences. Porter speaks of his works as the leading means by which continental Enlightenment thought influenced Britain, and adds, "Buffon's quantified estimates of the age of the Earth provoked controversy rather than acceptance, but his [two works] also ushered in an intellectual climate in which a long timescale was in principle acceptable."[220] Perhaps Buffon had been influenced by Whiston's year-long days, despite his disparagement of Whiston, and his use of similar terminology and ideas may constitute evidence of direct dependence on Needham.[221] Perhaps even De Maillet's ironic use of six 'days' suggested to Buffon the possibility of employing a hexaemeral guise. Buffon's catastrophism and periodization would in turn influence Cuvier; his uniformitarian principles Hutton; and his expansion of the Genesis days into ages established a popular trend. But any harmonization scheme destined to be truly persuasive in the nineteenth century would have to more specifically relate the geological ages either to the period hinted at in Gen. 1:2 or to the six days of creation themselves.

De Luc's Lettres

Buffon's pioneering day-age handling of the creation week looks partial and insincere, retaining merely "a whiff of hexameral idiom."[222] A more studied and sincere version and one of the best-known early day-age interpretations of Genesis was presented by the Genevan naturalist Jean-André de Luc (1727–1817), whose work was funded by his long-time appointment as 'reader' to England's Queen Charlotte, wife of George III. De Luc probably deserves to be included among the first true geologists, and used the term 'geology' in an almost modern sense to describe the cause and effect relationships of what had been called 'earth physics'.[223] His breadth of geological observation through field-work lends an empirical tone to his work, while his desire to find all-

[220] Porter, *Making of Geology*, 105, 159; Toulmin and Goodfield, *The Discovery of Time*, 149.

[221] For example the terms *écarter*, to 'depart' (from the literal sense of Genesis), and *échelle*, meaning 'scale': Buffon, *Les époques de la nature*, 1:63, 152.

[222] Kerry V. Magruder, "Thomas Burnet, Biblical Idiom, and Seventeenth-Century Theories of the Earth," in *Nature and Scripture in the Abrahamic Religions: Up to 1700*, ed. J.M. van der Meer and S. Mandelbrote, Brill's Series in Church History (Leiden: Brill, 2008), 486.

[223] See, respectively, Rudwick, *Bursting the Limits*, 133–35, 306.

encompassing and unifying explanatory principles identifies him with his geotheoretical forebears.[224]

De Luc's earliest letters, dating from 1773 forward, were first published as *Lettres physiques et morales sur les montaignes et sur l'histoire de la terre et l'homme* in 1778.[225] At this early stage, de Luc's geotheory had a simple, binary character, which radically distinguished the antediluvian earth, with its indefinitely long history, from the stable, post-diluvian earth bearing signs of its renovation in the recent past.[226] But by the time de Luc published a series of articles in the journal *Observations sur la Physique* (1790–93), "A multiplicity of revolutions now differentiated the former [antediluvian] world into a sequence of distinct stages in geohistory."[227] These geohistorical stages subtly suggested a correspondence with the days of the creation week, a correspondence made more explicit in the subsequent letters to Professor Blumenbach (1793–96).[228] So while de Luc's earliest *Lettres* predate Buffon's 1778 *Époques,* his seven-day Genesis-related scheme post-dates and probably depends on Buffon's work, since it replicates Buffon's humanistic twist on the creation week whereby the seventh day is the era of human domination, rather than of the divine rest.[229]

De Luc's works therefore constitute a geological *apologia* for the Mosaic writings, using certain geological "chronometers" to prove the recency of the present form of the earth's surface, and thus of the Mosaic cataclysm: "We cannot refer the birth of our continents, to a period more distant than that at which the Mosaic history fixes the deluge."[230] He represents the Deluge as involving an exchange of land

[224] Davies, *Earth in Decay*, 126, 137; Porter, *Making of Geology*, 201; Rudwick, *Bursting the Limits*, 150–58, 313; Collier, *Cosmogonies*, 264–65. On his employment as 'reader' to Charlotte, see Rudwick, p. 26.

[225] They were augmented and retitled as *Lettres physiques et morales sur l'histoire de la terre et de l'homme* (1779) : Rudwick, *Bursting the Limits*, 151–53. For a handy explanation of the confusing sequence of de Luc's publications, see Martin J.S. Rudwick, "Jean-André de Luc and Nature's Chronology," in *The Age of the Earth from 4004 BC to AD 2002*, ed. C.L.E. Lewis and S.J. Knell, GS Special Publications (London: The Geological Society, 2001), 55. Hence the different publication years in, for instance, Roberts, "Genesis Chapter 1," 43, 48.

[226] Rudwick, *Bursting the Limits*, 154ff., esp. 158; Rudwick, "Jean-André de Luc," 58; Porter, *Making of Geology*, 165.

[227] Rudwick, *Bursting the Limits*, 307, 310.

[228] Ibid., 329. It is the explicit correlation of the geological past with Genesis from these letters that is represented in de la Fite's translation: Rudwick, *Bursting the Limits*, 367.

[229] Ibid., 151; Rudwick, "Jean-André de Luc," 56.

[230] Jean André de Luc, *Letters on the Physical History of the Earth, Addressed to Professor Blumenbach: Containing Geological and Historical Proofs of the Divine Mission of Moses*, ed. Henry de la Fite (London: C.J.G. Rivington, 1831), 229, etc. GB, http://books.google.com/books?id=Q6UAAAAAMAAJ.

and sea, i.e. the collapse of the then-existing continents into the oceans, and the uplift of the ocean beds to form new continents.[231] This idea, as old as Aristotle, had also appeared in Buffon's work, and would significantly influence the conservative 'scriptural geology' of the early nineteenth century.[232] Yet natural processes prior to the Flood, de Luc was convinced from the stratigraphic evidence, had continued "for a considerable length of time." The Mosaic chronology imposed no limits here such as applied after the Flood.[233] The strata of the earth's crust had been laid down by chemical precipitation under the primordial oceans, in keeping with a Neptunist, Wernerian or falling-sea-level model of the earth's formation.[234]

De Luc believed that the days of Genesis 1 had to be figuratively interpreted, and asserted as early as 1793 that "he had long rejected any attempt to compress the whole early history of Earth into six literal days."[235] In preparing to recount the geological history of the earth in the letters to Blumenbach, he briefly offers and defends his view concerning these days:

> The operations … recited in the first chapter of Genesis, are there divided into six periods, called, in our translations, "days;" and upon the common interpretation of this word it is, that unbelievers have founded their most specious objections against Revelation. For with a slight knowledge of geology, it was easy to oppose many phenomena to a succession of such events as would have taken up only six of our days of twenty-four hours.[236]

De Luc argues that on the basis of the late appearance of the sun on Day 4, "The days in question … are not days of twenty-four hours, but certain portions of time of an indeterminate length." De Luc then turns quickly to his geological treatment, reluctant to be caught dwelling too long on the biblical text, and sets about "showing the astonishing conformity of our geological monuments with the whole of this sublime history, in its precise order; and that the attentive reader may

[231] Ibid., 42, 182–90 (within the letters themselves).

[232] On the connection with Aristotle, see Kelly, "Rise of Historical Geology," 219.

[233] De Luc, *Letters*, Introduction, 86, 89. Pages 86–117 of the introduction constitute a summary by de Luc's editor, de la Fite, of de Luc's views regarding the length of the days of creation as drawn from other sources, combined with supporting argumentation from ancient and recent authorities, from Origen and Augustine (see pp. 100f.) to James Parkinson (pp. 112–13).

[234] Gillispie, *Genesis and Geology*, 58. His thought also shows apparent influence from Burnet, as he often speaks of the 'ruins' of past catastrophes. His idea that the ocean basins and inclined strata formed when the earth's crust collapsed into eroded caverns is reminiscent of Steno's and of Le Cat's models. On the 'falling sea level' model, see Rudwick, *Bursting the Limits*, 173.

[235] Ibid.

[236] De Luc, *Letters*, 82.

notice this agreement (though henceforth I shall treat this subject only as it relates to natural history and physics) I shall divide into SIX PERIODS, the series of physical operations which have taken place upon our globe."[237]

Those physical operations begin as passive initial matter, incapable of any kind of self-assembly, is put into action by the creation of light in the first period.[238] Light is thus the agent ordained by God to drive the processes of creation.[239] The precipitation of the primary rocks (particularly granite) occupied the second period, producing the basic crust of the earth.[240] Subsequent aqueous processes undermined this crust, redepositing different rock types. This undermining process finally grew to catastrophic proportions, producing "the first general revolution that has left deep vestiges upon our globe; since it is that by which its surface first became divided into sea and dry land," though these original continents are long since gone. The early vegetation of this third period has gone to make up our present coal beds.[241] The fourth period saw the earth's own primordial fire principle running low, but the enormous phosphoric body of the sun reach its full light-generating capacity through its ongoing decomposition.[242]

The fifth period saw a change in the precipitating solution so that limestone, containing the relics of the earliest sea creatures, began to be deposited.[243] Further subsidence episodes altered the composition of the global solution, which precipitated distinctive rock types each time, while disruption and tilting of the existing strata produced the 'ruins' we now see.[244] Meanwhile, "In proportion as the atmosphere approximated to its present state, plants, and ... marine and terrestrial animals, in like manner approached still nearer and nearer to the species known at this day."[245] The sixth period witnessed the first existence and hence deposition of land animal fossils, "when the greater part of the stony strata ... had already suffered the catastrophes I have described in the preceding periods." Then de Luc briefly reiterates "that these SIX PERIODS bore a relation to the SIX DAYS mentioned in the first chapter of Genesis," so that "nature herself pays homage to that sacred

[237] Ibid., 83.

[238] Ibid., 83–93. Here we may notice affinities with the more chemically-oriented geotheories that prioritise the agency of light. The reference to self-assembly is effectively a refutation of Cartesian cosmology and its derivatives.

[239] De Luc, *Letters*, 81, 84. For many decades prior to de Luc a kind of 'chemical philosophy' had been popular that made light the great agent of chemical action.

[240] Ibid., 93–105.

[241] Ibid., 105–11.

[242] Ibid., 111–15.

[243] Ibid., 116ff.

[244] For the use of this term, see e.g. ibid., 119, 153.

[245] Ibid., 159–60.

and sublime history."[246] The last great catastrophic subsidence produced the stable globe that we presently see, that catastrophe being equivalent to the Deluge with which God vowed to "destroy them *with the earth*," that is, with the continents of the time, which fell into the sea while the present continents were uplifted.[247]

C.C. Gillispie thought that de Luc showed signs of "the burden of serving two masters," both acknowledging the principle of disallowing any biblical or other presuppositions from influencing what must be a purely inductive scientific process, but then seeking after the fact to show "how human beings were related to the earth, within a cosmology that related everything to God," and to reinforce the reliability and sanctity of "that sacred and sublime [Mosaic] history."[248] Gordon Davies called de Luc's work "a splendid example of the eighteenth century relapse from sense to nonsense."[249] But in the context of the period he was an innovator, combining Buffon's half-hearted strategy with better practical geological knowledge and a more serious attitude to the biblical text to produce a harmonistic model that influenced Cuvier, Jameson, and others. At de Luc's hands, "The Hexaëmeron had been rationalized into a directional naturalistic Earth history."[250] But this significant effort would suffer obsolescence as the religious presuppositions that undergirded de Luc's concordism were progressively filtered out of earth science: "the all-embracing character of his work, like that of other geotheorists, was passing out of fashion."[251]

Long Creation Days in the Late Eighteenth Century

Zöckler names several other important German advocates of periodic or day-age schemes in the late eighteenth century: J.D. Michaelis (1717–91), J.C. Döderlein (1746–92) and G. Hensler (d. 1791). Michaelis combined a ruin-restitution teaching with a creation week whose first three days were unusually long. Döderlein held his periodic day view in opposition to Eichhorn's nonconcordist portrayal of the six days as an edifying fiction. Hensler's exegetical strategy was to understand the terms 'evening', 'morning', 'day' and 'night' as collective ones, such that an indefinite series of evenings and mornings yielded

[246] Ibid., 173–80.

[247] Ibid., 182–272.

[248] Gillispie, *Genesis and Geology*, 56, 65–66; Martin J.S. Rudwick, "The Shape and Meaning of Earth History," in *God and Nature: Historical Essays on the Encounter between Christianity and Science*, ed. D.C. Lindberg and R. Numbers (Berkeley: University of California Press, 1986), 310–11; De Luc, *Letters*, 180; Rudwick, *Bursting the Limits*, 332.

[249] Davies, *Earth in Decay*, 138.

[250] Porter, *Making of Geology*, 201–202.

[251] Ibid.

each 'day' or period. Michaelis' example reminds us that during this exploratory stage for harmonizing interpretations, day-age, ruin-restitution, and the older long chaos interpretations were not yet felt to be mutually exclusive.[252]

In the English-speaking world, late eighteenth-century writers generally show openness to 'deep time' without always having a method (or else an inclination) to find harmony with Genesis 1. William Worthington awkwardly combines a rather literal exposition of Genesis 1 with a long chaos-based cosmogony, admitting that the formation of "the original shapeless mass of the earth ... would perhaps require many years, if not ages."[253] Bishop Richard Watson (1737–1816), in *An Apology for Christianity* (1776) maintains the recent arrival of the human race while denying "that there is any thing in the history of Moses repugnant to this opinion concerning the great antiquity of the earth."[254] Oliver Goldsmith's famous *History of the Earth* scrupulously avoids any reference to Genesis.[255] Scottish geologist and geotheorist James Hutton made no reference to Genesis but conceded the recency of the human race alone in his *Theory of the Earth* (1795). Hutton's cyclical theory of the earth was first published in the *Transactions of the Royal Society of Edinburgh* in 1788, and famously concludes that the geological evidence shows "no vestige of a beginning, – no prospect of an end."[256] John Whitehurst's 1778 geotheory, however, defends the biblical witnesses, with statements touching on the various days of creation that could be interpreted in periodic terms.[257] Day-age style views of Genesis 1 were probably not uncommon among educated Britons in the last half of the eighteenth century, but they held their peace until emboldened by Buffon's and de Luc's well publicized harmonizing schemes.

[252] Zöckler, *Geschichte*, 2:500–501, 513. A hint of a day-age teaching is visible in J.D. Michaelis, *Commentaries on the Laws of Moses*, trans. Alexander Smith, 4 vols. (London: printed for F.C. and J. Rivington, 1814), 3:158–59. Henry de la Fite claimed Michaelis' name as a precedent for de Luc's views: de Luc, *Letters*, 88, 101.

[253] W. Worthington, *The Scripture Theory of the Earth* (London: printed for J. and F. Rivington ... 1773), 29, ECCO.

[254] Watson, *Apology*, 257.

[255] Oliver Goldsmith, *An History of the Earth, and Animated Nature*, 8 vols., vol. I (London: printed for J. Nourse, 1774), ECCO. Roy Porter describes this work as "the classic embodiment of the popularization of eclectic Enlightenment views of the Earth," and "probably the most popular work of natural history in Enlightenment Britain": Porter, *Making of Geology*, 110–11.

[256] James Hutton, *Theory of the Earth: Investigation into Laws observable in the Composition, Dissolution, and Restoration of Land upon the Globe* (n.p.: Forgotten Books, 2007), 10, http://books.google.com/books?id=1bmiLkX5pPkC.

[257] E.g. also John Whitehurst, *An Inquiry into the Original State and Formation of the Earth Deduced from Facts and the Laws of Nature ...* (London: Cooper, 1778), 28, 80–83, ECCO.

At the very close of the century we find clearer examples of day-age thought in Britain.[258] Hutton's Aristotelian, timeless *Theory of the Earth* galvanized responses from de Luc (below), Philip Howard, whom Francis Haber identifies as a day-age advocate, and Irish mineralogist Richard Kirwan (1733–1812).[259] While Kirwan's essay against Hutton's theory that is included in his *Geological Essays* (1799) makes no reference to Genesis, the introductory section of the collected work defends the use of another source besides natural data, that is, historical testimony, and Kirwan means especially the divinely revealed testimony of Moses. The exact correspondence of this testimony with what can be known from observation confirms its reliability, and the natural inaccessibility of the content of this testimony, especially in a pre-geological age, confirms its divine origin.

Such favouring of written testimony as historical evidence over mute physical remains was often a factor in resistance to theoretical geology going into the nineteenth century.[260] We should observe, however, that Kirwan did not hold to a 'young earth' in the sense of modern creationism; as he explains his 'Neptunist' or diminishing ocean model of the earth's formation, wherein the strata precipitate from aqueous solution and the elevation of their embedded fossils indicates their relative time of creation, Kirwan several times emphasizes the considerable length of time required. "The regularity and uniformity of these strata strongly indicate a cause whose action was regular and uniform and long continued." The retreat of the sea "was not sudden, but continued for several ages," keeping in mind that the envisioned 'ages' could have had quite a modest scope.[261]

Kirwan's ensuing treatment of Genesis 1 represents a subtle day-age interpretation. He undertakes his hexaemeral interpretation only after articulating his geotheoretical model in order to show, after the fact as

[258] The Swiss de Luc had lived in England from 1773: Rudwick, *Bursting the Limits*, 151.

[259] Gillispie, *Genesis and Geology*, 44, 46, 49ff; Greene, *Death of Adam*, 76, 78, 80; Toulmin and Goodfield, *The Discovery of Time*, 154–55; Rossi, *Dark Abyss*, 118; Young, *Age of the Earth*, 48. The ensuing debate reveals itself in the definitive, two-volume, 1795 *Theory of the Earth*, where Hutton reports that one opponent says that he (Hutton) has "endeavoured to trace back the operations of this world to a remote period, by the examination of that which actually appears, contrary, as is alleged, 'to reason, and the tenor of the Mosaic history, thus leading to an abyss, from which human reason recoils'." Hutton, *Theory of the Earth*, 170, 175. Greene identifies this unidentified antagonist as Kirwan: Greene, *Death of Adam*, 80. On Philip Howard, see Haber, *Age of the World*, 192–93.

[260] Richard Kirwan, *Geological Essays* (London: D. Bremner, 1799), 433–99, ECCO. The anti-Huttonian essay is, 'Essay X. on the Huttonian Theory of the Earth.' Ibid., 4–6. On the favouring of textual witnesses, see the introduction to the following chapter.

[261] Ibid., 37–38; Rudwick, *Bursting the Limits*, 336; Rappaport, *Geologists*, 191–92.

it were, the perfect conformity of that account with the natural data. Kirwan perceives in Genesis 1 a series of geological events: (1) Initial creation (Gen. 1:1), which includes all the planets; (2) A great evaporation process, accompanied by the precipitation of solid rock from solution ('the/a spirit of God moved on the face of the waters', Gen. 1:2); (3) The formation of the mountains "in the bosom of the waters;"[262] (4) "The production of light" (Gen. 1:3f.); (5) "The production of the atmosphere (or 'firmament', Gen. 1:6f.); (6) The gathering of the waters to reveal dry land (Gen. 1:9f.); (7) The creation of fish (Gen. 1:20f.); (8) The creation of land animals (Gen. 1:24f.).[263]

"Here then," concludes Kirwan, "we have seven or eight geological facts, related by Moses on the one part, and on the other, deduced solely from the most exact and best verified geological observations, and yet agreeing perfectly with each other, not only in *substance*, but in the order of their succession."[264] Terrestrial formation is very much progressive, but this is in fact also true of the six-day structure of Genesis 1.[265] Kirwan finally supplements this concordance with a figurative interpretation of the word 'day'. The 'light' of Gen. 1:3, probably denoting volcanic 'flames', existed for a period that "Moses called *day*, evidently from its resemblance to *true* days, which could have only existed at a subsequent period, namely after the sun had gained its luminous powers."[266]

Indeed, thinks Kirwan, the facts of the earth's origin are in Genesis clothed in "mere anthropological phrases, suited to the conception of those to whom these facts were related." 'God said' signifies in each case "no more than that events naturally possible took place by virtue of the laws of their production."[267] Despite his frequent portrayal as a hard-nosed literalist, and his stout defence of the 'Mosaic writings' as an authoritative source of information, Kirwan's interpretation of the creation days is broad and figurative, involving a far-reaching accommodation principle, and his understanding of creation was naturalistic, notwithstanding his opposition to Hutton's eternalism.[268]

[262] It isn't certain whether this forms an element in the list, and may be the questionable item that leads to Kirwan's 'seven or eight geological facts' statement on p. 52.

[263] Kirwan, *Geological Essays*, 48–52.

[264] Ibid., 52.

[265] Ibid., 51.

[266] Ibid., 50.

[267] Ibid., 49–50.

[268] Gillispie, *Genesis and Geology*, 56. See Nicolaas Rupke's critique of Gillispie's historiography along similar lines: ibid., xii–xiii.

Conclusion

When the eighteenth century started, the possibility that the 'days' of Genesis 1 might be understood as much longer periods of time had already been floated, as we have seen. Whiston's long day scheme represented the persisting quest for a concord with Genesis, a quest already renounced by Burnet, virtually ignored by Leibniz, and perhaps parodied by de Maillet. John Witty meanwhile countered with his literal interpretation of the creation week, while Woodwardian diluvialism helped to maintain such literal approaches to the creation week during the early decades of the eighteenth century. But the tide of opinion turned away from diluvialism and towards the deep time of a diminishing ocean and/or a long history of volcanism. Moro offered a periodic day-based 'geology and Genesis' harmonization, and Augustine's figurative days were employed by Joseph Needham as an ecclesiastical license for a day-age interpretation of Genesis 1. Buffon, expediently, and then de Luc, sincerely, offered day-age concordism as an alternative to the vigorous semi-concordism of the ruin-restitution theory, while with Kirwan the day-age model took root afresh in the British sphere.

6

Nineteenth-Century Interpretation of the Days of Creation until the *Origin of Species* and *Essays and Reviews*

> The Sea of Faith
> Was once, too, at the full, and round earth's shore
> Lay like the folds of a bright girdle furl'd.
> But now I only hear
> Its melancholy, long, withdrawing roar,
> Retreating, to the breath
> Of the night-wind, down the vast edges drear
> And naked shingles of the world.
>
> Matthew Arnold, 'Dover Beach', c. 1851

Introduction

In this chapter I describe a nineteenth-century battle over concordism, the effort to bring Genesis and science into agreement, not in order to subscribe to the simplistic and discredited 'conflict thesis' which narrated a battle between science and religion (e.g. the Christian church) for the soul of the West, with science the victor. This black-and-white picture fails to do justice to the fact, for example, that many British scientists in the period prior to Darwin were clergymen themselves, often manifesting a sincere faith. The stressed atmosphere that often characterized the 'Genesis and geology' debates of the nineteenth century certainly indicates that some sort of conflict existed, but it was pluriform, with changing boundaries and agendas. Those who sought to establish a harmony between scientific research and the Bible, and specifically between geology and Genesis, debated those who believed such a program to be ill-conceived either because the two sources of knowledge did not really overlap, or because the information found in Genesis was now outmoded. The problem of biblically unmentioned or inexplicable natural data was coming to a head.[1] Resistance to the

[1] Haber, *Age of the World*, 35.

concordism that had been popular in the later eighteenth century was growing, and climaxed in a vigorous debate around 1860, the historical end-point of this study. Amidst this debate, the concordist or day-age interpretation of the creation week passed its peak in the mainstream scientific world, though it would live on in Christian circles. Meanwhile the semi-concordist gap theory, still motivated by the quest for agreement with scientific findings, would at times retain great popularity in the same circles and eventually become a standard position for early twentieth-century conservative Christians.

France and Germany had been centre-stage for the intellectual developments of the Enlightenment in the eighteenth century and had spawned the pioneering harmonizing schemes, the most sophisticated philosophies concerning creation and the historical criticism of the Bible. But the epicentre of efforts to relate Gen. 1:1-2:3 to the world's physical origin shifts to Britain in the first half of the nineteenth century. Partly because the English school of geologists were mostly clerics, and interested in seeking a place for the study of geology at twin institutions whose purpose was clerical training, Oxford and Cambridge Universities, Buckland and his fellows were motivated to seek a harmony between the Genesis text and geological findings. They did this at first, during the 1820s, by assuming that the biblical Flood was responsible for indications of 'diluvial' effects on the landscape in western Europe, and later by seeking strategies that would ultimately define the mostly separate spheres of biblical/human and geological history.[2]

Rupke reminds us that debates over geology and/or the concordist enterprise were complicated by differing views concerning what counted as historical evidence. An important classicist tradition of English scholarship, well-represented within the walls of Oxford, strongly relied on documentary evidence, that is, written testimony, to establish reliably the events of history. Monumental remains and the like ranked a poor second and could not interpret themselves; they could only be understood and historically located with the aid of written historical accounts. Therefore Christian convictions and classicist sympathies tended to reinforce one another in many educated minds in favour of biblical testimony.

Yet the gathering sense amongst geologists of earth's past 'narrative', of a geohistorical story that explained the strata and their embedded fossils, was essentially the product of inference from unwritten remains. For geologists, the impressions of deep time, species extinction, fossil progression and the like proved irresistible. But for classicists, inference could communicate nothing reliable about the past, while the testimony of Genesis stretched all the way back to creation, communicating

[2] Rupke, *Great Chain of History,* 5, 9, 17, 21, 51, 61–62, 204–205.

facts that were otherwise inaccessible. The reliability of its account was verified by other, albeit poorer ancient textual witnesses, for instance in the many flood legends related by other ancient cultures. With such written testimony on hand (though its eyewitness status and/or revelatory nature were open to question), such thinkers saw no need to abandon it in favour of the uncertain inferences of unreliable and arguably sinful human minds about the past. Reasoning by inference was far from being a universally-accepted method for discovering information about the past, and many thinkers were yet to be persuaded that history, human or terrestrial, fell within the province of science.[3]

The Emerging Impact of Biblical Criticism

A developing eighteenth-century continental trend towards applying literary criticism to the Bible had received one of its seminal treatments in Jean Astruc's (1684–1766) *Conjectures on Genesis* (1753), whose full title reminds us that Genesis particularly was the proving ground for early biblical source criticism.[4] Astruc theorized that Moses, in composing Genesis, had used pre-existing written sources, and Astruc offered a breakdown of these ostensible sources.[5] It was J.G. Eichhorn's more systematic articulation of this idea in his *Introduction to the Old Testament* (1780–83) that brought this approach to Genesis into mainstream scholarship.[6] He still treated the sources of Genesis as pre-Mosaic and argued for the superiority of the Genesis cosmogony among its ancient analogues, emphasizing the 'authenticity' (*Aechtheit*) of Genesis.[7] Yet his focus on literary history at the expense of theology embodied the general approach of the subsequent historical-critical tradition.[8] For historical criticism, the early chapters of Genesis, famous for the differential occurrence of the divine names or titles *Elohim* and *Yahweh*, would serve as the classic test piece.

[3] Ibid., 47–63.

[4] *Conjectures sur les mémoires originaux dont il paroît que Moyse se servit pour composer le livre de la Genèse* (Conjectures on the original memoirs which Moses apparently used to compose the book of Genesis)

[5] Jaki, *Genesis 1*, 191–92. Gerald Bray among others notes that the same idea has now been traced to a little-known German, H.B. Witter, writing in 1711: Bray, *Biblical Interpretation*, 240. Astruc's participation in early eighteenth century discussions about fossils is noted by Rappaport, *Geologists*, 96, 195.

[6] Reventlow incidentally discovers the same theory in a little-known manuscript of Herder's from the late 1760s. Reventlow, "Century of Enlightenment," 1044.

[7] Johann Gottfried Eichhorn, *Einleitung in das Alte Testament*, 4th ed., vol. III (Göttingen: Carl Eduard Rosenbusch, 1823), 71ff., 146, GB, http://books.google.com/books?id=L1IHAAAAQAAJ.

[8] Reventlow, "Century of Enlightenment," 1052.

Both source-critical analysis and Eichhorn's mythical perspective on the creation accounts were imported into the English-speaking world by Alexander Geddes (1737–1802).[9] His *Critical Remarks on the Hebrew Scriptures* (1800) shows an openness to the ruin-restitution model, as when he says of the creation of light in Gen. 1:3, "This was the first step to *recover* the earth from its desolate condition, and the commencement of the six days creation."[10] The progress of the creation week is meanwhile described in classic, 'forming out of chaos' terms, as the light of the sun slowly penetrates the primordial "thick darkness that *covered the face of the deep*." The earth takes its final form on Day 3, as Geddes exults, "How simply, but how beautifully, is all this expressed!"[11] Throughout the narrative God speaks "like a wise architect, who contrives, examines, and approves his plans and their execution."[12] Geddes then adds,

> A question here occurs, whether by each of the six days, above mentioned, is meant a natural day of twenty-four hours; or some other longer period, called, accommodatively, a *day?* Some modern world-makers, to give themselves room for a slow, progressive creation, make *one day* a period of 1000 years. Why not as well ten thousand, or a million?

But Geddes is no concordist, and to him, "plain it is that the Hebrew writer, whether he divided his creation into days for the sake of a certain order, as I really think he did; or believed that things happened literally as he relates them; his *day* and *night* cannot be any other than a common day, or ἡμερονύκτιον of twenty-four hours. At every other acceptation grammar and sense revolt."[13]

So despite a biblical cosmology that is based on the long chaos idea, and indications of a schematic view of the creation week, Geddes confesses the creation days to be twenty-four hours long. Whether the author believed the creation week literally or not, he certainly *expressed* himself in literal terms, in that the days do not stand allegorically for anything else, especially not periods of time. They are chiefly a heuristic device, intended "to establish the belief of one supreme God and Creator, in opposition to the various and wild systems of idolatry which then prevailed; and … to enforce the observance of a weekly

[9] Rogerson, *Old Testament Criticism*, 154–57; Bray, *Biblical Interpretation*, 236.

[10] Alexander Geddes, *Critical Remarks on the Hebrew Scriptures: Corresponding with a New Translation of the Bible … Volume I. Containing Remarks on the Pentateuch* (London: printed for the author by Davis, Wilks, and Taylor: and sold by R. Faulder; and J. Johnson, 1800), 1.14, ECCO. Italics mine. The context also reveals an aesthetic sensibility to the text that suggests the influence of J.G. Herder.

[11] Ibid., 1:17–18.

[12] Ibid., 1:15. See also p. 22, on Gen. 1:31.

[13] Ibid., 1:23.

Sabbath."[14] Geddes soon makes this apparent break between the biblical presentation and the physical reality explicit:

> Do I believe, then, that the narrative of Genesis is not a literally true narration? or that it is in all, or many of its parts, a pure allegory? I believe, neither the one nor the other: I believe it to be a most beautiful *mythos*, or philosophical fiction, contrived with great wisdom, dressed up in the garb of real history, adapted … to the shallow intellects of a rude barbarous nation; and perfectly well calculated for the great and good purposes for which it was contrived …[15]

The author of Genesis, rather than attempting a philosophical treatment that would have been opaque to his audience, described "a Creator resembling other artists." "A wiser system of cosmogony could not, certainly, be imagined.… Everything in it bears witness to the great sagacity … of the sapient inventor. The very circumstance of making God speak … was an admirable device to gain attention to his narrative, and respect to his theory."[16] Thus Geddes attributes the noble qualities of the passage not to divine inspiration but to an effective human author, and formalizes the separation of the narrative from the prehistoric reality to which it ostensibly corresponds by characterizing the creation story of Genesis as myth, as had Eichhorn.[17]

The mainstream English clerical reaction is typified by T.H. Horne's *Introduction to the Critical Study and Knowledge of the Holy Scriptures* (1818), when he insists,

> The style of these chapters, as indeed of the whole book of Genesis, is strictly historical, and betrays no vestige whatever of allegorical or figurative description.… Besides, if it be granted that Moses was an inspired lawgiver, it becomes impossible to suppose that he wrote a fabulous account of the creation and fall of man, and delivered it as a divine revelation, because that would have been little, if at all, short of blasphemy; we must therefore believe this account to be true.[18]

Geddes was ahead of his time, and he seems to have had little following in the English speaking world.[19] But he exemplifies the way

[14] Ibid., 1:26, 28.

[15] Ibid., 1:26.

[16] Ibid., 1:27–28.

[17] Geddes claims to have come to this belief independently of Eichhorn: ibid., 1:29.

[18] Horne, *Introduction*, 4:6–7. Naturally, reference to what Moses would do begs the question of authorship as it pertains to Geddes' own position. Horne seems to hold to a literal creation week, despite quoting Jameson's reference to "the periods of time, the six days of the Mosaic description": ibid., 1:591. His 1825 edition cites Granville Penn's 'vindication of the literal interpretation of the first chapter of Genesis,' with approval: ibid., 4:7.

[19] Like the German criticism of the time: Rogerson, *Old Testament Criticism*, 156–57.

that critical approaches to Genesis tended to minimize its authority and accuracy as a cosmogony, and thus to support a non-concordist interpretive approach that would not look for real prehistoric events or eras in Genesis 1.

The Day-Age Approach in Early Nineteenth-Century Britain and France

The debate over how the findings of natural science, especially geology, could be reconciled with the biblical narrative dominated nineteenth-century British study of Genesis.[20] Eventually the stand-alone nature of biological evolution and the purchase finally gained in the Anglophone world by biblical criticism would encourage different priorities in the study of Genesis, but at this stage of feverish interest in the earth sciences, many readers naturally brought to Genesis a consciousness of discoveries and ideas from geology and palaeontology. In a recent article on the scriptural geologists, Ralph O'Connor, of the University of Aberdeen, points out,

> [T]he Bible was still the most important book in early nineteenth-century British cultural life. Although liberal churchmen were busily instructing people that the Bible was not intended to teach facts about the natural world, the text of Genesis 1 appeared on the face of it to suggest otherwise, with its bald statements of what had been created when. For all but a growing minority, the Bible remained a vital touchstone for speculation about the natural world; conversely, any thoughtful reading of the first few chapters of Genesis necessarily involved reflections about the natural world.[21]

Biblical creation plays little part early in James Parkinson's (1755–1824) *Organic Remains of a Former World* (1804–11), whose conceptual matrix is initially strictly diluvial.[22] Having shifted by the time he published volume III to a more gradualist model of geological agency, Parkinson undertakes a Neptunist reading of Days 3, 5 and 6 of the Hexaemeron.[23] Having surveyed British sedimentary strata, Parkinson

[20] The sheer abundance of material also forces me to be more 'anglocentric' in this chapter than I would prefer. I would again refer the reader to Zöckler, *Geschichte* as still the most comprehensive coverage of continental science-oriented treatments of Genesis available for the first two-thirds of the century. I restrict myself here to some of the key English-speaking advocates of the concordist day-age approach.

[21] R. O'Connor, "Young-Earth Creationists in Early Nineteenth-Century Britain? Towards a Reassessment of 'Scriptural Geology'," *History of Science* 45 (2007): 391.

[22] James Parkinson, *Organic Remains of a Former World: An Examination of the Mineralized Remains of Vegetables and Animals of the Antediluvian World, Generally Termed Extraneous Fossils*, 3 vols. (London: J. Robson, 1804–11), 1:255.

[23] Ibid., 3:443. For more on the 'Neptunian' or falling-sea-level model associated with Abraham Werner, see the previous chapter.

concludes "that the formation of the exterior part of this globe, and the creation of its several inhabitants, must have been the work of a vast length of time." The separation of "the granitic and other primary rocks ... from the water" clearly fits the description in Day 3, while the creation of 'vegetables' on Day 3, the fish and birds of Day 5 and the land animals Day 6 all match the first substantial appearance of these groups in the geological column. Parkinson concludes with an air of pleasant surprise:

> From the whole examination a pleasing, and perhaps unexpected accordance appears between the order in which, according to the scriptural account, creation was accomplished, and the order in which the fossil remains of creation are found.... So close indeed is this agreement, that the Mosaic account is thereby confirmed in every respect, except as to the age of the world.[24]

So on a literal understanding of the word 'day', an unavoidable clash must still result between the creation account and the evidence of geology. "But if, on the other hand, the word day be admitted as figuratively designating certain indefinite periods, in which particular parts of the great work of creation were accomplished, no difficulty will then remain," though there be "little support in such a change from the critical expositors of this part of scriptural history." "Supposing," then, "the creation to have been performed in the order related in Genesis, ... it only becomes necessary to consider these periods as occurring at considerable indefinite lengths of time, to prove an exact agreement between that particular history and those phenomena which appear on examining the stratification of the earth."[25] Parkinson's is therefore one of the clearest yet presentations of the day-age approach to Genesis in the English-speaking world, while his tentativeness indicates the controversial nature of such a claim at this early point. His transition from a young-earth belief with a diluvial emphasis to a day-age one exemplifies the changing perspective of his intellectual generation in Britain.[26]

The science of palaeontology looks back with reverence to Georges Cuvier's (1769–1832) pioneering methods of comparative anatomy in the service of fossil reconstruction. He is sometimes also portrayed as a pioneer of the day-age interpretation, as when Mangenot says, "Cuvier ... had distinguished in the geological layers six epochs which corre-

[24] Ibid., 3:449–51, with quote on final page.

[25] Ibid., 3:451–53.

[26] Roberts, "Geology and Genesis Unearthed," unpaginated electronic edition. Rudwick's statement, "The accommodation of Genesis to a long timescale was itself highly traditional," I think a little overstated, especially for the British scene, and outside savant circles: Rudwick, *Bursting the Limits*, 497.

sponded to the six days of creation, but which were separated by violent catastrophes."[27] Zöckler, although acknowledging that Cuvier "makes less of an effort to go into a detailed harmonization of the mutual accounts," reports that Cuvier asserts, "The long-drawn-out sequence of earlier organic creatures ... offers certain clear agreements with the ascending series of creative acts described in Genesis."[28] There are no such explicit sentiments in Cuvier's *Discourse on the Revolutions of the Globe* (1812), where Cuvier endorses the Mosaic authorship of Genesis and alludes favourably to the Flood account but entirely passes over the Hexaemeron.[29]

The *Discourse* argues for a long earth history, a belief that was evidently far from uncontested, punctuated by large-scale catastrophes which intersect and subdivide that history, the last of which is geologically recent, separating the present system of life on earth from prior ones, and so described as to be readily identified with the deluge of Noah.[30] Cuvier pleads for the establishment of a fossil-based stratigraphic sequence, in contrast with the hopelessly speculative cosmogonies of preceding generations.[31] Reflecting on the systems of Burnet, Woodward and Whiston, Cuvier complains,

> It is easy to see, that though naturalists might have a range sufficiently wide within the limits prescribed by the book of Genesis, they very soon found themselves in too narrow bound; and when they had succeeded in converting the six days employed in the work of creation into so many periods of indefinite length, their systems took a flight proportioned to the periods, which they could then dispose of at pleasure.[32]

[27] Mangenot, "Hexaméron," 6:2341–42. More subtly, see Jaki, *Genesis 1*, 203–04.

[28] Zöckler, *Geschichte*, 2:505–06.

[29] The *Discourse* prefaces Cuvier's famous *Researches on Fossil Bones*. The original titles are *Discours sur les révolutions du globe et sur les changements qu'elles ont produits dans le règne animal* and *Recherches sur les ossemens fossiles de quadrupèdes, où l'on rétablit les caractères de plusieurs espèces d'animaux que les révolutions du globe paroissent avoir détruites*. I have used Georges Cuvier, *Essay on the Theory of the Earth*, ed. Robert Jameson, trans. R. Kerr (Edinburgh: W. Blackwood, 1813). I have also checked the edition used by Jaki, Georges Cuvier, *A Discourse on the Revolutions of the Surface of the Globe, and the Changes Thereby Produced in the Animal Kingdom* (Philadelphia: Carey & Lea, 1831), http://books.google.com/books?id=mqAaAAAAYAAJ. The change identified by Rudwick in editions of this work subsequent to 1821 do not affect the creation week: Martin J.S. Rudwick, *Worlds before Adam: The Reconstruction of Geohistory in the Age of Reform* (Chicago, London: University of Chicago Press, 2008), 18.

[30] On his argument for deep time, see Cuvier, *Theory of the Earth*, 131. Fossil preservation by means of sudden burial is one of his arguments for a complex, catastrophic earth history: ibid., 15–17.

[31] Ibid., 180–81.

[32] Ibid., 41.

Cuvier therefore demonstrates quite a jaundiced view of attempted reconciliations of earth history with the creation accounts, and seems disinclined to repeat their error. He connects the Mosaic record with the beginning of human rather than earth history.[33] By concentrating research on secondary strata, he thought the lapse into unfounded speculation about the earth's formation could be avoided, in favour of the much more reliable evidence from fossils.[34] So the 'Preliminary Discourse' provides evidence less of any intention to harmonize science and Genesis than of the fact that as "a man of the Enlightenment ... he always maintained that science and religion should be kept strictly separate."[35]

Yet Cuvier allowed himself to make comparisons between the geological record and the Mosaic creation account before a popular audience. Rudwick explains that Cuvier began a series of popular lectures at the Parisian Athénée des Arts in 1805 by asserting, "the fossil record conformed in broad outline to the creation story in Genesis, provided that there was the usual assumption that the biblical "days" were long stretches of time," an admission that Rudwick regards as made "almost casually and in passing," in order to make room for a genuine history of the earth.[36] And an 1830 journal article reported that another Parisian lecture by Cuvier featured the assertion,

> [Moses'] cosmogony especially, considered in a purely scientific view, is extremely remarkable, inasmuch as the order which it assigns to the different epochs of creation, is precisely the same as that which has been deduced from geological considerations. According to Genesis, after the earth and the heavens had been formed and animated by light, the aquatic animals were created, then plants, then terrestrial animals, and last of all man.[37] Now this is precisely what geology teaches us. In the deposites (*sic*) which have been first consolidated, and which, consequently are the deepest seated, there occur no organic remains; the earth, then, was therefore without inhabitants. In proportion as we approach the upper strata, we find appearing at first shells and remains of fishes, the remains of large reptiles, then bones of quadrupeds. As to the bones of the human race, they are met with only in alluvial deposites, in caves and in the fis-

[33] Ibid., 147–48.

[34] Ibid., 45, 54, etc.

[35] Cohn, *Noah's Flood*, 113; Greene, *Death of Adam*, 125. The verification of the biblical and other ancient flood accounts through the marks of a recent earth catastrophe form the limited exception to this rule, in the train of de Luc and another Frenchman, Dolomieu. But for Cuvier this reads more as a consultation with ancient literary witnesses than as any dabbling in religion. Cuvier, *Theory of the Earth*, 171; Rudwick, *Bursting the Limits*, 364.

[36] Rudwick, *Bursting the Limits*, 447, 454.

[37] It may be worth pointing out that this is *not* the biblical sequence at all, which puts vegetation first.

> sures of rocks; which shows that man made his appearance upon the earth after all the other classes of animals.[38]

This is apparently the clearest available concordist statement from Cuvier, but it still does not warrant regarding Cuvier as the founder of the day-age or periodist approach to Genesis, since his version probably derives from de Luc, just as his statements on the latest diluvial catastrophe imply a debt to de Luc's 'natural chronometers'.[39] It was by virtue of his great scientific authority that Cuvier's mostly inferred endorsement helped the periodic day cause, especially as harnessed by the Scottish Wernerian, Robert Jameson (1774–1854).[40] Jameson added extensive notes and a preface to an English translation of Cuvier's 1812 *Discourse*, and entitled it, *Essay on the Theory of the Earth*, making it sound like another of the speculative geotheories which Cuvier so disliked.[41] Jameson's preface supplements Cuvier's qualified diluvialism with a position on the creation week that is indebted to Whiston:

> Although the Mosaic account of the creation of the world is an inspired writing, and consequently rests on evidence totally independent of human observation and experience, it is still interesting ... to know that it coincides with the various phenomena observable in the mineral kingdom.... Even the periods of time, the six days of the Mosaic description, are not inconsistent with our theories of the earth.... The motions of the earth may have been slower during the time of [the earth's] formation than after it was formed, and consequently ... the day, or period between morn-

[38] Georges Cuvier, Baron, 1769–32, "Lectures on the History of the Natural Sciences," in *The Edinburgh New Philosophical Journal: Exhibiting a View of the Progressive Discoveries and Improvements in the Sciences and the Arts*, ed. Robert Jameson, William Jardine, and Henry Darwin Rogers (Edinburgh: A. and C. Black, 1830), 8:342, GB, http://books.google.com/books?id=sA0XAAAAYAAJ. This was cited by Robert Jameson in a subsequent article: Robert Jameson, "Remarks on Some of Baron Cuvier's Lectures on the History of the Natural Sciences, in Reference to the Scientific Knowledge of the Egyptians; of the Source from Whence Moses Derived his Cosmogony, and the General Agreement of that Cosmogony with Modern Geology," *Edinburgh New Philosophical Journal* 13 (1832): 41. It was then cited in turn via Jameson in Benjamin Silliman, "Suggestions Relative to the Philosophy of Geology as Deduced from the Facts and to the Consistency of Both the Facts and the Theory of This Science with Sacred History," in *An Introduction to Geology*, ed. Robert Bakewell (New Haven, CT: B. & W. Noyes, 1839), 554, GB, http://books.google.com/books?id=Ro9CAAAAIAAJ.

[39] Cuvier, "Lectures," 8:326–28.

[40] Gillispie, *Genesis and Geology*, 98–102.

[41] "[T]o put 'theory of the earth' into the title distorted Cuvier's whole project, for it replaced its primarily *geohistorical* goals with geotheory." Rudwick, *Bursting the Limits*, 510–11.

ing and evening, may have then been indefinitely longer than it is at present.[42]

Jameson is more of a pioneer of a systematic day-age interpretation than Cuvier.[43] He utilizes the harmonistic statement of Cuvier quoted above as the basis first of an exposition of Genesis 1 in geological (mainly biological) terms, and then of a table showing the harmony between Genesis and geology. The Hebrew term יוֹם *(yom)* or 'day' in Genesis 1 remains the interpretive crux. "A careful examination of the first chapter of Genesis itself, leads unavoidably to the conclusion, that our natural day of one revolution of the sun cannot be meant by it, for we find that no fewer than three of the six days had passed before the measure of our present day was established." Genesis 2:4 confirms "that the Hebrews used the term (yom) to express long periods of time," and Exod. 20:11 ought to be interpreted on this basis.[44] Jameson broadly describes the appearance of the different stages of life in progressive geological strata, with evident excitement at the 'coincidence' he perceives between Genesis and geology.[45] Wary of Francis Bacon's famous warning against unduly blending the studies of nature and divinity, Jameson claims to have treated each category using true Baconian induction, and to have discovered a correspondence that mutually confirms both. He believes that this permits the scientist to extract clues for his work from what he reads in Scripture.[46] Jameson was probably the most notable British day-age advocate in the nineteenth century, and was primarily responsible for the use of Cuvier's name to enhance the theory's authority.

There is further evidence for an increasing acceptance of the day-age solution in the Anglophone world of the early nineteenth century. Joseph Townsend (1739–1816), a clerical associate of the pioneering stratigrapher William Smith, defended a vaguely periodic understanding of the days of creation in *The Character of Moses Established for Ver-*

[42] Cuvier, *Theory of the Earth*, v–vii. I would suggest that had Cuvier said anything explicit (and not cynical) about the creation days in the body of his work, Jameson would gladly have utilised it.

[43] For their joint association with the theory in later writers, see e.g. John Pye Smith, *On the Relation between the Holy Scriptures and Some Parts of Geological Science* (New York: D. Appleton, 1840), 171, GB, http://books.google.com/books?id=QZUQAAAAIAAJ; Edward Hitchcock, *The Religion of Geology and Its Connected Sciences* (Boston: Phillips, Samson, and Company, 1851), 64; J.W. Dawson, *The Origin of the World, according to Revelation and Science*, 5th ed. (London: Hodder and Stoughton, 1888), 123.

[44] Jameson, "Remarks," 62–63.

[45] Jameson's scheme avoided mentioning, as Cuvier did in the context of the quote Jameson uses, that aquatic animals came before plants! Ibid.: 71–72.

[46] Ibid.: 73–74.

acity as an Historian (1813–15).[47] Townsend comments that the apparent diversification in fossil types as one ascends the strata "seems to indicate successive periods, and periods of uncertain length, which in scripture language, as it is conjectured, may have been denominated days." Although true days could not have existed prior to the sun's creation on Day 4, "yet, in perfect conformity to the prophetic language, the term *day* may be referred to *period* in general, without meaning to restrict the word to its present acceptation."[48] His attempt to debunk the recently claimed "antiquity of the present system, in opposition to the Chronology of Moses," indicates that the 'periods' he envisages were of quite limited scope.[49]

John Kidd (1775–1851) was thinking more expansively in his 1815 *Geological Essay*:

> And since the periods called days in the Mosaic history of Creation appear from the very terms of the history to have differed in their nature from what we now call by the same name, it is clearly impossible ... to define [their] measure ... and it is ... immaterial to our belief in the main point, whether they severally answer to only one, or to ten million revolutions of our globe.[50]

George S. Faber's (1773–1854) *Treatise on the Genius and Object of the Patriarchal, the Levitical, and the Christian Dispensations* (1823), seemingly melds the ancient, episodic catastrophes of Cuvier and de Luc with the world-week tradition to produce a periodic-day interpretation that takes the duration of human history (based on a short biblical chronology) as its guide for the length of each creative day. Because God's rest is unending, and follows the completion of creation, Faber understands Day 7 of creation to cover "a period commensurate with

[47] Joseph Townsend, *The Character of Moses Established for Veracity as an Historian: Recording Events from the Creation to the Deluge*, 2 vols. (Bath: Longman, Hurst, 1813, 1815). He is cited for this reason in de Luc, *Letters*, 101. See also M. Millhauser, "The Scriptural Geologists: An Episode in the History of Opinion," *Osiris* 11 (1954): 69.

[48] Townsend, *Character of Moses*, 1:411–12.

[49] Ibid., 1:431.

[50] J. Kidd, *A Geological Essay on the Imperfect Evidence in Support of a Theory of the Earth....* (Oxford: Oxford University Press, 1815), 13, GB, http://books.google.com/books?id=FGgUAAAAQAAJ. For a figure that stands vaguely aligned with the 'scriptural geologists' in Millhauser's 1954 article, this is quite a broad statement, and hardly a sample of biblical fundamentalism: Millhauser, "The Scriptural Geologists," 70. See Rudwick, *Bursting the Limits*, 537, 610. The famous English geologist of this period, William Buckland, in his early work, *Vindiciae Geologiae* (1819), shows an awareness of both the gap theory of Thomas Chalmers and the day-age option (citing Buffon's *Époques*): William Buckland, *Vindiciae Geologiae; or The Connexion of Geology with Religion Explained, in an Inaugural Lecture Delivered before the University of Oxford, May 15, 1819....* (Oxford: Oxford University Press, 1820), 31–33, National Library of Australia, http://nla.gov.au/nla.aus-vn2012561.

the duration of the created Universe," that is, "a period of not *less* duration than six millenaries." Therefore, "each of the six days must similarly and proportionately have been equivalent to a period equalling or exceeding six thousand years."[51] Faber is the first to have amplified an observation that God's rest continues until the present day into an estimation of the length of all seven creation days, with the first six understood as geological periods.

Faber is clearly compelled by the belief that the current strata and fossil record cannot be explained in terms of a literal creation week and single deluge. Noah's Flood cannot account for the many extinct species of land animals, all of whom should have been represented on the ark, nor the absence of human remains in the fossil record.[52] However, if we assume age-long creation days, "we shall ... find the very order of the fossil strata confirming in a most curious manner the strict accuracy of the Mosaical narrative."[53] Therefore, "The discoveries ... of our ablest physiologists afford ... positive and direct and palpable demonstration, that the six creative days *must* have been six periods of vast, though to us unknown, duration."[54] Faber goes on to offer an exposition of the creation week that combines a 'long chaos' cosmogonic model with a Wernerian aqueous precipitation of the different rock types. The abundant fossils and the evident disruption of the strata show evidence of the multiple 'revolutions' that occurred in the course of this creative week.[55] Faber frequently cites Cuvier's emphasis on 'successive epochs' for support and draws heavily on Parkinson to establish that the sequence of primitive rocks, then vegetation (especially as preserved in coal), fish, bird life, land animals, and finally man, is common both to the geological and biblical records, which on this interpretation exhibit a wonderful harmony.[56]

[51] George Stanley Faber, *A Treatise on the Genius and Object of the Patriarchal, the Levitical, and the Christian Dispensations*, 2 vols., vol. I (London: C. and J. Rivington, 1823), 1:115–17, GB, http://books.google.com/books?id=msgUAAAAYAAJ. Faber's argument in support of long creation days occupies an impressive fifty-six pages of the first volume.

[52] Ibid., 1:121–24.

[53] Ibid., 1:126.

[54] Ibid., 1:120–21. See also p. 145: "Moses teaches us, that the earth was brought into its present state, not instantaneously, but by a series of consecutive operations which he assigns to several different periods, each period being styled *a day*. "

[55] De Luc's final revolution that sees land and sea exchanged is misplaced when connected to the Flood of Noah, according to Faber, since the antediluvian geography of Gen. 2:10–14 corresponds to its post-diluvial equivalent, showing that the existing configuration of the earth's surface survived the Flood. Therefore the global revolutions that the geological record attests must be pushed backwards prior to human creation. Ibid., 1:134–40.

[56] Faber, *Treatise*, 1:149–55, 165–66. We might well infer Parkinson's influence here also.

The Gap Theory and Surviving Chaos Concepts

I have described the 'gap theory' and related ruin-restitution interpretation of Genesis 1 as 'semi-concordist' only, since they shoe-horn the geological ages into the 'formless and void' statement of Gen. 1:2, leaving little actual overlap between a scientific account of origins and the biblical text. They constituted a more vigorous alternative pair to the day-age approach early in this century. The day-age explanation had in its favour the impression that Genesis 1 explained the total origin of the world and not just its latest incarnation, and better fitted Exod. 20:8–11, while these alternative(s) did not require any perceived meddling with the meaning of 'day' in Gen. 1:1–2:3.

The gap theory read Gen. 1:2 as making passing reference to the entirety of pre-human earth history. Its cousin, the ruin-restitution hypothesis, may be distinguished as the spiritually-oriented version of the same reading, sometimes associated with continental theosophy, and certainly consistent with the older view of Episcopius and Limborch that attributed earth's ruin to angelic judgment.[57] This would leave the term 'gap theory' for the geologically-oriented version that maintained a literal creation week following the last great geological extinction event at the end of the Tertiary Era, or something similar. Harmonizing geologists clearly distinguished the two, and in the English-speaking world usually preferred the latter over the former.[58]

The geological version found a pioneering British advocate in Thomas Chalmers (1780–1847), an evangelical Scotsman, whose advocacy of the geologists' old earth was still daring in its time, but the gap theory offered a way of reconciling this to a literal interpretation of the creation week, to which the vast majority of Bible readers were still committed. He announced his deep time commitment in chemistry lectures dating from 1803–4, where he hinted at a temporal separation of the initial creation of Gen. 1:1 from the creation week that follows:

> By referring the origin of the globe to a higher antiquity than is assigned to it by the writings of Moses, it has been said that geology undermines our faith in the inspiration of the Bible.... This is a false alarm. The writings of Moses do not fix the antiquity of the globe. If they fix anything at all, it is only the antiquity of the species.[59]

[57] For a later example of the more spiritual version, see G.H. Pember, *Earth's Earliest Ages: And Their Connection with Modern Spiritualism and Theosophy* (London: Samuel Bagster & Sons, 1876; reprint, London: Hodder & Stoughton, 1893).

[58] Edward Hitchcock, "The Connection between Geology and the Mosaic History of Creation," *American Biblical Repository* 6 (1835): 312–19.

[59] Roberts, "Geology and Genesis Unearthed," n.p. See also Young and Stearley, *Bible, Rocks and Time*, 122.

In his commentary on Cuvier's newly-appeared *Theory of the Earth* in 1814, Chalmers offered a fuller explanation of this temporal break in connection with the Genesis account. He adamantly maintained, "We refuse to concede the literal history of Moses, or to abandon it to the fanciful and ever-varying interpretations of philosophers.... [W]e cannot consent to the stretching out of the days, spoken of in the first chapter of Genesis, into indefinite periods of time."[60] He suggested that Day 1 of creation be understood to begin from Gen. 1:3 rather than from Gen. 1:1, leaving us at liberty to place the original creation expressed in the latter verse as far back in time as is needed. "So Moses may, for any thing we know, be giving us the full history of the last great interposition, and be describing the successive steps by which the mischiefs of the last catastrophe were repaired."[61]

Chalmers' gap theory received an influential follow-up in *A Treatise on the Records of the Creation* (1816), written by John Sumner Bird (1780–1862), the eventual Archbishop of Canterbury. It was also the preferred solution of the early geologist William Conybeare (1787–1857), another Anglican clergyman, in his introduction to the 1822 geological textbook, *Outlines of the Geology of England and Wales*, and was famously advocated by William Buckland (1784–1856), especially in his Bridgewater Treatise, *Geology and Mineralogy, Considered with Reference to Natural Theology* (1836), leading to the general dominance of the gap theory in the British sphere at this time.[62] Nicholas Wiseman (1802–65), an English Roman Catholic cardinal from 1850, in his *Twelve Lectures on the Connection between Science and Revealed Religion* (1836), seems to prevaricate, but finally prefers the gap theory over the day-age alternative, although not treating them as mutually exclusive.[63]

The congregational scholar John Pye Smith (1774–1851) was the next great systematizer of the gap theory in the English-speaking world, and yet his constrained version from this historical distance seems to indicate a theory in trouble. His *On the Relation between The Holy Scriptures and Some Parts of Geological Science* (1839) shows a solid degree of competence in the geology of the day and an appreciation of

[60] Thomas Chalmers, "Remarks on Cuvier's Theory of the Earth; In Extracts from a Review of That Theory Which Was Contributed to 'The Christian Instructor' in 1814," in *Tracts and Essays: Religious and Economical*, Works (Edinburgh/London: published for Thomas Constable by Sutherland and Knox/Hamilton, Adams & co., 1848), 366–67, GB, http://books.google.com/books?id=s9orAAAAYAAJ.

[61] Ibid., 369–70.

[62] William Buckland, *Geology and Mineralogy Considered with Reference to Natural Theology*, 2 vols. (London: William Pickering, 1837; reprint, Philadelphia: Carey, Lea and Blanchard, 1937), 19–21. See Millhauser, "The Scriptural Geologists," 69–70.

[63] Nicholas Wiseman, *Twelve Lectures on the Connection between Science and Revealed Religion*, 6th ed., vol. I (London: Catholic Publishing and Bookselling Co. Ltd., 1859), 294–95.

its ramifications for biblical faith. Pye Smith limited not just the Deluge but the work of the creation week to a limited part of the terrestrial globe, thus arriving at the logical end-point of a trend towards the restriction of the scope of the creation account that had begun with its limitation to the solar system, as in Newton's correspondence, or the earth, as with Burnet.[64] This updated version of the gap theory was adopted by the American geologist Edward Hitchcock (1793–1864) in his *The Religion of Geology and Its Connected Sciences* (1851).[65] Though the gap theory would survive and even flourish anew towards the end of the nineteenth century, becoming the preferred choice of conservatives and fundamentalists for the interpretation of Genesis 1, Zöckler's conclusion is hard to avoid: "Pye Smith's restriction of the cosmogonic restitution-process to a relatively inconsiderable part of the earth's surface marked a partial abandonment of the restitution teaching."[66]

Moreover, despite the accumulating results of geological research and the appearance of thoroughly worked-out day-age and gap theory options before 1820, the more primitive interpretation of Gen. 1:2 in terms of an indefinite chaos that preceded six literal creation days persisted. This model differs from the much newer gap theory in the absence of any clear discernment of definite geological eras within the chaotic period. The events of the creation week remain the first actual formation of the earth, making this a 'chaos-constitution' rather than a 'ruin-restitution' understanding. That some writers have used the term 'chaos-restitution' for long chaos belief obscures the difference and thus falsely implies that repair of some damage to the terrestrial sphere was part of this model.[67]

This traditional interpretation of Genesis 1 characterizes the way Josef Haydn's oratorio *Die Schöpfung* (Creation) (1798) begins, as darkness and dark spiritual forces are driven away by the light of God's first command or *fiat* in Gen. 1:3:

[64] Pye Smith, *Relation*, 258.

[65] Hitchcock, *Religion of Geology*, 33–50, 56, 60–61, 66, etc. "That meaning which allows an intervening period between the creation of matter and the creation of light ... is entirely sufficient to remove all apparent collision between geology and revelation," pp. 60–61, is a sample statement.

[66] Zöckler, *Geschichte*, 2:533. This statement opens the section, 'Der beginnende Niedergang der Restitutionshypothese, seit Mitte der 40er Jahre' (The Beginning of the Decline of the Restitution-Hypotheses from the mid-1840s.) See also Hugh Miller, *The Testimony of the Rocks, or, Geology in Its Bearings on the Two Theologies, Natural and Revealed* (Edinburgh: Thomas Constable, 1857; reprint, Edinburgh: Nimmo, Hay & Mitchell, 1889), 121. For a more recent and more sweeping comment, see Philip Addinall, *Philosophy and Biblical Interpretation: A Study in Nineteenth-Century Conflict* (Cambridge: Cambridge University Press, 1991), 128.

[67] For an example of the latter usage and a general lack of clarity on this point, see Roberts, "The Genesis of John Ray," 147–50, 154.

URIEL	
Now the horrible shadows of the black darkness	Nun schwanden vor dem heiligen Strahle
Fade away before the holy beams;	Des schwarzen Dunkels gräuliche Schatten:
The first day arises.	Der erste Tag entstand.
Confusion yields, and order springs up;	Verwirrung weicht, und Ordnung keimt empor.
Petrified, the spirit-band of hell	Erstarrt entflieht der Höllengeister Schar
Flees down into the abyssal depths,	In des Abgrunds Tiefen hinab
To eternal night.	Zur ewigen Nacht.
CHOIR	
Despair, rage and terror accompany their fall,	Verzweiflung, Wut und Schrecken/ Begleiten ihren Sturz,
And a new world arises at God's word.	Und eine neue Welt/Entspringt auf Gottes Wort.[68]

Early nineteenth-century biblical commentaries still tended to take this line, for example the annotated Bible of Adam Clarke (1762?–1832). Clarke's Genesis section is more focused on astronomy than geology, with the solar system forming from a local chaos in a Cartesian vortex. "When this congeries of elementary principles was brought together, God was pleased to spend six days in assimilating, assorting, and arranging the materials, out of which he built up, not only the earth, but the whole of the solar system."[69] William G. Rhind, *The Age of the Earth Considered Geologically and Historically* (1838), defiantly proclaims,

> The idea of pre-Adamite strata containing organic remains … is at total variance with the narrative of Moses.… If the facts of geology … demand *an organized world* anterior in date to the present, we must renounce altogether the authority of Moses.… The utmost latitude, then, that the interpretation of the narrative of Moses will admit of, is, that an indefinite period of time may have elapsed between the first formation of the earth into a mass, and the commencement of the first of the days of creation, when light was elicited. In this period, the inorganic matter of the globe may have suffered change, but organized beings could have had no existence.[70]

[68] Prelude, 'The Introduction of the Chaos' (Die Vorstellung des Chaos), available in the original German at http://opera.stanford.edu/iu/libretti/schoepf.htm. Herder's influence seems unmistakeable.

[69] Adam Clarke, *The Holy Bible Containing the Old and New Testaments … with a Commentary and Critical Notes … Vol. 1: Genesis to Deuteronomy*, new ed. (New York: T. Mason, G. Lane, 1837), 30, http://books.google.com/books?id=1tgMAAAAIAAJ. The Genesis volume first appeared in 1810.

[70] W.G. Rhind, *The Age of the Earth Considered Geologically and Historically* (Edinburgh: Fraser, 1838), 77–82, 84, GB, http://books.google.com/books?id=cl4EAAAAQAAJ.

Sharon Turner in his much-reprinted *The Sacred History of the World* (1832) combines a long chaos with diluvialism in a popular amalgam when he places the formation of the primordial rocks in the gap prior to the creation week, retains literal, solar creation days, and attributes Secondary rocks to the antediluvian period and Tertiaries to the action of the Deluge itself.[71]

Granville Penn and the Geology of Moses

In the face of an exponential increase of natural data from geology, the two-century old long chaos interpretation of Genesis 1 was under pressure to step forward to either of the two main harmonizing options, the day-age or the gap theory. But some commentators struggled to see how the Genesis text, soundly interpreted, could truly permit either option. Some prevaricated in confusion, while others became devout non-concordists, turning away from mainstream science as currently practised altogether.

'Scriptural geology' has become the label for those nineteenth-century works that turned to the Bible exclusively, especially the early chapters of Genesis, for their defining framework for a science of geology, thanks to the title of a work by George Bugg.[72] This rather loose and eclectic assemblage of works shared the combination of commitment to an inerrant Bible with a young-earth chronology and a literal creation week, plus the strong preference for documentary evidence in historical reconstruction, of which they understood historical geology to be a subspecies.[73] This group of writers was largely ignored by last-generation writers such as C.C. Gillispie and Francis Haber.[74] Terry Mortenson has recently protested that the scriptural geologists have been rather arbitrarily defined out of the historical discussion as unqualified when at the time the line between amateur and professional geologists was very blurred indeed.[75] This remains true despite the clear

[71] Sharon Turner, *The Sacred History of the World: As Displayed in the Creation and Subsequent Events to the Deluge: Attempted to be Philosophically Considered, in a Series of Letters to a Son*, 2nd ed. (London: Longman, Rees, Orme, Brown, Green and Longman, 1832), 17–18, 25–26, 31, 35, 464–65, GB, http://books.google.com/books?id=ZJA5AAAAcAAJ.

[72] See George Bugg, *Scriptural Geology*, 2 vols. (London: Hatchland, 1826–7). Bugg seems to have bequeathed his title to the genre in which he was a pioneer.

[73] Rupke, *Great Chain of History*, 47; O'Connor, "Young-Earth Creationists," 366–67.

[74] T. Mortenson, *The Great Turning Point: The Church's Catastrophic Mistake on Geology before Darwin* (Green Forest, AZ: Master Books, 2004), 14–15; Haber, *Age of the World*, 204–205; Gillispie, *Genesis and Geology*, 152, 224, 248. See also Rupke's comments, p. x.

[75] Mortenson, *Great Turning Point*: 50–54.

tendenz in Mortenson's subtitle and at times in his treatment, but the situation is changing, as historians learn to take an interest not simply in the historical 'winners' whose line subtly leads down through time to … themselves, but also in those whose ideas did not prevail.[76]

Granville Penn (1761–1844) penned the defining work of the genre with *A Comparative Estimate of the Mineral and Mosaical Geologies* (1822). Penn's cosmogony partly resembles de Luc's, in that an exchange of land and sea at the Flood is fundamental to explaining the present form of the globe, and the occurrence of fossils of sea animals on land. Yet Penn regards de Luc as having sold out to an age-long, naturalistic development of the world, and insists on a short biblical chronology and literal creation days.[77] Penn believes that the sedimentary strata were deposited primarily between the creation week and the Flood in the depths of the ocean, and were exposed at the exchange of land and sea.[78] However, the initial division of the earth's surface into seas and continents is attributable to a (necessarily sudden and dramatic) revolution on Day 3 of creation, since the original earth was completely covered in water.[79]

Penn has no room for an indefinite chaos, which he regards as an intrusion from pagan tradition. Geology was no better as a source for primordial events: "It is … a *pure illusion* of the mineral geology, that it is able to point out, by mineral phenomena, a *period* antecedent to the *habitable state* of our globe."[80] Penn's system relies on the consideration of 'apparent age' at creation. Just as Adam would have to have been created with a mature appearance that would seem to imply, but would not really stem from, a process of organic growth, so plants and trees and even crystalline primary rocks would necessarily look as if they had a history, even though immediately created by God.[81] On this basis, natural objects provide no reliable data upon which their history can be inferred, no basis for reasoning by analogy from present processes.[82] Furthermore, the two great revolutions of Day 3 and the Deluge have destroyed the physical evidence of the nature of the antediluvian world.

[76] Rupke, "Foreword," in Gillispie, *Genesis and Geology*, viii–xiii; Rupke, *Great Chain of History*, 42–50.

[77] Granville Penn, *A Comparative Estimate of the Mineral and Mosaical Geologies*, 2nd, revised ed. (London: James Duncan, 1825), 99–101, GB, http://books.google.com/books?id=b7BAAAAAIAAJ.

[78] Silliman, "Philosophy of Geology," 552. Turner appears to follow him in this belief.

[79] Penn, *Comparative Estimate*, 206–23.

[80] Ibid., 67–68.

[81] Ibid., 71–77, 83–90, 96. I mean 'immediately' in the sense of 'without mediation' as well as 'instantly'.

[82] Ibid., 77–78, 109.

Penn concedes that Moses does not supply an entire geological system, but insists that he offers reliable geological facts which may form the basis for a true, 'Mosaical Geology,' obtained by Baconian principles of induction, and conforming to Newton's restriction of valid conclusions about nature to the present state of things.[83] In its determination to account for this present state by secondary causes alone, the mineral geology reveals its drift into a state of profanity. It is this determination alone that requires the expedient of untold past ages.[84] Penn is emphatic on the literal meaning of the 'days' involved, which in his second edition is laid out in opposition to Faber's six-thousand-year days.[85] After all, both Bacon and Newton held to a literal creation week without any qualms, says Penn.[86] His long exegesis of Gen. 1:1–2:3 constantly reiterates the inevitability of an appearance of age in first-created things, especially the crystalline granite, for whose truly 'primary' status Penn fights vigorously.[87]

The only reliable basis for a historical geology, then, is a textual witness provided by the Creator, that is, Genesis.[88] Rupke rightly highlights what we have clearly seen in Penn's case, "a belief in the [supreme] value of written documents as evidence in questions about the past," as the sole common denominator amongst the scriptural geologists who gathered to oppose Buckland and the English school of geologists. It was a firmly established principle amongst classicists of the day: "Questions about the history of the world, its chronology, its periodization, even its major physical vicissitudes ... were to be answered first and foremost from a study of ... written documents, the most reliable of which was believed to be the Bible."[89] So the history of planet Earth was perceived as a historical task, to be achieved by traditional historical means such as documentary study (hence the use of documentary metaphors by pioneering geologists).[90] In the case of creation, the sole qualified historian available could only be God himself, and Moses his amanuensis.

The chemist and physicist Andrew Ure's *A New System of Geology* (1829) also proclaimed that modern geology fell short of the Baconian/Newtonian scientific ideal, and that "The structure and revolutions of the earth, as explored by Geology, have opened a vast field, in

[83] Ibid., 33–34, 156–57, etc.

[84] Ibid., 117–21, 129.

[85] Ibid., 180, 186–87, 283–306.

[86] Ibid., 154–57, 180, 280–82.

[87] Ibid., 187, etc.

[88] Ibid., 151–52.

[89] Rupke, *Great Chain of History,* 47–48.

[90] Rudwick, *Bursting the Limits*, 194–203; Rupke, *Great Chain of History*, 111ff; Mortenson, *Great Turning Point*, 63.

which the champions of scepticism and revelation have latterly waged incessant warfare."[91] This situation demanded proof that the biblical and natural records were in harmony, and Ure undertook to show this seemingly independent of prior efforts. Rejecting the long and "ancient chaos" as "merely a mythological fiction," and inexplicable in the work of an almighty Creator, he asserted, "The demiurgic week, as it is called, is manifestly composed of six working days like our own, and a day of rest, each of equal length, and therefore containing and evening and a morning, measured by a rotation of earth around its axis."[92] He was emphatically young-earth, embracing the entire universe in the declaration, "neither Reason nor Revelation will justify us in extending the origin of the material system, beyond 6000 years from our own days."[93]

The following decade or two saw a raft of similar works published.[94] These works, while heirs to a literal interpretation of the creation days that went back to the Reformers and eventually to the more literal patristic interpreters, were a new phenomenon in the context of their time; influenced by the diluvialist heritage of John Woodward, but now facing a much more complex hypothetical geological history for the earth, they remained determined to incorporate the terrestrial past into the narrow frame of a traditional recent creation and biblical chronology. The chief schematic difference between this stance and the 'flood geology' of modern young-earth creationism is that here the secondary strata were normally attributed to aqueous deposition during the centuries of the antediluvian era, after which the Flood of Noah

[91] Ure, *New System*, xiii.

[92] Ibid., 11–12.

[93] Ibid., 15. Yet he, like Penn, was not a thoroughgoing diluvialist; the only geological remnant of the Flood was the widespread surface *diluvium* to which Buckland, Conybeare and Sedgwick also testified, while the Secondary and Tertiary strata were again attributed to the brief antediluvian period: ibid., 129ff., 341ff., 350ff.

[94] See for example George Fairholme, *General View of the Geology of Scripture: In Which the Unerring Truth of the Inspired Narrative of the Early Events in the World is Exhibited, and Distinctly Proved* (London: James Ridgway, 1833), GB, http://books.google.com/books?id=nbIAAAAAMAAJ; Henry Cole, *Popular Geology Subversive of Divine Revelation! A Letter to the Rev. Adam Sedgwick...Being a Scriptural Refutation of the Geological Positions and Doctrines Promulgated in His Lately Published Commencement Sermon* (London: Hatchard, 1834); Frederick Nolan, *The Analogy of Revelation and Science Established* (Oxford: J.H. Parker, 1833), GB, http://books.google.com.au/books?id=tyJAAAAAYAAJ; William Cockburn, *The Creation of the World* (London: Hatchard, 1840). Among secondary treatments, see Millhauser, "The Scriptural Geologists," 65–86; Roberts, *Evangelicals and Science*, 102–06; Stiling, "Scriptural Geology in America," in *Evangelicals and Science in Historical Perspective*, ed. D.N. Livingstone, D.G. Hart, and M.A. Noll (New York: Oxford University Press, 1999), 177–92. See also the section, 'The Opposition of the Anti-Geologists' in Roberts, "Geology and Genesis Unearthed. "

was often interpreted in terms of de Luc's land/sea exchange, as in Penn's case. But the scriptural geology phenomenon was largely over by 1840 in western Europe, leaving the gap theory as the most conservative option available for interpreters of the Genesis creation week, and 'young-earth' belief dormant and virtually undetectable in published literature for decades to come.

The Day-Age and Gap Theories in Early Nineteenth-Century America

Despite the advocacy of Jameson and others, the day-age method of harmonization could not rival the gap theory as the preferred approach to Genesis in Great Britain.[95] But Jameson's position was taken over virtually in its entirety by the respected American chemist Benjamin Silliman (1779–1864).[96] Silliman, at the beck of college president Timothy Dwight, was instrumental in establishing the natural sciences in the curriculum at Yale College from his appointment there in 1802, and also built up a busy lecturing circuit in which he assured audiences of the compatibility of science and biblical faith and displayed scientific principles using experimental demonstrations.[97]

In Silliman's modernized theory of the earth, chemical reactions in an initially uniform chaotic mixture produce a crust, an atmosphere and waters that surround the globe. Over time these produce the various sedimentary strata, in company with initially violent but steadily decreasing catastrophic action.[98] But Silliman admits that the findings of geology were still very new even to the educated, and hearers were shocked when told of "any other epochs ... than the creation and the deluge." The sense of a conflict between geology and Scripture, continues Silliman, "is founded upon the popular mistake ... that this

[95] Millhauser, "The Scriptural Geologists," 69.

[96] Silliman's harmonizing position appears most fully as a long appendix to his own edition of Robert Bakewell's *An Introduction to Geology* (1829). This appendix prompted the frustrated denial of the Mosaic authorship of the Pentateuch and thus the scientific authority of Genesis by a geology teacher who was compelled to use Bakewell as a textbook: Thomas Cooper, *On the Connection between Geology and the Pentateuch, in a Letter to Professor Silliman* (Boston: Abner Kneeland, 1837), GB, http://books.google.com/books?id=G8s0AAAAMAAJ. Silliman is described along with his concordist heirs J.D. Dana, A. Guyot and J.W. Dawson as "among the best North American geologists of the nineteenth century": Young and Stearley, *Bible, Rocks and Time*, 128.

[97] Leonard G. Wilson, ed., "Benjamin Silliman: A Biographical Sketch," in *Benjamin Silliman and his Circle: Studies on the Influence of Benjamin Silliman on Science in America* (New York: Science History Publications, 1979), 1–10; John C. Greene, "Protestantism, Science, and American Enterprise: Benjamin Silliman's Moral Universe," in *Benjamin Silliman and his Circle: Studies on the Influence of Benjamin Silliman on Science in America*, ed. L.G. Wilson (New York: Science History Publications, 1979), 11–27.

[98] Silliman, "Philosophy of Geology," 490–97.

world was formed substantially as we now see it ..."[99] "According to the popular understanding, the transition and secondary mountains with their coal beds, plants, and animals were ... formed ... in two or three natural days, which is incredible, because it is impossible."[100] The evident reworking of every part of the earth's crust makes it clear "that our planet, before it was inhabited by man, was subjected to a long course of formation and arrangement" to prepare it for living occupation.

But Silliman was encouraged to find, much as Parkinson had felt, "The order of the physical events, discovered by geology, is substantially the same as that recorded by the sacred historian," who only mentioned "the principal divisions of natural things, as they were successively created.[101] But if the two sources were in agreement regarding the *order* of events, what of the problem of the *time* apparently required for geological processes to produce the earth's present configuration? The production of all geological remains from one general deluge "is physically impossible, especially within the limits of time and under the circumstances assigned in the Mosaic account," and in fact even the 'diluvium' cannot all be attributed to the Flood.[102]

Silliman's solution is the periodic understanding of "*the divisions of time called days in the Genesis.*"[103] While "eminent biblical critics and divines" and common people alike were "tenacious ... of the common acceptance of the word day," and in fact "Moses himself probably understood the word day according to the popular signification," Silliman believes that the three days prior to the sun must necessarily be arbitrary measures of time, and that this in turn governs how the latter three days are to be taken. The way is open, then, "to interpret the word day in harmony with the facts of geology," making it possible "that the time should be sufficiently extended to render it physically possible that the events should happen."[104] The outstanding point of apparent discrepancy, that of time, was resolved.

Silliman's position doubtless gained wide exposure through its inclusion in North American editions of the geology texts of Bakewell and Mantell, and must have aided the acceptance of day-age concordism in North America. His widespread and ongoing lecturing activity, which

[99] Ibid. The United States public was trailing a little behind intellectual developments in Europe at this time: Rudwick, *Worlds before Adam*, 125.

[100] Silliman, "Philosophy of Geology," 568.

[101] Ibid., 538.

[102] Ibid., 549–51.

[103] Ibid., 554. He largely leaves the arguing of this case to an almost total reproduction of Jameson's above-mentioned article that drew on Cuvier's brief comments, pp. 554–66.

[104] Ibid., 566–68, 571.

"made him a national scientific figure," must also have widened the exposure of the day-age concordist strategy.[105] Yet resistance remained, and it was spearheaded, ironically, by one of Silliman's favourite and best students, the geologist Edward Hitchcock (1793–1864). As keen as Silliman to convince the American public of the value and validity of geology, and therefore to establish its compatibility with Christian Scripture, Hitchcock was initially undecided between harmonizing schemes. But by the time he published his greatest work of geology, his *Survey of Massachusetts* (1830), he had come down clearly in favour of the gap theory, and would hold to it lifelong.[106]

The next few years saw a flurry of publications in favour of the day-age theory on either side of the Atlantic: in 1830 Jameson published his embellished account of Cuvier's lectures (see above) along with one of his fullest presentations of the parallels between Genesis 1 and the geological record; Henry de la Fite of Trinity College, Oxford, published his translation of de Luc's letters to Professor Blumenbach (originally 1793–95) in 1831; and then Silliman drew on Jameson's explanation for his supplement to the 1833 American edition of Bakewell's geological text.[107] But in a key 1835 article, Hitchcock, having presented no less than thirteen ways of relating geology to creation in Genesis, spent more than thirty pages treating and finally rejecting the day-age interpretation, chiefly in debate with his mentor Silliman.[108] Yet Hitchcock agrees with Silliman that the central issue is "the chronological difficulty."[109] For Hitchcock, the gap theory, since it left the literalness of the creation days intact, while providing geology with the time it needed, was the preferable solution for harmonizing geology with

[105] Wilson, "Biographical Sketch," 8.

[106] Thus Hitchcock's shift paralleled that of William Buckland from the *Vindicae Geologiae* (1820) to his 1836 Bridgewater Treatise. P. Lawrence, "Edward Hitchcock: The Christian Geologist," *Proceedings of the American Philosophical Society* 116 (1972): 23, 27.

[107] Benjamin Silliman, "Supplement by the Editor," in *An Introduction to Geology: Intended to Convey a Practical Knowledge of the Science, and Comprising the Most Important Recent Discoveries, with Explanations of the Facts and Phenomena Which Serve to Confirm or Invalidate Various Geological Theories*, ed. B. Silliman and R. Bakewell (Hezekiah Howe, 1833); de Luc, *Letters*; Rupke, *Great Chain of History*, 40.

[108] Hitchcock, "Connection," 287–312. Silliman is addressed, for example, on pp. 301, 323, but quietly looms throughout as the nearest and greatest representative of the day-age view.

[109] Ibid., 261, 328.

Genesis.[110] Hitchcock was instrumental in making the gap theory the preferred option in the American sphere 1830–50.[111]

Hitchcock's article aroused the hackles of one of America's most noteworthy biblical scholars of this period, Moses Stuart (1780–1852), who could see no need for any harmonization of Genesis with science. Hitchcock may have been surprised: he had actually quoted Stuart sympathetically to close his case against the day-age option (although earlier in the article he had criticized his geological ignorance).[112] Stuart, who had studied with some of the great early nineteenth-century German biblical scholars, insisted that philology was the correct means to rightly understand the biblical text. Geology was of no relevance, since "the sacred writers did not compose their books with modern sciences in view," and "modern science not having been respected in the words of Moses, it cannot be the arbiter of what the words mean which are employed by him." For Stuart, divine inspiration of the Genesis text operated via Moses' own understanding, and we should not expect to find in Genesis an understanding of nature to which Moses could not have had access.[113] We should in fact, through philological study, establish what Moses meant in the context of his times, and reserve the question of the truthfulness of his meaning for a subsequent step.[114]

Stuart could in fact contemplate that some aspects of Moses' narration, grounded in the mindset of his age, might have become obsolete, such as the concept of a solid firmament (Gen. 1:7). This pertained merely to the manner of his narration, which was a time-bound phenomenon. However, the six-day duration of creation pertained not to the *manner* of Moses' narration but to the *facts* narrated, which could not fail.[115] It was plain to Stuart that "the language of Genesis chapter

[110] Ibid., 314–27. In his 1972 article, S.M. Guralnick completely misreads Hitchcock as advocating the day-age theory, but Lawrence is right to date Hitchcock's ownership of the gap theory from prior to 1830: Stanley M. Guralnick, "Geology and Religion before Darwin: The Case of Edward Hitchcock, Theologian and Geologist (1793–1864)," *Isis* 63 (1972): 532, 539; Lawrence, "Edward Hitchcock," 23, 27.

[111] Ronald L. Numbers, *Creation by Natural Law: Laplace's Nebular Hypothesis in American Thought* (Seattle: University of Washington Press, 1977), 89–91.

[112] Hitchcock, "Connection," 277–78, 312. Hitchcock, in his reply article, denied that there was any need for him to reply to Stuart's attacks on the day-age theory, since he had already disowned it in his own previous article: Edward Hitchcock, "Remarks on Professor Stuart's Examination of Gen. 1 in Reference to Geology," *American Biblical Repository* 7, no. 22 (1836): 459.

[113] Moses Stuart, "Critical Examination of Some Passages in Gen. I; with Remarks on Difficulties That Attend Some of the Present Modes of Geological Reasoning," *American Biblical Repository* 7, no. 21 (1836): 49–53.

[114] Ibid., 81–82.

[115] Ibid., 50, 80.

one could be understood in no other terms than those of six twenty-four [hour] days and a short age of the earth."[116]

Later in the same article Stuart succumbed to temptation, did essentially what he criticized Hitchcock for and wandered outside of his field of expertise to question some of the basic tenets of geology. Nevertheless, he had identified a problem with the harmonistic approach that had struck the popular Christian mind too: geological considerations seemingly suppressed or distorted the normal rules of biblical interpretation when it came to Genesis 1.[117] On the other hand, Stuart's commitment to what we would now recognize as 'grammatico-historical exegesis', with its commitment to reading the biblical authors according to their historical context, had more in common with his reading of German biblical scholars than with Hitchcock and with the typical 'person in the pew', who tended to read the Bible in a historically 'flat' way, sensing that God's inspired communications would sound the same in every age, unsullied by human ignorance.[118]

Mid-Century Developments in the Day-Age Theory

J.H. Kurtz (1809–90), "a professor of church history in the University of Dorpat," in his *The Bible and Astronomy* (1842) opened a hermeneutical door through which many subsequent interpreters would willingly walk.[119] His working premises are a curious continental mix of conservative ideas and critical elements that many English commentators of the day would have regarded as intolerable concessions. Kurtz was willing to concede, "Moses also may have had very physically errone-

[116] Stiling, "Scriptural Geology in America," 180. Compare Stuart, "Critical Examination," 73, 104. See also Moore, "Geologists and Interpreters of Genesis," 338–39; Bray, *Biblical Interpretation*, 286–87; R.W. Yarbrough, "Stuart, Moses *(1780–1852)*," in *HHMBI*, 368–72.

[117] Stuart, "Critical Examination," 73, 76–77, 81. For Hitchcock's reply, with some telling parries, see Edward Hitchcock, "Remarks," 448–87. See also Rodney Lee Stiling, 'The Diminishing Deluge: Noah's Flood in Nineteenth-Century American Thought,' PhD dissertation (ProQuest Dissertations and Theses), University of Wisconsin-Madison, 1991, 207–209.

[118] On Stuart's study of German scholars, see Richard Perry Tison, II., "Lords of Creation: American Scriptural Geology and the Lord Brothers' Assault on 'Intellectual Atheism'" (University of Oklahoma, 2008), 130–32, 216–20.

[119] The biographical detail is from Young and Stearley, *Bible, Rocks and Time*, 126. John Henry Kurtz, *The Bible and Astronomy: An Exposition of the Biblical Cosmology, and Its Relations to Natural Science*, trans. T.D. Simonton (Philadelphia: Lindsay & Blakiston, 1857), v, GB, http://books.google.com/books?id=BNk0AAAAMAAJ. This translation is based on the third German edition, which presented Kurtz's views as modulated through his debates with Delitzsch, Hofmann, J.P. Lange and others. And the translation itself omits parts of the original work, including a treatise on geology and the Bible, which would itself doubtless offer worthwhile insights.

ous views touching the nature of the starry heavens, or the structure of the earth, as he in the spirit of prophecy conceived the history of the creation of the heavens and the earth ... its design was wholly to impart religious knowledge."[120] To call Moses the author of the passage was rather conservative by this time in Germany, yet to lightly dispense with the infallibility of Scripture was a distinctly continental move. Indeed, Kurtz aligns himself with and quotes Eichhorn: "The Mosaic record ... is improperly called the history of the creation; it should be called a picture of the creation. Every feature of it appears to betray the pencil of the painter, not the pen of the historian."[121]

Kurtz therefore sought to combine the aesthetic viewpoint of Eichhorn and Herder with a measure of realism, and thus concordism, in his interpretation. For Kurtz, the Genesis account presents true, though not scientific, information which predates human witnesses and could only be known by means of, "objectively, *Divine revelation*, and, subjectively, *prophetic contemplation on the part of man*."[122] Whereas Delitzsch and many others imagined some kind of verbal communication from God to Adam or another early biblical figure, Kurtz thinks that the channel must have been visual, and thus pictorial, and he perceives the creation week as a series "of prophetico-historical tableaux, which are represented before the eye of the mind, scenes from the creative activity of God, each one of which represents some grand division of the great drama, some prominent phase of the development."[123] Genesis 1:1–2:3 thus constitutes a kind of 'retrospective prophecy' that is unique in Scripture, a point Kurtz' detractors used against him.[124]

In light of the visionary nature of this revelation, the question then arose, "whether the days of creation there mentioned are to be regarded as true, natural, common days of twenty-four hours, so that precisely six times twenty-four hours must have been spent in the creation and more complete formation of the earth and its whole organism—or whether this limitation existed only in the mind of the prophet, having no foundation in reality, so that the days are to be regarded as merely *prophetic* days, spaces or periods of time of indefinite length."[125] This

[120] Ibid., 24–26. More generally, Kurtz confessed that not only was the Bible not intended to communicate scientific information, but the inspired authors of Scripture "may very easily have been involved, as far as scientific knowledge is concerned, in the common and prevailing errors of their age," without detriment to religious truths: ibid., 23–24.

[121] Eichhorn, quoted in ibid., 110.

[122] Ibid., 79, 90–99, 107. The quotation falls on the latter page.

[123] Ibid., 110, 117, n.

[124] See the long argument with Delitzsch in a footnote, obviously representing a development post-dating the 1842 edition of the work: ibid., 115–18.

[125] Ibid., 116–18.

could be seen as an escape clause: if each 'day' stands for a visionary scene representing a stage in the world's development, any real reference to historical time could readily be abandoned. Kurtz seems to have unlocked a hermeneutical passage out of literal interpretation of the creation week.

Yet Kurtz himself does not take this way out. He thinks Delitzsch has too hastily embraced a day-age interpretation out of harmonistic motivations, and defends the priority of the biblical text. "How does the record itself regard the days of which it speaks?" If clearly as natural days, "neither Astronomy nor Geology has the right to a single word in the whole matter....We believe most firmly, that were this record explained merely on its own merits and with the aid of other scripture, and were there no outside ... influences at work, the days could only be regarded as natural days. But we also believe that natural science can be harmonized with the Bible."[126] The evening/morning language indicates "the occurrence of one regular, natural change of light and darkness," and Kurtz protests, "Surely it is not too literal an interpretation, to understand as proper, natural days, those that are described as such."[127] Yet the absence of the sun means that these first three days, and by extension the whole week, might have operated according to different laws, and not necessarily have been twenty-four hours long.

This cannot be rightly called a day-age view, but rather a literal day view with a little leeway.[128] The days remain physical ones of light and darkness. Kurtz in fact places his hope for harmonization of Genesis with science on the prevailing ruin-restitution view.[129] Vast periods of development prior to the six days of 'creation' may willingly be conceded to geology, "But never can geology convince us that the last preparation of the surface of the earth for the residence of man, must have required a time of either more or less than six days."[130] So Kurtz's vision theory of the creation days is an explanation of the manner by which primordial creation might have been revealed to a human prophet. But it also presented a means of escape from a realist approach to the chapter – a means unused by Kurtz himself, who adhered to the

[126] Ibid., 118–20, with quotations on the latter page.

[127] Ibid., 121, 125.

[128] Ibid., 122, 126. On the former page, he expressly defines Days 4–6 as twenty-four hour days. Zöckler credits J.D. Michaelis with such a view in combination with a ruin-restitution perspective: Zöckler, *Geschichte*, 2:513.

[129] Kurtz, *Bible and Astronomy*, 128–36. He leaves a decision between a long chaos, where Gen. 1:2 describes merely a hiatus in the work of creation, and a ruin-restitution view, where Gen. 1:2 represents a former world destroyed, unresolved at this point in the work, but clearly decides further along, pp. 232–38.

[130] Ibid., 426.

semi-concordist ruin-restitution model, but subsequently utilized by Hugh Miller and others.

Kurtz faced a circle of fellow German theologians who were sympathetic to the day-age scheme.[131] In *Die Genesis ausgelegt* (1852), Franz Delitzsch (1813–90) rejects Kurtz's visionary stance as too near the poetic approach of Herder and the mythopoetic approach of Eichhorn. The account in Gen. 1:1–2:3 comes across as strictly historical rather than prophetic, and critically speaking represents a priestly rather than prophetic tradition.[132] Delitzsch makes much of the literary structure of the Genesis week in terms of corresponding triads of days. He also airs Ewald's historical-critical idea that an original eight-act series had been squeezed into the present six-day scheme, although Delitzsch gives it a Trinitarian spin.[133] There also remains a cosmogonic aspect to Delitzsch's exegesis of the Genesis text, as he sees the supernatural production of light on Day 1 as initiating a natural sequence of subsequent creation events.[134]

Delitzsch agrees with Kurtz that external constraints should not shift the interpreter from literal days if this is the import of the passage.[135] Yet he finds exegetical indications that they are not so, including the familiar arguments from Gen. 2:4 and Ps. 90:4. Against the ruin-restitution hypothesis, his impression is: "For the unbiased mind, the creation account speaks of the creation of the universe, not of a mere re-creation of the earth and its solar system."[136] The watery deep of Gen. 1:2 contained no molluscs, fish or dinosaurs. "No, Genesis 1 recounts for us … the origin of the entire creation."[137] But convinced of the reality of deep time, Delitzsch feels forced to the conclusion that the creation days cannot be confined to the limits of the ordinary hu-

[131] These included J.P. Lange, J. Ebrard, J.C K. von Hofmann, and Franz Delitzsch: Zöckler, *Geschichte*, 2:540–43, 548; Bavinck, *In the Beginning*, 117. More generally on Hofmann and Delitzsch, see Rogerson, *Old Testament Criticism*, 104–20. Other continental figures often described as adherents of the day-age scheme for the first half of the nineteenth century are F. Krüger (1822), D.A. de Frayssinous (1825), Marcel de Serres (1838), F. de Rougemont (1841), Auguste Nicolas (1842), and G.B. Piancini (1851), and the names multiply after mid-century: Mangenot, "Hexaméron," 6:2342–43; Zöckler, *Geschichte*, 2:508. Franz's son, Friedrich, provoked a controversy with his 1902–1903 *Babel und Bibel*. Jaki seems to conflate the two, quoting the father as if he was the son: Jaki, *Genesis 1*, 223–24.

[132] Franz Delitzsch, *Die Genesis ausgelegt* (Leipzig/London: Dörffling & Franke/Williams & Norgate, 1852), 41–42, IA, http://www.archive.org/stream/diegenesisausge00deligoog.

[133] Ibid., 51–53.

[134] Ibid., 59. I have already mentioned that this idea had considerable currency in the modern period.

[135] Ibid., 60.

[136] Ibid., 63.

[137] Ibid., 66.

man week. "The creation days are creation periods," and human days merely reflect the greater types of the creative days of God.[138] Yet Delitzsch's stance does not represent a full-blown concordism, since he holds back from a specific parallelism with geology and palaeontology.[139] So in Germany as in Britain, day-age and ruin-restitution harmonizing schemes were in competition for the exegetical high ground, even as the concordist enterprise itself was at times questioned and qualified.[140]

The Scottish geologist Hugh Miller (1802–56) provided perhaps the most popular and persuasive compromise between the Genesis creation account and the maturing science of geology of the mid-nineteenth century.[141] Thus he best typifies the middle, concordist position between those who thought such a compromise was undesirable or impossible because geology had superseded Genesis, and those who thought that the 'deep time' conclusions of geology could not legitimately influence a perfectly sufficient Bible. Miller was responsible for elevating the day-age approach to a new level of popularity around mid-century, notably through his final publication. Although he had long promoted an argument from design in works like his popular *The Old Red Sandstone* (1841), and had contended with the transmutation of species in the *Vestiges* (1844) through his *Footprints of the Creator* (1849), it was in *The Testimony of the Rocks* (1857), completed just the day before his death by apparent suicide, that "he was at last in a position to attempt his grand reconciliation between the Biblical account of Creation and what geology had to tell on the basis of the fossils."[142]

[138] Ibid., 63.

[139] Ibid., 70, 76.

[140] Delitzsch is also much discussed for his shift in a more critical direction over time, witnessed in his Genesis commentaries as well as in his position on the authorship of Isaiah and so forth. Yet the shift does not seem to have affected his continued allegiance to a day-age position. See the fifth edition of his commentary: Franz Delitzsch, *A New Commentary on Genesis*, 2 vols., vol. I (Edinburgh: T&T Clark, 1888), 84–85, IA, http://www.archive.org/details/anewcommentgenes 00deliuoft. Young & Stearley refer to a change to a ruin-restitution position under Kurtz's influence, as something that shows up between the *New Commentary* and Delitzsch's *A System of Biblical Psychology* (Edinburgh: T&T Clark, 1899). But his death in 1890 does not leave much time for a change of heart after the *New Commentary*, although I have not checked the other work mentioned. See Young and Stearley, *Bible, Rocks and Time*, 127.

[141] Zöckler, *Geschichte*, 2:543–47; Millhauser, "The Scriptural Geologists," 80. Zöckler presents Miller's scheme fully and with obvious respect.

[142] David R. Oldroyd, "The Geologist from Cromarty," in *Hugh Miller and the Controversies of Victorian Science*, ed. Michael Shortland (Oxford: Clarendon, 1996), 104, also 90–92; James G. Paradis, "The Natural Historian as Antiquary of the World: Hugh Miller and the Rise of Literary Natural History," in *Hugh Miller and the Controversies of*

The preface to the reader acknowledges Miller's own migration to the day-age position. While he presents Chalmers' explanation of the gap theory with lingering admiration, he explains that according to his more recent researches in the upper part of the geological column, "No blank chaotic gap of death and darkness separated the creation to which man belongs from that of the old extinct elephant, hippopotamus, and hyaena."[143] Unsatisfied by Pye Smith's modification of the gap theory, which limited both creation and the Deluge to a limited region of the earth, Miller concludes that the theory, "Though perfectly adequate forty years ago, ... has been greatly outgrown by the progress of geological discovery, and is ... adequate no longer."[144]

Miller therefore begins his day-by-day survey of creation by stating his guiding proposition "that the days of the Mosaic creation may be regarded, without doing violence to the genius of the Hebrew language, as successive periods of great extent," since "the portion of time spoken of in the first chapter of Genesis as *six* days, is spoken of in the second chapter as *one* day."[145] Geology, in fact, need only account for the earth-oriented days of the creation week, Days 3, 5 and 6. Miller proceeds to do so, characterizing Day 3 as the era of the most prolific vegetation, the Palaeozoic Era.[146] His picturesque survey continues as he equates Day 5 with the Secondary Era and particularly its reptilian forms occupying sea, land (though unmentioned in Gen. 1:20–23) and air. The Tertiary Era, particularly characterized by mammalian life, or "the beasts of the field," corresponds to Day 6.[147] Each of these days has its particular 'evening' and 'morning', that is, its initial proliferation and its late stages of decline.[148]

Miller continues by suggesting that the mode of revelation of the creation week is visual rather than verbal, citing Kurtz's view that pre-human history and future history are likewise inaccessible to man except by Divine revelation, that is, through prophecy, and that "that record ... which occurs in the Mosaic narrative is simply *prophecy* described backwards."[149] Creation is revealed to the author by means of divinely granted visions of the typical earth of each of the six eras represented by the

Victorian Science, ed. Michael Shortland (Oxford: Clarendon, 1996), 136, 141; Millhauser, "The Scriptural Geologists," 80.

143 Miller, *Testimony of the Rocks*, xi. See similar statements on pp. 113, 120.

144 Ibid., 113.

145 This is despite "other philologers, such as the late Professor Moses Stuart, who take a different view. " Ibid., 123. See also p. xi.

146 Miller acknowledges that plants were not the first or only form of life in this era, but seeks to emphasize that they are its most noteworthy form of life.

147 Ibid., 124–28.

148 Ibid., 136–40.

149 Ibid., 147. The wording is Miller's.

days.[150] Miller re-creates in Miltonic terms the visionary experience of Moses, "in an untrodden recess of the Midian desert," seeing the type-scenes of creation pass, one after the other.[151] However, "The seven, or rather the six, exhibited scenes appear to be not [merely] symbolic or mystical … but truly representative of successive periods."[152]

The visionary mode of revelation accounts for the viewer's perspective that governs the narrative; things are described as they appear rather than as they objectively exist, particularly the appearance on Day 4 (through a clearing atmosphere) of the sun, moon and stars which had existed from Day 1.[153] One (convenient) hermeneutical implication of applying this generic rubric of 'prophecy' to the creation week for Miller is that, since prophecy is best interpreted in the light of its fulfilment, information from the sciences is the best resource for correct interpretation of the creation account![154]

Miller thus utilizes Kurtz's vision idea as a hermeneutical key that legitimizes a figurative, periodic reading of the creation days. Later in the work, Miller argues for the legitimacy of the concordist exercise against those who would dismiss either Genesis or geology or else see them as incapable of comparison. But he is forced to concede that "their grounds and objects [are] entirely different," presaging the serious disillusionment with the whole concordist enterprise witnessed in the same decade, as we will see shortly.[155] The durability of Miller's own legacy might be debated. Although David Oldroyd concludes, "after the publication of Darwin's *Origin* [just two years after that of *Testimony of the Rocks*], Miller's attempted reconciliation of science and Biblical revelation was quickly superseded and attention shifted elsewhere," we will see that the loss of confidence in the concordist enterprise hinted at above was well underway in various quarters prior to the *Origin*.[156] On the other hand, J.H. Brooke notes, "there is much of Hugh Miller in William Dawson," the Canadian scientist who fronted the concordist approach in North America until the dawn of the next century.[157]

[150] Ibid., 144–49.
[151] Ibid., 170–74.
[152] Ibid., 168, 170.
[153] Ibid., 152–53.
[154] Ibid., 158–59.
[155] Ibid., 339–40.
[156] Oldroyd, "Geologist from Cromarty," 108.
[157] John Hedley Brooke, "Like Minds: The God of Hugh Miller," in *Hugh Miller and the Controversies of Victorian Science*, ed. M. Shortland (Oxford: Clarendon, 1996), 174.

The Day-Age Views of Dana, Guyot and Dawson

While the debate over the meaning of the creation days and the reconcilability of Genesis with science went on in Europe, in North America the day-age position pioneered by Silliman took hold afresh on the imaginations of some of the leading Christian scientists (especially geologists) of the mid-nineteenth century as an alternative both to the seemingly unsustainable literal option of strict conservatives and to the sceptical dismissal of Genesis from those at the other extreme. Several prominent American scientists exemplify this effort to secure a non-literal approach to the days of creation as a warrant for scientific undertakings.

Arnold Guyot (1807–84), a Swiss-born professor of geography and geology at Princeton University, finally published his long-held Genesis-based cosmogonic model, *Creation, or, The Biblical Cosmology in Light of Modern Science* in the year of his death. But the content of an 1852 lecture series by Guyot was publicized by an admirer, E.O. Means, and Guyot's ideas were influential at this earlier stage.[158] Means' article describes the current perception of "an *apparent* conflict between the [biblical] record and science," and identifies several crux issues, the age of the earth being the key difficulty.[159] The simple denial of deep time is by now untenable, says Means, with the Flood and/or the antediluvian period expected to do an impossible amount of geological work.[160] Of the harmonizing options, including an intermittent day theory that has literal twenty-four hour creation days separated by vast spans of time, Means prefers the day-age option as propounded by Guyot.[161]

> The first verse describes the creation of all things; the second represents matter in its chaotic state. Then come what may be called the great days of creation, or cosmogonic days, the six working days of the Creator, ending with a day of rest. These six days are subdivided into two series of three days each. In the first three days, the creation of inorganic matter takes place ; in the second three, the creation of organic beings, ending with man. The last day in each series is subdivided again, containing two works,

[158] Means talks about the original lectures at the opening of the second part of the article: John O. Means, "The Narrative of the Creation in Genesis," *Bibliotheca Sacra and the American Biblical Repository* 12 (1855): 324.

[159] Ibid.: 85, 101–05.

[160] Ibid.: 106–12.

[161] Ibid.: 112–22, 130. Means' dependence upon Guyot in this two-part article gradually becomes apparent as it proceeds, until it is quite explicit.

– the second work in each case constituting the 'germ' of the higher order to follow.[162] Thus plants are the 'germ' of the coming organic order of Days 4–6, while man represents the germ of a higher, moral order yet to come. While Days 4–6 equate to the major geological periods, with Day 5 ending with the catastrophe that closed the Secondary (i.e. Cretaceous) Period, Days 1–3 really characterize the earth's formation from gaseous original matter in terms of Laplace's nebular hypothesis. The evenings along the way signify the 'revolutions' that have broken up this otherwise ascending pattern of development, and that in the case of life, have required new creations to replace the orders of life made extinct.

If it be objected that "that Moses could have conceived no such scientific system, and therefore he could not have taught it," which was exactly Stuart's point, Guyot's view of revelation allows that God may incorporate into such a prophetic communication far more than the mouthpiece (Moses) or the audience can comprehend at the time. The nebular hypothesis is what allows this fuller meaning to be unravelled.[163] Just as the diminishing ocean model of the earth's development represented the altered form of the long chaos belief adopted by many geological pioneers, the nebular hypothesis represented the same 'development out of chaos' concept applied to the cosmos, and for Guyot and others it also suggested a process where heat was at least as important an agent as water.[164]

James Dwight Dana (1813–95) advocated and extended Guyot's day-age approach to Genesis 1.[165] Dana was a leading nineteenth-century geologist, and both student and son-in-law to Benjamin Silliman, the pioneer American day-age theorist.[166] Like Guyot, Dana fully incorporates the nebular hypothesis into the earliest stages of his day-age scheme, which is similarly broken up by Cuvieran 'revolutions' and follows the same idea of earth's steady refrigeration from a molten state.[167] Dana's scheme, like Miller's, emphasizes the broad correspond-

[162] Ibid.: 325.

[163] Ibid.: 128–29, 336–37. On this point and for the relationship of Guyot to Dana, see Numbers, *Laplace's Nebular Hypothesis*, 91–94.

[164] Means, "Narrative of the Creation," 328.

[165] Dana makes this dependence explicit at James Dwight Dana, *Science and the Bible: A Review of "The Six Days of Creation" of Prof. Tayler Lewis. From the Bibliotheca Sacra for January 1856* (Andover: W.F. Draper, 1856), 110, 116, GB, http://books.google.com/books?id=xNE0AAAAMAAJ. Dana also refers to the article just reviewed as expressing Guyot's views.

[166] Stiling, "Scriptural Geology in America," 186.

[167] Dana, *Science and the Bible*, 115; James Dwight Dana, *Manual of Geology: Treating of the Principles of the Science, with Special Reference to American Geological History...* Rev. ed. (Philadelphia: T. Bliss, 1866), 741–44, GB, http://books.google.com/books?id=

ence between the sequence in Genesis and the earth's nebulous origin, the formation of continents, the early role of vegetation in removing carbon dioxide from the atmosphere and infusing it with oxygen, and the great ages of fishes, reptiles and mammals in turn.[168] There is the same consciousness of parallelism between Days 1–3 and Days 4–6 that we saw with Guyot.[169]

While this scheme requires a 'little flexibility' toward the biblical text on the part of the exegete, Dana asserts its clear superiority to the only other viable harmonizing option, the gap theory, since geology has now disproven any global "return to chaos."[170] Dana conceives of the progressive sophistication of life, matching the ascending shape of Genesis 1, as a unity in the plan of God (as per Louis Agassiz) rather than one of organic descent, although he often uses the term 'evolution' and seems to typify a generation of thinkers that, despite renouncing transmutation of species, was unwittingly tending in a Darwinian direction.[171] In the meantime, Dana's status as "the premier nineteenth-century American geologist" ensured the popularity of the day-age strategy over the next few decades among educated American Christians.[172]

John William Dawson (1820–99), a Canadian geologist who was a devout Presbyterian, offered the first of his many publications on science and religion with *Archaia* (1860).[173] Dawson's primary achievement was to synthesize various elements from prior positions into a detailed and defining presentation of the day-age view for the late nineteenth century.[174] Dawson utilizes the *aeon* concept of Tayler Lewis (see below) and his idea that the naming of the first day in Gen. 1:4 is intended "as a plain and authoritative declaration *that the day of creation*

kLsQAAAAIAAJ&dq. See again Numbers, *Laplace's Nebular Hypothesis*, 94–99; Moore, "Geologists and Interpreters of Genesis," 338–39.

[168] Dana, *Science and the Bible*, 112–28; Dana, *Manual of Geology*, 742–46; Zöckler, *Geschichte*, 2:547–48.

[169] Means, "Narrative of the Creation," 325.

[170] Dana, *Science and the Bible*, 108–09.

[171] Ibid., 109, 112, 122. "The development of the plan of creation, while by successive creations, was in accordance with the law of evolution, as Agassiz has explained, that is, progress from the simple to the complex, from comprehensive unity to multiplicity through successive individualizations." Dana, *Science and the Bible*, 123–24.

[172] The phrase is from Young and Stearley, *Bible, Rocks and Time*, 128. A similar comment appears in Ramm, *Science and Scripture*, 145.

[173] This was later revised as *The Origin of the World according to Revelation and Science* (1877), the latter featuring a desperate delaying action against transmutation that is absent from the earlier work. See Stiling, "Diminishing Deluge," 294; Numbers, *Laplace's Nebular Hypothesis*, 100.

[174] This notwithstanding the belated publication of Guyot's ideas in Arnold Guyot, *Creation; or, The Biblical Cosmogony in the Light of Modern Science* (Edinburgh: T&T Clark, 1883). See Numbers, *Laplace's Nebular Hypothesis*, 94.

is not the day of popular speech."[175] With Dana and Guyot he uses the nebular hypothesis to explain the chaotic beginning of the earth and understands that geology contributes the key clue that the Genesis days are not literal.[176] These and other borrowings give Dawson's conclusions about the creation days a 'synthesized' feel:

> Moses may have seen these wondrous events in vision – in visions of successive days – under the guise of which he presents geological time.... The doctrine of day-periods ... harmonises with the progressive nature of the work, the evidence of geology, and the cosmological notions of ancient nations.... Each great creative aeon may have extended through millions of years.[177]

Dawson lived to the threshold of the new century, and through his many similar publications represented a bastion among mainstream scientists for the concordist approach and continued reception of the authority of Genesis.[178]

The Idealist Alternative to Realist Concordism

Dana's *Science and the Bible* arose out of his ongoing debate with a man Philip Schaff called "one of the ablest and most learned classical and biblical scholars of America," Tayler Lewis (1802–77).[179] Lewis still held to Chalmers' gap theory in *Nature, Progress, Ideas* (1850), but by 1855 his position had changed, and he wrote *The Six Days of Creation*, "the most exhaustive nineteenth-century exegetical study of Genesis 1," from a non-literal day point of view.[180] This intriguing and original work defies neat categorization and reflects the traditional influences of ancient classical literature, the church fathers and Renaissance cosmogonies, but deliberately resists the influence of 'modern science'. Its dominant theme is that the days of creation should not be interpreted literally. In fact, the extraordinary nature of the days is a natural *a priori* expectation created by the narrative itself, not "a forced resort to avoid

[175] Dawson, *Origin of the World*, 76, 124–25, 128–33. Dawson adopts this terminology without taking on Lewis' underlying metaphysic. Rodney Stiling identifies an increasing dependence on Lewis' ideas with successive editions of the work: Stiling, "Diminishing Deluge," 255–56.

[176] Dawson, *Origin of the World*, 112–22, 138.

[177] Ibid., 152–53.

[178] Stiling, "Scriptural Geology in America," 186.

[179] Johann Peter Lange and Tayler Lewis, *Genesis: or, The First Book of Moses, Together with a General Theological and Homiletical Introduction to the Old Testament*, trans. Tayler Lewis and A. Gosman, A Commentary on the Holy Scriptures: Critical, Doctrinal, and Homiletical, ed. P. Schaff (New York: Scribner, 1869), vi, IA, http://www.archive.org/details/genesisorthefirs00languoft.

[180] Millhauser, "The Scriptural Geologists," 80–81; Young and Stearley, *Bible, Rocks and Time*, 129.

a scientific difficulty."[181] "Our object, then, is not ... to reconcile science and the written revelation, or to assume any real or apparent controversy between them. They are to be regarded as belonging to two distinct spheres, as having, in fact, nothing to do with each other."[182] We are reminded here that there was such a phenomenon as 'believing non-concordism', a rejection of the concordist enterprise that stemmed neither from scepticism nor from a strict literalism.

The narrative element of the Genesis text that urges a non-literal understanding of the days is once again the passing of three sunless creation days, which are clearly differentiated by this textual signal from the ordinary diurnal phenomenon. "The days were anomalous.... The Bible does not teach that the creative days were twenty-four hours long."[183] Prior to the sun there was no twenty-four hour paradigm for a day at all; the more fundamental meaning of 'day' is related to periodicity or cyclicity.[184] And cycles are very much at home in Lewis' strongly Platonist view of the world. With respect to creation, this cyclicity is married to 'time's arrow' to yield an ascending spiral from chaos to order that is strongly reminiscent of Joseph Needham's.[185] In this idealist reading, once evidenced in Augustine's transitional interpretation of Genesis 1, 'evening' represents initial non-being or matter without form, and 'morning' represents a coming into being or form.

> Each of the great creative times or days, we have regarded as characterized by two divisions ... one may be called the natural, the other the supernatural, one the night of nature's rest, whether we regard it as a steady ongoing, or as a period of decay and torpor after a preceding growth, the other the morning of God's new working, when the Word again goes forth, and the old slumbering nature is awaked to a higher energy, and made to co-operate in the production of a higher organization, or a higher order of being.[186]

[181] Tayler Lewis, *The Six Days of Creation; or, The Scriptural Cosmology, with the Ancient Idea of Time-Worlds, in Distinction from Worlds in Space* (Schenectady, NY: G.Y. Van Debogert, 1855), 7, http://books.google.com/books?id=CUvOViSeGDAC.

[182] Ibid., 43. Yet the Bible's truth is not limited to purely religious or moral spheres, according to Lewis, but it speaks authoritatively upon whatever it addresses, including physical topics: ibid., 13–15, 43.

[183] Ibid., 6–7, 12.

[184] Ibid., 74. The most thorough argument for periodic days after the introductory chapters is in chs. 13 and 14, pp. 151–83.

[185] Needham's obscurity makes dependence unlikely. Instead, people who interpret Genesis 1 from a Platonist point of view down through the centuries tend to instinctively come to the same sorts of conclusions. The expression 'time's arrow' is Stephen Jay Gould's.

[186] Lewis, *Six Days of Creation*, 233.

Lewis explicitly draws on the cyclicity of Plato's *Politicus*, wherein God stirs up creation, then allows it to coast under natural momentum until it degenerates to the edge of a new chaos, at which point God salvages it again. We may find in Plato's "anacyclical revolutions something like the natural and supernatural times we have regarded as shadowed forth in the evening and morning of the Mosaic account."[187] He believes that the references to *aeons* (τοὺς αἰῶνας) in Heb. 1:2; 11:3 actually speak of these great creative cycles.[188]

A Platonist dualism leads Lewis to locate the creation days on an 'upper register' of the divine or eternal realm; they are really not of this physical world at all.[189] Scripture calls the steps in the world's ascent from chaos to order 'days', but "certainly they could have been no common days, no common nights, no common mornings. This, we think, must appear from the whole spirit and aspect of the strange account. They were God's days, his ימי עולם or *dies eternitatis.* They were the morning and evening intervals of his creative periods, as much beyond our diurnal cycles as his ways are above our ways."[190] Thus the human week acts as the antitype of the greater week and rest of God.[191] But as with Augustine's more recent admirers, Lewis grants the work days of God a chronological aspect lacking in Augustine's treatment by making them 'ages' of earth time.[192]

Lewis reveals further roots going back through the Renaissance to Plato when he pictures the world as a 'growth' (φύσις) from a seminal form, employing Augustine's concept of 'seminal principles' (λόγοι σπερματικοί) and Plato's living world, or ζῶον (*zōon*).[193] The earth produces plant life very naturally, being organic itself, and the world's creation occurs through (divinely initiated) growth and decay phases.[194] Lewis therefore regards the theory of transmutation of species favourably, hesitating only where humankind is in view.[195] Moses Stuart, too, had casually suggested that living species readily tend to alter into others, out of a similarly organic view of the earth, to Hitchcock's dis-

[187] Ibid., 244–45. Lewis seeks to justify his use of Plato on page v of the preface.

[188] Ibid., 7–9.

[189] I draw the term from the 'upper register cosmogony' of the similarly Platonist framework view of Meredith Kline, as seen in Meredith G. Kline, "Space and Time in the Genesis Cosmogony," *PSCF* 48, no. 1 (1996): 2–15.

[190] Lewis, *Six Days of Creation*, 99–100.

[191] Ibid., 10. This was a point that Delitzsch made: see above.

[192] Ibid., 156. We might note a resemblance here to the approach of the Cambridge Platonist Henry More.

[193] Ibid., 224–30, 307–308.

[194] Ibid., 193–211, 238–41. He curiously seems to shunt the appearance of vegetation into Day 5 of creation to suit the requirements of his scheme: compare pp. 121ff. and pp. 193ff.

[195] Ibid., 246–52.

may.[196] This is not what we might expect, as historian of science Morgan Sherwood pointed out in the case of Lewis: the conservative biblical exegete in each case defends a stance that is amenable to biological evolution against the mainstream Christian scientist.[197] We stand warned against assuming that the lines of debate or the boundaries of viewpoints concerning Genesis, creation and the natural world lay in the past where they lie today.

And all of this metaphysical complexity underlies an apparently conservative re-emphasis upon the language of the Genesis text itself; a failure to understand the 'phenomenal' nature of this language has led to the misstep of taking the creation days literally.[198] "We have God's eternal *facts* of creation, revealed to Moses in their chronological order through *conceptions* familiar to Moses."[199] Why do we get an attack of literalism when it comes to Genesis 1, protests Lewis, perceiving a literal week or a solid firmament, when we seem to handle figurative or anthropomorphic language elsewhere in the Bible?[200] Despite his protests, a subtle harmonistic motive still influences Lewis' exegesis; understanding the world's origin as 'generation', he comments at one point, "would demand the long periods, of which geology is supposed to suggest."[201] In any case, Lewis' Bible-prioritizing exegesis of Gen. 1:1–2:3 incorporates a fascinating and complex mixture of philosophical influences, and defends an idealist rendition of the day-age viewpoint as conservative Christian orthodoxy.

The fact that both Dana and Lewis effectively adhered to variants of the same, day-age stance on the creation week bids us ask again about the nature of their strong disagreement. Certainly Dana's stance favoured the physical cause-and effect reasoning of the scientist, and Lewis' Platonist metaphysic seemed very strange to him. Nor could he comprehend Lewis' hostility to science when his exegetical outcome was so similar to his own: "Is it not a marvel that a learned Professor should accord, in his cosmogony, with the views of science in all their grander points, and yet lose no opportunity to denounce science: should adopt, with science, the idea of indefinite periods for days, and

[196] Stuart, "Critical Examination," 66–67, 88–89; Hitchcock, "Remarks," 482–85.

[197] Morgan B. Sherwood, "Genesis, Evolution, and Geology in America before Darwin: The Dana-Lewis Controversy, 1856–1857," in *Toward a History of Geology*, ed. C.J. Schneer (Cambridge, MA: M.I.T. Press, 1969), 312.

[198] Lewis, *Six Days of Creation*, i–ii, 1–4.

[199] Ibid., 36, also 34, 20ff., and frequently.

[200] Ibid., 112.

[201] Ibid., 16–17. See also pp. 98, 120, 178, 194, 242 as a sample of other references to geology.

then pick a quarrel because geologists make the days, he thinks, too long … ?"[202]

But there was a kind of epistemological turf-war occurring. Lewis' book represented a program of demarcating spheres of knowledge, an enterprise entirely consistent with that of Moses Stuart in his controversy with Hitchcock a generation earlier. Like Stuart, Lewis emphasizes that philological scrutiny is the path to accurate interpretation of the Bible, unbiased by external influences.[203] Scientific theories trespassed in a sphere not their own when they began to pressure theologians and biblical scholars into certain exegetical outcomes. In this tussle over 'intellectual jurisdiction', says Morgan Sherwood, "Lewis would not concede to science the right of biblical interpretation." This was "the central disagreement in the controversy."[204] Similarly John Greene: "Lewis's basic aim was to protect the doctrine of the inspiration of the Bible from being undermined by superficial reconciliations in which the language of Scripture was perpetually reinterpreted to make it agree with the ever-changing discoveries and theories of science."[205]

Another idealist view of the creation days stemmed from Harvard mathematician Benjamin Peirce (1809–1880). According to an advocate, Peirce treats Genesis 1 as the first of three great divine revelations.[206] In this first one, the creation of everything in nature is represented "as the work of six successive periods, using an order of time to express order of importance, or order of thought … the days' works have no real reference to time, but are only a figure to represent the successive movements of the prophet's own mind looking at the works of God."[207] Nevertheless "the transitions will be natural, and correspond to a chronological order," namely, that suggested by La-

[202] Dana, *Science and the Bible*, 105. Lewis' alternate set of priorities can be seen in the title of a work of response to Dana's critique, Tayler Lewis, *The Bible and Science; or, The World-Problem* (Schenectady, NY: G.Y. Van Debogert, 1856). Lewis has reversed Dana's title to signify opposing priorities.

[203] Lewis, *Six Days of Creation*, i, 1, 11, 15, 266.

[204] Sherwood, "Genesis, Evolution, and Geology," 312–14; Stiling, "Diminishing Deluge," 216.

[205] John C. Greene, "Science and Religion," in *The Rise of Adventism: Religion and Society in Mid-Nineteenth-Century America*, ed. E.S. Gaustad (New York: Harper & Row, 1974), 60–63, with quotation on p. 63.

[206] T[homas] H[ill], "The First Chapter of Genesis," *Christian Examiner* 59 (1855): 383–84. This source and an analysis are found in Numbers, *Laplace's Nebular Hypothesis*, 102, 160.

[207] H[ill], "The First Chapter of Genesis," 387, 390.

place's hypothesis for the earlier creation days, and by geology for the later days.[208]

This clumsy tactic juxtaposed two very different long creation day approaches: Dana's and Guyot's version inspired by scientific concordism, and an idealist scheme with clear affinities to that of Tayler Lewis. Lewis' own thoroughgoing idealist scheme remained influential, according to historian Rodney Stiling, to the end of the century.[209] It was an interpretation that looked like a day-age one, but was so different from the science-influenced version that a vast gulf separated Lewis from Dana. It shared the organicist and Platonist sympathies of Popkin's seventeenth-century 'third force', and of Joseph Needham in the eighteenth, in a philosophical synthesis that looks positively otherworldly today except to the mystically or Platonically-inclined.

Conservative Anti-Concordism in the 1850s

Each noteworthy concordist work published in the early to mid-nineteenth century usually prompted at least one reactive work of the scriptural geology type. One example from the American scene, *The Epoch of Creation* (1851) by Eleazar Lord (1788–1871), New York capitalist, railroad magnate and amateur theologian trained at the College of New Jersey (Princeton), was a response to Hitchcock's *Religion of Geology* of the same year, and also took aim at Miller's *Footprints of the Creator* (1849) and Pye Smith's restricted gap theory.[210] A defining, early pronouncement in Lord's work sounds as though it was based on the Westminster Confession: "In all our reasonings, this great fact, that in the beginning God created and completed the heavens and the earth in the space of six days, is to be regarded as a starting point, like a first truth in philosophy, or an axiom in geometry."[211]

Lord did not sense the weight of geological evidence in favour of the earth's antiquity. He had no faith in the method, so fundamental to geology, of understanding past processes by analogy with those operating in the present.[212] God's moral or redemptive purposes are the sole

[208] 'Another secondary explanation' looks at the anti-polytheistic, anti-eternalistic, anti-animistic polemical purposes of the chapter. Ibid., 392–93.

[209] Stiling, "Diminishing Deluge," 255–56.

[210] For these biographical details, see Tison, "Lords of Creation," 45–60.

[211] Eleazar Lord, *The Epoch of Creation: The Scripture Doctrine Contrasted with the Geology Theory* (New York: Charles Scribner, 1851), xiii, GB, http://books.google.com/books?id=dbMAAAAAMAAJ.

[212] He really only accepted the validity only of one ancestor of the geology of his day, the eighteenth-century German speciality of 'geognosy', which simply sought to analyse present rock structures and did not seek causal explanations at all. See the explanation of the term 'geognosy' in its eighteenth-century context in Rudwick, *Bursting the Limits*, 84–99. The title of his brother's work of a few years later is indica-

rationale for the world's existence in Lord's eyes, and he cannot imagine the point of an immensely long pre-history bereft of moral human subjects.[213] "The theory of [earth's] remote antiquity is no part of the science, but … merely an inference … a conjecture" arising from naturalistic assumptions.[214] The process of sedimentation naturally understood would of course take "inconceivable rounds of time" to produce the present strata, but one should not assume that the sedimentary rocks were naturally formed, although if one is determined to look for causes, the Flood is a perfectly good one that has a moral purpose.[215] The problem is, "The geologist … assumes that this existing structure and condition were caused by the slow operation of physical causes, and thence infers that the globe was created at an epoch inconceivably earlier than the "six days," and thereby contradicts the plain import of the inspired account of the creation." As long as God had moral reasons for accomplishing this work miraculously and quickly, "there is nothing in the existing structure and condition of these formations inconsistent … with the inspired account of the work of creation as having taken place in the six days of the Mosaic narrative."[216]

Having protested especially against the gap theory, Lord concludes, "The first verse of the first chapter of Genesis … is part of the narrative of the creation of all things in the space of six days; and if geology…teaches that the earth was created at an earlier epoch than man, it can neither derive any countenance from the first verse of Genesis, nor be reconciled with the narrative of the six days."[217] There is no mistaking which source of information is to be disregarded in the light of this irreparable breakdown. There is no need to delve into Lord's attempt to demonstrate the foolishness of geology on its own terms, which founders through his own ignorance of the subject.[218] He himself adopts a Woodwardian, diluvial model of the earth's past along with an

tive: David Lord, *Geognosy, or The Facts and Principles of Geology against Theories* (New York: Franklin Knight, 1855).

[213] Lord, *Epoch of Creation*, 84ff., 143ff., 168ff.

[214] Ibid., 95.

[215] Ibid., 99–100, 229–39. Lord's diluvialism is similar to Woodward's a long before, only that he visualizes a paradise-like world whose enormously deep and rich soil was torn up and redeposited in the Deluge.

[216] Ibid., 157. Lord also questions the presumption by which the geologist will more readily doubt the intention of the literal meaning of the Genesis text than to question his own naturalistic assumptions and therefore his conclusions about great age from the sedimentary deposits: ibid., 37.

[217] Ibid., 54.

[218] For instance, he assumes that according to standard geology all sedimentary strata must be derived from presently protruding 'primary' rocks, requiring those 'primary' mountains to have had an average original elevation of about forty miles: ibid., 105. See pp. 94–114 for various examples.

'apparent age' argument in order to preserve the literal meaning of Genesis 1, appearing reluctant to comprehend strata and fossils as historical clues in any sense.

Lord's brother, David, held a position nearer that of Granville Penn, in that natural processes had produced the sediments and fossils in the antediluvian ocean basins, whose subsequent uplift would produce the fossil-bearing continents upon which we now live.[219] That his chief opponents are gap theory supporters befits the emergence of this work shortly before the resurgence of the day-age viewpoint associated with Hugh Miller, Dana and Lewis in the late 1850s. Stiling, interestingly, defines Eleazar and David Lord, along with their associate, the physician Martyn Paine, as "nothing less than the last American generation of 'Scriptural Geologists'."[220] They were prominent representatives of Moses Stuart's principle that geology should not define how Genesis is interpreted, and Eleazar in fact had studied under Stuart at one time.[221] Like Stuart, they wandered ill-prepared and somewhat hypocritically into geological apologetics, crossing the epistemological boundary whose transgression by geologists they sought to forbid.

A better-informed but no more successful approach to the question from the conservative side appears in the (in)famous *Omphalos* (1857) of Philip Gosse (1810–88), a work that constitutes essential reading for understanding contemporary debates over creation.[222] Gosse takes special creation to a kind of logical extreme.[223] The logic is sound (granted Gosse's assumptions) and the outcome so consistent and yet so unsatisfactory, that the entire enterprise of opposing the reality of the evidence of earth's geological history in the name of creation takes on a starkly surreal character.[224]

[219] Tison, "Lords of Creation," 353–54, 387; Stiling, "Diminishing Deluge," 277.

[220] Ibid., 284–85.

[221] Tison, "Lords of Creation," 14, 46.

[222] For a biographical perspective on Philip Gosse and on his thought, see Edmund Gosse, *Father and Son: Biographical Recollections*, 4th ed. (New York: Charles Scribner's Sons, 1908).

[223] His son Edmund writes, "In truth, [his father's theory] was the logical and inevitable conclusion of accepting, literally, the doctrine of a sudden act of creation. " Ibid., 115.

[224] Gosse could be accused at points of begging the question, however, as where he says, "If, then, the existence of retrospective marks, visible and tangible proofs of processes which were prochronic, was so necessary to organic essences … is it absurd to suggest the *possibility* … that the world itself was created under the influence of the same law, with visible tangible proofs of developments and processes, which yet were only prochronic?" Philip Gosse, *Omphalos: An Attempt to Untie the Geological Knot* (London: John Van Voorst, 1857), 350–51, GB, http://books.google.com/books?id=acwQAAAAIAAJ. For a brief, rather unsympathetic synopsis on this work, see R.J. Berry, "Did Darwin Dethrone Humankind?," in *Darwin, Creation and the Fall:*

Gosse's thesis is not argued on the basis of Genesis, whose authority by now counted for little, but played an important role in Genesis-and-science debates. The essence of Gosse's argument is that since the organic reproductive cycle has no beginning, and assuming that an organism stems from the creative work of God, there is no natural entry point for God's creative action, but creation must constitute an 'irruption' into the cycle, which would then continue predictably from that point.[225] It follows that the infinite repetitions of the cycle chronologically prior to that point of 'irruption' would appear to have left their mark on the freshly created organism. Hence the work's title, since a newly created mature man would have a navel or *omphalos* that implied a reproductive cyclic history that had never actually occurred.[226]

Gosse spends much of his book considering various organic structures that must inevitably imply such a past the instant they were created. The theoretical past of such an organic chain he calls 'prochronic' history, history before time.[227] This 'history' only exists in the ideal realm, in the mind of God.[228] So Gosse's logic depends not only on a biblical doctrine of special creation and commitment to a young earth, but also on a cyclical, organic, Platonist world-picture. The implication for geology and palaeontology is that any object viewed, such as a sedimentary rock layer or a fossil, might belong to this prochronic time and not be a true historical artefact.[229] This denies all validity to the method of making inferences about the past on analogy with the present, and if fully adopted would destroy any basis for the historical sciences and make an illusion of the material world outside of the present and any event recorded by memory.[230]

Having established by many examples the difficulty of imagining special or direct creation *without* appearance of age, Gosse concludes

Theological Challenges, ed. R.J. Berry and T.A. Noble (Nottingham: InterVarsity, 2009), 42 n. 30.

[225] Ibid., 123. See his 'postulates', ibid., 110f.

[226] Gosse, *Omphalos*, 274, 334, 351, and frequently.

[227] We might compare the 'proleptic time' of seventeenth-century chronologer Joseph Scaliger: McCalla, *Creationist Debate*, 32.

[228] Gosse, *Omphalos*, 345–46, 370.

[229] Ibid., 347.

[230] The conservative French writer Chateaubriand had rebuffed claims to the earth's antiquity the same way: "This has been answered a hundred times in this way, *God was obliged to create and did without doubt create the world with all the marks of antiquity [vétusté] … that we observe in it.*" F.-R. Chateaubriand, *Génie du Christianisme*, vol. 14, Oeuvres Choisies de M. de Chateaubriand (Paris: Pourrat Frères, 1834), 136, GB, http://books.google.com/books?id=BaEGAAAAQAAJ; Roberts, "Genesis Chapter 1," 43. E.O. Means claimed that Chateaubriand had extended this 'appearance of age' argument to ancient cities revealed by archaeology! Means, "Narrative of the Creation," 108.

triumphantly by quoting Exod. 20:11, "IN SIX DAYS JEHOVAH MADE HEAVEN AND EARTH, THE SEA, AND ALL THAT IN THEM IS."[231] His argument, while not based on Genesis, is clearly meant as a defence of its literal interpretation. Yet by describing at length and in a sense admitting the reality of the geological evidence for deep time, while resorting to his appearance of age argument to reconcile this apparent evidence to recent creation in a literal week, Gosse had effectively exposed both the reality of the geological evidence and the absence of a viable explanation that could avoid compromising either (some) biblical or geological testimony.

A continental counterpart to these American and British examples, the confessional Lutheran C.F. Keil (1807-88), takes a very conservative position in his entry on Genesis in the commentary series co-authored with Franz Delitzsch – more conservative, certainly, than Delitzsch's own Genesis commentary. While Delitzsch subscribed to deep time and took a day-age stance, Keil still disputes the reliability of the geological evidence.[232] He also staunchly rejects any real concordance with other ANE cosmogonies, any literary parallelism between Days 1–3 and Days 4–6 such as Herder claimed, and any allusion in Gen. 2:3 to the Israelite Sabbath, such that reinforcement of the latter should have been the motivation behind the account's construction.[233] Against Kurtz' 'tableau' idea, Keil maintains that the tone of the account is fundamentally historical, so that we are intended to accept "as actual truth," not just the fact of God's creation of all, "but also the description of the creation itself in all its several stages."[234]

In relation to the creation week, Keil maintains, "If the days of creation are regulated by the recurring interchange of light and darkness, they must be regarded not as periods of time of incalculable duration, of years or thousands of years, but as simple earthly days." Even if the earth's rotation was slower in those earliest days, we are still talking about solar days, and there is "no essential difference between the first three days and the last three, which were regulated by the rising and setting of the sun." Keil refuses to "make interpretation dependent upon natural science, because the creation lies outside the limits of empirical and speculative research."[235] He reverses the tendency of concordist exegetes by allowing the apparent normalcy of Days 4–6 to

[231] Gosse, *Omphalos*, 372.

[232] Keil, "The First Book of Moses (Genesis)," 41–44. See Rogerson, *Old Testament Criticism*, 112, n. 125, on Keil's authorship of this volume.

[233] Keil, "The First Book of Moses (Genesis)," 38–41.

[234] Ibid., 37, 45.

[235] Ibid., 51–52, incl. footnotes.

be determinative for the nature of the creation days overall, rather than making the non-solar Days 1–3 determinative for the rest.[236]

Despite Keil's entrenchment, Germany would be the birthplace of the 'history of religions' approach to the OT, which by the dawn of the twentieth century would see Franz Delitzsch's son Friedrich relativize Israelite religion amongst that of its neighbours in the context of the 'Babel/Bibel' controversy. Meanwhile Hermann Gunkel would pioneer the form-critical approach to the OT, notably in his 1901 Genesis commentary. Keil therefore appears from a modern perspective to have been standing against a tide that had long turned against his literal approach.

Harmony or Variance: The Concordist Debate in the 1850s

While concordist efforts were still quite popular in Great Britain and the United States, the developing stream of biblical 'higher criticism', the eighteenth-century Romantic imagination of a childlike, intuitive, ANE grasp of the world, expressed by Herder and Eichhorn, and a burgeoning consciousness of other ancient literature related to Genesis were converging to produce a rather schizoid perspective on the Genesis cosmogony. By this I mean that the creation account of Gen. 1:1–2:3 had become on the one hand material for literary-critical source analysis, and on the other hand a poetic carryover from the infancy of humanity, to be interpreted literally and simply on an aesthetic level. It could not be regarded as imparting any useful information about the actual, historical origin of the earth. This removed any basis for the concordist enterprise; there was nothing in Gen. 1:1–2:3 really suitable to be reconciled with scientific inferences about the world's origin.

Peter von Bohlen (1796–1840), a German educator who taught mainly at Königsberg and spent his last few years in England, offered such a viewpoint in his 1835 work whose first volume appeared in English translation, *Introduction to the Book of Genesis,* in 1855.[237] Von Bohlen interpreted Genesis 1:1–2:3 as one of many similar ANE works, which included the Persian *Avesta* and the Hindu *Institutes of Menu* and Vedas. Because it derives from this common mythical milieu, it is a mistake to "strive, as many naturalists and geologists have done to wearisomeness, to verify minutely a simple and childlike myth, but rather let us seek to understand and comprehend the meaning of

[236] Ibid., 69. This extrapolation approach is clearly a two-edged sword, and its use in one direction begs the question about the opposite possibility.

[237] The original title is *Die Genesis historisch-kritisch erläutert.*

the whole."[238] The person who takes the account literally and seeks a natural harmony with Herschel's discoveries, 'Buffon's hypothesis', Michaelis' calculations of light from the stars or Frayssinous' central heat, loses "all sense for poetry and antiquity" as well as "all feeling for the pious and elevating object of the writer." More tasteless again is the person "who derives each step of the narrative through inspiration from the Deity, in order that this cosmogony 'may far exceed everything that we know from the wise men of the ancient world.'"[239]

The Genesis cosmogony for von Bohlen is just one amongst equals, and on some points is outshone by its rivals, as in the creation of worlds by the mere thought of the Deity in the Hindu Vedas.[240] Lacking any motivation to seek reconciliation of the Genesis text with the natural science of his day, von Bohlen simply understands the days of creation as literal days: "We cannot ... agree with Hensler and Frayssinous, to assign longer periods to the single acts of creation, although Genesis would then completely coincide with the Zend representation, but we must strictly adhere to the natural days of the text."[241] He sees the point of the passage in terms akin to Eichhorn: "The consecration of the seventh day is the point upon which the whole narrative really turns, as well as the systematic division of creation into days of labour; so that in fact it appears as if the [first] cosmogony itself had been only described in order to give importance to the Sabbath."[242]

Such German critical ideas were achieving greater penetration of the British mind by the 1850s than they had earlier in the century.[243] Baden Powell had already, in *Connexion of Natural and Divine Truth* (1838), taken a similar line. Whereas the scriptural geologists rejected the harmonistic enterprise for its biblical compromises on the basis of an unreliable and/or faithless geology, Powell rejected it on the basis of the Bible's unreliability in scientific matters, and this despite his clear admiration for the creation account. He reproved the preferred option of that time, the gap theory, as "totally at variance with the obvious tenour of the whole style of description," which reads instead as a first-

[238] Peter von Bohlen, *Historical and Critical Illustrations of the First Part of Genesis* (London: Longman, Green, Longman, and Roberts, 1862), 4, GB, http://books.google.combooks?id=rBkVAAAAYAAJ.

[239] Ibid., 1:5. The inner quotes are present in the original text, but without any identifying citation. Such a statement could have come from almost any concordist or conservative commentator on Genesis from the preceding century.

[240] Ibid., 1:10–11.

[241] Ibid., 1:21.

[242] Ibid., 1:20. This Sabbath element confirms a late, post-Mosaic date for Genesis, since it is Mesopotamian in origin: ibid., 1:2.

[243] John Rogerson says that English audiences finally saw "what a German critical work of the de Wettian era of criticism was really like" with the 1855 English translation of von Bohlen's Genesis commentary. See Rogerson, *Old Testament Criticism*, 175.

time creation out of nothing, and is far from "bearing the most remote reference to any anticipations of geological discoveries."[244] If the writer of Genesis had meant to communicate the outlines of modern geology through the text of Genesis 1 by employing figurative language, then he singularly failed, since "no one has ever imagined the secret meaning of the description till the present day."[245]

Having renounced any compulsion to find a harmony, Powell acknowledges the 'days' of the creation week as ordinary days with ordinary evenings and mornings.[246] But these days for Powell pertain to the author's conception and not any external reality, and it is here that Powell, in tune with the mythical approach to Genesis 1 emerging from Germany, goes beyond the majority of his English-speaking contemporaries. When geology and the Genesis narrative are compared, "there is an *insuperable discrepancy* in the most material points of the description," with its special creation of the entire world by divine power in a sudden, interposing way, and its alignment of terrestrial and human chronology. We the readers ought to "honestly ... allow that we cannot reconcile the description to the facts."[247] We may be permitted "to regard the first chapter of Genesis as embodying what were the commonly received ideas among the Jews.... The entire description being thus divested of the attributes of a real history ... can therefore only be regarded as having been designed for the more powerful enforcement of [the Sabbath] institution on the Jews."[248] "If the representation cannot have been designed for *literal history*, it only remains to regard it as having been intended for the better enforcement of its objects in the language of *figure* and *poetry*."[249]

Powell's dissolution of the privileged place of the Genesis text and his mythical reception of the creation narrative had already aroused Pye Smith's warning, "The rash and harsh language of Mr. Powell has betrayed him into great inconsistency with his own sacred professions and obligations."[250] By the 1850s there was greater alarm in the British Christian mind over the implications of science and the findings of biblical higher criticism, such that Powell's briefer restatement of his

[244] Baden Powell, *The Connexion of Natural and Divine Truth; or, The Study of the Inductive Philosophy Considered as Subservient to Theology* (London: John W. Parker, 1838), 251–54, GB, http://books.google.com/books?id=bWMOAAAAQAAJ.

[245] Ibid., 246–48.

[246] Ibid., 250.

[247] Ibid., 254–55.

[248] Ibid., 257.

[249] Ibid., 260. The humble possessive adjective 'its' here is significant: the Genesis text has its own intention, or at most reflects an author's intention, but divine intention has ceased to play a role.

[250] Pye Smith, *Relation*, 168–70.

views in an essay collection in 1855 quickly provoked several responses. Powell reprised his earlier views in an essay "On the Unity or Plurality of Worlds."[251] While some deluded minds were still trying to construct biblical geologies, he said, sane minds had abandoned literal belief in the narrative. The fact is, "the whole tenor of geology is in entire contradiction to the cosmogony delivered from Sinai." Yet while "the narrative, as a whole, as it cannot be received as *historical*, may be regarded as a *poetical*, representation." Where difficulties arise in the Bible's physical statements, it is because "the sacred writers...may fairly be understood as speaking *conformably to the existing state of knowledge*." Powell reiterates that figurative interpretation is permissible "if ... in any instance the letter of the narrative or form of expression may be found *irreconcileably at variance with physical truth*." The phrase 'at variance', which recurs elsewhere in this collection of Powell's essays, was destined to become a bone of contention.[252]

The phrase 'at variance' also appears in the 'Preliminary Essay' to M. M. Kalisch's *Historical and Critical Commentary on the Old Testament* (1858). Kalisch's driving argument is "that the results of the natural sciences are at variance with the Biblical narrative, especially with regard to the Age of the World, the Creation in Six Days, and the Formation of the Solar System and the Universe."[253] Therefore theology and biblical exegesis should avoid attempts to influence scientific outcomes, while exegesis in turn should avoid forcing on "the Hebrew historian...our modern systems of philosophy."[254] The Genesis account is not a vision, nor a myth, nor an apology, nor a hieroglyph, but a simple prose narrative; however, while it attempts to furnish a history of the physical creation of the world, "it expresses facts which the researches of science cannot sanction, and which were the common errors of the ancient world."[255] The general tone of Kalisch's commentary, while 'critical' in the scholarly sense, is not derogatory, and shows that even in an apparently reverent mind, criticism of the Bible and disillusionment with concordism were leading increasing

[251] For the following series of quotations, see Baden Powell, *Essays on the Spirit of the Inductive Philosophy, the Unity of Worlds, and the Philosophy of Creation* (London: Longman, Brown, Green, and Longmans, 1855), 304–307, GB, http://books.google. com/books?id=FkYnAAAAMAAJ.

[252] The essay is titled, 'On the Philosophy of Creation': ibid., 441.

[253] M.M. Kalisch, *A Historical and Critical Commentary on the Old Testament with a New Translation: Genesis. English Edition* (London: Longman, Brown, Green, Longmans, and Roberts, 1858), 31, http://books.google.com/books?id=QwUXAAAAYAAJ. Kalisch is admittedly a Jewish commentator, but Jewish and Christian critical treatments of the OT/Hebrew Bible sometimes differed very little in this era.

[254] Ibid., 31, 41.

[255] Ibid., 40.

numbers to affirm an 'irreconcilable contradiction' between Genesis and, in particular, geology.

Yet there were still voices advocating the real concordance between Genesis 1 and the Bible. Hugh Miller's *Testimony of the Rocks* aside, the concordist cause saw several fightbacks prompted directly by Powell's restated opinions. *Sermons in Stone* (1856) by Dominick McCausland was certainly prompted by Powell's essay:

> The Author is sensible that where so many of high talent and deep research have failed to identify the Record of Nature with the Record of Moses, a prejudice must prevail to induce the majority of Readers to distrust *any elucidation* of the subject, and ... to acquiesce in the hasty and dogmatic assertion of the Author of "The Unity of Worlds," that they are wholly at variance.[256]

The opening pages of Donald Macdonald's *Creation and the Fall* (1856) also lament Powell's declaration of "the irreconcilable contradiction between the whole view opened to us by Geology, and the narrative of the creation in the Hebrew Scriptures."[257]

Another 1856 work, J.H. Pratt's *Scripture and Science not at Variance,* lists five modern, and initially painful, changes to the interpretation of Genesis 1 brought about through interaction with science, from each of which, Pratt's thesis is to show, "Scripture once more emerges ... unhurt."[258] The first was the vast antiquity of the earth, the second "the Existence of Animals and Plants prior to the six days' work," and the third "The Existence of the Sun before the Fourth Day." The fourth was death before Adam (so that Paul's argument in Romans 5 must have concerned human death only), and the fifth was Pye Smith's restriction of the sphere of the creation week to a limited area of the earth's surface. Pratt describes an awkward outcome:

> The discoveries of botany and zoology, in conjunction with those of geology, are said to call upon us to believe that the work of the six days refers not to the whole surface of the globe, but only to that region of it where man was created, and his descendants dwelt in the first ages of the

[256] Dominick McCausland, *Sermons in Stones; or, Scripture Confirmed by Geology* (London: Richard Bentley, 1856), vii, GB, http://books.google.com/books?id=aEMDAAAAQAAJ.

[257] Donald Macdonald, *Creation and the Fall: A Defence and Exposition of the First Three Chapters of Genesis* (Edinburgh: Thomas Constable, 1856), 5, IA, http://www.archive.org/stream/creationfalldefe00macd. He reports that the same phrase was heard used in a London pulpit: ibid., [v] n. 1.

[258] J.H. Pratt, *Scripture and Science Not at Variance: or, The Historical Character and Plenary Inspiration of the Earlier Chapters of Genesis Unaffected by the Discoveries of Science* (London: Thomas Hatchard, 1856), 56, GB, http://books.google.com/books?id=rqYCAAAAQAAJ.

world … [a demand] which at first seems so utterly opposed to the letter of Scripture.[259]

Yet Pratt soon concedes with Pye Smith that creation, like the Flood, was a localized event, while in other areas of the globe the existing flora and fauna had lived on into the present era. After what sounds like a series of reluctant concessions to a stronger opponent, Pratt ironically asks how any would-be philosopher can still claim "that Scripture and Science can be at variance."[260] Despite rash pronouncements like Powell's, the ordinary believer can be confident that science and Scripture will always agree, even in the face of the new theories of development (i.e. evolution).[261] While the gap theory in Pye Smith's limited version supported Pratt's Pyrrhic victory, Macdonald and McCausland had bet on the day-age approach to the problem. Addinall describes the palpable tension in these works, reflecting the strain of dealing with "the increase of scientific discovery, and the persistent threat of German scholarship."[262] The strain would only worsen with the publication of *Essays and Reviews*.

The Climax of the Debate over Concordism around 1860

The publication of the controversial *Essays and Reviews* in 1860, a collection of seven essays, mostly by Anglican clergymen, marked a watershed for the penetration of continental biblical criticism into the English sphere. In Rogerson's words, "Its importance lies … in the way in which it indicates a growing tide of opinion against traditional orthodox opinions; a readiness of liberals to come out into the open."[263] That this higher-critical trend impinged upon interpretation of the Genesis cosmogony may be seen in the inclusion of an essay by C.W. Goodwin, 'Mosaic Cosmogony.'[264] Yet Goodwin's essay shows little sign of any developed historical-critical method of exegeting Genesis; Goodwin simply points out "that in reality two distinct accounts [of creation] are given us in the book of Genesis," produced by two different writers.[265] Goodwin's discussion otherwise simply belongs to the familiar 'Genesis and geology' debate, and the rejection of con-

[259] Ibid., 56–69, with quotation on final page.
[260] Ibid., 71.
[261] Ibid., 75.
[262] Addinall, *Philosophy and Biblical Interpretation*, 65, 67–68.
[263] Rogerson, *Old Testament Criticism*, 209.
[264] To Rogerson it is the standout essay in the collection. Ibid., 214; Bray, *Biblical Interpretation*, 288.
[265] C.W. Goodwin, "On the Mosaic Cosmogony," in *Essays and Reviews* (London: John W. Parker and Son, 1860), 217.

cordism is his key point, quietly buttressed by but not dependent on the new critical perspective.

Goodwin initially offers a brief survey of the picture of the earth's origin by means of the nebular hypothesis of cosmic origins and the very long history of the earth brought to light by geology and palaeontology.[266] Then he surveys the content of Gen. 1:1–2:3, in order "to inquire, whether this account can be shown to be in accordance with our astronomical and geological knowledge." Goodwin believes that the account is characterized by "simple grandeur," but not by a poetic style, and in no way invites a mystical interpretation. It reads very plainly, and is neither difficult to understand, nor "simply leaves out details which modern science supplies." "It is manifest that the whole account is given from a different point of view from that which we now unavoidably take."[267]

Goodwin goes on to survey in detail the main harmonizing options that were available, first confronting the gap theory as expounded by William Buckland in his Bridgwater Treatise (1836): "It is plain, from the whole tenor of the narrative, that the writer contemplated no such representation as that suggested, nor could any such idea have entered into the minds" of the first hearers.[268] Such conciliatory schemes imply that the Genesis account functioned as an impenetrable riddle for its earliest human audiences. Goodwin concedes to Hugh Miller's day-age scheme "a superficial resemblance in the Mosaic account to that of the geologists," but objects that the 'evenings' and 'mornings' of the Genesis text give the lie to having each day stand for an age. "We need only substitute the word 'period' for 'day' in the Mosaic narrative to make it very apparent that the writer at least had no such meaning, nor could he have conveyed any such meaning to those who first heard his account read."[269] The essential problem with the concordist approach is, "We are asked to believe that a vision of creation was presented to [the writer] by Divine power ... which vision inevitably led him to give a description which has misled the world for centuries, and in which the truth can now only with difficulty be recognised."[270] Goodwin poignantly adds:

> It would be difficult for controversialists ... to admit more explicitly that the Mosaic narrative does not represent correctly the history of the universe up to the time of man ... the task proposed is to evade the plain

[266] Ibid., 212–17.

[267] Ibid., 217–23.

[268] Ibid., 228–30.

[269] Ibid., 240. Tayler Lewis made the same substitution in various OT texts to establish the opposite point: Lewis, *Six Days of Creation*, 156.

[270] Goodwin, "Mosaic Cosmogony," 247, 249.

> meaning of language, and to introduce obscurity into one of the simplest stories ever told, for the sake of making it accord with the complex system of the universe which modern science has unfolded.[271]

Goodwin believes that such accord is not achievable. The Hebrew creation narrative belongs to an earlier day, "a human utterance, which it has pleased Providence to use in a special way for the education of mankind," a tool belonging to the religious infancy of humanity.[272] Since it is clearly intended to be read according to its plain sense, the narrative must be labelled factually false. "It can scarcely be said that this chapter is not intended in part to teach and convey at least some physical truth, and taking its words in their plain sense it manifestly gives a view of the universe adverse to that of modern science." Further, the Bible's value "as a book of religious instruction" is not to be maintained "by striving to prove it scientifically exact … but by the frank recognition of the erroneous views of nature which it contains."[273]

But despite Goodwin's own apparent admiration for the creation narrative, it is not clear how an age infatuated with the burgeoning discoveries of the natural sciences (as Goodwin himself evidently is) could retain its faith in the value of an ancient writing, traditionally held as divinely inspired, that failed in this most important area.[274] Goodwin seems unaware that his rather persuasive presentation virtually consigns the Genesis account, whose value he himself would seemingly still want to defend, to the shelf of endearing but outdated religious documents of ancient cultures. His essay aroused multiple responses, some conservative and strongly opposed, some effectively conceding many of the points Goodwin made to a significant degree.

Beginning at the conservative end, T.R. Birks, Anglican clergyman, graduate of and eventually Professor of Moral Philosophy at Cambridge, wrote his apologetic *The Bible and Modern Thought* (1861).[275] In an appendix devoted to 'Genesis and Geology', Birks defends the gap theory, citing recent research by the geologist D'Orbigny. "What reason can there be for deserting the literal sense of the days, in order to replace it by the immense disproportion of day periods … ?"[276] "On the literal view of the six days, however, the explanation is simpler, and less dependent on doubtful questions of science."[277] Birks' use of

[271] Ibid., 249–50.
[272] Ibid., 250–53.
[273] Ibid., 208–09, 211.
[274] For Goodwin's attitude to scientific discoveries, see ibid., 209, 211.
[275] The biographical detail is from http://www.hymnary.org/person/Birks_TR.
[276] T.R. Birks, *The Bible and Modern Thought* (London: Religious Tract Society, 1862), 509, GB, http://books.google.com.au/books?id=WDc-AAAAcAAJ.
[277] Ibid., 501.

language is indicative of the situation for this debate by this time: the gap theory represents the conservative option that permits literal acceptance of the creation days. That it might be possible to deny deep time and retain an entire universal creation in six days does not enter the equation.

In his reply to Goodwin, A. McCaul, "the professor of Hebrew and Old Testament at King's College, London," emphasized that Genesis 1 is historical in nature, rather than poetic, prophetic, or visionary.[278] McCaul combines a ruin-restitution understanding with periodic creation days. He believes that Moses denominates the combined pairs of light and dark periods as days "to mark the distinctive breaks in the progress of the development of the world."[279] The first three days in particular are not solar days but "days of the Lord, God's days.... But though the Mosaic language implies that the six days of which he speaks are six periods of time, it does not follow that they are to be identified with the six periods commonly received in geology," since Moses' audience could not have understood such information. In terms of this qualified concordism, "the first two days may, for all we know, incorporate the whole Primary–Tertiary sequence; ... the third day presents the dry land in its present state, with its flora differing from the preceding geological stages."[280] Genesis 1 actually anticipates many points of modern science, such as the reality of a definite 'azoic' phase in the earth's early history, a feature that McCaul can only attribute to divine inspiration.[281] McCaul's denial that Genesis 1 communicates a scientific scheme, combined with a determination to show its scientific accuracy where it does speak of the natural world, reveals an unresolved hermeneutical tension in his concordist approach.[282]

The writer of the essay, 'The Creative Week' in the apologetic *Replies to Essays and Reviews,* G. Rorison, is more consistently non-concordist, and more sympathetic to Goodwin.[283] McCaul's principle, "The six days are days of the Lord," is actually more consistently implemented by Rorison than by McCaul, leading to a non-concordist

[278] A. McCaul, "The Mosaic Record of Creation," in *Aids to Faith. A Series of Theological Essays*, ed. W. Thomson (London: D. Appleton, 1862), 229–31, GB, http://books.google.com/books?id=B1kXAAAAYAAJ. For the quoted content see Rogerson, *Old Testament Criticism,* 215.

[279] McCaul, "Mosaic Record," 247. See pp. 231–41 for his ruin-restitution position, and pp. 241–50 for his periodic days. See also Millhauser, "The Scriptural Geologists," 80, n. 28. Rudwick points out that Buffon's scheme worked the same way: Rudwick, *Bursting the Limits*, 143.

[280] McCaul, "Mosaic Record," 250.

[281] Ibid., 250–70. On the azoic phase, see p. 268.

[282] McCaul's semi-idealist, semi-concordist hybrid approach is not too different from those of Tayler Lewis and Benjamin Peirce, a few years prior.

[283] Zöckler, *Geschichte*, 2:494.

and quite non-historical approach to Gen. 1:1–2:3; "God's week is mystical; man's week is literal."[284] Rorison makes much of the parallelism between Days 1–3 and Days 4–6 of creation, and characterizes the account, despite its narrative dress, as "the oldest and sublimest poem in the world."[285] "Respect the parallelism, cease to ignore the structure, allow for the mystic significance of the number seven, and all perplexities vanish." Within this perspective the individual days of creation become poetic 'stanzas' or 'strophes', "lamps and land-marks of a creative sequence ... a mystic drapery, a parabolic setting, – shadowing by the sacred cycle of seven the truths of an ordered progress."[286]

Rorison therefore essentially adopts the ideal, ontological, cognitive understanding of Herder and Henry More, both of whom Rorison quotes in this context. From this idealist stance, Rorison is scathing about the entire concordist enterprise, whether involving gap or day-age options.[287] He interprets Gen. 1:1–2:3 against the background of other ancient cosmogonies, culminating in the best representative of these – yes, Ovid's *Metamorphoses*.[288] Yet Genesis does make definite truth claims according to Rorison, such as the origin of the distinctive forms of life, especially of human beings, by divine will, not simply by blind natural law.[289] He postulates a progressive creation model: "the strata of the earth are the register of divine acts strictly creative and supernatural," revealing "an ordered progress culminating at last in man," who constitutes a revelation of God and the climax of "the evolution of ancient nature."[290] True Christian faith involves adherence to the supernatural and to divine revelation, and since the *Essays and Reviews* represents an attack on the Bible by its friends, Goodwin should declare whether he, too, accepts the supernatural (for example the resurrection of Christ) and the reality of divine revelation.[291]

The example of Rorison and those of Lewis and Peirce in the United States suggest that the dilemmas of the concordist position encouraged a revival of idealist interpretation of Gen. 1:1–2:3. Cambridge astronomer James Challis, famously involved in controversy over the

[284] G. Rorison, "The Creative Week," in *Replies to Essays and Reviews* (Oxford/London: John Henry and James Parker, 1862), 291.

[285] Ibid., 288.

[286] Ibid., 290.

[287] Ibid., 242, 285–87.

[288] Ibid., 259–66.

[289] Ibid., 258.

[290] Ibid., 279–81. Note that once again, 'evolution' as used here does not yet connote transmutation, although it does connote a progressive sequence.

[291] This would be to side with Owen and Whewell against Powell and Darwin. Ibid., 292–94.

discovery of Neptune in 1846,[292] in *Creation in Plan and Progress* (1861) also presents a day-age concordism tempered by an idealist element: "[T]he Scriptural account of the *creation* is not a narrative of facts, but a communication to us of the scheme of the *creation* as framed originally in the mind of the Creator." The narrative dress of this scheme makes reference "to successive intervals of time" the only practical means of communication. "The enumeration of days serves the purpose of presenting the parts in a certain order, which, quite irrespective of the lengths of the days, may correspond with the order of developement."[293] The narrative from Gen. 2:6 represents the realization of this divine plan in actual history.[294] The ideal nature of the prior narrative, indicated by the reference to vegetation before its appearance in Gen. 2:4–5, explains why the correspondence with geological eras is not as exact as we might expect.[295]

Before the controversy over *Essays and Reviews* had fully subsided, John William Colenso (1814–83), Bishop of Natal in South Africa, published the first part of *The Pentateuch and the Book of Joshua Critically Examined* (1862). John Rogerson eulogizes the work, saying, "It is difficult not to regard it as the most remarkable achievement by a British scholar in the field of Old Testament criticism in the nineteenth century."[296] It represented the strongest advocacy of German critical scholarship yet seen in the English-speaking world, and critical methods are much more prominent in Colenso's handling of Genesis than they were in Goodwin's essay. While his source analysis itself does not directly impact his exegesis of the creation narrative, the critical implications of the composite nature of the Genesis narrative prove important.[297]

Colenso's initial consideration of the character of Genesis is undertaken on the basis of internal evidence alone, temporarily excluding the issue of potential contradictions between the Genesis narrative "and the results of Science".[298] Having demonstrated to his own satisfaction the composite nature of Genesis 1–11, and finding the sources irreconcilable with one another at various points, and otherwise contain-

[292] Donald J. Fernie, "The Neptune Affair," *American Scientist* 83, no. 2 (1995): 116–19.

[293] Challis, *Creation*, 58–59.

[294] Ibid., 56.

[295] Ibid., 54–55. Note the reappearance of a point that supported Augustine's idealist interpretation.

[296] Rogerson, *Old Testament Criticism*, 232.

[297] Colenso regarded Gen. 1:1–2:3 as "manifestly *Elohistic*, the work of one hand throughout," the distinction between Elohistic and Priestly sources having not yet come into common usage at that time. John W. Colenso, *The Pentateuch and Joshua Critically Examined* (London: Longmans, Green, and Co., 1870), 294.

[298] Ibid., 278.

ing 'difficulties, contradictions, improbabilities, impossibilities,'[299] Colenso concludes,

> We are now, then, free to consider the accounts of these miracles and supernatural appearances, which are recorded in the Pentateuch, and especially the stories of the Creation, the Fall, and the Deluge, in the light of Modern Science ... comparing them ... with what we *certainly know* to be true from other sources. For the Light of Modern Science ... is a gift of God.[300]

This new revelation of God now takes the authoritative role, functioning as Colenso's critical yardstick by which to judge biblical accuracy. His target is the teaching that upholds "the Bible in all its parts, and the Pentateuch especially, as a divinely infallible record of absolute historical truth."[301] The persistence of the teaching that 'Scripture and Science' are not 'at variance'[302] demands that Colenso "show, as plainly as possible, [the] utter groundlessness" of such assertions, that so the progress of scientific enquiry may not again be checked, as it was in days ... gone by."[303]

The partial exegesis of Gen. 1:1–2:3 that follows takes the text quite literally and straightforwardly, always with the agenda of showing the artificial and contorted nature of harmonistic interpretations.[304] A plain reading of verse 1 discovers that, "as the first act of that continuous six days' work, of which man was to be the last, 'God created the Heaven and the Earth'," as Exod. 20:11 states, leaving "absolutely no room" for Chalmers' 'gap'. This creation, a biblical chronology implies, occurs "about *six thousand years ago*. But Geology teaches that the earth has been in existence for hundreds of thousands – perhaps millions – of years." The creation days, "cannot...denote *six geological* ages... they are, in the meaning of the writer, six common days of twenty-four hours."[305] This is confirmed by the appointment of sun and moon to regulate day and night. "But Geology shows that the Earth was not brought into its present form in six days, but by continual changes through a long succession of ages," and that in a sequence that differs

[299] A search back over Part Four to this point reveals only the odd comment on internal discrepancies, most of which pertain to the Flood narrative. Regarding the 'two creation accounts' in Genesis 1–3, he has only spoken in general terms of 'remarkable discrepancies' or variation between them, without elaborating: ibid., 295, 304.

[300] Ibid., 313.

[301] Ibid.

[302] This is apparently a reference to Pratt, *Scripture and Science*. Pratt's work also features in Goodwin's refutations in 'Mosaic Cosmogony'.

[303] Colenso, *Pentateuch and Joshua*, 314.

[304] Ibid., 316–24.

[305] Ibid., 317.

from Genesis, ruling out the day-age option.[306] Denial of death before the Fall and the teaching that the sun and moon pre-existed Day 4 of creation cannot be sustained.[307] "The statements of both the Elohist and Jehovist...cannot be regarded as historically true, being contradicted in their literal sense, again and again, by the certain facts of modern Science."[308]

The value of the Hexaemeron, then, does not consist in its literal meaning taken as scientific or historical statement. "These stories of the first chapters of Genesis, whatever they may teach of Divine Eternal Truth ... are in their present form and structure mythical descriptions, where the narrative is an imaginative clothing for ideas."[309] Colenso finds here three such principles of truth: "(i) God is the Creator and Preserver of all things; (ii) Man is made in the image of God; (iii) All that God has made is very good." These are indeed revealed truths, he affirms, as people everywhere instinctively recognize upon hearing them.[310] The existence of similar creation stories, especially those including a set of six or seven periods, shows that, in Delitzsch's words, "The author ... has expressed in words an old tradition already existing."[311] Colenso detects evidence of a universal revelation from God: "The mind of man, in all ages and in all countries, musing upon the origin of all things, has been led by a Divine instinct to the same grand conclusions."[312]

Genesis 1:1–2:3, then, is one witness among others to a universal revelation by God of certain basic theological truths, grasped everywhere by common human intuition. It is certainly not the exclusive or inerrant vehicle of this revelation according to Colenso. Continued defence of Gen. 1:1–2:3 as a literally, historically, scientifically true record of creation only threatens to bring Christianity into deeper disrepute in a time when "the plainest facts of Natural Science ... are now brought home, by the extension of education, to every village ...

[306] Ibid., 318.

[307] Colenso argues, "It is a mere evasion of the plain meaning of these words, to say that Elohim made the Sun and Moon to *appear* first only on the fourth day," an argument common to both the harmonizing positions. Cf. Rorison, "The Creative Week," 254–55. Colenso argues that death had to be part of the prehistoric existence of animals since many of them were carnivorous in their very makeup: Colenso, *Pentateuch and Joshua*, 323–24.

[308] Ibid., 278.

[309] Ibid., 314.

[310] Ibid., 324. This confidence in a universal religious instinct in humanity is a mark of the confident liberal Christianity of the period.

[311] Ibid., 326. He proposes that the seven-day week stems naturally from the division of the lunar month into its four phases, fractions aside (since the lunar month is about 29½ days long), p. 327.

[312] Ibid.

in the land."[313] We witness in Colenso the fusion of historical-critical and scientific (or scientistic) perspectives in a joint internal/external deflation of the traditional Christian attitude to Scripture. His presentation demonstrates again that the most conservative and the most critical biblical interpreters tended to share a literal understanding of the days of creation, while those in the middle, who respected both the Bible and the fundamental soundness of sciences like geology, often resorted to more figurative interpretations of the creation week in the interest of achieving harmony between the two.[314]

Postlude: Darwin's *Origin of Species* and Debates over Genesis 1 after 1860

Our detailed survey of the interpretation of the creation week of Gen. 1:1–2:3 has come to a close with the concordist controversy centred in Britain. But incidental notices in some of the last-mentioned works of the growing influence of the 'developmental hypothesis', or what we might call biological evolution, raise the question, "What was the impact of Darwin's *Origin of Species* (1859) on debates over Genesis 1?" Put briefly, its impact was not prominent in the first few years after its publication in the works that I have studied. R.J. Berry asserts, "Darwin's arguments were quickly accepted," but his example is an endorsement in Frederick Temple's Bampton Lectures, delivered in 1884 and published in 1885. I found that works relating the Bible to science from around 1860–62 as a rule did not mention Darwin's theory at all, suggesting delayed penetration at a popular level.

Let us consider a few examples. Baden Powell writes very favourably of the transmutation (i.e. evolution) idea *prior* to Darwin's *Origin*, citing Darwin on a minor point.[315] But writing in 1860, Goodwin, though a non-concordist, sounds more cautious than Powell, noting that the transmutation hypothesis has not yet persuaded the majority of naturalists.[316] Rorison resists transmutation firmly, and Birks reviles it as

[313] Ibid., 324.

[314] For an Australian example of wholesale adoption of the biblical criticism advocated by Colenso and a completely skeptical position on concordism between Genesis and science, see Richard Davies Hanson, 1805–76, "Science and Theology: A Paper Read before the Adelaide Philosophical Society," in *Law in Nature, and Other Papers, Read before the Adelaide Philosophical Soc[iety] and the South Australian Institute* (Adelaide: W.C. Rigby, 1865), 52–67; Richard Davies Hanson, 1805–76, "On Some Relations of Science and Scripture," in *Law in Nature, and Other Papers, Read before the Adelaide Philosophical Soc[iety] and the South Australian Institute* (Adelaide: W.C. Rigby, 1865), 68–77.

[315] Powell, *Essays*, 401, 408, 410, 426, etc. For the citation of Darwin, see p. 343.

[316] Goodwin, "Mosaic Cosmogony," 214–15.

atheistic, but neither mentions Darwin.[317] Only when J.P. Lange, originally writing in 1864, notes but attempts to limit the implications of Darwin's work, do we begin to feel that Darwin's theory is beginning to significantly affect the discussion of Gen. 1:1–2:3.[318] In Germany, however, a young Otto Zöckler responded early and thoroughly to Darwin's publication, making his name by forging a conservative theological response to Darwinism.[319]

In his book, *The Post-Darwinian Controversies* (1979), James Moore drew attention to 'the Victorian crisis of faith,' and thought of Darwinism as the primary catalyst, but the way he phrases one troubling question of the time shows that its causes predate Darwin: "If creation did not proceed according to the record in the first chapters of Genesis, … can the Bible be trusted to provide inerrant knowledge in other matters?"'[320] While Darwinism may have aggravated the nineteenth-century British crisis of faith, reservations regarding the literal statements in Genesis about the physical world predated Darwin's *Origin* by two centuries or more, if we think of Henry More's *Conjectura cabbalistica*, Galileo's 'Letter to the Grand Duchess Christina', and Hobbes' *Leviathan*.[321] And many of the crux issues in the 'Victorian crisis of faith', e.g. the trivial span of human existence in the context of geological time and the potential for humanity to share the extinction of the great species of the past, do not directly depend on Darwinian belief. Two classic literary products of this crisis, Tennyson's *In Memoriam A.H.H.*, with its cry over Nature's qualmless extinction of individuals and whole species, and Matthew Arnold's 'Dover Beach', observing the retreat of the 'sea of faith' over the 'naked shingles of the world', were both published prior to Darwin's famous work.[322]

[317] Rorison, "The Creative Week," 280; Birks, *The Bible and Modern Thought*, 516.

[318] Lange and Lewis, *Genesis*, 190. See also Lewis' anti-Darwinian comment on p. 183, perhaps a reaction to Darwin's seeming materialism.

[319] Gregory, *Nature Lost?*, 119–29.

[320] James R. Moore, *The Post-Darwinian Controversies: A Study of the Protestant Struggle to Come to Terms with Darwin in Great Britain and America, 1870-1900*. Cambridge: Cambridge University Press, 1979, 113. For the connection of this Victorian crisis of faith to Darwinism, see pp. 13–14, 102–103, 110, etc.

[321] Hobbes' reservations were indirect, but his doubts about the Mosaic authorship of the Pentateuch naturally cast doubt on the genuineness and therefore inspiration and reliability of Genesis.

[322] Both works became available in or near 1850. Dennis Dean, "'Through Science to Despair': Geology and the Victorians," in *Victorian Science and Victorian Values: Literary Perspectives*, ed. J. Paradis and T. Postelwait, Annals of the New York Academy of Sciences (New York: The New York Academy of Sciences, 1981), 121–23. For easy access to these two poems, see http://theotherpages.org/poems/arnold01.html#1 and http://theotherpages.org/poems/books/tennyson/tennyson01.html. See poems 55 and 56.

"The publication of Darwin's *Origin of Species* in 1859," says Philip Addinall, "aggravated what was already becoming a very difficult situation for defenders of the faith.... The fearful spectacle of a world entirely explicable in naturalistic terms had taken another and massive step towards realization."[323] His subsequent comment that the acceptance of evolution in the modern sense made it "impossible to accept the details of Genesis chapters 1 and 2 at their face value" unfortunately lapses into same problem as Moore's.[324] While special, direct acts of creation understood as instantly performed, the 'fixity of species', and the teaching of the image of God in human beings in Gen. 1:1–2:3 faced a hard new challenge in Darwin's *Origin,* I would argue that the difficulties raised for Christianity by Darwinism were principally theological rather than exegetical in nature.[325] Modern, naturalistic 'evolution' entered debates over Genesis on the coat-tails of geology, and before that, of astronomy, as yet another ratcheting up of the cognitive pressure from a naturalistic, empirical science.

Therefore the Darwinian challenge to Genesis was not essentially new; the challenges to a theology of purpose in nature and to human uniqueness and similitude to God were the fundamental issues. For Christian opponents of Darwinism like Charles Hodge, "the fundamental question was not the incompatibility of Darwinism with the Mosaic account of creation nor the prospect of kinship with apes but the negative consequences of Darwinism for theism."[326] By the time Darwin's *Origin* gained full sway in the Western mind, the debate over the Genesis cosmogony, and the meaning of its creation days, had already passed its peak.

Dean's article shows that this crisis had already achieved a mature state by 1859: Dean, "Science to Despair," 111–24.

[323] Addinall, *Philosophy and Biblical Interpretation*, 196.

[324] Ibid., 197.

[325] Even the earlier debate over transmutation sparked by the *Vestiges of a Natural History of Creation* (1844) made little use of the Genesis account. Neither the *Vestiges*, nor Miller's 1847 *Footprints of the Creator*, nor Adam Sedgwick's greatly enlarged fifth edition of *A Discourse on the Studies of the University* (1850) allude much to Genesis, instead carrying the debate on natural and theological grounds. See Adam Sedgwick, *A Discourse on the Studies of the University of Cambridge. The Fifth Edition, with Additions, and a Preliminary Dissertation* (London: John W. Parker, 1850), GB, http://books.google.com/books?id=aQhCAAAAIAAJ.

[326] D.C. Lindberg and R.L. Numbers, eds., *God and Nature: Historical Essays on the Encounter between Christianity and Science* (Berkeley: University of California Press, 1986), 14.

7

The Shape of the History of Christian Interpretation of Genesis 1:1–2:3

> The Earthlings appear to take great interest in a book they call The Bible.... The book appears to be a source of profound wisdom and great debate.... The book suggests that the universe was created in seven days, including one full day devoted to rest, which might explain the Earthlings' tendency to laze around at the end of the working week, although it appears The Creator bucked human tradition by not celebrating his efforts by consuming 14 or more beers.[1]

I have surveyed the interpretation of the days of the creation week in Gen. 1:1–2:3 from the beginning of Christian interpretation down to 1860. Naturally, the story does not stop there, and indeed the main lines of interpretation persisted with fluctuating fortunes, whether concordist, non-concordist, literal or ideal, physical, metaphysical or mystical. This interesting and relevant next stage of the history of interpretation is better covered in OT introductions and Genesis commentaries than the period discussed here, not to mention histories of science and religion. To conclude this study I will review the interpretive history in terms of its continuity with modern interpretation (i.e. 'depth') and areas of discontinuity ('difference'), then draw some conclusions concerning the history of interpretation of this influential text ('trajectory') and the present day utilization of that long tradition.

A Story of Depth

This history reveals the *depth* of modern biblical hermeneutics. It enhances our insights into the long intellectual pedigree that lies behind any present reader's perspective. Only a few fundamentally different philosophical views of the world are available to the thinker in any age; therefore the same essential classes of thought constantly recur in dif-

[1] Trent Dalton, "Life from Mars," *The Courier-Mail*, Monday, January 5 2009, 27.

ferent guises, and the same is true with regard to interpretive perspectives towards Gen. 1:1–2:3. In one recurring choice, the reader of this part of Genesis has always been faced with the choice whether to interpret the days of creation literally, or figuratively, or both.

This choice is already apparent in the patristic age, when Alexandrian Christians in the allegorical tradition of Philo felt their natural inclination to interpret the creation week figuratively confirmed by the philosophical difficulties of the literal sense. The Antiochenes and Cappadocians, however, felt that something critical would be lost in so doing, and felt obliged to defend the inherent, timely 'sequence' of the biblical story back to the very beginning in Genesis 1. A quirky third option arose from the marriage of these two: an allegorical interpretation of the creation week in reference to the whole scope of human, redemptive history, although this 'world-week' or prophetic interpretation was a perspective on human history, not on terrestrial creation.

The two poles of literal or figurative interpretation may correspond to a philosophical polarity: the basic difference between a realist, time-conscious, this-worldly orientation, where the physical or sense-perceptible world is understood as the primary object of interest, and an idealist, atemporal, other-worldly orientation that seeks to look beyond sense-perceptible data to the true, invisible realities. Where idealism thrived, with its focus on 'being', allegorical or idealist perspectives on Genesis took the creation days as significant gateways into vital ontological realities. Where realism prevailed in the sense just outlined, there was a sensitivity to 'becoming', to change and historical process, and support for interpreting the creation days as real time intervals. For much of the period covered here, these polar alternatives corresponded roughly to Platonism versus Aristotelianism; Platonism strongly influenced patristic interpretation, favouring an allegorical creation week in many minds, reviving periodically to influence medieval, Renaissance and even modern treatments of Genesis, while the Aristotelian revival dating from the thirteenth century, and the rediscovery of Jewish scholarship, seems to have aided the subsequent turn toward the literal sense.

Theology played a significant role here too, as we might expect. The perfect, changeless God at the top of the ontological tree in Greek philosophy was beyond the influence of time and the vicissitudes of material existence. His power was absolute; how could he need any passage of time to achieve his creative will? Why, for that matter, would commands fulfilled instantaneously be separated by twenty-four hour intervals? Many philosophically-astute fathers such as Augustine could only imagine creation as instantaneous, direct, and unmediated. In modern theological lingo, creation was the ultimate interventionist act of an interventionist God. It made sense therefore if it was unique, required and had no preparatory conditions, underwent no inherent development, and by the (unmentioned) close of Day 7, was complete.

But some Christian thinkers who were alert to the sheer historical texture of the Judaeo-Christian Scriptures, and to the free will of God more than to his philosophically necessary attributes, might more easily acknowledge the sense of a creation that manifested a temporal order, appearing sequentially according to the purposes of God.[2] Some believed that God had delegated to certain elements of creation a role in assisting his creative work, perhaps implied in statements like, "Let the land produce vegetation" (Gen. 1:11). They allowed scope for natural cause-and-effect within the creative process, and were more willing to accommodate the developmental view of the world that has dominated more recent centuries. To them, the growth of living things and even the human individual suggested that God sometimes chose to create gradually, although for most of the period we have reviewed, a literal six-day creation constituted the more gradual creation option! For others, biblical creation, rather than being absolute and complete, became one episode in the story of origins, the making of merely the present phase of world history, or a single turn of an endless cycle.

Another issue that remains consistently relevant throughout this story is the nature and sources of knowledge. The standing of the creation week as an account of the origins of the world and of humanity depended on the place of written testimony or texts in one's epistemology, and on the nature of this particular text in one's theology of revelation. The authority of Genesis' account of origins hung on its status as a revelatory text, a transmission of truth from the true God. When perceived as a divinely inspired text, it could be expected to reveal truth about the world that was fully reliable and perhaps unmatched by any other source. If its authority instead stemmed from its sheer antiquity, a tempting idea for the Renaissance classicist, then other ancient creation myths such as Ovid's *Metamorphoses* or Plato's *Timaeus* might legitimately be brought in alongside of Genesis to help craft one's understanding of the world's origin.

The scientific revolution was really founded on the conviction that God had authored a second work beside the 'Book of Scripture', and that was the 'Book of Nature'. To use these terms together was to imply that natural objects and phenomena could 'tell' a story or com-

[2] On the highly relevant polarity of necessitarian/intellectualist and voluntarist theology, particular with reference to the Modern era, see John Henry, "Palaeontology and Theodicy: Religion, Politics and the Asterolepsis of Stromness," in *Hugh Miller and the Controversies of Victorian Science*, ed. M. Shortland (Oxford: Clarendon, 1996), 151–70.

municate truth in a manner comprehensible to reason. It was an endorsement of the empirical enterprise, the quest to gather data from nature to form an implicit picture of the past. Where both 'Books' were taken seriously, and derived from the one author, a lone God, the strong instinct of many Christian thinkers was to attempt to reconcile them wherever they seemed to coincide, such as in their respective indications of how the world came to be. That is, the concordist enterprise of the modern era, seen for example in the 'Genesis and geology' debates, rested on the understanding that God exists and communicates truth, or at least that his truth is accessible to humans via multiple channels.

Unsurprisingly, then, the main interpretive options for reconciling Genesis and knowledge of nature and its history today have relatively deep roots, much deeper than the twentieth century. Day-age (i.e. truly concordist) schemes date back to the mid-1600s, being cited and rejected by Matthew Hale and enshrined in a constrained form in Whiston's year-long days. Semi-concordist schemes, the ruin-restitution and gap theory hypotheses, have clear precedents almost as far back as the mid-1700s. The long-chaos belief as applied to the initial formlessness of the world prior to the actions of the creation week, the natural parent of both semi-concordist alternatives, held sway in the eighteenth century and can be traced back through its seventeenth-century re-emergence and right back through the Middle Ages into the patristic era and to classical literature.

But some figures in our story believed truth was available from other sources again. A stubborn minority believed that God revealed cosmic truths to a few privileged individuals directly, namely themselves, usually with the associated responsibility to share their mystical insights with the world. The influence of figures such as Eriugena, Böhme and Swedenborg was surprisingly great. This mystical stream has functioned as a radicalizing influence in Genesis interpretation over the centuries, injecting the Neoplatonism of Pseudo-Dionysius through Eriugena in the ninth century, an apocalyptic world-week interpretation through Joachim of Fiore in the thirteenth, a fairly plain Gnosticism into the Renaissance cauldron through Böhme, and a suggestion of the dispensability of a written revelation through the Quakers in seventeenth-century England and Holland.[3]

One basic hermeneutical question that is posed, then, is whether a biblical text should be interpreted as a stand-alone entity, or with reference merely to other parts of the scriptural canon? Or should its interpretation be comparative, considering its links to the human world beyond with its culture, history, and literature? To the natural world

[3] Popkin, *Third Force*, 355–57.

that can seemingly testify through the senses to its present rules of operation and to its formative history? The interpretive story told here might suggest that the biblical Hexaemeron came out of the contest of truth battered and bruised, but what alternative was there? The account of truth that sits alone on the sidelines has already proved its redundancy. It is in the public square that truth proves its mettle.

A Story of Difference

However, this is also a story of *difference*, something often overlooked by modern readers of Genesis who have combed the interpretive tradition for authoritative precedents for their own viewpoint. To attempt to line up past thinkers behind a modern literal creation week, framework hypothesis, or day-age viewpoint is to oversimplify the interpretive 'playing fields' of the past. There is really no popular creation week interpretation in existence today that truly resembles Augustine's model, despite how often his ghost is summoned up.[4] He did not even remotely propose or periodize any pre-human history, and even a quasi-Platonist scheme such as Meredith Kline's lacks Augustine's angelic content.[5] It is equally mistaken to recruit patristic world-week thought in support of day-age concordism, as if it was exclusive of a short world chronology or of an accompanying literal creation week, or as if it concerned pre-human history.

It is the neglect of these distinctions that permits wrong-headed, sweeping generalization such as, "All [the ante-Nicene fathers who wrote on Genesis] accepted that *yôm* could mean 'a long time period.' The majority explicitly taught that the Genesis creation days were extended time periods (something like a thousand years per *yôm*)."[6] The opposing writers in the same work announce,

> The historic Christian tradition ... has viewed these days mainly as normal days because it has viewed the Genesis account as historical. No significant debate existed on the matter before the nineteenth century because the plainest and most straightforward reading of the text had no sustained challengers.[7]

[4] E.g. John P. Dickson, "The Genesis of Everything: An Historical Account of the Bible's Opening Chapter," *ISCAST Online Journal* 4 (2008): 5.

[5] Kline, "Genesis Cosmogony," 2–15.

[6] Hugh Ross and Gleason L. Archer, "The Day-Age View," in *The Genesis Debate: Three Views on the Days of Creation*, ed. D. Hagopian (Mission Viejo, CA: Crux, 2001), 125–26.

[7] J. Ligon Duncan, III and David W. Hall, "The 24-Hour View," in *The Genesis Debate: Three Views on the Days of Creation*, ed. D. Hagopian (Mission Viejo, CA: Crux, 2001), 22.

This blanket generalization is nearly as superficial as the claims it opposes and manifests a glaring ignorance of the early Modern rise of science, Augustine's perennial influence and Aristotle's periodic resurgence through the medieval period down through Reformation times on the other. All of this serves as a warning against an unvetted eagerness to recruit ancestral support for modern viewpoints without an accompanying willingness to do the serious historical research required.

Non-literal interpretations of the days of Genesis formed a sustained minority strand throughout the period in view in this study. But the modern reader rarely possesses the philosophical exposure to appreciate the warp and woof of a strongly Platonist Genesis interpretation such as those of Eriugena, Joseph Needham or Tayler Lewis. And the organic view of the world so basic to the Genesis interpretations of Needham and William Hobbs and J.G. Herder's *Ideen* is much less familiar among Genesis readers than a mechanistic, Newtonian world-picture. The Gnosticism behind Böhme's mysteries is unknown to many Genesis readers today, despite its historical recurrence. Even the almost exclusively christological, and therefore allegorical, way of reading Genesis 1 that characterized Anastasius of Sinai or Isidore of Seville may be strikingly unfamiliar other than to a Catholic scholar.

Sometimes we encounter unexpected alignments, such as the support for evolutionary organic development *before* Darwin by the biblical conservatives Moses Stuart and Tayler Lewis, in *opposition* to the anti-evolutionary stance of the mainstream science of their time. And medieval and Reformation-era scholars were divided over which creation view was more safely orthodox: a gradual (six-day) creation that better handled the Genesis text and majority patristic opinion, or an instantaneous creation that shut down any suggestion that matter contained its own, inherent developmental potential, or pre-dated Genesis 1. Such 'difference' in hermeneutical landscapes makes it incumbent upon us to study the history and thinking of the different eras concerned, in aid of a better-informed appreciation of their approaches to this and other biblical texts.

One further interpretive 'difference' may need special highlighting. Whereas in the modern era the biblical text has primarily been understood literally in Protestant circles, and as having one primary meaning anchored in the intention of the original author, and isolated using historical-grammatical methods, it was considered not just possible, but desirable through much of the period covered here to find more than one meaning in a text such as Gen. 1:1–2:3. The classical and medieval Christian thinkers perceived a reality of multiple levels, some of which related to the visible world and some to the invisible, spiritual world. Many, indeed, were conscious of the superiority of the spiritual realms to the physical. This inclined them towards allegorical interpretation, which allowed them to penetrate beyond the physical 'veil' of the text.

But these two kinds of interpretation were not usually mutually exclusive. The same interpreter could and usually did hold a literal, cosmological interpretation of the Genesis text alongside a series of allegorical interpretations, classically one related to human physical development, one more significantly to personal spiritual ascent by stages towards God, and one prophetic scheme, the world-week outline of human history. These might jockey for priority in each writer's scheme, but we must recognize that they usually co-existed in the patristic mind and almost always in the medieval mind.

Along with this goes another difference. Whereas until the advent of postmodern thought the modern era has sought textual meaning in the intention of the human author, encouraging us to seek a single meaning, most Christian interpreters historically have read the biblical text as originating in the mind of the divine Author. As Augustine explained in *On Christian Doctrine*, God is perfectly able to encase plural meanings in the biblical text according to the needs of its various readers. Textual polyvalence is no postmodern invention; it has been the rule rather than the exception for two thousand years of Christian interpretive history, though interpretive license was normally to be bounded by reverence for the 'Rule of Faith', the church's consensus understanding of gospel truth.

A Story with a Trajectory: The Influential Career of Genesis 1

The Genesis account of the six days of creation and seventh day of God's rest was well placed to take a prominent place in the thinking of the early church, thanks to its placement at the head of the Hebrew canon, its global scope and cosmogonic subject matter, its theological importance, the narrative form that integrated it with subsequent biblical history, its intrinsic connection to one of the Ten Commandments, and even, initially, the new cultural importance of the seven-day week. Gen. 1:1–2:3 swelled in importance just as Christianity inherited the mantle of cultural leadership from the declining Roman Empire. As the medieval era opened, Genesis had become established as the essential point of reference for discussions of the world's creative origin, for the initial step of human redemptive history, for Trinitarian theology, and for the Christian view of nature and of humanity's place therein. Many philosophical currents swept the medieval intellectual scene, and the early chapters of Genesis remained one of their key testing-grounds, retaining a divine 'right of reply' to all. The Hexaemeron framed the medieval view of the world's origin and constitution.

The abundant Genesis commentaries of the Renaissance/Reformation period could embrace any and every topic; the Hexaemeron was the fountainhead and framework of all knowledge, whether cosmic, terrestrial, historical or devotional. "Part of the importance of Genesis in the Renaissance pattern of thought was that it gave the only authoritative account of the beginning of things. It filled what would otherwise have been a cultural vacuum. In the sixteenth century the account of creation in Genesis as it is expanded in the commentaries had no serious competitors."[8] The same was true of the encyclopaedic mirror literature, or the universal histories – Genesis had the cultural dominance.

Yet Renaissance inquisitiveness turned to re-examine ancient, non-biblical textual sources just as Portuguese, Spanish and Dutch ships discovered unknown new lands. Soon telescopes, in league with changing astronomical theory, revealed the immense scale of the cosmos, straining the Christian-Aristotelian world-picture inherited from the Middle Ages. And the willingness to question received authority implicit in the Reformation fuelled budding criticism of the authorship and authenticity of the Mosaic writings. Yet Gen. 1:1–2:3 survived the transition to the heliocentric system of Newton, and eighteenth-century Christianity rebounded from scepticism about the Bible in parts of the West, so that Genesis was still normally called the work of Moses in Britain and America well after 1800. It was the investigation of (and speculation about) the earth and intimations of its long and complex past that brought matters to a head for the biblical creation week.

The new genre of geotheory was born out of a strange marriage of the Bible, pagan cosmogonic speculation, and the stirrings of scientific inquiry. Thomas Burnet bypassed the creation week altogether, while Newton's protégé William Whiston offered his influential year-long creation day scheme to the world, and John Ray wondered about the impact of the expanding testimony of fossils and strata upon the traditional world chronology. Woodward's diluvial model initially explained the new data, diverting pressure from the prevailing literal creation week, although many thinkers prefixed a long chaotic period to it under classical influences such as that of Ovid's *Metamorphoses*.

Yet the growing perception of the earth's antiquity and the sheer complexity of the geological record increasingly forced thinkers to seek harmonization with the creation week of Genesis by treating the days as long prehistoric periods and/or by subdividing the primordial chaos into geological eras. Indeed the very idea of the earth's formation out of the elements of an initial chaos by natural processes suggested a pro-

[8] Williams, *Common Expositor*, 266.

cess taking much longer than a week, an impression only strengthened as empirical research revealed the earth's complex stratigraphy. Harmonistic motivations had by the end of the eighteenth century produced the mature day-age and gap or ruin-restitution theories, both able to accommodate any amount of time that geology should require. For many scientifically-informed Christian thinkers, one of these two options provided a satisfactory compromise stance requiring only a minor concession over the language of the 'days' of creation. Yet a significant sector of English-speaking society remained sceptical of 'deep time' and naturalistic reasoning generally, and produced a large number of works of scriptural geology that defended a literal creation week, a catastrophic Deluge and a short biblical chronology.

It was increasingly felt, as the nineteenth century continued, that the details of geology were not being read out of the Genesis text, but in fact being read into it. The sheer depth, complexity and contingency of geological history defied the ability of any concise description to embrace it, yet its reality was tangible.

But the biblical text gave no clear indication that the earth had existed for vast ages prior to human creation, and indeed the simple, six-day description of Genesis 1 seemed to militate against this idea. Both harmonizing interpretations seemed to take liberties with the Genesis text that threatened the definition of literal interpretation. Day-age interpretation remained faithful to the common-sense impression that Genesis 1 spoke of the original creation of the world as a whole, provided it could allow the sun, moon and stars to pre-exist Day 4. Thus it represented the fullest realization of the concordist enterprise – earth history and Gen. 1:1–2:3 fully coincided.

By contrast, the semi-concordist gap theory prided itself on retaining literal creation days, avoiding the forced rendering of the word 'day'. Yet it lacked convincing exegetical warrant for referring the creation narrative only to the current state of the earth's existence, and placed an enormous interpretive load on a lone phrase in Gen. 1:2. And importantly, it flew in the face of the fourth commandment (Exod. 20:11) assertion that the Lord had made heaven, earth, the seas and all their contents in six days. Idealist interpretation of Genesis 1 made a modest comeback, aided by its ability to excuse itself from concordist obligations, but could only interest those still convinced of the authority of Genesis. But many studious eyes that would in another era have teased apart biblical terms for meaning were focused now on the natural world and the nature of the human being.

The inroads of the continental mythical perspective on Gen. 1:1–2:3 after mid-century aggravated a general scepticism about the whole concordist undertaking and provided a warrant for the more sceptically inclined to disregard the text's apparently dated cosmogony. A noble yet flawed human product, a monument to the history of the religious development of man, or at least intended to communicate solely moral or spiritual rather than scientific truths, its harmony with modern (enlightened) human discoveries should never have been expected. Far separated from the scriptural geologists in their respect for the literal truth of the Bible, holders of this mythical perspective ironically shared with them an antagonism for the concordist enterprise. But their concessions on the reliability of scripture seemed grave from many Christians' point of view, provoking multiple defences of the authority and relevance of the hexaemeral account in a flurry of writing climaxing around 1860, the end-point of this study.

The concordist debate therefore peaked before Darwin's brand of evolution took hold in the popular mind. The fact that the biological theory of evolution found an (apparent) explanatory mechanism in Darwin's natural selection perhaps aggravated the tension over Genesis 1, since it did not lie easily with the instruction that living things had arisen in their distinctiveness by the direct will of God, commissioned to reproduce 'after their kind', or that humans uniquely bore God's image.[9] But issues of divine purpose and design, anthropology and a dynamic versus a static biosphere bore on Christian theology and philosophy more directly than on the text of Genesis. I agree with John Rogerson's recent statement: "Whatever impact that *On the Origin of Species* may have had on the scientific community and the general public, its effect on the interpretation of the opening chapters of Genesis was surprisingly minimal."[10] The waning of the intellectual dominance of the Hexaemeron is largely a pre-Darwinian story.

The reign of Gen. 1:1–2:3 over the worldview of the West, long contested, was finally overthrown in debates concerning geology. Having long supplied the framework for knowledge of truths natural and supernatural, Genesis 1 was driven to the margins of what counted as knowledge. Concordist efforts ultimately lacked the resources to bridge the epistemological gap between the world of nature and the authorized biblical text. The various options for interpreting the creation week, the day-age and gap theories, literal, and ideal or symbolic approaches all survived the transition into the twentieth century. But they survived in the conversations of a subculture, voices in the ghetto. Separate communities developed according to whether their primary authority was an inspired Bible or scientific consensus. Their dialects

[9] David Wilkinson, "Did Darwin Dethrone Humankind?," in *Darwin, Creation and the Fall: Theological Challenges*, ed. R.J. Berry and T.A. Noble (Nottingham: Inter-Varsity, 2009), 19.

[10] John Rogerson, "What Difference Did Darwin Make?," 75.

diverged, and they in time lost the ability to communicate with each other, making reconciliation increasingly unlikely. Genesis 1, the explanatory keystone of the worldview of Christendom, had lost its spell over the West as a whole. The remorseless erosion of its hegemony after the Reformation is a telling instance of the yet-unfinished 'breakdown of the medieval synthesis'.[11] Yet the West is not the world, some non-Western cultures' perspectives on the Genesis cosmogony are very different, and often less jaded, than that of the West.[12] We ought to remember that the story of the career of this seminal biblical text is not yet fully told, much like the story of the world whose creation it narrates.

Re-utilizing the Interpretive Tradition

Contemporary scholars approach this text with a range of agendas. Some have sought the meaning of Gen. 1:1–2:3 (1) within an exilic historical setting,[13] or (2) in its literary context, perceived as head of the Hebrew canon and prologue to the Torah,[14] or (3) in its cultural context, as describing God's construction of a world-temple.[15] The popularity of literary approaches to the Bible has led to (4) increased efforts to identify the genre of Genesis 1.[16]

[11] Almond, *Adam and Eve*, 214; Green, *Renaissance and Reformation*, 28; Williams, *Common Expositor*, 268. We are reminded that this breakdown can be seen as originating earlier: Leff, *Dissolution*, 145–47. It could be argued that the crisis over Aristotelianism in the thirteenth century, or even experiments with Neoplatonism in the twelfth, represent the beginning of the 'dissolution of the medieval outlook'.

[12] See for example David Tuesday Adamo, "The Genesis Creation Accounts: An African Background," in *Genesis*, ed. A. Brenner, A.C.C. Lee, and G.A. Yee, *Texts/Contexts* (Minneapolis: Fortress, 2010), 25–33.

[13] Louise Schottroff, "The Creation Narrative: Genesis 1.1–2.4a," in *A Feminist Companion to Genesis*, ed. A. Brenner (Sheffield: Sheffield Academic Press, 1993), 25.

[14] Ian Hart, "Genesis 1:1–2:3 as a Prologue to the Books of Genesis," *Tyndale Bulletin* 46, no. 2 (1995): 315–36; Yair Hoffman, "The First Creation Story: Canonical and Diachronic Aspects," in *Creation in Jewish and Christian Tradition*, ed. H. Graf Reventlow and Y. Hoffman, JSOT Sup (London: Sheffield Academic Press, 2002), 50–52.

[15] Weinfeld, "Sabbath, Temple," 501–12; Michael Welker, "Creation, Big Bang," 173–87; Walton, *Lost World*.

[16] This is a very widespread theme, but just to mention a few, see Frank Polak, "Poetic Style and Parallelism in the Creation Account (Genesis 1.1–2.3)," in *Creation in Jewish and Christian Tradition*, ed. H. Graf Reventlow and Y. Hoffman, 2–31; Richard H. Moye, "In the Beginning: Myth and History in Genesis and Exodus," *Journal of Biblical Literature* 109 (1990): 577–98; Waltke, "Literary Genre," 2–10; J.I. Packer, "Hermeneutics and Genesis 1–11," *Southwestern Journal of Theology* 44, no. 1 (2001): 13–16.

And yet these discussions are often geared to refute concordist approaches to Genesis 1.[17] John Rogerson complained in 1997 that the shadow of modern science looms over most discussion of Gen. 1:1–2:3.[18] Many popularly oriented publications either promote or oppose young-earth creationist belief, while others defend a day-age concordist position, or non-concordist approaches like the framework hypothesis.[19] Especially for members of believing communities, the choice between literalism, concordism and a harmonious kind of non-concordism remains a real issue. One reason is that they are faced with more than one apparently authoritative source of truth. They are assured, primarily by those who do not share their faith, either that their biblical source is redundant, which simply sounds scornful and hostile, or that their biblical source does not overlap in any way with scientific claims about the world.

Yet it still looks to the average believer as if the scientific community and the Genesis text, plainly read, both speak of the emergence or appearance of the natural world, and not in very compatible ways. And so the tension remains, and the parties in creation-evolution debates, loyal to different authorities and often operating with different epistemologies, talk past each other with insufficient appreciation of the nature of the cultural and intellectual gulf that has been widening between them for centuries. Meanwhile the believer who reveres the Bible and can also appreciate the rationale behind scientific endeavours continues to seek an integrated yet faithful explanation of the origin of our world.

[17] Dickson, "The Genre of Genesis 1"; Waltke, "Literary Genre," 8–9; Conrad Hyers, "The Narrative Form of Genesis 1: Cosmogonic, Yes; Scientific, No," *Journal of the American Scientific Affiliation* 36 (1984): 208–15; C.H. Pinnock, "Climbing out of a Swamp: The Evangelical Struggle to Understand the Creation Texts," *Interpretation* 43 (1989): 143–55.

[18] John W. Rogerson, "Genesis 1–11," *Currents in Research: Biblical Studies* 5 (1997): 68–71.

[19] E.g., in favour of young-earth creationism, James B. Jordan, *Creation in Six Days: A Defense of the Traditional Reading of Genesis One* (Moscow, Idaho: Canon, 1999); Douglas F. Kelly, *Creation and Change: Genesis 1.1–2.4 in the Light of Changing Scientific Paradigms* (Fearn, Ross-shire: Mentor, 1997). Opposed to creationism are McCalla, *Creationist Debate*; Robert T. Pennock, *Tower of Babel: The Evidence Against the New Creationism* (Cambridge, MA: MIT Press, 2000). Along framework hypothesis lines, see Kline, "Genesis Cosmogony," 2–15. For a presentation of 'anthropomorphic' creation days, see C. John Collins, *Genesis 1–4* (Phillipsberg, NJ: P&R Publishing, 2006). For related positions within a single debate, see Carol A. Hill, "A Third Alternative to Concordism and Divine Accommodation: The Worldview Approach," *PSCF* 59, no. 2 (2007): 129–34; Paul H. Seely, "Concordism and a Biblical Alternative: An Examination of Hugh Ross's Perspective," *PSCF* 59.1 (2007): 37–45; David F. Siemens, Jr., "Extended Humpty Dumpty Semantics and Genesis 1," *PSCF* 59.3 (2007): 194–200.

Such a quest sometimes drives present-day interpreters of Gen. 1:1–2:3 to delve into the Christian interpretive tradition in a quest for ancient insights and authoritative precedents for present stances, though this is a well-established habit in Catholic, Reformed and Eastern Orthodox traditions. Augustine and other respected figures of Christian tradition are often recruited for the benefit of competing literal and figurative understandings of the creation days.[20] Since such treatments often display a superficial understanding of the mindset and circumstances of ancient Christian thinkers, it might help to briefly reflect on the historical background to three popular contemporary Evangelical interpretations of the creation week of Gen. 1:1–2:3: the day-age or concordist view, the framework view, and the literal creation week associated with 'young-earth creationism'.

Nothing meaningfully like the day-age view existed before the Reformation. Augustine's instantaneous creation week was non-temporal, while the world-week idea, sometimes mistaken for a day-age view, was an allegorical transfer of the meaning of the creation days across to human history that paralleled their literal understanding. Even Methodius' unique melding of these two, so that creation lasted through human history, was still not a *pre-historic* day-age teaching. Henry More's pregnant suggestion in *Conjectura cabbalistica* (1653), "all might be made at once, or in such periods of time, as is most suitable to the nature of the things themselves," represents the earliest possible hint of long creation days that I have found.[21] We saw Matthew Hale in 1667 resisting the clearly available option of periodic creation days,[22] and Newton considering it in 1681. Other writers around 1700 employ the long day option, most clearly Halley, the little-known Hobbs, and Whiston more formally in his 1696 *New Theory*. Anton Lazzaro Moro's 1740 *De' Crostacei* was another significant step forward for this theory. Buffon's half-hearted use of the scheme in his 1778 *Époques* gave it scientific respectability, while from 1790, de Luc's more sincere version began to penetrate British Christianity, as seen in Kirwan and especially Parkinson. But a formal, detailed, geologically-oriented day-age theory is best attributed to Robert Jameson, channelling as he did the apparent endorsement of Cuvier.[23]

This established, day-age strategy drew, perhaps unconsciously, on the long-running habit of dividing up the past using a hexaemeral framework, yielding a 'world-week', but now its original content,

[20] In Hagopian, ed., *Genesis Debate*, Augustine is discussed on 43 out of 307 pages.

[21] More, *Conjectura cabbalistica*, 148.

[22] Hale, *Primitive Origination*, 307.

[23] Rudwick pointed out that the French geologist Soulavie also used a six-part geological scheme in his *Natural History of Southern France* (1780–84): Rudwick, *Bursting the Limits*, 220.

(salvific) human history, was replaced by geological history. It came with patristic license in the limited sense that Augustine had demonstrated the possibility of non-literal interpretation of the days of creation. The geological periodization of history was doubtless encouraged through the example of Noah's Flood as a catastrophic boundary between past and present eras of earth history, and reborn with the assistance of a resurgent Platonism that was strongly biased toward ideal creation days. The new astronomy of Newton provided the platform upon which Whiston introduced the long creation day to the world. The emergence of 'deep time' added a new urgency to its eighteenth-century development, while it breathed the air of the concordist assumption of a generous overlap in content and kind between biblical and naturally-obtained facts.

The roots of the twentieth-century 'framework hypothesis' are more subtle. Its focus is literary rather than historical, treating the days of creation as a cognitive or heuristic framework, and highlighting the literary arrangement of the two parallel sets of three days. It may comprehend the creation week as an anthropomorphism that describes the divine creative work in human terms and may think of 'God's work week' as operating on a higher ontological plane.[24] The creation week becomes a metaphorical description of God's work using the analogy of the familiar, human working week.

E.J. Young attributed this position to a 1924 work by Dutchman Arie Noordtzij.[25] Yet it seems to have analogues in nineteenth-century non-concordism, the aesthetic creation week of Herder and others in late eighteenth-century Germany, the literary appreciation of the form of Gen. 1:1–2:3 that dates back to medieval scholasticism and beyond, and the Platonism that emphasized the merely analogous correspondence of divine and human modes of working. There is therefore a measure of truth to the claim, "The modern framework interpretation builds upon Augustine's figurative interpretation of the days," while it seems to me to overstate the case to continue, "and is in fundamental continuity with it."[26] The framework hypothesis is one modern-day heir to the non-literal, ideal tradition of creation week interpretation, and at its heart, unlike the day-age position, is non-concordist, in that the metaphorical language of Genesis 1 does not favour concrete chronological comparisons with scientific inferences about earth history.

Then we have the literal interpretation associated now with young-earth creationism rather than with the gap theory as it was around

[24] Collins, "Anthropomorphic Days," 109–30; Kline, "Genesis Cosmogony," 2–15.

[25] Edward J. Young, "The Days of Genesis," *WTJ* 25 (1963): 3.

[26] Lee Irons and Meredith G. Kline, "The Framework View," in *The Genesis Debate: Three Views on the Days of Creation*, ed. D. Hagopian, 224.

1860. Advocates see themselves as simply faithfully maintaining the orthodox Christian position that existed since early church times, while critics counter, "[T]his interpretation is only a century old and was codified in the North American context of the post-Darwinian controversies."[27] The truth lies somewhere in the middle. Contemporary creation-week literalism is the natural descendant of a long literal tradition that goes back to the Antiochenes and the course mostly taken by Basil. 'Literal', albeit rather metaphysical creation days were often held in complementary combination with the spiritual senses in the Middle Ages, with the nearest example to modern literalism coming from the hand of Andrew of St. Victor. The early Reformers and the Jesuit scholars plainly defended literal days against Augustine and Cajetan. English Protestantism after 1600 was avowedly literal, including the Westminster divines and in every instance I have read prior to Henry More's 1653 work, reflecting the continental Protestant heritage. Ralph O'Connor emphasizes this long view when he writes, "The allegorical approaches taken by some Church Fathers had opened a door for old-earth cosmologies ... but interpretations grounded in a literal reading went back to Eusebius and Jerome, the founders of sacred chronology."[28]

One point of novelty, though, is that the diluvialism that invariably accompanies young-earth creationism today essentially dates to John Woodward's attribution of fossil burial to Noah's Flood (1695), so that this combination of a literal creation week and a young earth with a fossil-conscious geological diluvialism is a little over 300 years old.[29] The modern position is most like the scriptural geology of the early 1800s. Though Ralph O'Connor cautions against labelling nineteenth-century scriptural geologists as 'young-earth creationists' in the modern sense, Stiling points to intersections between the nineteenth- and twentieth-century versions, saying, "Twentieth-century flood geology proved to be essentially the same as nineteenth-century Scriptural Geology: both advocated a literal six-day creation, a short age of the earth, and the idea that all of the fossil-bearing strata were formed during or shortly after the Flood," though he denies any genetic link between them.[30] (In fact, Penn, Fairholme and some others attributed strata formation to the antediluvian period, rather than to the Deluge

[27] David Wilkinson, "Reading Genesis 1–3 in the Light of Modern Science," in *Reading Genesis after Darwin*, ed. S.C. Barton and D. Wilkinson (New York: Oxford University Press, 2009), 134.

[28] O'Connor, "Young-Earth Creationists," 360.

[29] Remembering that the view that fossils were real organic remains was just achieving dominance at the time through thinkers like Woodward.

[30] O'Connor, "Young-Earth Creationists," 365, 396 n. 57; Stiling, "Scriptural Geology in America," 187–88.

itself, but the difference is not critical.) The two groups share a conservative attitude towards the biblical text and a confidence in its inalienable right and infallible competence to speak on facts of nature.

My feeling is that literal creation week belief did not completely expire in the mid-1800s, despite its general absence from published literature, but survived in certain streams of Christian theology, certain denominations and certain sects, especially, I would suggest, outside the halls of scholarship.[31] Ronald Numbers is correct, I believe, when he says, "No doubt many Christians, perhaps most, remained unpersuaded by the geological evidence of the earth's great age and continued to believe in a recent creation in six literal days, but these people rarely expressed their views in books and journals."[32] Davis Young has recently demonstrated how in Dutch Reformed circles Herman Bavinck's wariness of geology in his *Geereformeerde Dogmatiek* (1895–1901) paved the way for the blank rejection of an old earth in favour of a literal six-day creation by Valentine Hepp (around 1930) and by Louis Berkhof in his influential *Reformed Dogmatics* (1932).[33] The receptivity of conservative US Lutherans to George McCready Price's (1870–1963) version of creation in a literal week suggests too that the literal, young-earth creation belief represented by Keil's 1861 Genesis commentary survived in Lutheran circles.[34] And Adventist pioneer and prophetess Ellen G. White (1827–1915) made a literal creation week indispensable to Adventism as early as 1864.[35]

I would therefore imagine the twentieth-century 'flood geology'/young-earth creationism of Price, Henry Morris and others as possibly a survival, something of a mutation, perhaps, from nineteenth-century Genesis-based pious literalism, via a fine, low-level 'cobweb' of person-to-person links among common Christians by which such tight and literal fidelity to Genesis 1 was transmitted, perhaps nurtured

[31] Tison, "Lords of Creation, ", 5–6.

[32] Ronald Numbers, *The Creationists: From Scientific Creationism to Intelligent Design*, Expanded ed. (Cambridge, MA: Harvard University Press, 2006), 30.

[33] Davis A. Young, "The Reception of Geology in the Dutch Reformed Tradition: The Case of Herman Bavinck (1854–1921)," in *Geology and Religion: A History of Harmony and Hostility*, ed. M. Kölbl-Ebert, GS Special Publications (Bath: The Geological Society, 2009), 289–300. On p. 297, Young does note that Hepp directly cited George McCready Price, but the thrust of Young's essay shows that suspicion of the idea of an old earth was carried over whole and seemingly unchecked from Bavinck by Hepp and Berkhof; I would suggest that Price simply supplied an articulated rationale for its complete rejection. Note: subsequent editions of Berkhof's *Reformed Dogmatics* went under the title of *Systematic Theology*.

[34] Numbers, *The Creationists*, 118, 124–25, etc.; Keil, "The First Book of Moses (Genesis)," 51–52, 69.

[35] Numbers, *The Creationists*, 88–90, 462 n. 465; Jim Gibson, "Issues in 'Intermediate Models' of Origins," *Journal of the Adventist Theological Society* 15.1 (2004): 82.

by travelling popular speakers, in the Bible conference movement that was popular around 1900 in the United States, and in similar social settings.

But while literal interpretation of the creation week itself has not shifted a great deal, the Western world has certainly shifted in cultural and intellect terms, radically changing the context of literal interpretation. To cite the support of pre-modern and Reformation thinkers for literal interpretation, or for that matter, Miller or Buffon for a concordist one, demands this kind of contextual qualification. Andrew Louth's comment concerning Darwin would apply as well or better if the word 'geology' were substituted for Darwin's name, when he warns of

> ... the danger of imagining that those who want to ignore Darwin are simply continuing the traditional account of what Christians have always believed. In reality, interpreters of Genesis who ignore ... Darwin ... are *reacting against* Darwin, and their reading of Genesis is ... much affected by that reaction..."[36]

A change in context effectively changes the entire picture. Present-day adherence to a literal creation week implies a stance toward geology, biology and science generally that ancient interpreters could not have imagined, much less chosen. The literalism of the approach of, say, the Westminster divines to the creation week is beyond doubt; but the historical situation in which they maintained such literalism is utterly beyond retrieval, too. In that sense, present-day literalism is a new phenomenon.

Genesis 1:1-2:3 remains an arresting narrative of vast scope and a transcendent quality and timeless versatility that are not found in its ANE analogues.[37] In light of the interest it continues to attract and also the renewed popularity of recourse to historical precedent in Christian and Jewish tradition, I would call all participants in debates over Gen. 1:1–2:3 and biblical creation generally to a more thorough, intelligent and even honest use of Christian traditional sources. Ancient writers wrote with motivations and worldviews that many of their modern recruiters do not always fully comprehend. Such 'difference' has yielded an irony: the bulk of Christian history saw commentators labouring to explain why God took so long as six days to create the world, while those inclined to naturalistic accounts showed how this passage of time permitted the unfolding of creation events according to a natural cause

[36] Louth, "Six Days of Creation," 39.

[37] There are some provocative ideas along these lines in P. van Inwagen, "Genesis and Evolution," in *Reasoned Faith: Essays in Philosophical Theology*, ed. E. Stump (Ithaca, NY: Cornell University Press, 1993), 103–08.

and effect sequence.[38] But in recent times a literal creation week has become the province of those opposing naturalism, and emphasizing that God does *not* need time to perform his creative work. Six-day creationism has in this sense become the new instantaneous creation.

[38] E.g. Thierry of Chartres, "Tractatus de sex dierum operibus," 557–62 (*Tractatus* 5–17).

Bibliography

[Claudius of Turin]. "In Genesim." In *PL*, vol. 50, 893–1048.

[Jamieson]. *A Critical and Practical Exposition of the Pentateuch, with Notes, Theological, Moral, Philosophical, Critical, and Historical* ... London: Printed for J. & P. Knapton, 1748. ECCO.

Abegg, Martin, Jr., Peter Flint, and Eugene Ulrich. *The Dead Sea Scrolls Bible: The Oldest Known Bible Translated for the First Time into English.* Edinburgh: T&T Clark, 1999.

Abelard, Peter. "Expositio in hexameron." In *PL*, vol. 178, 731–84.

Adamo, David Tuesday. "The Genesis Creation Accounts: An African Background." In *Genesis*, edited by Athalya Brenner, Archie Chi-Chung Lee and Gale A. Yee. Texts/Contexts, 25–33. Minneapolis: Fortress, 2010.

Adams, John. *A View of Universal History, from the Creation to the Present Time....* 3 vols. Vol. I. London: printed for G. Kearsley, 1795. ECCO.

Addinall, Philip. *Philosophy and Biblical Interpretation: A Study in Nineteenth-Century Conflict.* Cambridge: Cambridge University Press, 1991.

Ainsworth, Henry. *Annotations upon the First Book of Moses, called Genesis.* [Amsterdam]: Imprinted [by Giles Thorp], 1616.

Albert the Great. *B. Alberti Magni ... Opera omnia.* Edited by E. Borgnet. Vol. 32: Summa theologiae pars secunda. Paris: L. Vivès, 1895, http://albertusmagnus.uwaterloo.ca/webPages/downloading.html.

Albritton, Claude C. *The Abyss of Time.* San Francisco: Freeman, 1980.

Alcuin. "Interrogationes et responsiones in Genesin." In *PL*, vol. 100, 515–70.

Alexandre, Monique. *Le Commencement du livre Genèse I-V: La version grecque de la Septente et sa réception.* Christianisme Antique. Paris: Beauchesne, 1988.

Almond, Philip C. *Adam and Eve in Seventeenth-Century Thought.* Cambridge: Cambridge University Press, 1999.

———. "Adam, Pre-Adamites, and Extra-Terrestrial Beings." *Journal of Religious History* 30, no. 2 (2006): 163-74.

Altaner, B., and A. Stuiber. *Patrologie.* 9th ed. Freiburg: Herder, 1978.

Ambrose, Saint, Bishop of Milan. "De Cain et Abel." In *PL*, vol. 14, 315–59.

———. *Hexameron, Paradise, and Cain and Abel.* Translated by John J. Savage. Fathers of the Church, a New Translation, 42. New York: Catholic

University of America Press, 1961. Reprint, Ann Arbor, MI: UMI, 1997.

Anastasius of Sinai. "Anagogicarum contemplationum in Hexaemeron ad Theophilum libri undecim." In *PL*, vol. 89, 851–1078.

Andrew of St. Victor. *Expositionem super Heptateuchum*. Corpus Christianorum, continuatio mediaevalis, 53. Turnholt: Brepols, 1986.

Angelom of Luxeuil. "In Genesim." In *PL*, vol. 115, 107–244.

Anselm. "Why God Became Man." In *A Scholastic Miscellany: Anselm to Ockham*, edited by Eugene R. Fairweather, 100–83. The Library of Christian Classics: Ichthus Edition. Philadelphia: Westminster, 1982.

Aquinas, Thomas. *Summa Theologiae: Latin Text and English Translation*. Edited by Thomas Gilby. 60 vols. Vol. 10: Cosmogony (1a. 65–74). Translated by William A. Wallace. London: Blackfriars in conjunction with Eyre & Spottiswoode, 1964–76.

Arbuthnot, J. *An Examination of Dr Woodward's Account of the Deluge*. London: printed for C. Bateman ... , 1697.

Armstrong, G.T. *Die Genesis in der Alten Kirche. Die drei Kirchenväter, Justinus, Irenäus, Tertullian*. Beiträge zur Geschichte der biblischen Hermeneutik. Tübingen: J.C.B. Mohr (Paul Siebeck), 1962.

Arnold of Bonneval. "De operibus sex dierum." In *PL*, Vol. 189, 1513–70.

Ashworth, William B., Jr. "Catholicism and Early Modern Science." In *God and Nature: Historical Essays on the Encounter between Christianity and Science*, edited by D.C. Lindberg and R.L. Numbers, 136–66. Berkeley: University of California Press, 1986.

Athanasius. "Against the Arians (Orationes contra Arianos IV.)." In *NPNF*[2], Vol. 4, 303–447.

———. "Orationes tres contra arianos." In *PG*, vol. 26, 12–468.

Augustine. "The City of God." In *NPNF*[1], vol. 2, 1–511.

———. *Confessions*. Translated by R.S. Pine-Coffin. Harmondsworth: Penguin, 1961.

———. *The Literal Meaning of Genesis*. Translated by John Hammond Taylor. 2 vols. Ancient Christian Writers, 41, 42. New York: Newman Press, 1982.

———. *On Genesis: Two Books on Genesis Against the Manichees and On the Literal Interpretation of Genesis: An Unfinished Book*. Translated by S.J. Roland J. Teske. Fathers of the Church, a New Translation, 84. Washington, DC: The Catholic University of America Press, 1991.

Avitus. "De Mosaicae Historiae Gestis." In *PL*, vol. 70, 323ff.

Babington, Gervase. *Certaine Plaine, Briefe and Comfortable Notes upon Everie Chapter of Genesis*. London: for Thomas Charde, 1592.

Backus, I., ed. *The Reception of the Church Fathers in the West*. 2 vols. Leiden: Brill, 1997.

———. "Ulrich Zwingli, Martin Bucer and the Church Fathers." In *RCFW*, vol. 2, 627–60.

Bacon, Francis. "The New Atlantis." In *Ideal Commonwealths*. New York: P.F. Collier and son, 1901, http://oregonstate.edu/instruct/phl302/texts/bacon/atlantis.html.

Banderier, G. "A 'Fortunate Phoenix'? Renaissance and Death of the Hexameron (1578–1615)." *Neuphilologische Mitteilungen* 102, no. 3 (2001): 251–67.

Barker, William S. "The Westminster Assembly on the Days of Creation: A Reply to David W Hall." *WTJ* 62, no. 1 (2000): 113–20.

Barr, James. "Why the World Was Created in 4004 BC: Archbishop Ussher and Biblical Chronology." *Bulletin of the John Rylands Library* 67 (1985): 575–608.

Basil of Caesarea. "Hexaemeron." In *NPNF*², vol. 8, 51–107.

———. *Homélies sur l'Hexaemeron.* Translated by Stanislas Giet. 2nd ed. Sources chrétiennes, 26. Paris: Éditions du Cerf, 1968.

Bavinck, Herman. *In the Beginning: Foundations of Christian Theology.* Translated by John Vriend. Edited by John Bolt. Grand Rapids: Baker, 1999.

Beaumont, John. *Considerations on a Book Entitled the Theory of the Earth.* London: printed for the author, and are to be sold by Randal Taylor ... 1693.

Bede. *On Genesis.* Translated by Calvin Kendall. Translated Texts for Historians, 48. Liverpool: Liverpool University Press, 2008.

Berndt, R. "The School of St. Victor in Paris." In *HB/OT*, vol. I, bk 2, 467–95.

Berry, R.J. "Did Darwin Dethrone Humankind?" In *Darwin, Creation and the Fall: Theological Challenges*, edited by R.J. Berry and T.A. Noble, 30–74. Nottingham: InterVarsity, 2009.

Birks, T.R. *The Bible and Modern Thought.* London: Religious Tract Society, 1862. GB, http://books.google.com.au/books?id=WDc-AAAAcAAJ.

Bischoff, Bernhard, and Michael Lapidge, eds. *Biblical Commentaries from the Canterbury School of Theodore and Hadrian.* Cambridge Studies in Anglo-Saxon England, 10. Cambridge: Cambridge University Press, 1994.

Blount, Charles. *The Oracles of Reason: Consisting of 1. A Vindication of Dr. Burnet's Archiologiae. 2. The Seventh and Eighth Chapters of the Same. 3. etc.* London: n.p., 1693. Reprint, New York: Garland, 1979.

Böhme, Jakob. *Mysterium magnum, or An Exposition of the First Book of Moses called Genesis...* London: printed and are to be sould by Lodowick Lloyd... 1656. EEBO.

———. *Aurora. That is, the day-spring. Or dawning of the day in the Orient or morning-rednesse in the rising of the sun. That is the root or mother of philosophie, astrologie & theologie from the true ground...* Translated by John Sparrow. London: printed by John Streater, for Giles Calvert, etc., 1656. EEBO.

Bonaventure. *Collations on the Six Days.* Translated by J. de Vinck. Paterson, NJ: St Anthony Guild Press, 1970.

Bonner, G. "Augustine as Biblical Scholar." In *The Cambridge History of the Bible.* Vol. 1, *From the Beginnings to Jerome*, edited by P.R. Ackroyd and C.F. Evans, 541–563. Cambridge: Cambridge University Press, 1970.

Bossuet, Jacques-Bénigne. "Discourse on Universal History." In *Classic European Historians*, edited by Orest Ranum. Chicago: University of Chicago Press, 1976.

Bougerol, Jacques-Guy. "The Church Fathers and Auctoritates in Scholastic Theology to Bonaventure." In *RCFW*, vol. 1, 289–335.

———. "The Church Fathers and the Sentences of Peter Lombard." In *RCFW*, vol. 1, 113–64.

Bouteneff, Peter C. *Beginnings: Ancient Christian Readings of the Biblical Creation Narratives*. Grand Rapids: Baker Academic, 2008.

Bouwsma, William J. *Concordia Mundi: The Career and Thought of Guillaume Postel (1510–1581)*. Edited by Oscar Handlin. Harvard Historical Monographs, 33. Cambridge, MA: Harvard University Press, 1957.

Bowler, Peter J. *Evolution: The History of an Idea*. Berkeley: University of California Press, 1984.

Bradley, Ritamary. "Backgrounds of the Title Speculum in Mediaeval Literature." *Speculum* 29, no. 1 (1954): 100–15.

Bray, Gerald. *Biblical Interpretation: Past and Present*. Downers Grove: InterVarsity, 1996.

Brenz, Johannes. *Explicatio Geneseos, inchoata primo die septembris, anno salvatis 1553*. Tübingen: Excudebat Georgius Gruppenbachius, 1576. CPT.

Briggs, Richard S. "The Hermeneutics of Reading Genesis after Darwin." In *Reading Genesis after Darwin*, edited by Stephen C. Barton and David Wilkinson, 57–71. New York: Oxford University Press, 2009.

Bromiley, Geoffrey W. *Historical Theology: An Introduction*. Grand Rapids: Eerdmans, 1978.

Brooke, John Hedley. "Genesis and the Scientists: Dissonance among the Harmonizers." In *Reading Genesis after Darwin*, edited by Stephen C. Barton and David Wilkinson, 93–109. New York: Oxford University Press, 2009.

———. "Like Minds: The God of Hugh Miller." In *Hugh Miller and the Controversies of Victorian Science*, edited by Michael Shortland, 171–86. Oxford: Clarendon, 1996.

Browne, Sir Thomas. *Religio Medici the Fourth Edition, Corrected and Amended...* London: printed by E. Cotes for Andrew Crook ... 1656. EEBO.

Bruns, P. "Severian of Gabala." In *DECL*, 531–32.

———. "Theodore of Mopsuestia." In *DECL*, 562–64.

Buckland, William. *Geology and Mineralogy Considered with Reference to Natural Theology*. 2 vols. London: William Pickering, 1837. Reprint, Philadelphia: Carey, Lea and Blanchard, 1937.

———. *Vindiciae Geologiae; or The Connexion of Geology with Religion Explained, in an Inaugural Lecture Delivered before the University of Oxford, May 15, 1819....* Oxford: Oxford University Press, 1820, National Library of Australia, http://nla.gov.au/nla.aus-vn2012561.

Budge, E.A.W., ed. *The Book of the Cave of Treasures*. London: Religious Tract Society, 1927.

Buffon, Georges Louis Leclerc, Comte de. Barr's Buffon. *Buffon's Natural History, Containing a Theory of the Earth, a General History of Man, ... From the French. With Notes by the Translator.* 10 vols. Vol. I. London: printed by J.S. Barr, 1792. ECCO.

———. *Les époques de la nature*. 2 vols. Paris: de l'Imprimerie royale, 1780. GB, http://books.google.com/books?id=d4sNAAAAQAAJ.

Bugg, George. *Scriptural Geology*. 2 vols. London: Hatchland, 1826–27.

Bultmann, Christoph. "Creation at the Beginning of History: Johann Gottfried Herder's Interpretation of Genesis 1." *JSOT* 68 (1995): 23–32.

———. "Early Rationalism and Biblical Criticism on the Continent." In *HB/OT*, vol. 2, 875–901.

Burnet, Thomas. *Archeologiae philosophicae, sive Doctrina antiqua de rerum originibus*. London: typis R. Norton, 1692.

———. *Doctrina antiqua de rerum originibus: or, An Inquiry into the Doctrine of the Philosophers of All Nations, concerning the Original of the World....* London: printed for E. Curll, 1736.

———. *The Sacred Theory of the Earth, containing an Account of the Original of the Earth, and of All the General Changes which It Hath Already Undergone, or Is to Undergo, till the Consummation of All Things*. Glasgow: R. Urie, 1753. GB, http://books.google.com/books?id=-aQvAAAAYAAJ.

Cajetan, Thomas de Vio. *Opera omnia quotquot in Sacrae Scripturae expositionem reperiuntur. Vol. 1, Commentarii illustres planeque insignes in Quinque Mosaicos libros, Thomae de Vio Caietani, Cardinalis S. Xisti, in Quinque libros Mosis, iuxta sensum literalem, commentarii: et primum in Genesim*. Rome, 1531. Reprint, Hildesheim: Georg Olms Verlag, 2005. GB, http://books.google.com/books?id=OwW0VNRfxHYC. Accessed June, 2009, preview no longer accessible online.

Calmet, Augustin. *Commentarius litteralis in omnes libros Veteris et Novi Testamenti. Tomi primi pars prima*. Paris: chez Pierre Emery, 1707. Reprint, Venice: Typis Sebastiani Coleti, 1767.

———. *Histoire universelle, sacrée et profane: Depuis le commencement du monde jusqu'à nos jours*. Vol. I. Strasbourg: Jean Renaud Doulssecker, 1735.

Calvin, John. *Genesis*. The Geneva Series of Commentaries. London: Banner of Truth, 1965.

Cantor, Petrus. *Glossae super Genesim. Prologus et Capitula 1–3*. Translated by Agneta Sylwan. Studia Graeca et Latina Gothoburgensia, 55. Göteborg: Acta Universitatis Gothoburgensis, 1992.

Capito, Wolfgang. *Hexemeron Dei opus explicatum...* Strassburg: Per Wendelinum Rihelium, 1539. CPT.

Carmichael, Calum M. *The Story of Creation: Its Origin and Its Interpretation in Philo and the Fourth Gospel*. Ithaca: Cornell University Press, 1996.

Cartwright, Christopher. *Electa thargumico-rabbinica; sive, annotationes in Genesin....* London: Typis Guil. Du-gard: Impensis Sam. Thomson ad insigne equi candidi, in Coemeterio Paulino, 1648. CPT.

Catcott, Alexander. *Remarks on the Second Part of the Lord Bishop of Clogher's Vindication of the Histories of the Old and New Testament....* London: sold by E. Withers, etc., 1756. ECCO.

Catharinus, Ambrosius. *Enarrationes R.P.F. Ambrosii Catharini politi senensis archiepiscopi Compsani in quinque priora capita libri Geneseos*. Rome: apud Antonium Bladum caerae apostolicae typographum, 1552. Reprint, Ridgewood, NJ: Gregg Press, 1964.

Chadwick, Henry. "Augustine." In *A Dictionary of Biblical Interpretation*, edited by R.J. Coggins and J.L. Houlden, 65–69. London: SCM, 1990.

———. *Augustine*. Past Masters, ed. Keith Thomas. Oxford: Oxford University Press, 1986.

Challis, James. *Creation in Plan and Progress*. Cambridge: Macmillan, 1861. GB, http://books.google.com/books?id=3e4rAAAAYAAJ.

Chalmers, Thomas. "Remarks on Cuvier's Theory of the Earth; In Extracts from a Review of That Theory Which Was Contributed to 'The Christian Instructor' in 1814." In *Tracts and Essays: Religious and Economical*, 347–72. Works, 12. Edinburgh/London: published for Thomas Constable by Sutherland and Knox/Hamilton, Adams & co., 1848. GB, http://books.google.com/books?id=s9orAAAAYAAJ.

Charlesworth, James H., ed. *The Old Testament Pseudepigrapha*. Vol. I: *Apocalyptic Literature and Testaments*. Garden City, NY: Doubleday, 1983.

———, James H., ed. *The Old Testament Pseudepigrapha*. Vol. II. Garden City, NY: Doubleday, 1985.

Chateaubriand, F.-R. *Génie du Christianisme*. Vol. 14. Oeuvres Choisies de M. de Chateaubriand. Paris: Pourrat Freres, 1834. GB, http://books.google.com/books?id=BaEGAAAAQAAJ.

Chenu, M.-D., ed. *Nature, Man and Society in the Twelfth Century: Essays on New Theological Perspectives in the Latin West*. Chicago: University of Chicago Press, 1968.

Childs, Brevard. *Introduction to the Old Testament as Scripture*. Philadelphia: Fortress Press, 1979.

Chrysostom, John. *Homilies on Genesis 1–17*. Translated by R. C. Hill. Fathers of the Church, a New Translation, 74. Washington, DC: Catholic University of America Press, 1985.

———. "In Genesim (homiliae 1–67)." In *PG*, Vol. 53, 21–385.

Clarke, Adam. *The Holy Bible Containing the Old and New Testaments...with a Commentary and Critical Notes... Vol. 1, Genesis to Deuteronomy*. New ed. New York: T. Mason, G. Lane, 1837, http://books.google.com/books?id=1tgMAAAAIAAJ.

Clayton, Robert. *A Vindication of the Histories of the Old and New Testament. Part II. Wherein the Mosaical History of the Creation and Deluge is Philosophically Explained...* Dublin/London: reprinted for W. Bowyer, and sold by R. Baldwin, and M. Cooper, etc., 1754. ECCO.

Clement of Alexandria. "Eclogae ex Scripturis propheticis." In *PG*, Vol. 9, 697–728.

———. "The Stromata." In *ANF*, Vol. 2, 299–568.

———. *Stromata Buch I–VI*. Translated by Otto Stählin. Die griechischen christlichen Schriftsteller der ersten Jahrhunderte. Berlin: Akademie-Verlag, 1985.

Clüver, Dethlev. *Geologia sive philosophemata de Genesi ac structura globi terreni, oder: Natürliche Wissenschafft von Erschaffung und Bereitung der Erd-kugel: Wie nemlich nach Mosis und der ältesten Philosophen Bericht aus dem Chao, durch mechanische Gesetze der Bewegungen, die Erde sey herfür gebracht worden....* Hamburg: Liebezeit, 1700.

Cockburn, William. *The Creation of the World*. London: Hatchard, 1840.

Cohen, Jeremy. *Be Fertile and Increase, Fill the Earth and Master It: The Ancient and Medieval Career of a Biblical Text*. Ithaca, NY: Cornell University Press, 1989.

Cole, Henry. *Popular Geology Subversive of Divine Revelation! A Letter to the Rev. Adam Sedgwick ... Being a Scriptural Refutation of the Geological Positions and Doctrines Promulgated in His Lately Published Commencement Sermon.* London: Hatchard, 1834.

Colenso, John W. *The Pentateuch and Joshua Critically Examined.* London: Longmans, Green, and Co., 1870.

Colet, John. *Letters to Radulphus on the Mosaic Account of Creation [microform]: Together with Other Treatises.* Edited by Joseph Hirst Lupton. London: G. Bell, 1876. IA, http://www.archive.org/details/MN41730ucmf_0.

Collier, Katherine B. *Cosmogonies of Our Fathers. Some Theories of the Seventeenth and Eighteenth Centuries.* New York: Columbia University Press, 1934. Reprint, New York: Octagon Books, 1968.

Collingwood, R.G. *The Idea of History.* Oxford: Clarendon, 1946.

Collins, C. John. *Genesis 1–4.* Phillipsberg, NJ: P&R Publishing, 2006.

———. "How Old Is the Earth? Anthropomorphic Days in Genesis 1:1–2:3." *Presbyterion* 20 (1994): 109–30.

Colson, F. H. *The Week: An Essay on the Origin and Development of the Seven-Day Cycle*: Cambridge University Press, 1926. Reprint, Westport, CT: Greenwood Press, 1974.

Comenius, Johann Amos. *Naturall Philosophie Reformed by Divine Light, or, A Synopsis of Physicks by J.A. Comenius....* London: printed by Robert and William Leybourn, for Thomas Pierrepont, at the Sun in Pauls Church-yard, 1651. EEBO.

Comestor, Peter. "Historia Scholastica." In *PL*, Vol. 198, 1053–1722.

Congar, Yves M.-J. "Le thème de *Dieu-Createur* et les explications de l'Hexameron dans la tradition chrétienne." In *L'Homme devant Dieu: Mélanges offerts au Père Henri de Lubac*, vol. I, 189–222. Theologie 56–58. Paris, 1963–64.

Cooper, Thomas. *On the Connection between Geology and the Pentateuch, in a Letter to Professor Silliman.* Boston: Abner Kneeland, 1837. GB, http://books.google.com/books?id=G8s0AAAAMAAJ.

Cowper, William. *The Task: A Poem. In Six Books. To which is Added, Tirocinium: or, A Review of Schools.* New ed. Philadelphia: printed for Thomas Dobson, etc., 1787. GB, http://books.google.com/books?id=StE0AAAAMAAJ.

Crehan, F.J. "The Bible in the Roman Catholic Church from Trent to the Present Day." In *The Cambridge History of the Bible.* Vol. 3, *The West from the Reformation to the Present Day*, edited by S. L. Greenslade, 199–237. Cambridge: Cambridge University Press, 1963.

Croft, Herbert. *Some Animadversions upon a Book Intituled The Theory of the Earth.* London: printed for Charles Harper... 1685. EEBO.

Cross, F.L., and E.A. Livingstone, eds. *The Oxford Dictionary of the Christian Church.* 2nd. rev. ed. Oxford: Oxford University Press, 1983.

Crouse, Robert D. "The Meaning of Creation in Augustine and Eriugena." In *Tenth International Conference on Patristic Studies, Oxford, 1987*, edited by Elizabeth A. Livingstone, 229–34. Studia Patristica, 12. Leuven: Peeters, 1989.

Cuvier, Georges, Baron, 1769–1832. *A Discourse on the Revolutions of the Surface of the Globe, and the Changes Thereby Produced in the Animal Kingdom.* Philadelphia: Carey & Lea, 1831, http://books.google.com/books?id=mqAaAAAAYAAJ.

———. *Essay on the Theory of the Earth.* Translated by R. Kerr. Edited by Robert Jameson. Edinburgh: W. Blackwood, 1813.

———. "Lectures on the History of the Natural Sciences." In *The Edinburgh New Philosophical Journal: Exhibiting a View of the Progressive Discoveries and Improvements in the Sciences and the Arts,* edited by Robert Jameson, William Jardine and Henry Darwin Rogers, Vol. 8, 326–50. Edinburgh: A. and C. Black, 1830. GB, http://books.google.com/books?id=sA0XAAAAYAAJ.

Cyprian of Carthage. "Exhortation to Martyrdom, Addressed to Fortunatus." In *ANF*, vol. 5, 496–507.

Cyril of Alexandria. "Glaphyra." In *PG*, vol. 69, 9–678.

Dahan, Gilbert. "Genres, Forms and Various Methods in Christian Exegesis of the Middle Ages." In *HB/OT*, vol. I, bk 2, 196–236.

Daley, Brian E., ed. *Gregory of Nazianzus.* Early Christian Fathers. London: Routledge, 2006.

Dalton, Trent. "Life from Mars." *The Courier-Mail,* Monday, January 5 2009, 27.

Dana, James Dwight. *Manual of Geology: Treating of the Principles of the Science, with Special Reference to American Geological History ...* Rev. ed. Philadelphia: T. Bliss & co., 1866. GB, http://books.google.com/ books?id=kLsQAAAAIAAJ&dq.

———. *Science and the Bible: A Review of "The Six Days of Creation" of Prof. Tayler Lewis. From the Bibliotheca Sacra for January 1856.* Andover: W. F. Draper, 1856. GB, http://books.google.com/books?id=xNE0AAAAMAAJ.

Daniélou, J. *The Theology of Jewish Christianity.* Translated by John A. Baker. The Development of Christian Doctrine before the Council of Nicaea. London: Darton, Longman and Todd, 1964.

Danielson, D.R. "The Great Copernican Cliché," *American Journal of Physics* 69 no. 10 (2001): 1029–35.

Davies, Gordon L. *The Earth in Decay: A History of British Geomorphology, 1578–1878.* London: Macdonald, 1968.

Davies, Philip. "Reading the Bible Intelligently." *Relegere: Studies in Religion and Reception* 1, no. 1 (2011): 145–64.

Dawson, J.W. *The Origin of the World, according to Revelation and Science.* 5th ed. London: Hodder and Stoughton, 1888.

Day, Allan J. "Adam, Anthropology and the Genesis Record - Taking Genesis Seriously in the Light of Contemporary Science." *Science & Christian Belief* 10 no. 2 (1998): 115–43.

de Luc, Jean André. *Letters on the Physical History of the Earth, Addressed to Professor Blumenbach: Containing Geological and Historical Proofs of the Divine Mission of Moses.* Edited by Henry de la Fite. London: C.J.G. Rivington, 1831. GB, http://books.google.com/books?id=Q6UAAAAAMAAJ.

de Margerie, Bertrand. *An Introduction to the History of Exegesis*. Vol. 1, *The Greek Fathers*. Petersham: Saint Bede's, 1993.

de Wette, Wilhelm Martin Leberecht. *A Critical and Historical Introduction to the Canonical Scriptures of the Old Testament*. Translated by Theodore Parker. 2 vols. Boston: Charles C. Little and James Brown, 1843.

Dean, Dennis. "The Age of the Earth Controversy: Beginning to Hutton." *Annals of Science* 38 (1981): 435–56.

———. ""Through Science to Despair": Geology and the Victorians." In *Victorian Science and Victorian Values: Literary Perspectives*, edited by J. Paradis and T. Postelwait, 111–36. Annals of the New York Academy of Sciences, 360. New York: The New York Academy of Sciences, 1981.

Declerck, José H., ed. *Eustathii Antiocheni, patris Nicaeni, opera quae supersunt omnia*. Corpus christianorum series Graeca, 51. Turnhout: Brepols, 2002.

Delitzsch, Franz. *Die Genesis ausgelegt*. Leipzig: Dörffling & Franke/London: Williams & Norgate, 1852. IA, http://www.archive.org/stream/diegenesisausge00deligoog.

———. *A New Commentary on Genesis*. 2 vols. Vol. 1. Edinburgh: T & T Clark, 1888. IA, http://www.archive.org/details/anewcommentgenes00deliuoft.

———. *A System of Biblical Psychology*. Edinburgh: T&T Clark, 1899.

Descartes, René. *Principles of Philosophy*. Edited by Valentine Rodger Miller and Reese P. Miller. Dordrecht: D. Riedel, 1983.

———. *The World and Other Writings*. Edited by Stephen Gaukroger. Cambridge Texts in the History of Philosophy. New York: Cambridge University Press, 1998.

Devréesse, R. *Les anciens commentateurs grecs de l'Octateuque et des Rois*. Studi e Testi. Vatican City: Biblioteca apostolica vaticana, 1959.

Dickson, John P. "The Genesis of Everything: An Historical Account of the Bible's Opening Chapter." *ISCAST Online Journal* 4 (2008): 1–18.

———. "The Genre of Genesis 1." Centre for Public Christianity, http://www.publicchristianity.com. Accessed September, 2008. (No longer accessible at this address.)

Diderot, Denis. "Mosaïque et chrétienne philosophie." In *Encyclopédie, ou dictionnaire raisonné des sciences, des arts et des métiers*, edited by Denis Diderot and Jean le Rond D'Alembert, Vol. 10, 741–45. Paris: Briasson, David, Le Breton, Durand, 1765. ARTFL Encyclopédie Projet (winter 2008 edition), Robert Morrissey (ed.), University of Chicago, http://artfl.uchicago.edu/cgi-bin/philologic31/getobject.pl?c.78:16.encyclopedie1108.

Didymus the Blind. *Sur la Genèse*. Translated by Pierre Nautin. 2 vols. Sources chrétiennes, 233, 244. Paris: Les Éditions du Cerf, 1976.

Dillenberger, John. *Protestant Thought and Natural Science*. Notre Dame, IN: University of Notre Dame Press, 1960,

Dionysius the Carthusian. *Doctoris Ecstatici D. Dionysii Cartusiani in Sacram Scripturam Commentaria ... Tomus I. In Genesim, Et Exodum (I–XIX)*. Monstrolii: Cartusiae Sanctae Mariae de Pratis, 1896.

Doane, A.N. *The Saxon Genesis: An Edition of the West Saxon Genesis B and the Old Saxon Vatican Genesis.* Madison, Wis.: University of Wisconsin Press, 1991.

Dodd, William. *A Commentary on the Books of the Old and New Testament.* 3 vols. Vol. I. London: printed for R. Davis, L. Davis, and T. Carnan and F. Newbery, Jr., 1770.

Döpp, Siegmar, and Wilhelm Geerlings, eds. *Dictionary of Early Christian Literature.* New York: Crossroad, 2000.

Douglas, J.D., ed. *The New International Dictionary of the Christian Church.* Grand Rapids: Zondervan, 1996.

Dracontius, Blossius Aemilius. *Oeuvres.* Edited by Claude Moussy and Colette Camus. 4 vols. Vol. I. *Louanges de Dieu [De laudibus dei], Livres I et II.* Paris: Belles lettres, 1985.

Drobner, Hubertus R., ed. *Opera Exegetica in Genesim, Volume 1: Gregorii Nysseni in Hexaemeron,* Gregrorii Nysseni Opera. Leiden: Brill, 2009.

Du Bartas, Guillaume de Salluste. *Du Bartas His Deuine Weekes and Workes ...* Translated by Joshua Sylvester. 3rd ed. London: Humfrey Lounes... 1611. EEBO.

Duffield, G.E. "Colet, John (c.1466–1519)." In *The New International Dictionary of the Christian Church,* edited by J. D. Douglas and Earle E. Cairns, 239. Grand Rapids: Zondervan, 1978.

Duguet, Jacques Joseph, and Joseph Vincent Bidel d'Asfeld. *Explication litterale de l'ouvrage des six jours mêlée des reflexions morales.* Brussels: Francois Foppens, 1731, http://books.google.com.au/books?R6cGAAAA QAAJ.

Duhem, P. *To Save the Phenomena: An Essay on the Idea of Physical Theory from Plato to Galileo.* Translated by Edmund Doland and Chaninah Maschler. Chicago, University of Chicago Press, 1969.

Dünzl, F. "Gregory of Nyssa." In *DECL,* 263–68.

Eichhorn, Johann Gottfried. *Einleitung in das Alte Testament.* 4th ed. Vol. 3. Göttingen: Carl Eduard Rosenbusch, 1823. GB, http://books.google.com/books?id=L1IHAAAAQAAJ.

Elders, Leo J. "Thomas Aquinas and the Fathers of the Church." In *RCFW,* vol. 1, 337–66.

Ephraem Syrus. *Hymnen de nativitate (Epiphania).* Edited by Edmund Beck. Corpus scriptorum Christianorum orientalium, 186/187. Louvain: Secretariat du Corpus SCO, 1959.

———. "Hymns on the Nativity." In *NPNF*[2], vol. 13, 221–62.

———. *Selected Prose Works.* Edited by Kathleen E. McVey. Fathers of the Church, a New Translation, 91. Washington, D.C.: Catholic University of America Press, 1994.

Episcopius, Simon. *M. Simonis Episcopii institutiones theologicae, privatis lectionibus Amstelodami traditae.* Edited by Étienne de Courcelles. Amsterdam: Ex typographico Ioannis Blaeu, 1650. CPT.

"The Epistle of Barnabas." In *The Apostolic Fathers: Greek Texts and English Translations of Their Writings,* edited by Michael W. Holmes, 271–327. Grand Rapids: Baker, 1999.

Eriugena, Johannes Scotus. *Periphyseon (De divisione naturae) Liber Tertius*. Translated by I.P. Sheldon-Williams. Scriptores Latini Hiberniae, 11. Dublin: The Dublin Institute for Advanced Studies, 1981.

Eusebius of Caesarea. *The History of the Church from Christ to Constantine*. Translated by G.A. Williamson. Harmondsworth: Penguin, 1965.

Eusebius of Emesa. *Eusèbe d'Émèse*. Vol. 1, *Commentaire de l'Octateuque*. Edited by V. Hovhannessian. Venice: Bibliothèque de l'Académie Arménienne de Saint Lazare, 1980.

Evans, Gillian R. *The Language and Logic of the Bible: The Earlier Middle Ages*. Cambridge: Cambridge University Press, 1984.

———. *The Language and Logic of the Bible: The Road to Reformation*. Cambridge: Cambridge University Press, 1985.

———. "Masters and Disciples: Aspects of Christian Interpretation of the Old Testament in the Eleventh and Twelfth Centuries." In *HB/OT*, vol. I, bk 2, 237–60.

Evans, J.M. *'Paradise Lost' and the Genesis Tradition*. Oxford: Clarendon, 1968.

Faber, George Stanley. *A Treatise on the Genius and Object of the Patriarchal, the Levitical, and the Christian Dispensations*. 2 vols. Vol. I. London: C. and J. Rivington, 1823. GB, http://books.google.com/books?id= msgUAAAAYAAJ.

Fairholme, George. *General View of the Geology of Scripture: In Which the Unerring Truth of the Inspired Narrative of the Early Events in the World is Exhibited, and Distinctly Proved*. London: James Ridgway, 1833. GB, http://books.google.com/books?id=nbIAAAAAMAAJ.

Fernie, Donald J. "The Neptune Affair." *American Scientist* 83, no. 2 (March-April 1995): 116–19.

Fesko, J. V. "The Days of Creation and Confession Subscription in the OPC." *WTJ* 63 (2001): 235–49.

Fludd, Robert. *Mosaicall philosophy Grounded upon the Essentiall Truth, or Eternal Sapience / written first in Latin and afterwards thus rendred into English by Robert Fludd, Esq*. London: printed for Humphrey Moseley ... 1659. EEBO.

———. *Utriusque Cosmi Maioris scilicet et Minoris Metaphysica, Physica atque Technica Historia*. Oppenheim, 1617.

Frei, Hans. *The Eclipse of Biblical Narrative: A Study in Eighteenth and Nineteenth-Century Hermeneutics*. New Haven: Yale University Press, 1974.

Frishman, Judith, and Lucas van Rompay, eds. *Book of Genesis in Jewish and Oriental Christian Interpretation: A Collection of Essays*. Louvain: Peeters, 1997.

Froehlich, Karlfried. "Christian Interpretation of the Old Testament in the High Middle Ages." In *HB/OT*, vol. I, bk 2, 496–558.

———, and Margaret T. Gibson, eds. *Biblia Latina cum Glossa Ordinaria: Facsimile Reprint of the Editio Princeps Adolph Rusch of Strassburg 1480/81*. 4 vols. Vol. I. Turnhout: Brepols, 1992.

Fuhrer, T. "Diodorus of Tarsus." In *DECL*, 174–76.

———. "Eustathius of Antioch." In *DECL*, 219–20.

Fuller, John G.C.M. "Before the Hills in Order Stood: The Beginning of the Geology of Time in England." In *The Age of the Earth from 4004 BC to*

AD 2002, edited by C.L.E. Lewis and Simon J. Knell, 15–24. GS Special Publications, 190. London: The Geological Society, 2001.

Galilei, Galileo. "Letter to Madame Christina of Lorraine, Grand Duchess of Tuscany, Concerning the Use of Biblical Quotations in Matters of Science." In *Discoveries and Opinions of Galileo*, edited by Stillman Drake, 173–216. Garden City, NY: Doubleday, 1957.

Gallus, Cyprianus. "Genesis. (Authorship Uncertain)." In *The Writings of Tertullian, Vol. III, with the extant works of Victorinus and Commodianus*, edited by Alexander Roberts and James Donaldson, 293–300. Ante-Nicene Christian Library, 18. Edinburgh: T&T Clark, 1880.

———. "Incerti Auctoris Genesis." In *PL*, vol. 2, 1097–1101.

Geddes, Alexander. *Critical Remarks on the Hebrew Scriptures: Corresponding with a New Translation of the Bible ... Volume I. Containing Remarks on the Pentateuch.* London: printed for the author by Davis, Wilks, and Taylor: and sold by R. Faulder; and J. Johnson, 1800. ECCO.

Geerlings, W. "Augustine." In *DECL*, 61–81.

Gennadius. "In Genesin Fragmenta." In *PG*, vol. 85, 1623–64.

Gibbons, Nicholas. *Questions and Disputations concerning the Holy Scripture....* London: imprinted by Felix Kyngston, 1601. EEBO.

Gibert, Pierre. "The Catholic Counterpart and Response to the Protestant Orthodoxy." In *HB/OT*, vol. II, 758–73.

Gibson, Jim. "Issues in "Intermediate" Models of Origins." *Journal of the Adventist Theological Society* 15, no. 1 (2004): 71–92.

Gibson, Margaret T. "The Place of the Glossa Ordinaria in Medieval Exegesis." In *Ad Litteram: Authoritative Texts and their Medieval Readers*, edited by Mark D. Jordan and Kent Emery, 5–27. Notre Dame Conferences in Medieval Studies, 3. Notre Dame, IN: University of Notre Dame Press, 1992.

Giere, Samuel D. "A New Glimpse of Day One: An Intertextual History of Genesis 1.1–5 in Hebrew and Greek Texts up to 200 CE." PhD diss., University of St. Andrews, 2007.

Gignoux, Ph., ed. *Homélies de Narsaï sur la Création.* Patrologia Orientalis, 34. Turnholt: Brepols, 1968.

Gill, John. *An Exposition of the Old Testament, ... Vol. I. Containing, I. Genesis. II. Exodus. III. Leviticus. IV. Numbers.* London: printed for the author; and sold by George Keith, 1763–65. ECCO.

Gillispie, C.C. *Genesis and Geology: A Study in the Relations of Scientific Thought, Natural Theology and Social Opinions in Great Britain, 1790–1850.* New York: Harper & Row, 1951. Reprint, with a foreword by Nicolaas A. Rupke and a new preface by the author, Cambridge, MA: Harvard University Press, 1996.

Goldsmith, Oliver. *An History of the Earth, and Animated Nature.* 8 vols. Vol. 1. London: printed for J. Nourse, 1774. ECCO.

Goodwin, C.W. "On the Mosaic Cosmogony." In *Essays and Reviews*, 207–53. London: John W. Parker and Son, 1860.

Gordis, Robert. "The Heptad as an Element of Biblical and Rabbinic Style." *Journal of Biblical Literature* 62, no. 1 (1943): 17–26.

Gosse, Edmund. *Father and Son: Biographical Recollections*. 4th ed. New York: Charles Scribner's Sons, 1908.

Gosse, Philip. *Omphalos: An Attempt to Untie the Geological Knot*. London: John Van Voorst, 1857. GB, http://books.google.com/books?id= acwQ AAAAIAAJ.

Gould, Stephen Jay. *Time's Arrow, Time's Cycle. Myth and Metaphor in the Discovery of Geological Time*. Harvard: Harvard University Press, 1987.

———, ed. *Eight Little Piggies*. London: Jonathan Cape, 1993.

Green, V.H.H. *Renaissance and Reformation: A Survey of European History between 1450 and 1660*. 2nd ed. London: Edward Arnold, 1964.

Greene-McCreight, K.E. *Ad Litteram: How Augustine, Calvin, and Barth Read the "Plain Sense" of Genesis 1–3*. Issues in Systematic Theology, 5. Frankfurt am Main: Lang, 1999.

Greene, John C. "Protestantism, Science, and American Enterprise: Benjamin Silliman's Moral Universe." In *Benjamin Silliman and his Circle: Studies on the Influence of Benjamin Silliman on Science in America,* edited by Leonard G. Wilson, 11–27. New York: Science History Publications, 1979.

———. "Science and Religion." In *The Rise of Adventism: Religion and Society in Mid-Nineteenth-Century America*, edited by Edwin S. Gaustad, 50–68. New York: Harper & Row, 1974.

———. *The Death of Adam: Evolution and Its Impact on Western Thought*. Ames: Iowa State University Press, 1959.

Gregory, Frederick. "The Impact of Darwinian Evolution on Protestant Theology in the Nineteenth Century." In *God and Nature: Historical Essays on the Encounter between Christianity and Science*, edited by D.C. Lindberg and R.L. Numbers, 369–90. Berkeley: University of California Press, 1986.

———. *Nature Lost? Natural Science and the German Theological Traditions of the Nineteenth Century*. Cambridge, MA: Harvard University Press, 1992.

Gregory of Nazianzus. "Carmina dogmatica." In *PG*, vol. 37, 397–522.

———. *On God and Man: The Theological Poetry of St. Gregory of Nazianzus*. Edited by Peter Gilbert. Popular Patristics. Crestwood, NY: St. Vladimir's Seminary Press, 2001, http://books.google.com/books?id= 2ngq3Bd_YuMC.

———. "Orationes 38, 44." In *PG*, vol. 36, 312–33, 608–21.

Gregory of Nyssa. "Explicatio apologetica in Hexaemeron." In *PG*, vol. 44, 61–124.

Gregory the Great. *S. Gregorii Magni moralia in Iob libri XXIII–XXXV*. Edited by Marci Adriaen. Vol. 143B. Corpus Christianorum series Latina. Turnholt: Brepols, 1985.

Grew, Nehemiah. *Cosmologia Sacra: or A Discourse of the Universe as It Is the Creature and Kingdom of God....* London: W. Rogers, 1701. ECCO.

Griggs, Tamara. "Universal History from Counter-Reformation to Enlightenment." *Modern Intellectual History* 4 (2007): 219–47.

Grosseteste, Robert. *On the Six Days of Creation*. Translated by C.F.J. Martin: Oxford University Press, 1996.

Grotius, Hugo. "Annotationes in Vetus Testamentum." In *Hugonis Grotii Opera omnia theologica in tres tomos divisa : ante quidem per partes, nunc autem conjunctim & accuratius edita.* London: Prostant venalia apud Mosem Pitt, 1679. EEBO.

Guralnick, Stanley M. "Geology and Religion before Darwin: The Case of Edward Hitchcock, Theologian and Geologist (1793–1864)." *Isis* 63 (1972): 529–43.

Guyot, Arnold. *Creation; or, The Biblical Cosmogony in the Light of Modern Science.* Edinburgh: T. & T. Clark, 1883.

H[ill], T[homas]. "The First Chapter of Genesis." *Christian Examiner* 59 (1855): 379–98.

Haber, Francis Colin. *The Age of the World: Moses to Darwin.* Baltimore: Johns Hopkins Press, 1959.

Hagopian, David, ed. *The Genesis Debate: Three Views on the Days of Creation.* Mission Viejo, CA: Crux, 2001.

Hale, Matthew. *The Primitive Origination of Mankind, Considered and Examined according to the Light of Nature.* London: printed by William Godbid for William Shrowsbery, 1677. EEBO.

Hall, Christopher. *Reading Scripture with the Church Fathers.* Downers Grove: InterVarsity, 1998.

Hall, David W. "What Was the View of the Westminster Assembly Divines on the Creation Days?" In *Did God Create in Six Days?*, edited by Jr. Joseph A. Pipa and David W. Hall, 43–54. Taylors, SC: Southern Presbyterian Press, 1999. Reprint, Tolle Lege Press, 2005.

Halley, Edmund. "An Attempt to find the Age of the World by the Saltness of the Sea." In *The Philosophical Transactions (from the year 1700 to the year 1720) Abridg'd and Dispos'd under General Heads. Vol V. containing Part I. The Anatomical and Medical Papers, Part II. The Philological and Miscellaneous Papers*, edited by Henry Jones, 216–19. London: G. Strahan, etc., 1721, http://books.google.com/books?id=o1AV AAAAQAAJ.

Hamilton, Victor P. *The Book of Genesis Chapters 1–17.* Grand Rapids: Eerdmans, 1990.

Hanson, R.P.C. "Biblical Exegesis in the Early Church." In *The Cambridge History of the Bible.* Vol. 1, *From the Beginnings to Jerome*, edited by P.R. Ackroyd and C.F. Evans, 412–53. Cambridge: Cambridge University Press, 1970.

Hanson, Richard Davies, "On Some Relations of Science and Scripture." In *Law in Nature, and Other Papers, Read before the Adelaide Philosophical Soc[iety] and the South Australian Institute*, 68–77. Adelaide: W.C. Rigby, 1865.

———. "Science and Theology: A Paper Read before the Adelaide Philosophical Society." In *Law in Nature, and Other Papers, Read before the Adelaide Philosophical Soc[iety] and the South Australian Institute*, 52–67. Adelaide: W.C. Rigby, 1865.

Harrison, Peter. *The Bible, Protestantism, and the Rise of Natural Science.* Cambridge, UK: Cambridge University Press, 1998.

———. "'Science' and 'Religion': Constructing the Boundaries." *Journal of Religion* 86, no. 1 (2006): 81–106.

Hart, Ian. "Genesis 1:1–2:3 as a Prologue to the Books of Genesis." *Tyndale Bulletin* 46, no. 2 (1995): 315–36.

Hauser, Alan J., and Duane F. Watson, eds. *A History of Biblical Interpretation.* Grand Rapids: Eerdmans, 2003.

Haydn, Joseph, and Gottfried van Swieten. "Die Schöpfung: Oratorium in drei Teilen." 1798.

Hearne, Thomas. *Ductor Historicus: or, A Short System of Universal History, and an Introduction to the Study of It.* 2nd ed. 2 vols. Vol. I. London: printed for Tim. Childe... 1704–05. ECCO.

Heidel, Alexander. *The Gilgamesh Epic and Old Testament Parallels.* 2nd ed. Chicago: University of Chicago Press, 1949.

Helmont, Jean Baptiste van, 1577–1644. *Oriatrike, or, Physick Refined.* London: printed for L. Loyd, 1662. EEBO.

Henry, John. "Palaeontology and Theodicy: Religion, Politics and the Asterolepsis of Stromness." In *Hugh Miller and the Controversies of Victorian Science*, edited by M. Shortland, 151–70. Oxford: Clarendon, 1996.

Henry, Matthew. *Exposition of the Old and New Testaments*, 1708–10. CCEL, http://www.ccel.org/ccel/henry/mhc1.Gen.ii.html.

Herder, Johann Gottfried. *Älteste Urkunde des Menschengeschlechts.* 2 vols. Vol. I. Riga: J.F. Hartknoch, 1774.

———. *Reflections on the Philosophy of the History of Mankind: Abridged, and with an Introduction, by Frank E. Manuel.* Chicago: University of Chicago Press, 1968.

Hess, Richard S. "God and Origins: Interpreting the Early Chapters of Genesis." In *Darwin, Creation and the Fall: Theological Challenges*, edited by R.J. Berry and T.A. Noble, 86–98. Nottingham: InterVarsity, 2009.

Hidal, Sten. "Exegesis of the Old Testament in the Antiochene School with its Prevalent Literal and Historical Method." In *HB/OT*, vol. I, bk 1, 543–68.

Hilary of Poitiers. "De Trinitate." In *PL*, vol. 10, 25–472.

———. "De Trinitate or On the Trinity." In *NPNF*[2], vol. 9, 31–234.

Hill, Carol A. "A Third Alternative to Concordism and Divine Accommodation: The Worldview Approach." *PSCF* 59, no. 2 (2007): 129–34.

Hippolytus. *Commentarium in Danielem.* Translated by M. Lefèvre. Sources chrétiennes, 14. Paris: Éditions du Cerf, 1947. TLG.

———. "On Daniel." In *ANF*, vol. 5, 177–94.

———. *Refutatio omnium haeresium.* Translated by Paul Wendland. Die griechischen christlichen Schriftsteller der ersten drei Jahrhunderte, 26. Hildesheim: Georg Olms Verlag, 1977.

———. *The Refutation of All Heresies ... with Fragments from his Commentaries on Various Books of Scripture.* Translated by J.H. Macmahon and S.D.F. Salmond. Ante-Nicene Christian Library, 6. Edinburgh: T&T Clark, 1878.

Hitchcock, Edward. "The Connection between Geology and the Mosaic History of Creation." *American Biblical Repository* 6 no. 18 (1835): 261–332.

———. *The Religion of Geology and Its Connected Sciences*. Boston: Phillips, Samson, and Company, 1851.

———. "Remarks on Professor Stuart's Examination of Gen. 1 in Reference to Geology." *American Biblical Repository* 7, no. 22 (1836): 448–87.

Hobbes, Thomas. *Leviathan*. Revised student ed. Cambridge Texts in the History of Political Thought. Cambridge: Cambridge University Press, 1996.

Hobbs, R. Gerald. "Pluriformity of Early Reformation Scriptural Interpretation." In *HB/OT*, vol. II, 452–511.

Hobbs, William. *Earth Generated and Atomized*. Edited by Roy Porter. London: British Museum/Ithaca: Cornell University Press, 1981.

Hodge, B.C. *Revisiting the Days of Genesis*. Eugene, OR: Wipf & Stock, 2011.

Hoffman, Yair. "The First Creation Story: Canonical and Diachronic Aspects." In *Creation in Jewish and Christian Tradition*, edited by Henning Graf Reventlow and Yair Hoffman, 32–53. JSOT Sup, 319. London: Sheffield Academic Press, 2002.

Holsinger-Friesen, Thomas. *Irenaeus and Genesis: A Study of Competition in Early Christian Hermeneutics*. Journal of Theological Interpretation Supplements. Winona Lake: Eisenbrauns, 2009.

Honorius Augustodunensis. "Hexaemeron." In *PL*, vol. 172, 253–66.

Horne, Thomas Hartwell. *An Introduction to the Critical Study and Knowledge of the Holy Scriptures*. 4th ed. 4 vols. Philadelphia: E. Little, 1825. GB, http://books.google.com.au/books?id=icFCAAAAIAAJ.

Hudson, Wayne. *The English Deists: Studies in Early Enlightenment*. The Enlightenment World: Political and Intellectual History of the Long Eighteenth Century. London: Pickering & Chatto, 2009.

Hugh of Amiens. "Tractatus in hexaemeron." In *PL*, vol. 192, 1247–56.

Hugh of St. Victor. *Hugh of Saint Victor on the Sacraments of the Christian Faith*. Translated by J. D. Deferrari. Cambridge, MA: The Mediaeval Academy of America, 1951.

Hughes, George, 1603–67. *An Analytical Exposition of the First Book of Moses*. n.l.: n.d., 1672. EEBO.

Hutchinson, John. *Moses's Principia. Of the Invisible Parts of Matter; of Motion: of Visible Forms …* London: J. Bettenham, 1724.

Hutton, James. *Theory of the Earth: Investigation into Laws observable in the Composition, Dissolution, and Restoration of Land upon the Globe*. n.p.: Forgotten Books, 2007, http://books.google.com/books?id=1bmiLkX5pPkC.

Hyers, Conrad. "The Narrative Form of Genesis 1: Cosmogonic, Yes; Scientific, No." *Journal of the American Scientific Affiliation* 36 (1984): 208–15.

Indicopleustes, Cosmas. *Cosmae Aegyptii Monarchi Christiana Topographia, Sive Christianorum Opiniode Mundo*. In *PL*, vol. 88, 51–476.

Irenaeus. "Against Heresies." In *ANF*, vol. 1, 309–567.

Isidore of Seville. "Sancti Isidori Hispalensis Episcopi chronicon." In *PL*, vol. 83, 1017–58.

———. "Sancti Isidori Hispalensis Episcopi mysticorum expositiones sacramentorum seu quaestiones in Vetus Testamentum. In Genesin." In *PL*, vol. 83, 207–88.

Jacob, Christoph. "The Reception of the Origenist Tradition in Latin Exegesis." In *HB/OT*, vol. I, bk 1, 682–700.

Jacob of Sarug. "On the Establishment of Creation, Memra One, The First Day." In *Biblical Interpretation*, edited by J.W. Trigg, 184–202. Wilmington, DE: Michael Glazier, 1988.

Jaki, Stanley. *Genesis 1 through the Ages*. New York: Thomas More Press, 1992.

James, F.A., III. "Vermigli, Peter Martyr *(1499–1562)*." In *HHMBI*, 239–45.

Jameson, Robert. "Remarks on Some of Baron Cuvier's Lectures on the History of the Natural Sciences, in Reference to the Scientific Knowledge of the Egyptians; of the Source from Whence Moses Derived his Cosmogony, and the General Agreement of that Cosmogony with Modern Geology." *Edinburgh New Philosophical Journal* 13 (1832): 41–75.

Jansma, T. "L'Hexameron de Jacques de Sarug." *L'Orient syrien* 4 (1959): 3–42, 129–162, 253–84, 451–521.

Jerusalem, J.F.W. *Betrachtungen über die vornehmsten Wahrheiten der Religion*. 3 vols. Vol. II, part 2. Braunschweig: Fürstl[ich?] Waisenhaus = Buchhandlung, 1779, http://books.google.com/books?id=_VBbAAAA QAAJ.

Joachim of Fiore. *Liber de concordia Novi ac Veteris Testamenti*. Edited by E. Randolph Daniel. Transactions of the American Philosophical Society, 73 pt. 8. Philadelphia, Pa.: American Philosophical Society, 1983.

Jobling, David Kenneth. "'And Have Dominion ...': The Interpretation of Old Testament Texts Concerning Man's Rule over the Creation (Genesis 1:26, 28, 9:1–2, Psalm 8:7–9) from 200 B.C. to the Time of the Council of Nicea." Th.D. Dissertation, Union Theological Seminary, 1972.

John of Damascus. "Exposition of the Orthodox Faith." In *NPNF*[2], vol. 9, 1–101.

Jordan, James B. *Creation in Six Days: A Defense of the Traditional Reading of Genesis One*. Moscow, Idaho: Canon, 1999.

Jorink, Eric. "'Horrible and Blasphemous': Isaac La Peyrère, Isaac Vossius, and the Emergence of Radical Biblical Criticism in the Dutch Republic." In *Nature and Scripture in the Abrahamic Religions: Up to 1700*, edited by Jitse M. van der Meer and Scott Mandelbrote, 429–50. Leiden: Brill, 2008.

Josephus. "Antiquities." In *Josephus: Complete Works*, 1736. Reprint, Grand Rapids: Kregel, 1960.

Julius Africanus. "The Extant Fragments of the Five Books of the Chronography of Julius Africanus." In *ANF*, vol. 6, 130–38.

Kalisch, M.M. *A Historical and Critical Commentary on the Old Testament with a New Translation: Genesis. English Edition*. London: Longman, Brown, Green, Longmans, and Roberts, 1858, http://books.google.com/books?id=QwUXAAAAYAAJ.

Kant, Immanuel. *Universal Natural History and Theory of the Heavens*. Translated by Stanley L. Jaki. Edinburgh: Scottish Academic Press, 1981.

Kearney, Eileen F. "Peter Abelard as Biblical Commentator: A Study of the Expositio in Hexaemeron." In *Petrus Abaelardus (1079–1142)*, 199–210. Trier: Paulinus-Verlag, 1980.

Keil, C.F. "The First Book of Moses (Genesis)." In *Commentary on the Old Testament. 1. The Pentateuch*, edited by C.F. Keil and F. Delitzsch, 33–414. Edinburgh: T&T Clark, 1866. Reprint, Grand Rapids: Eerdmans, 1973, http://books.google.com/books?id=F6NkmPGJKvIC.

Keill, John. *An Examination of Dr. Burnet's Theory of the Earth*.... Oxford: printed at the Theater, 1698.

Kelly, Douglas F. *Creation and Change: Genesis 1.1–2.4 in the Light of Changing Scientific Paradigms*. Fearn, Ross-shire: Mentor, 1997.

Kelly, Joseph F. "Bede's Use of Augustine for His *Commentarium in Principium Genesis*." In *Augustine: Biblical Exegete*, edited by Frederick van Fleteren and Joseph C. Schnaubelt, 189–96. New York: Peter Lang, 2001.

Kelly, Sister Suzanne. "The Rise of Historical Geology in the Seventeeth Century." In *Toward a History of Geology*, edited by Cecil Schneer, 214–25. Cambridge, MA: MIT Press, 1969.

Kidd, J. *A Geological Essay on the Imperfect Evidence in Support of a Theory of the Earth*.... Oxford: Oxford University Press, 1815. GB, http://books.google.com/books?id=FGgUAAAAQAAJ.

Kim, Yoon Kyung. *Augustine's Changing Interpretations of Genesis 1–3: From De Genesi Contra Manichaeos to De Genesi Ad Litteram*. Lewiston, NY: Edwin Mellen Press, 2006.

Kirkconnell, W., ed. *The Celestial Cycle*. Toronto: University of Toronto Press, 1952. Reprint, New York: Gordian, 1967.

Kirwan, Richard. *Geological Essays*. London: D. Bremner, 1799. ECCO.

Klaaren, Eugene M. *The Religious Origins of Modern Science: Belief in Creation in Seventeenth Century Thought*. Grand Rapids: Eerdmans, 1977.

Klauck, Hans-Josef, Bernard McGinn, Paul Mendes-Flohr, Choon-Leong Seow, Hermann Spieckermann, Barry Dov Walfish, and Eric Ziolkowski, eds. *The Encyclopedia of the Bible and Its Reception*. Berlin: De Gruyter, 2009-.

Kline, Meredith G. "Space and Time in the Genesis Cosmogony." *PSCF* 48, no. 1 (1996): 2–15. www.asa3.org/ASA/PSCF.html.

Knight, Mark. "*Wirkungsgeschichte*, Reception History, Reception Theory." *Journal for the Study of the New Testament* 33, no. 2 (2010): 137–146.

Köpf, Ulrich. "The Institutional Framework of Christian Exegesis in the Middle Ages." In *HB/OT*, vol. I, bk 2, 148–79.

Krey, Philip D.W., and Lesley Smith, eds. *Nicholas of Lyra: The Senses of Scripture*. Studies in the History of Christian Thought, 90. Leiden: Brill, 2000.

Kronholm, T. *Motifs from Genesis I–XI in the Genuine Hymns of Ephrem the Syrian with Particular Reference to the Influence of Jewish Exegetical Tradition*. Coniectanea Biblica OT, 11. Lund: CWK Gleerup, 1978.

Kugel, James L., and Rowan A. Greer. *Early Biblical Interpretation*. Library of Early Christianity, 3. Philadelphia: Westminster Press, 1986.

Kurtz, John Henry. *The Bible and Astronomy: An Exposition of the Biblical Cosmology, and Its Relations to Natural Science*. Translated by T.D. Simonton. Philadelphia: Lindsay & Blakiston, 1857. GB, http://books.google.com/books?id=BNk0AAAAMAAJ.

La Peyrère, Isaac de, 1594–1676. *Men before Adam: Or A Discourse upon the Twelfth, Thirteenth and Fourteenth Verses of the Epistle of the Apostle Paul to the Romans*. London: n.p., 1656. EEBO.

Lactantius. "The Divine Institutes." In *ANF*, vol. 7, 9–223.

Laistner, M.L.W. "Some Early Medieval Commentaries on the Old Testament." *Harvard Theological Review* 46 (1953): 27–46.

Lambert, W.G., A.R. Millard, and Miguel Civil, eds. *Atra-Hasis: The Babylonian Story of the Flood with the Sumerian Flood Story*. Oxford: Oxford University Press, 1969.

Lampe, G.W.H. *Patristic Greek Lexicon*. Oxford: Clarendon, 1961–68.

Lange, Johann Peter, and Tayler Lewis. *Genesis: or, The First Book of Moses, Together with a General Theological and Homiletical Introduction to the Old Testament*. Translated by Tayler Lewis and A. Gosman. A Commentary on the Holy Scriptures: Critical, Doctrinal, and Homiletical, ed. Philip Schaff. New York: Scribner, 1869. IA, http://www.archive.org/details/genesisorthefirs00languoft.

Lapide, R.P. Cornelius a. *Commentaria in Scripturam Sacram. Tomus primus: in Pentateuchum Mosis*. Paris: Ludovicus Vivès, 1859. IA, http://www.archive.org/stream/commentariainsc00lapigoog.

Lavallee, Louis. "Augustine on the Creation Days." *Journal of the Evangelical Theological Society* 32 (1989): 457–64.

———. "Creeds and the Six Creation Days." *Impact* 235 (Jan 1993).

Lawrence, P. "Edward Hitchcock: The Christian Geologist." *Proceedings of the American Philosophical Society* 116 (1972): 21–34.

Layton, B., et al. *Nag Hammadi Codex II, 2–7* ... 2 vols. The Coptic Gnostic Library/Nag Hammadi Studies, 20, 21. Leiden: Brill, 1982.

Le Clerc, Jean, 1657–1736. *In Genesin*. Mosis Prophetae Libri Quinque. Amsterdam, 1710.

Leff, G. *The Dissolution of the Medieval Outlook: An Essay on the Intellectual and Spiritual Change in the 14th Century*. New York: New York University Press, 1976.

Leibniz, Gottfried Wilhelm. *Protogaea*. Translated by Claudine Cohen and Andre Wakefield. Chicago: University of Chicago Press, 2008.

Lenglet Dufresnoy, Nicolas. *Chronological Tables of Universal History, Sacred and Profane, Ecclesiastical and Civil; from the Creation of the World* ... London: printed for A. Millar, etc., 1762. ECCO.

Leonardi, Claudio. "Aspects of Old Testament Interpretation in the Church from the Seventh to the Tenth Century." In *HB/OT*, vol. I, bk 2, 180–95.

Letham, Robert. "'In the Space of Six Days': The Days of Creation from Origen to the Westminster Assembly." *WTJ* 61, no. 2 (1999): 149–74.

Lewis, C.L.E., and Simon J. Knell, eds. *The Age of the Earth from 4004 BC to AD 2002*. GS Special Publications, 190. London: Geological Society, 2001.

Lewis, Jack P. "The Days of Creation: An Historical Survey of Interpretation." *Journal of the Evangelical Theological Society* 32 (1989): 433–55.

Lewis, Neil. "Robert Grosseteste and the Church Fathers." In *RCFW*, vol. 1, 197–229.

Lewis, Tayler. *The Bible and Science; or, The World-Problem*. Schenectady, NY: G. Y. Van Debogert, 1856.

———. *The Six Days of Creation; or, The Scriptural Cosmology, with the Ancient Idea of Time-Worlds, in Distinction from Worlds in Space*. Schenectady, NY: G.Y. Van Debogert, 1855, http://books.google.com/books?id=CUvOViSeGDAC.

Liddell, Henry G., and Robert Scott. *Greek-English Lexicon*. 9th ed. Oxford: Clarendon Press, 1940.

Lightfoot, John. *A Chronicle of the Times, and the Order of the Texts of the Old Testament*. London: John Clark, 1647. EEBO.

———. *The Whole Works of the Rev. John Lightfoot: Master of Catharine Hall, Cambridge*. 13 vols. Edited by John Rogers Pitman. London: printed by J.F. Dove, 1822. GB, vol. II URL: http://books.google.com/books?id=mAIUAAAAQAAJ. vol. IV URL: http://books.google.com/books?id=HQMUAAAAQAAJ.

———. *A Few, and New Observations upon the Booke of Genesis*. London: printed by T. Badger, 1642. EEBO.

Limborch, Philip van. *Theologia Christiana*, 1686. CPT.

Lindberg, David C. "Science and the Early Church." In *God and Nature: Historical Essays on the Encounter between Christianity and Science*, edited by D.C. Lindberg and R.L. Numbers, 19–48. Berkeley: University of California Press, 1986.

———, and Ronald L. Numbers, eds. *God and Nature: Historical Essays on the Encounter between Christianity and Science*. Berkeley: University of California Press, 1986.

Linder, Robert D. "Abelard (Abailard), Peter (1079–1142)." In *The New International Dictionary of the Christian Church*, edited by J.D. Douglas, 3. Grand Rapids: Eerdmans, 1996.

Linnaeus, Carl. "Oratio de Telluris habitabilis incremento (1744)." In *L'Équilibre de la Nature*, edited by Camille Limoges, 29–55. L'Histoire des Sciences: Textes et Études. Paris: Librarie Philosophique J. Vrin, 1972.

———. *Philosophia botanica*. Vienna: Ioannis Thomae Trattner, 1755.

Loewenstamm, S.E. "The Seven-Day Unit in Ugaritic Epic Literature." *Israel Exploration Journal* 15 (1965): 122–33.

Lombard, Peter. "Sentences." In *PL*, vol. 192, 521–964.

Lord, David. *Geognosy, or The Facts and Principles of Geology against Theories*. New York: Franklin Knight, 1855.

Lord, Eleazar. *The Epoch of Creation: The Scripture Doctrine Contrasted with the Geology Theory*. New York: Charles Scribner, 1851. GB, http://books.google.com/books?id=dbMAAAAAMAAJ.

Louth, Andrew, ed. *Genesis 1–11*. Edited by Thomas C. Oden. Ancient Christian Commentary on Scripture. Downers Grove, IL: InterVarsity, 2001.

———. "The Six Days of Creation according to the Greek Fathers." In *Reading Genesis after Darwin*, edited by Stephen C. Barton and David Wilkinson, 39–55. New York: Oxford University Press, 2009.

Lovejoy, A. *The Great Chain of Being*. Cambridge, MA: Harvard University Press, 1936. Reprint, New York: Harper, 1960.

Luther, Martin. *Lectures on Genesis: Chapters 1–5*. Edited by J. Pelikan. 8 vols. vol. I. St. Louis: Concordia, 1958.

Lyell, Charles. *Principles of Geology*. London: John Murray, 1830–33. Reprint, Philadelphia: James Kay, Jun. and Brother, 1837. GB, http://books.google.com/books?id=AOcJAAAAMAAJ.

Macdonald, Donald. *Creation and the Fall: A Defence and Exposition of the First Three Chapters of Genesis*. Edinburgh: Thomas Constable and Co., 1856. IA, http://www.archive.org/stream/creationfalldefe00macd.

MacLeish, Kenneth. "Legacy from the Age of Faith." *National Geographic*, December 1969, 857–82.

Magruder, Kerry V. "Thomas Burnet, Biblical Idiom, and Seventeenth-Century Theories of the Earth." In *Nature and Scripture in the Abrahamic Religions: Up to 1700*, edited by Jitse M. van der Meer and Scott Mandelbrote, 451–90. Leiden: Brill, 2008.

Maillet, Benoît de. *Telliamed: or, Discourses between an Indian Philosopher and a French Missionary, on the Diminution of the Sea, the Formation of the Earth, the Origin of Men and Animals....* London: T. Osborne, 1750. ECCO.

Mandelbrote, Scott. "Biblical Hermeneutics and the Sciences, 1700–1900: An Overview." In *Nature and Scripture in the Abrahamic Religions: 1700–Present*, edited by J.M. van der Meer and S. Mandelbrote, 3–37. Leiden: Brill, 2008.

———. "Isaac Newton and Thomas Burnet: Biblical Criticism and the Crisis of Late Seventeenth-Century England." In *The Books of Nature and Scripture*, edited by R. Popkin and J. Force, 149–78. Dordrecht: Kluwer, 1994.

Mangenot, E., ed. "Hexaméron." In *Dictionnaire de théologie catholique*, vol. VI, 2325–54. Paris: L. Letouzey, 1920.

Marston, Justin. "Jewish Understandings of Genesis 1 to 3." *Science & Christian Belief* 12 (2000): 127–50.

Martyr, Justin. "Apologia." In *Die ältesten Apologeten*, edited by E.J. Goodspeed, 26–77. Göttingen: Vandenhoeck & Ruprecht, 1915. TLG.

———. "The First Apology." In *ANF*, vol. 1, 163–87.

Matter, E. Ann. "The Church Fathers and the Glossa Ordinaria." In *RCFW*, vol. 1, 83–111.

Maurus, Rabanus. "Commentaria in Genesim." In *PL*, vol. 107, 439–670.

McCalla, Arthur. *The Creationist Debate: The Encounter between the Bible and the Historical Mind*. London: Continuum, 2006.

McCaul, A. "The Mosaic Record of Creation." In *Aids to Faith. A Series of Theological Essays*, edited by W. Thomson, 189–238. London: D. Appleton, 1862. GB, http://books.google.com/books?id=B1kXAAAAYAAJ.

McCausland, Dominick. *Sermons in Stones; or, Scripture Confirmed by Geology*. London: Richard Bentley, 1856. GB, http://books.google.com/books?id=aEMDAAAAQAAJ.

McKim, Donald K., ed. *Historical Handbook of Major Biblical Interpreters*. Leicester, England; Downers Grove, IL: InterVarsity Press, 1998.

McVey, Kathleen. "The Use of Stoic Cosmogony in Theophilus of Antioch's Hexaemeron." In *Biblical Hermeneutics in Historical Perspective: Studies in Honor of Karlfried Froehlich on His Sixtieth Birthday*, edited by Mark S. Burrows and Paul Rorem, 32–58. Grand Rapids: Eerdmans, 1991.

Means, John O. "The Narrative of the Creation in Genesis." *Bibliotheca Sacra and the American Biblical Repository* 12 (1855): 83–130, 323–38. http://books.google.com.au/books?id=P08XAAAAYAAJ.

Melanchthon, Philip. "Commentarius in Genesin." In *Philippi Melanthonis opera quae supersunt omnia*, edited by C.G. Bretschneider, Vol. 13, 761–92. Corpus Reformatorum. Halle: C.A. Schwetschke, 1846.

———. *Philippi Melanthonis opera quae supersunt omnia*. Translated by Charles H. Hill. Edited by C.G. Bretschneider and H.E. Bindseil. Vol. 21. *Loci theologici*. Corpus Reformatorum. Brunswick: C.A. Schwetschke and Son, 1854. GB, http://books.google.com/books?id= x6QMAAAAIAAJ.

Mercerus, Johannes. *In Genesim Commentarius*. Geneva: ex typographia Matthaei Berjon, 1598.

Mersenne, Marine. *Quaestiones celeberrimae in Genesim, cum accurata textus explicatione*. Paris: sumptibus Sebastiani Cramoisy, 1623.

Mesguich, Sophie Kessler. "Early Christian Hebraists." In *HB/OT*, vol. II, 254–75.

Methodius of Olympus. "The Banquet." In *ANF*, vol. 6, 309–55.

———. "Fragments on Creation." In *The Writings of Methodius, Alexander of Lycopolis, Peter of Alexandria, and Several Fragments*, 176–82. Ante-Nicene Christian Library, 14. Edinburgh: T&T Clark, 1883.

Michaelis, J.D. *Commentaries on the Laws of Moses*. Translated by Alexander Smith. 4 vols. London: printed for F.C. and J. Rivington, 1814.

Miller, Hugh. *The Testimony of the Rocks, or, Geology in Its Bearings on the Two Theologies, Natural and Revealed*. Edinburgh: Thomas Constable, 1857. Reprint, Edinburgh: Nimmo, Hay & Mitchell, 1889.

Millhauser, M. "The Scriptural Geologists: An Episode in the History of Opinion." *Osiris* 11 (1954): 65–86.

Milton, John. *Paradise Lost*, 1667. Reprint, Books That Have Changed Man's Thinking; Geneva: Edito-Service S.A., n.d.

Mirandola, Pico della. *On the Dignity of Man, On Being and the One, Heptaplus*. Translated by P.J.W. Miller. Indianopolis: The Library of Liberal Arts, 1965.

Moore, James R. "Geologists and Interpreters of Genesis in the Nineteenth Century." In *God and Nature: Historical Essays on the Encounter between Christianity and Science*, edited by D.C. Lindberg and R.L. Numbers, 322–50. Berkeley: University of California Press, 1986.

———. *The Post-Darwinian Controversies: A Study of the Protestant Struggle to Come to Terms with Darwin in Great Britain and America, 1870–1900.* Cambridge: Cambridge University Press, 1979.

More, Henry. *Conjectura cabbalistica.* London: James Flesher, 1653. EEBO.

Mortenson, T. *The Great Turning Point: The Church's Catastrophic Mistake on Geology – before Darwin.* Green Forest, AZ: Master Books, 2004.

Moye, Richard H. "In the Beginning: Myth and History in Genesis and Exodus." *Journal of Biblical Literature* 109 (1990): 577–98.

Mulholland, J. Derral. "Book Review: Planets and Their Inhabitants, a review of Planets and Planetarians by Stanley L. Jaki," *Journal for the History of Astronomy* 11 (1980): 68–69.

Muller, R.A. "Lightfoot, John (1602–1675)." In *HHMBI*, 208–12.

Musculus, Wolfgang. *In Genesim Mosis plenissimi commentarii.* Basel: per Ioannes Heruagios, 1554. Reprint, Microform: Inter Documentation Co., Zug, Switzerland, 1985.

Narsai of Nisibis. "On the Expression, "In the Beginning," and Concerning the Existence of God." In *Biblical Interpretation*, edited by J. W. Trigg, 203–20. Message of the Fathers of the Church, 9. Wilmington, DE: Michael Glazier, 1988.

Needham, Joseph, and Lazzaro Spallanzani. *Nouvelles recherches physiques et métaphysiques sur la nature et la religion, avec une nouvelle théorie de la terre, et une mesure de la hauteur des Alpes*...par M. de Needham. 2 vols. Vol. 2. London/Paris: Lacombe, 1769. ECCO.

Neil, W. "The Criticism and Theological Use of the Bible 1700–1950." In *The Cambridge History of the Bible.* Vol. III, *The West from the Reformation to the Present Day*, edited by S.L. Greenslade, 238–93. Cambridge: Cambridge University Press, 1963.

Nellen, H.J.M. "Growing Tension between Church Doctrines and Critical Exegesis of the O.T." In *HB/OT*, vol. II, 802–26.

Neuschäfer, B. "Didymus the Blind." In *DECL*, 172–74.

Newton, Isaac. *Correspondence.* Edited by H.W. Turnbull et al. Cambridge: published for the Royal Society at the University Press, 1960.

Nolan, Frederick. *The Analogy of Revelation and Science Established.* Oxford: J.H. Parker, 1833. GB, http://books.google.com.au/books?id= tyJAAAAAYAAJ.

Norris, John M. "Augustine's Interpretation of Genesis in the *City of God* XI–XV." In *Fourteenth International Conference on Patristic Studies*, edited by F. Young, M. Edwards and P. Parvis, 207–11. Oxford: Peeters, 2006.

Norris, Richard A., Jr. "Augustine and the Close of the Ancient Period of Interpretation." In *A History of Biblical Interpretation*, edited by Alan J. Hauser and Duane F. Watson, 380–408. Grand Rapids: Eerdmans, 2003.

North, John D. "Chronology and the Age of the World." In *Cosmology, History, and Theology*, edited by Wolfgang Yourgrau and Allan D. Breck, 307–33. New York: Plenum Press, 1977.

Numbers, Ronald L. *Creation by Natural Law: Laplace's Nebular Hypothesis in American Thought.* Seattle: University of Washington Press, 1977.

———. *The Creationists: From Scientific Creationism to Intelligent Design*. Expanded ed. Cambridge, MA: Harvard University Press, 2006.

O'Connor, R. "Young-Earth Creationists in Early Nineteenth-Century Britain? Towards a Reassessment of 'Scriptural Geology'." *History of Science* 45 (2007): 357–403.

Oetinger, Friedrich Christoph, 1702–82, and Julius Hamberger. *Die Theologie aus der Idee des Lebens abgeleitet und auf sechs Hauptstücke zurückgeführt*. Stuttgart: J.F. Steinkopf, 1852. GB, http://books.google.com/books?id=d3orAAAAYAAJ.

O'Loughlin, Thomas. "Christ as the Focus of Genesis Exegesis in Isidore of Seville." In *Studies in Patristic Christology*, edited by Thomas Finan and Vincent Twomey, 144–62. Dublin: Four Courts, 1998.

Oldroyd, David R. "The Geologist from Cromarty." In *Hugh Miller and the Controversies of Victorian Science,* edited by Michael Shortland, 76–121. Oxford: Clarendon, 1996.

Opitz, Peter. "The Exegetical and Hermeneutical Work of John Oecolampadius, Huldrych Zwingli and John Calvin." In *HB/OT*, vol. II, 407–51.

Origen. *Contra Celsum*. Translated by Henry Chadwick. Cambridge: Cambridge University Press, 1953.

———. "Fragmenta in Genesim." In *PG*, vol. 12, 61–146.

———. *Homilies on Genesis and Exodus*. Translated by Ronald E. Heine. Fathers of the Church, a New Translation, 71. Washington, DC: Catholic University of America Press, 1981.

———. *On First Principles*. Translated by George William Butterworth. Edited by Paul Koetschau. Gloucester, MA: Smith, 1973.

Osbourne, Catherine. *Rethinking Early Greek Philosophy*. London: Duckworth, 1987.

Otten, Willemien. "The Texture of Tradition: The Role of the Church Fathers in Carolingian Theology." In *RCFW*, vol. 1, 3–50.

Packer, J.I. "Hermeneutics and Genesis 1–11." *Southwestern Journal of Theology* 44, no. 1 (2001): 4–21.

Paradis, James G. "The Natural Historian as Antiquary of the World: Hugh Miller and the Rise of Literary Natural History." In *Hugh Miller and the Controversies of Victorian Science,* edited by Michael Shortland, 122–50. Oxford: Clarendon, 1996.

Pareus, David. *In Genesin Mosis commentarius*. Frankfurt: In Officine Ionae Rhodii, 1609.

Parker, Andrew. *The Genesis Enigma: Why the Bible is Scientifically Accurate*. New York: Dutton Adult, 2009.

Parker, Benjamin. *A Survey of the Six Days Works of the Creation*. London: printed for the author; Benjamin Stichall; and sold by R. Baldwin and J. Jefferies, 1745.

Parkinson, James. *Organic Remains of a Former World: An Examination of the Mineralized Remains of Vegetables and Animals of the Antediluvian World, Generally Termed Extraneous Fossils*. 3 vols. London: J. Robson, 1804–11.

Patrick, Simon. *A Commentary on the First Book of Moses, Called Genesis*. London: Ri. Chiswell, 1695.

Patton, C. "Creation, Fall and Salvation: Lyra's Commentary on Genesis 1–3." In *Nicholas of Lyra: The Senses of Scripture*, edited by Philip D.W. Krey and Lesley Smith, 19–43. Leiden: Brill, 2000.

Pember, G.H. *Earth's Earliest Ages: And Their Connection with Modern Spiritualism and Theosophy*. London: Samuel Bagster & Sons, 1876. Reprint, London: Hodder & Stoughton, 1893.

Penn, Granville. *A Comparative Estimate of the Mineral and Mosaical Geologies*. 2nd, revised ed. London: James Duncan, 1825. GB, http://books.google.com/books?id=b7BAAAAAIAAJ.

Pennock, Robert T. *Tower of Babel: The Evidence Against the New Creationism*. Cambridge, MA: MIT Press, 2000.

Pererius, Benedictus. *Commentariorium et disputationum in Genesim, tomi quatuor, continentes historiam Mosis ab exordio mundi*. Cologne: apud Antonium Hierat, 1601. Reprint, vol. CA-29, series Catholic Reformation, Inter Documentation Co., Zug, Switzerland.

Perkins, William. *An Exposition of the Symbole or Creed of the Apostles, according to the Tenour of the Scripture, and the Consent of Orthodoxe Fathers of the Church. The Workes of that Famous and Worthy Minister of Christ, in the Universitie of Cambridge, Mr. William Perkins*. London: printed by John Legatt, Printer to the Universitie of Cambridge, 1616. CPT.

Petavius, Dionisius. *The History of the World: Or, An Account of Time*. London: printed by J. Streater ... 1659. EEBO.

———. "De sex primorum mundi dierum opificio." In *Dogmata Theologica Dionysii Petavii*, vol. IV, 123–508, 1650. Reprint, Paris: L. Vivès, 1866. GB, http://books.google.com/books?id=ewwND6aisfgC.

Petit, F. *Catenae Graecae in Genesim et in Exodum*. vol. I, *Collectio Coisliniana in Genesim*. Corpus christianorum, series graeca, 15. Turnhout: Brepols, 1986.

Philo. "Allegorical Interpretation, I." In *The Works of Philo*, edited by C. D. Yonge, 25–37. Peabody, MA: Hendrickson, 1993.

———. "On the Creation." In *The Works of Philo: Complete and Unabridged*, 3–24. Peabody, MA: Hendrickson, 1993.

Philoponus, Johannes. *De opificio mundi*. Translated by G. Reichardt. Leipzig: G.B. Teubner, 1897. TLG.

Pietersma, Albert, and Benjamin G. Wright, eds. *A New English Translation of the Septuagint and the Other Greek Translations Traditionally Included under That Title*. New York: Oxford University Press, 2007.

Pike, Samuel. *Philosophia Sacra: or, The Principles of Natural Philosophy. Extracted from Divine Revelation*. London: printed for the author, and sold by J. Buckland ... 1753. ECCO.

Pinnock, C.H. "Climbing out of a Swamp: The Evangelical Struggle to Understand the Creation Texts." *Interpretation* 43 (1989): 143–55.

Pisides, Georgius. "Hexaemeron sive Cosmopoeia." In *PG*, vol. 92, 1426–1580.

Pluche, Noël Antoine. *The History of the Heavens, Considered according to the Notions of the Poets and Philosophers, Compared with the Doctrines of Moses ...* 2 vols., vol. II. London: printed for J. Osborn... 1740. ECCO.

Polak, Frank. "Poetic Style and Parallelism in the Creation Account (Genesis 1.1–2.3)." In *Creation in Jewish and Christian Tradition*, edited by Henning Graf Reventlow and Yair Hoffman, 2–31. JSOT Sup, 319. London: Sheffield Academic Press, 2002.

Pollard, Arthur. "Cambridge Platonists." In *The New International Dictionary of the Christian Church*, edited by J.D. Douglas and Earle E. Cairns, 183. Grand Rapids: Zondervan, 1996.

Popkin, Richard H. "Cartesianism and Biblical Criticism." In *Problems of Cartesianism*, edited by Thomas M. Lennon, John M. Nicholas and John W. Davis, 61–81. Kingston and Montreal: McGill-Queen's University Press, 1982.

———. *Isaac La Peyrère (1596–1676)*. Leiden: E.J. Brill, 1987.

———. *The Third Force in Seventeenth-Century Thought*. Leiden: E.J. Brill, 1992.

Porter, Roy. *The Making of Geology: Earth Science in Britain 1660–1815*. Cambridge: Cambridge University Press, 1977.

Powell, Baden. *The Connexion of Natural and Divine Truth; or, The Study of the Inductive Philosophy Considered as Subservient to Theology*. London: John W. Parker, 1838. GB, http://books.google.com/books?id= bWMOAAAAQAAJ.

———. *Essays on the Spirit of the Inductive Philosophy, the Unity of Worlds, and the Philosophy of Creation*. London: Longman, Brown, Green, and Longmans, 1855. GB, http://books.google.com/books?id= FkYnAAAAMAAJ.

Pranger, Burcht. "Sic et Non: Patristic Authority between Refusal and Acceptance: Anselm of Canterbury, Peter Abelard and Bernard of Clairvaux." In *RCFW*, vol. 1, 165–93.

Pratt, J.H. *Scripture and Science Not at Variance: or, The Historical Character and Plenary Inspiration of the Earlier Chapters of Genesis Unaffected by the Discoveries of Science*. London: Thomas Hatchard, 1856. GB, http://books.google.com/books?id=rqYCAAAAQAAJ.

Pritchard, James B., ed. *Ancient Near Eastern Texts Relating to the Old Testament*. Third, supplemented ed. Princeton: Princeton University Press, 1969.

Proba. "Centones Virgiliani." In *PL*, vol. 19, 803–18.

Procopé, J.F. "The Christian Exegesis of the Old Testament in the Alexandrian Tradition." In *HB/OT*, vol. I, bk 1, 478–542.

Procopius of Gaza. "Commentarii in Genesin." In *PG*, vol. 87, 21–512.

Proctor, Everett. *Christian Controversy in Alexandria: Clement's Polemic against the Basilideans and Valentinians*. American University Studies. Series 7, Theology and Religion, 172. New York: P. Lang, 1995.

Pseudo-Eustathius. "Commentarius in Hexameron." In *PG*, vol. 18, 707–94.

Pseudo-Hilary. "S. Hilarii in Genesim ad Leonem Papam." In *Cypriani Galli Poetae Heptateuchos accedunt incertorum de Sodoma et Iona et ad senatorem carmina et Hilarii quae feruntur in Genesin, de Maccabaeis atque de Euangelio*, edited by R. Peiper, 231–39. Corpus Scriptorum Ecclesiorum Latinorum Vienna: Tempsky, 1881. IA, http://www.archive.org/stream/corpusscriptorum24cypruoft.

Puckett, D.L. "Calvin, John (1509–1564)." In *HHMBI*, 171–79.

Pye Smith, John. *On the Relation between the Holy Scriptures and Some Parts of Geological Science.* New York: D. Appleton, 1840. GB, http://books.google.com/books?id=QZUQAAAAIAAJ.

Quasten, J. Patrology: *The Golden Age of Greek Patristic Literature.* 4 vols. Westminster: Spectrum, 1960.

Ralegh, Sir Walter. *The History of the World,* 1614. Reprint, The Works of Sir Walter Ralegh, Kt., vol. 2, London: Burt Franklin, 1829.

Rappaport, Rhoda. *When Geologists Were Historians 1665–1750.* Ithaca, NY: Cornell University Press, 1997.

Ray, John. *Further Correspondence of John Ray.* Edited by Robert W.T. Gunther. Ray Society Publications, 114. London: printed for the Ray Society, 1928.

———. *Three Physico-Theological Discourses.* London: printed for Sam Smith, 1693.

Remigius of Auxerre. *Remigii Autissiodorensis expositio super Genesim / cura et studio Burton Van Name Edwards.* Corpus Christianorum, continuatio mediaevalis, 136. Turnhout: Brepols, 1999.

Reventlow, Henning Graf. *The Authority of the Bible and the Rise of the Modern World.* Philadelphia: Fortress, 1985.

———. “Towards the End of the ‘Century of Enlightenment’: Established Shift from *Sacra Scriptura* to Literary Documents and Religion of the People of Israel.” In *HB/OT,* vol. II, 1024–63.

‘Review of The Testimony of Natural Theology to Christianity by Thomas Gisborne (London, 1818),’ *Quarterly Review* 41 (January 1819), 54.

Rhind, W.G. *The Age of the Earth Considered Geologically and Historically.* Edinburgh: Fraser & co., 1838. GB, http://books.google.com/books?id=cl4EAAAAQAAJ.

Richard of St. Victor. “Excerptionum allegoricarum libri XXIV “ In *PL,* Vol. 177, 191–284.

Richardson, John, 1580–1654. *Choice Observations and Explanations upon the Old Testament....* London: printed by T.R. and E.M. for John Rothwell, 1655. EEBO.

Rivetus, Andraeus. *Theologicae et scholasticae exercitations centum nonaginta in Genesin.* Leyden, 1633.

Robbins, Frank. *The Hexaemeral Literature: A Study of the Greek and Latin Commentaries in Genesis.* Chicago: University of Chicago Press, 1912.

Robbins, Gregory Allen, ed. *Genesis 1–3 in the History of Exegesis: Intrigue in the Garden.* Lewiston: Edwin Mellen, 1988.

Roberts, H. *Biblical Epic and Rhetorical Paraphrase.* Liverpool: Francis Cairns, 1985.

Roberts, Jonathan. “Introduction.” In *The Oxford Handbook of the Reception History of the Bible,* edited by Michael Lieb, Emma Mason and Jonathan Rowland, 1–8. Oxford: Oxford University Press, 2006.

———, and Christopher Rowland. “Introduction.” *Journal for the Study of the New Testament* 33, no. 2 (2010): 131–36.

Roberts, Michael. *Evangelicals and Science.* Greenwood Guides to Science and Religion, ed. Richard Olson. Westport, CT/London: Greenwood Press, 2008.

———. "Genesis Chapter 1 and Geological Time from Hugo Grotius and Marin Mersenne to William Conybeare and Thomas Chalmers (1620 to 1825)." In *Myth and Geology*, edited by L. Piccardi and W.B. Masse, 39–49. GS Special Publications, 273. London: The Geological Society, 2007.

———. "The Genesis of John Ray and His Successors." *Evangelical Quarterly* 74, no. 2 (2002): 143–63.

———. "Geology and Genesis Unearthed." *Churchman* 112, no. 3 (1998): 225–55 http://home.entouch.net/dmd/geolandgenesis.htm.

Robinson, Thomas. *New Observations on the Natural History of This World of Matter and This World of Life ... Grounded upon the Mosaick System of the Creation and the Flood....* London: printed for John Newton ... 1696. EEBO.

Roger, Jacques. *The Life Sciences in Eighteenth-Century French Thought.* Translated by Robert Ellrich. Edited by Keith Rodney Benson. Stanford: Stanford University Press, 1998. GB, http://books.google.com/books?id=_LY1bpIsrEgC.

Rogerson, John W. "Genesis 1–11." *Currents in Research: Biblical Studies* 5 (1997): 67–90

———. *Old Testament Criticism in the Nineteenth Century: England and Germany.* London: SPCK, 1984.

———. "What Difference Did Darwin Make? The Interpretation of Genesis in the Nineteenth Century." In *Reading Genesis after Darwin*, edited by Stephen C. Barton and David Wilkinson, 75–91. New York: Oxford University Press, 2009.

Rogland, Max. "*Ad Litteram:* Some Dutch Reformed Theologians on the Creation Days." *WTJ* 63 (2001): 211–33.

Romeny, R.B. ter Haar. "Eusebius of Emesa's Commentary on Genesis and the Origins of the Antiochene School." In *The Book of Genesis in Jewish and Oriental Christian Interpretation: A Collection of Essays*, edited by Judith Frishman and Lucas van Rompay, 125–42. Louvain: Peeters, 1997.

Rorison, G. "The Creative Week." In *Replies to Essays and Reviews*, 277–346. Oxford/London: John Henry and James Parker, 1862.

Rosenmüller, Johann Georg. *Antiquissima telluris historia.* Ulm: Jo. Conradi Wohleri, 1776. GB, http://books.google.com/books?id=j38UAAAAQAAJ.

Ross, Alexander. *The First Book of Questions and Answers upon Genesis.* London: Nicholas Okes, 1620.

Rossi, Paolo. *The Dark Abyss of Time. The History of the Earth and the History of the Nations from Hooke to Vico.* Chicago: University of Chicago Press, 1984.

Roth, W.M.W. "The Numerical Sequence X/X+1 in the Old Testament." *Vetus Testamentum* 12 (1962): 300–11.

Rousselet, Jean. "Grégoire de Nysse, avocat de ... Moïse." In *In Principio: Interprétations des premiers versets de la Genèse*, edited by Paul Vignaux, 95–113. Paris: Études Augustiniennes, 1973.

Rowecamp, G. "Acacius of Caesarea." In *DECL*, 4.

Rudwick, Martin J.S. *Bursting the Limits of Time: The Reconstruction of Geohistory in the Age of Revolution*. Chicago and London: University of Chicago Press, 2005.

———. "Jean-André de Luc and Nature's Chronology." In *The Age of the Earth from 4004 BC to AD 2002*, edited by C.L.E. Lewis and Simon J. Knell, 51–60. GS Special Publications, 190. London: The Geological Society, 2001.

———. "The Shape and Meaning of Earth History." In *God and Nature: Historical Essays on the Encounter between Christianity and Science*, edited by David C. Lindberg and Ronald Numbers, 296–321. Berkeley: University of California Press, 1986.

———. *Worlds before Adam: The Reconstruction of Geohistory in the Age of Reform*. Chicago, London: University of Chicago Press, 2008.

Rupert of Deutz. *De sancta Trinitate et operibus eius*. Edited by R. Haacke. Corpus Christianorum, continuatio mediaevalis, 21, 23. Turnholt: Brepols, 1971.

Rupke, Nicolaas. *The Great Chain of History: William Buckland and the English School of Geology (1814–1849)*. Oxford: Clarendon, 1983.

Russel, Jeffrey B. *Inventing the Flat Earth*. New York: Praeger, 1991.

Ryken, Leland. "Paradise Lost and its Biblical Epic Models." In *Milton and Scriptural Tradition*, edited by James H. Sims and Leland Ryken, 43–81. Columbia, MO: University of Missouri Press, 1984.

Saak, Eric Leland. "The Reception of Augustine in the Later Middle Ages." In *RCFW*, vol. 1, 367–404.

Sachau, E. *Theodori Mopsuesteni fragmenta Syriaca*. Lipsiae (Leipzig): sumptibus Guilelmi Engelmann, 1869.

Schaff, Philip. *The Creeds of Christendom*. 3 vols. Grand Rapids: Baker, 1966 [1877].

Scholten, Clemens. "Weshalb wird die Schöpfungsgeschichte zum naturwissenschaftlichen Bericht: Hexaemeronauslegung von Basilius von Cäsarea zu Johannes Philoponos." *Theologische Quartalschrift* 177, no. 1 (1997): 1–15.

Schottroff, Louise. "The Creation Narrative: Genesis 1.1–2.4a." In *A Feminist Companion to Genesis*, edited by A. Brenner, 24–38. Sheffield: Sheffield Academic Press, 1993.

Schulz-Flügel, Eva. "The Latin Old Testament Tradition." In *HB/OT*, vol. 1, bk 1, 642–62.

Schulze, Manfred. "Martin Luther and the Church Fathers." In *RCFW*, vol. 2, 573–626.

Schwanke, Johannes. "Luther on Creation." *Lutheran Quarterly* 16, no. 4 (2002): 1–20.

Schwarte, K.H. "Victorinus of Pettau." In *DECL*, 596–97.

Sedgwick, Adam. *A Discourse on the Studies of the University of Cambridge. The Fifth Edition, with Additions, and a Preliminary Dissertation*. London: John W. Parker, 1850. GB, http://books.google.com/books?id=aQhCAAAAIAAJ.

Seely, Paul H. "Concordism and a Biblical Alternative: An Examination of Hugh Ross's Perspective." *PSCF* 59, no. 1 (2007): 37–45

Severian of Gabala. "Homilies on Creation and Fall." In *Commentaries on Genesis 1–3*, edited by Robert C. Hill and Michael Glerup. Ancient Christian Texts, 1–94. Downers Grove: InterVarsity, 2010.

———. "In mundi creationem." In *PG*, vol. 56, 429–500.

Sherwood, Morgan B. "Genesis, Evolution, and Geology in America before Darwin: The Dana-Lewis Controversy, 1856–1857." In *Toward a History of Geology*, edited by Cecil J. Schneer, 305–16. Cambridge, MA: M.I.T. Press, 1969.

Shuckford, Samuel. *The Sacred and Prophane History of the World Connected, from the Creation of the World to the Dissolution of the Assyrian Empire...* 3 vols. vol. I. London: printed for R. Knaplock... 1728–30. ECCO.

Siegert, Folker. "Early Jewish Interpretation in a Hellenistic Style." In *HB/OT*, vol. I, bk 1, 130–98.

Siemens, David F., Jr. "Extended Humpty Dumpty Semantics and Genesis 1." *PSCF* 59, no. 3 (2007): 194–200.

Silliman, Benjamin. "Suggestions Relative to the Philosophy of Geology as Deduced from the Facts and to the Consistency of Both the Facts and the Theory of This Science with Sacred History." In *An Introduction to Geology*, edited by Robert Bakewell, 461–579. New Haven, CT: B. & W. Noyes, 1839. GB, http://books.google.com/books?id=Ro9CAAAAIAAJ.

———. "Supplement by the Editor." In *An Introduction to Geology: Intended to Convey a Practical Knowledge of the Science, and Comprising the Most Important Recent Discoveries, with Explanations of the Facts and Phenomena Which Serve to Confirm or Invalidate Various Geological Theories*, edited by Benjamin Silliman and Robert Bakewell, 389–466. New Haven: Hezekiah Howe, 1833.

Simon, Richard. *A Critical History of the Old Testament*. London: Walter Davis, 1682. EEBO.

Simonetti, Manlio. *Biblical Interpretation in the Early Church: An Historical Introduction to Patristic Exegesis*. Translated by J.A. Hughes. Edinburgh: T&T Clark, 1994.

Skarsaune, Oskar. "The Development of Scriptural Interpretation in the Second and Third Centuries – except Clement and Origen." In *HB/OT*, vol. I, bk 1, 373–442.

Smalley, Beryl. *The Study of the Bible in the Middle Ages*. Oxford: Blackwell, 1952.

Smith, Jonathan Z. "Ages of the World." In *The Encyclopedia of Religion*, edited by Mircea Eliade, vol. I, 128–33. New York: Macmillan, 1987.

Smolinski, Reiner, ed., *Biblia Americana: Cotton Mather*. Grand Rapids: Baker, 2010.

Snavely, I.L., Jr. "Zwingli, Ulrich *(1484–1531)*." In *HHMBI*, 249–55.

Speiser, O. *Genesis*. Anchor Bible. Garden City, NY: Doubleday, 1964.

Spinoza, Baruch. *Tractatus Theologico-Politicus*. Translated by Samuel Shirley. Leiden: E.J. Brill, 1989.

Stackhouse, Thomas. *A New History of the Holy Bible, from the Beginning of the World, to the Establishment of Christianity....* 2nd rev. ed. 2 vols. vol. I. London: printed for Stephen Austen, 1742–44. ECCO.

Steiner, Rudolf. *Genesis: Secrets of Creation: The First Book of Moses: Eleven Lectures Given in Munich, 16–26 August 1910.* Forest Row: Rudolf Steiner Press, 2002.

Steneck, N.H. *Science and Creation in the Middle Ages: Henry of Langenstein on Genesis.* Notre Dame: University of Notre Dame Press, 1976.

Steno, Nicolaus. *The Prodromus of Nicolaus Steno's Dissertation concerning a Solid Body Enclosed by Process of Nature within a Solid.* Translated by John Garrett Winter. University of Michigan Humanistic Series/Contributions to the History of Science. New York: Macmillan, 1916. Reprint, New York: Hafner, 1968.

Sterling, E.S. "Philo." In *Dictionary of New Testament Background*, edited by Craig A. Evans and Stanley E. Porter, 789–93. Downers Grove: InterVarsity, 2000.

Steuchus, Eugubinus Augustinus. *Cosmopoeia, vel de mundano opificio, expositio III capitum Genesis, in quibus de creatione tractat Moses* ... Sebast. Gryphius, 1535.

Stevens, Martin and John Block Friedman, "Arnold Ledgerwood Williams," *The Chaucer Review* 7 (1973): 229–33.

Stiling, Rodney Lee. "The Diminishing Deluge: Noah's Flood in Nineteenth-Century American Thought." PhD diss., The University of Wisconsin, 1991.

———. "Scriptural Geology in America." In *Evangelicals and Science in Historical Perspective*, edited by D.N. Livingstone, D.G. Hart and Mark A. Noll, 177–92. New York: Oxford University Press, 1999.

Stinger, Charles. "Italian Renaissance Learning and the Church Fathers." In *RCFW*, vol. 2, 473–510.

Stordalen, Terje. "Genesis 2,4: Restudying a Locus Classicus." *Zeitschrift für die Alttestamentliche Wissenschaft* 104 (1992): 163–77.

Stuart, Moses. "Critical Examination of Some Passages in Gen. I; with Remarks on Difficulties That Attend Some of the Present Modes of Geological Reasoning." *American Biblical Repository* 7, no. 21 (1836): 46–106.

Suarez, Francisco. "Tractatus de opere sex dierum." In *Francisci Suarez opera omnia*, edited by D.M. André, vol. III, 1–460. Paris: L. Vivès, 1856. GB, http://books.google.com/books?id=a7sWAAAAQAAJ.

Suidas. *Suidae Lexicon.* Edited by Ada Adler. 4 vols., vol. IV. Stuttgart: in aedibus B.G. Teubneri, 1967-.

Swan, John. *Speculum Mundi or A Glasse Representing the Face of the World....* 4th ed. London: printed by J.R. for John Williams, 1670. EEBO.

Swedenborg, Emanuel. *Arcana Coelestia: The Heavenly Arcana Contained in the Holy Scripture* ... New York: Swedenborg Foundation, 1982.

Swift, Jonathan. *Travels into Several Remote Nations of the World* ... by Lemuel Gulliver.... Dublin, 1727. ECCO.

Sylwan, A. "Petrus Comestor, Historia Scholastica: une nouvelle édition." *Sacri Erudiri* 39 (2000): 345–82.

Taylor, Kenneth L. "Buffon, Desmarest and the Ordering of Geological Events in Époques." In *The Age of the Earth from 4004 BC to AD 2002*, edited by C.L.E. Lewis and Simon J. Knell, 39–50. GS Special Publications, 190. London: The Geological Society, 2001.

ten Napel, E. "Some Remarks on the Hexaemeral Literature in Syriac." In *IV Symposium Syriacum (Groningen, 1984)*, edited by H.W.J. Drijvers, R. Lavenant, C. Molenburg and G.J. Reinink, 57–69. Orientalia Christiana Analecta, 229. Roma: Pont. Institutum Studiorum Orientalium, 1987.

Tertullian. "Against Hermogenes." In *ANF*, vol. 3, 477–502.

Teske, Roland J. "The Genesis Accounts of Creation." In *Augustine through the Ages: An Encyclopedia*, edited by O.S.A. Allan D. Fitzgerald, 379–81. Grand Rapids/Cambridge: Eerdmans, 1999.

Theodore of Mopsuestia. "Fragmenta alia in Genesin." In *PG*, vol. 66, 633–46.

Theodoret of Cyrrhus. "Quaestiones in Octateuchum." In *PG*, vol. 80, 76–528.

Theophilus of Antioch. "Theophilus to Autolycus." In *ANF*, vol. 2, 85–127.

Thierry of Chartres. "Tractatus de sex dierum operibus." In *Commentaries on Boethius by Thierry of Chartres and His School*, edited by N. M. Häring. Toronto: Pontifical Institute of Medieval Studies, 1971.

Tison, Richard Perry, II. "Lords of Creation: American Scriptural Geology and the Lord Brothers' Assault on "Intellectual Atheism"." PhD diss., University of Oklahoma, 2008.

Tonneau, R.M. *Sancti Ephraem Syri in Genesim et in Exodum Commentarii*. Corpus scriptorum Christianorum orientalium, 152/153. Louvain: Peeters, 1955.

Toulmin, Stephen, and June Goodfield. *The Discovery of Time*. London: Harper & Row, 1965.

Townsend, Joseph. *The Character of Moses Established for Veracity as an Historian: Recording Events from the Creation to the Deluge*. 2 vols. Bath: Longman, Hurst, 1813, 1815.

Trigg, Joseph W. "The Apostolic Fathers and Apologists." In *A History of Biblical Interpretation*, edited by Alan J. Hauser and Duane F. Watson, 304–33. Grand Rapids: Eerdmans, 2003.

———, ed. *Biblical Interpretation*. Message of the Fathers of the Church, 9. Wilmington, DE: Michael Glazier, 1988.

Trompf, Gary W. *The Idea of Historical Recurrence in Western Thought: From Antiquity to the Reformation*. Berkeley: University of California Press, 1979.

Turner, Laurence A. *Genesis*. Readings. Sheffield: Sheffield Academic Press, 2000.

Turner, Sharon, 1768–1847. *The Sacred History of the World: As Displayed in the Creation and Subsequent Events to the Deluge: Attempted to be Philosophically Considered, in a Series of Letters to a Son*. 2nd ed. London: Longman, Rees, Orme, Brown, Green and Longman, 1832. GB, http://books.google.com/books?id=ZJA5AAAAcAAJ.

An Universal History, from the Earliest Account of Time to the Present.... 20 vols. vol. I. Dublin, 1744–47. ECCO.

Ure, Andrew. *A New System of Geology....* London: Longman, Rees, Orme, Brown, & Green, 1829, http://books.google.com.au/books?id=MULPAAAAMAAJ.

Ussher, James. *The Annals of the Old Testament. From the Beginning of the World.* London: printed by E. Tyler, for J. Crook ... and for G. Bedell ... 1658. EEBO.

Vaccari, Ezio. "European Views on Terrestrial Chronology from Descartes to the Mid-Eighteenth Century." In *The Age of the Earth from 4004 BC to AD 2002*, edited by C.L.E. Lewis and Simon J. Knell, 25–38. GS Special Publications, 190. London: The Geological Society, 2001.

VanderKam, J.C. "Jubilees." In *Dictionary of New Testament Background*, edited by Craig A. Evans and Stanley E. Porter, 600–603. Downers Grove/Leicester: InterVarsity, 2000.

Van Fleteren, Frederick. "Principles of Augustine's Hermeneutic: An Overview." In *Augustine: Biblical Exegete*, 1–32. New York: Peter Lang, 2001.

van Inwagen, P. "Genesis and Evolution." In *Reasoned Faith: Essays in Philosophical Theology*, edited by Eleonore Stump. 93–127. Ithaca, NY: Cornell University Press, 1993.

Van Oort, Johannes. "John Calvin and the Church Fathers." In *RCFW*, vol. 2, 661–700.

van Rompay, Lucas. "Antiochene Biblical Interpretation: Greek and Syriac." In *The Book of Genesis in Jewish and Oriental Christian Interpretation: A Collection of Essays*, edited by Judith Frishman and Lucas van Rompay, 103–23. Louvain: Peeters, 1997.

———. "The Christian Syriac Tradition of Interpretation." In *HB/OT*, vol. I, bk 1, 612–41.

———. "Development of Biblical Interpretation in the Syrian Churches of the Middle Ages." In *HB/OT*, vol. I, bk 2, 559–77.

van Ruiten, Jacques T.A.G.M. *Primaeval History Interpreted: The Rewriting of Genesis 1–11 in the Book of Jubilees.* Supplements to the Journal for the Study of Judaism. Leiden: Brill, 2000.

van Winden, J.C.M. "Hexaemeron." In *Reallexikon fur Antike und Christentum*, Vol. 14, 1250–69. Stuttgart: Anton Hiersemann, 1988.

Vermigli, Pietro Martire, 1499–1562. *In Primum Librum Mosis, qui vulgo Genesis dicitur.* Zurich: Christophorus Froschauer, 1579.

Victor, Claudius Marius. "Alethia." In *Commodianus; Claudius Marius Victorius*, edited by P.F. Hovingh, 115–93. Corpus Christianorum Series Latina, 128. Turnholt: Brepols, 1960.

———. "Commentariorum in Genesin libri tres." In *PL*, vol. 61, 937–70.

Victorinus of Pettau. "On the Creation of the World." In *ANF*, vol. 7, 341–43.

Vignaux, Paul, ed. *In Principio: interprétations des premiers versets de la Genèse.* Paris: Études Augustiniennes, 1973.

Vincent of Beauvais. *Speculum quadriplex, sive, Speculum maius.* 4 vols. Graz: Akademische Druck- und Verlagsanstalt, 1964–65.

Vogt, H.J. "Origen." In *DECL*, 444–51.

von Bohlen, Peter. *Historical and Critical Illustrations of the First Part of Genesis.* London: Longman, Green, Longman, and Roberts, 1862. GB, http://books.google.com/books?id=rBkVAAAAYAAJ.

von Rad, Gerhard. *Genesis.* Revised ed. Old Testament Library. London: SCM, 1972.

von Zittel, Karl Alfred. *History of Geology and Palaeontology to the End of the Nineteenth Century*. Translated by Maria M. Ogilvie-Gordon. London: Walter Scott, 1901. GB, http://books.google.com/books?lr=&id=0z28AAAAIAAJ.

Walker, George. *The History of the Creation*. London: printed for John Bartlet ... 1631.

Wall, William. *Critical Notes on the Old Testament....* London: printed for C. Davis, 1734. ECCO.

Waltke, Bruce. "The Literary Genre of Genesis, Chapter One." *Crux* 27 (1991): 2–10.

Walton, John H. *The Lost World of Genesis One: Ancient Cosmology and the Origins Debate*. Downers Grove, IL: IVP Academic, 2009.

Warren, Erasmus. *Geologia: or, A Discourse concerning the Earth before the Deluge*. London: R. Chiswell, 1690.

Watson, Richard. *An Apology for Christianity in a Series of Letters, Addressed to Edward Gibbon, esq., Author of The Decline and Fall of the Roman Empire*. Cambridge: printed by J. Archdeacon printer to the University, for T. and J. Merrill, and J. Woodyer ... 1776. GB, http://books.google.com/books?id=3MAvt_UW4XwC.

Weinfeld, Moshe. "Sabbath, Temple, and the Enthronement of the Lord – The Problem of the Sitz im Leben of Genesis 1:1–2:3." In *Mélanges bibliques et orientaux en l'honneur de M. Henri Cazelles*, edited by André Caquot and Mathias Delcor, 501–12. Kevelaer: Butzon und Bercker, 1981.

Welker, Michael. "Creation, Big Bang or the Work of Seven Days?" *Theology Today* 52, no. 27 (1995): 173–87.

Wenham, Gordon J. *Genesis 1–15*. Word Biblical Commentaries 1. Waco, TX: Word, 1987.

Wesley, John. *Explanatory Notes on the Old Testament*. 3 vols. vol. I. Bristol: Wm. Pine, 1765, http://jcsm.org/StudyCenter/wesley_commentary/genesis.htm.

Westermann, Claus. *Genesis*. 3 vols., vol. I. Minneapolis: Augsburg, 1984–86.

"Westminster Confession of Faith, with Amendments by The Presbyterian Reformed Church of Australia." Strathpine North, QLD, Australia: Covenanter Press, 1982.

Wevers, John W. "The Interpretative Character and Significance of the Septuagint Version." In *HB/OT*, vol. I, bk 1, 84–107.

———, ed. *Septuaginta Vetus Testamentum Graecum. Vol. I: Genesis*. Göttingen: Vandenhoeck & Ruprecht, 1974.

Whewell, William. *History of the Inductive Sciences*. 3 vols. London: John W. Parker, 1837.

Whiston, William. *A New Theory of the Earth, from its Original, to the Consummation of All Things....* London: R. Roberts, 1696. EEBO.

White, Andrew Dickson. *A History of the Warfare of Science with Theology in Christendom*. 2 vols. New York: D. Appleton, 1896.

White, John, 1575–1648. *A Commentary upon the Three First Chapters of the First Book of Moses called Genesis*. London: printed by John Streater ... 1656. EEBO.

Whitehurst, John. *An Inquiry into the Original State and Formation of the Earth Deduced from Facts and the Laws of Nature ...* London: Cooper, 1778. ECCO.

Wicbod. "Liber quaestionum super librum Genesis ex dictis sanctorum partum ..." In *PL*, vol. 96, 1105–68.

Wicks, Jared. "Catholic Old Testament Interpretation in the Reformation and Early Confessional Eras." In *HB/OT*, vol. II, 617–48.

Wilkinson, David. "Did Darwin Dethrone Humankind?" In *Darwin, Creation and the Fall: Theological Challenges*, edited by R.J. Berry and T.A. Noble, 15–29. Nottingham: InterVarsity, 2009.

———. "Reading Genesis 1–3 in the Light of Modern Science." In *Reading Genesis after Darwin*, edited by Stephen C. Barton and David Wilkinson, 127–44. New York: Oxford University Press, 2009.

Willet, Andrew. *Hexapla in Genesin.* Cambridge: John Legat, 1605. EEBO.

Williams, Arnold L. *The Common Expositor: An Account of the Commentaries on Genesis 1527–1633.* Chapel Hill: University of North Carolina Press, 1948.

Williams, Thomas. "Biblical Interpretation." In *The Cambridge Companion to Augustine*, edited by Eleonore Stump and Norman Kretzmann, 59–70. Cambridge: Cambridge University Press, 2001.

Wilson, Leonard G., ed. "Benjamin Silliman: A Biographical Sketch." In *Benjamin Silliman and his Circle: Studies on the Influence of Benjamin Silliman on Science in America,* 1–10. New York: Science History Publications, 1979.

Wise, Michael, Martin Abegg, Jr., and Edward Cook. *Dead Sea Scrolls: A New Translation.* Rydalmere: Hodder & Stoughton, 1998.

Wiseman, Nicholas. *Twelve Lectures on the Connection between Science and Revealed Religion.* 6th ed. Vol. I. London: Catholic Publishing and Bookselling Co. Ltd., 1859.

Witty, William. *An Essay towards a Vindication of the Vulgar Exposition of the Mosaic History of the Creation of the World.* London: J. Wyat, 1705. ECCO.

Woodward, John. *An Essay Toward a Natural History of the Earth ...* London: R. Wilkin, 1695. Reprint, Arno Press, 1978.

Worthington, W. *The Scripture Theory of the Earth.* London: printed for J. and F. Rivington ... 1773. ECCO.

Wright, David F. "Augustine: His Exegesis and Hermeneutics." In *HB/OT*, vol. I, bk 1, 701–30.

Wright, J.W. "Genealogies." In *Dictionary of the Old Testament: Pentateuch*, edited by T. Desmond Alexander and David W. Baker, 345–50. Downers Grove: InterVarsity, 2003.

Yarbrough, R.W. "Stuart, Moses *(1780–1852).*" In *HHMBI*, 368–72.

Yarchin, W. "Biblical Interpretation in the Light of the Interpretation of Nature: 1650–1900." In *Nature and Scripture in the Abrahamic Religions: 1700–Present*, edited by J.M. van der Meer and S. Mandelbrote, 41–82. Leiden: Brill, 2008.

Young, Davis A. "The Contemporary Relevance of Augustine's View of Creation." *PSCF* 40, no. 1 (1988): 42–45 www.asa3.org/ASA/PSCF.html.

———. "The Reception of Geology in the Dutch Reformed Tradition: The Case of Herman Bavinck (1854–1921)." In *Geology and Religion: A History of Harmony and Hostility*, edited by Martina Kölbl-Ebert, 289–300. GS Special Publications, 310. Bath: The Geological Society, 2009.

———. "Scripture in the Hands of Geologists." *WTJ* 49 (1987): 1–34, 257–304.

———, and Ralph Stearley. *The Bible, Rocks and Time: Geological Evidence for the Age of the Earth*. Downers Grove: InterVarsity, 2008.

Young, Edward J. "The Days of Genesis." *WTJ* 25 (1963): 1–34, 143–71.

Young, Frances. "Alexandrian and Antiochene Exegesis." In *A History of Biblical Interpretation*, edited by Alan J. Hauser and Duane F. Watson, 334–54. Grand Rapids: Eerdmans, 2003.

Zahlten, Johannes. *Creatio Mundi: Darstellungen der sechs Schöpfungstage und naturwissenschaftliches Weltbild im Mittelalter*. Stuttgarter Beiträge zur Geschichte und Politik, 13. Stuttgart: Klett-Cotta, 1979.

Zanchius, Hieronymus. *De operibus Dei intra spacium sex dierum creatis opus*. Neustadt, 1591. Reprint, Hanover, 1597.

Zerubavel, Eviatar. *The Seven Day Circle: The History and Meaning of the Week*. New York: The Free Press, 1985.

Zöckler, Otto. *Geschichte der Beziehungen zwischen Theologie und Naturwissenschaft: mit besondrer Rücksicht auf Schöpfungsgeschichte*. 2 vols. Gütersloh: C. Bertelsmann, 1877–79.

Zwingli, H. *Farrago annotationum in Genesim, ex ore Huld. Zuinglii per Leonem Iudae & Casparem Megandrum exceptarum*. Edited by Rudolph Gwalther and Leo Jud. Opera D. Huldrychi Zuinglii, vigilantissimi Tigurinae ecclesiae antistitis. Zurich: Christoph Froschauer, 1545. CPT.

Index of Primary Text Authors, Ancient Figures and Movements Named for Figures

Index of Modern Authors (select)

Index of Subjects

Index of Scripture and Other Ancient Texts

Apocryphal/ Deuterocanonical Works

New Testament

Pseudepigrapha

Qumran

Ancient and Classical Texts

Ancient Near Eastern Epics

Jewish